Dreamweaver® CS4 All-~~In-One~~ For Dummies®

D0004845

To Do This: (Action)	Press: (PC Shortcut)	Press: (Mac Shortcut)
Create a new document	Control+N	Command+N
Open an existing document	Control+O	Command+O
Save an open document	Control+S	Command+S
Close an open document	Control+W	Command+W
Close all open documents	Control+Shift+W	Command+Shift +W
Quit Dreamweaver	Control+Q or Alt+F4	Command+Q or Opt+F4
Undo	Control+Z or Alt+Backspace	Option+Delete
Redo	Control+Y or Control+Shift+Z	Command+Y or Command+Shift+Z
Cut	Control+X or Shift+Delete	Command+X or Shift+Delete
Copy	Control+C or Shift+Insert	Command+C or Shift+Insert
Paste	Control+V	Command+V
Paste Special	Control+Shift+V	Command+Shift+V
Select All	Control+A	Command+A
Find and Replace	Control+F	Command+F
Open the Preferences Panel	Control+U	Command+U
Refresh Design View	F5	F5
Make Selected Text Bold	Control+B	Command+B
Make Selected Text Italic	Control+I	Command+I
Apply Paragraph Formatting to Selected Text	Control+Shift+P	Command+Shift+P
Apply Heading Formatting (H1-H6) to Selected Text	Control+1 through 6	Command+1 through 6

(continued)

For Dummies: Bestselling Book Series for Beginners

Dreamweaver® CS4 All-in-One For Dummies®

Cheat Sheet

To Do This: (Action)	Press: (PC Shortcut)	Press: (Mac Shortcut)
Add New Paragraph	Return	Return
Add a Line Break 	Shift+Return	Shift+Return
Insert a Non-Breaking Space	Command+Shift+ Spacebar	Command+Shift+ Spacebar
Move object or text	Drag selection to new location	Drag selection to new location
Copy object or text	Control-drag selection to new location	Option-drag selection to new location
Select a word	Double-click	Double-click
Select a row	Triple-click	Triple-click
Run a Spell Check	Shift+F7	Shift+F7
Open the Help Window	F1	F1
Zoom In	Control+=	Command+=
Zoom Out	Control+-	Command+-
Preview in Primary Browser	F12	Option+F12
Preview in Secondary Browser	Shift+F12 or Control+F12	Command+F12
LiveView	Alt+F11	Option+F11

Toggle Display	PC Shortcut	Mac Shortcut
Rulers	Control+Alt+R	Command+Option+R
Guides	Control+;	Command+;
Visual Aids	Control+Shift+I	Command+Shift+I
Grid	Control+Alt+G	Command+Option+G
Page Properties	Control+J	Command+J

Copyright © 2009 Wiley Publishing, Inc.
All rights reserved.

Item 9180-8.

For more information about Wiley Publishing, call 1-800-762-2974.

For Dummies: Bestselling Book Series for Beginners

Dreamweaver® CS4
ALL-IN-ONE
FOR
DUMMIES®

by Sue Jenkins and Richard Wagner

WILEY

Wiley Publishing, Inc.

Dreamweaver® CS4 All-in-One For Dummies®

Published by
Wiley Publishing, Inc.
111 River Street
Hoboken, NJ 07030-5774

www.wiley.com

Copyright © 2009 by Wiley Publishing, Inc., Indianapolis, Indiana

Published by Wiley Publishing, Inc., Indianapolis, Indiana

Published simultaneously in Canada

For general information on our other products and services, please contact our Customer Care Department within the U.S. at 800-762-2974, outside the U.S. at 317-572-3993, or fax 317-572-4002.

For technical support, please visit www.wiley.com/techsupport.

Wiley also publishes its books in a variety of electronic formats. Some content that appears in print may not be available in electronic books.

Library of Congress Control Number: 2008938867

ISBN: 978-0-470-39180-8

Manufactured in the United States of America

10 9 8 7 6 5 4 3 2 1

WILEY

About the Authors

Sue Jenkins is a Web and graphic designer, illustrator, photographer, teacher, and writer, and the owner and creative director of Luckychair (www. luckychair.com), a full-service design studio serving companies across the U.S. since 1997. When not designing, this Adobe Certified Expert/Adobe Certified Instructor teaches three-day courses in Dreamweaver, Illustrator, and Photoshop at Noble Desktop in New York City. In addition to this Dummies book, Sue is the author of *Web Design: The L-Line, The Express Line to Learning* (Wiley), *How To Do Everything Illustrator CS4* (McGraw-Hill), and the upcoming *Web Design All-in-One For Dummies* (Wiley). Sue can also be seen as the software instructor in three of ClassOnDemand's (www.class ondemand.com) Adobe Training DVDs, namely *Dreamweaver for Designers* (winner of a 2007 Bronze Telly Award), *Designer's Guide to Photoshop*, and *Designer's Guide to Illustrator*. Sue lives with her husband and son in Pennsylvania.

Richard Wagner is an experienced Web designer and developer as well as author of several Web-related books. These books include *Building Facebook Applications For Dummies, Professional iPhone and iPod touch Programming, XSLT For Dummies, Creating Web Pages All-In-One For Dummies, XML All-In-One For Dummies, Web Design Before & After Makeovers*, and *JavaScript Unleashed* (1st, 2nd ed.). Before moving into full-time authoring, Richard was vice president of product development at NetObjects. He was also inventor and chief architect of the award-winning NetObjects ScriptBuilder. A versatile author with a wide range of interests, he is also author of *The Expeditionary Man* and *The Myth of Happiness*.

Dedication

In loving memory of Buddy and Lizzy.

— Sue Jenkins

Authors' Acknowledgments

A special thank-you goes to my agent, Matt Wagner, for yet another great opportunity; to Linda Morris and Jeff Noble for their impeccable editing throughout all of the changes to the beta software; to all the people working in Composition Services at Wiley to make this book look good; to senior acquisitions editor, Bob Woerner, for his care and management of this project; and to my coauthor, Rich Wagner, who generously stepped in to revamp books VII, VIII, and IX on this project despite his overbooked schedule. Thank you to my friends in New York City, and to Scott Carson and my fellow co-workers and instructors at Noble Desktop: You make every trip to Manhattan a special one. Thanks to my parents for bringing me into the world and to my sisters and their partners and children for always being just a phone call away. I'd also like to thank my husband, Phil, and son, Kyle, for their love, support, and patience while I spent most of our summer at the keyboard.

— Sue Jenkins

I would like to thank Linda Morris for her flawless management of this book from start to finish. Thanks also to Jeff Noble for his technical insights to ensure the accuracy of the book.

— Richard Wagner

Publisher's Acknowledgments

We're proud of this book; please send us your comments through our online registration form located at www.dummies.com/register/.

Some of the people who helped bring this book to market include the following:

Acquisitions and Editorial

Project Editor: Linda Morris

Executive Editor: Bob Woerner

Copy Editor: Linda Morris

Technical Editor: Jeff Noble

Editorial Manager: Jodi Jensen

Editorial Assistant: Amanda Foxworth

Sr. Editorial Assistant: Cherie Case

Cartoons: Rich Tennant
(www.the5thwave.com)

Composition Services

Project Coordinator: Kristie Rees

Layout and Graphics: Reuben W. Davis, Christin Swinford, Ronald Terry, Christine Williams, Erin Zeltner

Proofreader: Evelyn C. Gibson

Indexer: Estalita Slivoskey

Publishing and Editorial for Technology Dummies

Richard Swadley, Vice President and Executive Group Publisher

Andy Cummings, Vice President and Publisher

Mary Bednarek, Executive Acquisitions Director

Mary C. Corder, Editorial Director

Publishing for Consumer Dummies

Diane Graves Steele, Vice President and Publisher

Composition Services

Gerry Fahey, Vice President of Production Services

Debbie Stailey, Director of Composition Services

Contents at a Glance

Table of Contents

Introduction

*W*hen professional Web designers want to build a Web site, they nearly always pick Dreamweaver. With more than 80 percent of all designers using it, Dreamweaver is definitely the top dual-platform (PC and Mac) Web design software application on the market today.

What makes Dreamweaver so great is the combo WYSIWYG *(What You See Is What You Get)* coding interface that allows you to build HTML files containing text, graphics, and other media, all the while seeing the page layout and its code as you create pages in Dreamweaver's Design and Code views.

Dreamweaver accurately generates all the HTML, CSS, and JavaScript source code needed for Web developers to create HTML- and XHTML-compliant Web pages. No more sweating intricate coding issues such as merging table cells, creating rollover effects, and applying CSS to text. In addition, Dreamweaver integrates well with Fireworks, for roundtrip graphic editing, and Contribute CS4, for Web site maintenance and the publishing of content changes by a nondesigner.

Dreamweaver CS4 enhancements include a better coding environment, integrated support for JavaScript, CSS, server-side scripting, and accessibility standards-compliant code. You'll also find improved dynamic content creation tools for connecting to databases, such as MySQL, and working with a variety of scripting technologies including PHP, ASP, JSP, ASP.NET, and ColdFusion. In addition, you can easily integrate XML content with both XSL and the Spry framework for Ajax. The program contains all the tools you need to streamline page development, and many of the tools are customizable through the Preferences dialog box.

Use *Dreamweaver CS4 All-in-One For Dummies* as your complete guide to the exciting world of Web design.

About This Book

This is a reference book, which means you can jump around from chapter to chapter reading whatever section you want as the need arises. Don't feel locked into the idea of reading the book from cover to cover. In fact, think of each minibook as its own little reference zone where each zone is split into chapters about performing specific tasks in Dreamweaver CS4.

Everything you find in this book is written so you don't have to wade through complicated technical help files or have to commit anything to memory. To keep things simple, you'll find detailed, step-by-step, easy-to-follow instructions. When more technical information is needed to clarify a particular process, it's often set apart from the main text in sidebars or noted in the margins with a Technical Stuff icon.

The bottom line is that we want to make you comfortable with Dreamweaver CS4 and hope that you'll continue to use this book frequently and consider it the main resource of your Web-design library.

Conventions Used in This Book

To help with new terms and concepts, the following typographical rules or *conventions* are used in this book:

✦ **New terms:** New terms are set apart with italics. For example:

Dreamweaver CS4 comes with the commonly used JavaScripts, which it refers to as *behaviors,* ready to insert into your pages from the Behaviors panel.

✦ **Placeholder text:** Text that is a placeholder is set in italic. For example, in the phrase

```
Type username here
```

username is a placeholder for your actual username, so it is set in italic.

✦ **Code samples:** We include short code samples in monospaced text within the paragraph, like this: `<img src"logo.gif">`. We set longer code samples apart from the text, like this:

```
<frameset rows="80,*" cols="*" frameborder="NO"
    border="0" framespacing="0">
  <frame src="top.html" name="topFrame" scrolling="NO"
    noresize title="topFrame">
```

For the times when we want to draw your attention to particular parts of code samples, we indicate the important parts in bold, as in this example: `<div id="`**sidebar**`"></div>`.

✦ **Reader entry:** Anything you need to type is in boldface.

✦ **Cross-platform:** Whenever PCs and Macs have different shortcuts, we include both the Windows equivalent (right-click) and the Mac equivalent (Control+click).

✦ **Web addresses:** Web addresses are set apart in monofont, such as `www.adobe.com`.

What You Don't Have to Read

You don't have to read any part of this book that doesn't interest you. For example, if you never intend to use Fireworks, skip that chapter! And if you see a sidebar that covers more technical information than you care to know, pass it by. The main thing is that you know what is available and only read what is useful to you.

Assumptions About You

With only a general idea of the kinds of people who will buy this book, we must make certain broad assumptions about all our readers to write this book with enough specificity for each of you. Therefore, we assume that you're a human being living on planet Earth who knows how to operate a computer and visit Web sites on the Internet, and has a desire to create Web sites using Dreamweaver. Beyond that, we presume no prior knowledge of Web design, HTML, JavaScript, CSS, or Dreamweaver.

How This Book Is Organized

This book is divided into nine minibooks, each of which is further divided into relevant chapters organized by topic. Each minibook relates to the most important concepts in Dreamweaver.

Book 1: Getting Started

Begin your trip into the world of Web design with a look around the Dreamweaver workspace and a review of site design. Then find out how to create and manage sites in Dreamweaver — an important step that enables you to take full advantage of Dreamweaver's automated features.

Book II: Mastering the Basics

Book II shows you everything you need to know to create new documents; add and format text on a page; insert graphics and create rollover buttons; convert text and graphics into clickable links to other Web pages; add movies, sound, and other media files to your pages; add tables for organizing content; and build fantastic forms for collecting data from visitors.

Book III: Working Like the Pros

Book III walks you through the process of styling your pages with Cascading Style Sheets (CSS), building sites using Dreamweaver templates, and using Library items. You also find out about using server-side includes, creating and using code snippets, and recording and saving custom commands with the History panel. The final chapter in this minibook contains information on using Dreamweaver with Fireworks for roundtrip image optimization.

Book IV: Energizing Your Site

When you're ready to add more zing and pizzazz to your pages, turn to Book IV. Here you find out how to work with layers instead of tables, create opportunities for visitor interactivity by adding JavaScript behaviors to objects on your pages, work with Spry effects and Spry widgets, and design pages built with frames. The final chapter in this minibook shows you all about the benefits of XHTML and how to configure Dreamweaver to write XHTML-compliant code.

Book V: Publishing Your Site

Book V shows you how to run Dreamweaver's reports and use other tools to test and fix any errors before you publish your site. You also find out how to select and set up a remote connection to your host server and transfer files to the remote site.

Book VI: Working Collaboratively

Adobe's Contribute CS4 is a software program that allows nondesigners to edit and update content on live Web pages through a special interface — all without needing to know any HTML or Dreamweaver. Book VI contains information on setting up, connecting to, and managing a Contribute site.

Book VII: Building Web Applications

This minibook discusses how to select and add Web and application servers along with how to configure, edit, and delete database connections. When working with databases, troubleshooting problems is important, so we also discuss resolving permission problems, database connection issues, and error messages.

Book VIII: Making Pages Dynamic

In this minibook, you find out how to define data sources and make them available for use in your dynamic pages. We also show you how to add simple dynamic data to your Web pages, as well as create HTML tables for your recordsets, navigate through your recordsets, and dynamically control them. In addition, you discover how to test the functionality of your dynamic site by using Dreamweaver's Live Data view. This minibook also includes a chapter on working with ColdFusion components, adding Web services to your site, and putting custom server behaviors to work.

Book IX: Developing Applications Rapidly

Book IX shows you how to build master and detail pages, search and results pages, and record insert, update, and delete pages. We also get into more complicated territory, such as calling ASP command objects, working with JSP prepared statements, and using stored procedures. Finally, you find out how to restrict site access.

Icons Used in This Book

To make your experience with the book easier, you'll find a handful of icons in the margins of the book to indicate particular points of interest.

Tip icons alert you to interesting techniques or hints that can save you time and effort.

The Remember icon is a friendly cue about things to keep in mind when performing certain tasks or important information that can benefit you in understanding how Dreamweaver works.

Any time you see the Warning icon, watch out! Paragraphs marked with this icon include important information that will help you avoid common design mistakes and steer clear of trouble.

Occasionally we include some technical information that, while interesting to some, is not essential reading for everyone. Nevertheless, consider at least glancing at the text marked with the Technical Stuff icon just in case it applies to your situation.

Where to Go from Here

Read through the Table of Contents to find what interests you. Otherwise, consider the following jumping-off topics:

+ For an overview of Dreamweaver in general and the new features in Dreamweaver CS4 in particular, go to Book I.

+ For information about working with text, graphics, and links, read Book II.

+ For information on using Cascading Style Sheets, see Book III.

+ To discover how to work with layers, use JavaScript behaviors, and work with Spry framework widgets, see Book IV.

+ For information on publishing your site, see Book V.

+ For details about working collaboratively with a team, see Book VI.

+ For instructions on building Web applications, go to Book VII.

+ To build dynamic Web pages, read Book VIII.

+ For information on rapid application development, see Book IX.

Beyond this book there are loads of valuable Dreamweaver resources on the Internet to help you build Web sites. The following is a sample of some useful sites you'll find out there:

Adobe Resources

Dreamweaver Support Center: `www.adobe.com/support/dreamweaver/`

Dreamweaver Exchange: `www.adobe.com/cfusion/exchange/index.cfm?event=productHome&exc=3&loc=en_us`

Author Resources

Luckychair: `www.luckychair.com`

Standards, Guidelines, and Initiatives

World Wide Web Consortium (W3C): `www.w3.org`

Web Accessibility Initiative: `www.w3.org/WAI/`

Dreamweaver Extensions

Project Seven: `www.projectseven.com`

Hot Dreamweaver Fever: `www.hotdreamweaver.com`

Kaosweaver: `www.kaosweaver.com`

Web Developer Resources

Web Monkey: `www.webmonkey.com`

W3 Schools: `www.w3schools.com`

JavaScript Resources

Dynamic Drive DHTML Scripts: `www.dynamicdrive.com`

EarthWeb JavaScripts: `http://webdeveloper.earthweb.com/webjs/`

JavaScript Source: `http://javascript.internet.com`

CSS Resources

W3C's CSS: `www.w3.org/Style/CSS/`

CSS Zen Garden: `www.csszengarden.com`

Sitepoint CSS Reference: `http://reference.sitepoint.com/css`

W3Schools CSS Tutorial: `http://w3schools.com/css/default.asp`

CSS Beauty: `www.cssbeauty.com`

Free CSS Templates: `www.freecsstemplates.org`

Book I
Getting Started

The 5th Wave   By Rich Tennant

"As a web site designer I never thought I'd say this, but I don't think your site has enough bells and whistles."

Contents at a Glance

Chapter 1: Cruising Around the Dreamweaver CS4 Workspace

In This Chapter

✔ Getting to know the Dreamweaver workspace

✔ Understanding the panels and Properties inspector

✔ Setting Dreamweaver preferences

✔ Finding help in the Help files, tutorials, and Reference panel

A basic understanding of the Dreamweaver workspace can greatly assist you with using the program. If you're familiar with Dreamweaver but new to Dreamweaver CS4, use this chapter as a review of the workspace basics.

This chapter provides a general overview of the workspace and Document window, a review of the panels and Properties inspector, a quick look at setting preferences, and tips on how and where to find Dreamweaver help.

Choosing a Workspace Layout

When launching Dreamweaver for the very first time, the program automatically opens and displays the newly updated default Designer layout. After the program is open, you can switch to any of the other available layout options through Dreamweaver's Window➪Workspace Layout menu, or by clicking on the new Workspace Switcher menu button on the workspace's Application bar.

With the release of CS4 (which uses the new OS Widget Library (OWL) interface that is darker gray and more angular than prior versions of Dreamweaver), the workspace options are now nearly identical for both Windows and Macintosh platforms. The only slight differences include the location of the main menu, some keyboard shortcuts, the order and placement of items on the new Application bar, and an integrated workspace area for the Mac that completely hides the desktop, as indicated in Table 1-1.

Table 1-1   Windows versus Mac Workspace Differences

Description	Windows	Macintosh
Location and order of contents on the new Application Bar	At the top of the application window, includes an App icon, Workspace Switcher button, Main Menus, App Controls (Layout Widget, Site Control, Web Widget, Workspace Switcher, and UI Search Field), and right-aligned OS Window Controls	At the top of the application window, includes an App icon, Workspace Switcher button, App Controls (Layout Widget, Site Control, Web Widget, Workspace Switcher, and UI Search Field), and left-aligned OS Window Controls
Location of Main Menu	Moved to inside the Application Bar	Still located at the top of the Main monitor
Integrated workspace with no desktop visibility	Yes	Yes

With this new integrated workspace, all Dreamweaver users, regardless of platform, now have equal access to the same workspace layouts! Here's a closer look at each of the different layout options:

✦ **App Developer:** Select this layout to have the Databases, Bindings, Behaviors, Files, Assets, and Snippets panels docked on the left with the Document window displaying in the center and no Properties inspector.

✦ **App Developer Plus:** Select this layout to have the App Developer panels mentioned above docked on the left, the Document window set to Split Code view in the center, the Properties inspector below the code, and the iconic view of the Insert, CSS Styles, and AP Elements panels docked along the right. Click the double arrows at the top of the panel dock to expand and collapse the panel as needed.

✦ **Classic:** This layout most closely mirrors the default Designer layout setup from previous CS versions of Dreamweaver. The right edge of the screen displays the docked panels, while the rest of the workspace is composed of the Insert panel across the top, the Document window in Split Code view below that, and the Properties inspector along the bottom. In all other CS4 layouts, the Insert panel opens inside at the top of the dock area. Remember, all the panels can be docked and undocked (free floating) giving you the flexibility of setting up your workspace to your liking.

✦ **Coder:** Select this layout to have the Files, Assets, and Snippets panel groups display on the left — similar to Macromedia HomeSite, Macromedia ColdFusion Studio, and other programming software applications — with the Document window display in Code view in the center of the screen.

✦ **Coder Plus:** Identical to the Coder but also includes the iconic view of the Insert, CSS Styles, and AP Elements panels docked along the right.

✦ **Designer:** Select this layout to have the Insert, CSS Styles, AP Elements, Files, and Assets panels docked on the right with the Document window in Split code view in the center, and the Properties inspector along the bottom.

✦ **Designer Compact:** Select this layout to have the iconic Insert, CSS Styles, AP Elements, Files, and Assets panels docked along the right, with the Document window in Split code view in the center, and the Properties inspector along the bottom.

✦ **Dual Screen:** Select this layout if you have a secondary monitor to the left or right of your primary monitor. Initially the panel dock displays on the left monitor while the Document window and code view display on the right; however, you can customize this setup if you prefer working with a different configuration.

Each of these workspace layouts are designed to assist you with particular tasks. Choose an Application Developer layout if you'll be developing applications, select a Coder option if you'll be working only with code, select a Designer layout if you'll be working with the WYSIWYG editor (Design view) and Code editor, pick the Classic option if you're already a Dreamweaver user but not ready to start using the new Designer layout, and when working with two monitors, choose the Dual Screen layout. If you're still unsure of which one to use, we recommend you select the Designer option.

Getting to Know the Dreamweaver Workspace

As most Dreamweaver users are designers, we'll explore the workspace using the Designer layout, which consists of the Application bar at the top of the screen, the Document window in the center, the panel dock and panels on the right, and the Properties inspector along the bottom, as shown in Figure 1-1 for Windows and Figure 1-2 for Macintosh. All of these elements work together to assist you with adding and modifying the content in an open document.

Coding toolbar

Document toolbar   Document tab   Code view   Insert panel

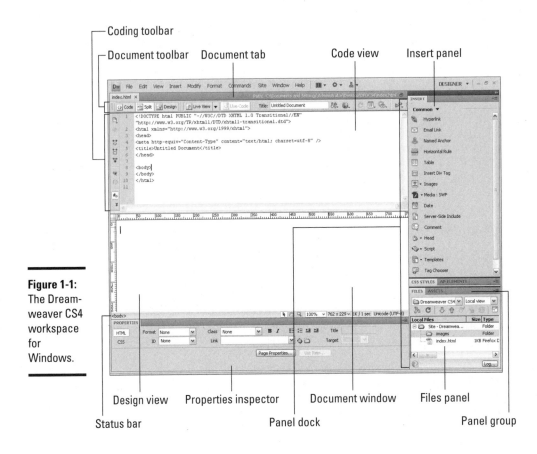

Figure 1-1:
The Dream-
weaver CS4
workspace
for
Windows.

Design view   Properties inspector   Document window   Files panel

Status bar   Panel dock   Panel group

You find these elements in the Dreamweaver workspace:

✦ **Welcome Screen:** When you launch Dreamweaver, the Welcome Screen, which is automatically enabled, appears in the open workspace area any time no files are open. The Welcome Screen (shown in Figure 1-3) contains quick links to create new documents and open recent files, and provides Web links to the Dreamweaver Exchange and to a library of Adobe training videos. In addition, you'll find links to "Getting Started" and "New Features" both of which will be helpful for new users and users seeking quick details about what's new in CS4.

Hide and show the Welcome Screen by adjusting the Show Welcome Screen check box in the General category of the Preferences dialog box. (See "Setting Dreamweaver Preferences," later in the chapter, for more on the Preferences dialog box.)

Coding toolbar

Document toolbar   Document tab   Code view   Panel dock   Insert panel

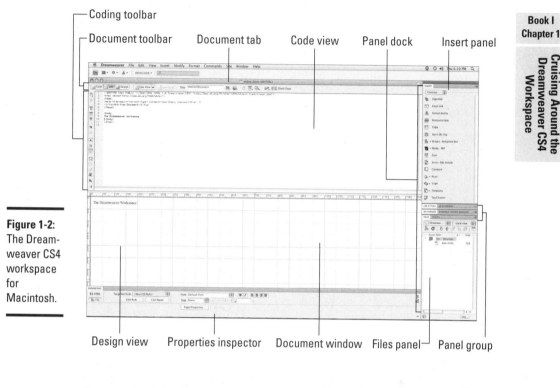

Figure 1-2:
The Dream-
weaver CS4
workspace
for
Macintosh.

Design view   Properties inspector   Document window   Files panel   Panel group

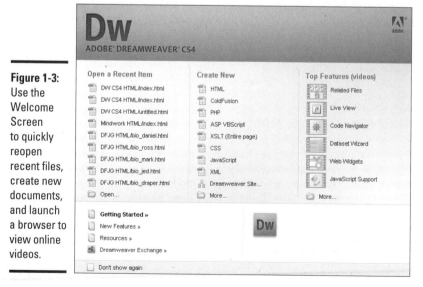

Figure 1-3:
Use the
Welcome
Screen
to quickly
reopen
recent files,
create new
documents,
and launch
a browser to
view online
videos.

✦ **Application bar:** The Application bar layout differs slightly between Windows and Mac platforms (see Figures 1-1 and 1-2), but their contents are the same. The bar includes the Dreamweaver logo, a Layout menu for selecting different code and design views, an Extend Dreamweaver button for accessing the Dreamweaver Exchange, a site button for quickly managing new and editing existing Dreamweaver sites (see Book I, Chapter 3), and a Workspace layout menu for toggling between the different workspace layout options.

✦ **Insert panel:** The Insert panel has been moved from its bar position at the top of the Document window to its own panel at the top of the panel dock. The Insert panel displays a variety of buttons for quickly adding objects such as images and tables into an open file. You can find a more in-depth description of it in the "Using the Insert panel" section, later in the chapter.

✦ **Document window:** This window shows the active document as you create and edit it. View the document in Code, Split (half code/half design), or Design view.

✦ **Document toolbar:** This toolbar is located at the top of every open document just beneath the document's title tab. The toolbar includes the Code, Split, and Design view buttons as well as quick links for other features like the new Live View and Live Code settings. For more on the different buttons and icons, check out the "Document toolbar" section, later in this chapter.

✦ **Coding toolbar:** This toolbar, which adds special quick-coding buttons to the left edge of the Code view area, are particularly useful to programmers. Shortcut buttons include options to collapse and expand lines of code, add or remove line numbers and comment tags, and highlight invalid code, among several others. Toggle this toolbar on and off by choosing View⇨Toolbars⇨Coding. Remember, the Coding toolbar is visible only in Code or Split view.

✦ **Standard toolbar:** This toolbar has shortcut links to common tasks from the File and Edit menus such as New, Open, Browse in Bridge, Save, Save All, Print, Cut, Copy, Paste, Undo, and Redo. To toggle this toolbar on and off, choose View⇨Toolbars⇨Standard.

✦ **Style Rendering toolbar:** This toolbar has shortcut buttons to show how a design would look using different media types, presuming the page uses CSS (Cascading Style Sheets) specific to those media types. For instance, the <body> tag may have different CSS attributes for handheld devices, such as a BlackBerry, versus screen media, such as a browser. The right-most button on this toolbar toggles CSS on and off in Design view. To view this toolbar, which appears in the open Document window below the Document toolbar, choose View⇨Toolbars⇨Style Rendering.

To find out more about CSS in general, see Book III, Chapter 1. To find out more about CSS for media in particular, visit the World Wide Web Consortium at www.w3.org/TR/CSS21/media.html.

✦ **Properties inspector:** The properties inspector is docked under the document window at the bottom of the screen. The contents of this inspector change according to the object or text selected in your document. Select an object in Design or Code view, and then add or change properties in the Properties inspector. See "Using the Properties inspector," later in this chapter, for a more detailed description of its capabilities.

✦ **Files panel:** Use the Files panel, located at the bottom of the panel dock, to access and manage all your site files and folders. For a more in-depth description of this panel, page ahead to "Working with the Files panel," later in this chapter.

✦ **Tag selector:** This status bar area is at the bottom of the open Document window. Here you see the hierarchy of tags around a selection or wherever you have placed the insertion point on the page. Click any tag in the Tag selector to quickly select that tag and its contents. This tool is extremely handy when adding CSS to objects in a document.

✦ **Panel groups:** Within the panel dock, related panels are combined together into a single panel group with individual tabs. A more in-depth description follows later in the chapter in the section "Accessing panels and panel groups."

Exploring the Document Window

The Document window is made up of several parts, some of which are always visible, whereas others can be toggled on and off. The following section describes features of the Document window including the Document tab bar, the Document toolbar, the rulers, grids, and guides, and the status bar.

Document tab bar

The Document tab bar is located directly under the Application bar and displays the document filename tab and path of an open file. When multiple files are open, the tabs of every open file display from left to right inside the tab bar. If you'd prefer to see the documents in a particular order, you can drag and drop them into the desired position. When space permits, the blank area to the right of the tab(s) is used to display the local path of the currently active open document. When multiple files are open and there isn't room enough to display the local path of the open file, hovering your mouse over the document's filename tab reveals the local path.

Document toolbar

The Document toolbar (shown in Figure 1-4), located at the top of every open document, just below the Application and Document tab bars displays options and details associated with the active document.

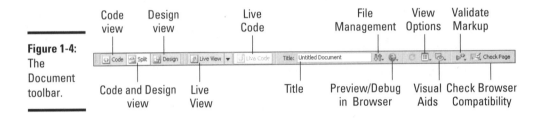

Figure 1-4:
The Document toolbar.

The Document toolbar has buttons that display different views of your page, as well as quick links for other features such as adding a page title and previewing the page in a browser. When you hover your mouse over each of them, a handy tool tip appears giving you the button's name and function. Click the buttons to select options from their submenus:

✦ **Code view:** Use this setting to hand-code and edit HTML, JavaScript, server-side coding (for example, PHP, ASP, or CFML), and other code in the open Document window. The code is colored for easier development, but you can change that as well if you are visually impaired or just prefer a certain color palette The default display font for text inside Code view is 9-pt Courier, but you can change it in the Fonts category of Dreamweaver's Preferences.

✦ **Design view:** This *WYSIWYG* (What You See Is What You Get) editor displays a visual rendering of all the code contained between the <body> tags of the open document. Manipulate text and other objects in this view by selecting, editing, and applying properties to the content. Although similar to what you see in a browser window, this view cannot display many interactive code elements, such as links or JavaScript, so be sure to test the page in a browser or use the Live View button.

✦ **Split view:** The best of both worlds, use Split view to simultaneously see both Design and Code views in the open Document window. Resize the two panes by clicking and dragging the divider bar between them.

Note: If the contents of an open document exceed the visible area of the workspace in any of the three views above, scroll bars appear to help you scroll to the hidden areas of the page.

Four additional layout options are available, but these are only accessible through the Layout menu button on the Application bar:

✦ **Split Code view:** Use Split Code view to simultaneously see two different Code views of the same open document. Both panes can be resized by clicking and dragging the divider bar between them.

✦ **Design View on Top:** Code view can sit on the top or bottom of the screen. To change the Code view position from the default location above the Design view to below it, select this option from the Application bar Layout menu or click the View Options button on the Document toolbar and select Design View on Top.

✦ **Split Vertically:** Both the Split Code and the Code and Design views can have their horizontally split panels converted to vertically split panels by selecting the Split Vertically option from the Application bar Layout menu.

✦ **Design View on Left:** After you choose Split, the code in Code and Design view appears on the left whereas Design view appears on the right side of the Document window. To flip the code view to the right side of the Document window, select Design View on Left from the Application bar Layout menu.

✦ **Live View:** New in CS4, this option allows you to see your code, along with any dynamic content, *live* in Design view by choosing View➪Live View. To help with troubleshooting display issues, use the options from the Live View menu to freeze or disable JavaScript, disable plug-ins, switch between a Testing Server for Document Source or Local Files for Document links, and access and modify the HTTP Request settings.

✦ **Live Code:** When Live View is enabled, click the Live Code button to select objects in Design view and quickly identify the corresponding code.

For more information about working with live data in Live View and Live Code, and planning dynamic pages, see Book VIII.

✦ **Title:** Enter a title for your page here, which displays in the browser's title bar. You may also type a title directly into the code.

For open documents that have been edited but not saved, Dreamweaver adds an asterisk next to the filename in the Document filename tab as a visual reminder of the document's unsaved status. Save the document, and the asterisk goes away.

✦ **File Management:** Select a function from the file management drop-down list.

✦ **Preview/Debug in Browser:** Preview or debug the open file in any browser listed in the drop-down list. Add browsers through the Preferences dialog box.

✦ **Server Debug:** Click here to see a report of the page to help with debugging in ColdFusion. This button only appears when a managed site uses a ColdFusion test server.

✦ **Refresh Design View:** Refresh the document's Design view after making changes in Code view. Code view changes don't automatically appear in Design view unless you save the file, press F5, or click this button.

✦ **View Options:** The View Options menu offers settings for turning on and off the grid, rulers, guides, and header bar, among other options. Here you can also flip the position of Design view from top to bottom with the Split view.

✦ **Visual Aids:** The Visual Aids menu lets you toggle on and off various tools to assist you with page layout including CSS Layout Box Model, CSS Layout Outlines, Table Borders, and Invisible Elements, among others.

✦ **Validate Markup:** Click this button to validate code within the current file, current site, or selected files. You can validate markup against doc-types selected in the Validator category of Dreamweaver's Preferences, and results can include the display of errors, warnings, and messages.

✦ **Check Page:** This tool checks the open file for cross-browser compatibility. The Results panel displays the errors, if any.

Rulers

Rulers, which appear along the top and left edges of the Document window, are great tools to assist you with the measurement and placement of objects in your document. Rulers can display in pixels, inches, or centimeters. The ruler's X/Y coordinates, which represent the 0/0 measurement mark for the horizontal and vertical axes and are located by default at the top-left edge of the file, can be moved to any location in the open Document window by clicking and dragging the origin square at the top-left edge of the rulers, and then releasing the origin point anywhere inside the visible Document window. The X/Y coordinates then jump to 0/0 at that new position. To reset the X/Y coordinates to the default location at the top-left edge of the Document window, choose View⇨Rulers⇨Reset Origin. Toggle rulers on and off by choosing View⇨Rulers⇨Show.

Grids

Use the grid to assist with laying out content in Design view. Because the grid lines extend in regular intervals through the entire document, from left to right and from top to bottom, you can use them as guides for exact positioning of objects in your document, as shown in Figure 1-5. For best alignment, turn on the Snap to Grid option by choosing View⇨Grid⇨Snap to Grid. Control the grid settings, such as grid coloring and spacing, with the Grid Settings dialog box by choosing View⇨Grid⇨Grid Settings. Hide and show grids by choosing View⇨Grid⇨Show Grid.

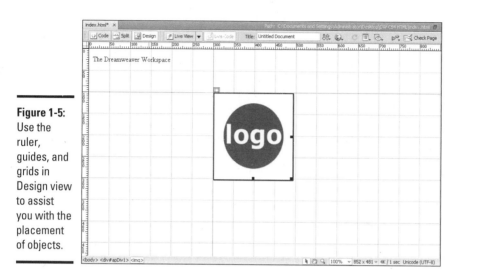

Figure 1-5:
Use the
ruler,
guides, and
grids in
Design view
to assist
you with the
placement
of objects.

Guides

Guides are horizontal and vertical guide lines that you can drag into the
open Document window to assist you with the measurement and placement of objects. For example, you may want to place the top-left edge of a
layer at exactly 150 pixels in from the left edge of the Document window. A
guide placed at the 150-pixel vertical mark with the Snap to Guide option
enabled would allow you to snap the layer to the guide at that position.
Dreamweaver's guides work like the guides in Adobe Photoshop and
Illustrator; they are visible on-screen in the work environment but aren't visible in print or on a Web page.

To create guides, first turn the rulers on (as described in the earlier section "Rulers") and then click and drag guides out from the top and left
ruler bars. When the guide is in the desired position, release the guide
onto the document. Lock or unlock guides as needed for easy repositioning or quick removal by dragging the guide back onto the ruler bar. Choose
View➪Guides➪Snap to Guides to have elements snap to guides when positioning objects, such as layers, inside the Document window. Quickly hide
and show guides by choosing View➪Guides➪Show Guides.

Status bar

Dreamweaver's Status bar (shown in Figure 1-6) includes many handy features. The Tag selector is on the bottom-left edge of the Document window
and allows for easy tag and tag content selection. On the bottom-right edge,
the status bar shows the current size (in pixels) of the Document window,
as well as a file size and estimated file opening time reflecting the file preferences for projected site visitors. For example, an open document may

display 760 x 420 and 27K/4 sec, meaning that the current page is optimized for a monitor with a resolution set to 800 x 600, has a 27K file size, and would take 4 seconds to load in a browser on a computer using a 56K modem.

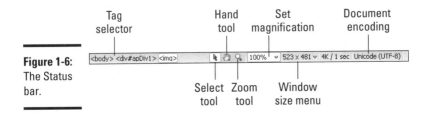

Figure 1-6:
The Status
bar.

You can resize the Document window to a predetermined size to approximate the inside of a browser window for testing purposes. On the Download Size/Download Time drop-down list, select a window size or choose the Edit Sizes option to create and save custom size settings.

In addition, the status bar includes magnification tools to assist you with editing page content:

✦ **Select tool:** Use the Select tool to select content in the Document window. This is the default tool for selecting objects in your file in Design view. For example, single-click an image to select it with the Select tool.

✦ **Hand tool:** Use the Hand tool in conjunction with a Zoom view to move the section of the page you're viewing in the Document window. For example, at 1600% view, the Hand tool allows you to reposition what you see in the Document window at that magnification.

✦ **Zoom tool:** The Zoom tool allows you to zoom in and out of the Design view window. Select the tool and click in the Document window to zoom into the page. Press Alt (Windows) or Option (Mac) and click again to zoom out. Double-click the Zoom tool button to return to 100% view.

✦ **Set Magnification menu:** The Magnification menu displays Zoom settings in percentages from 6% to 6400%. Select a preset magnification view from the drop-down list or type a number in the percentage field and click Enter (Windows) or Return (Mac) to view the page with a custom magnification.

Understanding the Panels and Properties Inspector

Dreamweaver uses panels to help you organize, select from, and modify content, as well as provide access to common features and functions. The main panels are the Insert panel, Files panel, and the Properties inspector. With the exception of the Properties inspector, all panels are located inside the panel dock area, either individually or inside a panel group. You can, however, open, resize, reposition, undock, redock, and close any of the panels and panel groups as desired.

The Panel dock

The dock is a fixed rectangular area at the left and/or right edge of the workspace (depending on your selected layout) that contains the currently open panels and panel groups. Each dock can be shown in *expanded* or *collapsed* mode by clicking on the double-arrows in dark gray bar at the top of the dock.

✦ **Expanded mode:** When the dock is expanded, the individual panels can either be individually expanded (showing the panel's contents) or collapsed (showing just the panel's tab).

✦ **Collapsed mode:** When the dock is collapsed, the panels appear in iconic mode with just an icon and panel name.

All panels have common features making them easy to understand:

✦ **Options menu:** Each panel has an Options menu at the top-right corner of the panel. Use the Options menus to access panel-specific tasks.

✦ **Expand/Collapse:** Double-click the panel tab to expand and collapse the panel or panel group window.

✦ **Repositioning:** Reposition panels by clicking and dragging on the panel tab. Panels can be reordered within a panel group, repositioned inside and outside of panel groups within the dock, and moved outside the dock to become free-floating panels.

✦ **Resizing:** To resize the height of docked panels, place your cursor on top of the divider line between two panels. When the cursor turns into a double-sided arrow, click and drag to resize the panels. To resize undocked panels, place your cursor at any edge of the panel window. When the cursor turns into a double-sided arrow, click and drag to resize the panel.

Accessing panels and panel groups

Dreamweaver has many panels to help you get the job done, most of which you can open and close via the Window menu.

Panel groups are sets of related panels combined together as separate tabbed layers on a single panel, either inside or outside the dock. Access each panel by clicking the tab at the top of the panel group. For example, the CSS panel group displays both the CSS Styles and the AP Elements panels; to see the AP Elements panel in that panel group's window, click the AP Elements tab.

Create new and modify existing panel groups by dragging and dropping panels into their new locations as desired. Expand and collapse panel groups by double-clicking on any of the tabs in the group. If docked to the right or left side of the Dreamweaver workspace, you can undock panels or entire panel groups by clicking on tab of a panel or on the gray unused area next to the panel tabs within a panel group, and dragging the panel or panel group to the new location, either inside or outside the dock.

When rearranging panels outside of the dock, panels can sometimes get hidden behind each other. If a panel marked as open on the Window menu seems to have disappeared, try choosing Window⇨Workspace Layout⇨Reset to neatly rearrange the open panels and closed any hidden and free-floating panels.

Using the Insert panel

The Insert panel (shown in Figure 1-7) has gray buttons for adding common *objects,* such as tables, images, and media, into an open document. As you hover your mouse over the buttons, the colors on them become visible. If you'd prefer to see color icons instead, select the Color Icons option from the Insert panel's options menu. Each button, when pressed, automatically adds the correct code to your page for the object or action selected. For instance, to insert an image, click the image icon (and select the desired graphic) and the appropriate HTML code is added to your page, as in <img src="logo.gif">. Though adding objects this way is fast and easy, you can also add the same objects to your page using the Insert menu.

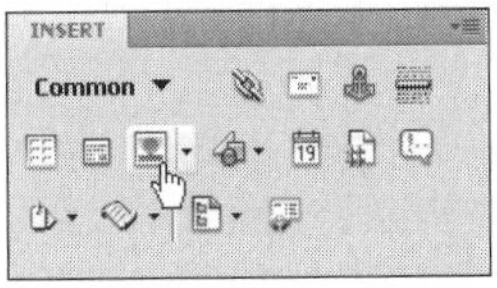

Figure 1-7:
The Insert
panel.

By default, the Insert panel displays the icons and labels for each of the options within the different available categories, such as Common, Layout, or Data. You can also choose to display the icons without the labels by selecting Hide Labels from the panel's category dropdown menu. Expand and collapse the Insert panel into and out of tab mode by double-clicking the panel's tab. The panel also has an Options menu at the top-right edge, from which you can hide and show labels and access help files.

To add any of the objects or assets in the Insert panel to an open document, select one of the categories (Common, Layout, Forms, and so on) and then do one of the following:

✦ Click a button to insert the object.

✦ Click the down arrow on a button and select an option from the button's dropdown menu.

Some of the buttons insert an object (or perform an action) automatically, whereas others open object- or action-specific dialog boxes prompting you to select a file or add attributes or parameters to the object or action. When inserting objects from the Insert panel into Code view instead of Design view, you may also encounter the Tag editor. In that case, enter the appropriate information and click OK to add the object to your page.

Using the Properties inspector

The Properties inspector is the panel to use for adding formatting and other attributes or properties to selected objects in your document.

The most versatile of all the panels, the Properties inspector's contents change according to the object or text selected in Code or Design view. For instance, when text is selected on your document, the Properties inspector displays options for adding properties to text; when a graphic is selected, the inspector displays options for adding properties to images, as shown in Figure 1-8. This works for most object selections; the main thing to remember is that you must select the desired object or content *before* adding properties.

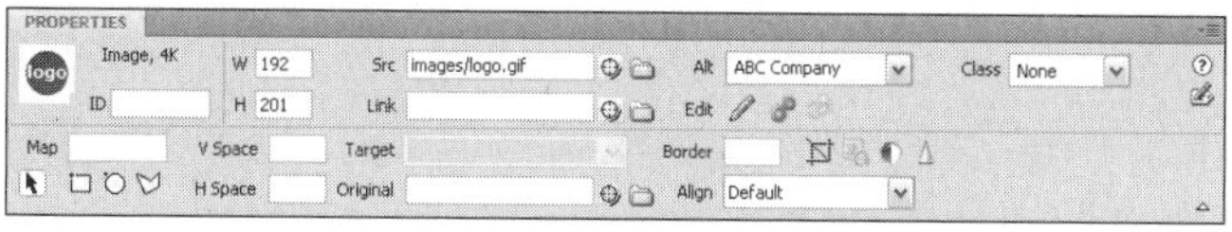

Figure 1-8:
When an image is selected, the Properties inspector displays options for adding image properties.

Working with the Files panel

Use the Files panel to manage (organize, select, and open) all your site files and folders, view both remote and local file listings, access other files on your hard drive, and manage sites within Dreamweaver.

Rather than relying upon your Explorer window (Windows) or Finder (Mac) to find and open files, create a "managed site" (see Book I, Chapter 3) for each project you work on in Dreamweaver and use the Files panel to locate and open all of your site files; your life will be much easier when you centralize this task to the Files panel.

The Files panel displays in its collapsed mode in the Designer workspace, and when displaying a "managed" site, it lists all the files and folders of the specified directory. You can also expand the panel into two panes to show both local and remote site views in one window; see the following list for details.

At the top of the Files panel, two drop-down menus assist you with site management tasks. These two menus, Site Management and Site View, are shown in Figure 1-9. Here's the lowdown on these menus:

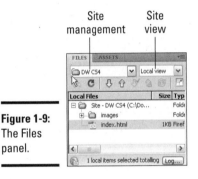

Figure 1-9:
The Files panel.

+ **Site Management:** This menu lists all the managed sites you've created in Dreamweaver. A site becomes *managed* when you define a folder on your local computer for the HTML files of a specific project, and tell Dreamweaver where to find that folder. You need to create a managed site for each project you work on in Dreamweaver. To create a new managed site, scroll down to the bottom of this menu and select Manage Sites to open the Manage Sites dialog box. For more information on creating a managed site, see Book I, Chapter 3.

+ **Site View:** When the Files panel is collapsed, use the Site View menu to toggle among four views:

  • **Local:** Select this view to see the file structure of the local managed site. You may also use this view to see both local and remote sites with the Files panel split into two panes. Use the Expand/Collapse button to toggle between viewing one and two panes. By default, the local site appears in the right pane and the remote site appears in the left, but you can modify this in the Site category of Dreamweaver's Preferences if you'd prefer having the local pane appear on the left, like many older FTP programs do.

- **Remote:** Select this view to see the file structure of the remote site. A remote site is a version of your local site sitting on a hosting server accessible from the internet. You must set up a remote site in advance to see the remote site files.

- **Testing:** This view shows a directory listing of both the testing server and local site files. You must set up a testing server in advance to see the testing server site.

- **Repository:** This feature is used when Dreamweaver is setup to use Subversion, a version control application. Selecting this options invokes the Version Control context menu, inside which files can be compared, viewed, and reverted.

Beneath the drop-down lists are a series of helpful buttons to aid with transferring files to and from a remote server. Book V, Chapter 4 covers these buttons, which are Connect/Disconnect, Refresh, Get Files, Put Files, Check Out Files, Check In Files, and Expand/Collapse.

Use the Files panel Options menu to create new files and folders by choosing File⇨New File or File⇨New Folder. New files and folders automatically are added to the bottom of the Files panel with the name *untitled* for easy renaming. To use the Files panel to quickly open a file, double-click a filename or drag and drop a file into the workspace.

In addition to the features-rich Options menu at the top of the panel, the bottom of the Files panel has a Log button to open the background file activity log, and a status bar, which displays important file data for individual selected files, such as title, creation date and time, and file size.

Customizing the Workspace

The Dreamweaver workspace is highly customizable, so you can create a work environment that best meets your needs and then save the layout for future use. The panels, for instance, are docked to their respective locations, but you can reposition and resize them by clicking and dragging them by their tabs. When you create and save a custom layout, all the panel locations, groupings, sizes, and expanded/collapsed states are saved along with the Document window and application window sizes and positions.

Here's how to work with a custom layout:

✦ To save a custom layout, choose Window⇨Workspace Layout⇨New Workspace. Give your layout a name and click OK.

✦ To open and use a saved layout, choose Window⇨Workspace Layout and then select the layout name.

✦ To rename a saved layout, choose Window➪Workspace Layout➪Manage Workspaces, select the layout from the listing in the Manage Workspace Layouts dialog box, and click the Rename button.

✦ To delete a selected layout, choose Window➪Workspace Layout➪Manage Workspaces, select the layout from the listing in the Manage Workspace Layouts dialog box, and click the Delete button.

✦ To revert a layout to its default settings and arrangement, choose Window➪Workspace Layout➪Reset.

Setting Dreamweaver Preferences

You can modify many settings in Dreamweaver's Preferences dialog box to further customize your workspace and workflow. To access the Preferences dialog box, choose Edit➪Preferences (Windows) or Dreamweaver➪Preferences (Mac).

The Preferences dialog box offers several categories for customization. Select a category from the list on the left to reveal that category's preference settings on the right side of the dialog box. Figure 1-10 shows the Preferences dialog box with the General category selected.

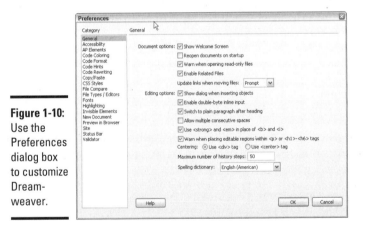

Figure 1-10: Use the Preferences dialog box to customize Dream-weaver.

Many of the category settings can stay as they are. In some instances, however, you may choose to modify the settings to improve your work experience. You can find entries throughout this book that reference the Preferences settings and suggest ways to customize specific categories.

Finding Help

We all need help from time to time and the best place to find it (for Dreamweaver, at least) is through the options inside the Help menu. There you find links that open special dialog boxes or browser windows revealing a variety of help topics. Read about these topics in more detail in the following sections.

To find help for a specific Dreamweaver feature, click the Help button, which looks like a little question mark, found in most dialog boxes and panels. Upon clicking the button, the Adobe Help Viewer window opens to display information for the most closely related topic. For instance, to find out more about setting properties on graphic files, select an image inserted in a document and then click the Help button in the Properties inspector. The Help Viewer window opens automatically to a Setting Image Properties page.

Using Dreamweaver Help (F1)

The most resourceful link on the Help menu by far is Dreamweaver Help, which launches the Dreamweaver CS4 Resources Web site where you can search for help by topic or any keyword. In addition to being extremely thorough and helpful, most results also contain quick links to related topics as well as related online resources such as tutorials and videos.

You must have a live Internet connection to access the online help files, which can be launched by choosing Help➪Dreamweaver Help, by pressing F1, or by visiting `http://help.adobe.com/en_US/Dreamweaver/10.0_ Using/index.html`.

Search the Help files by selecting a category along the left and drilling down into the topic area you want to learn more about. When you select a topic on the left, the details of the topic will appear on the right side of the window. You can also search for specific topics by typing keywords into the Search field. Results are listed by order of relevance. You may then select the topic that most matches your query to view the results of your search. In addition, when viewing a topic, use the navigation buttons to go forward and backward within the topic area.

Working with the Reference panel

The Reference panel displays reference information for all the markup languages, programming languages, accessibility standards, and CSS you can use when building your Web site.

Open this panel by choosing Help➪Reference. The panel opens as a tab within the Results panel, alongside other helpful tools, such as Search and Validation, that are covered in later chapters. Select a book from the panel's

Book drop-down list to display information from that reference book, as shown in Figure 1-11. Each entry contains descriptions and examples of the styles, tags, and objects in your code.

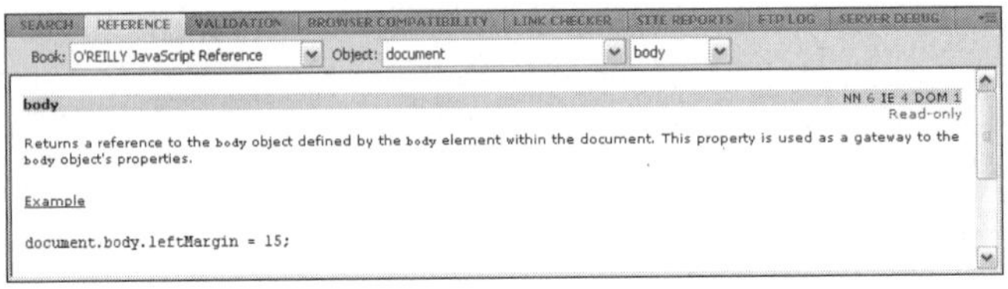

Figure 1-11:
Select a reference book.

To reference a specific tag, keyword, or attribute in Code view, do one of the following:

✦ Right-click (Windows) or Control+click (Mac) the item and choose Reference from the context menu.

✦ Place the insertion point in a tag, keyword, or attribute and press F1.

If the reference contains an example you want to copy and paste into another document, select it from the Reference panel and copy it using the context or Options menu in the panel.

Visiting the Dreamweaver Support Center

Several of the Help menu links launch browser windows for online Adobe Support for Dreamweaver users. The entire Adobe Web site gets updated regularly and includes tips, updates, examples, and detailed information on advanced topics, so check the site often.

To help you find specific destinations within Adobe's online Help Resource Center, Dreamweaver provides quick access to the following locations through the Help menu:

✦ **Spry Framework Help:** This option launches the Spry Framework for Ajax online developers guide.

✦ **ColdFusion Help:** This option launches the Adobe ColdFusion online documentation.

✦ **Dreamweaver Exchange:** Go to the Dreamweaver Exchange page where you can search for, purchase, and download free Dreamweaver extensions.

✦ **Manage Extensions:** Launch the Dreamweaver Extension Manager for help installing, removing, and submitting extensions to/from the Adobe Exchange.

✦ **Dreamweaver Support Center:** Launch the Dreamweaver Support Center Web page for searching the Adobe Dreamweaver Knowledge Base, located at www.adobe.com/support/dreamweaver/.

✦ **CSS Advisor:** Launch the CSS Advisor section of the Adobe Developer Connection Web site, where you'll find detailed information on all things CSS including browser compatibility, solutions and workarounds to common display issues, and comments from the Adobe community.

✦ **Adobe Online Forums:** Open a page providing access to several Adobe Web-based and newsreader-based online forums, where you can talk with other Dreamweaver users about Dreamweaver topics and technical issues.

✦ **Adobe Training:** Launch the Adobe Training & Certification Web page detailing authorized training and certification programs. Adobe offers self-paced and instructor-led courses, books, links to authorized continued learning facilities, and details about professional certification programs.

✦ **Registration:** Connect to the Internet to register your product online.

✦ **Updates:** Automatically connect to www.adobe.com to check for software updates.

✦ **Adobe Product Improvement Program:** Sign up for Adobe's Product Improvement program where, with your permission, Adobe automatically receives information about your usage to help with improving future versions of the software.

Chapter 2: Planning and Designing Your Site

In This Chapter

✔ Figuring out who your audience is

✔ Taking a look at the site design

✔ Adding graphics to your design

*P*utting a Web site on the Internet involves more than figuring out how to build Web pages. Creating a site that people actually use requires careful planning and design, based on site visitors' expectations and your (or your client's) Web site goals.

Planning a good Web site involves conducting market research, defining business needs, making decisions about Web-based technology, discussing search engine optimization and accessibility, gathering and organizing content, setting a budget and signing contracts, purchasing a hosting plan, and designing and optimizing graphics. Discussing all these topics in detail is beyond the scope of this book; instead, this chapter focuses on a few key aspects of Web design that you need to think about. If you want more in-depth information on Web design, check out Sue Jenkins's Web design book, *Web Design: The L Line, The Express Line to Learning* (Wiley).

Whether designing a site for yourself, your company, or freelance clients, the overall planning and design process is relatively the same. This chapter discusses knowing your audience, reviewing design considerations, and designing a successful site.

Understanding the Web Design Workflow

Building a Web site has a logical workflow. The different stages of the Web design workflow are as follows:

> Define > Design > Build > Test > Launch

Each stage requires cooperation from all parties involved — including the client, designers, and programmers — because each is responsible for different parts of the process. Table 2-1 shows who should be involved with each step of the workflow process.

Table 2-1	Web Design Workflow			
Define	Design	Build	Test	Launch

Typically, the client provides content, the designer (you) creates the design and builds the site, the programmer adds dynamic functionality, everyone gets involved in testing, and finally, the site gets published to the Internet.

Knowing Your Audience

The ultimate aim of a Web site is to meet the audience's needs and, at the same time, achieve the client's mission. Both the client and you (the designer) need to have knowledge of the target market, an understanding of the demographics of the target audience, and a good overview of the existing online competition.

Defining the client's expectations

Use the client's mission statement as a starting point to define its goals for the Web site. If the client doesn't have a mission statement, you need to ask some questions to help define the goals. For example, what does the client hope to achieve with the Web site? Here are some goals the client may have for the site:

✦ Provide information to current and potential customers

✦ Generate leads

✦ Sell products and services

✦ Provide information to the general public

When defining the Web site goals, consider the three most important aspects about the business that make it unique and beneficial to customers. The look of the site should be largely determined by the industry and Web site needs, and the organization of the site should be defined by the content being delivered.

Exploring the audience's expectations

Market research is one of the best ways to determine site visitors' expectations. Here's the information you need to assemble:

✦ The target demographic.

✦ The target visitors' Web browsing habits. Determine whether they are seeking products, information, or a consultation, or have information to share with others.

✦ The target visitor's bandwidth capabilities. Not all Internet users have access to high speed Internet, especially visitors from across the globe. If this is a consideration, a fast-loading Web page will be one of your main priorities.

✦ The target visitor's Internet browsing equipment. Some of your visitors may want to view your site on mobile devices in addition to using an Internet browser, which means you may need to develop separate mobile content or mobile-ready Web pages.

✦ The amount of money they have available to spend on the client's products or services.

✦ Whether the target audience prefers to purchase online or shop in a bricks-and-mortar store.

Collecting this information can help you determine the design direction, layout, and structure of the site. For instance, if the site is aimed at a worldwide audience, you may need to consider language and cultural issues.

You can find Web sites for every conceivable industry in the world, so a good place to start the design process when creating a new Web site is to review what's already on the Internet. Do a general online search for companies in the same industry world- or country-wide. Then do additional searches for competition in the same general geographic region, such as statewide, countywide, and citywide. Think about design, usability, budget, timeframe, and technical issues. Look at the competitors' sites and take notes about what works and what doesn't with regard to content and layout.

After gathering data about competitors' sites, draw diagrams and design ideas, write copy, and make a list of key points that the site should address. You may even want to generate a preliminary site map of all the sections of your new site based on your research of competitor's sites, client feedback, and so on. A clear understanding of the target audience helps define the site's organization and structure.

Examining Issues That Impact the Site Design

When you're designing a Web site, whether for yourself or for a client, keep in mind these three main components to any Web project:

✦ **Time:** Decide when you can deliver the job.

✦ **Cost:** Determine how much the project is going to cost.

✦ **Scope:** Determine what you hope to achieve.

Most projects begin with some kind of specific limitations with regard to these project components. One frequent limitation has to do with budget; a client may specify that they hope to pay a particular fee for a new Web site that achieves the defined scope and is delivered by a specific time. Although that may be an ideal goal, achieving all three components of the Web project may not be feasible. For example, if a project needs to be delivered in a short time frame, the project fee may need to increase, or if the client only has X dollars to pay for the project, only parts of the scope may be met. Obviously, the three Web project components have a strong dependency between them; if the project fee, time frame, and scope are in synch, all three can be achieved. However, if limits are placed on any one of the components, a compromise may need to be reached.

When you're considering the best way to transmit a message on a Web site, you need to take into account several site design considerations, including design, usability, accessibility, copyright, budget, and technicality. For instance, is the new site selling a product or service, is it a nonprofit organization, or is it a personal Web site? Decide whether the new site will be a *brochureware* site (a print brochure in Web format), or if it will have any dynamic functionality for gathering information, selling products, or providing password-protected content.

Before beginning any Web project, spend some time reflecting on the following site concepts:

- ✦ **Design:** The visual design of the page is the most important aspect of the site. Not only does the look help communicate the information contained on the page, but it also says a lot about the client, the product or service being sold, the professionalism of the person (or team) who designed it, and the site owner's level of professionalism and competence.

  The design itself should be simple with a clear navigation plan. The navigation scheme and company logo or other identifying icon should appear on every page in the same general location, allowing easy access to the home page at all times. You want visitors to move through the site easily and find what they're looking for as quickly as possible.

  Programs such as Adobe Photoshop have a ton of neat features for designing graphics and integrating into a Web site. However, sometimes beginners get carried away and lose focus on the overall design in favor of showing off the fancy effects they have learned. For instance, there is no need for text with a drop shadow, inner bevel, inner glow, outer glow, and a gradient overlay. The same applies to Adobe Flash; it's great you can create animations and buttons that fade on mouse up and mouse down, but if a visitor can't figure out how to navigate the Web site, the design will suffer.

- ✦ **Usability:** Consider in advance how users will interact with the pages and the Web site as a whole. Is the site easy to understand and navigate? Can users access information quickly and is it formatted logically in an easy-to-read way? You need to clearly define the main idea of each page.

Keep text short and to the point and include links and graphics relevant to the rest of the site. Above all, proofread the site for spelling errors and double-check links. If you have the time, consider asking another designer, a friend, or family member for their quick feedback about usability issues. Often times they may be able to point out something obvious you have missed or attempt to use a feature differently than you had imagined.

✦ **Accessibility:** Making a site accessible to people with visual, auditory, motor, and other disabilities has implications for a site's design. Consider adding text navigation links instead of (or in addition to) graphical links for visitors with browsers that don't support graphics or visitors using disability software such as speech readers and text viewers. Dreamweaver has tools that let you author accessible content. See the "Designing Web sites with accessibility" sidebar in this chapter for more information about accessibility issues.

Perhaps Ed Tittel, author of *HTML, XHTML, & CSS For Dummies* (Wiley), said it best on his book's companion Web site (`www.edtittel.com /html4d6e/index.php?option=com_content&view=article&id= 73:web-site-accessibility&catid=31:general&Itemid=41`): "If you have a small vanity site and simply don't care about making its content accessible to those with reading or vision impairments, then perhaps site accessibility doesn't matter . . . to you. But for any kind of site that may eventually wish to reach a broader audience, or whose sponsor wants to attract government business at any level (most cities, counties, states, and the feds all require their vendors to offer accessible sites to users of their products or services), accessibility isn't an option — it's a mandate."

✦ **Copyright:** Make sure that any graphics, text, music, video, and other media you add to the site is original or legally licensed to avoid copyright infringement. In other words, assume everything online is copyrighted unless otherwise stated.

✦ **Budget:** You need to know the budget defined for the project so you can appropriately allocate time to designing and building, and possibly even maintaining, the site. Extra costs may also be incurred for hosting, training, and other Web site needs. Plan, too, for the cost of the project changing scope due to revision requests by the client. Changes can also affect the timeline, so be sure to build in extra time as a cushion for the unexpected. This happens all too often so be prepared for hourly cost increases and/or contract addendums.

✦ **Technical:** You have many technical considerations when designing and building a Web site that affect how visitors experience the site, including the browsers and operating systems the site supports, whether the site will use any dynamic functionality, and whether the site requires a secure server for data protection. For instance, information collected from visitors needs to be kept secure and protected.

Also, the coding and database for the dynamic functionality, if any, depends on the Web server type (linux/unix servers use PHP/mySQL and Microsoft servers use .NET and SQL databases) so designers and developers need to plan accordingly.

Before building the site, you need to decide upon other issues that affect the overall design of the site, including monitor resolution, browser optimization, and breadth of content. We discuss these issues in detail in the sections that follow.

Monitor resolution

When visitors come to your Web site, how much of the Web site design they see in their browsers is somewhat determined by the elements within their browser, like the address bar, navigation buttons, status bar, and scroll bars, and their monitor resolution setting. Monitor resolutions can be set anywhere from 600 x 400 to 2560 x 2048. The smaller the numbers, the larger the site appears in the monitor display; the larger the numbers, the smaller the site appears.

Currently, most monitors come with a factory preset resolution of 1024 x 768 or higher. Nevertheless, because you have no control over what monitor resolutions visitors will have, consider doing some advanced market research to find out who your audience will be, and what monitor resolution they're likely to have. This information helps you determine the ultimate width of your Web site design. For a few years, the standard was to design a Web site for a monitor set to 800 x 600 resolution. However because less than 10% of all Internet traffic uses that resolution anymore, the new standard is to design for monitors optimized for 1024 x 768 and higher resolution settings. That said, because a design at 1024 x 768 pixels would be too wide to fit in a browser window with the aforementioned browser widgets, the design would need to be a little smaller — about 955 x 600 pixels — to fit without invoking horizontal scrollbars.

For a great discussion about designing for multiple screen sizes, check out the whitepaper titled "Screen Size Matters" by Catalyst Group Design at www.catalystgroupdesign.com/cofactors/upload/catalyst_ resolution_whitepaper.pdf.

TECHNICAL STUFF

Designing Web sites with accessibility

When designing Web sites, you need to consider whether the audience will include people with visual and other disabilities. If so, you should add accessibility features, such as image labels and keyboard shortcuts, to your site. Dreamweaver has the tools that let you author accessible content that complies with government guidelines. In addition, Dreamweaver supports designers who need accessibility features themselves to create accessible sites.

To turn on Accessibility features in Dreamweaver, which prompts you to add Accessibility tags and attributes to objects when they are inserted onto a page, follow these steps:

1. Choose Edit➪Preferences (Windows) or Dreamweaver➪Preferences (Mac).

   The Preferences dialog box opens.

2. Choose the Accessibility category on the left to reveal the accessibility options on the right.

3. Next to the Show Attributes When Inserting option, choose the content that you want to be prompted for.

   For example, to always be prompted to add accessibility tags or attributes to images inserted on a page, select the Images option.

4. For Web designers with disabilities who are using Dreamweaver to create Web pages, consider the following options:

Enable the Keep Focus option to access an accessibility panel after you open it. This is a good option for Web designers using screen readers who need accessibility settings to create Web pages in Dreamweaver.

Consider disabling the Off-Screen Rendering option if using a screen reader. This option is turned on by default but may cause conflicts for designers using screen readers.

5. Click OK to accept the new preferences.

In addition to these accessibility features, Dreamweaver comes with several sample Web page designs that comply to accessibility standards. To access these sample designs, choose File➪New to open the New Document dialog box, and choose an accessible page design from the Blank Page category.

If you do use accessibility settings on your Web pages, be sure to run an accessibility report to test your page or site against the government's Section 508 guidelines as part of the testing process prior to publishing your site. See Book V, Chapter 1 for more about testing.

To find out more about Accessibility initiatives, visit the Web sites for both the World Wide Web Consortium Web Accessibility Initiative (www.w3.org/wai) and Section 508 of the Federal Rehabilitation Act (www.section508.gov).

Browser optimization

Another issue to consider is browser optimization. Taking a look at browser trends can give you insight into important design considerations, such as layout size and CSS (Cascading Style Sheets) support. For example, currently the most popular browser is Internet Explorer (IE), the most used operating system is Windows XP, and the most common monitor display setting is 1024 x 768.

The W3 Schools Web site lists browser and operating system usage statistics on a monthly basis dating back to 2003. Examples are shown in Tables 2-2 and 2-3. For the most current browser optimization statistics, visit www.w3schools.com/browsers/browsers_stats.asp.

Table 2-2				Browser Usage Statistics			
2008	*IE 7*	*IE 6*	*IE 5*	*Firefox*	*Mozilla*	*Safari*	*Opera*
June	27.0%	26.5%	0.5%	41.0%	0.5%	2.6%	1.7%

Table 2-3				Operating System Usage Statistics			
2008	*Windows XP*	*Windows 2000*	*Windows 98*	*Windows Vista*	*Windows 2003*	*Linux*	*Mac*
June	74.6%	2.6%	0.2%	10.0%	1.9%	3.7%	4.8%

In a perfect world all Web sites would function flawlessly on all browsers, however this rarely happens without significant effort. There most definitely are subtle differences to how a Web site is interpreted by different browsers from the things like the actual layout and placement of images and text, font sizes, or even the functionality of forms. This fact is extremely frustrating for beginners and seasoned designers, but underlines the importance of proper testing, validation, checking compatibility and accessibility. Remember to design and test for the majority of your audience; although it would be nice if the Web site works on all browsers, spending three months past your deadline fixing bugs on a Web site for some random non-name browsers with .05% of the browser market isn't an effective use or your time.

Content

Before building a Web site, you (or your client) need to create and gather content and other site assets. Content gathering includes writing text and creating or licensing image, sound, and video files. It's important to gather these assets in advance so that you don't have to stop site development repeatedly to create or find any missing content.

Gathering content is a big undertaking, even for the smallest sites, so unless you're also being compensated by your client as the project/content manager, this process should be the *client's* sole responsibility *before the project begins;* otherwise, you may be blamed for significant delays, even though you're not the one holding up the project. Before you sign contracts, make sure you reinforce the idea that it's the client's responsibility to gather the content before you start the project timeclock. Trust us: You'll be glad you did.

After you've gathered the content, organize everything electronically in a place that's easily accessible when it comes time to build the site. For example, you may decide to create a folder on your computer called Websites, and in that folder create a subfolder for the client. Inside the client's folder, you may create several additional subfolders for all the different assets, as shown in Figure 2-1.

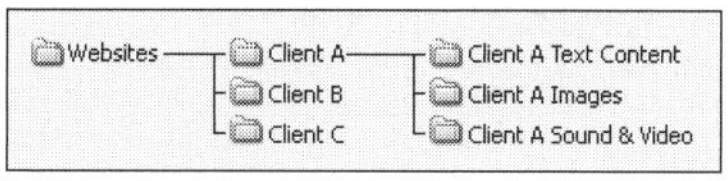

Figure 2-1:
Organize file
assets into
folders.

Planning the Site Layout

You can save time by planning and designing the site layout before working in Dreamweaver. A consistent layout and design helps create a good user experience. Site layout applies to the look of all the pages on the site, as well as how the pages are logically arranged and how they interact with each other. This phase is where you're creating the site's *architecture,* or structure.

With regard to the layout of the pages themselves, consider designing a mock-up that has fixed as well as editable areas. Dreamweaver allows you to create templates and library items for page layouts and elements that are consistent on every page. For instance, the navigation element may be at the top of every page, with an area for subnavigation on the left margin, and page-specific content in the center of the page below the navigation.

As you create the design, think about the site visitors' experience:

✦ Visitors should be able to move from page to page with ease. Therefore, navigation should be consistent throughout the site.

✦ Visitors should know where they are inside the site and how to return to the home page. Use indexes and subnavigation to assist visitors with finding information. Also provide a method for contacting the company in case a visitor wants to communicate with the company.

After you gather and organize your data, you may want to create some HTML *wireframe* pages to help organize the site's structure. A wireframe is a tree diagram or flowchart of a Web site that includes all its pages. Each wireframe indicates links between pages but doesn't typically include any reference to the design of the site or the content on any of the specific pages. You can create additional wireframes for the individual pages to assist with the organization of content on the page, in advance of having real content.

To create a wireframe for your Web site, consider using a graphics program such as Adobe Illustrator or Adobe Photoshop, or a diagramming program such as Microsoft Visio. In addition to labeling each page on the wireframe, these programs have the tools you need to customize the diagram with graphic elements, color, text, specific fonts, and other information.

To find out more about wireframes, check out the SitePoint article by Matt Beach at `www.sitepoint.com/article/wire-frame-your-site`.

After creating a wireframe and prior to building the site in Dreamweaver, you may also want to create a mock-up or *comp* of the site design on paper or in a graphics program such as Adobe Photoshop, Adobe Illustrator, or Adobe Fireworks. A key benefit to designing a mock-up in a graphics program is that after the client approves the mock-up, you can use it to generate many if not all of the graphics.

A mock-up differs from a wireframe in that the mock-up is a design of the site that contains all the graphical information for the Web site layout including company identity, navigation, headers, text, and other graphics. In other words, the mock-up should have all the elements the client has requested for the site. For instance, clients may tell you that they "want the logo on the top of the page, the navigation below that, an area for links to frequently accessed pages, and a section for a photo gallery." In response to these needs, you plan the layout of the page and the site. Then you show the mock-up to the client to make sure the design meets their needs.

Both the creation of the mockup and the wireframe/sitemap are critical elements to planning a successful Web site. Giving the client the opportunity to see the design (mockup) and the site structure (wireframe/sitemap) *before* the site gets built provides both parties with the opportunities to hash out ideas and agree upon the final design. The designer then has a good understanding of the Web site project and the exact design the client is expecting so there are no misunderstandings later on.

Designing and Optimizing Graphics

After the design is finalized, the next step is to slice and optimize graphics. *Slicing* and *optimizing* describe the process of dividing a large flat mock-up into individual pieces, or *graphics,* that are then compressed into GIF, JPEG, or PNG graphics and reassembled on the Web page, much like the pieces of a puzzle.

The number of graphics overall should be limited to ensure the page loads quickly in a browser. If you're considering rollover button functionality and other interactive features on the site, create the graphics for these elements at this stage of the process, in advance of optimization.

Before adding graphics to Web pages, you need to compress them, because in their native format (PSD, PDF, AI, EPS, TIFF, and so on), the file sizes are much too large to download over the Internet.

When compressing images for the Web, you can choose from three graphics formats: GIF, JPEG, and PNG, as shown in Table 2-4. Web browsers have widely supported GIF (Graphics Interchange Format) and JPEG (Joint Photographic Experts Group) for years: however, the PNG (Portable Network Graphic) has more recently gained in popularity and is now also widely supported. Nonetheless, due to some browser incapability issues, you may still want to be careful when using PNG files. For example, IE6 interprets transparent PNG files into a wonderful shade of baby blue!

Each format uses a different compression format to crunch data and create smaller file sizes. With all formats, the compression goal is to achieve the best image quality possible while reducing the file size. Fortunately, because the Web displays images at low resolution (72 ppi or *pixels per inch*), most of the loss in image quality from the compression is hard to see on screen.

Table 2-4	Graphics File Formats	
Format	*Is Best For*	*What It Supports*
GIF	Images with large flat areas of color	Maximum of 256 colors (8-bit); both animation and background transparency
JPEG	Photographs and graphics with lots of color and gradient blends	Millions of colors (24-bit), but not animation or transparency
PNG	Recommended for replacing GIFs by the W3C, supports images with large flat areas of color	PNG-8, maximum of 256 colors (8-bit); PNG-24, millions of colors (48-bit); background transparency, but not animation

Use an image-compression program such as Adobe Fireworks or an old copy of Adobe ImageReady (CS2 and earlier), or the built-in compression engine within Adobe Photoshop or Adobe Illustrator as of CS3, to optimize the images. Most applications allow you to slice, optimize, and export graphic files and HTML. Other compression programs and plug-ins are also available, such as Spinwave (`www.spinwave.com`), BoxTop (`www.boxtopsoft.com`), and Equilibrium's Debabelizer (`www.equilibrium.com`).

Whichever program you choose, be sure to consult the program's Help files for further instruction on image sizing and optimization.

Chapter 3: Creating and Managing Sites

In This Chapter

✔ **Understanding how Web sites are put together**

✔ **Setting up a managed site the basic way**

✔ **Setting up a managed site with the advanced method**

✔ **Keeping track of multiple sites**

A Web site is a group of pages that are linked together and share common features such as design, content, and purpose. Dreamweaver enables you to organize all the pages and assets of your site in one convenient location. To take advantage of Dreamweaver's great site-management features, such as uploading files and managing links among many others, first you need to create a *managed* site in Dreamweaver. When managing your site, you'll likely adopt a general Web site structure and opt for either a root-level or document-level organization for your files.

In this chapter, you find out how to create a managed Web site, gain an understanding of root-level and document-level site organization, review the settings in the Site Definition dialog box, and discover how easy it is to manage multiple sites in Dreamweaver.

Understanding General Web Site Structure

Before you manage your first Dreamweaver Web site, you need to be familiar with the general Web site structure and have a basic understanding of the different types of root level organization, as discussed in the sections that follow.

Web site structure

Web sites typically consist of two or three basic parts:

✦ **The local folder:** This folder, also called the *local root folder*, holds all the files, images, and other assets of a managed site. The root level, simply put, is the top level or starting point a browser uses for finding objects within a Web site. The local folder typically sits somewhere on your computer's hard drive, though it may also be on a mapped drive or network server. Wherever it resides, you must specify the location of the local root folder in the Site Definition dialog box (see Book V, Chapter 3).

✦ **The remote folder:** This folder is where you publish your site, typically on a remote Web server. For example, when you purchase a Web hosting plan, you're essentially renting a parking space for your Web site in the virtual parking lot of the Internet. That space is on the host's remote Web server. You'll be transferring files to the remote folder from the local folder to ensure the published Web site is functional and up to date. You can choose from many options when you're setting up the remote folder. See Book V, Chapter 3 for more info on setting up a remote folder.

✦ **The testing server folder:** This folder is where Dreamweaver processes dynamic data to create dynamic content and connect with a database while you create and test your site. Your testing server can be on the local computer, a development or staging server, or a production server. We don't recommend that you use the remote folder for the testing server folder because you can run into some problems. See Book VII, Chapter 1 to set up your testing server.

Root-level organization

After deciding on the general Web site structure for your site, the next step is to determine how to organize and link the files to one another relative to the *root* (top-level) folder.

Each page on a Web site has its own unique address or URL (Uniform Resource Locator), such as `http://www.adobe.com/products/dream weaver/index.html`. When you make a *local link* (a link from one file to another on the same site), however, you don't generally need to specify the entire URL of the file you're linking to. Instead, you just need to set the relative path, which is the path from the current file or the site's root folder to the linked file. For instance, to link from an about.html page to a contact.html page, both of which sit at the root level of a URL, the local link code would look like this: `<a href="contact.html">Contact Us</a>`.

You can use three types of link paths:

✦ **Document-relative paths:** This type of link specifies the path and name of the document being linked to, such as about.html or photogallery/ MollySurfing.html. The general idea behind document-relative paths is that you don't need to add the *absolute* (full) URL including http:// for them to work because all the files being linked to reside either at the root level or inside a subfolder of the local root folder.

Using the Pacific Surf site structure shown in Figure 3-1 to create a document-relative path to a file inside a subfolder at the root level, add a forward slash after the folder name containing the file you want to link to, as in the path

```
photogallery/MollySurfing.html
```

Figure 3-1:
This site
uses
document
relative
paths.

```
☐ 📁 Site - Pacific Surf
  ⊞ 📁 images
  ⊞ 📁 Library
  ☐ 📁 photogallery
        📄 JasmineSmiling.html
        📄 JasmineSurfing.html
        📄 KimAndJeff.html
        📄 MollySurfing.html
  ⊞ 📁 Templates
        📄 about.html
        📄 contact.html
        📄 index.html
```

This path tells the browser to move down a level in the folder hierarchy, from the root level into the photogallery folder to find a file called MollySurfing.html. If you were then to add a text link from the MollySurfing.html page to the about.html page, you'd add two periods and a slash (`../`) before the filename, as in `../about.html`. The `..` tells the browser to move up a level in the folder hierarchy. Table 3-1 shows different folder scenarios which might help you understand the path structure a little better.

Table 3-1	Linking Explained
Link From A To B	*Link example*
From index.html to about.html	about.html
From about.html to MollySurfing.html	/photogallery/MollySurfing.html
From MollySurfing.html to KimAndJeff.html	KimAndJeff.html
From MollySurfing.html to contact.html	../contact.html

REMEMBER Be sure to save new files before creating document-relative paths to ensure that the path is saved correctly. Otherwise, you may see a temporary path starting with `file://` in the code until the file gets saved and Dreamweaver can update all the temporary paths to relative paths.

✦ **Site root-relative paths:** Links using site root-relative paths display the path and name of the document being linked to, but they direct the browser to begin searching for the path by starting at the root level of the site. To indicate this, you include a forward slash before the first folder or filename in the link code, as in the following two examples:

```
/contact.html
/services/widgets.html
```

The forward slash stands for the site's root folder. Use these paths for large sites sitting on several servers, a site that has multiple hosts, or sites that use server-side includes (SSIs), as described in Book III, Chapter 3.

✦ **Absolute paths:** An absolute path is the full URL to the linked document, as in

```
http://www.example.com/services/widgets.html
```

You must use absolute paths for files that sit on other servers, such as a link to purchase a specific *For Dummies* book from Amazon.com or a link that takes you to a particular page on a blog site. Using absolute paths is somewhat discouraged for local site pages because links on files moved from one domain name or folder location to another get broken. So unless you have a particular reason for using absolute paths, try to use document-relative paths for local links whenever possible.

Setting Up a Site with a Wizard

Setting up a managed site simply means defining a local site on your computer so that Dreamweaver knows where to save documents and find files related to that site. You'll want to create a managed site for each project that you work on so that you can open and edit site-specific files from the Files panel. Always try to define or manage a site before you start development to ensure the site takes advantage of Dreamweaver's great site management features, such as sitewide filename change support and the sitewide link checker.

Dreamweaver provides you with two easy ways to create a managed site. The Basic method uses a wizard with step-by-step prompts, and the Advanced method lets you manually set all the local, remote, and testing folder settings as well as other category options. If you're new to Dreamweaver, we encourage you to use the wizard. If you'd rather go the advanced route, check out the later section, "Setting Up a Site Using the Advanced Method," for details.

To set up a Dreamweaver site using the wizard, follow these steps:

1. **Choose Site⇨Manage Sites.**

You can also launch the wizard by selecting Manage Sites from the Site Management drop-down list in the Files panel. To bypass the Manage Sites dialog box completely, select Site⇨New Site and skip ahead to step 3.

The Manage Sites dialog box opens, as shown in Figure 3-2.

Figure 3-2:
The Manage
Sites dia-
log box.

2. **Click New, and then from the drop-down list that appears, select Site.**

   The Site Definition dialog box opens.

3. **Select the Basic tab.**

   Figure 3-3 shows the Basic Wizard. The wizard walks you through the steps for setting up a new site.

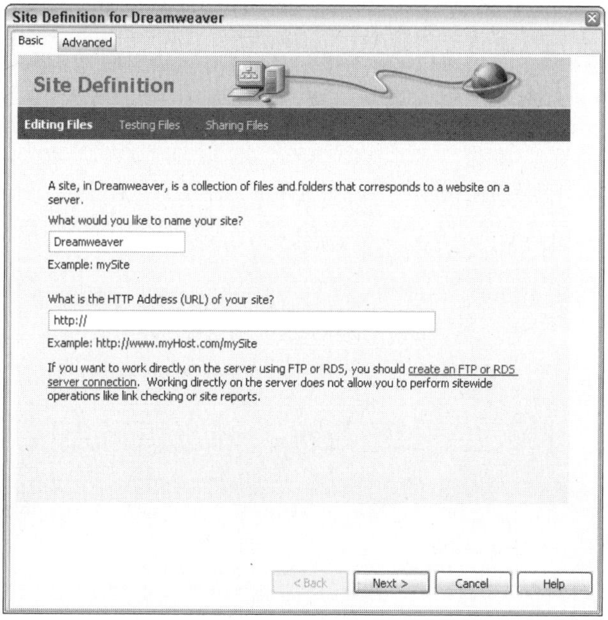

Figure 3-3:
The first screen of the Basic Wizard.

4. **Provide a name for your site and enter the site's HTTP Address (URL); then click the Next button.**

   The name you enter here is totally arbitrary and can be anything you like to help remind you what the file is called on your local computer. For instance, you may want to name the site after the client, such as Acme Widgets, or when the client name is really long (such as Dreamweaver For Dummies All-in-One Desk Reference For Dummies) use an abbreviation, such as DFDAIO.

5. **Decide whether you want to work with a server technology:**

   • No, I do not want to use a server technology: Select this option and click Next.

   • Yes, I want to use a server technology: Select a server technology from the drop-down list and click Next.

If you're unsure of whether you need this or not, click No for now. You can always come back later and add server information. For more information about choosing and setting up server technology, turn to Book V, Chapter 3.

6. **Choose whether to edit local copies of your files before uploading or work directly on the server using a local network. In addition, specify the location on your computer where the files for this site will be stored (this site's *local root folder*). Click Next.**

Though it is an option here, we do not recommend that you work or edit directly on the server, as this means you'd be changing your live Web site without testing. This is a terrible idea for beginners and experts alike.

Dreamweaver may attempt to fill in the location on your computer based on the site name you used in Step 1. If this is not what you want, click the folder icon next to the text field to browse for and select the correct folder on your local computer.

7. **Select a method of connection to your remote server. The bottom half of this screen changes to match the method you select. Click Next.**

For example, if you plan on connecting using Local/Network settings, enter the path to the folder on the server where the files will be stored.

For a complete explanation of each of these options, see Book V, Chapter 3.

8. **If you selected a remote server option, choose whether to enable the Check In/Out feature for this site. Click Next.**

When this option is enabled, only one person at a time can check files out. You must also select a method for how Dreamweaver handles files upon check-out and enter your name and e-mail address.

9. **A summary of the site settings appears, for your review, as shown in Figure 3-4.**

Use the Back button to return to a previous screen if you need to make any changes.

10. **Click the Done button to accept the settings and close the Basic Wizard.**

11. **Click the Done button in the Manage Sites dialog box.**

The Manage Sites dialog box closes, and the newly defined site in Dreamweaver opens, displaying all the existing files, if any, in the root folder in the Files panel.

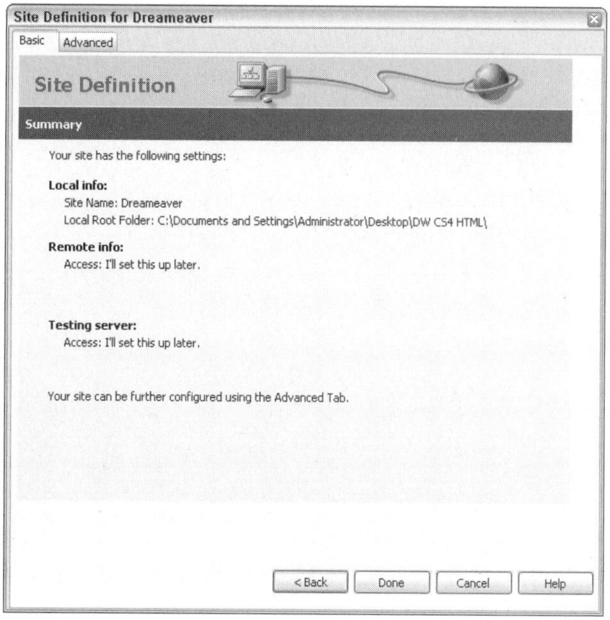

Site Definition for Dreameaver

Basic | Advanced

Site Definition

Summary

Your site has the following settings:

Local info:
　　Site Name: Dreameaver
　　Local Root Folder: C:\Documents and Settings\Administrator\Desktop\DW CS4 HTML\

Remote info:
　　Access: I'll set this up later.

Testing server:
　　Access: I'll set this up later.

Your site can be further configured using the Advanced Tab.

[< Back]　[Done]　[Cancel]　[Help]

Figure 3-4:
Review your
settings and
click Done
to accept
them.

If your server or work computer is not backed up regularly, seriously consider making a local backup copy of your site before you modify it each time. Having backups is a great practice, one that can serve you well when mistakes are made, data gets lost, or you need to revert to a previous version.

Setting Up a Site Using the Advanced Method

If you're an experienced designer, you'll probably want to use the Advanced tab of the Site Definition dialog box to specify managed-site settings. To start working quickly, you can set up just the local folder for now; you can return to the Site Definition dialog box at any time to add remote and testing folder information. That said, if you already have all the information you need to set up your site, entering everything at once may be easier.

Technically, it's only necessary to fill out the Local Info category to begin building a site and the Remote Info category if you also intend to use Dreamweaver to upload your site to a remote server. You can complete the remaining categories as needed. We discuss how to set up a remote server in Book V, Chapter 3.

To get your site up and running locally, follow these steps:

1. **Choose Site➪New Site.**

   The Site Definition dialog box opens.

2. **Select the Advanced tab.**

   The Advanced tab of the Site Definition dialog box appears, as shown in Figure 3-5.

3. **In the Site Name field, enter the name of your site.**

   Picking a name that matches the name of the client or indicates your site's purpose is best, such as ABC Company or My Blog.

4. **Verify that the Local Root Folder field points to a directory in your local Web root directory.**

   To keep your files organized, add the myblog folder (\myblog\), for example, onto the end of your Web root so that all files related to this site are in their own Web-accessible folder. This isn't required, but it keeps you from having a mess of unrelated files in your Web root.

5. **Leave the Default Images Folder field blank.**

   Because this is a new site, there is no folder created yet to store all your images inside of. You can either create that folder now, or add one later after the site is managed. Most images folders are named **images** or **img**.

Changing the link path

By default, Dreamweaver uses the document-relative path for links. If you would rather use site root-relative paths for links, you need to modify the Local Info settings during the site-management process. To change from the default document-relative path setting to site root-relative paths, follow these steps:

1. Choose Site➪Manage Sites.

   The Manage Sites dialog box opens.

2. Double-click the site you want to modify from the list.

   The Site Definition dialog box opens.

3. Click the Advanced tab at the top of the dialog box.

4. In the Local Info category, change the Links relative to setting from Document to Site Root.

This step doesn't change the paths of existing links, but does apply to any new links created in Dreamweaver.

When using site root-relative paths, the pages don't appear when you preview the files in a browser. Browsers don't recognize site roots — servers do. To preview the paths in a browser while working in Dreamweaver, choose Edit➪Preferences (Windows) or Dreamweaver➪Preferences (Mac) to open the Preferences dialog box. Then select the Preview Using Temporary File option in the Preview in Browser category.

6. **Select Document as the Links Relative To setting.**

   This option builds links in your sites that reference other files by their positions relative to the active file. It allows you to easily move your site to a different directory.

7. **In the HTTP Address field, type** http://localhost/*directoryname*, **where** *directoryname* **is the directory in your local Web root directory from Step 5**.

   For example, if you're using the directory recipe under your Web root, enter **http://localhost/myblog**.

8. **Leave the Use Case-Sensitive Link Checking check box unchecked.**

   This option tells Dreamweaver not to worry about the case of names in links.

9. **Leave the Enable Cache check box selected.**

   This option speeds up working with files in Dreamweaver.

10. **Click OK in the Site Definition dialog box.**

11. **Click the Done button in the Manage Sites dialog box.**

    Your site opens, displaying all the existing files (if any) in the root folder in the Files panel.

The following sections describe the other categories, in case you're filling them in.

Remote Info

After specifying the local folder, fill in the Remote Info category information. The remote folder is the place to store files for collaboration, testing, production, and deployment. If the Web server is running on your local computer, you don't need to set up the remote folder as long as the specified local folder points to the same file. See Book V, Chapter 3 for more info on setting up a remote folder.

Testing Server

In the Testing Server category, specify the location where you want your dynamic pages processed. In other words, this folder is an alternative location where you can test your files on a server with an identical database setup, without having to deploy the files to the live site while they're still under development. The testing server can be on your local computer, or on a staging, development, or production server. Check out Book VII, Chapter 1 if you need to set up a testing server.

Version Control

The Version Control category is where you can setup remote access to a server running Subversion software inside which the site's files can be viewed, compared, and reverted to previous versions of the site. If you're not using Subversion software for version control, ignore this setting. Otherwise, see Book V, Chapter 3 for details on Version Control set up.

Cloaking

Cloaking prevents specified files and folders from being included in a variety of site operations, such as site file synchronization between local and remote servers. For example, you may want to cloak large movie files or Design Notes folders from being uploaded each time you update site files to the remote server. For more details on how to enable site cloaking, see Book V, Chapter 3.

Design Notes

Dreamweaver lets you create and share Design Notes about site files, which are then stored in a separate location. Enable this feature when communicating within a design team or workgroup about a shared managed site. You can attach Design Notes to documents, templates, images, Flash movies, ActiveX controls, and applets. Refer to Book VI, Chapter 1 for details on Design Notes.

File View Columns

In the expanded Files panel, Dreamweaver displays file and folder details in columns next to the filenames. You can customize which file and folder details show up there by making changes to the File View Columns category. For instance, you can hide and show, add and delete, reorder, share, and rename column settings. Find out more about defining File View Columns in Book VI, Chapter 1.

Contribute

When creating a site for use with Adobe Contribute software, you must enable Contribute compatibility before administering the site in Dreamweaver. The Contribute category allows you to enter Administration settings. See Book VI, Chapters 2 and 3 for the lowdown on using Dreamweaver with Adobe Contribute.

Templates

By default, the Template Updating option is set to *not* rewrite document relative paths. To turn this feature off, deselect the check box here. To learn more about the joys of working with Templates, turn to Book III, Chapter 2.

Spry

If desired, you could specify the folder location for Spry assets. However, by default a folder named SpryAssets is preset to drop into the local root folder if and when any Spry assets are used on the site. Don't change this unless you really know what you're doing. You can learn more about working with Spry in Book IV, Chapter 2.

Managing Multiple Sites

Because you create a new managed site for each project you work on in Dreamweaver, keeping track of all your sites is relatively easy. You can view a list of all your managed sites as follows:

+ **Files panel:** The Files panel lists the files from a selected managed site. To change from viewing one site's files to another site's files, select the desired site by choosing it from the list of managed sites.

+ **Manage Sites dialog box:** Choose Site➪Manage Sites to open the Manage Sites dialog box. Select your desired site from the list and click the Done button to switch to the selected site and see that site's files listed in the Files panel. You may briefly see the Opening Site and Uploading Site Cache dialog boxes as Dreamweaver opens the selected site.

Duplicating sites

Create exact duplicate copies of any existing defined site by clicking the Duplicate button in the Manage Sites dialog box. Dreamweaver copies all the settings and creates the new site with the same filename appended with the word *copy*. For example, if duplicating a site called Company ABC, the name of the new duplicate managed site would be Company ABC copy until you rename it.

This doesn't copy the actual files. It just creates a new site setting within Dreamweaver, which you can then modify. Often, you'll also want to duplicate the local folder and all its files so you have a new copy to work on in Dreamweaver.

Exporting and importing sites

Dreamweaver allows you to save and reopen sites as XML files using the Import and Export buttons. In other words, you'll export a site with all its settings as an XML file and then import the site with the same settings later, either on the same machine or on another machine. This method is handy to get a new computer up and running with all the sites you're currently managing.

Exporting sites

To save a site as an XML file, follow these steps:

1. **Choose Site⇨Manage Sites to open the Manage Sites dialog box.**

2. **Select one or more sites and click the Export button.**

   Use Control+click (Windows) or ⌘+click (Mac) to select multiple files.

3. **Browse to, select, and save the location for the export of each site.**

   The exported file gets saved as an XML file with the .ste file extension.

Importing sites

To import previously exported XML files back into Dreamweaver, follow these steps:

1. **Choose Site⇨Manage Sites to open the Manage Sites dialog box.**

2. **Click the Import button.**

3. **Browse to and select one or more sites with the .ste file extension for importing.**

   Use Control+click (Windows) or ⌘+click (Mac) to select multiple files.

4. **Click Open to begin the importing process.**

   The Manage Sites dialog box lists the site name when the import process is complete.

Removing sites from the managed-sites list

When removing sites, keep in mind that sites listed in the Manage Sites dialog box are merely pointers to the location of files on the specified computer and not the actual files and folders themselves. Therefore, removing a site from the managed-sites list removes *only* the location information Dreamweaver needs to work on the files in the specified site.

As a backup, before you remove a managed site from the listing, you may want to export the site using the Export steps mentioned above. That way you'll have a copy handy should you ever need to import it into Dreamweaver.

To remove your site from Dreamweaver, select your site from the Manage Sites dialog box and click the Remove button. Dreamweaver gives you the *You cannot undo this action* message. Don't be unnerved; if you accidentally delete a managed site from the list, you can just re-create it.

Book II

Mastering the Basics

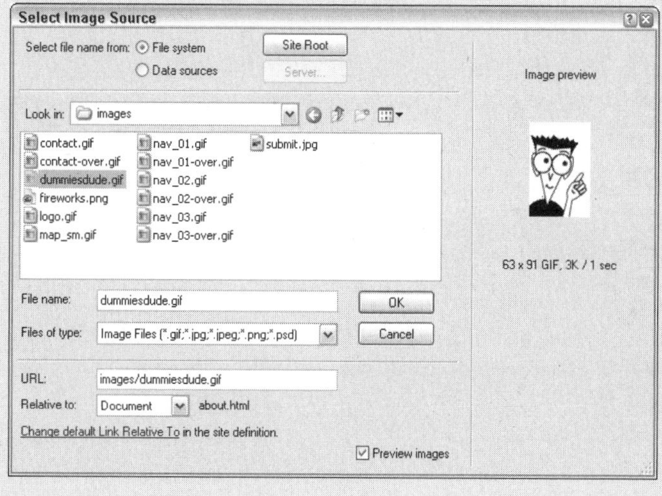

Contents at a Glance

Chapter 1: Creating Documents

C reating documents is the basis for everything you'll do for the Web. Dreamweaver provides several ways to create them, several types of new documents to choose from, and even several premade "design files" to use as starting points for your own designs.

This chapter explores document types, document creation, document saving, and document opening. You also discover how to set page properties, work with invisible page elements, and import Word and Excel files (Windows only).

Creating a New Document

In Dreamweaver CS4, as in Dreamweaver MX, MX 2004, and 8, the default Welcome Screen appears in the workspace when you launch the program. The Welcome Screen allows you to open existing files from a list of the nine most recent documents, create new files by file type (such as HTML, CSS, or PHP), jump directly to the Site Definition dialog box to manage a new site, and launch a browser to watch the top featured videos from Adobe. com. If you don't see the Welcome Screen when you launch the program, you can enable it by following the steps in the "Enabling the Welcome Screen" sidebar.

When the Welcome Screen is visible (shown in Figure 1-1), the quickest way to create a new blank document is to click one of the file types in the Create New column. Click the HTML link, for instance, and a new untitled Document window opens, complete with basic HTML structural code, ready for adding content and saving with a filename and extension.

To create a new document, follow these steps:

1. **Choose File⇨New to launch the New Document window, shown in Figure 1-2.**

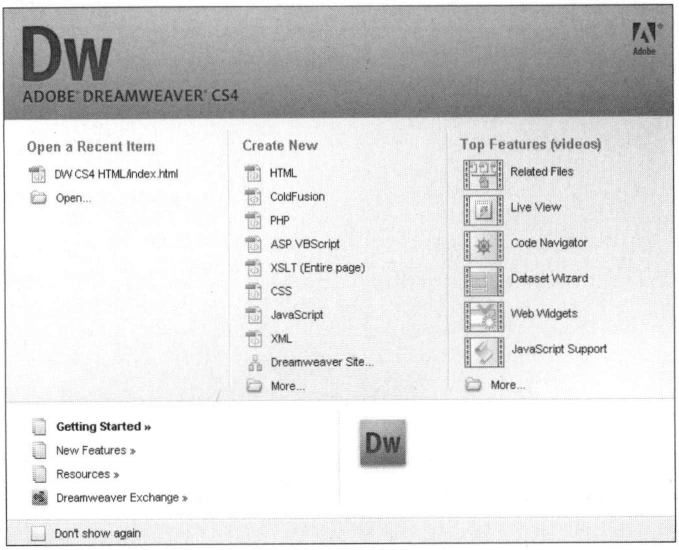

Figure 1-1:
Use the
Welcome
Screen
to quickly
create new
documents.

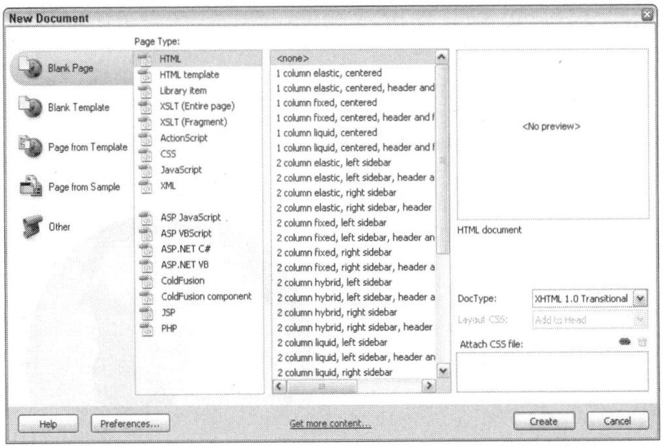

Figure 1-2:
Select a
category,
page type,
layout, and
document
type (DTD)
from the
General tab.

This dialog box is divided into various columns to assist you with selecting the desired file type, such as a blank page or page from template. In this chapter, we discuss the blank, sample, and other page options; Book III, Chapter 2 shows you how to work with templates.

2. **In the column on the left, select the type of document you want to create.**

The default document type is set to Blank Page.

3. **In the Page Type column, select the desired document type, such as HTML or CSS.**

   Take some time to explore the different layout options, when applicable, in each category. Dreamweaver supplies you with a nice group of blank documents and sample design files to use as a starting point for your own projects. For example, the Blank Page category for the HTML page type has several prewritten code layout options for you to choose from. You'll also find several CSS color schemes in the CSS Style Sheet folder of the Page from Sample category, each filled with preset colors, fonts, and sizes for you to use as is or as a starting point for further development.

   Beginners may want to select one of the preset layout options that include prewritten HTML and CSS layouts as a starting point to customizing the code. Then, later, as you get more familiar with Dreamweaver, it will be easier to create blank HTML pages and write your own CSS.

4. **(Optional) To set default document preferences for all new documents (such as document type, file extension, and encoding) click the Preferences button at the bottom of the New Document window. When finished, click OK to close the Preferences Window and continue setting options for your new document.**

   The Get More Content link at the bottom of the New Document dialog box takes you to Adobe's Exchange Web site where, after you register, you can download more design files and plug-ins to enhance your copy of Dreamweaver. (See Book IV, Chapter 2 for more on the Dreamweaver Exchange.)

5. **Select an option from the DocType (DTD) drop-down list.**

   The default document type is currently XHTML 1.0 Transitional, but you can also choose from any of the other options available in the drop-down list including the HTML 4.01 Transitional DTD.

   When a DTD is specified here, Dreamweaver automatically writes the DTD code at the top of your new document above the opening <html> tag, and at times may append the <html> tag itself, like this:

   ```
   <!DOCTYPE html PUBLIC "-//W3C//DTD XHTML 1.0 Transitional//EN" "http://
       www.w3.org/TR/xhtml1/DTD/xhtml1-transitional.dtd">
   <html xmlns="http://www.w3.org/1999/xhtml">
   ```

   If you're unsure of which one to pick, either leave the setting at XHTML 1.0 Transitional for XHTML or select the HTML 4.01 Transitional option for HTML. For a more detailed discussion of XHTML, turn to Book IV, Chapter 4.

6. **After you make all your selections from the New Document window, click the Create button.**

   The new file opens in the Document window.

Enabling the Welcome Screen

You can enable and disable the Welcome Screen through Dreamweaver's Preferences. To turn on the Welcome Screen (after disabling it by checking the Don't Show Again box at the bottom of the Welcome Screen), follow these steps:

1. Choose Edit⇨Preferences (Windows) or Dreamweaver⇨Preferences (Mac).

   The Preferences dialog box opens.

2. Select the General Category to reveal general category options.

3. Select the Show Welcome Screen check box in the Document Options area on the right. Then click OK.

Dreamweaver displays the Welcome Screen in the center of the workspace.

Saving Documents

When saving a document, give the file a unique name with the appropriate file extension and save it to the root level of the managed site folder.

To save a new file, follow these steps:

1. **Choose File⇨Save.**

The Save As dialog box opens.

Be sure you select File⇨Save and not File⇨Save As. The Save command automatically prefills the file name with the proper extension (`untitled.html`) whereas the Save As command leaves the extension off (`untitled`), forcing you to remember to add it in. If you do forget, Dreamweaver should add the extension to your file name for you.

2. **In the Save As dialog box, navigate to the folder where you want to save the new file.**

Remember to save your file in a managed Dreamweaver site. If you haven't managed your site yet, turn to Book I, Chapter 3.

3. **Type the name of your file in the File Name text box.**

When naming the file, consider using all lowercase letters and avoid using special characters such as ñ or ö, spaces, or punctuation, such as periods or slashes. Though filenames can be any length in Windows, keep filenames under 29 characters in length to avoid Mac OS issues (31 characters is the published Mac character length recommendation).

Changing the default file extensions

In versions of Dreamweaver earlier than Dreamweaver 8, the default extensions for all document types were listed in an external XML file. To change the default extension, you had to manually open the XML file and edit the code by hand. Thankfully, since Dreamweaver 8, you may now change the default HTML file extension right in the Preferences dialog box. (To change any of the other document type file extensions — though you'll probably never need to do so — you still open the XML file.)

To edit the default document type and preferences, follow these steps:

1. Choose Edit⇨Preferences (Windows) or Dreamweaver⇨Preferences (Mac) to launch the Preferences dialog box.

2. Click the New Document category on the left.

3. On the right, change the preferences as needed for default document, extension, document type definition (DTD), and encoding.

4. Click OK when you're done.

The new default file extensions work immediately for all newly created documents.

By default, Dreamweaver assigns a default file extension to your untitled document, which for HTML files can be either .html or .htm (see the "Changing the default file extensions" sidebar for instructions on setting the default file extension). Regardless of which extension you choose to work with, be consistent and use the same extension throughout your entire Web site. The extension on the filename ensures the files display correctly in a browser window. If needed, choose a different file type from the Save as Type drop-down list.

4. **Click Save.**

   After the file has been named and saved, you can continue saving new changes to the file by choosing File⇨Save. This overwrites the previously saved version with the same file name.

After you initially save your document, you have some additional options when saving it in the future. For instance, you can save a copy of the file, save several files at once, or revert to a previous version of the file, as described in the following sections.

Saving a copy of a file

You can save changes to documents after the initial save with their existing name and location, thereby overwriting the previous version of that file. You can also save a file as a copy using the Save As command.

To save a copy of the file using Save As, follow these steps:

1. **Choose File⇨Save As.**

   The Save As dialog box opens.

2. **In the Save As dialog box, navigate to the folder where you want to save a copy of the file.**

   You can save a copy of the file with the same or different filename in a new folder, or save a copy of the file with a different filename in the same folder.

3. **Enter a different filename in the File Name text box.**

4. **Click Save.**

Saving multiple documents at once

Another saving command that can often come in handy is Save All. This command saves all the open documents in the workspace with one command.

To save all the open files at once, choose File⇨Save All. If any open documents are unsaved, the Save As dialog box opens for each unsaved file. For each unsaved file, enter filenames with file extensions and navigate to the folder you want to save the file to. Then click the Save button.

If Save All is a function you intend to perform often, create a custom keyboard shortcut for the Save All command! See Book III, Chapter 4 for details.

Reverting to a previous version of a file

Inevitably, a time comes when you need to revert to the last saved version of a file. During each work session, Dreamweaver allows you to revert to the previously saved version, whether that's the state the file was in when you opened it, or the state the file was in three minutes ago when you saved your updates.

Follow these steps to refer to the previous version of a file:

1. **Choose File⇨Revert.**

   A dialog box opens and asks if you want to discard any changes you've made to the current file and revert to the previous version.

   If your Revert command is grayed out, you may have already saved the file with any updates, so there is nothing to revert to. If you haven't saved yet, however, the Revert option is selectable.

2. **Click Yes to revert; click No to cancel.**

This function works only during the current Dreamweaver session. When you close Dreamweaver and restart it, you can no longer revert to a previous version of a file.

Opening Existing Files

After creating, saving, and closing a file, you can reopen it at any time for editing in Dreamweaver. Furthermore, you can open any existing Web page or text-based file in Dreamweaver, even when it was created in another program. Other file types you can open in Dreamweaver include JavaScript (.js), CSS (.css), XML (.xml), and text files (.txt). However, you can't open Word (.doc) files directly in Dreamweaver.

Here's how to open an existing file:

1. **Choose File⇨Open.**

The Open dialog box appears.

2. **Navigate to and click the file you want to open.**

3. **Click Open.**

The file opens in the Document window. With HTML files, you can choose Code, Split, or Design view for editing purposes. However, by default, JavaScript, CSS, and text files open in Code view. (See Book I, Chapter 1 for more on these views.)

You can also open files by double-clicking the file in the Files panel or by pressing Ctrl+O (Windows) or ⌘+O (Mac) to launch the Open dialog box where you can navigate to and open a file.

If the file you open is a Microsoft Word file that's been saved as a Microsoft Word HTML file, you need to clean up the Microsoft markup. Choose Commands⇨Clean Up Word HTML to have Dreamweaver remove all the unnecessary Microsoft markup. For more information, check out Book V, Chapter 2.

**Book II
Chapter 1**

Creating Documents

Setting Page Properties

Dreamweaver lets you set the page formatting properties for a single page in the Page Properties dialog box (see Figure 1-3). Formatting options include setting the page's default appearance (font family, size, color, background color, background image, and so on) and margin spacing; define CSS link styles and headings; enter the page title, DTD, and other encoding options, and specify a tracing image. Any page can have its own property settings, and you can modify these settings at any time.

In Dreamweaver CS4, page properties settings are added to the page as either inline HTML formatting tags or as CSS (Cascading Style Sheet) markup in the head area of the page. To find out more about CSS, turn to Book III, Chapter 1.

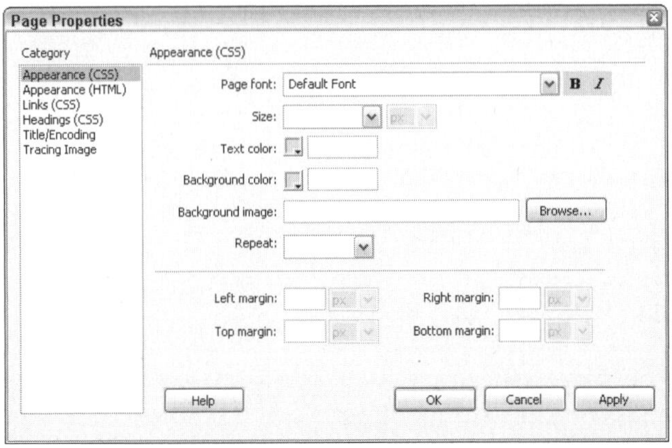

Figure 1-3:
Set the
appearance
and other
properties
of a page.

To access the Page Properties dialog box from any open document, use one of the following methods:

◆ Click the Page Properties button in the Properties inspector.

◆ Press Ctrl+J (Windows) or ⌘+J (Mac).

◆ Choose Modify⇨Page Properties.

After you open the Page Properties dialog box, select the layout and formatting properties that you need from the Appearance (CSS), Appearance (HTML), Links (CSS), Headings (CSS), Title/Encoding, and Tracing Image categories.

Understanding Invisible Page Elements

When certain HTML code, such as JavaScript or comment tags, needs to be in the body of the page even though it shouldn't be displayed in the browser, Dreamweaver hides that code in Design view with little yellow icons called *invisible elements.* That way, rather than seeing an entire swatch of JavaScript code in Design view, Dreamweaver inserts the invisible element to show where the code sits in Code view. Grab the invisibles by their icons if you need to move, edit, or delete them.

By default, about half the available invisible elements are enabled and appear in Design view when you choose View⇨Visual Aids⇨Invisible Elements. A check mark next to Invisible Elements means it's turned on; without the check, the Visual Aid is turned off.

You may notice that content in Design view shifts slightly when the invisible elements appear. Therefore, for precision with layout, you may need to toggle the invisibles on and off; if you prefer to leave them on, preview your page in a browser often to test the accuracy of the layout.

Use the settings in the Preferences dialog box to further control which invisible elements appear in Design view. For instance, you may want to show an invisible icon for named anchors but not line breaks. Table 1-1 provides a brief description of all the invisible elements.

To change the Invisible Elements preferences, follow these steps:

1. Choose Edit↷Preferences (Windows) or Dreamweaver↷Preferences (Mac).

The Preferences dialog box opens.

2. Click the Invisible Elements category.

On the right side of the dialog box, as shown in Figure 1-4, you see a list of invisible elements.

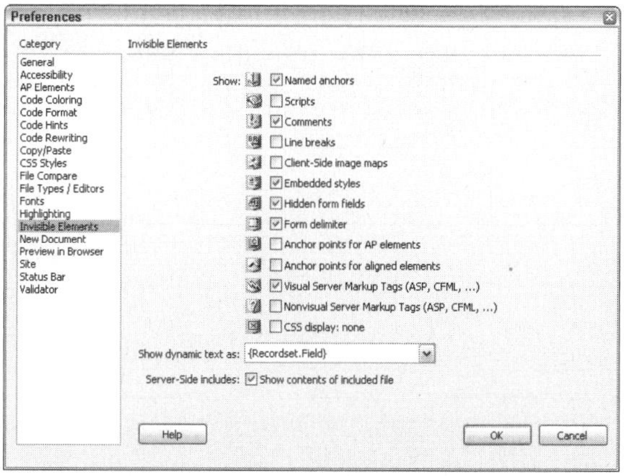

Figure 1-4:
The
Preferences
dialog box
with the
Invisible
Elements
options.

3. Place a check mark next to the name of each invisible you want to show on your pages in Design view.

4. Click OK.

Your changes take effect immediately. Modify these settings at any time by reopening the Preferences dialog box.

You can add some invisibles, like comments or named anchors, to your document with the buttons on the Common area of the Insert panel. With the invisible element selected in Design view, you can edit its contents in the Properties inspector.

Table 1-1	Invisible Elements
Invisible Element	*What Its Yellow Icon Hides in the Code*
Named Anchors	Marks the spot where each named anchor (`a name=""`) sits in the code.
Scripts	Marks the spot where JavaScript or VBScript sits in the body part of the file. The invisible element spans from the opening to closing `<script>` tags and includes the entire contents of the script. Edit the content of the script in Code view and change the language, source, and type in the Properties inspector by selecting the invisible element icon in Design view. ***Note:*** Script invisibles don't appear for inline JavaScript or JavaScript URLs.
Comments	Marks where you find HTML comments. Edit the comments in the Properties inspector by selecting the invisible element icon in Design view.
Line Breaks	Shows icons for every line break (` ` or ` `) in the code. Select the invisible element icon to move or delete the break.
Client-Side Image Maps	Marks the spot of each client-side image map in the code.
Embedded Styles	Marks the spot where CSS is embedded in the body of the file rather than in the head of the file or in an external CSS. Technically, `<style>` tags should only be in the head, although Dreamweaver lets you manually put them in the body.
Hidden Form Fields	Shows an icon for every instance of a hidden form field with the type attribute `"hidden"`.
Form Delimiter	This invisible element appears as part of the `<form>` tag and displays in Design view as a red dotted border to show where you can insert form elements. This feature is a good one to leave on, as you must insert form fields inside the dotted line for the form to work properly.
Anchor Points for AP Elements	Shows an icon to visually represent each AP element (layer) in the file. You can position the AP element itself anywhere on the page, while the icon typically sits at the top-left corner. Click the AP element icon to see the AP element's contents.
Anchor Points for Aligned Elements	Marks the spot where code can have the `align` attribute, including tables, images, plug-ins, and applets.
Visual Server Markup Tags and Non-Visual Server Markup Tags	These invisibles mark the spot where server markup tags, such as ASP and ColdFusion, sit in the code even though they don't display in the Document window.

Invisible Element	What Its Yellow Icon Hides in the Code
CSS Display: none	Shows the location of page content that has been hidden with the CSS property, display: none, in any linked or embedded CSS file.
Show Dynamic Text As	This option shows dynamic text in the format of {Recordset:Field}. To prevent long values from distorting page formatting, change the display setting here to {}.
Server-Side Includes	When enabled, this option makes pages show the contents of any SSI include file(s).

Importing Tabular Data Files

Tabular data files are delimited text files containing records that are separated or *delimited* by a specified character, such as a tab or comma, that doesn't appear in the data. You can create delimited text files with most spreadsheet and database programs such as Microsoft Excel and Access.

After you convert an Excel or database file into a delimited text file, you can import it into a Web page with Dreamweaver. During the import process, you select the delimiter type that you originally used to separate the data. The delimiter is used to separate data into individual table cells. This gives you a new level of control over your imported data that wasn't available before!

To import a tabular data file, follow these steps:

1. **Choose File⇨Import⇨Import Tabular Data.**

The Import Tabular Data dialog box opens, shown in Figure 1-5.

2. **Browse to and select the file to import.**

3. **From the Delimiter drop-down list, choose the delimiter type used when the file was saved.**

Select from Colon, Comma, Semicolon, Tab, and Other. If Other, enter the character that was used as the delimiter.

4. **(Optional) Enter other settings as desired to format the table that will hold the imported data.**

5. **Click OK.**

After importing, save your page and edit the imported data as you need.

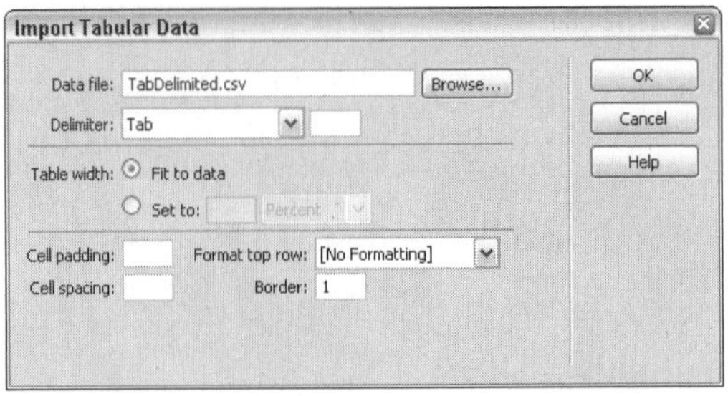

Figure 1-5:
The Import
Tabular
Data dialog
box.

Importing Word and Excel Files (Windows Only)

Windows users can import Word and Excel files right into any new or existing Dreamweaver page. During the import process, Dreamweaver automatically strips the Microsoft files of unnecessary code including style formatting and converts the content into HTML code. The only cautionary restriction is that the file must be smaller than 300K after importing.

Follow these steps to import the entire contents of a Word or Excel file:

1. **Choose File⇨Import and then choose either Word or Excel.**

2. **In the Import File dialog box, browse for and select the file to open and click Open to begin the import.**

Figure 1-6 shows the Import Word Document dialog box.

If your computer alerts you that the server is busy and that the action cannot be completed because another program is busy, click the Switch To or Retry button to correct the problem and import the file.

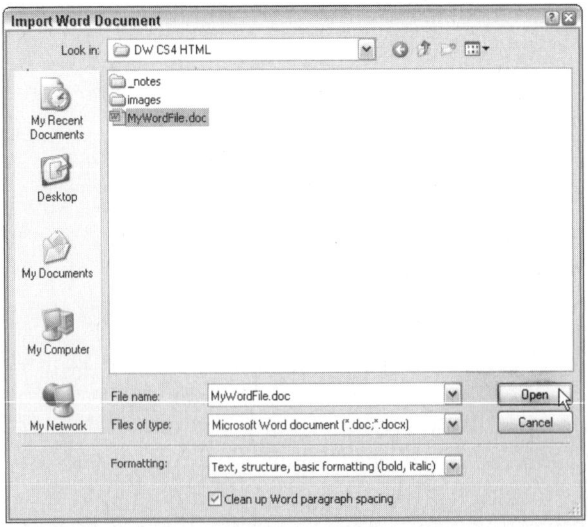

Figure 1-6:
Import a
Word file
with the
Import Word
Document
dialog box.

3. **Edit the imported data as you need.**

   You're making changes in the new document and not altering the original Microsoft file.

4. **Choose File⇨Save.**

To include only part of a Microsoft file and preserve formatting, paste the portion of the file you want directly in the Web document.

Chapter 2: Working with Text

In This Chapter

✔ Adding, editing, and removing text

✔ Inserting text with the Paste and Paste Special commands

✔ Using the Properties inspector

✔ Creating inline style sheets

✔ Creating bulleted and numbered lists

✔ Searching with Find and Replace

*A*dding text to your pages in HTML is as easy as typing in a word processing document or text editor. You can insert, change, or delete text, as well as style, order, and structure it. You can even paste text from another file into an open Dreamweaver Document window.

Text is the keystone of all Web pages. In fact, a Web page is simply a text file (that may also contain other objects, such as images and tables) that uses a set of HTML tags and CSS markup to describe to a browser how to format and display the text. Use text to describe a company's products or services, provide contact information, make important facts and figures available to visitors, tell stories, and more. In addition, text on a Web page is searchable by search engines, which means what you add to a page should be easy to read and understand.

This chapter covers everything you need to know about working with text including adding, editing, and removing copy; using the Properties inspector to create inline CSS; making lists; and using the Find and Replace tool for robust text and code editing.

Adding Text

You can type text directly into the Document window in either Design or Code view. To begin adding text in Design view, open any new or existing document and place your cursor at the point where you want to add the text; then, begin typing. In Code view, you can add text straight to the code anywhere inside the opening and closing `<body>` tags, including inside table cells, `<div>` tags, and `<span>` tags.

In Design view, when you select a word, sentence, or paragraph, the corresponding code also gets selected in Code view, and when you select content in Code view, that content also gets selected in Design view. You can switch freely between typing text in Design and Code views.

As you add text to your page and leave your mouse hovering over the workspace in Design or Code view, you may notice a small square gray icon with a ship's steering wheel appear. This is the icon for the Code Navigator tool, which pops up to provide you with quick access to the CSS rules and other code sources that affect your selection (or the content near your cursor when no selection is active). To find out more about the Code Navigator, see Book III, Chapter 1.

Editing Text

To edit text, select the text you want to edit and start typing. By selecting the text first, you automatically overwrite the text in the selection when you type. Make a selection by double-clicking a word to select the whole word, or triple-clicking a word to select an entire block of text.

When selecting with a triple-click in Design view, only the copy gets selected. However, when triple-clicking in Code view, both the content and the content's HTML container tags get selected.

If, however, the content between any two tags includes any unnecessary breaks in the text (not including <br> or <p> breaks), the triple-click in Code view only selects a single line rather than the entire content block between the two tags. If that happens, clean up the code by removing any unnecessary spacing between characters and try the triple-click again.

Text containers include <body>, <p>, <h1> through <h6>, <div>, <span>, <td>, and <li> among others. If a paragraph of text is contained inside a paragraph tag, the opening and closing <p> tags aren't selected along with the text in Design view, but they are selected in Code view, as shown in the following examples.

When triple-clicking a word inside a paragraph in Design view:

```
Hot cross buns! Hot cross buns! One a penny two a penny - Hot cross buns!
```

When triple-clicking a word inside a paragraph in Code view with no unnecessary breaks in the content:

```
<p>Hot cross buns! Hot cross buns! One a penny two a penny - Hot cross buns!</p>
```

When triple-clicking a word inside a paragraph in Code view with an unnecessary break in the content, in this case the break is after the second instance of the word *buns!*:

```
<p>Hot cross buns! Hot cross buns!
```

Removing Text

To remove text, select it and delete it by pressing Delete or Backspace on the keyboard or by choosing Edit⇨Clear or Edit⇨Cut from the main menu to clear or cut the selection. The keyboard shortcut for the Cut command is Ctrl+X (Windows) or ⌘+X (Mac)Pasting Text from Another File

When pasting data into Dreamweaver from a Word document, Web site, or other word processing file, Dreamweaver often preserves that document's formatting when you use the regular Paste command. Formatting, including font face, size, and alignment, transfers to the file with the copied text. If you want to preserve formatting, choose Copy⇨Paste.

On the other hand, if you want to have some control over how the pasted copy gets formatted, follow these steps:

1. **Copy the text you want to paste and then choose Copy⇨Paste Special.**

The Paste Special dialog box opens, as shown in Figure 2-1.

2. **Select one of the following paste options:**

- **Text only:** Paste the copied text as unformatted text. Any formatting attributes copied from the original source file, including line and paragraph breaks, bold or italics, font size, and font color, is stripped.

- **Text with structure:** Paste the copied text with its existing paragraph structure, including line and paragraph breaks, lists, and tables. Its formatting attributes, such as bold or italics, are not included.

- **Text with structure plus basic formatting:** Paste the copied text with pre-existing structure and HTML formatting, including paragraphs, line breaks, and tables, and basic text markup using tags such as `<h1>`, `<strong>`, `<em>`, and `<hr>`.

- **Text with structure plus full formatting:** Paste the copied text into Dreamweaver with all its original structure, HTML formatting, and pre-existing internal CSS data. This option does not include the copying of styles that come from sources external to the copied file, such as an external CSS file, or from any programs that don't allow style information to be copied to the Clipboard.

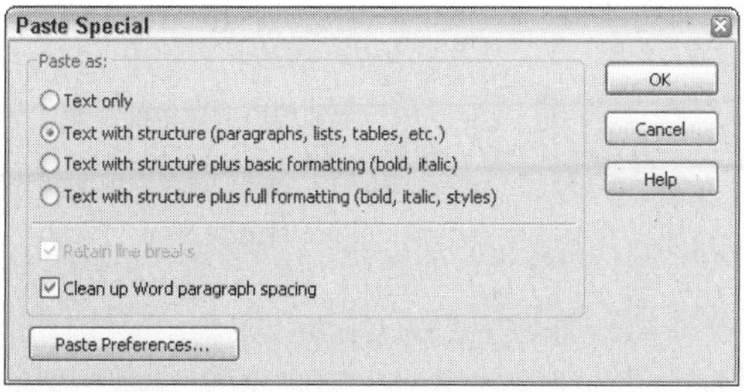

**Book II
Chapter 2**

Working with Text

Figure 2-1:
Set formatting preferences for pasted text.

3. **Check the Retain Line Breaks option.**

   Enable this option to keep pre-existing line breaks, or disable this option to remove the unwanted line breaks that some applications add at the ends of each line of text. This option is not available for the Text Only option. Note: If this option is grayed out, click the Paste Preferences button to edit the default settings in the Copy/Paste category of the Preferences dialog box.

4. **Check the Clean Up Word Paragraph Spacing option.**

   Enable this option when using the Text with Structure and Text with Structure plus Basic Formatting options to remove extra spaces between paragraphs in the pasted text.

5. **Click OK.**

   The copied text is pasted into your document with the selected settings.

The paste preferences you select in the Paste Special dialog box remain in effect until you change them, so feel free to change them as often as needed.

Setting Text Properties in the Properties Inspector

The Properties inspector is context specific, so when you're adding text to the page, it displays options for formatting and linking text. The Properties inspector has two different tabs or views; one for HTML and one for CSS. To toggle between the two tabs, click the HTML or CSS button at the left edge of the panel.

Within the HTML tab, as shown in Figure 2-2, you can specify font format such as Paragraph or H1, add bold or italics tags, set a CSS class or ID, create lists, indent or outdent text, and enter hyperlink information. These settings, or *styles*, are applied immediately to selected content, and you can change them at any time.

Figure 2-2:
The Properties inspector displays HTML formatting options for selected text.

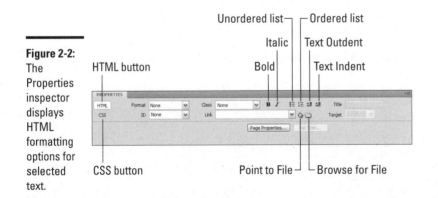

In the CSS tab, shown in Figure 2-3, settings include specifying a targeted rule, selecting the font family, size, and color, adding bold or italics, and setting font alignment. You can also quickly access a CSS rule in the CSS Styles panel for any selected content by clicking the CSS Panel button, and edit that rule, if desired, by clicking the Edit Rule button.

When you add Bold or Italic formatting by clicking the B or I button in the Properties inspector, Dreamweaver writes the newer standards-compliant <strong> and <em> (for emphasis) tags into the code instead of the former <b> and <i> tags. This is because <b> and <i> are formatting tags, whereas <strong> and <em> are structural tags. Both tags format text, but structural tags can also provide clues about the text's importance that can help improve search engine rankings by emphasizing important keywords or phrases as well as complying with Web accessibility guidelines to improve the way screen readers interpret text on a page with speech inflections. Though browsers still support the old <b> and <i> tags, we recommend you only use the newer <strong> and <em> tags.

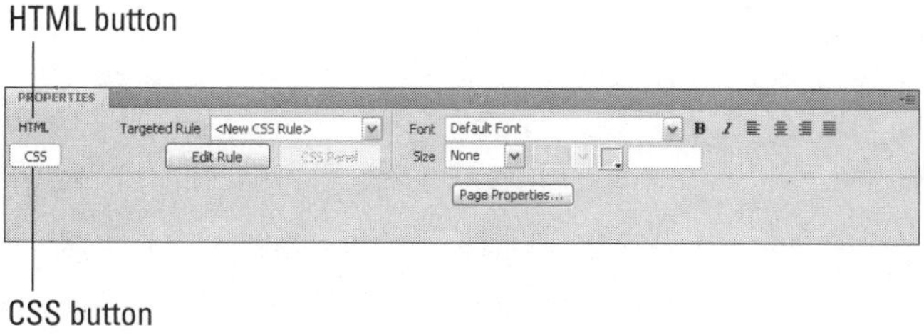

Figure 2-3:
The Properties inspector also displays CSS formatting options when text is selected.

HTML button

CSS button

PROPERTIES							
HTML	Targeted Rule	<New CSS Rule>	▾	Font	Default Font	▾	**B** *I* ≣ ≣ ≣ ≣
CSS		Edit Rule	CSS Panel	Size	None ▾	▾ ▯	
			Page Properties...				

HTML Properties Inspector

Here's an overview of the text options in the Properties inspector when the HTML tab is selected:

✦ **Format** lets you choose the paragraph style that's applied to the selected text. Styles include none, paragraph <p>, preformatted <pre>, or headings <h1> through <h6>.

✦ **ID** lets you select an ID from any linked or internal CSS style sheet. An ID identifies the contents of a tag pair with a unique name, which can then be formatted and positioned with CSS.

✦ **Class** shows a list of custom styles on the internal and/or attached external CSS, if any. Select and apply a style by name, remove a style attribute by selecting None, or launch dialog boxes to rename a style or attach an external style sheet to the open document. When no style is applied, the drop-down list appears blank or says None, and when multiple styles are applied, the drop-down list is blank.

✦ **Bold** adds the `<strong>` tags around selected text to emphasize the selection with boldness.

✦ **Italic** adds the `<em>` tags around selected text to emphasize the selection with italics.

✦ **Link** adds hypertext links to selected text or graphics. To add a link, select the text or graphic in either Design or Code view and do one of the following:

- Type the URL or filename of the link in the Link text field.

- Click the folder button to browse for and select a file by name.

- Click and drag the Point to File button onto the name of the file in the Files panel. Release the button, and Dreamweaver writes the filename in the Link text field for you. This is a great feature that both saves time and helps you avoid typos!

- Drag and drop a file from the Files panel into the Link text box.

To create a text or image link before you know what the final URL or filename will be, enter **#** or **`javascript:;`** in the Link text box.

✦ **Unordered List** converts the selected text into a bulleted list.

✦ **Ordered List** converts the selected text into a numbered list.

✦ **Text Outdent** and **Indent** uniformly apply indenting and outdenting to lists and blocks of text inside container tags such as `<p>`. Click the Indent and Outdent buttons in the Properties inspector to add and remove margin spacing evenly around the selected text. You can also apply indents and outdents from the main menu or the context menu. Indenting regular text adds the `<blockquote>` tag around a selection, while outdenting removes the tag. By contrast, clicking the Indent and Outdent buttons with list text creates sublists using `<ol>` or `<ul>` and `<li>` list tags. You can then format your multitiered lists with CSS to apply font styles and control margin spacing.

Indenting with the `<blockquote>` tag typically adds about 40 pixels of uniform padding on the left and right margins and a little extra white space above and below. For better control over your content, consider using CSS to create a custom style that indents your content without the need for `<blockquote>` tags.

✦ **Title** adds a title attribute to a selected hyperlink for enhanced accessibility for visitors using assistive devices. Titles also can be used to improve search engine listings and rankings.

✦ **Target** specifies where the linked page opens, whether in the same browser window, another browser window, or a frame inside a frameset. Without adding a target, the default setting is to open the linked page in the same browser window. Choose _blank to display the linked page in a new browser window, _self to open it in the same browser window, _parent to open the file in the parent frameset or the same frame as the link, or _top to open the file in the full browser, breaking any pre-existing frames. (Though frames aren't a best practice in web design anymore, you can learn more about using frames, see Book IV, Chapter 3). The Target option appears grayed out until you activate it by entering a link in the Link field.

✦ **List Item** allows you to specify a list type from a dialog box. For unordered lists, choose a list style of circle, disc, or square. For ordered lists, choose from numbers (1, 2, 3), upper (I, II, III) or lowercase (i, ii, iii) roman numerals, and upper (A, B, C) or lowercase (a, b, c) letters. The list item button remains grayed out until you create a list on your page and place your cursor anywhere inside, but not selecting, part of the list.

✦ **Page Properties** opens the Page Properties dialog box, from which you can modify the properties of the currently open page, including the default font face, size, and color, background color, and margin spacing. (See Book II, Chapter 1 for details on the Page Properties dialog box.)

CSS Properties Inspector

When the CSS tab on Properties inspector is selected, use the following text formatting options:

✦ **Targeted Rule** lists options in the drop-down menu for adding a new rule, and applying a CSS class, or removing a CSS class from selected text:

- **New CSS Rule:** Select to launch the New CSS Rule dialog box.

- **New Inline Style:** Select to add inline CSS style formatting to selected text using the options within the Properties inspector.

- **Remove Class:** Select to strip CSS styles applied to selected text.

- **Custom Style:** Select a custom style by its name from the list to apply the desired custom class style to selected text.

✦ **Edit Rule** launches the CSS Rule Definition dialog box for the CSS style applied to selected text (or the CSS style applied to text surrounding the current location of your cursor), inside which you may make adjustments to that CSS style.

✦ **CSS Panel** opens or expands the CSS Styles panel when it is unopened or collapsed in the panel dock area.

✦ **Font** shows a list of font sets to choose from to apply to the selected text. In a font set, if the first font is unavailable on the visitor's computer, the second font is used for onscreen display. If the second font is unavailable, the third font is used, and so on. When you select a font set, the New CSS rule dialog box will open so you can create your own custom class, tag, or ID style with the "font-family" style to your style sheet, as in "font-family: "Arial Black", Gadget, sans-serif;".

✦ **Bold** launches the New CSS Rule dialog box so you can create your own custom class, tag, or ID style with the "font-weight: bold;" style to your style sheet.

✦ **Italic** launches the New CSS Rule dialog box so you can create your own custom class, tag, or ID style with the "font-style: italic;" style to your style sheet.

✦ **Left, Center, Right,** and **Justify Align** launches the New CSS Rule dialog box so you can create your own custom class, tag, or ID style with the "text-align: left", "text-align: right", "text-align: center", or "text-align: justify" style to your style sheet. The custom style will then be automatically applied to your selection.

✦ **Size** launches the New CSS Rule dialog box so you can create your own custom class, tag, or ID style with the "font-size: n unit;" style to your style sheet, as in "font-size: 36px;" which will automatically be applied to your selection. The size can be set in pixels (px), points (pt), inches (in), centimeters (cm), millimeters (mm), picas (pc), ems (em), exs (ex), or percentages (%). Because fonts render uniformly on both platforms when specified in pixels, pixels are currently the preferred measure for specifying precise font sizes. Alternately, percentages and ems are also popular proportional sizing units.

Table 2-1 lists descriptions for all the acceptable units of measure. Enter an exact number and unit, or select from preset sizes ranging from xx-small to xx-large.

✦ **Text Color** turns the selected text to the specified RGB color by launching the New CSS Rule dialog box so you can create your own custom class, tag, or ID style with the "color: #hexvalue" style to your style sheet. The custom style will then be automatically applied to your selection. To select a hexadecimal color, type a color name, such as **aqua** into the text field next to the Text Color box, or enter a hexadecimal number, such as **#000000** for black. Click the Text Color box to pick a color from the Web-safe color palette or the System Color Picker (it's the rainbow colored circle button at the top of the Web-safe color palette).

✦ **Page Properties** opens the Page Properties dialog box, from which you can modify the CSS properties of the currently open page, including the default font face, size, and color, background color, and margin spacing in the Appearance (CSS), Appearance (HTML), Links (CSS), and Headings (CSS) categories. (See Book II, Chapter 1 for details on the Page Properties dialog box.)

Table 2-1	Units of Measure
Unit of Measure	*Description*
px	Pixels.
pt	Points. One point is equal to $1/12$ inch.
pc	Picas. A pica is equal to 12 points.
%	Percentage.
in	Inches.
cm	Centimeters.
mm	Millimeters.
em	A proportional unit of measure that equals the point size of the current font. For example, if the current font is 10 point, 1.2 em is equal to 12 points.
ex	A proportional unit of measure that equals half the point size of the current font. For example, if the current font is 10 point, 1.2 ex is equal to 6 points.

Creating Inline Styles

By default, Dreamweaver writes internal or external CSS instead of HTML to add text formatting to your pages (see Book III, Chapter 1 for a full discussion of Cascading Style Sheets).

However, you can add inline CSS styles using the New Inline Style Targeted Rule on the CSS area of the Properties inspector, which writes code similar to this:

```
<p style="font-family: Georgia, 'Times New Roman', Times, serif">This is how a
    sentence gets marked up with an inline style.</p>
```

For inline CSS style markup, set the Targeted Rule to New Inline Style, and use the Properties inspector's font, size, color, bold, italic, list, and align fields to add inline formatting to the page (as described in the preceding section). Then, if you need to add list formatting, indenting, outdenting, or a link, you can toggle to the HTML side of the Properties inspector to that information. For example, bold linked text looks like this:

```
<a href="http://www.google.com"><strong>Google</strong></a>
```

Hexadecimal numbers and the Web-safe palette

Colors on a Web page, whether used to format page properties, text, table cells, or other objects, display in a browser by using special color codes called hexadecimal numbers. These numbers are actually a set of three hexadecimal number pairs where each digit in a pair represents a value for red, green, and blue, as in #RRGGBB. A number symbol (#) always precedes the six digits when they appear in the HTML or CSS code, and each digit can have a value from 0–F (0–9 and A–F), as in #CC33FF. On the 0–F scale, 0 has a null value and F has the highest value of 15. The biggest value for any of the RGB pairs is FF, which is equal to 255 in the normal decimal system. This means, for example, that a value of #00FF00 yields the highest amount of green possible.

Web-safe colors refer to the 216 colors that can accurately display in Web browsers on both Mac and PC computers with 8-bit monitors. These browser-safe colors use only the following hexadecimal values: 00, 33, 66, 99, CC, and FF. In addition to using the hexadecimal

values, you can also specify Web-safe colors using a color name, such as **cornflowerblue, crimson,** or **plum.**

To make specifying a color in Dreamweaver easy, click in the Text Color box in the Properties inspector to choose a color from the Web-safe palette or the System Color Picker, or if you happen to know it, type the hex value or name of the color.

You can find a listing of all the acceptable color names along with a swatch with their color and hexadecimal equivalents at www. w3schools.com/html/html_ colornames.asp.

Of course, these days — with monitors capable of rendering millions of colors — using a Web-safe color is no longer the critical issue it was in the early days of the internet. Nonetheless, knowing about the Web-safe palette and understanding how to use it can really help you to use color successfully on the Web.

When choosing a font, select one that is available for any site visitor (whether using Mac OS or Windows). Here's an acceptable list of fonts to choose from when specifying the font face for your HTML text:

Arial	*Verdana*	*Helvetica*	*Times*
Times New Roman	Courier	Courier New	Georgia
Geneva	PalatinoPalatino LinotypeTahoma		
Trebuchet	Serif	Sans-serif	

For additional information about browser-safe fonts in general and a thorough list of fonts that come preinstalled in Windows and Macintosh computers, check out `www.websitenotes.com/websitenotes-37-2004` `1220BrowserSafeFonts.html` or `www.ampsoft.net/webdesign-1/` `WindowsMacFonts.html`.

To help further with font selection, Dreamweaver allows you to select *font sets* to style your text. Font sets are lists of fonts that browsers read and use to display text. The browser looks for the first font listed in the set and renders the page using that font face. If the first font listed is unavailable, the browser searches for the next font in the list, and so on. Most font sets end with either serif or sans-serif, which are standard to all computers. A typical font set is Arial, Helvetica, Sans-serif. The benefit of using font sets instead of a single font is that if a single font is not found on the computer viewing the page, the text on that page displays with the browser's default font face. With a font set, you have more control over which fonts are tried — and hopefully used — to display the text on the page.

To set the default font face, size, and color for an entire Web site, create an external Cascading Style Sheet, as described in Book III, Chapter 1.

Inserting Special Characters

From time to time, you may need to access special characters such as © or ® or ñ when typing text in the Document window. Although you could look up the HTML code for the appropriate character and then type it in Code view, Dreamweaver lets you choose many of the commonly used symbols found in other programs. All special characters are represented in HTML with a name or number. Dreamweaver calls each of these an entity. For instance, you can code the copyright symbol with `&copy;` or `&#169;`.

If you need to use the greater- and less-than brackets in your text and don't want HTML to interpret them as tags, use the entity symbols: `&gt;` for greater than (>) and `&lt;` for less than (<).

To add a special character to an open file, follow these steps:

1. **Place your cursor in the position you want to add the special character.**

   Single-click in Design view or Code view to place the insertion point in the right position.

2. **Choose Insert⇨HTML⇨Special Characters. Then from the flyout menu, choose from the list of commonly used special characters.**

3. **If you don't see the character you want to use, choose Other at the very bottom of the flyout menu.**

   The Insert Other Character dialog box, shown in Figure 2-4, appears.

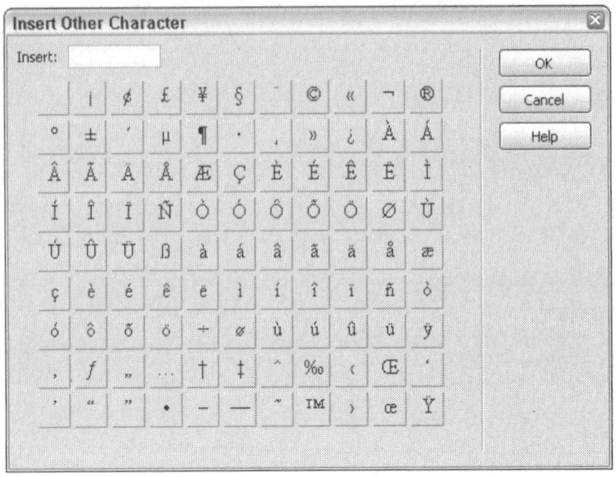

Insert Other Character

Insert: [   ]

OK
Cancel
Help

Figure 2-4:
Add special
characters
to your
page.

4. **Select the character you want and click OK to insert that character.**

   You can also copy and paste the HTML code from the Insert field at the top of the Special Characters dialog box. For instance, the HTML code for the Euro currency sign is `&#8364;`.

For a great list of commonly used unicode symbols, see `www.w3schools.com/tags/ref_entities.asp`.

Creating Lists

Lists are classified as either *unordered* or *ordered:*

+ **Unordered:** A bullet precedes all the list items. The style of the bullet can be a bullet (a solid circle), a circle (a hollow disc), or a small square. Dreamweaver only lets you choose a bullet or a square, however, so to use the circle style, you need to modify the code by hand.

   ```
   <ul type="disc|circle|square">
   ```

+ **Ordered:** The list type can be Numbered (1, 2, 3), Roman Uppercase (I, II, III), Roman Lowercase (i, ii, iii), Alphabet Uppercase (A, B, C), or Alphabet Lowercase (a, b, c).

   ```
   <ol type="A|a|I|i|1">
   ```

   In addition to the number type, ordered lists can have a starting value different than 1. For example, to start an ordered list using Alphabet uppercase at the letter J, add the start value of 10 (J is the 10th letter) to the `<ol>` tag:

   ```
   <ol type="A" start="10">
   ```

   To add a start value to a list item `<li>` tag instead of the ordered list `<ol>` tag, use the value attribute instead of the start attribute:

   ```
   <li value="10">
   ```

If you don't specify a list type, the default unordered list is bulleted with a solid circle, and the default ordered list is numbered (1, 2, 3). To learn how to customize the look of your bulleted lists with custom graphics and formatting, turn to Book III, Chapter 1.

To convert selected text into list format, follow these steps:

1. **Select the text you want to convert to a list.**

   You can also type your first entry, convert it to a list format, and then continue adding items. Dreamweaver automatically continues to format your list.

2. **Click the Unordered or Ordered List button in the HTML area of the Properties inspector.**

   The Unordered List button looks like a bulleted list, and the Ordered List button looks like a numbered list (refer to Figure 2-2).

3. **Deselect the text by clicking the cursor inside any of the list items.**

   When the list is deselected, the List Item button becomes active in the Properties inspector.

4. **Click the List Item button in the Properties inspector.**

   The List Properties dialog box opens.

5. **Select a list type.**

6. **Click OK to close the List Properties dialog box.**

To change the list type of an existing list, place your cursor anywhere inside the list and choose another list type from the List Properties dialog box. You can also convert unordered lists into ordered lists, and vice versa. The list buttons in the Properties inspector are toggle buttons allowing you to add and remove list formatting to selected text as needed.

Editing with the Find and Replace Tool

The Find and Replace dialog box is a powerful editing tool. For example, you could use the Find and Replace Tool to search for all instances of a copyright date of '2008' and replace them with '2009'. Use this feature to find and replace text or source code in a selection, in an open document, for a specified folder, or for the currently managed site. This is a great tool for replacing filenames, stripping out unnecessary tags, adding or removing site root-relative path formatting, and replacing entire blocks of code with other content.

The following sections explain how to search for specific tags and attributes, search for text in specific tags, save and reuse search strings, and search using regular expressions.

Searching for tags and attributes

The most common use of the Find and Replace tool is to search for and modify specific tags and attributes. For example, you may need to find all instances of the old `<font>` tag and strip them from the code, or you may need to find all occurrences of the word *Principle* and replace them with the word *Principal*. Whatever your need, the general find and replace method is the same. The differences are where you're searching, what you're searching for, and what you want to do with the results when you find them.

Follow these steps to search for specific tags or attributes:

1. **Open the file you want to search in, or select the document or folder you want to search in the Files panel.**

2. **Choose Edit⇨Find and Replace.**

   The Find and Replace dialog box opens, as shown in Figure 2-5.

3. **Select the files to be searched from the Find In drop-down list.** These are your options:

   • **Selected Text** searches only in text selected in the open document.

   • **Current Document** searches the open file.

   • **Open Documents** searches any file that's open in the workspace.

   • **Folder** searches only in the specified folder.

   • **Selected Files in Site** searches only the files and folders selected in the Files panel.

   • **Entire Current Local Site** searches an entire local or remote site.

4. **Select a search type from the Search drop-down list.**

   • **Source Code** searches for specific HTML code or tags.

   • **Text** searches for specific words or word combinations ignoring HTML. For example, searching for `the perfect car` would match both `the perfect car` and `the <strong>perfect </strong>car`.

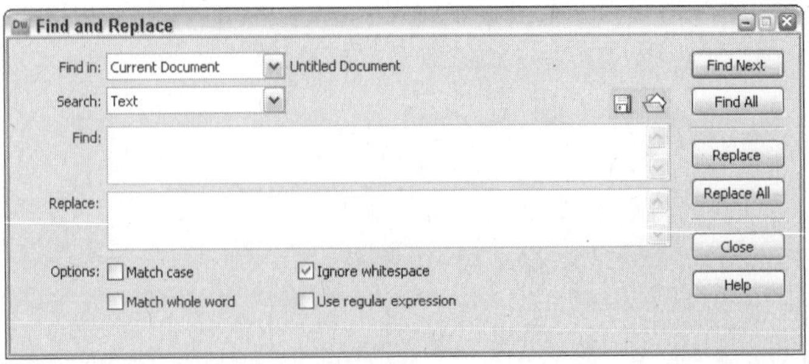

Figure 2-5:
Find and replace items including text, source, code, and specific tags.

- **Text (Advanced)** searches for specific text inside or outside of tags. For instance, searching for apple pie and specifying Inside Tag and the <b> tag would only find the first instance of the words apple pie: *I wanted to eat* <b>apple pie</b> *for breakfast but my mother told me I had to wait until dinner. Who made her the apple pie rule queen?*

- **Specific Tag** searches for specific tags, their attributes, and those attribute values, such as all <td> tags with align set to bottom: <td align="bottom">.

To search for a Return character, add line breaks in the search query by pressing Shift+Enter (Win) or Shift+Return (Mac). Just be sure to turn off the Ignore White Space option if regular expressions are not part of the search. Doing so ensures the search finds a Return and not a <br> or <p> tag.

Book II Chapter 2

Working with Text

5. **Enter additional options as needed to further define the search:**

   - **Match Case** matches upper and lowercase letters as defined. For example, if you search for Chocolate Cake, you won't find chocolate cake.

   - **Ignore Whitespace** reads any white space except <p> and <br> tags as a single space for the purposes of matching items in your search. With the option turned on, me and you would match me and you and me   and you, but not meandyou. This option is not available when using regular expressions, so if you use them, you need to write the expression to ignore white space.

   - **Match Whole Word** searches for text matching a whole word or phrase, similar to the regular expression search for strings starting and ending with \b.

   - **Use Regular Expression** forces specific characters and strings like \b or ? to be interpreted as regular expression *operators*. See the upcoming section "Using regular expressions in your searches" for more information on regular expressions.

When starting a search from within Code view, Dreamweaver may let you know that it's synchronizing views before beginning the search. If that happens, click OK to continue.

6. **Search for your text by clicking the appropriate button:**

   - **Find Next** jumps from each found instance to the next, and if searching in multiple documents, jumps from one document to the next.

   - **Find All** opens the Results panel and displays search results.

   - **Replace** replaces your search criteria with your replacement text in the To field. Click Find Next to move to the next instance.

   - **Replace All** finds all instances of your search criteria and replaces them with your replacement text in the To field.

You can't undo these commands, so be sure to perform a backup of your files prior to replacing all, or just be really, really careful that you're replacing what you want to be replacing.

7. Click the Close button when finished.

Press F3 (Windows) or ⌘+G (Mac) to search for the same criteria again without launching the Find and Replace dialog box.

You can also click the "Save Report" icon (the disk) on the search results panel and save the results as an XML file, which you can drag into Microsoft Excel and view a nice chart. This is handy for showing bosses and clients how many text items were replaced.

Searching for text in specific tags

When searching in code for specific tags, you may find including attributes is helpful as a way to narrow the search. Dreamweaver lets you search not only for specific tags, but also for the attributes of those tags and the attribute values, as shown in Figure 2-6.

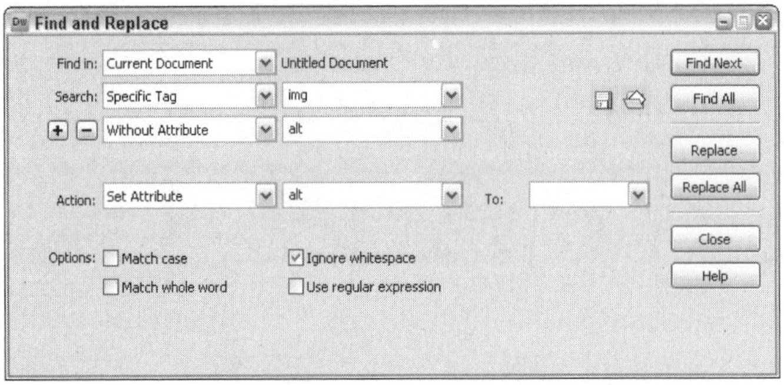

Figure 2-6: Search for attributes in specific tags.

For instance, to ensure all your images have `alt` attributes for W3 accessibility compliance, you may need to search for all the `<img>` tags without `alt` attributes. You can set parameters to add the attribute with an empty value (`alt=" "`) by leaving the To field blank.

To search for text in specific tags, follow Steps 1 through 3 from the previous section and continue with these steps:

1. From the Search drop-down list, select Specific Tag.

2. Click the plus (+) button to add a tag modifier (optional):

- **With Attribute** lets you specify the attribute type and attribute value of the tag to be a match.

- **Without Attribute** lets you specify that a particular attribute is not in the search to be considered a match.

- **Containing** lets you specify either text or a tag that must be present in the specific tag to be a match.

- **Not Containing** lets you specify that certain text or a tag must not be in the first tag to be a match.

- **Inside Tag** lets you specify that a tag must be found inside the first tag to be a match.

- **Not Inside Tag** lets you specify that a tag must not be found inside the first tag to be a match.

Note: When the search does not need any tag modifiers, click the minus (–) button to remove any pre-existing tag modifiers.

3. **To further limit the search, repeat Step 2.**

4. **If replacing content, choose an action from the Action menu and input additional information as prompted:**

   - **Replace Tag & Contents** prompts you to enter Replace With information for the new tag and contents.

   - **Replace Contents Only** prompts you to enter Replace With information for the contents of the specified tag.

   - **Remove Tag & Contents** removes the selected tag and everything in between.

   - **Strip Tag** will completely remove specified tags but not their content.

   - **Change Tag** prompts you to select another tag type from a drop-down list.

   - **Set Attribute** lets you select a tag and specify its attribute, if any.

   - **Remove Attribute** prompts you to select an attribute to be removed from the specified tag.

   - **Add Before Start Tag** lets you enter data to add before the specified start tag.

   - **Add After End Tag** lets you enter data to add after the specified end tag.

   - **Add After Start Tag** lets you enter data to add after the specified start tag.

   - **Add Before End Tag** lets you enter data to add before the specified end tag.

5. **Search for your text by clicking the appropriate button:**

   - **Find All** opens the Results panel and displays search results.

   - **Find Next** jumps from each found instance to the next, and if searching in multiple documents, jumps from one document to the next.

- **Replace** replaces your search criteria with your replacement text in the To field. Click Find Next to move to the next instance.

- **Replace All** finds all instances of your search criteria and replaces them with your replacement text in the To field.

6. **Click the Close button to exit the Find and Replace dialog box.**

Saving and reusing searches

When creating complex search parameters, you may need to reuse a search in the future. To save a search to reuse later, enter the desired search options and click the Save Query icon, which looks like a floppy disk and is located near the Find Next button. When prompted, name the search with the .dwr file extension, browse to the location where you want to save the search, and click Save.

To use a saved search, launch the Find and Replace dialog box and click the Load Query icon, which looks like an open folder with a page being filed inside it. In the Load query dialog box, navigate to the folder where you saved the search, select it, and click Open. After it's loaded, click any of the Find or Replace buttons.

Using regular expressions in your searches

Regular expressions are patterns made up of letter, symbol, and number combinations used in searches to help narrow search terms. Dreamweaver allows for use of regular expressions in your searches if you want to use them. Common regular expression characters include the following:

- ✦ /d: Matches a single digit between 0 and 9.

- ✦ ^: Matches at the start of the line.

- ✦ /b: Matches at a word boundary.

For example, to compile a search for a specific e-mail address (info@ companyname.com) in the entire Web site, your search criteria is the following:

- ✦ Look for the specific tag, in this case, <a>.

- ✦ The tag must contain text including the regular expression, in this case, ^info.

- ✦ Replace the text with the e-mail address.

Take a look at Figure 2-7 to see this search.

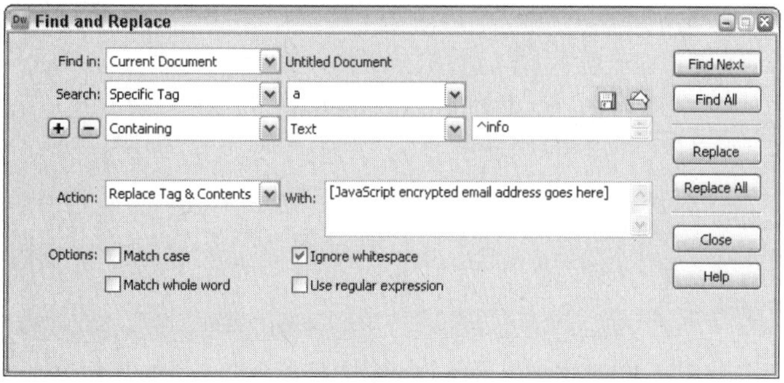

Figure 2-7:
Search
using
regular
expressions.

To find out more about regular expressions, visit `www.regular-expressions.info/` or see the "Introduction to Regular Expressions in Dreamweaver" article on the Dreamweaver Developer Center Web site at `www.adobe.com/devnet/dreamweaver/articles/regular_expressions.html`.

Chapter 3: Inserting Graphics

In This Chapter

✔ **Inserting, editing, deleting, and moving images**

✔ **Setting image attributes**

✔ **Adding interactive elements, such as rollover images and image maps**

Graphics give a Web page personality. They help create the look and feel that represents the product, service, company, or person the Web site is for. Graphics are great for navigation buttons, logos, photographs, icons, buttons, background images, illustrations, and more.

For Web sites, you're limited to certain types of graphics. The three main types of graphics supported by most browsers are GIF (pronounced JIF, like the peanut butter, though some people say GIF with a hard G as in *gate*), PNG (pronounced Ping), and JPEG or JPG (pronounced J-peg). Each format takes high-resolution images and compresses the data to keep file sizes smaller than their high-resolution counterparts. Because most browsers can only support 72 pixels per inch for on-screen display, you need to reduce your Web graphics to 72 pixels per inch. Fortunately, what is lost in resolution is made up for in reduced file sizes.

When optimizing your images for the Web, GIF and PNG-8 files are best used for graphics with large, flat areas of color with a maximum of 256 colors, while JPEGs and PNG-24s support millions of colors and are best used for photographs and images with gradients. While the PNG-24 file format is far superior to the PNG-8 format, PNG-24 files are not yet fully supported by Internet browsers. As such, this chapter limits discussion of PNG files to the PNG-8 format.

This chapter presumes your graphics are optimized in the GIF, PNG-8, or JPG format and are ready to insert into your Web page. Besides inserting images, you find out how to edit, delete, and move graphics, set image attributes such as borders, create rollover buttons and image maps, build an image-based navigation bar, and work with graphics and HTML generated in Adobe Fireworks.

Inserting Images in Your Web Page

As with many features of Dreamweaver, you have several ways to add images to a Web page. Oftentimes, the insertion method you choose is simply determined by where the mouse happens to be on-screen. For instance, if your mouse is closest to the Files panel, you'll probably insert the image from there.

 Before you begin adding images to your Web page, be sure you save all your graphics into an images folder at the root level of your managed Web site. If the folder doesn't exist yet, create it so you can place all your graphic files inside it. Organizing your graphics into a common folder can help you keep track of files as the site grows.

When inserting your images, whatever method you choose, Dreamweaver automatically writes the code for you, including the path where the image is. If the image is outside the managed site folder, Dreamweaver may prompt you to copy the graphic file into the current managed site. Furthermore, whenever the Select Image Source dialog box appears, you can select File System to pick a graphic from a folder, or choose Data Source to specify a dynamic image source.

Using the Insert panel

The easiest way to insert images is by using the Images pull-down menu on the Common category of the Insert panel. The pull-down menu remembers the last button selected and displays that button's icon, but by default, the Image button appears. To insert an image, follow these steps:

1. **Click the Insert Image menu button in the Common category of the Insert panel and select the Image button.**

The Image button looks like a little tree in a grassy field.

When the button on the menu displays the image type you need, you can click it to insert a graphic. Otherwise, use the pull-down menu to select the type of image you want to insert.

The Select Image Source dialog box opens (shown in Figure 3-1) where you can navigate to and select the graphic you want to insert. The dialog box has a panel to display the files by name and a preview area including an image preview, image dimensions, format, size, and probable loading time.

2. **Select the image you want to insert and click OK.**

The image appears on the page.

Select Image Source

Select file name from: ⊙ File system   [Site Root]
                      ○ Data sources   [Server...]

Image preview

Look in: 🗀 images

📄 contact.gif   📄 nav_01.gif   📄 submit.jpg
📄 contact-over.gif   📄 nav_01-over.gif
📄 dummiesdude.gif   📄 nav_02.gif
🖼 fireworks.png   📄 nav_02-over.gif
📄 logo.gif   📄 nav_03.gif
📄 map_sm.gif   📄 nav_03-over.gif

63 x 91 GIF, 3K / 1 sec

File name: dummiesdude.gif   [OK]
Files of type: Image Files (*.gif;*.jpg;*.jpeg;*.png;*.psd) ▾ [Cancel]

URL: images/dummiesdude.gif
Relative to: Document ▾ about.html
Change default Link Relative To in the site definition.
                                    ☑ Preview images

Figure 3-1:
Use the Select Image Source dialog box to select an image to insert.

If you have Accessibility options activated in Dreamweaver's Preferences, the Image Tag Accessibility Attributes dialog box appears to add accessibility attributes for Alternate text and a long description. Enter one or both accessibility attributes. At the minimum, it's highly recommended that you add Alternate text to describe the image in 50 characters or less. The Alt attribute you enter is read by browser screen-reader software used by the visually impaired. For the long description, enter a filename or URL to a page that has a longer description of that image. Then click OK. To bypass Accessibility options and insert the image, click Cancel. To discover more about designing Web sites with accessibility, see Book I, Chapter 2.

You can also drag and drop the Image button from the Insert panel into the open file in either Design or Code view. Believe it or not, you can even drag and drop an image from the desktop into an open Dreamweaver document.

When working in an unsaved file, Dreamweaver writes a `file:///` reference to the image, but converts that reference to the document-relative path upon saving the file. For instance, before saving your file, the image path may look like this:

```
<img src="file:///C|/Documents and Settings/Administrator/My Documents/ Clients/
    ClientX_HTML/images/logo.gif" width="200" height="200" alt="logo" />
```

But after saving the file, the path may look like this:

```
<img src="images/logo.gif" width="200" height="200" alt="logo" />
```

Using the Insert menu

Use the Insert menu as an alternate method of inserting images. Choose Insert⇨Image to insert an image. As with the Insert panel method described in the preceding section, navigate to and pick the image to insert from the Select Image Source dialog box.

Using the Assets panel

To use the Assets panel to insert images, you must define your site first (see Book 1, Chapter 3 for details) and make sure you've placed all the optimized graphics for the site into an images folder at the root level of the managed site. After defining the site, click the Images button located at the top-left corner of the Assets panel (as shown in Figure 3-2) to see a list of images. The Assets panel has a preview window that shows a thumbnail of any selected graphic file in the managed site. Beneath the preview window, graphics are listed alphabetically by name and also show file dimensions in pixels, file size in KB, file type (GIF, PNG, JPG, and so on), and the full path and filename of the image.

To insert an image from the Assets panel, select the image and do one of the following:

+ Click the Insert button at the bottom of the panel.

+ Drag and drop the image into the page at the desired location.

Images button   Preview window

Figure 3-2:
The Assets panel displays images.

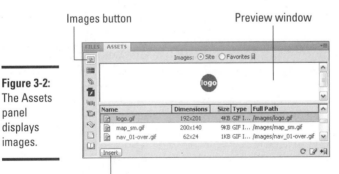

Insert button

Using the Files panel

To add images to an open document from the Files panel, simply select, drag, and drop the chosen image into the desired location on the page. If you have Accessibility preferences enabled, the Image Tag Accessibility Attribute dialog box opens and prompts you to enter accessibility attributes for the image. Enter those values and click OK, or click Cancel to bypass accessibility options and insert the image without the Alt and Long Description attributes.

Editing, Deleting, and Moving Inserted Images

After you insert the image, you can do many things with it:

+ **Edit:** Select the image to modify any of the image attributes or replace the image with another image in the Properties inspector. For the lowdown on modifying image attributes, see the section "Setting Image Attributes with the Properties Inspector," later in the chapter.

+ **Delete:** Select the image and press Delete or Backspace, or choose Edit➪Clear or Edit➪Cut.

+ **Move:** In Design view, drag the image to its new location and release the mouse button. You can also cut and paste the image in both Design and Code views.

Using an Image Placeholder When a Graphic Isn't Ready

Placeholder images are great to use if you know you need graphics in parts of your layout but the graphics aren't ready yet. Placeholder images can be any size in pixels, and the width and height attributes display in the center of the placeholder image itself.

Image placeholders don't display in browser windows and are intended for use in the Dreamweaver environment only. Therefore, before launching a Web page or site, be sure to replace any image placeholders with the desired GIF, PNG, or JPEG files.

To insert a placeholder image, follow these steps:

1. **Select the Image Placeholder option from the Image drop-down menu in the Common category of the Insert panel.**

The button has an image of two tiny squares overlapping; one has a picture of a tree on it and the other has a big grayed out X.

You can also choose Insert➪Image Objects➪Image Placeholder.

The Image Placeholder dialog box opens, as shown in Figure 3-3.

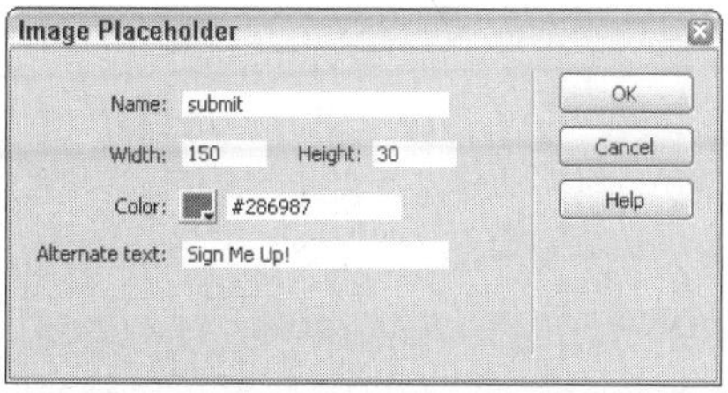

Figure 3-3:
Set Image
Placeholder
attributes.

Image Placeholder	
Name: submit	OK
Width: 150 Height: 30	Cancel
Color: #286987	Help
Alternate text: Sign Me Up!	

2. **Enter the placeholder image attributes: Name, Width, Height, Color, and Alternate Text. The Name field is used to create both name and id attributes, which will be used later for identifying the graphic with CSS and JavaScript.**

The color attribute should either match the surrounding layout or the predominant color of the graphic, because code for this color attribute will be added to your placeholder image and it will not be removed when you replace the placeholder with the real image. If the color is a contrasting color, and you don't remove the style code manually after inserting the real image, site visitors may see that contrasting color momentarily as the image loads in their browser. Here's an example of placeholder code:

```
<img name="portrait" src="" width="300" height="200" alt=""
    style="background-color: #00FF99">
```

To choose a color, click the button to the right of Color and choose your color from the pop-up palette. The hexadecimal number then appears in the text box to the right. You can also type a color name, such as **green**, or enter a hexadecimal number, such as **#ff9933.** (See Book II, Chapter 2 for more about using hexadecimal numbers.)

In Figure 3-3, the placeholder name is `submit`, the width is 150, the height is 30, the color is #286987, and the Alternate text is `Sign Me Up!`

3. **Click OK.**

The placeholder image is inserted on the page.

In Code view, you see the following HTML for the example:

```
<img src="" alt="Sign Me Up!" name="submit" width="150" height="30"
    id="submit" style="background-color: #266984" />
```

Figure 3-4 shows how this image looks in Design view. The image placeholder displays the name, dimensions, and color you input in the dialog box.

When you're ready to replace the placeholder image with the real image, double-click the placeholder image in Design view to open the Select Image Source dialog box, select the replacement image, and click the OK button. The `name`, `id`, `background color`, and `alt` attributes from the placeholder image remain, while the source of the image and its width and height get updated with the new file name.

Figure 3-4:
A
placeholder
image.

submit (150 x 30)

Setting Image Attributes with the Properties Inspector

After you insert an image into your document, you'll want to add other markup and possibly style attributes to the image. Most of the attributes can be added to the image through the Properties inspector, including applying any custom CSS styles you may have already created or intend to create. (See Book III, Chapter 1 for the lowdown on creating style sheets.)

Suppose, for example, you insert an image called `logo.gif` into a Web page. Select the image to apply attributes. As shown in Figure 3-5, a thumbnail of the image displays in the top left of the Properties inspector, along with the file size in K, width and height sizes, image source, ID, and Alternate text. If your Properties Inspector also displays a Photoshop or Fireworks icon in the Edit area, you can click that icon to open the selected graphic in that program for editing.

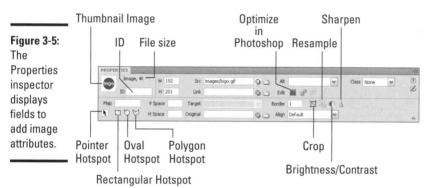

Figure 3-5:
The Properties inspector displays fields to add image attributes.

Thumbnail Image — ID — File size — Optimize in Photoshop — Resample — Sharpen

Pointer Hotspot — Oval Hotspot — Polygon Hotspot — Crop — Brightness/Contrast

Rectangular Hotspot

If you can't see all the image properties shown in Figure 3-5, click the expander arrow in the bottom-right corner of the Properties inspector.

Naming your images

First and foremost, it's a good idea to name all your images so you can quickly apply Dreamweaver behaviors, JavaScript, CSS, and/or VBScript to them later. To name your images, select the graphic and enter a name in the Name field of the Properties inspector (refer to Figure 3-5).

Specifying the width and height of images

By default, when images are inserted onto a page, Dreamweaver reads image dimensions, writes them into the code in pixels, and displays them in the W and H fields of the Properties inspector. Although Dreamweaver inserts dimensions in pixels, you can adjust the dimensions to percentages. When specifying sizes in percentages, be sure to add the % symbol after the number, as in 80%. In the example image, the logo graphic is 192 x 201 pixels. If the image gets resized, the new image dimensions appear in the W and H fields.

Resizing and resetting images

Resize images by either dragging the resize handles located on the left, bottom, and bottom-left corners of the selected image or by entering new image dimensions in the W and H fields on the Properties inspector. Once an image is stretched or scrunched beyond its normal size, the Reset Size button appears between the W and H fields in the Properties inspector and the W and H values appear in bold. To revert to an image's normal size, click the Reset Size button.

It's a good idea — especially if you're scaling up — to create new graphics with an external image-editing program rather than resize them in Dreamweaver. Inserting correctly sized images reduces browser download time as well as helps to maintain the integrity of the image as it appears elsewhere on the site.

Adding vertical or horizontal padding

To push the edges of a graphic away from surrounding text, you may want to add padding to your images. In the past, designers would use the V Space and H Space HTML markup fields to add uniform vertical or horizontal padding. For vertical padding above and below the image, enter pixels in the V Space field. For horizontal padding on the left and right sides of the image, enter pixels in the H Space field.

A better method of adding padding to images is to use CSS, especially because it allows you to apply non-uniform padding around an image, such as padding on just the top and left sides. See Book III, Chapter 1 to learn more about CSS.

Adding image links

The Properties inspector has a Link field to enter the filename or full path of a page or document the graphic can link to. To add a link to an image, select the image and enter the filename and/or path, including file extension, in the Link field. For alternate link options and detailed instructions on linking, see Book II, Chapter 4.

Adjusting targets

When an image contains a link, the Target field becomes active to set the browser frame or browser window into which the linked file should load. When unspecified, the default target for all links is _self. In other words, when you click a link in a browser window, the linked document opens in the same browser window. If that's what you want to happen when clicking the link, leave the Target field blank. Otherwise, to specify that the link opens a new window for displaying the linked page, select _blank from the Target drop-down list. (You can read more on setting link targets in Book II, Chapter 4.)

Specifying the original file

The Original field allows you to specify the location and filename of the original file used to create the optimized Web graphic. Once specified, you can quickly edit that file in the image editor you specify in the External Editors preferences by clicking the Edit application icon next to the Link field. See the "Using the image-editing buttons" section below to find out more about editing web graphics in Dreamweaver.

Adding image borders

By default, images with no links have no borders, but they can have black borders of any pixel width using HTML markup. Images with links have a border that takes on the properties of text links. For example, if the default text link color is blue, a linked image has a blue border.

Although adding an HTML border may seem like a great advantage, the major drawback to it is that you can't choose a different border color through the Properties inspector. (Similar to Henry Ford and his Model-T: "You can buy it in any color, as long as it's black.") Technically, the border color can be the same color as surrounding text color, so you could control the border color with the old <font> tag if for some reason you don't want to use CSS, as in the following example:

```
<p><font color="#CC0066">This text is pink, which means the image will have the
    same border color. <img src="images/logo.gif" width="192" height="201"
    border="1"></font></p>
```

The major browsers don't consistently support this method, so be sure to test it if you intend to use it.

Although you could add a simple HTML border on your images by entering a number for the width of the border in the Border field in the Properties inspector, a better method is to create a custom CSS style. CSS borders can be any color or thickness, one of a handful of different styles, and applied to any or all of the image's four sides. Turn to Book III, Chapter 1 to redefine tags and create custom styles in Cascading Style Sheets.

Providing Alternate text

When accessibility features are enabled in Dreamweaver's Preferences, you can add accessibility attributes to your images as you insert them onto your pages. However, when the accessibility features are disabled, be sure to

Book II
Chapter 3

Inserting Graphics

add these attributes manually to your images through the Properties inspector before publishing the Web site. The two most important accessibility attributes for images are Alternate text and a Long Description. Alternate text, or *Alt text,* is useful for site visitors who use text-only browsers, have their browsers set to manually download images, or use speech synthesizer software to read the descriptions of the image. In some browsers, Alt text appears in place of the images when images are downloading and when the mouse pointer hovers over an image. Furthermore, some search engines use Alt text to help determine site ranking by presuming the words used in Alt text are more relevant and important than text found in <meta> tags.

You can make Alt text as brief as one word or as long as a paragraph, though you should enter a complete, meaningful sentence rather than a list of keywords. If you want to provide a longer description for your image, you can also include a Long Description attribute that links to a separate Web page containing the longer description. The code for an image with both Alternate text and a Long Description looks something like this:

```
<img src="images/brooklynbridge.jpg" alt="The Brooklyn Bridge" width="400"
    height="300" border="10" longdesc="bridge.html" />
```

Aligning images

You can align selected images in two different ways, one using HTML markup, and the other using CSS, which is the more modern, standards-compliant, W3C (World Wide Web Consortium) recommended practice.

✦ **HTML: Wrap elements — such as text — around the image:** Select an option from the Properties inspector Align drop-down list (shown in Figure 3-6). When no alignment is specified, the default alignment is Left. This alignment method adds the align attribute to the <img> tag.

✦ **CSS: Make images float to the left or right of text or other objects on the page:** Apply a custom style to an image by selecting the style by name from the Class drop-down list (shown in Figure 3-6).

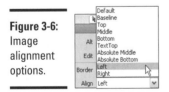

Figure 3-6:
Image
alignment
options.

With CSS, each style can have multiple properties, or rules. For example, you can create a style that adds a 1-pixel border, 5 pixels of padding, and right alignment to an image:

```
<style type="text/css">
<!--
.alignright {
   padding: 5px;
   border: 1px solid #000033;
   clear: right;
   float: right;
}
-->
</style>
```

Using the image-editing buttons

Dreamweaver has seven tools for editing images without the need to launch an external image editor. You can use these editing tools on any GIF or JPEG file inserted on a page. The following seven image-editing tools are located under the Alt field in the Properties inspector whenever you select an image on a page in Design or Code view (refer to Figure 3-5):

✦ **Edit:** Launches the default image-editing program. Specify an image editor in the File Types/Editors category of the Preferences dialog box. Choose Edit⇨Preferences (Windows) or Dreamweaver⇨ Preferences (Mac).

✦ **Edit Image Settings:** Launches the Image Preview dialog box, inside which you can make several simple adjustments to the selected image. The dialog box has two tabs, Options and File. In the Options tab, you can adjust the image format and quality; add image smoothing, progressive browser display, and sharpening color edges; set a matte color; remove unused colors, crop down the image, and view RGB values for the image showing in the preview window. Essentially, the dialog box works like a mini Web graphics optimization program. In the File tab, you can adjust the image scale and export area.

✦ **Update from Original:** When the original file that was used to create the optimized graphic is specified in the original field of the Properties inspector, you can click this button to make adjustments to the selected image using the original source file instead of the optimized graphic.

✦ **Crop:** Allows you to crop the graphic. Clicking this button opens an alert dialog box that warns you about the permanence of any changes you make. Click OK in the alert dialog box to continue. Cropping handles then appear around the image that allow you to crop the image. Press Enter (Windows) or Return (Mac) to accept the cropping.

✦ **Resample:** Allows you to resample a resized image to improve the quality of the image at the new size. This feature appears only after you resize an image. Try, though, to keep resampling to a minimum (especially resampling up) as this process can degrade the quality of the image. If you really need a graphic at a different size, create a new graphic in an image-editing program.

✦ **Brightness/Contrast:** Allows you to adjust the brightness and contrast of the image. Like the Crop tool, clicking the Brightness/Contrast button opens an alert dialog box that warns you about the permanence of any changes you make to the image. Click OK in the dialog box to continue and a Brightness/Contrast dialog box appears. Move the sliders in the dialog box to the left or the right to increase or decrease the brightness and contrast. Click OK to accept the new settings or Cancel to close the Brightness/Contrast dialog box without changes.

✦ **Sharpen:** Adjusts the overall image contrast and edge pixel clarity. The Sharpening dialog box uses a sliding scale of 0–10 to adjust the image sharpness; the higher the number, the more intense the image's definition or sharpness.

Creating Interactive Images

Besides inserting the occasional static graphic here and there on a Web page, Dreamweaver greatly simplifies the process of adding interactive image options on a Web page, including creating rollover images, image maps, and navigation bars, and adding Fireworks HTML to an existing Web page.

The following sections discuss these interactive techniques. All the interactive image buttons are accessible from the Common category of the Insert panel, as shown in Figure 3-7.

Image button

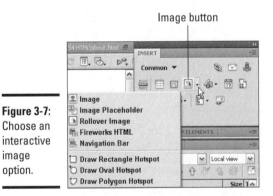

Figure 3-7: Choose an interactive image option.

Adding rollover images

Rollover images are graphics that change to a different image in a browser window when a visitor moves the mouse over the image. To make a rollover button, you need two graphics — one for the normal state and one for the over state — that are exactly the same pixel width and height but that look different enough that a visitor will notice the rollover effect.

Dreamweaver lets you create rollover images by inserting JavaScript into the code that tells a browser to display one image for the normal state and another image for the mouseover state.

Before creating your rollover images in Dreamweaver, optimize the graphics for both normal and rollover states and place, give them similar names, such as nav01.gif and nav01-over.gif, and save them in an images folder at the root level of your managed site. Make sure both images have the same image dimensions in pixels so that the over state image does not get distorted during mouseover.

To create rollover images, follow these steps:

1. **Place the insertion point in the Document window where you want the rollover image to go.**

The spot you click in the Document window is where the rollover image will appear on the page.

2. **Click the Image button in the Common category of the Insert panel and choose Rollover Image from its drop-down list (refer to Figure 3-7).**

Or choose Insert⇨Image Objects⇨Rollover Image.

The Insert Rollover Image dialog box opens, as shown in Figure 3-8.

3. **Enter an image name, browse to and select the graphics to use for both the original and rollover images, add Alternate text, and a filename or URL for a link to another file.**

By default, the Preload Rollover Image option is enabled. This option adds JavaScript to the page that tells the browser to preload this graphic into the browser's cache as the page is loading. When this happens, the over state graphic is ready to appear by the time a visitor places the mouse on the rollover graphic's normal state.

4. **Click OK.**

Dreamweaver inserts the original image and writes all the JavaScript necessary to perform the rollover function. JavaScript is attached to the `<img>`, `<head>`, and `<body>` tags.

**Book II
Chapter 3**

Inserting Graphics

Figure 3-8:
Specify a
rollover
image.

Insert Rollover Image

Image name:	contact	OK
Original image:	images/contact.gif	Browse...
Rollover image:	images/contact-over.gif	Browse...
	☑ Preload rollover image	Cancel
Alternate text:	Contact Us	Help
When clicked, Go to URL:	contact.html	Browse...

To preview or test JavaScript behaviors in Design view, click the Live View button on the Document toolbar, or choose File➪Preview in Browser to test the rollover effect in a browser. You can tell the rollover effect is working properly by positioning the mouse over the rollover button.

Creating image maps

An image map is an image that has shaped regions or *hotspots* defined by pixel coordinates in the code that can have a behavior (such as a hyperlink) assigned to it. When a visitor clicks the hotspot, an action occurs (for example, another page opens). Hotspots can be rectangular, oval, or polygonal in shape. The following example shows how image maps are defined in the code for a hotspot in the shape of a circle:

```
<img src="images/logo.gif" width="192" height="201" border="1"
    usemap="#Map1"><map name="Map1" id="Map1"><area shape="circle"
    coords="97,98,75" href="#">
```

Images can have multiple hotspots as well as multiple behaviors assigned to a hotspot. For instance, you may have a photograph of a map of the United States and want to turn each state's shape into a unique hotspot linking to information elsewhere on the site specific to that state. (See Book IV, Chapter 2 for more on behaviors.)

You can draw hotspots on a selected image using the Rectangular Hotspot, Oval Hotspot, and Polygon Hotspot tools in the Properties inspector beneath the image thumbnail (refer to Figure 3-5). You can adjust the hotspot border with another tool, the Pointer Hotspot.

Here's how to create a hotspot on a graphic:

1. **Select the image in Design view.**

   By selecting the image in Design view, you activate the image hotspot options in the Properties inspector.

2. **In the Properties inspector, enter a name for the image map in the Map field.**

   If unspecified, image maps get assigned a default name such as Map1, Map2, Map3, and so on. If creating multiple image maps in the same document, definitely use separate map names for each.

3. **Select a hotspot tool and draw a hotspot shape on the image:**

   - **Rectangular:** Drag and release the mouse to create an enclosed rectangular shape.

   - **Oval:** Drag and release the mouse to create an enclosed oval shape.

   - **Polygon:** Create a non-uniform polygonal shape by selecting this tool and clicking the image multiple times to insert anchor points for the hotspot shape. Click the pointer tool to finish the shape.

To select these hotspot tools, click one of the buttons in the bottom-left corner of the Properties inspector (see Figure 3-9).

4. **Use the Pointer Hotspot tool to select the hotspot and assign `link`, `target`, and `alt` attributes.**

When the hotspot is selected, the Properties inspector displays fields for assigning a link, link target, and Alternate text to the hotspot. You can also adjust the anchor points of the hotspot shape with the Pointer Hotspot tool.

5. **Deselect the hotspot and/or image by clicking away from the image with the Pointer Hotspot tool in Design view.**

Figure 3-9 shows an image with a hotspot.

6. **To continue adding hotspots on the same image, select another hotspot tool and repeat Steps 2 through 5.**

Book II
Chapter 3

Inserting Graphics

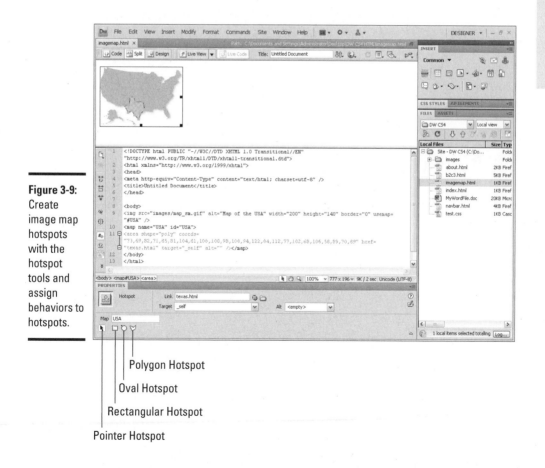

Figure 3-9:
Create image map hotspots with the hotspot tools and assign behaviors to hotspots.

Polygon Hotspot

Oval Hotspot

Rectangular Hotspot

Pointer Hotspot

Inserting a navigation bar with images

Creating a simple vertical or horizontal navigation bar in Dreamweaver has never been easier. From the Insert Navigation Bar dialog box (Insert⇨Image Objects⇨Navigation Bar), you can specify and organize all the nav bar elements at the same time.

Follow these steps to create and insert a navigation bar with images:

1. **Click the Image button in the Common category of the Insert panel and choose Navigation Bar from its drop-down list (refer to Figure 3-7).**

   Or choose Insert⇨Image Objects⇨Navigation Bar.

   The Insert Navigation Bar dialog box opens, as shown in Figure 3-10.

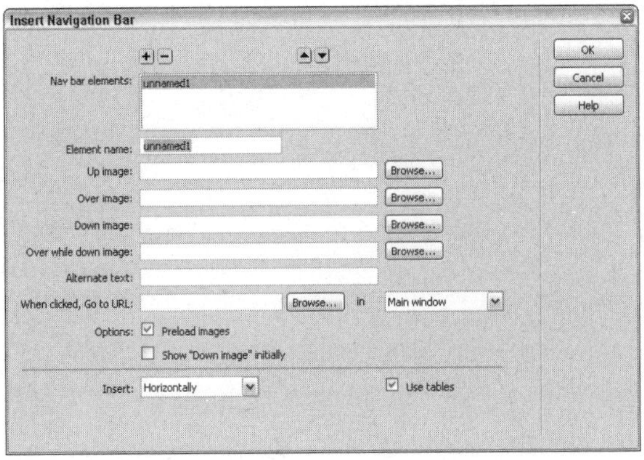

Figure 3-10: Create a custom graphic navigation bar with the Insert Navigation Bar dialog box.

2. **For the first rollover graphic on the navigation bar, enter the following information:**

   - **Element Name:** Enter the name of the button.

   - **Up Image:** Select an image for the button's normal *up* (nonclicked) state.

   - **Over Image:** Select an image for the button's mouseover state.

   - **Down Image (optional):** Select an image for the button's *down* state, which appears when a visitor clicks the button.

   - **Alternate Text:** Enter a text description for the button, such as **About Us** or **Contact us for more information**. Alternate text displays as the images are downloading and is read aloud by any screen-reader software used by the visually impaired. It may also appear in some browsers as pop-up text when the cursor is placed over the graphic.

- **When Clicked, Go to URL:** Select the page that is the target of the button.

3. **Select any other options you need.**

4. **To add additional rollover buttons to the navigation bar, click the Add Item (+) button and repeat Steps 1 through 3.**

5. **To remove a button from the navigation bar, click the Remove Item (–) button.**

6. **To reorder the navigation bar elements, select a button name from the Nav Bar Elements listing and click the Move Item Up In List and Move Item Down In List arrows to reposition the element in the list.**

7. **When you're satisfied with the navigation bar, click OK.**

Dreamweaver inserts the new navigation bar (see Figure 3-11) and all attending JavaScript. The navigation bar, essentially, is a single row or column table with a series of hyperlinking rollover buttons in each cell.

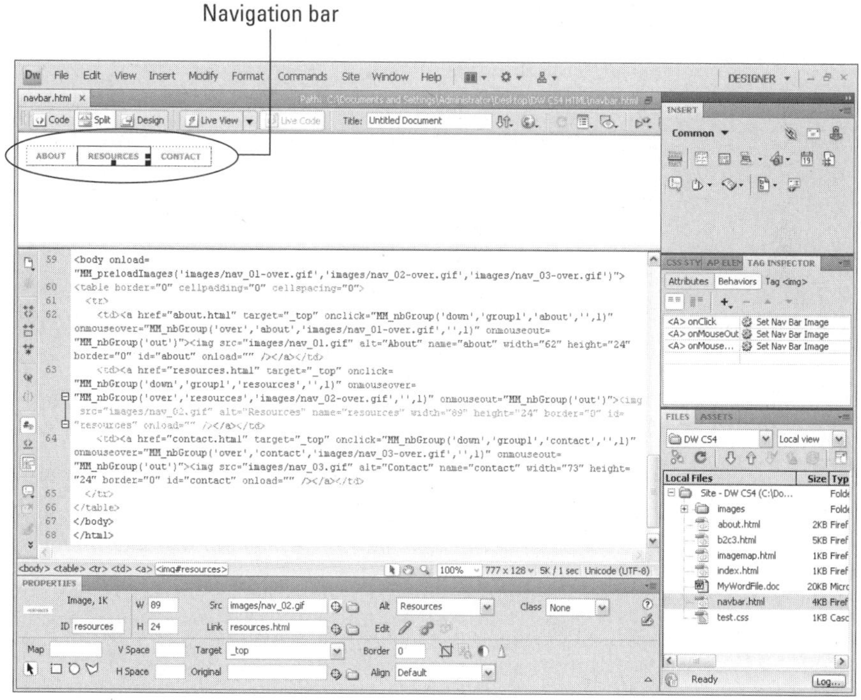

Navigation bar

Figure 3-11:
Create horizontal or vertical navigation bars with your own custom graphics.

Only one navigation bar can exist at a time on any one page, but it can be modified if you need to add, edit, or remove a rollover button. To make adjustments to an existing navigation bar, do one of the following to open the Modify Navigation Bar dialog box:

✦ Click the Navigation Bar button on the Common area of the Insert panel.

✦ Select the navigation bar in the Document window and choose Modify➪Navigation Bar.

Inserting Fireworks HTML

Fireworks lets you create, slice, and optimize images for the Web, and because it's an Adobe program, it integrates beautifully with Dreamweaver. One of the main things you can do with Fireworks is create a page layout and then export the file as an HTML page including images and rollover effects. After you export the file, you can import it into Dreamweaver. Dreamweaver lets you quickly add design elements, such as animated rollovers, pop-up menus, and other images, generated by Fireworks into an open document. Fireworks has an export command that lets you specify which Dreamweaver managed site folder to place the code into so you can easily import the code into Dreamweaver when you're ready.

To import Fireworks content into an open Dreamweaver document, follow these steps:

1. **Click in the page to place the insertion point where you want to add the Fireworks HTML.**

2. **Click the Image button in the Common category of the Insert panel and choose Fireworks HTML from its drop-down list (refer to Figure 3-7).**

You can also choose Insert➪Interactive Images➪Fireworks HTML.

The Insert Fireworks HTML dialog box opens, as shown in Figure 3-12.

3. **Browse to and select the Fireworks HTML file that you want to import.**

To have Dreamweaver delete the Fireworks HTML after inserting it on your page, click the Delete File After Insertion check box.

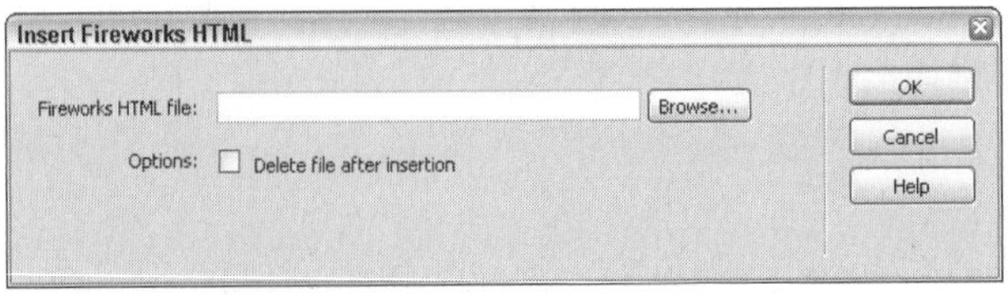

Figure 3-12:
Insert
Fireworks
HTML.

Insert Fireworks HTML	
Fireworks HTML file: [_____] [Browse...]	[OK] [Cancel] [Help]
Options: ☐ Delete file after insertion	

4. **Click OK.**

   Dreamweaver imports the HTML, graphics, and any associated JavaScript to support rollover effects and other interactivity.

   For more on using Dreamweaver with Fireworks, see Book III, Chapter 5.

Chapter 4: Making Links with Text and Images

In This Chapter

- ✔ Making links with text
- ✔ Making links with images
- ✔ Creating e-mail links
- ✔ Editing and deleting links
- ✔ Hand-coding with the Tag Chooser

Web pages become a Web site when they are joined together by hyperlinks. Hyperlinks (often called just *links*) convert nearly any content — including text or graphics — into clickable pointers that lead the site visitor through other pages on a site, winding through text and graphics along the way.

Links can point to another Web page on the same site, another page on a different Web site, a section of the same or another page, PDF, Word or PowerPoint document, graphic, sound file, movie, Zip or SIT file, or downloadable software. They can open a blank e-mail message with the recipient's address already in place, or they can be temporary placeholders for behaviors and scripts to attach to.

You can add, edit, or remove links from a page at any stage of the site building process. Though they look like working links inside of the Dreamweaver Document window, they don't work when you click them there, so be sure to launch a browser window by pressing F12 (Window) or Option+F12 (Mac) or click the Live View button to test the functionality and accuracy of your links.

This chapter takes an in-depth look at the different kinds of links that you can create in Dreamweaver.

Understanding Hyperlinks

You can create four types of hyperlinks in Dreamweaver:

✦ **Regular:** Links pages together by converting content, including text and graphics, into hyperlinks.

✦ **E-mail:** Launches a computer's default e-mail program and prompts the site visitor to send e-mail to the e-mail address in the link.

✦ **Named anchor:** Takes the site visitor to a link location embedded on the same page as the link or to an anchor link location embedded on another page.

✦ **Temporary:** There are two kinds of temporary links, called *null* and *script* links that convert selected content into undefined links for adding detailed link information or behaviors at a later time.

Before adding links, be sure you understand the difference between document-relative, absolute, and site root-relative paths as the link syntax varies slightly depending on the path type. Turn to Book I, Chapter 3 for a general discussion about paths.

One of the fastest ways to add links to your page is to select some text, graphic, or object on the page and enter the link information in the Link field in the Properties inspector. Type the link by entering the filename or full URL, including `http://` and the file extension. After you enter the link, the Target field becomes activated. Then, you can select a target for the link (see the "Setting Link Targets" section in this chapter).

In the HTML view of the Properties inspector, there are two buttons (shown in Figure 4-1) to the right of the Link text that also allow you to add links to any selected text, graphic, or object on the page. Both methods are faster and more accurate (since there's no typing involved) ways of linking files:

Figure 4-1: The Properties inspector helps you add links.

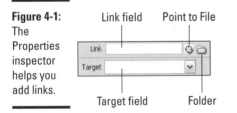

Link field   Point to File

Target field   Folder

✦ **Folder:** Click the folder button to open the Select File dialog box. Browse to and select the file you want to link to, and then click OK and Dreamweaver writes the link of the filename into the Link field. Enter any target information in the Target field.

✦ **Point to File:** Click this button and drag the pointer icon to a file listed in the Files panel. Release the mouse when the cursor is on top of the desired file and Dreamweaver writes the link of the filename into the Link field. Enter your target information in the Target field. The Point to File button also works for selecting named anchors on a page.

To test a link, you must launch a browser window. Here's how to open a browser to test your link:

✦ To preview an open page, press F12 (Windows) or Option+F12 (Mac) to launch your primary browser or press Control+F12 (Windows) or Command+F12 (Mac) to launch your secondary browser (see Book V, Chapter 1 to specify a primary and secondary browser). The currently open document opens in a browser window.

✦ To preview a file listed in the Files panel, right-click (Windows) or Control+click (Mac) the file, choose Preview in Browser, and choose the browser type from the list.

To open a locally linked file inside Dreamweaver, either highlight the link in the Dreamweaver document window and choose Modify➪Open Linked Page, or press Ctrl (Windows) or ⌘ (Mac) and double-click the link to open the linked document in Dreamweaver's Document window.

All links use the <a> tag plus one or two different attributes to convert selected text or graphics into links. The next few sections give separate descriptions and examples of the four link types.

**Book II
Chapter 4**

**Making Links with
Text and Images**

Creating Text Links

You can create text links from a word, phrase, sentence, paragraph, or even an entire page worth of text. The link code surrounds a selection of text and converts it into a clickable hyperlink. Text links use the <a> tag with the href attribute. The href attribute stands for *Hypertext REFerence,* and the attribute points either to a file at the root level of the defined site or to an external Web page by including the http:// and full path to that page. The target attributes, which tell the browser whether to open the link in the same or another browser window, also go inside the opening <a> tag.

This example link opens the Google home page in a new window:

```
<a href="http://www.google.com" target="_blank">Search on Google</a>
```

This example opens an About page in the same browser window:

```
<a href="about.html" target="_self">About Us</a>
```

To create a text link, follow these steps:

1. **Choose Insert⇨Hyperlink or click the Hyperlink button on the Common category of the Insert panel, which looks like a chain link.**

   The Hyperlink dialog box opens, as shown in Figure 4-2.

2. **Enter the following information in the dialog box:**

   • **Text:** Enter the text you want to make into a link, such as **Learn More** or **Contact Us.**

   • **Link:** Type the path and filename of the linked page. If the linked page is on the same site, enter only the filename, such as **contact. html**. However, if the linked page is external to the current site, enter the full URL including the `http://`, as in **http://www.dummies.com.**

   • **Target:** By default, linked pages automatically open in the same browser window. To override this setting, select **_blank** to have the link open in a different browser window. See the "Setting Link Targets" section for more about other target settings.

   • **Title:** Add a description for the link. The title appears as a tool tip in some browsers when a visitor mouses over the link. In addition, it can both improve visitor accessibility and assist in better search engine indexing and ranking.

   • **Access Key:** Add a one-letter keyboard equivalent that the visitor can use in combination with the Tab key to select the link in the browser. Once selected, the visitor can press Enter (Windows) or Return (Mac) to visit that linked page.

   • **Tab Index:** Add a number for the tab order of this link, relative to other links on the page. The tab order, which defines the order of accessible elements on a page using the Tab key, begins at the top of the browser window and moves downward from left to right, as when reading a book.

3. **Click OK.**

   Dreamweaver adds the link to the page.

Making Image Links

Image links work the same way text links do, but instead of surrounding text, the link code surrounds an image.

Here's an example of a link to visit Google using a GIF file:

```
<a href="http://www.google.com" target="_blank"><img src="images/googlelogo.
    gif"></a>
```

Here's an example of a link to a page at the root level of a defined site using an About Us graphic:

```
<a href="about.html"><img src="images/aboutus.gif"></a>
```

To create an image link, select the image on the page in Design view and type the filename or path of the linked page into the Link field in the Properties inspector. If desired, add a link target to define where the linked page will open.

When you add a link to an image, the borders around the image become hyperlinks. To remove the link border from your linked image, set the border property on the Properties Inspector to 0.

You can also create an image link the same way you create a text link. See the previous section to find out how to do so.

Inserting E-Mail Links

E-mail links, when clicked in a browser window, tell the site visitor's computer to launch the computer's default e-mail program, open a blank e-mail message window, and populate the Send To field with the e-mail address in the link. E-mail links use the `<a>` tag with the `href` attribute just like text links do, but instead of listing the `//` before the filename, an e-mail link uses the `mailto:` attribute before the e-mail address (`mailto:` is a URL just like `http://` is), like this:

```
<a href="mailto:me@example.com">me@example.com</a>
```

To create a standard HTML e-mail link, follow these steps:

1. **Choose Insert⇨E-mail Link to launch the E-mail Link dialog box.**

   Or, in the Common category of the Insert panel, click the E-mail Link button, which looks like an envelope.

2. **In the Text field, enter the text that will appear in the browser window as linked text, such as** Contact Us **or** contact@company.com. **In the E-Mail field, enter the e-mail address for the link, such as** contact@company.com.

3. **Click OK.**

   Dreamweaver writes the e-mail link code into the page.

Adding an e-mail address to a Web page using this type of HTML e-mail link makes the e-mail address vulnerable to spam bots and spam spiders that crawl the Web in search of anything that has the `me@example.com` format or for links containing the `mailto:` attribute. For encryption ideas, check out the nearby sidebar "Encrypting e-mail addresses" or search online to find more about e-mail encryption.

Encrypting e-mail addresses

E-mail addresses are very vulnerable to being harvested by spam-gathering software and then sold to zillions of spam lists. To better protect your e-mail address, encrypt your e-mail address or use some other form of hiding the e-mail address so it can't be electronically harvested or easily obtained.

Try these suggestions for hiding or encrypting e-mail links on Web pages:

- Encrypt your e-mail address with a JavaScript encryption software application. Several freeware and shareware versions are available, including Email Riddler at `www.dynamicdrive.com/email riddler/;` do a search for **Email Address Encryptor** to find others.

- Enter your e-mail address in Code view using URL code entities for all the special characters. For example, `me@example.com` becomes `me%40example%2Ecom`.

  Visit the W3Schools Web site (`www.w3schools.com/tags/ref_urlencode.asp`) to convert your e-mail address into URL unicode.

- Include your e-mail address on the page but don't turn it into a link. Your e-mail address is still vulnerable, but less so than as a standard e-mail link.

For a great article about e-mail harvesters and the countermeasures you can take to fight them, read Tim Williams's take on e-mail at `www.u.arizona.edu/~trw/spam/`.

Creating Named Anchor Links

Named anchor links are great for creating links that jump to another location on the same page, or to a specific part of another page within the same website. Use named anchor links for FAQ lists, Table of Contents, Indexes, Back to Top links, and other page elements where internal linking would be useful.

Creating a named anchor requires two steps:

1. **Lay down and name the anchor in the spot you want to link to.**

2. **Make a link that points to the named anchor you just laid down.**

Say you have a page with two FAQs and you want to list the questions at the top of the page and the answers in sequence below the questions. The text on your page may look something like this:

1. Question

2. Question

1st Question Answer
Answer to question. Answer to question. Answer to question. Answer to question. Answer to question.

2nd Question Answer
Answer to question. Answer to question. Answer to question. Answer to question. Answer to question.

To link each question to its answer, you create a named anchor right before each answer and then link to it. This type of link is called a named anchor because it uses the name attribute of the <a> tag. You'll notice, however, that the code for named anchors includes both name and id attributes:

```
<a name="Q1" id="Q1"></a>
```

The name and id attributes have the same values so that they share the same domain value space, which means you could use either one when specifying the link to the anchor. For example, you can create an anchor using the name attribute, as the following example shows:

```
<a name="Q1">1st Question Answer</a>
```

or turn another element into an anchor using the id attribute, as this example shows:

```
<h1 id="Q1">1st Question Answer</h1>
```

Once the anchor is laid down, the link to the anchor is the same:

```
<a href="#Q1">Go to question 1 answer </a>
```

Dreamweaver tries to simplify the process by including both name and id attributes in the code whenever you create a named anchor.

The following sections cover the two-step process for creating a named anchor.

Step 1: Lay down the named anchor

Remember to create your page with all the text before creating the named anchors. Then lay down your anchors at each of the destination points. For example, in a FAQ list, you want to place the anchors right before the text for each answer in the list.

To lay down a named anchor, follow these steps:

1. **Click the Named Anchor button, which looks like a golden anchor, in the Common category of the Insert panel or choose Insert⇨Named Anchor.**

   The Named Anchor dialog box appears, as shown in Figure 4-3.

Figure 4-3:
The Named
Anchor
dialog box.

Named Anchor	
Anchor name:	OK
	Cancel
	Help

2. **Enter a name for your anchor and click OK.**

   Try not to use any spaces or funny characters in your anchor names, and do not put any anchors inside a layer.

   In Design view, your named anchor displays as a little yellow invisible element to mark where the named anchor sits in the code.

   If you don't see the invisible element in Design view, be sure the Invisible Elements Visual Aids option is enabled in the Document window and that the invisible elements in the Preferences dialog box are set to show named anchors. To see visual aids, choose View⇨Visual Aids⇨Invisible Elements.

Step 2: Link to the named anchor

Creating the link to the named anchor uses the href attribute just like standard text and image links, but it has one unique twist: Instead of linking to a filename or URL, the link name attribute is preceded by a number symbol (#) to tell the browser to look for the named anchor on the same page, like this:

```
<p><a href="#Q1">1. Question</a></p>
```

To create a link to a named anchor, do one of the following:

✦ Select the text that will become the link, and in the Link field of the Properties inspector, type the number symbol (#) followed by the anchor name, as in **#Q1**. Alternately, you can use the Point to File feature in the Properties Inspector to point to the named anchor.

✦ Select the text that will become the link, and choose Insert⇨Hyperlink, which opens the Hyperlink dialog box (refer to Figure 4-2), from which you can select the named anchor from the Link drop-down list. (See the previous section "Creating Text Links" for details.)

You can also use named anchor links when linking from one page to another by typing the number symbol (#) followed by the anchor name after the name of the file being linked to. For example, if you want a visitor to click a link in one page and go right to a particular section of another page, your link may look something like this:

```
<a href="contact.html#wholesale">Learn more about Wholesale Pricing</a>
```

In this example, the visitor is taken to a named anchor destination called wholesale within the page called contact.html.

Creating Temporary Links

The most common types of links are the links you create to other files and named anchors, but you can add other link types to a page:

✦ **Script:** These links call JavaScript functions or run JavaScript code to provide information to the site visitor without having to leave the page, such as when a JavaScript alert box opens. JavaScript links can also do other page processing duties, such as form validation, when the visitor interacts in some way with the page, like clicking a particular button. For an excellent tutorial on JavaScript, go to www.w3schools.com/js/default.asp.

✦ **Null:** These empty links don't go anywhere but still treat the text or object like a link. Once created, you can use null links to attach behaviors to the text and objects on the page. (You can find more about behaviors in Book IV, Chapter 2.)

To create a script link, follow these steps:

1. **Select the text, graphic, or object in Design view.**

2. **Enter javascript: (the word** *javascript* **followed by a colon) into the Link field in the Properties inspector, followed by a JavaScript or function call.**

For instance, to create a JavaScript link that closes the currently open browser window, type the following text in the Link field:

```
javascript:parent.close();
```

The script for the link appears in the code like this:

```
This is a <a href="javascript:parent.close();">Close</a> link.
```

where the JavaScript code appears between double quote marks as a value of the `href` attribute. If you need to include double quote marks as part of your script, be sure to add escape marks before your double quotes, as `\"This link goes to the home page\"`.

To create a null link, do one of the following:

✦ Select the text, graphic, or object in Design view and enter **javascript:;** (the word *javascript* followed by a colon, followed by a semicolon) into the Link field in the Properties inspector.

✦ Select the text or graphic and enter a number symbol (#) in the Link field in the Properties inspector.

Some browsers jump to the top of the page when a number sign is used as a null link; therefore, the JavaScript null link is preferred.

Whenever you're ready to convert the temporary link into a permanent link, replace the temporary link with the appropriate filename or URL.

Setting Link Targets

After adding a link to text or a graphic, you can assign a *target* in the Target field of the Properties inspector. The target defines where the linked file opens, whether in a specific frame of a frameset, the same browser window, or a new browser window. When unspecified, the linked page typically opens in the same browser window. For further details see the Setting Text Properties with the Properties Inspector section in Book II, Chapter 2.

Editing and Deleting Links

Links aren't set in stone after you create them; you can edit and even delete them at any time you see fit. You can even edit all instances of a single link used on several pages of your site at the same time.

Editing links

To edit a link after inserting it into your page, select the link — whether it's a text, graphic, or object link — and then do either of the following:

✦ Edit or replace the link text using the Property inspector.

✦ Choose Modify⇨Change Link. The Select File dialog box opens, allowing you to search for and select another file for the link.

Dreamweaver has a great feature that allows you to change a link throughout an entire managed site (for instance, change the August newsletter link to a September newsletter link). To do this, follow these steps:

1. **Select a file in the Files panel and then choose Site⇨Change Link Sitewide.**

The Change Link Sitewide dialog box opens, as shown in Figure 4-4, with the filename you selected in the Change All Links To box.

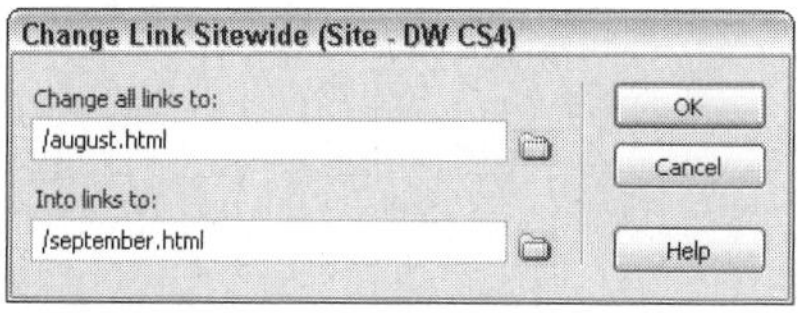

**Book II
Chapter 4**

**Making Links with
Text and Images**

Figure 4-4:
The Change
Link
Sitewide
dialog box.

Change Link Sitewide (Site - DW CS4)

Change all links to:
/august.html

Into links to:
/september.html

OK
Cancel
Help

2. **Enter the new filename in the Into Links To box and click OK.**

The Update Files dialog box appears showing a list of files that will be changed.

3. **Click the Update button to convert all those links in the site. Click the Don't Update button if you change your mind.**

Deleting links

To delete an existing link, do one of the following:

✦ Select the link text, graphic, or object and remove the link attributes from the Link field in the Properties inspector.

✦ Select the link text, graphic, or object and choose Modify⇨Remove Link.

✦ Delete the opening and closing link tag code by hand in Code view.

Using the Tag Chooser

The Tag Chooser is a special place you can go to find and insert tags on your page. The Tag Chooser bills itself as "A collection of Markup Language Tags." That's because, in addition to all the HTML tags, the Tag Chooser contains tags for several other markup languages including CFML, ASP, JSP, ASP.NET, PHP, and WML. You'll learn more about how to use these correctly in Books VII, VIII, and IX.

What's more, each language is housed in its own tag library folder and has its tags categorized into logical subfolders to help you find the right tag. For example, if you're looking for a tag to add an iframe, or inline frame, to your page, you'd open the HTML Tags Language folder, and search for the tag in the Page Elements category, as shown in Figure 4-5. When you select a tag in the panel on the right side of the dialog box, the Tag Info panel at the bottom of the dialog box reveals tag reference information such as syntax and tag usage.

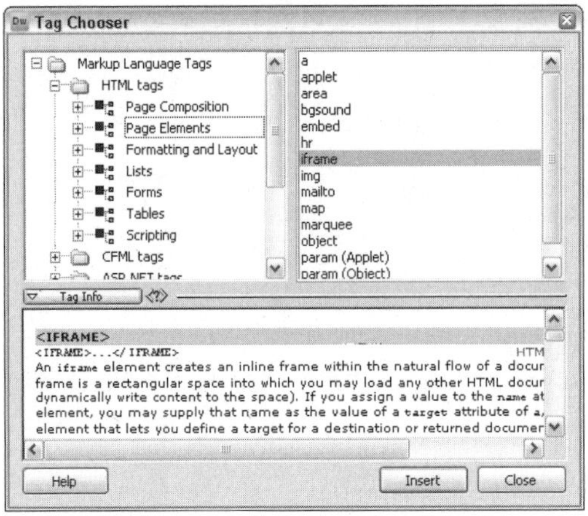

Figure 4-5: Find and insert specific markup language tags with the Tag Chooser dialog box.

To use the Tag Chooser, follow these steps:

1. **Choose Insert⊏>Tag.**

   The Tag Chooser dialog box opens, as shown in Figure 4-5. This dialog box provides access to all the tags in a variety of markup languages.

2. **Select the language folder you want to use in the left pane of the dialog box and navigate to that folder's subcategories to find the type of tag to insert.**

   Expand folders as needed to narrow down the tag search.

3. Search the right pane for the specific tag you want to insert.

Tags in each subcategory are listed in the right pane of the dialog box, and descriptions for each tag appear in the bottom panel of the dialog box, below the button that says Tag Info. If you don't see the description panel, click the Tag Info button so that it's arrow points downward.

4. To insert a tag on your page, select the tag and click the Insert button, or simply double-click on the tag name.

If the tag is listed in the right pane with angle brackets surrounding it (such as <u></u>), it's inserted in your document. All other tags, however, need additional information.

If the tag needs more information, the Tag Editor dialog box opens. Figure 4-6 shows an example of the Tag editor set to insert properties for the <iframe> tag.

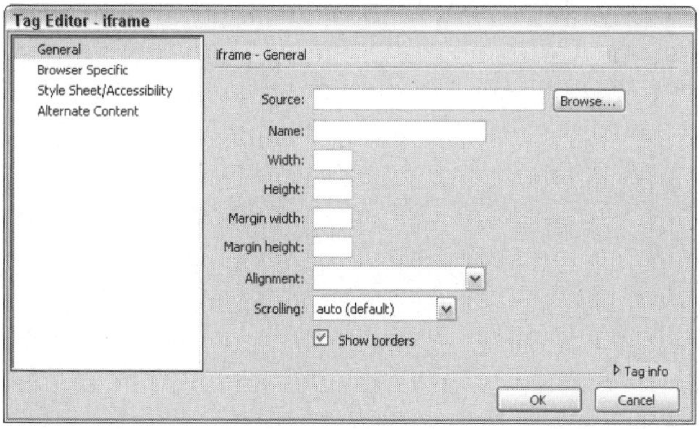

Tag Editor - iframe

General
Browser Specific
Style Sheet/Accessibility
Alternate Content

iframe - General

Source: [   ] [Browse...]
Name: [   ]
Width: [   ]
Height: [   ]
Margin width: [   ]
Margin height: [   ]
Alignment: [▼]
Scrolling: [auto (default) ▼]
☑ Show borders

▷ Tag info

[OK] [Cancel]

Figure 4-6:
Enter tag details in the Tag Editor.

5. Enter the tag and attribute details.

The Tag editor is context specific, meaning it displays all the property fields available for the selected tag. If you're unsure of what to add in any field, leave it blank for now because you can always edit the tag through the Properties inspector at a later time.

If the Tag editor displays multiple categories, such as General, Browser Specific, and Style Sheet/Accessibility, look at those category options and add any tag attributes as desired.

6. Click OK in the Tag editor.

The selected tag is inserted onto your page.

7. To add more tags to your page, repeat Steps 2 through 6. Otherwise, click the Close button to close the Tag Chooser.

Coding Links by Hand

If you happen to know the HTML markup syntax, by all means feel free to hand-code your links. Simply go right into Code view and type away. Just be sure you remember to close your link tags with the closing </a> tag. Table 4-1 shows examples of the link types.

Table 4-1	Sample Links
Link Type	*Link Example*
Hyperlink with text, including `target` attribute and link to file on same site	`<a href="about.html" target="_self"> About Us</a>`
Hyperlink with text, including `target` attribute and full path of link	`<a href="http://www.google.com" target="_blank">Google</a>`
Hyperlink with graphic, including `target` attribute and link to file on same site	`<a href="about.html" target="_self"><img src="images/about.gif"></a>`
Hyperlink with graphic, including `target` attribute and full path of link	`<a href="http://www.google.com" target="_blank"><img src="images/google.jpg"></a>`
E-mail link	`<a href="mailto:me@example.com">me@example.com</a>`
Named anchor	`<a name="anchor1" id="anchor1"></a>` (Anchor laid down) `<a href="#anchor1">Go to Anchor 1</a>` (Link to anchor)
Named anchor laid down that includes a `target` attribute and the full path to a link	`<a name="anchor1" id="anchor1" href="http://www.example.com">Link to the home page</a>`

Chapter 5: Adding Flash, Movies, Sound, and More

In This Chapter

✔ Adding Flash SWFs

✔ Adding FlashPaper and Flash Video (FLV)

✔ Inserting Shockwave movies, Java applets, and ActiveX controls

✔ Working with Netscape Navigator plug-ins

✔ Adding other video and sound

You've probably seen Web sites that include Flash intros, MPEG videos, MP3 songs, QuickTime movies, and other various kinds of sound and video plug-ins. Dreamweaver makes it easy to insert these media clips, adjust the attributes that determine how the media displays on a Web page, and, if applicable, change how the user can interact with it.

This chapter shows you how to add Flash, movies, sound, and other media types to a Web page. You also find a brief discussion about acceptable sound file formats and the differences between linking and embedding video and sounds.

Flash Elements You Can Add to Your Web Site

Your basic Flash movie uses the most common SWF file format, but you can add other Flash elements to your Web pages. Before you begin adding them, however, you need to understand the subtle differences between the different Flash file formats:

✦ .fla, or *Flash files,* are Flash movies. These are the original, editable source files for creating SWF files.

✦ .swf files (pronounced *swiff*) are compressed, portable versions of .fla files that you can preview in Dreamweaver and play in browsers. Flash buttons and Flash text also use SWF files. These files are not editable as the original FLA files are.

✦ .swt are Flash template files that allow you to change information in SWF files. For example, a button created in Flash might use SWT files to let you generate multiple buttons with different text.

Adobe's Dreamweaver Exchange has many button templates available for download at www.adobe.com/cfusion/exchange/ us. After you download them from the Web site, save the templates into your computer's Dreamweaver/Configuration/Flash Objects/Flash Buttons folder.

✦ .swc are Flash element files or special SWF files that make customizable Rich Internet applications.

✦ .flv, or *Flash video files,* play movies that have encoded audio and video data that allows the free Flash player to play them. For example, a Windows Media or QuickTime video could be encoded with special software into FLV files for viewing in a Flash player. Flash's Video Encoder, which is integrated with Flash (www.adobe.com), and Sorensen Squeeze (www.sorensonmedia.com) are two recommended encoders. To discover more about the process of encoding videos, visit www.adobe. com/devnet/video/.

To add Flash movies, Flash video, and FlashPaper to your site, you must first create the SWF, FLV, and FlashPaper files in Flash.

Flash is a great tool, but beginners should be aware that it can be misused on the Web. Before you add Flash movies to your Web site, do a little research to become aware of both the benefits (animation, sound, interactivity) and the drawbacks (search engines ignore Flash movies so it's not good for SEO; many Web visitors dislike Flash; beginners tend to overuse it) of Flash.

Inserting Flash Movies (SWFs)

Inserting Flash movies into your Web page in Dreamweaver is a simple two-step process. Before you can insert a Flash movie in Dreamweaver, however, you must first create the movie in the Flash program and save it as an SWF file. Check out *Adobe Flash For Dummies* (Wiley) by Finkelstein and Leete if you need help preparing your Flash movie.

Adding a Flash movie to your page

To add a Flash movie (SWF) to a Web page, follow these steps:

1. **Place your cursor where you want the Flash movie to appear on your Web page.**

2. **Choose Insert⇨Media⇨Flash.**

You can also click the Media button in the Common category of the Insert panel and select Flash from its drop-down list.

The Select File dialog box opens.

3. **Select the Flash SWF movie file you want to insert on the page and click OK.**

Note: If you enabled Accessibility options in Preferences, the Object Tag Accessibility Attributes dialog box appears prompting you to add a title, access (shortcut) key, and tab index number to the SWF file. Enter those attributes and click OK or click Cancel to add the SWF file without the Accessibility attributes.

Dreamweaver embeds the movie with all the Flash HTML code needed for the movie to play in most major browsers by including the <object> tag for Microsoft ActiveX controls, hidden comments to identify the different parts of the code, and HTML that prompts visitors using browsers with older versions of the Flash player to download the current version. The code, as in the following example, shows how an SWF file called flashsample.swf would be embedded on a page:

**Book II
Chapter 5**

Adding Flash, Movies, Sound, and More

```
<object id="FlashID" classid="clsid:D27CDB6E-AE6D-11cf-96B8-444553540000"
    width="550" height="250">
  <param name="movie" value="flashsample.swf" />
  <!-- Next object tag is for non-IE browsers. So hide it from IE using IECC. -->
  <!--[if !IE]>-->
  <object type="application/x-shockwave-flash" data="flashsample.swf" width="550"
    height="250">
    <!--<![endif]-->
    <param name="quality" value="high" />
    <param name="wmode" value="opaque" />
    <param name="swfversion" value="8.0.35.0" />
    <!-- This param tag prompts users with Flash Player 6.0 r65 and higher to
    download the latest version of Flash Player. Delete it if you don't want
    users to see the prompt. -->
    <param name="expressinstall" value="Scripts/expressInstall.swf" />
    <!-- The browser displays the following alternative content for users with
    Flash Player 6.0 and older. -->
    <div>
      <h4>Content on this page requires a newer version of Adobe Flash Player.</
      h4>
      <p><a href="http://www.adobe.com/go/getflashplayer"><img src="http://www.
      adobe.com/images/shared/download_buttons/get_flash_player.gif" alt="Get
      Adobe Flash player" width="112" height="33" /></a></p>
    </div>
    <!--[if !IE]>-->
  </object>
  <!--<![endif]-->
</object>
<script type="text/javascript">
<!--
swfobject.registerObject("FlashID");
//-->
</script>
```

Dreamweaver displays the embedded Flash movie on the page in Design view as a gray placeholder box with a tabbed blue outline (see Figure 5-1). The tab displays the file format (swf), file name, and an eye icon that toggles visibility between the movie and the download information visitors without Flash installed will see. The Document window doesn't automatically preview the Flash movie; however, you can preview it both inside and outside of Dreamweaver.

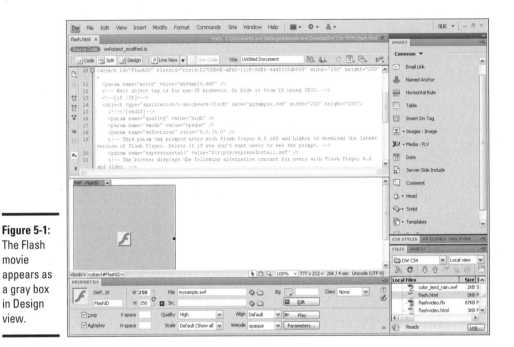

Figure 5-1:
The Flash movie appears as a gray box in Design view.

To preview the Flash movie, select the Flash movie in Design view and do one of the following:

✦ Click the Play button in the Properties inspector. Click Stop to stop the preview.

✦ Click the Live View button on the Document bar to watch the movie, as you would in a browser window. Click Live View again to stop the preview.

✦ Press F12 to preview the movie in a browser window.

Setting Flash movie attributes

After inserting the movie onto the page, select the Flash placeholder in Design view and use the Properties inspector to set the movie attributes. If you don't see all the movie properties, click the expander arrow in the bottom-right corner of the Properties inspector.

✦ **Flash ID:** Input the movie ID. The default name is FlashID.

✦ **Loop:** If you check this option, your SWF movie plays continuously in the browser; leave it unchecked, and your movie plays once and then stops. Note: If the movie itself contains a loop, it will play continuously regardless of whether the Loop option is checked or unchecked.

✦ **Autoplay:** Starts playing the movie automatically when the page loads in a browser window. This option is on by default.

✦ **W** and **H:** The size should automatically match the size of the movie; however, you may change it by entering different values here.

✦ **V Space** and **H Space:** Set white space in pixels above and below, and on both sides, left and right, of the movie.

✦ **File:** Specifies the path of the Flash .swf file. Browse for and select the file using the folder button, Point to File pointer, or type in the path.

✦ **Src:** Specifies the location of the original Flash .fla file used to create the .swf file. Browse for and select the file using the folder button, Point to File pointer, or type in the path to the desired file.

✦ **Quality:** This setting deals with *anti-aliasing,* or smoothing, of the movie during playback. The higher the setting, the smoother the movie, but also the potentially slower the movie displays. By contrast, low settings load faster but look less crisp. Auto Low and High options improve appearance or emphasize quality, respectively.

✦ **Scale:** Determines how the movie fits into the pixel sizes displayed in the W and H text boxes:

 • **Default (Show all):** The entire movie displays at 100 percent.

 • **No Border:** Maintains the original movie dimension aspect ratio but fits the movie, without borders, into the sizes set in the W and H text boxes, which means that any parts of the movie that extend beyond the W and H settings are cut off.

 • **Exact Fit:** Squishes the movie into the specified dimensions, regardless of the original size of the movie.

✦ **Align:** Sets the alignment of the movie relative to the page.

✦ **Wmode:** Sets the Wmode for the SWF file in the browser window, which helps prevent conflicts with DHTML page elements like Spry widget. Choose from any of the following:

 • **Window:** Forces the SWF on top of all page elements.

 • **Opaque:** The default setting, allows DHTML elements to flow on top of the SWF.

 • **Transparent:** Forces DHTML elements to appear behind the SWF. This is often a problem when combining Flash with DHTML menus. If you're menu falls behind the Flash movie, switch the Wmode to Opaque or Window.

✦ **Bg Color:** Adds a background color behind the movie. This color displays only if and when the movie is not playing.

✦ **Edit:** Provides access to the source FLA file for the SWF movie when Flash is loaded on the same computer. If no Flash application is detected, this button is disabled.

✦ **Reset Size:** This button only appears next to the W and H fields when the original size of the SWF file has been modified. Click to revert the SWF file to its original movie size.

✦ **Play/Stop:** Starts and stops movie previews within Design view.

✦ **Parameters:** Opens a dialog box where you can enter more parameters for the movie if the movie has been created to accept these parameters.

✦ **Class:** Applies CSS to a movie, such as styles with border, positioning in the browser, or alignment attributes.

Inserting FlashPaper

Adobe's (formerly Macromedia) FlashPaper software converts any printable document, such as a Word or Excel file, into either a FlashPaper SWF file or PDF (Portable Document Format) file. Like PDFs, anyone can open FlashPaper SWFs in a browser; unlike PDFs, anyone can view FlashPaper online without needing to link to another file or open another browser window. FlashPaper also allows a user to see all the pages in the document, as well as zoom in and out, search, and print.

For more information on FlashPaper, see the Adobe Web site at www. adobe.com/products/flashpaper/.

To insert a FlashPaper document in your Web page, follow these steps:

1. **Open a document and place the insertion point where you want the FlashPaper to appear.**

2. **Choose Insert⇨Media⇨FlashPaper.**

You can also choose the FlashPaper button from the Media drop-down list in the Common category of the Insert panel.

The Insert FlashPaper dialog box appears, as shown in Figure 5-2.

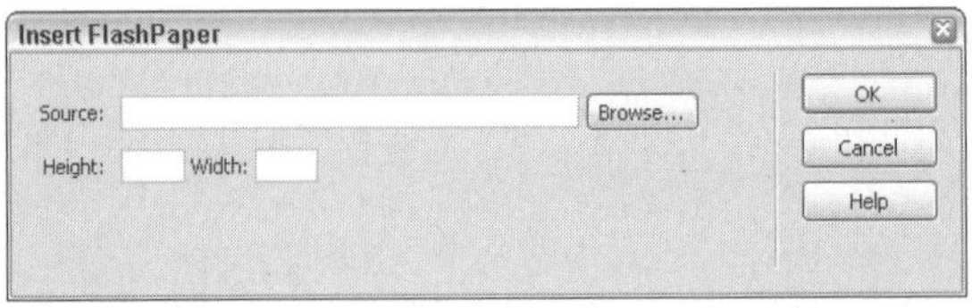

Figure 5-2:
The Insert Flash Paper dialog box.

3. **In the Source field, select a FlashPaper document.**

4. **Set the width and height of the FlashPaper object in pixels.**

   FlashPaper scales the document to fit the width and height.

5. **Click OK to insert the FlashPaper on your page.**

   The Flash object appears on the page as a gray placeholder box. To set additional attributes for the FlashPaper object (which are the same as other Flash elements as described earlier in this chapter), select it and enter attributes in the Properties inspector.

To preview the FlashPaper object and test the functionality of the FlashPaper toolbar, select the FlashPaper placeholder and click the Play button in the Properties inspector. Click Stop to stop the preview. You can also preview the file in Dreamweaver by pressing the Live View button on the Document toolbar, or by pressing F12 to preview the document in a browser window.

Inserting Flash Video

**Book II
Chapter 5**

**Adding Flash,
Movies, Sound, and
More**

Flash video is different from a regular Flash movie in that a Flash video uses the FLV file format and allows you to add prerecorded video to a Web page in a format that most visitors can view with the free Adobe Flash player. A Flash movie, by comparison, is more of a limited animation clip delivered on the Web using the SWF file format.

Flash videos start as captured video, which can be in many formats, including Avid Xpress DV, Adobe After Effects, Apple QuickTimePro, and Apple Final Cut Pro. Once captured, the video gets encoded into the Flash Video format (FLV). You can then decide on a delivery mechanism and add the video to your Web site.

You need to acquire the video and encode it into the FLV format, or at least obtain the FLV files prior to adding them to your site. Once a Flash video has been encoded, you can add it to your page using the Dreamweaver Insert Flash Video command. This tool enables you to add Flash video to your pages without using the Flash program, and it enables browsers to play the inserted Flash video with playback controls.

Find out more about Flash video from the Adobe Learning Guide, including tips on encoding video with Flash CS4 and other programs, at www.adobe. com/devnet/flash/articles/video_guide.html.

When inserting the video, you can select two options for the video type: Progressive Download and Streaming. The decisions you make for inserting Flash video vary slightly depending on which type you choose:

✦ **Progressive Download Video** downloads the FLV file to the user's computer and plays it there. The benefit of FLV is that the video starts to play during the download.

✦ **Streaming Video** streams the Flash video and plays it in the browser window. Streaming video typically buffers for a few seconds before playback to help the playback be smooth rather than bumpy. Streaming also requires the file to be served by your own Flash Media Server or a hosted server running Flash Video Streaming Services.

These types of streaming servers aren't common to most basic servers, so be sure to check with your Webhost for recommendations.

To insert Flash video using the Progressive Download Video type, follow these steps:

1. **Open a document and place the insertion point where you want the Flash video to appear.**

2. **Choose Insert⊏ゝMedia⊏ゝFLV.**

You can also click the Media: FLV button in the Common area of the Insert panel.

The Insert FLV dialog box appears, as shown in Figure 5-3.

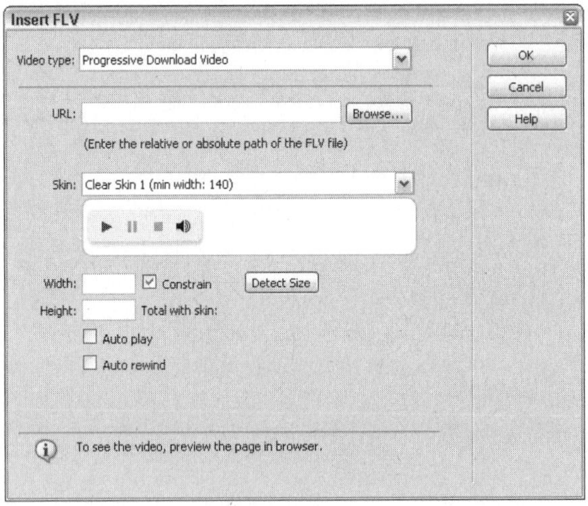

Figure 5-3:
The Insert FLV dialog box set to Progressive Download Video.

3. **Select Progressive Download Video as the video type.**

4. **Set the following options:**

- **URL:** Enter the relative or absolute path of the FLV file. Or click the Browse button to choose a FLV file. For absolute paths, type the complete URL including http://, as in **http://www.mySampleSite. com/video.flv**. If you're using a Mac, you must use an absolute path when FLV files sit more than two levels up from the HTML file the video is inserted on.

  Note: The FLV files must contain metadata in order to work properly as a video player. Many encoders automatically add metadata to the FLV files, but some do not.

- **Skin:** Select an appearance for the video player from the Skin drop-down list. A preview window displays an approximation of how each option looks.

- **Width** and **Height:** Enter a dimension in pixels for both the width and height of the FLV file. Click the **Detect Size** button to have Dreamweaver attempt to automatically read the FLV file dimensions; if the dimensions are unreadable, manually enter W and H sizes. The Total with Skin dimensions displayed after the dimensions are detected represent the total W and H of the FLV file plus the W and H of the chosen skin.

- **Constrain:** This option is enabled by default and ensures that the aspect ratio between the width and height of the FLV movie is maintained.

- **Auto Play:** Enable this option to have the video begin playing as soon as the Web page loads in the browser window.

- **Auto Rewind:** Enable this option to have the video playback return to the start position when the video reaches the end.

5. **Click OK to close the dialog box and insert the Flash video on your page.**

   Along with the appropriate code for inserting the FLV file, the code also includes version detection that prompts visitors to download a newer version of the free Adobe Flash Player, should their browser's version be out of date.

   A video SWF file and SWF skin are created to play the video in a browser. These files are added to the same directory as the HTML file the video has been inserted in. In the example shown in Figure 5-4, these files are called Clear_Skin_3.swf and FLVPlayer_Progressive.swf.

   You must also upload these skin files to your server for the video to play properly. Dreamweaver automatically uploads these files as dependents during the FTP as long as you agree to upload dependent files during the upload process

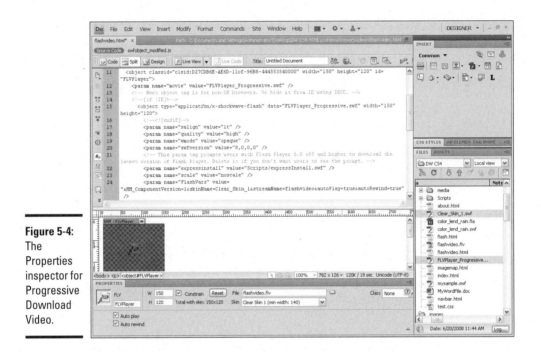

After inserting the FLV, you can modify some of the Flash video settings, such as Auto Play, Auto Rewind, and the Skin, in the Properties inspector (see Figure 5-4).

To insert Flash video using the Streaming Video type, follow these steps:

1. **Open a document and place the insertion point where you want the Flash video to appear.**

2. **Choose Insert➪Media➪FLV.**

You can also click the Media: FLV button in the Common area of the Insert panel.

The Insert FLV dialog box appears, as shown in Figure 5-5.

3. **Select Streaming Video as the video type.**

4. **Set the following options:**

- **Server URI:** Enter the server, application, and instance names in the form, as in `rtmp://www.mySite.com/application_name/instance_name`.

- **Skin:** Select an appearance for the video player from the Skin drop-down list. A preview window displays an approximation of how each option looks.

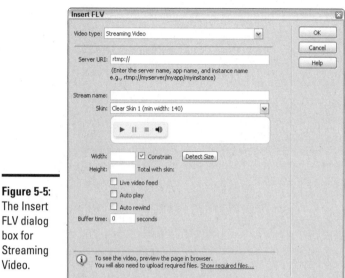

Figure 5-5:
The Insert
FLV dialog
box for
Streaming
Video.

- **Width** and **Height:** Enter a dimension in pixels for both the width and height of the FLV file. Click the **Detect Size** button to have Dreamweaver attempt to automatically read the FLV file dimensions; if the dimensions are unreadable, manually enter W and H sizes. The Total with Skin dimensions displayed after the dimensions are detected represent the total W and H of the FLV file plus the W and H of the chosen skin.

- **Constrain:** This option is enabled by default and ensures that the aspect ratio between the width and height of the FLV movie is maintained.

- **Live Video Feed:** Enable this option only when the video feed is live. When live, the player plays a live video streamed from the server. The name in the Stream Name text box is the name of the live video feed. Because a viewer can't manipulate live video, only the volume control appears on the skin. Furthermore, the Auto Play and Auto Rewind options are also inoperable with live video.

- **Auto Play:** Enable this option to have the video begin playing as soon as the Web page loads in the browser window.

- **Auto Rewind:** Enable this option to have the video playback return to the start position when the video reaches the end.

- **Buffer Time:** This is the time it takes, in seconds, before the video begins to play in a browser. By default, the buffer is set to 0, but you can increase the number of seconds to have the player pause before the video begins to play, which may be helpful for sites that have occasional bandwidth issues when visitor traffic is high. When Auto Play is enabled, however, the buffer time is ignored.

5. **Click OK to close the dialog box and insert the Flash video on your page.**

   Along with the appropriate code for inserting the FLV file, Dreamweaver includes version detection markup that prompts visitors to download a newer version of the free Adobe Flash Player, should their browser's version be out of date.

   A video SWF file and SWF skin are also created to play the video in a browser. You must upload the SWF files to your Web server and the ASC file to the Flash Communication Server for the video to play properly. Dreamweaver automatically uploads these files as dependents when transferring files with FTP as long as you agree to upload dependent files during the upload process.

Flash videos may require different players depending on which codec the video was created with. For more information about Flash video, visit the Flash Developer Center at `www.adobe.com/devnet/flash/` and read the Flash Video with Dreamweaver tutorial by Jen deHaan at `www.adobe.com/devnet/flash/articles/flv_tutorial.html`.

Adding Shockwave Movies, Java Applets, and ActiveX Controls

In Dreamweaver, you can add Shockwave movies, Java applets, ActiveX controls, and other sound and video files to any open, saved file. If the object you want to add is not one of these types, use a Netscape Navigator plug-in instead (as described in the section "Adding Netscape Navigator Plug-ins," later in the chapter). You need to prepare these objects in advance before inserting them on your page. Table 5-1 describes the type of objects you can add to your Web page.

Table 5-1	Media Types
Media Type	*Description*
Shockwave Movie	Adobe's standard for interactive multimedia files on the Web, typically created from compressed Adobe Director files. Shockwave movies download fast and can display in browsers with the appropriate free Shockwave player.
Java Applet	Lightweight applications *(applets)* generated with the Java programming language that are inserted onto Web pages.
ActiveX Control	Formerly called OLE controls, these media files are reusable components that behave like Netscape browser plug-ins. They run only in Windows versions of Internet Explorer. You can assign these controls additional attributes and parameters in Dreamweaver.

Media Type	Description
QuickTime Movie	A movie format created with Apple's QuickTime program that can include video, audio, and other bitstreams, such as images and animations.
Netscape Navigator Plug-in	A plug-in, or helper application, that allows a Netscape Navigator browser to display multimedia content (audio, video, animation, virtual reality, and 3D objects) in a range of file formats. Plug-ins include RealPlayer, QuickTime, and MP3 files, among many others.

Follow these steps to insert a media object:

1. Choose Insert⇨Media and select the desired media type (Shockwave, Applet, ActiveX, or Plug-in) from the submenu.

Or click the Media button in the Common category of the Insert panel to select the media type from its drop-down list.

The Select File dialog box appears.

2. Browse to and select a source file, and set any parameters for the media file.

For the lowdown on adding parameters for media files, see the nearby sidebar "Controlling media objects with parameters."

To insert a media placeholder and bypass having to select a source file or set any preferences (though the Tag Accessibility dialog box may still pop up when Accessibility features are enabled), press and hold Control (Windows) or Option (Mac) while inserting the media object. For example, to insert a placeholder for a plug-in without selecting the plug-in file, press and hold Control or Option and choose Insert⇨Media⇨Plug-in, or click the Plug-in button in the Media drop-down list in the Common category of the Insert panel.

3. Click OK to insert the media.

If you've enabled Accessibility options in Preferences, the object's Tag Accessibility Attributes dialog box appears prompting you to add a title, shortcut *(access)* key, and tab index options to the media file. Enter those attributes and click OK, or click Cancel to add the media file or placeholder without the Accessibility attributes.

Setting Shockwave movie properties

Shockwave movies, which are compressed multimedia files created with Adobe Director, are embedded into a page in a similar fashion and have the same options as Flash files. Though often confused with Flash files, they are not Flash.

To specify the properties for Shockwave movies, select the movie place-holder in Design view and apply attributes to it from the Properties inspector. See the earlier section "Setting Flash movie attributes" for a description of each property.

Setting Java applet properties

You can also add Java applets to HTML files with Dreamweaver. Java (not to be confused with JavaScript, a scripting language) is a programming language that creates *applets,* or little applications.

After inserting the applet on the page, select the applet placeholder and set the applet attributes in the Properties inspector (see Figure 5-6):

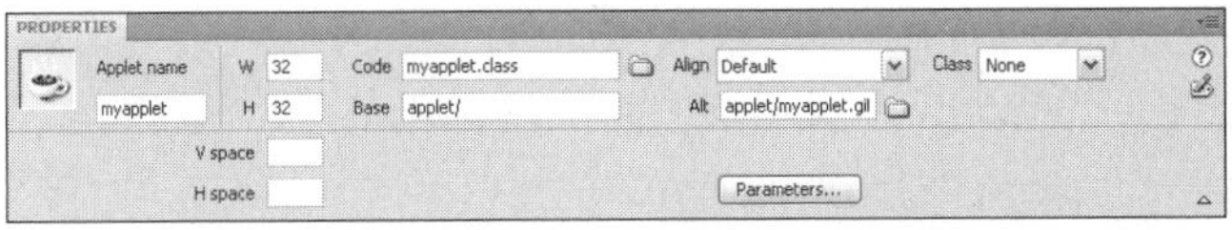

Figure 5-6:
Set properties for a Java applet.

+ **Applet Name:** Enter the applet name in the text box.

+ **W** and **H:** Set the width and height of the applet in pixels.

+ **V Space** and **H Space:** Set white space in pixels above and below, and on both sides, of the applet.

+ **Code:** When you select the applet, this field gets filled in automatically. To change the Java applet source file, click the folder button or type a different filename.

+ **Base:** If you selected a file in the Code field, the location or path of the applet displays in this box.

+ **Align:** Set the alignment on the applet relative to the page.

+ **Alt:** Set alternative content and specify a graphic file that displays if the user's browser doesn't support Java applets or has Java disabled. You can also insert Alt text instead of a graphic. When you add an image, the `<img>` tag gets inserted between the opening and closing `<applet>` tags. To specify both an image and Alt text, insert the image first, and then add the alt attribute to the `<img>` tag in Code view:

```
<applet code="myapplet.class" codebase="applet/" width="32" height="32">
  <img src="applet/myapplet.gif" width="32" height="32" alt="Spinning
    Counter" />
</applet>
```

✦ **Class:** Apply CSS to an applet.

✦ **Parameters:** Click the Parameters button to enter more parameters for the applet. See the upcoming sidebar "Controlling media objects with parameters" for more info about setting parameters.

If you don't see all these properties, click the expander arrow in the bottom-right corner of the Properties inspector.

Setting ActiveX control properties

Formerly known as OLE controls, *ActiveX controls* are mini-applications that behave like browser plug-ins and can be reused as often as you need. The ActiveX object lets you add attributes and parameters for an ActiveX control in a user's browser.

Book II
Chapter 5

Adding Flash, Movies, Sound, and More

Controlling media objects with parameters

With most media objects, the Properties inspector includes a Parameters button when you're specifying properties for that media object. Parameters are special values for Shockwave movies, Java applets, ActiveX controls, Netscape Navigator plug-ins, and Flash SWF files. These values are attached to the `<object>`, `<embed>`, and `<applet>` tags in the code, and usually set specific attributes for the type of media object being added to the page. For instance, a Shockwave movie can have a URL parameter that is part of the `<embed>` tag as the following line of code shows (where `swURL` is the name and `file-name.html` is the value of the parameter):

```
<embed src="swmovie.dcr" height="100"
       width="100" swURL="filename.
       html">
```

To find out what attributes you can add to an object, see the documentation for the media object you're inserting. Whatever parameters you do add, the process for adding them is the same.

To add parameters to media objects, follow these steps:

1. Select the media file placeholder in Design view.

2. Click the Parameters button in the Properties inspector.

   The Parameters dialog box opens, shown in the following figure.

3. Enter a value for the parameter. Click the plus (+) button to add a parameter or the minus (–) button to remove a parameter.

4. Enter the parameter name in the Parameter column and the value in the Value column.

5. Repeat steps 3 and 4 to add or remove parameters as needed.

(continued)

(continued)

6. To reorder the parameters, click the up and down arrow buttons.

7. Click OK when you're done setting all the parameters.

You can also view the assigned attributes of any selected media object by viewing the Attributes tab of the Tag Inspector panel. There you can add, edit, and delete attributes like src, width, and height.

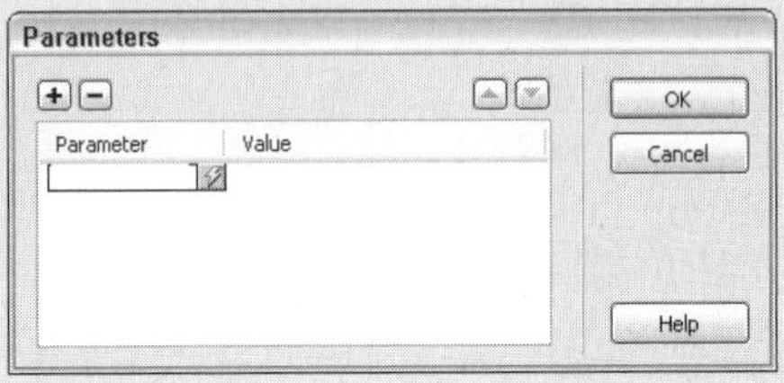

> **Parameters**
>
> `+` `−`   `▲` `▼`   **OK**
>
> | Parameter | Value |
> | --- | --- |
> | | |
>
> Cancel
>
> Help

WARNING!

ActiveX controls run on Windows with Internet Explorer, but not on IE on a Mac or in any Netscape browser, so use them with consideration.

Select the ActiveX control placeholder in Design view, and set the attributes of the `<object>` tag and the parameters of the ActiveX control in the Properties inspector (see Figure 5-7).

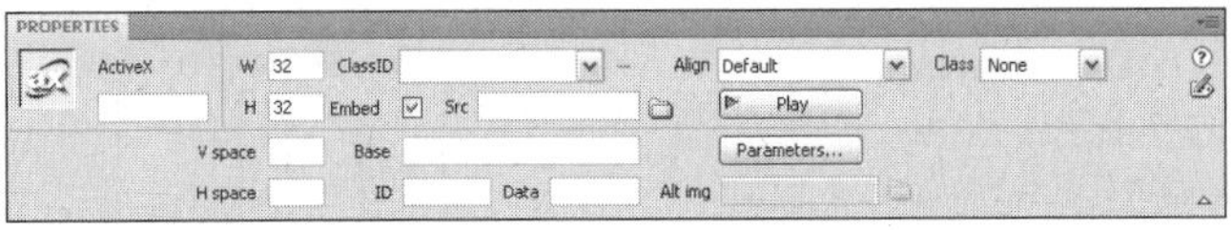

Figure 5-7:
Set properties for the ActiveX control.

PROPERTIES

ActiveX   W 32   ClassID   Align Default   Class None   ?
           H 32   Embed ✓ Src   ▶   Play
    V space   Base   Parameters...
    H space   ID   Data   Alt img

✦ **ActiveX:** Enter the name of the ActiveX media file in the ActiveX text box in the top-left corner of the Properties inspector. The name assists with scripting the object.

✦ **W** and **H:** Set the width and height of the object in pixels.

✦ **V Space** and **H Space:** Set white space in pixels above and below, and on both sides, of the object.

✦ **ClassID:** Select a value from the drop-down list or type a value for the ClassID, such as RealPlayer or Shockwave for Flash. This field identifies the control to the browser. If the browser can't find the ActiveX control specified, it tries to download it from the URL listed in the Base field.

✦ **Embed:** Activate the Netscape Navigator plug-in equivalent of the ActiveX control using the `<embed>` tag within the `<object>` tag. ActiveX property values assigned in Dreamweaver are applied to their Netscape Navigator plug-in equivalents.

✦ **Src:** If you enabled the Embed option, type or browse to and select the data file for a Netscape Navigator plug-in. If you don't specify a filename, Dreamweaver attempts to find the value using the other ActiveX properties.

✦ **Base:** Identify the URL with the ActiveX control. If the control is not already installed on the user's computer, IE prompts the user to download it. Without the proper ActiveX control installed, the browser can't display the object.

✦ **ID:** Set the ID for the ActiveX control to load. If you don't have information for this parameter, leave this field blank.

✦ **Data:** Set the data file for the object to load in the browser. Some ActiveX controls, such as RealPlayer, don't use this parameter. Leave the field blank if you don't have information for this parameter.

✦ **Alt Img:** Specify a graphic file to display if the user's browser doesn't support the `<object>` tag. The Embed option must be unchecked to use this feature.

✦ **Align:** Set the alignment of the object relative to the page.

✦ **Class:** Apply CSS to an object.

✦ **Parameters:** Click this button to enter more parameters for the ActiveX control. See the sidebar "Controlling media objects with parameters" for more info about setting parameters.

Adding Netscape Navigator Plug-ins

Typical plug-ins for Netscape Navigator (the precursor to Firefox and other non-IE browsers) include QuickTime movies, RealPlayer content, and MP3s. If you want to insert an object that is *not* a Flash, Shockwave, applet, or ActiveX object, try inserting it on your page with the Netscape Navigator plug-in. You can create your own content or get it from another source, and then use Dreamweaver to insert the file into your HTML page. To insert a Netscape Navigator plug-in, follow the steps in the earlier section "Adding Shockwave Movies, Java Applets, and ActiveX Controls" and choose the Plug-in option in Step 1.

Setting Netscape Navigator plug-in properties

After adding the Netscape Navigator plug-in object, select the plug-in place-holder in Design view and set its properties in the Properties inspector (see Figure 5-8). Here are your options:

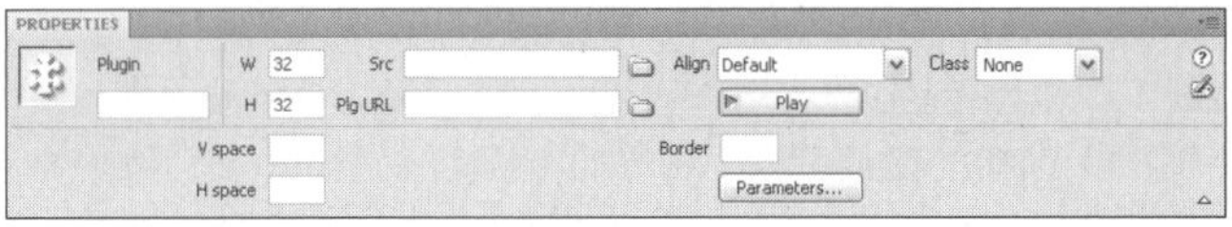

Figure 5-8:
Set
properties
for the
plug-in.

+ **Plug-in ID/Name:** Enter the name in the Plug-in text box in the top-left corner of the Properties inspector.

+ **W and H:** Set the width and height of the plug-in object in pixels.

+ **V space** and **H space:** Set white space in pixels above and below, and on both sides, of the plug-in object.

+ **Src:** If you selected a source file for the plug-in when you inserted it, this field is already filled in. If not, identify the source data file of the plug-in by typing the filename or click the folder button to browse to and select the file.

+ **Plg URL:** Specify the URL where users can download this plug-in. If the user's computer doesn't have the plug-in, the browser downloads it from this URL.

+ **Border:** Add a black border, in pixels, around the entire plug-in.

+ **Align:** Set the alignment of the object relative to the page.

+ **Class:** Apply CSS to an object.

+ **Parameters:** Click the Parameters button to enter more parameters for the Netscape Navigator plug-in. See the sidebar "Controlling media objects with parameters" for more info about setting parameters.

Playing Netscape Navigator plug-ins

Dreamweaver lets you preview movies and animations that use Netscape Navigator plug-ins (but not ActiveX controls) in Design view. As long as you've installed the appropriate plug-ins, you can play previews of all the plug-ins at once or play them separately.

Be sure to also test the plug-ins in as many browsers as possible to ensure your site visitors have the most consistent experience viewing them. A fantastic online testing site is www.browsershots.org.

Here's how to preview movies and animations with Netscape Navigator plug-ins:

✦ **To preview a single movie or animation:** Select a media file inserted on the page and click the Play button in the Properties inspector. The media file plays in Design view.

Or choose View➪Plug-ins➪Play.

✦ **To preview all the media files on a single document:** Choose View➪ Plug-ins➪Play All. All the media files on the same page play. Alternately, you can try to preview the plug-ins by clicking the Live View button on the Document toolbar.

✦ **To stop playing the media files:** Click the Stop button in the Properties inspector. For multiple media files, you can also choose View➪Plug-ins➪Stop All. For Live View previews, click the Live View button again to toggle out of Live View.

If for some reason the plug-in content does not play in the Document window, try the following troubleshooting tips:

✦ Be sure the plug-in is installed on the test computer and that the plug-in content is compatible with the plug-in version installed. For instance, if a movie runs with QuickTime V7, but only the QuickTime V5 player is installed, the movie won't play.

✦ Open the Configuration/Plug-ins/UnsupportedPlug-ins.txt file in a text editor to see if the plug-in is listed. This file automatically adds problematic plug-ins to the list.

✦ Check the computer to see if enough memory is allocated to run the file. Many plug-ins need an extra 2 to 5MB of memory just to run! That said, most modern operating systems don't use memory allocation, so this issue may be more applicable for Mac OS9, Windows 95, and earlier operating systems.

Acceptable Sound File Formats

There are several common sound file formats, each with their own set of benefits and drawbacks. Here are the most common file formats:

✦ **.mp3 (Motion Picture Experts Group Audio, or MPEG-Audio Layer-3):** This sound file compresses files so they are much smaller in size. The quality is very good — even close to CD quality if recorded and compressed in the right way. One of the great things about this format is the ability to stream data so the user doesn't have to wait for the entire file to download before listening to it. Most podcasts are MP3 or ACC.

One possible drawback is the overall file size, which can get pretty big, making download times on a dialup connection seem impossible. The user's computer must have helper applications, such as iTunes, QuickTime, RealPlayer, or Windows Media Player, to play MP3 files.

✦ **.qt, .qtm, .mov, or QuickTime:** This format is great because it can contain both sound and video. Developed by Apple, it's the default sound/video player for Macintosh computers. PCs can play QuickTime files too, but the user needs to download and install the free QuickTime player first. The encoding formats supported by QuickTime include JPEG, MPEG, and Cinepak.

✦ **.ra, .ram, .rpm, or Real Audio:** Like MP3s, this format allows for streaming audio data. It also compresses files, but into even smaller file sizes than MP3s. Visitors would need to download and install the RealPlayer application to play these files. That said, Real Audio is on the decline so you might want to shy away from using Real Audio.

✦ **.wav (Waveform Extension):** These files have good sound, are widely supported by browsers, and don't need any special plug-ins to play. They tend to have very large file sizes, so sound clips need to be small enough to add to Web pages. Most computers allow you to record your own WAV files in some way with a microphone.

✦ **.midi or .mid (Musical Instrument Digital Interface):** These files are intended for instrumental music only. Small files can provide long sound clips, too. The sound quality, however, is dependent on the sound card on the user's computer. Like WAV files, most browsers support MIDI files and they don't require special plug-ins. The biggest drawback to MIDI files is that you can't easily record with them; they must be synthesized using specific software and hardware.

✦ **.aif (Audio Interchange File Format, or AIFF):** Like the WAV format, these sound files have good sound, are supported by most browsers, and don't need plug-ins to play. AIFF files can be recorded to CDs and tapes using a microphone through your computer, but because of their large file sizes, sound clips need to be small enough to add to Web pages.

If you come across another file format that you want to use on your Web page, check with the format creator's technical help files to find out about browser support.

Adding Other Video and Sound to a Page

Dreamweaver supports adding sound to a Web page. There are many types of sound files and formats, such as .wav, RealPlayer, and .mp3, as described in the preceding section.

Before you decide on a format and how to add the sound to your page, consider the audience, the file size, the sound quality, and the different ways browsers support these files because different browsers handle sound files very differently. If you're trying to create a consistent experience for your visitors — regardless of their browser type — consider adding the sound to a Flash SWF file rather than having it linked or embedded to the page. Ultimately, testing the sound and video files in multiple browsers is the best way to decide what to add and how to add it.

Linking versus embedding video

You can link or embed your prepared video files (non-Flash) to a Web page, depending on the video format and preferred method of display. That means you can set up the video to download to the user's desktop, or embed it in the page so it streams in the browser while downloading.

Book II
Chapter 5

Adding Flash,
Movies, Sound, and
More

Follow these steps to link or embed a short video in your page:

1. **Add the video clip to your site folder.**

   Video clips often use the MPEG or AVI file format.

2. **Link or embed the clip to your page by doing one of the following:**

   - **Linking:** Type the text you want to appear on your page (such as **Download Video**), select that text, and in the File text field in the Properties inspector, type the video filename with extension, or click the folder button to browse for and select the video file.

   - **Embedding:** Follow the steps in the earlier section, "Adding Shockwave Movies, Java Applets, and ActiveX Controls."

     Streaming video requires that the user's computer has a helper application, such as RealMedia, Windows Media, or QuickTime, for the video to play.

Be sure to upload the video file to the server along with the file it's linked to so the site visitor can download or watch the video.

Linking versus embedding sound

Linking to a sound file is the best way to add sound to a Web page because it allows users to decide for themselves whether they want to listen to the file in advance of hearing it.

Embedding sound, by contrast, adds the sound directly into a Web page so it plays automatically, as long as the user's computer has the right plug-in. Embedded files can play background music, for instance. Sound plug-ins often embed volume control as well as On/Mute control.

Although both methods are possible, the more widely used practice is to embed sound in a Flash file, which avoids the need for visitors to download a bunch of different plug-ins.

Linking to a sound file

To add a link to a sound file on a Web page, follow these steps:

1. **Select the image or text you want to use as the link to the audio file.**

2. **In the Properties inspector, type the filename in the Link text box, or click the folder button to browse for and select the audio file you want to use.**

Be sure to upload the sound file to the server along with the file it's linked to so the site visitor can access the sound file. This method makes the sound file available to the widest audience.

Embedding a sound file

To embed a sound file on a Web page, follow these steps:

1. **In Design view, place the insertion point on the page where you want to embed the file.**

2. **Choose Insert⇨Media⇨Plug-in.**

   Or click the Media button in the Common category of the Insert panel and choose Plug-in from its drop-down list.

   The Select File dialog box appears.

3. **Browse to and select the sound file you want to insert.**

4. **Click OK to insert the sound file.**

After inserting the sound object, select the sound placeholder object in Design view and enter values in the attribute fields in the Properties inspector. The Width and Height values, for example, determine the size of the audio controls displayed in the browser window.

Be sure to upload the sound file to the server along with the file it's embedded in so the site visitor can hear and play the sound file.

Launching a Media External Editor

Dreamweaver allows you to launch many external editors for a variety of media types if you need to edit those media files while working within Dreamweaver. For example, you can launch Fireworks to modify GIF files,

Photoshop to modify JPG files, and oXygen or Altova XMLSpy to modify XML files. Launching an external editor from within Dreamweaver to edit most media types is a simple process that requires only a few simple steps.

First, you need to associate the media file type with the editor on your computer. To so do, follow these steps:

1. **Choose Edit⇨Preferences (Windows) or Dreamweaver⇨Preferences (Mac) and then choose the File Types/Editors category in the Preferences dialog box, as shown in Figure 5-9.**

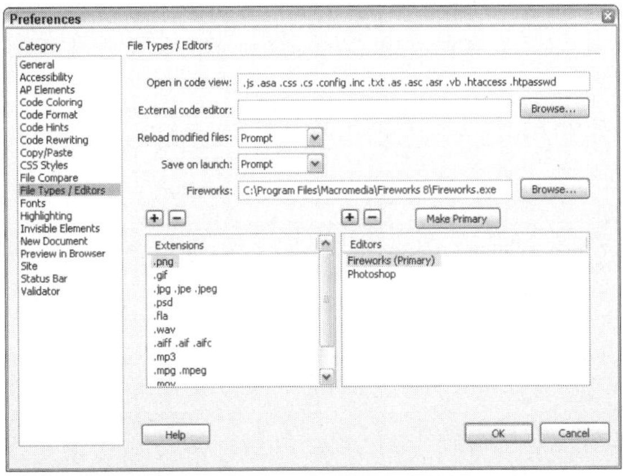

Book II
Chapter 5

Adding Flash, Movies, Sound, and More

Figure 5-9:
The File Types/ Editors Preferences.

2. **Select the file extension in the Extensions panel to see any associated editors in the Editors panel.**

For example, in Figure 5-9, the .png extension is associated with the Fireworks editor, which is also the primary editor.

3. **If needed, add or change extension types by clicking the plus (+) or minus (–) button. To make an editor the primary editor, click the Make Primary button.**

4. **When you finish, click OK to save your changes.**

After you establish the file types/editor preferences, double-click the media file in the Files panel to start the external media editor. The primary editor associated with that media type opens.

If you'd prefer to occasionally not use the primary editor to edit the media file, right-click (Windows) or Control+click (Mac) the media file from the Files panel or from within Design view and choose Open With or Edit With from the context menu.

Chapter 6: Organizing Data with Tables

In This Chapter

✔ Creating tables

✔ Using table visual aids

✔ Formatting tables and table cells

✔ Adding content to table cells

✔ Importing tabular data

With the increasing popularity of CSS layout and CSS best practices, table-based Web sites are becoming less and less common. Most Web designers have switched to a CSS layout model, which is widely recognized as being more flexible than table-based layout. (See Book IV, Chapter 1 to learn more about layers-based Web sites.)

That said, tables themselves are still a great way to organize tabular data and other content, like a listing of store locations or detailed product information, in a visually pleasing way. HTML tables can have as many rows and columns as needed, and additional tables can be nested inside other table cells ad infinitum for more complex layouts. Tables are made up of one or more rows, and each row has one or more cells. The cells make up columns, and though the columns are not explicitly defined in HTML, Dreamweaver allows you to manipulate rows, columns, and cells.

As far as styling goes, tables can have borders, background colors, background images, and be aligned relative to the page. Their individual table cells can also have similar attributes. Furthermore, table content can include text, graphics, links, movies, sound, and other plug-ins, and each of those can have their own formatting or style attributes.

This chapter guides you through the process of inserting, editing, and deleting tables, formatting and adding content to them, plus some general tips for using tables to improve the overall look and feel of a page.

Creating Tables

Though creating Web page layouts with CSS and *AP Elements*, or *layers*, is the preferred method of design these days, you can still use tables for laying out and organizing other content. It's also important to understand how tables have been used in the past for layout, as you may someday inherit a Web site built with a tables-based layout and need to convert it to layers, or at the very least edit the content within it.

To add a table to your page, simply insert the table in an open file in the Dreamweaver Document window and format the table and content inside the cells according to a predetermined design or your own personal aesthetic. For instance, you can create a table that organizes UPS second-day air shipping rates by state and number of units sold. (see Figure 6-1).

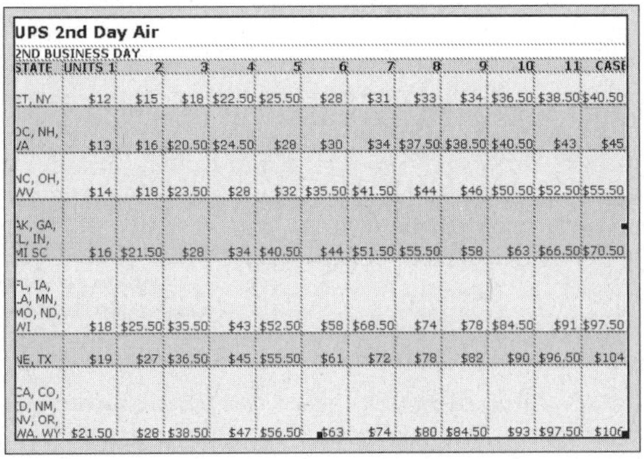

UPS 2nd Day Air

2ND BUSINESS DAY

STATE	UNITS 1	2	3	4	5	6	7	8	9	10	11	CASE
CT, NY	$12	$15	$18	$22.50	$25.50	$28	$31	$33	$34	$36.50	$38.50	$40.50
DC, NH, VA	$13	$16	$20.50	$24.50	$28	$30	$34	$37.50	$38.50	$40.50	$43	$45
NC, OH, WV	$14	$18	$23.50	$28	$32	$35.50	$41.50	$44	$46	$50.50	$52.50	$55.50
AK, GA, IL, IN, MI SC	$16	$21.50	$28	$34	$40.50	$44	$51.50	$55.50	$58	$63	$66.50	$70.50
FL, IA, LA, MN, MO, ND, WI	$18	$25.50	$35.50	$43	$52.50	$58	$68.50	$74	$78	$84.50	$91	$97.50
NE, TX	$19	$27	$36.50	$45	$55.50	$61	$72	$78	$82	$90	$96.50	$104
CA, CO, ID, NM, NV, OR, WA, WY	$21.50	$28	$38.50	$47	$56.50	$63	$74	$80	$84.50	$93	$97.50	$106

Figure 6-1: Use tables to organize content within a page.

When your table contains a lot of text, it's best to fix the width of the table cell to a readable size, usually 500 pixels wide or less. To contain text inside a fixed area of the page, insert a fixed-width table with one row and one column and paste the content inside the table cell. When opened in a browser window, the text then wraps inside the cell boundaries instead of expanding and collapsing with the edges of the browser window.

In the Layout category of the Insert panel, shown in Figure 6-2, you can choose from two layout modes when working with tables:

- **Standard:** By default, Dreamweaver uses Standard mode, which shows tables as a grid of rows and columns.
- **Expanded:** For even easier editing, try using the Expanded mode, which adds temporary cell padding and cell spacing for more precise selections.

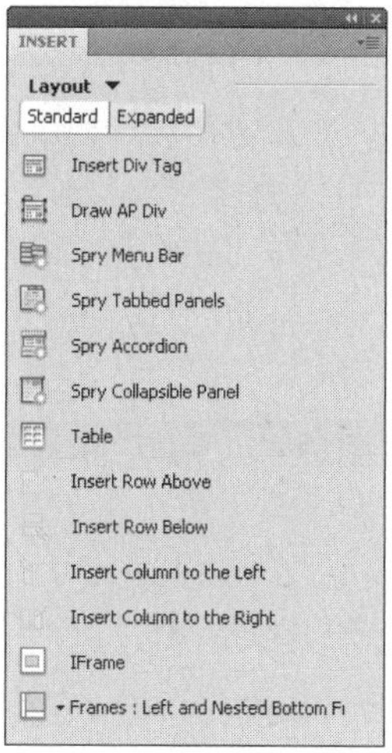

Figure 6-2:
The Layout category of the Insert panel.

To switch layout modes, click the desired Layout mode button in the Layout category of the Insert panel. You can also switch modes by choosing View⇨Table Mode and then selecting a layout mode option from the submenu.

In the following sections, you find out how to insert a basic table in your Web page.

Inserting a basic table in your page

To create a basic table in Dreamweaver, follow these steps:

1. **Place your cursor where you want the table to appear on the page.**

2. **Choose Insert⇨Table.**

You can also click the Table button on the Layout category of the Insert panel.

The Table dialog box appears, as shown in Figure 6-3.

3. **Specify the following attributes for the new table:**

- **Rows** and **Columns:** Enter the number of rows and columns for your table.

- **Table Width:** Enter a fixed width in pixels or a percentage width between 1 and 100 percent.

- **Border Thickness:** Enter the size, in pixels, for the table border. If left blank, the border displays as if it was set to 1 pixel. To remove a border completely, set the thickness to 0.

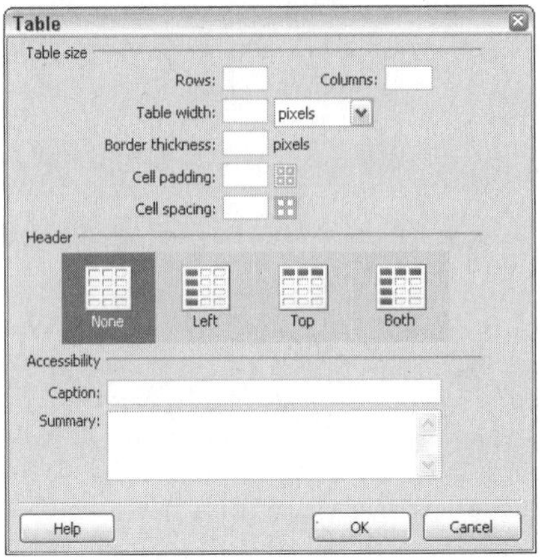

Figure 6-3:
Set table options before adding a table to the page.

- **Cell Padding:** Enter a number in pixels to increase the space between the cell's walls and its contents. If left blank, the cell padding displays as if it was set to 1 pixel. To remove cell padding completely, set the size to 0.

- **Cell Spacing:** Enter a number in pixels to increase the walls of the table between the cells. If left blank, the cell spacing displays as if it was set to 2 pixels. To remove cell spacing completely, set the size to 0.

4. **(Optional) Choose a header for the table.**

   The content in header rows or columns format differently than content in other table cells. In addition, screen readers identify the content in header rows or columns differently to assist visually impaired visitors in understanding the content in the table.

5. **In the Accessibility area, fill in the following fields:**

   - **Caption:** This is a title for the table, which appears outside of the table, directly on top of the first table row.

   - **Summary:** Add a description for your table. This information is added to the opening Table tag and hidden from view in a browser, but is read by screen readers.

6. **When you finish, click OK to create your table.**

   Dreamweaver adds the table to your page with the specified settings.

7. **Add content to your table cells.**

   You can insert text, graphics, media, and other files in a table cell — anything that can exist on a page can also be placed and formatted in a table cell. For details, see the "Inserting Text and Images in Table Cells" and "Formatting Individual Table Cells" sections.

After inserting the table, you can also nest tables inside the table's individual cells. To nest a table inside a table cell, place your cursor inside the table cell and repeat Steps 2 through 7.

Turning On Table Visual Aids

Creating tables can sometimes be a tricky business, so Dreamweaver created some interesting visual aids. They help you select table cells, columns, and rows, edit the tables themselves, and view table attributes such as cell widths in pixels or percentages.

By default, the visual aids for tables should already be on; however, you can toggle them on and off by choosing View➪Visual Aids➪Table Widths and/or View➪Visual Aids➪Table Borders. You see a check mark when the aids are enabled, and no check mark when they're turned off. You can also turn Visual Aids on and off through the Visual Aids menu of any open Document window. Figure 6-4 shows an example of a table with and without Table Visual Aids.

Book II
Chapter 6

Organizing Data
with Tables

Visual Aids

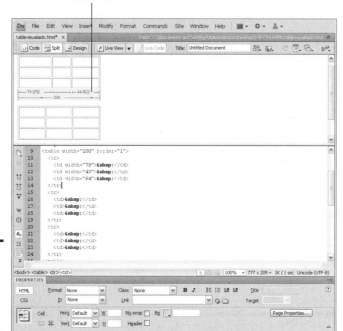

Figure 6-4:
A table with and without visual aids enabled.

When Table Visual Aids are turned on, Dreamweaver shows a table header menu, which displays table widths and column widths when the table is selected or the cursor is somewhere inside the table. Next to the widths you see tiny green arrows that, when clicked, quickly access a few of the table-related commands.

If two numbers are specified for the width dimensions, check the HTML code to ensure that the column widths add up to the total table width. For instance, one column's width may be set to 100 pixels, but after adding a long sentence or large graphic, the cell stretches to 300 pixels. The first number (100) is the HTML-specified cell width, and the number in parentheses (300) is the visual width as displayed on-screen. Fix the table dimensions in the code by clicking the table header menu and selecting Make All Widths Consistent. Then preview the page in a browser window (F12 (Windows) or Option+F12 (Mac)) to test for visual accuracy.

Formatting Tables with the Properties Inspector

After creating a table, you can set formatting options for the whole table, or for specified rows, columns, or cells, in the Properties inspector.

To select a table to format it, do one of the following:

✦ Click on the table's outer edge.

✦ With your cursor anywhere inside of the table, click the table tag on the Quick Tag Editor bar at the bottom of the Document window.

When a table is selected, selection handles appear on the right-center, bottom-center, and bottom-right corners of the table, and the Properties inspector displays table formatting options, as shown in Figure 6-5.

Table formatting attributes are totally optional. Use them in any combination to format tables in harmony with the data contained in them and the overall look of the Web site design. When adding formatting to a table, keep in mind that cell formatting takes precedence over row formatting, which takes precedence over table formatting. In other words, a cell with a background color displays that color in the browser even if the row or entire table has a different background color attribute.

Also keep in mind that most of the decorative table styling should be applied with CSS. You can apply those custom CSS styles along with other formatting using the Properties inspector.

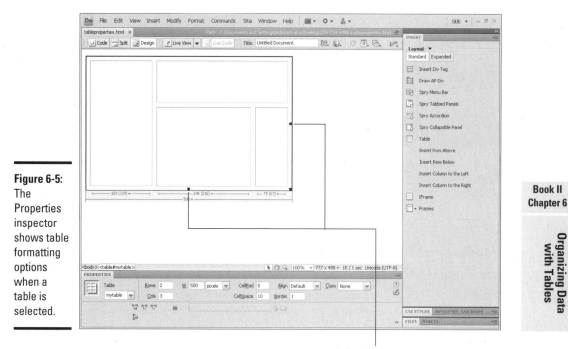

Figure 6-5:
The
Properties
inspector
shows table
formatting
options
when a
table is
selected.

Selection handles

The Properties inspector includes these table formatting options:

✦ **Table ID:** Input the table name. IDs are now used instead of name
  attributes for easier assignment of CSS, Dreamweaver behaviors, and
  JavaScript events. You don't need to name all your tables, but adding
  Table IDs to each of your tables is a more Web standards compliant way
  of coding, and it also helps you keep better track of them when you do.

✦ **Rows** and **Cols:** Change the numbers in the Rows and Cols fields to
  adjust the table rows and columns accordingly (see the "Adding Rows
  and Columns to a Table" section).

✦ **W:** Adjust the width of the table in pixels or percentages. Widths are
  generally specified for tables automatically, while the height field is typically left blank so that the overall height is determined by the contents
  of the table. When specifying dimensions in percentages, the width is
  relative to the open browser window or containing cell. For instance,
  W=80% (or in the code view, width="80%") means the table expands to
  80 percent of the open browser window, or 80 percent of a containing
  cell if the table is nested inside another table.

- ✦ **Border:** Add a border to the outer edges of a table. By default, the Border field is blank. Enter any number from 0 to 750. Borders without a border color attribute appear beveled.

  For better borders, create a custom CSS style. See Book III, Chapter 1 to learn more about Cascading Style Sheets.

- ✦ **Class:** Apply a custom style from an internal or external CSS to style tables or table cells with background colors, borders, and background images, among other things.

To gain further control over the look of your tables, consider adding cell padding, cell spacing, and cell alignment attributes:

- ✦ The **CellPad** field adds uniform spacing in pixels inside all the cells in a table, padding cell contents away from the cell walls.

- ✦ The **CellSpace** field adds uniform spacing in pixels to the walls of the cells in the table.

- ✦ The **Align** field determines where the table sits relative to other content on the page. The browser determines the default alignment, but most browsers have the default set to Left. To ensure the table aligns properly, select Left, Center, and Right from the drop-down list.

By default, the CellPad and CellSpace fields are blank, which has the equivalent of 2 pixels, respectively. To remove the default spacing attributes, enter **0** in both fields.

Merging and Splitting Rows and Columns

Editing rows and columns in Dreamweaver is a dream come true! Adobe has made splitting and merging cells so easy that you might never want to go back to hand-coding your tables (although hand-editing tables after they're built can often be faster than editing through the Properties inspector and Design view).

It's important to understand what's happening to the code when you split or merge cells. For example, when merging two cells in a row into one cell, the two cells are combined by making the first cell span across two columns, using the colspan attribute in the <td> tag:

```
<table width="300" border="1">
  <tr>
   <td colspan="2">Merged Cells</td>
  </tr>
  <tr>
   <td>Bottom Left</td>
   <td>Bottom Right</td>
  </tr>
</table>
```

By contrast, when merging two cells in a column, those cells actually span across two rows, this time using the `rowspan` attribute in the `<td>` tag:

```
<table width="300" border="1">
   <tr>
     <td rowspan="2">Merged Cells</td>
     <td>Right Top</td>
   </tr>
   <tr>
     <td>Right Bottom</td>
   </tr>
</table>
```

Figure 6-6 shows examples of what a merged row and a merged column look like in Design view, compared to normal tables with no merged cells.

**Book II
Chapter 6**

**Organizing Data
with Tables**

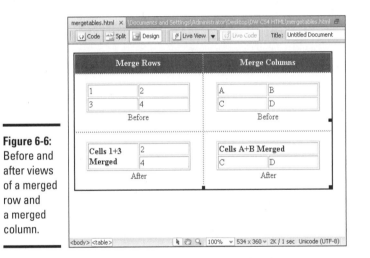

Figure 6-6:
Before and after views of a merged row and a merged column.

Seems simple enough, but this process can get very confusing the more complex your tables get. Imagine having to figure it out and code it by hand! Thankfully, Dreamweaver handles all this merging and splitting with ease — in fact, Dreamweaver makes everything about designing Websites a breeze by giving you the option of working in either Code or Design views. In the past, people had to actually code everything by hand! The following sections explore ways to split and merge cells as well as add rows and columns.

You can merge or split any number of cells using buttons on the Properties inspector. For instance, you may want to select all the cells in a particular row and merge them into one wide cell, or take one cell somewhere in the table and split it into three cells.

If you forget which button is which (merge or split) in the Properties inspector, hover your cursor over the button to read the tool tip description. Merge says *Merges selected cells using spans* and Split says *Splits cell into rows or columns.* The merge button has two boxes that look like they are being combined or pushed together, whereas the split button has two boxes being pushed away or separated from one another.

Merging cells

To perform a merge, follow these steps:

1. **Select the cells that you want to combine by clicking and dragging across several cells.**

   Selected cells must be *contiguous,* or touching, as well as evenly matched horizontally and vertically (in the shape of a rectangle) for the merge to work. If the selection is unbalanced in some way, the merge button is grayed out. As long as the merge button is active, the merge can take place with the selection.

2. **Click the Merge Selected Cells button in the lower-left corner of the Properties inspector.**

   Dreamweaver merges the selected cells into a single cell.

To remove a merge, place your cursor inside a single cell and do one of the following:

✦ Choose Modify⇨Table⇨Decrease Row Span to merge the selected cell into the cell below it.

✦ Choose Modify⇨Table⇨Decrease Column Span to merge the selected cell into the cell to the right of it.

Splitting a cell

To split a cell, follow these steps:

1. **Place the cursor inside the cell you want to split.**

2. **Click the Split cell button in the Properties inspector.**

   You can also choose Modify⇨Table⇨Split Cell.

   The Split Cell dialog box opens, shown in Figure 6-7.

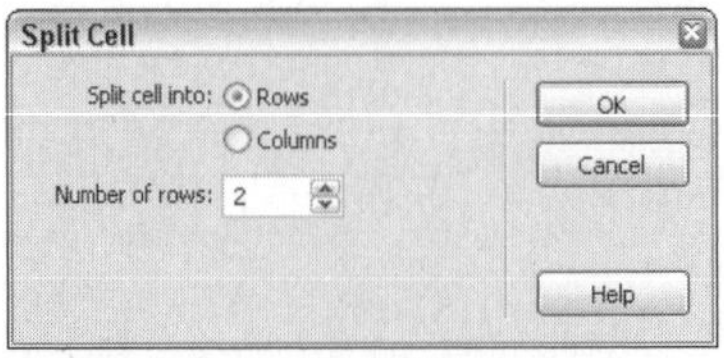

Figure 6-7:
The Split
Cell dialog
box.

Split Cell	
Split cell into: ⦿ Rows	OK
○ Columns	Cancel
Number of rows: 2	
	Help

3. **Select Rows or Columns as the Split Cell Into type and enter a number for the split in the Number Of field.**

4. **When you're finished, click OK.**

Dreamweaver splits the cell.

Setting Table Width and Heights

When first creating a table, the overall size of the table is determined by the pixels or percentages settings in the width field. Both pixels and percentage settings split cells and rows evenly but without adding exact pixel dimensions into the W field for each row or column. The reason for this is that most table cells use their contents to determine their size. However, sometimes you need to fix a table, table row, table column, or table cell's dimensions.

When the need arises, select an entire row or column, or place your cursor inside any cell to modify the dimensions of the cells, and then enter width attributes in pixels or percentages in the Properties inspector.

Alternately, you can specify the exact width and height of a table, table row, column, or cell using Cascading Style Sheets.

Take care when manually entering W cell sizes to your cells because if the math doesn't add up right, the table may not display accurately in a browser window. Therefore, be sure each row or column adds up to 100 percent or the total amount of pixels specified for the table. For example, in a table with two columns that is 200 pixels wide, check to see that the total cell width equals 200 (100 pixels wide each). Unequal columns can be any size as long as they equal 200, as in the following code where 85 is the width for the first column and 115 is the width for the second column:

```
<table width="200" border="1" cellpadding="5">
  <tr>
    <td width="85" rowspan="2">Coffee</td>
    <td width="115">Regular</td>
  </tr>
  <tr>
    <td>Decaffeinated</td>
  </tr>
</table>
```

Adding Rows and Columns to a Table

When adding rows and columns, all the contents in each of the cells are duplicated right along with the new row or column.

Adding a row

To quickly add a row to a table:

+ To **add a row above** a certain row, place your cursor inside a cell and choose Insert⇨Table Objects⇨Insert Row Above. You can also insert a row above a selected cell by clicking the Insert Row Above button in the Layout category of the Insert panel.

+ To **add a row below** a certain row, place your cursor inside a cell and choose Insert⇨Table Objects⇨Insert Row Below. You can also insert a row below a selected cell by clicking the Insert Row Below button in the Layout category of the Insert panel.

Adding a column

To quickly add a column to a table:

+ To **add a column to the left** of a certain column, place your cursor inside a cell and choose Insert⇨Table Objects⇨Insert Column to the Left. You can also insert a column to the left of a selected cell by clicking the Insert Column to the Left button in the Layout category of the Insert panel.

+ To **add a column to the right** of a certain column, place your cursor inside a cell and choose Insert⇨Table Objects⇨Insert Column to the Right. You can also insert a column to the right of a selected cell by clicking the Insert Column to the Right button in the Layout category of the Insert panel.

Adding multiple rows or columns

When adding columns, the rightmost column gets duplicated and added to the right edge of the table. When adding rows, the bottom row gets duplicated and added to the bottom of the table.

To add multiple rows or columns, place your cursor inside the cell next to where you want to add the rows or columns, and follow these steps:

1. **Choose Modify⇨Table⇨Insert Rows or Columns.**

The Insert Rows or Columns dialog box opens, shown in Figure 6-8.

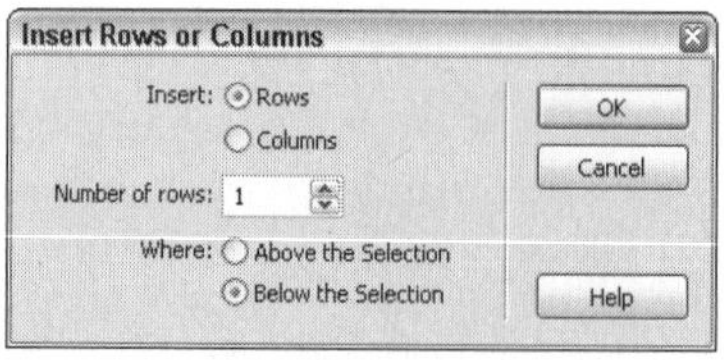

Figure 6-8:
The Insert
Rows or
Columns
dialog box.

2. **Select either the Rows or Columns option button, enter the number of rows or columns that you want to insert, and select either the Above the Selection or the Below the Selection option button.**

3. **When you finish setting the options, click OK.**

   Dreamweaver inserts the specified number of rows or columns into your table.

Deleting rows and columns

Delete rows and columns quickly with any of these methods:

✦ Place your cursor inside a cell of the row or column to be deleted and choose Modify⇨Table⇨Delete Column or Delete Row.

✦ Select an entire row or column and press Ctrl+X (Windows) or ⌘+X (Mac), or choose Edit⇨Cut.

✦ Select an entire row or column and click the Delete or Backspace key.

Inserting Text and Images in Table Cells

Add text and graphics to table cells just as you'd add them to a page. Click inside the cell and begin typing to add text or use the Insert panel to add an image (see Book II, Chapter 3). Insert other media to table cells in the same way by browsing for and selecting the media that you want to insert.

You can also paste contents from other sources — such as a word processing document — into a cell. Apply text and graphics formatting attributes with the Properties inspector or with the help of CSS. (See Book III, Chapter 1 for more on CSS.)

Formatting Individual Table Cells

In addition to standard text formatting options, the cells themselves can have specific formatting attributes, which are slightly different from formatting options for an entire table. If you don't see cell formatting options in the Properties inspector, click the down expander arrow in the bottom-right corner to reveal the cell's formatting area.

Format several cells at once or one at a time depending on your needs using any of these formatting options in the Properties inspector (see Figure 6-9):

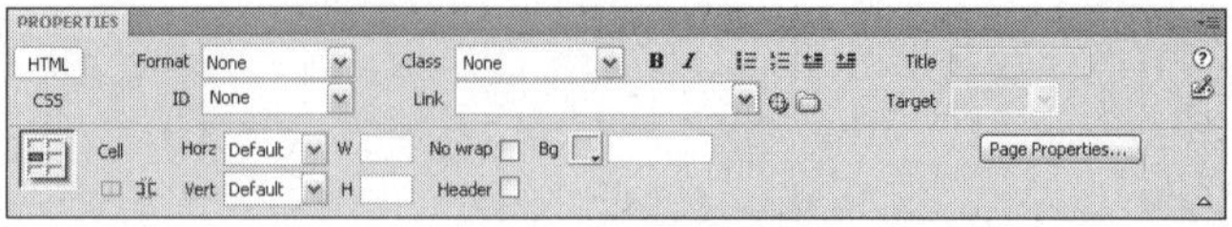

Figure 6-9:
Set cell
properties.

◆ **Horz** and **Vert:** Stands for Horizontal and Vertical alignment options for any cell, row, or column. The default horizontal alignment is Left for regular cells and Center for header cells. Horizontal alignment options include Left, Center, and Right. Vertical alignment options include Top, Middle, Bottom, and Baseline. Both dimensions also have a Default option, which aligns the contents of the cells left and center.

◆ **W** and **H:** Set the width and height for an entire selection. Enter dimensions in pixels or percentages. Or, for more control, use CSS to set the dimensions of individual cells.

◆ **No Wrap:** Forces text or other content in that cell to not wrap, thereby pushing out the cell walls and adjusting the cell sizes if the content extends beyond the cell's specified size. Use this feature for addresses or other information that needs to be all on one line.

◆ **Header:** Turns any regular cell into a header cell by converting the `<td>` tag into a `<th>` tag. Table headers have preset formatting attributes to help set their content apart from the rest of the content in the table. Headers are typically only used on the top row or left column of a table.

◆ **Bg Color:** Sets the background color of a cell or set of selected cells. Background cell colors sit on top of, or *hide,* a table background color. To specify a background color, click the color picker icon and select a color or enter the hexadecimal number preceded with a # (number sign) in the Bg Color field, as in **#FF3300**. If you forget to add the # before the hex value, the color may not appear in different browsers. Alternately, you can use CSS to style your cells with background colors, borders, and images.

Changing Table Measurements from Pixels to Percentages

Another great feature Dreamweaver provides when working with tables is the ability to convert a table's measurements from pixels to percentages, and vice versa. This is especially useful when you want the flexibility of adjusting a table with percentages but need to convert to fixed pixel widths before publishing.

To change table measurements from pixels to percentages (or vice versa), select the entire table and choose a convert option from the submenu when you select Modify⇨Table. Or, for even faster conversions, use the table property conversion buttons located in the Properties inspector, as shown in Figure 6-10.

Clear   Convert
Column   Table
Widths   to Pixels

Figure 6-10:
The table
property
conversion
buttons.

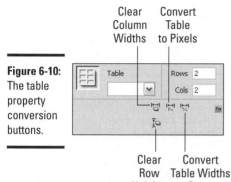

Clear   Convert
Row   Table Widths
Heights   to Percent

A description of each is provided in the following list:

✦ **Clear Column Widths:** Completely removes any width attributes from column cells in the entire table.

✦ **Convert Table Widths to Pixels:** Converts all table widths from percentages to fixed pixels.

✦ **Convert Table Widths to Percent:** Converts all table widths from fixed pixels to percentages.

✦ **Clear Row Heights:** Completely removes any width attributes from row cells in the entire table.

✦ **Convert Table Heights to Pixels:** Converts all table heights from percentages to fixed pixels.

✦ **Convert Table Heights to Percent:** Converts all table heights from fixed pixels to percentages.

Importing Tabular Data

Dreamweaver now swiftly imports tabular data saved as tab delimited .txt files and converts it into HTML tables! This is great news to anyone who's ever tried to paste table data from Microsoft Excel or Access into an HTML page. Windows users can import Excel files directly into Dreamweaver (File⇨Import⇨Excel Document) or import tabular data as described below. Mac users, however, can't import Excel files into Dreamweaver, and must therefore (for now) use the Import Tabular Data command.

To insert tabular data, choose File⇨Import⇨Tabular Data. The Import Tabular data dialog box opens, where you can enter the filename of the tab delimited data file, set the delimiter type, and perform other table formatting. Turn to Book II, Chapter 1 for more info about importing tables.

Sorting Information in a Table

Another great Dreamweaver table tool is the Sort Table command. Though normally you'd sort your data prior to inputting it in a table in Dreamweaver, you may want to improve the order of the information in your table after populating the table cells. Use this sort command to sort your alphabetical or numerical table data in either an ascending or descending order, such as alphabetizing a list of client names or store addresses, or ordering a list of items by their unique ID numbers.

Because Dreamweaver can only sort data along a single column of data, this feature does not work on tables with colspan or rowspan attributes. Therefore, you should perform this task before you merge or split any cells in your table. The sorting command physically changes the order of the content in your tables.

With the table filled with your data selected, follow these steps to sort the information in the table:

1. **Choose Commands⇨Sort Table.**

The Sort Table dialog box, shown in Figure 6-11, opens.

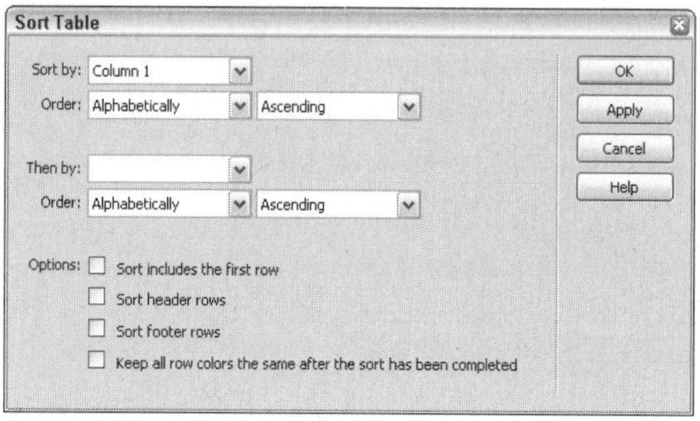

Figure 6-11:
Select table
sorting
options.

2. **In the Sort By drop-down list, select which column you want to sort by.**

For example, if your table has two columns, select either Column 1 or Column 2.

3. **In the two Order drop-down lists, choose whether you want to sort the column alphabetically or numerically and in ascending (A to Z or 1 to 100) or descending (Z to A or 100 to 1) order.**

To alphabetize a list, select Alphabetically and Ascending to sort your data from A to Z.

4. **In the Then By list, choose another column number for a secondary sort, or leave the field blank.**

   This option offers a second level of organization for your sort. For example, you may want to sort a list of names by last name and then by first name.

5. **In the Options area, further refine your results:**

   - **Sort Includes the First Row:** Select this option if your table doesn't include headings, so the first row of data gets included in the sort. If your table does include headings, leave this option disabled.

   - **Sort Header Rows:** This option sorts all the rows in the table's `thead`, separate from the sorting of the data in the rest of the table. To find out about the `<thead>` tag, open the Reference panel by choosing Help⇨Reference.

   - **Sort Footer Rows:** This option sorts all the rows in the table's `tfoot`, separate from the sorting of the data in the rest of the table. To find out about the `<tfoot>` tag, open the Reference panel by choosing Help⇨Reference.

   - **Keep All Row Colors the Same After the Sort Has Been Completed:** Select this option to have any row attributes stay with the data after the sort. This option doesn't work well with tables formatted with alternating row colors; rather, this feature is best for tables that have row attributes specific to the content in each row.

6. **To see the sorting results before committing to them, click the Apply button. If you're satisfied with the result, click OK. Or to exit without sorting, click Cancel.**

   If you like the new ordering, save the changes to the table.

If you want to immediately revert the table contents to the order it was in prior to the sort command, choose Edit⇨Undo Sort Table.

Working with Tables Created by Other Programs

If you want to harness the power of another program to do much of the table organization for you — especially with regard to graphics — several Web optimization programs can help you convert your graphic layouts from flattened artwork or layered files to a tables-based or CSS-layers-based HTML file with sliced graphic images in each of the table cells or layers. Most notable are ImageReady (which is being phased out by Adobe in favor of using the built-in Save For Web & Devices dialog box inside Photoshop and Illustrator) and Fireworks, but other programs do essentially the same thing.

In fact, there are now several Web services, like MarkUpNow.com and psd2html.com that, for a modest fee, gladly convert your flat artwork into standards-compliant, cross-browser compatible, valid page layouts complete with optimized graphics, XHTML, CSS, and sometimes JavaScript!

When using an optimization program yourself, you'll probably use a slice tool to cut the graphic into slices, which in turn get converted into individual GIF, PNG, or JPEG files upon optimization. Many of these programs also allow you to add JavaScript behaviors to the slices including rollover button behavior, animation, and graphical styles or effects. After all these extras have been applied to the slices in the optimization program, all the slices (or selected slices) can be optimized and converted into HTML and CSS-ready files. Typical options for exporting optimized graphics from an optimization program include HTML and Images, Images only, CSS Layers, and HTML only. After the optimization process is complete, you can bring the HTML files and graphics into Dreamweaver for further editing.

For ImageReady-or Fireworks generated HTML files, which typically include an index.html page and an attending images folder, move or copy these files to a logical location on the local computer. Many Web designers organize their Web files into one master folder containing separate HTML folders for each Web site, as in the following example:

```
Hard Drive/Clients/ClientA/A_HTML
Hard Drive/Clients/ClientB/B_HTML
Hard Drive/Clients/ClientC/C_HTML
```

After the exported files are in the appropriate folder on your computer, define (manage) a new Dreamweaver site, as described in Book I, Chapter 3. Taking this step is essential to ensuring that you have access to all of Dreamweaver's managed-site tools. From within the managed site, open the individual ImageReady- or Fireworks-generated HTML files and apply further formatting, links, and so on.

Using Fireworks-generated HTML is slightly different and more sophisticated than ImageReady and other optimization programs. For more about Fireworks HTML and how to use it in Dreamweaver, see Book III, Chapter 5.

Chapter 7: Building Fabulous Forms

In This Chapter

✔ **Putting together a form**

✔ **Adding fields to your form**

✔ **Performing form validation with JavaScript**

✔ **Performing form validation with Spry assets**

*F*orms are a great tool for collecting information from site visitors. Forms allow users to request information, send comments and questions, sign up for services or newsletters, fill out an online application, or enter payment information for purchasing products or services.

Before building a form for your Web page, spend some time figuring out what data you need to collect and consider how to organize that data logically so your form is easy to understand and navigate. As a best practice, try to keep the form length down and only request information that you really need. Otherwise, you risk people leaving the page.

Forms, by default, are not secure documents. If you need your forms to be secure — a must if you're collecting confidential personal information such as a credit card or password — speak to your host provider about purchasing an SSL (Secure Sockets Layer) digital security certificate of some kind. SSL encrypts data and provides secure connections for e-commerce and communication so your site visitors can feel confident that their personal information is protected and safe. VeriSign (www.verisign.com), GeoTrust (www.geotrust.com), and Thawte (www.thawte.com) are the most popular SSL encryption certificates.

Another option is using a third-party online credit card processing service, such as PayPal or Authorize.net, which, for a minimal transaction fee, takes on the risks of liability that comes with credit card processing.

You can do many other things to make your forms secure, such as creating a secure login script, using cookies, and creating XForms with XML, but that falls a little beyond the scope of this book. To find out more about Web security in general, visit the VeriSign, GeoTrust, and Thawte Web sites. For more on XForms, visit the W3C (www.w3.org/TR/xforms) and W3Schools (www.w3schools.com/xforms/default.asp) Web sites.

In this chapter, you find out how to create fabulous forms, validate them with JavaScript, and submit them to your server for processing.

Organizing Data in Your Form

Although you can't nest forms inside other forms, you can have multiple forms on a page, if needed. To organize your form data, use tables, line breaks, paragraph breaks, and CSS formatting, just as you would anywhere else on the page to make the form collection fields and labels look good.

One of the best ways to organize your form is to use a table. (See Book II, Chapter 6 for the lowdown on creating tables.) Although you can build your form in any order, it's often easier to add all your form labels first before adding form fields. For instance, in a two column, multi-row table, enter form labels for name, address, city, state, ZIP, phone, e-mail, and so on down the left column of cells, and then add all the form fields down the right column. By labeling all the form fields, the users know what information to input or select from. Figure 7-1 shows a simple form requesting billing information to make a purchase.

Check box   Text fields

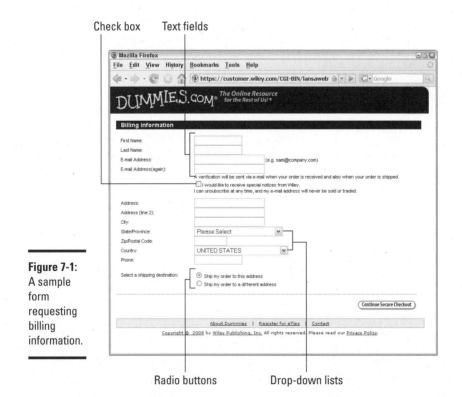

Radio buttons   Drop-down lists

Figure 7-1:
A sample form requesting billing information.

For more complex data collection needs, feel free to nest tables within tables to further help with organization. For instance, you may have a section of the form that describes an event as well as listing the event's location and date. If the data needs to be broken up into categories, it may benefit from being organized inside a nested table.

Creating a Fabulous HTML Form

This section describes how to create an HTML form. If you want to use Dreamweaver to make dynamic Web forms, turn to Book VIII, Chapter 4 for more information.

Book II
Chapter 7

When creating a form, you start by adding the `<form>` tag to an open document. If you forget the `<form>` tag, Dreamweaver prompts you to add it when you insert your first form field. Nevertheless, inserting the `<form>` tag yourself before you build your form is a good habit to get into.

Building Fabulous Forms

When a visitor enters information into your form and clicks the Submit button, the data needs to go somewhere for processing. In most cases, that somewhere is a server-side script or program, so be sure to check with your host provider about what their Web server can handle so you choose the correct scripting language. Forms are often processed with ASP, PHP, CGI, and ColdFusion scripts. The script or program then processes the data and responds by returning information back to the user, performing an action based on the form's instruction (like sending the user to a Thank You page), or sending an e-mail directly to a specified e-mail recipient. Host providers often have a forms processing method available as part of your hosting package, so be sure to check with your host provider for details and instructions.

To create a form and link it to a script, follow these steps:

1. **Place the cursor where you want the form to appear on the page.**

2. **Choose Insert➪Form➪Form.**

You can also click the Form button (which looks like a little square with a dotted red outline) in the Forms category of the Insert panel.

In Design view, the `<form>` tag appears on your page as a dotted red line in the shape of a large rectangle. In Code view, the inserted form tag looks like this:

```
<form name="form1" method="post" action=""></form>
```

If you don't see the dotted red line, which Dreamweaver considers an *invisible element* that appears in Design view but doesn't show up in the browser, choose View➪Visual Aids and check that invisible elements are enabled.

After you create the `<form>` tag, the Properties inspector displays the form formatting options, as shown in Figure 7-2.

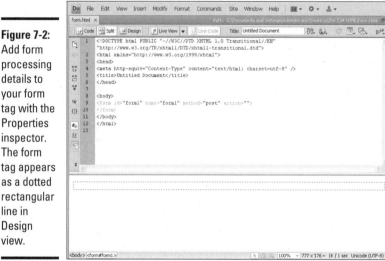

Figure 7-2:
Add form
processing
details to
your form
tag with the
Properties
inspector.
The form
tag appears
as a dotted
rectangular
line in
Design
view.

3. **Give your form a unique name by typing it in the Form ID text box in the Properties inspector.**

   Names are important if you plan to add JavaScript or VBScript to control the form in some way. If you forget to name the form, or don't need to add scripting, Dreamweaver uses the form*n* syntax to name your forms, where *n* is equal to the number of each form that is added to a page, such as id=form2.

4. **In the Action field, click the folder button to browse to and select the script or file that will process the collected data in the form.**

   If the script is on the server, type the path to that script. For example, many forms use CGI scripts located inside a CGI folder on the server, like this script where the name email.pl should be replaced with the actual name of your script filename:

   ```
   <form name="form1" method="post" action="cgi-bin/email.pl"></form>
   ```

   By default, the form field is inserted with the following information:

   ```
   <form name="form1" method="post" action=""></form>
   ```

   The CGI script is something that your host provider or system administrator provides you.

5. **Choose a method for transmitting collected form data to the server from the Method drop-down list:**

   • **Default** uses the browser's default setting to send the data. Because the default is usually — but not always — the GET method, it's better to specify GET or POST rather than using the default.

- **GET** adds the value of the collected data to the URL requesting the page, making this URL bookmarkable, and therefore vulnerable to hackers. Also, because URLs can only have a maximum of 8192 characters, this method is not useful for long forms. GET is best for repeatable, stateless form applications.

- **POST** hides the form data inside the HTTP request, preventing the collected data page from being bookmarked. The data, however, is not encrypted (it's also vulnerable to hackers), so be sure to use a secure connection to a secure server, especially if you're collecting personal information such as credit cards, usernames, and passwords.

6. **(Optional) In the Enctype drop-down list, choose the MIME encoding type of the data being sent to the server.**

   By default, this field is blank. Select application/x-www-form-urlencode as the default type for the POST method, or when adding a file-upload field to a form, select the multipart/form-data MIME type.

   If you're unsure of what to select here, leave the field blank and check with your host provider or system administrator for assistance.

7. **Set the target browser location for any returned data or documents in the Target drop-down list:**

   - **_blank:** Display the returned document or data in a new browser window.

   - **_self:** Display the returned data in the same window.

   - **_top:** Use the current open window even if other windows are open.

   - **_parent:** Use the parent window of the current file.

You have now completed the preliminary steps for adding a form to your page. The dotted red line marks the boundaries of your form. Within this border, you can add *form objects,* such as text fields, check boxes, radio buttons, lists, menus, and so on, as described in the next section. If you plan to organize your form objects inside a table, now is the time to add the table to your page. (See Book II, Chapter 6 for details on creating tables.)

Adding and Labeling Form Fields

Dreamweaver calls all the form input fields *form objects*. These are what you use to collect data from the site visitor. The following sections provide descriptions for adding each of the form objects to your form and customizing them with their respective property setting options.

Text fields

Use text fields to collect text or numerical data, such as a name, address, telephone number, e-mail address, or password.

Inserting a text field

To insert a text field in your page, follow these steps:

1. **Place your cursor inside the form area on your page where you want to insert a text field.**

   For example, if you've already inserted form tags and created a table inside the form tags with labels to indicate the data you will be collecting in the form, place your cursor in the table cell (next to the cell containing the first form label) where you intend to insert the first text field.

   If you haven't yet created a form, see the earlier section, "Creating a Fabulous HTML Form."

2. **Choose Insert⇨Form⇨Text Field.**

   You can also click the Text Field button in the Forms category of the Insert panel.

   If form accessibility preferences are turned on, the Input Tag Accessibility Attributes dialog box opens, prompting you to enter accessibility attributes to the form field. Complete the dialog box and click OK to insert the image or press Cancel to insert the field without accessibility attributes.

3. **In the TextField box in the Properties inspector, enter a name/ID for the text box.**

   All text fields need a unique name for the form to work properly. Names can contain numbers and letters as well as the underscore character, but can't include any spaces or special characters. Figure 7-3 shows an example of a form layout including the form tag (red dotted outline), form labels (Name, Address, Phone, and so on), and form fields to collect data. The Properties inspector shows the properties for the Address field, as shown in Figure 7-3.

   This text field name is the variable that stores the value of the field (which is the data the user inputs), and is sent to the server for processing. For example, a text field with the name `Address` and corresponding input by a user of `123 Main St.` may be returned to you as `Address=123 Main St.`

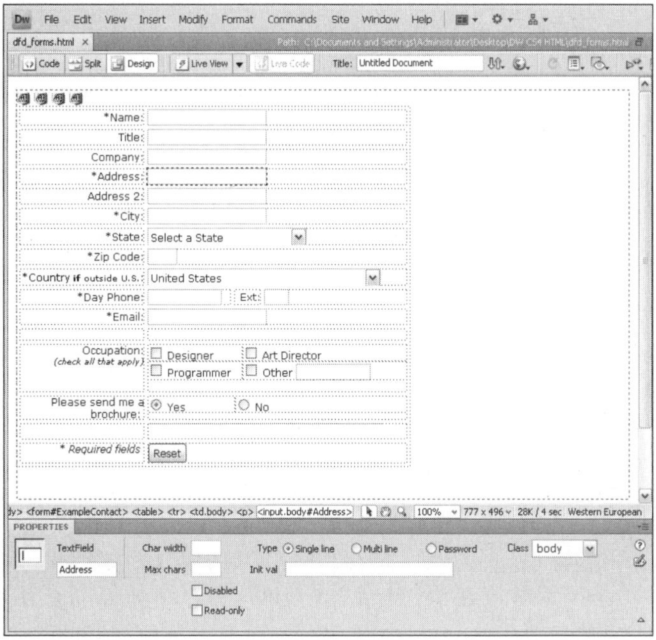

Figure 7-3:
Add properties to selected form fields with the Properties inspector.

4. **In the Type area, indicate whether you want the text field to be a single-line, multi-line, or password field:**

    *   **Single Line** uses the `<input>` tag with the `type=text` attribute.

    *   **Multi Line** creates multi-line text input fields. Multi-line fields use the `<textarea>` tag with the `cols` attribute for character width and the `rows` attribute for number of lines.

    *   **Password,** which uses the `<input>` tag with the `type=password` attribute, makes asterisks or bullets appear when typing inside the form field in a browser. The data, however, is not encrypted. To provide encryption, talk to your host provider about buying an SSL certificate.

    Figure 7-4 shows examples of the three types of text fields.

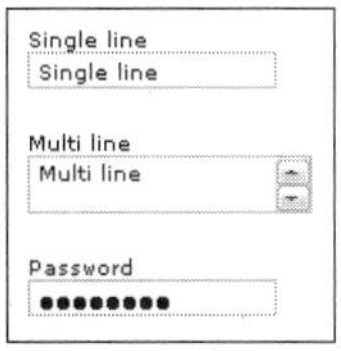

Figure 7-4:
Three types of text fields.

5. **In the Char Width box, enter the maximum number of characters that you want displayed in the text field.**

   This determines the width of the text input field. Additional characters may be accepted, but not displayed, depending on the value entered in the Max Chars field. Controlling the width of an input field with CSS is better than inputting a number here in the HTML code because different browsers interpret this attribute in different ways.

6. **In the Max Chars field, enter the maximum number of characters that can be entered into the text field.**

   This is especially useful for limiting phone numbers to ten digits, ZIP codes to five digits, or other data that requires a limited number of characters. If a visitor enters more characters than defined by this field, the browser tells the computer to make an alert sound.

7. **In the Num Lines box (for multi-line only), the height is determined by the number of lines entered here, such as 4 for a multi-line text field that is four lines high.**

8. **(Optional) In the Init Val box, enter any text that should appear inside the form object when the page loads.**

   This text can then be replaced with information from the user.

9. **(Optional) From the Class drop-down list, choose a CSS to apply to the form object.**

   For example, you may have created a custom CSS for all your text input fields. Choose the style from the menu to apply it.

Inserting a text area

A text area object is exactly the same as a text field object set to multi-line, only you don't need to set the Multi-line type in the Properties inspector yourself. Like the text field object, the text area object has fields for you to specify character width and number of lines as well as entering any initial value text to appear inside the field when the page loads and setting the wrap preferences, as described in the preceding section.

Hidden fields

For times when you need to hide information from the site visitor while providing information about the form to the server during form processing, or for when you want to store information entered by a user, add hidden fields to your form. For example, you can use a hidden field to specify an e-mail address or subject with an input name and value such as the following:

```
<input name="recipient" type="hidden" id="recipient" value="contact@example.com">
<input name="subject" type="hidden" id="subject" value="usercomments">
```

To insert a hidden field in your form, open your document and follow these steps:

1. **Place your cursor inside the form area on your page where you want to insert a hidden field.**

   Hidden fields are typically placed right after the opening `<form>` tag.

   If you haven't yet created a form, see the earlier section, "Creating a Fabulous HTML Form."

2. **Choose Insert⇨Form⇨Hidden Field.**

   You can also click the Hidden Field button in the Forms category of the Insert panel.

   The Properties inspector, shown in Figure 7-5, shows the properties for the hidden field.

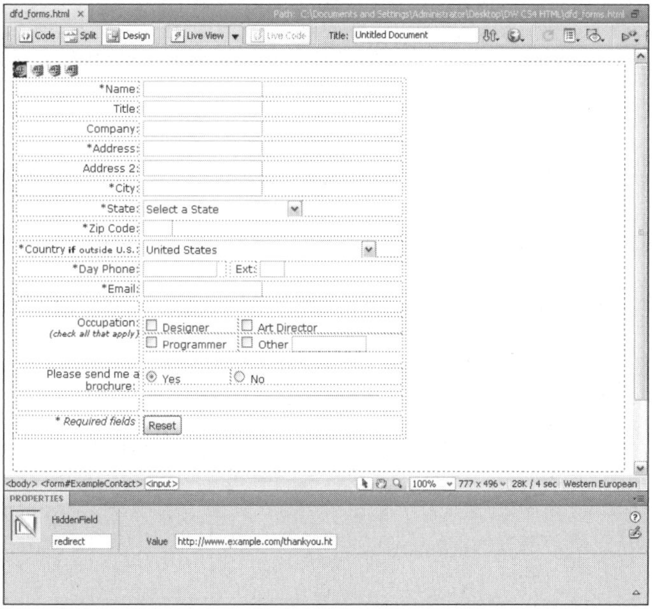

Figure 7-5:
Use the Properties inspector to set the name and value of hidden fields.

3. **In the HiddenField box in the Properties inspector, enter a name/ID for the field.**

   The name/ID labels the hidden field, such as Redirect, Recipient, Subject, or Title.

4. **In the Value field, enter a sentence, e-mail address, URL, or other information.**

The following are examples of hidden fields, including type (hidden) name, and value:

```
<input type="hidden" name="Redirect" value="http://www.example.com/
    thankyou.html">
<input type="hidden" name="Recipient" value="info@example.com">
<input type="hidden" name="Subject" value="Brochure Request">
```

Check boxes

Check box fields allow users to specify multiple responses when presented with a single question. You can add as many check boxes to the form as you want to support the question being asked. Figure 7-6 shows an example with four check boxes.

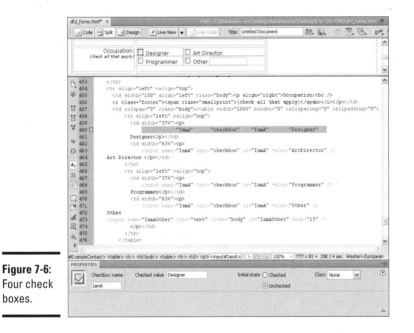

Figure 7-6:
Four check boxes.

To insert a check box in your form, follow these steps:

1. **Place your cursor inside the form area on your page where you want to insert a check box.**

   If you haven't yet created a form, see the earlier section, "Creating a Fabulous HTML Form."

2. **Choose Insert⇔Form⇔Checkbox.**

   You can also click the Checkbox button in the Forms category of the Insert panel.

3. **In the Properties inspector, enter a name for the check box in the Checkbox Name field and a value in the Checked Value field.**

   When listing multiple questions with check boxes on a form, be sure to give each check box set a unique name to identify it within the form. The name must not have any spaces or special characters in it, but the checked value can contain letters, numbers, and spaces, as in the following:

   ```
   <input name="chkGrapes" type="checkbox" value="Likes grapes"
       checked="checked"> Grapes
   <input name="chkBanana" type="checkbox" value="Likes bananas"
       checked="checked"> Bananas
   <input name="chkApple" type="checkbox" value="Likes apples"> Apples
   ```

4. **Select the initial state of the check box to be either checked or unchecked.**

5. **Repeat Steps 2 through 4 to insert additional check boxes.**

Book II
Chapter 7

Building Fabulous Forms

Another way of adding checkboxes to your forms is to use the Checkbox Group button, which launches a dialog box to build an entire check box group rather than making buttons one at a time. All the same rules apply to check box groups as to check box buttons with the added benefit of having Dreamweaver write `<label>` tags for you to identify the text associated with the check box button. When you launch the Checkbox Group dialog box, simply enter labels and values for each button, name the group, and select a layout type.

To insert a check box group in your form, follow these steps:

1. **Place your cursor inside the form area on your page where you want to insert a check box group.**

   If you haven't yet created a form, see the earlier section, "Creating a Fabulous HTML Form."

2. **Choose Insert➪Form➪Checkbox Group.**

   You can also click the Checkbox Group button in the Forms category of the Insert panel.

   The Checkbox Group dialog box opens (see Figure 7-7).

3. **In the Checkbox Group dialog box, enter a name for the Checkbox button Group in the Name field.**

   The group name identifies all the buttons as belonging to the same group and adds the same name attribute (such as `name="magazines"`) to each button.

4. **In the Label column, type a label for each check box button in the group.**

   Each item in the list represents a button in the check box group.

   To add new buttons, click the plus (+) button. To remove any buttons, select the item to be removed from the list and click the minus (–) button.

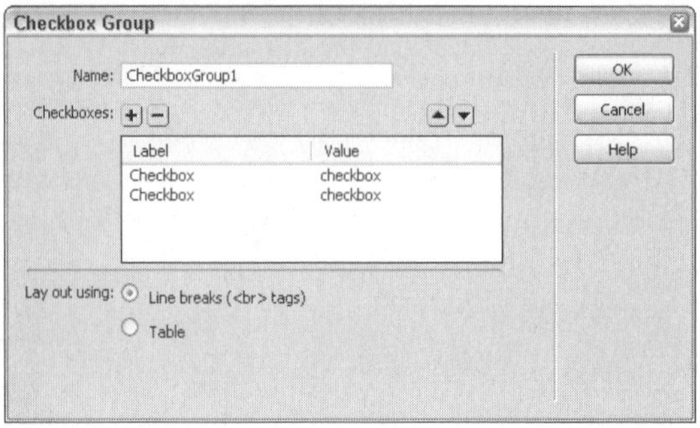

Figure 7-7:
The
Checkbox
Group
dialog box
lets you
quickly build
and insert
checkbox
groups.

Checkbox Group

Name: CheckboxGroup1

Checkboxes: [+] [−]   [▲] [▼]

Label	Value
Checkbox	checkbox
Checkbox	checkbox

Lay out using: ⊙ Line breaks (
 tags)
               ○ Table

OK
Cancel
Help

To reorder the buttons listed in the group, select a button from the list and click the up or down arrows.

5. **In the Value column, type a checked value for each check box button in the group.**

   The checked value represents the value that is submitted as the selected choice for this radio group, such as a particular magazine.

6. **Choose Line Breaks or Table as the layout option for the checkbox group.**

   The buttons that are inserted onto your page can be separated by line breaks or by table cells.

7. **Click OK to insert the check box group on the page.**

8. **Select one (or more) of the buttons in the group to be checked by default by entering the initial state as checked in the Properties inspector.**

   Use the Properties inspector to make further adjustments to the check box buttons in the group.

Radio buttons

Radio button fields allow users to specify either/or choices when presented with a question. You can have as many radio buttons as you want for any question, but the user can only select one answer.

Inserting radio buttons one at a time

To insert a radio button in your form, follow these steps:

1. **Place your cursor inside the form area on your page where you want to insert a radio button.**

   If you haven't yet created a form, see the earlier section, "Creating a Fabulous HTML Form."

2. Choose Insert⇨Form⇨Radio Button.

You can also click the Radio Button icon in the Forms category of the Insert panel.

3. In the Properties inspector, enter a name for the radio button in the Radio Button field and enter a value in the Checked Value field.

A group of radio buttons must have the same name but different values to make the selection mutually exclusive. Therefore, provide the same name to each radio button in your list and add a word in the Checked Value field to match the question being asked. You should also set one of the radio button's initial state value to checked. For instance, if asking people to choose their preference for beef, chicken, or vegetarian, the name for each radio button would be meal and the value for each is equal to the individual meal choice, and if they fail to make a selection on their own, they'll get beef, as in the following example:

```
<input type="radio" name="meal" value="beef" checked="checked">
<input type="radio" name="meal" value="chicken">
<input type="radio" name="meal" value="vegetarian">
```

Figure 7-8 shows how to configure the radio buttons using the Properties inspector.

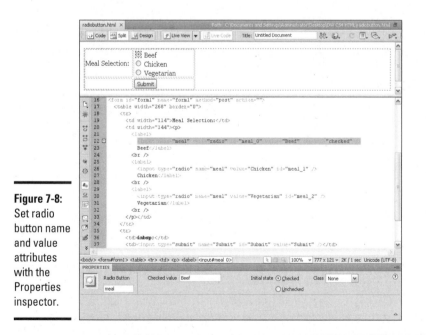

Figure 7-8: Set radio button name and value attributes with the Properties inspector.

4. Select an option to set the initial state of the radio button to checked or unchecked.

The radio button doesn't actually show a check mark; rather, it displays with a small dot in the center to indicate that it's been *checked* (selected).

Book II
Chapter 7

Building Fabulous Forms

5. **Repeat Steps 2 through 4 to insert additional radio buttons.**

   Make sure that radio buttons are always used in sets of two or more. Then be sure to only check one radio button as checked by default; if you specify more than one button with a checked value, it can create problems with data collection.

Inserting a group of radio buttons

The Radio Group button launches a helpful dialog box to help build an entire radio group all at once rather than creating a group of buttons one button at a time. In a group, only one option can be selected, whereas with individual buttons you could theoretically select them all. Selecting multiple buttons defeats the purpose because radio buttons are intended to be used as either/or selection fields. All the same rules apply to radio groups as to radio buttons with the added benefit of having Dreamweaver write <label> tags for you to identify the text associated with the radio button. When you launch the Radio Group dialog box, simply enter labels and values for each button, name the group, and select a layout type.

To insert a radio group in your form, follow these steps:

1. **Place your cursor inside the form area on your page where you want to insert a radio group.**

   If you haven't yet created a form, see the earlier section, "Creating a Fabulous HTML Form."

2. **Choose Insert⇨Form⇨Radio Group.**

   You can also click the panel.

   The Radio Group dialog box opens (see Figure 7-9).

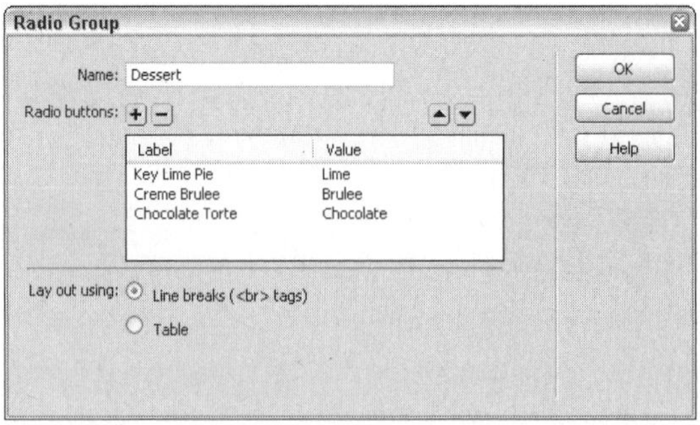

Figure 7-9:
Create
a group
of radio
buttons all
at once.

3. **In the Radio Group dialog box, enter a name for the radio button Group.**

   The group name identifies all the buttons as belonging to the same group and adds the same name attribute (such as `name="dessert"`) to each button.

4. **In the Label column, type a label for each radio button in the group.**

   Each item in the list represents a radio button in the radio group.

   To add new buttons, click the plus (+) button. To remove any buttons, select the item to be removed from the list and click the minus (–) button.

   To reorder the buttons listed in the group, select a button from the list and click the up or down arrows.

5. **In the Value column, type a checked value for each radio button in the group.**

   The checked value represents the value that is submitted as the selected choice for this radio group.

6. **Choose Line Breaks or Table as the layout option for the radio group.**

   The buttons can be separated by line breaks or by table cells.

7. **Click OK to insert the radio group on the page.**

8. **Select one of the buttons in the group to be checked by default by entering the initial state as checked in the Properties inspector.**

   Use the Properties inspector to make further adjustments to the radio buttons in the group.

Lists and menus

The List/Menu form object creates both list and menu type form fields. Use this object to provide a list or menu that allows users to make a selection within the form, such as a state or country.

To insert a list or menu in your form, follow these steps:

1. **Place your cursor inside the form area on your page where you want to insert a List/Menu object.**

   If you haven't yet created a form, see the earlier section, "Creating a Fabulous HTML Form."

2. **Choose Insert⇨Form⇨List/Menu.**

   You can also click the List/Menu button in the Forms category of the Insert panel.

   If you enabled Accessibility features, the Input Tag Accessibility Attributes dialog box opens. Complete the dialog box and click OK to insert the List/Menu object or press Cancel to insert the field without accessibility attributes.

3. **Click the List Values button in the Properties inspector.**

   The List Values dialog box opens. You use this dialog box to add labels and values to your list or menu (see Figure 7-10).

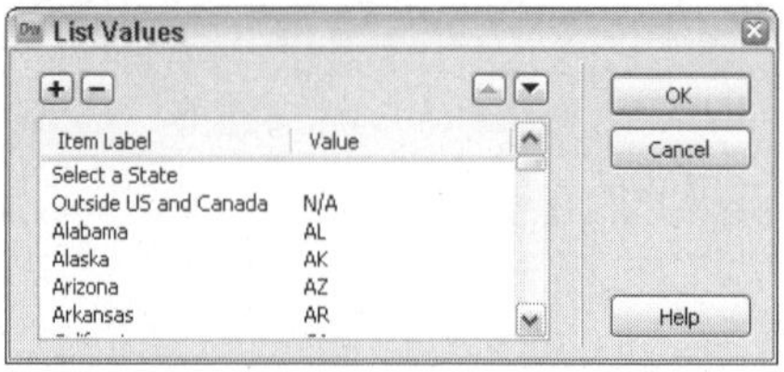

Figure 7-10:
Add labels
and values
to lists and
menus.

- **Item Label:** This text appears as a selection in the list.

  To add new list items, click the plus (+) button. To remove any items from the list, select the item to be removed and click the minus (–) button. To sort items, select an item from the list and click the up or down arrow.

- **Value:** This value is returned with the collected data when the item is selected, as in CA for California.

  After you add all the items to your list, click OK to close the List Values dialog box.

4. **With the list/menu object still selected, select a list Type in the Properties inspector.**

   Choose List to make a drop-down list or Menu to make a box that displays the options to choose from.

5. **In the Height box (for List type only), enter a number to represent the number of lines to be displayed in the list.**

   If the contents of the box exceed the box height, scroll bars appear.

6. **(Optional) Click the Allow Multiple Selections option to allow users to Shift-click when making multiple selections from the list or menu.**

7. **In the Initially Selected field, select any one item in the list/menu to display as the initial item, such as Select a State.**

Jump menus

Use jump menus to create a list of items that a visitor can select from, and once selected tell the browser to jump to another page or URL. Jump menus automatically add the necessary JavaScript behaviors required to instruct the browser to go to another page. This type of menu can be a useful tool for quick navigation on a Web site.

To find out how to set up a jump menu, see Book IV, Chapter 2.

Image fields

The Image Field option inserts an image into the form, for times you may prefer to use your own graphic for a Submit button or other form input field.

Images in forms become clickable Submit buttons by default, unless you apply a different JavaScript to the image.

To add an image field to your form, follow these steps:

1. **Place your cursor inside the form area on your page where you want to insert an image field.**

If you haven't yet created a form, see the earlier section, "Creating a Fabulous HTML Form."

2. **Choose Insert⇨Form⇨Image Field.**

You can also click the Image Field button in the Forms category of the Insert panel.

The Select Image Source dialog box appears.

3. **Browse to and select the image you want to add to the form.**

If you enabled Accessibility features, the Input Tag Accessibility Attributes dialog box opens. Complete the dialog box and click OK to insert the image or press Cancel to insert the field without accessibility attributes.

The image is inserted onto your page, as shown in Figure 7-11.

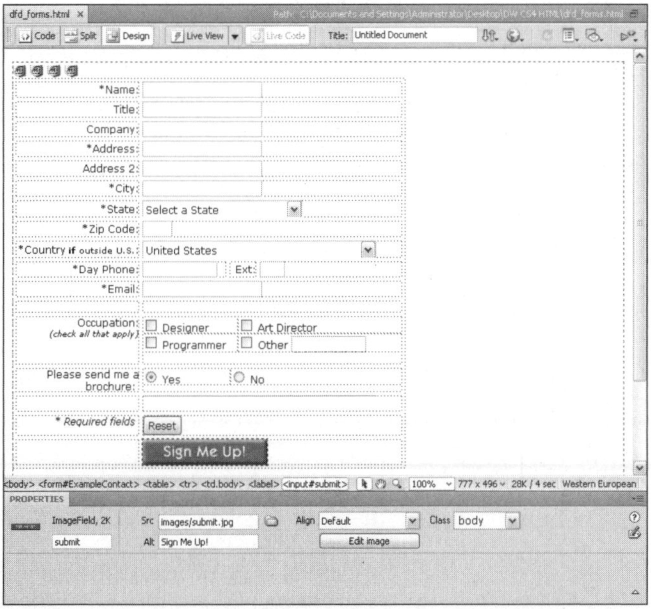

Book II
Chapter 7

Building Fabulous Forms

Figure 7-11: With the Image Field form object, you can use your own graphics.

4. **In the Alt field in the Properties inspector, enter Alternate text for the image.**

   Typically, the text in the Alt field mirrors the text on the button graphic.

5. **(Optional) From the Align drop-down list, select an alignment option for the graphic.**

   Alignment options include Default, Top, Middle, Bottom, Left, and Right.

6. **(Optional) From the Class drop-down list, choose a CSS style to apply to the form object.**

   For example, you may have created a custom CSS style for all your text input fields. Choose the style from the menu to apply it.

7. **In the ImageField field, enter Submit or Reset to use the image as a Submit or Reset button.**

   Alternatively, you can give your button a unique name to use the button with a JavaScript behavior. For example, you can create a button that, when a visitor presses it, runs a script to launch a pop-up window.

File upload fields

Add a file field to your form when you want to allow visitors to search for a file on their own computers and upload it to the server. When adding a file field, Dreamweaver inserts a text field with a Browse button next to it.

To use a file field on a Web page, you must make sure your server has a server-side script that can accept this type of data submission. File fields require the POST method for transmitting files from the browser to the server. Select enctype="multipart/form-data" as the encryption type for the form. The data is posted to the address in the form's action field; you can use a regular HTTP URL as the value as long as your application has the right server permissions to be able to write files accepted this way.

Be sure to test this feature in your target browsers before publishing the page, as the file field displays very differently in different browsers: Safari, Internet Explorer, Opera, and Firefox all have very unique ideas about how to handle this field, including how much space they take up and what words are displayed.

To insert a file field in your form, follow these steps:

1. **Place your cursor inside the form area on your page where you want to insert a file field.**

   If you haven't yet created a form, see the earlier section, "Creating a Fabulous HTML Form."

2. **Choose Insert⇔Form⇔File Field.**

   You can also click the File Field button in the Forms category of the Insert panel.

If you enabled Accessibility features, the Input Tag Accessibility Attributes dialog box opens. Complete the dialog box and click OK to insert the file field, or press Cancel to insert the field without accessibility attributes.

3. **In the Properties inspector, enter the following attributes:**

- **`FileField Name`:** Enter the name for the file field.

- **`Char Width`:** Enter a number of characters to set the width of the file field.

- **`Max Chars`:** Enter the maximum number of characters that a visitor can enter into the file field.

- **`Class`:** If you've created a custom CSS style to format this field, select it by name from the Class drop-down list.

Book II
Chapter 7

Building Fabulous
Forms

Buttons

Add a form button to your form for visitors to click when they're ready to submit data or trigger other form processing operations. Typical form buttons are labeled as Submit, Reset, or Send, but you can create buttons with other labels that perform other tasks such as calculating shipping charges based on a user's geographical zone.

To create a button, follow these steps:

1. **Place your cursor inside the form area on your page where you want to insert a form button.**

If you haven't yet created a form, see the earlier section, "Creating a Fabulous HTML Form."

2. **Choose Insert⇨Form⇨Button.**

You can also click the Button icon in the Forms category of the Insert panel.

If you enabled Accessibility features, the Input Tag Accessibility Attributes dialog box opens. Complete the dialog box and click OK to insert the button, or press Cancel to insert the button without accessibility attributes.

The Properties inspector shows the properties for the button, as shown in Figure 7-12.

3. **In the Button Name field in the Properties inspector, enter a name for your button.**

4. **In the Value field, enter the text to appear on the button face.**

For instance, if you want a button that says Join Mailing List, type **Join Mailing List**.

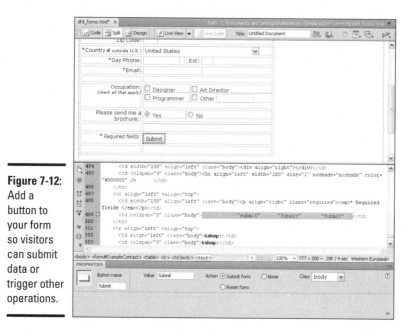

Figure 7-12:
Add a
button to
your form
so visitors
can submit
data or
trigger other
operations.

5. **(Optional) From the Class drop-down list, select a custom CSS style to apply to the button.**

6. **Choose an action from the Action field:**

   • **Submit:** This default form button type submits the collected data to a script or processing application on the server. Submit buttons can have any label as long as the Action type in the Properties inspector is set to Submit.

   • **Reset:** A Reset form button clears the form fields by returning the form to its original state. You can label reset buttons with any text. Choose the Action type in the Properties inspector to reset the form.

   • **None:** A third option creates a button with customized text that you can attach a behavior to, such as a Go button for a jump menu. Select None as the Action type in the Properties inspector and apply a JavaScript behavior using the Behaviors panel (see Book IV, Chapter 2 for more about behaviors).

Label tags

The `<label>` tag is used for enhancing accessibility attributes. When the `<label>` tag wraps around another form item, not only can screen-reader software read the label, but a *focus rectangle* surrounds both the label and form field in some browsers, which allows the user to click anywhere inside the text and form field area to select it. This grouping is especially helpful when using radio buttons and check boxes!

If you label your objects without the <label> tags, the label isn't associated with the form object, as in the following sample code:

```
<input name="Dessert" type="radio" value="Apple" checked="checked" />Apple
    Crumble
```

With the <label> tags, however, the label is associated with the form object, as in the following:

```
<label><input name="Dessert" type="radio" value="Apple" checked="checked" />Apple
    Crumble</label>
```

If you've enabled Accessibility preferences, the Input Tag Accessibility Attributes dialog box automatically appears any time you insert a form object on your page. There you can wrap your object with the <label> tag.

To insert a <label> tag in your form after you add objects to your form, follow these steps:

1. **Place your cursor inside the form area on your page where you want to insert a <label> tag.**

   If you haven't yet created a form, see the earlier section, "Creating a Fabulous HTML Form."

2. **Choose Insert⇨Form⇨Label Field.**

   You can also click the Label Field button in the Forms category of the Insert panel.

   The <label> tag is inserted into your page code, as shown in Figure 7-13.

If you're adding a <label> tag to an existing form object, such as a check box or radio button, check the code to ensure that the label for the form object sits between the opening and closing <label> tags.

Fieldset tags

A <fieldset> tag is used as a container for other form objects. Use fieldsets to define multiple fields into logical groups within the form. For instance, one fieldset may include text input fields for name and e-mail information, and another fieldset may include username and password information (see Figure 7-14).

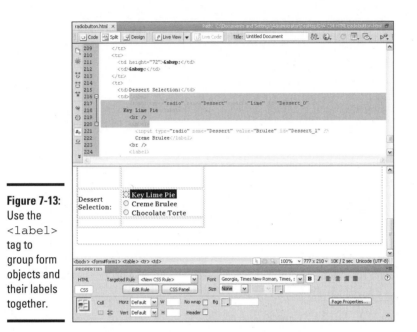

Figure 7-13:
Use the
`<label>`
tag to
group form
objects and
their labels
together.

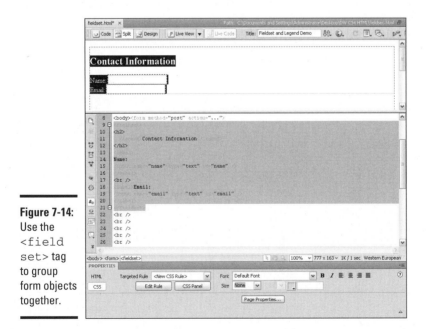

Figure 7-14:
Use the
`<field set>` tag
to group
form objects
together.

You can use the `<legend>` tag with the `<fieldset>` tag to label each field set, as in the following example:

```
<form method="post" action="...">
<fieldset>
<h2>
  <legend>Contact Information</legend>
</h2>
<label>
Name:
<input name="name" type="text" id="name" />
</label>
<br />
<label>Email:
<input name="email" type="text" id="email" />
</label>
</fieldset></form>
```

These tags create a very interesting look in a browser. Figure 7-15 shows how the example appears in Firefox on a PC.

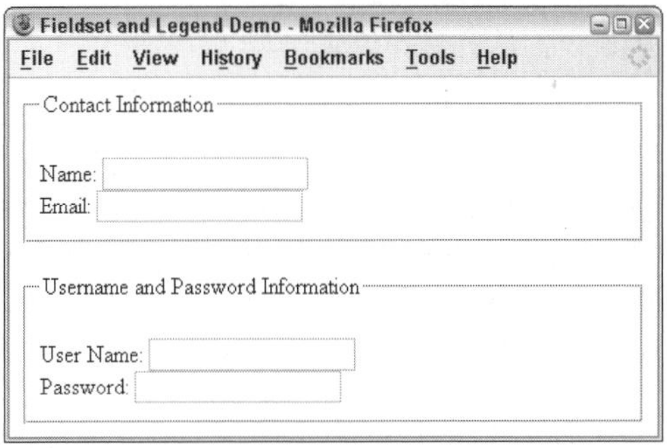

Book II
Chapter 7

Building Fabulous Forms

Figure 7-15: The `<field set>` and `<legend>` tags format form data in a unique way.

To insert `<fieldset>` and `<legend>` tags, follow these steps:

1. **Open a file containing a form in which you want to insert `<field-set>` and `<legend>` tags.**

If you haven't yet created a form, see the earlier section, "Creating a Fabulous HTML Form."

2. **Select all the form elements that you want to group inside the `<fieldset>` tags.**

3. **Choose Insert➪Form➪Fieldset.**

You can also click the Fieldset button in the Forms category of the Insert panel.

The Fieldset dialog box opens.

4. **In the Fieldset dialog box, enter a name for the legend and click OK.**

   The legend is like a heading for the objects grouped inside the `<fieldset>` tags.

   Dreamweaver wraps the selected content with `<fieldset>` and `<legend>` tags. After the `<fieldset>` and `<legend>` tags have been added to your code, you can style the content with CSS.

As an alternative to the legend and fieldset tags, consider using `div` tags and CSS, which provide greater control for spacing, margins, background, colors, fonts, and so on.

Validating a Form with JavaScript

If you've ever filled out a form and gotten a pop-up message back from your browser that says you filled out the form incorrectly or that you missed entering data in a field, you've witnessed form validation in action. Validation can be performed dynamically with PHP, ASP, JSP, or ColdFusion code. However, for most non-dynamic sites, a simple JavaScript Validate Form action does the trick.

The Validate Form behavior cross-checks all the fields against the validation rules you specify to ensure that the user entered the data correctly. This way, you can check the form on the client side for completion and accuracy before the server collects the data.

You can attach validation events to as many fields in the form as you want. A couple of validation events are

✦ **onBlur:** Validates individual fields as the form is being completed

✦ **onSubmit:** Reviews the entire form input data all at once

To validate a form with the Validate Form action, follow these steps:

1. **To validate the entire form, select the form's `<form>` tag, or to validate an individual field, select that form object.**

2. **Open the Behaviors panel (which is technically a tab on the Tag Inspector panel) by choosing Window⇨Behaviors.**

3. **Click the plus (+) button in the Behaviors panel and choose Validate Form from the Add Behavior pop-up menu.**

   The Validate Form dialog box opens, as shown in Figure 7-16, showing a list of all the named fields in your form.

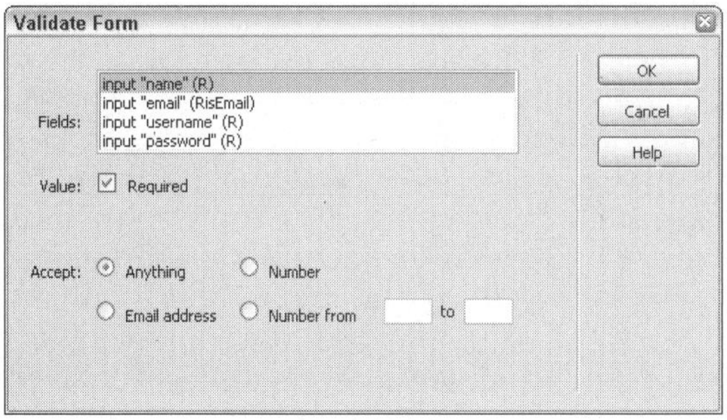

Figure 7-16:
The Validate
Form dialog
box.

4. **Select a form input field from the Named Fields listing, and then choose a setting for it:**

   - **Value Required:** Enable this option when the field must contain data of some kind, rather than stay blank.

   - **Accept Anything:** If this option is selected, the selected field must also be set to Required so that a user can input any type of data into the form field.

   - **Accept Email Address:** Select this option to have the validation script verify that the field contains the @ symbol.

   - **Accept Number:** Select this option to have the validation script check that this field contains numbers only.

   - **Accept Number From/To:** When this option is selected, you can specify a range for acceptable numbers.

   When validating the entire form, you must set a value and accept an option for each field in the form.

5. **Repeat Step 4 for every form input field in your form.**

6. **Click OK.**

Dreamweaver adds the Form Validation JavaScript code to the `<form>` and `<head>` tags. When validating an entire form, the onSubmit validation event automatically displays next to the Validate Form Events menu in the Behaviors panel. If validating only a single field, the default validation event is either `onBlur` or `onChange`.

Validating a Form with Spry Assets

Like JavaScript validation, Spry validation is another cool new way to validate your forms, only this way uses the more advanced tools in the Spry framework. The Spry framework, which you find out more about in Book IV, Chapter 2, is a library of JavaScript that helps Web designers with a basic understanding of HTML, CSS, and JavaScript build XLM rich Web pages that provide more interactive experiences for site visitors.

Spry validation form fields, or *widgets*, include the Text Field, Textarea, Checkbox, Select (Menu), Password, Confirm, and Radio Group. To use these widgets, you need to insert the Spry fields into your form instead of inserting the regular HTML form field tags. After you've inserted these Spry fields, you'll customize how each field validates data, and if desired, modify the look and feel of how the field appears in the browser, as all of the Spry Validation widgets are styled with an external CSS file (such as SpryAssets/ SpryValidationTextField.css) that is automatically added to the root level of your managed site when you insert the first Spry Validation form field. In addition to the CSS file, an adjoining JavaScript file is also added to your managed site (such as SpryAssets/SpryValidationTextField.js).

To get the most use out of the Spry Validation form fields you need a firm understanding of HTML, CSS, and JavaScript. Spry widgets are more advanced Dreamweaver tools intended for the experienced Dreamweaver user. As such, the following information includes general guidelines for using the Spry Validation tools. For detailed online help and infor- mation about working with Spry Validation, see `help.adobe.com/ en_US/Dreamweaver/10.0_Using/WS2442184F-3DF4-4240-96AF- CC6D792E2A62a.html`.

All of the Spry Validation widgets are located at the bottom of the Forms cat- egory of the Insert panel, as shown in Figure 7-17.

Figure 7-17: Insert Spry Validation form fields from the Forms category of the Insert panel.

All of the Spry Validation fields can be inserted in the same way. What is different about each of them is how they are styled and the kind of interactive opportunities they offer to site visitors. For example, with the Spry Validation Text field, visitors can be prompted to enter the correct date format and see an error message ("Invalid format" or "The value is required") when the format entered does not match the formatting hint you provided or no input is made to the field, as shown in Figure 7-18.

Figure 7-18:
Visitors are prompted to enter data correctly.
A. Hint activated.
B. Correctly entered data. C. Incorrect data entered.
D. Missing data in required field.

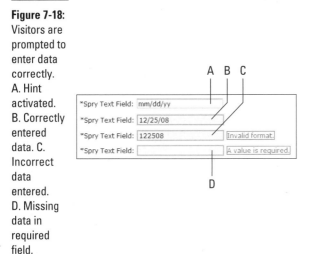

A B C

D

As you insert each of the Spry Validation fields, Dreamweaver saves a linked SpryAssets CSS and JavaScript file into your managed site. These files must be uploaded to the server along with the page(s) using the Spry Validation fields for the Spry Validation form fields to function properly in a browser.

To insert any of the Spry Validation Fields into your page, follow these steps:

1. **Place your cursor inside the area in your form where you want to insert a Spry Validation Field.**

2. **Click the desired Spry Validation Field button on the Forms category of the Insert panel.**

If the Input Tag Accessibility Attributes dialog box opens, complete the fields and click OK.

The selected Spry Validation Field is automatically added to the page in the specified location. The Spry Validation form fields look like their regular HTML form field counterparts, except the Spry versions are surrounded by a blue outline and tab that identifies the form field as a Spry Validation form field.

You can also insert any of the Spry Validation form fields by selecting Insert⇨Spry⇨ and then choosing the desired option from the submenu.

3. **Select the new Spry Validation field in Design view to customize the field in the Properties inspector.**

   Like the normal form field, you can set parameters for the Validation field with the Properties inspector.

4. **Select the Validation field's tab to set the validation Type and Format in the Properties inspector.**

   When you click the Validation field's tab, a different set of information appears in the Properties inspector. You'll need to set the correct type and format to match the data you intend to collect from site visitors, such as a phone number, currency, dates, or credit card information.

   For a complete listing of Types and Formats, see `help.adobe.com/ en_US/Dreamweaver/10.0_Using/WS455A2B6C-8E96-4879-8195- 4B47394B9BA3a.html`.

5. **Specify when the validation event will occur.**

   Select Blur, Change, and/or Submit. Select as many as you like, or disable them all.

   • **Blur:** The field validates when the user clicks outside the field.

   • **Change:** The field validates while the user enters text inside the field.

   • **Submit:** The field validates when the user submits the form.

6. **Set other options as required by the Validation field.**

   For example, when you select the Spry Validation Text Field tab, other options include setting the minimum and maximum number of characters, min and max values, whether to display preview widget states, change required status of a field, create a hint, or block invalid characters.

After the Spry Validation field is inserted and its properties are set in the Properties inspector, the field's style and error message (if any) can be customized in the CSS. Finding the right field can be a bit tricky on your own, so be sure to consult the online help files to ensure you're editing the correct CSS style.

To find the correct CSS and learn more about advanced styling, go to `www. adobe.com/go/learn_dw_spryselect_custom`.

Book III

Working Like the Pros

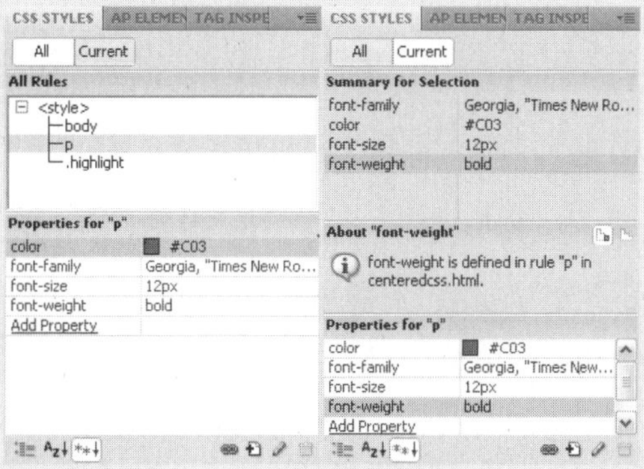

Contents at a Glance

Chapter 1: Looking Good with Cascading Style Sheets (CSS)

In This Chapter

✔ **Understanding Cascading Style Sheets**

✔ **Creating internal and external style sheets**

✔ **Creating new CSS styles**

✔ **Editing, renaming, and deleting styles**

✔ **Attaching Design Time Style Sheets**

✔ **Using the Code Navigator**

Cascading Style Sheets (CSS) are a recommended standard from the World Wide Web Consortium (W3C) to provide Web designers with more control over the layout and appearance of HTML and XML files. Cascading Style Sheets perform a similar function as formatted text in a word processor. You can set default formatting for particular styles such as paragraphs and headings. You can also create your own custom styles for text, graphics, tables, and more, plus create styles that control the format and position of block-level assets like margins and borders.

With CSS, you can control things like

- ✦ Fonts, font sizes, font styles, and font colors
- ✦ Line spacing and letter spacing
- ✦ Margins, padding, indenting, and outdenting
- ✦ Background images and colors
- ✦ Border style, width, and color
- ✦ List and link formatting
- ✦ Size, alignment, positioning, and visibility of elements on the page
- ✦ Page breaks, filters, and cursor visual effects

Dreamweaver CS4 formats text with Cascading Style Sheets (CSS) as the default text styling method (instead of HTML tags), as CSS has been implemented in all modern browsers including Microsoft Internet Explorer, Safari, Firefox, Opera, Netscape Navigator, and Mozilla.

You'll enjoy these benefits with CSS:

✦ Style sheets separate content from the style and formatting information.

✦ Style sheets simplify HTML code and file size (because all the styling information is contained in one location — either the head of the file or in an external style sheet — rather than inline with the text) without compromising the structure of the content.

✦ Style sheets give you more control over the presentation of your pages.

✦ Using style sheets means your HTML files have faster download times across multiple browsers.

✦ You have a centralized location for the Web site design, so you can change an entire site's look by changing just one file.

✦ Site visitors with disabilities have better access to pages using CSS.

✦ Older browsers can still view pages.

This chapter presents an overview of Cascading Style Sheets, including the difference between internal, external, and inline style sheets. You discover the three general types of styles and how to create, edit, rename, and delete your own CSS using the Dreamweaver CSS Styles panel. You also find a full explanation of the categories of the CSS Rule Definition dialog box, plus when and how to use Design Time CSS.

Understanding Cascading Style Sheets (CSS)

In the early days of the Internet, how the content looked was largely the work of specialized formatting tags used inside the HTML code, such as `<font face="Arial" size="2">`, which would instruct a browser to display the text in a specific font (Arial) and size (2). With the advent of HTML 4 in late 1997, however — which began supporting Cascading Style Sheets and scripting, among other great enhancements — most formatting is now written with style sheets, either inside the HTML document itself or outside the document in an external style sheet file.

Cascading Style Sheets (CSS) separate form from content by taking control over the appearance of the text through specification of font style, font size, text color, and alignment, as well as positioning and additional formatting attributes for other elements such as images, tables, layers (called AP Elements in Dreamweaver), and forms. HTML can now primarily be used for organizing content, whereas the external CSS typically has all the formatting and positioning instructions.

One of the great benefits of separating form from content with CSS style sheets is that when you need to make formatting changes, rather than modifying the style attributes inside the HTML code for every page, you only need to edit the CSS file. As you find out in the following sections, CSS code can be placed in any of three locations: *inline* with the HTML, *internal* in the head of your HTML file, or as an *external* file that is linked to all the pages on your site. External CSS is the preferred method of professional Web designers because it is the most organized and flexible way to format content.

For example, a sentence using the old `<font>` tag with face, size, and color attributes looks like this:

```
<p><font="Verdana, Arial, Helvetica" size="2" color="#990000">Do an Internet
   search to find the best restaurants in your neighborhood.</font></p>
```

In comparison, using a style sheet that defines a custom style called .restaurants with attributes of Verdana, 12px, #990000 looks like this:

```
<style type="text/css">
<!--
.restaurants {
    font-family: Verdana, Arial, Helvetica, sans-serif;
    font-size: 12px;
    color: #990000;
}
-->
</style>
```

and when applied to the same sentence, the sentence code simply looks like this:

```
<p class=""restaurants">Do an Internet search to find the best restaurants in
   your neighborhood.</p>
```

When you place the CSS in an external file, you can simply upload the revised CSS to the hosting server to change the look of your entire site. By contrast, when HTML styles are used and you want to make a site wide change, all the pages on the site must be modified before uploading to the server.

Another great feature about CSS is that style sheets allow you to somewhat control what site visitors see when they visit your page regardless of the platform they are browsing in. Like the old HTML tags, CSS styles override default browser font face and font size settings, but in a much cleaner way.

Exploring Different Style Sheet Types

Dreamweaver CS4 uses CSS, rather than HTML tags, as the default method for editing text. If you like, you can still use HTML tags for styling your text by applying attributes to selected content through the HTML tab on the Properties inspector, or of course, by hand editing the code with the old HTML tags. The trend, however, is to use CSS.

You can place your style sheet information in three different locations, relative to the HTML code, that allow it to work properly:

✦ **Inside the document.** You can create an internal style sheet through the CSS Styles panel and automatically add styles in between the `<head>` tags of the document through the CSS tab of the Properties inspector.

✦ **Outside the file in a separate CSS file.** You can create an external style sheet through the CSS Styles panel and then link it to your document.

✦ **Inline, putting the CSS markup right next to the HTML.** You need to know the proper syntax to add inline CSS so you can manually type the style code in the HTML.

You can use all three style sheet types (internal, external, and inline) in combination with one another. For instance, you may have some internal styles and an external style sheet linked to the same document, plus an inline style or two throughout the code. You may even use multiple style sheets on a page or in an entire site, if it suits your needs. Just remember that whatever styles are closest to the content typically (though not always) take precedence over styles that are farther away.

Internal styles

After adding text to a Web document, you can apply certain styling attributes to your text with the formatting options on the HTML and CSS tabs of the Properties inspector. The options on the HTML tab add HTML markup to your code, and the options on the CSS tab add CSS markup to either the head area of your open document or to an external style sheet. Figure 1-1 shows the HTML tab options and Figure 1-2 shows the formatting settings on the CSS tab.

Figure 1-1:
The HTML formatting options in the Properties inspector.

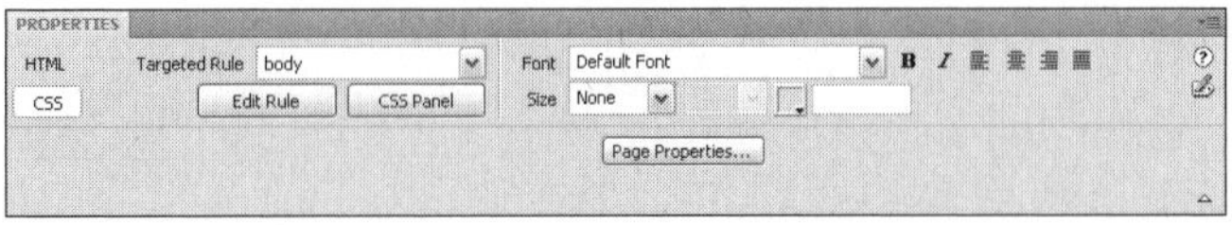

Figure 1-2:
The CSS
formatting
tab in the
Properties
inspector.

The HTML Properties inspector settings add formatting tags to the HTML code:

Format   ID

Class   Link

Bold (Strong)   Italic (Em)

Unordered List Ordered List

Indent/Outdent   List Item

The CSS Properties inspector settings add CSS markup to either the `<head>`
of the open page or to an external CSS file:

Targeted Rule Font

Bold   Italic

Font Size   Font Color

Align (Left/Center/Right/Justified)

WARNING! As you may have noticed, both tabs on the Properties inspector include a
Page Properties button, which applies CSS formatting only to the currently
active page. If you're new to CSS, ignore this button for now and concentrate
on figuring out how to apply CSS to your pages through the CSS Styles panel.

Any time you use the CSS properties, Dreamweaver automatically writes the
style sheet code to either your HTML, right before the closing `<head>` tag of
the page or to an external style sheet, which can be a new blank CSS file that
you create on the fly, or an existing CSS file that you specify before adding a
new style rule to it.

TIP One major benefit of using CSS is that you can build your own master CSS
file and then use it again and again on each project, customizing the fonts,
colors, styles, and so on, to match the each project's design. See `http://`
`www.crucialwebhost.com/blog/master-stylesheet-the-most-`
`useful-css-technique/` for a great example of this.

When adding internal CSS to the file, for example, if you select the Arial font
from the Font drop-down menu in the CSS Properties inspector, you are
prompted to create a custom CSS style, such as `.saleprice`, or specify the

HTML tag that will be redefined with the new font, such as the `<p>` tag for all paragraphs. After you create the new style, the following style sheet code is added to your HTML document between the `<head>` tags:

```
<style type="text/css">
<!--
.saleprice {font-family: Arial, Helvetica, sans-serif}
-->
</style>
```

The style sheet markup begins and ends with the `<style>` tag. Nested between those are opening and closing comment tags (`<!--` and `-->`), which *comment out* (hide) the style attributes so that older browsers don't display them as text in the body of the page. Comment tags are used to insert text in your code that isn't displayed in a browser. Between the comment tags is where the style attributes go.

Styles you apply with the CSS Properties inspector use the unique names you provide for them, such as `.saleprice` and `.sidebarheader`. Between the comment tags, you can list as many styles as you need to style the page. Each time you style content with the CSS Properties inspector, you are prompted to add a new custom style to the internal or external style sheet. After your new custom styles are added to the internal or external style sheet, the Targeted Rule menu in the Properties inspector (refer to Figure 1-2) displays those styles by name and preview. You can also apply your custom CSS styles to selected content using the Class menu on the HTML Properties inspector.

When adding internal CSS styles to the open document, be aware that those internal CSS styles only alter the contents on that particular page. To use a single style sheet for multiple pages on a Web site, you must create an external style sheet, described next.

External styles

External styles refer to style descriptions saved in a single separate, external file with the .css file extension. External style sheets are often named after the company or project they're used with, or with some acronym or abbreviation relative to the Web site, such as monkey.css for a site about monkeys, although some designers simply refer to their CSS files as style.css so that every project uses the same naming convention.

The external style sheet needs to link to the HTML pages using a special line of code. When the link is present and the page is displayed in a browser window, the browser interprets and displays the page's contents using the external style sheet information. You place the link to the external style sheet inside the `<head>` tag of the document with the `href` attribute referencing the location and filename of the CSS, as in this example:

```
<link href="monkey.css" rel="stylesheet" type="text/css" />
```

External style sheet styles use the same syntax and formatting as internal style sheets to define styles with one tiny exception: The styles in an external style sheet do not need to be surrounded by the `<style>` and `<!--comment-->` tags that internal styles require. Furthermore — and this is what makes external style sheets so powerful — external style sheets are best when working with a multipage Web site because a single external style sheet can control the formatting for all the pages on the site. For example, if you need to change the style attributes of all the Heading 1s (`<h1>`) sitewide, you only need to modify the one external style sheet to make all the pages conform to the new style definitions!

Inline styles

Occasionally, you may need to add an inline style to a document rather than using internal or external style sheets. For example, if you're creating an HTML e-mail, you might use tables instead of CSS layers, but still use inline styles for text formatting because many e-mail programs prefer to interpret HTML tags over CSS for layout and positioning. What's more, when the style data is inline with the content, a visitor can also read the mail offline and view it styled as you intended.

Inline style descriptions are written inside the code, surrounding the selected text, oftentimes appending whatever existing tag is closest to the content to be styled, or by adding a `<span>` tag with the style attribute, as in the following two examples:

```
<p style="font-size: 12px; color: #990000; ">Inline styles are "in line" with the
    text.</p>
<p>This example uses the span tag to selectively apply a <span style="font-size:
    12px; color: #990000; ">custom style</span> to selected text.</p>
```

To add an inline style to your page, follow these steps:

1. **Select the word or words you'd like to apply an inline style to.**

   For example, you may want to style the words 'On Sale Now!'.

2. **On the CSS Properties inspector, select <inline style> from the New Rule section of the Targeted Rule menu.**

   Essentially, you'll be formatting the `style` tag attribute in a similar way to how the old `<font>` tag used to be coded.

3. **Apply the desired font, size, and color attributes to the selected text, as well as bold, italics, and alignment settings, if desired.**

   When the inline style is applied to an entire paragraph, the style markup is added to the opening `<p>` tag, like this:

   ```
   <p style="font-family: Georgia, 'Times New Roman', Times, serif; font-weight:
       bold; color: #F63; font-size: 16px;">On Sale Now!</p>
   ```

When the inline style is applied to a single word or selection of words inside a paragraph, the style markup surrounds the selected text using the <span> tag, like this:

```
<p>We have thousands of products <span style="font-family: Georgia, 'Times New
    Roman', Times, serif; font-size: 16px; font-weight: bold; color: #F63;">On
    Sale Now!</span></p>
```

Working with the CSS Styles Panel

Use the CSS Styles panel to create and manage your internal and external style sheets. If the panel is not visible, open it by choosing Window➪CSS Styles. Though applying styles is typically done through the Properties inspector, we strongly recommend using the CSS Styles panel instead of the Properties inspector for creating and editing all your CSS.

The Dreamweaver CS4 CSS Styles panel has many enhancements from versions prior to CS3, including multiple panes. Resize panes by clicking and dragging the divider line between the panes up or down until they are the size you want.

Two buttons appear at the top of the panel: All and Current, as shown in Figure 1-3, each of which display different views of the CSS Styles panel. The following sections discuss these views in detail.

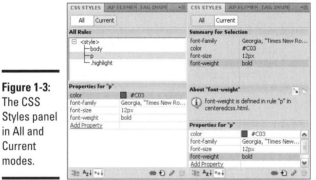

Figure 1-3: The CSS Styles panel in All and Current modes.

All mode

Click the All button and the CSS Styles panel splits into two panes:

✦ **All Rules:** The top pane displays a list of all the styles attached to, or contained inside of, the currently selected open document.

✦ **Properties:** Select a style in the top pane, and the bottom pane displays its specific attributes. You can quickly make a change to an existing property or add more properties by clicking the Add Property link.

Current mode

Click the Current button and the CSS Styles panel divides into three panes:

✦ **Summary for Selection:** The top pane shows an attributes summary of the currently selected style. Properties display in order of specificity. Class styles have higher specificity than tag selectors.

✦ **About/Rules:** You can toggle this area to display data in two views by clicking the buttons on the top-right edge of the section's title bar. The left About button displays information about a selected property (such as Color is defined in an inline style attribute in index.html), whereas the right Rules button shows the style name and the tag in the code the selected style is applied to (such as `<.onsale> <span>` or `<inline style> <p>`).

✦ **Properties:** The bottom pane displays the attributes of the selected style in an editable format. Make a change to a property or add more properties by clicking the Add Property link.

CSS Styles panel viewing buttons

The bottom edge of the CSS Styles panel (as shown in Figure 1-4) displays buttons that are shared by both All and Current views and allow you to select from different viewing and editing options.

Book III
Chapter 1

Looking Good with
Cascading Style
Sheets (CSS)

Figure 1-4:
These buttons display viewing and editing options.

Attach Style Sheet   Edit Rule

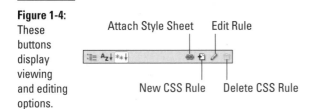

New CSS Rule   Delete CSS Rule

The panel's bottom right edge displays four buttons:

✦ **Attach Style Sheet** launches the Attach External Style Sheet dialog box to select an external style sheet to link to or import to the current file, as well as to specify the desired media type(s) the attached CSS should be associated with.

✦ **New CSS Rule** opens the New CSS Rule dialog box for naming, choosing a selector type, and specifying the location for the new style rule.

✦ **Edit Rule** opens the CSS Rule definition dialog box when a style is selected in the CSS Styles panel.

✦ **Delete CSS Rule** permanently removes a selected rule or property from the CSS Styles panel, as well as any formatting from elements to which it was applied. It doesn't, however, delete references in the HTML markup to that style.

The panel's bottom left edge displays three buttons that change how the listing in the Properties pane of the panel are displayed:

✦ **Show Category View** splits CSS properties into nine categories: Font, Background, Block, Border, Box, List, Positioning, Extensions, and Tables, Content, Quotes. Each category's properties are displayed in expandable list format. You can expand and collapse the list by clicking the plus (+) or minus (–) button next to the category name. Properties in each category are listed alphabetically with set properties sorted on top in blue text.

✦ **Show List View** shows CSS properties in descending alphabetical order with set properties in blue text at the top of the list.

✦ **Show Only Set Properties** shows only set properties. This is the default view.

In all the CSS Styles panel views, any set properties display in blue text while the rest appear in black text unless they are irrelevant properties (when the rule is not inherited by the style or is overridden by another style), which display with a red strikethrough line. In addition, irrelevant rules contain explanatory pop-up messages that you can see when you hover your mouse over the rule.

Understanding CSS Style Types

All Cascading Style Sheet rules are written in two-part syntax consisting of the selector and the declaration:

✦ The *selector* is the name of the style, which could be a tag like <p> or <h1>, or a custom name, such as `.tableheader`.

✦ The *declaration* specifies all the style's elements, such as font face, size, color, and so on. Rules can contain multiple declarations as long as each is separated by a semicolon (;) as shown in the example below.

Here's an example of a CSS rule where p is the selector and everything inside the curly brackets ({}) is the declaration:

```
p {
font-family: Verdana, Arial, Helvetica, sans-serif;
font-size: 12px;
color: #993300;
}
```

Notice that the declarations themselves have two parts separated by a colon (:): the property (such as color) and the value (such as #993300). In the rule for p in the preceding example, a style has been defined for all <p> tags, meaning that all content in the document between any pair of opening and closing <p> tags displays as Verdana, 12px, and #993300 (which is the hexadecimal code for a deep brick red color). (To find out more about *hex* colors, see Book II, Chapter 2.)

The *cascading* part of Cascading Style Sheets refers to the capability of adding multiple style declarations to the same rule as well as applying multiple rules to the same elements. For instance, you can have one rule define the style of text and another rule define the margin and line spacing around it. In a greater sense, however, the term refers to the ability to use multiple style sheets and multiple style inheritances in a cascading way that determines which styles take precedence over the others. To find out more about CSS cascading rules, see the About.com article on CSS types at webdesign. about.com/od/css/f/blcssfaqcascade.htm.

In addition to hand coding, Dreamweaver provides you with two different ways to create CSS styles for your documents:

✦ **Properties inspector:** As we mentioned previously, you can automatically create and add internal, externally linked, or inline styles to your page when styling selected content using the CSS Properties inspector.

✦ **CSS Styles panel:** Using the CSS Styles panel (as described in the section "Adding a Style to a New or Existing Style Sheet") you can add internal or external styles to your files by accessing the full library of style properties inside the CSS Rule Definition dialog box.

Before you begin creating your styles, you need to be familiar with the different style types. You can create four general types of styles using the CSS Styles panel: Custom styles, ID styles, Tag redefines, and Compound CSS selectors. Each type modifies different parts of the HTML, as described in the following sections.

Custom styles (Class)

If you want to selectively style content, use custom styles. For instance, in the sentence, "When collecting seashells, remember to bring a bucket or other container with you," you could create a custom style for the word *seashells*. That custom style might look something like this:

```
.seashells {
    font-family: Verdana, Arial, Helvetica, sans-serif;
    font-size: 12px;
    color: #3366CC;
    font-style: italic;
}
```

Book III
Chapter 1

Looking Good with
Cascading Style
Sheets (CSS)

Custom style names, whether placed on internal or external style sheets, must have a period (.) before the style name to display properly in a browser window. Dreamweaver lists, in preview form, all custom styles in the Targeted Rule and Class drop-down lists in the Properties inspector.

To apply the custom style to a document, select the content in Design view, and select the custom style from the Targeted Rule or Class drop-down lists in the Properties inspector. Dreamweaver modifies the selection by surrounding it with the `<span>` tag with the designated class attribute, as the following example shows:

```
<p>When collecting <span class="seashells">seashells</span> remember to bring a
    bucket or other container with you.</p>
```

Figure 1-5 shows how this sentence looks in Design and Code views.

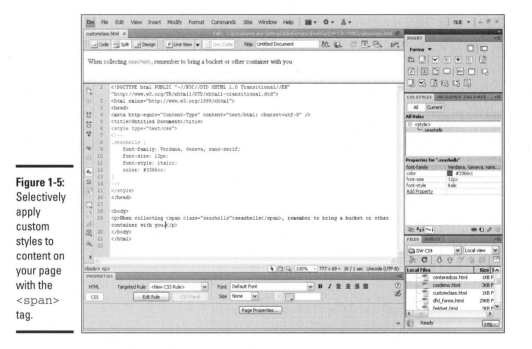

Figure 1-5: Selectively apply custom styles to content on your page with the `<span>` tag.

ID styles (ID)

Use the ID styles to create custom styles that are automatically applied to any object on the page with the ID matching the ID style name.

To illustrate, say you have an AP Element (layer) filled with a listing of different models of low-flow showerheads, like the one shown in Figure 1-6. If you then give the table an ID attribute of "showerheads", using the syntax `id="showerheads"`, and create a style using the syntax `#showerheads`, that ID style is automatically applied to the table. As long as the ID style name is proceeded with the number symbol (#), the style is automatically applied to the object with a matching ID. This is different from CSS styles, which must be hand-applied to selections using the Targeted Rule or Class menu on the Properties inspector.

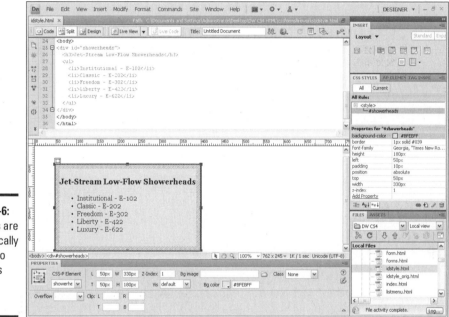

Figure 1-6:
ID Styles are automatically applied to elements with the same ID.

**Book III
Chapter 1**

Looking Good with Cascading Style Sheets (CSS)

Here's an example how an ID style is written in the CSS:

```
#showerheads {
    font-family: Georgia, "Times New Roman", Times, serif;
    background-color: #BFEBFF;
    border: 1px solid #039;
    position: absolute;
    width: 330px;
    height: 180px;
    z-index: 1;
    left: 50px;
    top: 50px;
    padding: 10px;
    }
```

And here is what the HTML markup would look like:

```
<div id="showerheads">
    <h3>Jet-Stream Low-Flow Showerheads</h3>
    <ul>
        <li>Institutional - E-102</li>
        <li>Classic - E-202</li>
        <li>Freedom - E-302</li>
        <li>Liberty - E-422</li>
        <li>Luxury - E-622</li>
    </ul>
</div>
```

CSS tag redefines

You can use *tag redefine CSS styles*, created with the CSS Styles panel, to modify the preformatted look of existing HTML tags, such as the <p>, <h1>, and <td> tags. For example, the Heading 1 tag (<h1>) is preformatted to be large and bold, using whatever font styles the browser's default H1 setting are set to display it in. By redefining the tag in the CSS, you can force content styled with the <h1> tag to display with your chosen style attributes, such as 36 pixels, Verdana, navy blue, and bold:

```
h1 {
    font-family: Verdana, Arial, Helvetica, sans-serif;
    font-size: 36px;
    color: #000033;
    font-weight: bold;
}
```

Whatever properties or tags you don't redefine in the CSS, however, remain set at the browser defaults.

Compound styles

Compound styles are like the muscles of CSS, where you can create some really amazing layout and formatting styles. The only drawback is that compound styles can seem a bit complicated for the beginner. The W3C (www.w3.org/TR/REC-CSS1) has technical definitions of all the things you can achieve with CSS and these *advanced selectors*, but if you're new to CSS, these instructions may be difficult to understand. For a more basic breakdown, try reading the Advanced Selectors article by Ross Shannon on the HTMLSource Web site at www.yourhtmlsource.com/stylesheets/advancedselectors.html.

The most common use of the Compound selector type is to modify the color of links. The default link color for browsers is royal blue, and the default visited link color is purple. If those colors don't blend well with the colors of your Web site, create custom link colors with the Compound style type.

What's more, in addition to changing the link and visited link colors, style sheets allow you to add two additional link states to your links:

✦ The hover state, for when you mouse over the link.

✦ The active state, for when you actually click the link.

The order in which you create these link states is important. Create the normal link state first, and then the visited state, and then the hover and active states. A different order may cause the links to not work properly. If you have trouble remembering the order, try using the mnemonic "LoVe HAte" for Link, Visited, Hover, Active.

When added to a style sheet, the following code changes the link color for each of the states using a hexadecimal value for the color:

```
a:link {
    color: #990000;
}
a:visited {
    color: #ff0000;
}
a:hover {
    color: #6600cc;
}
a:active {
    color: #000000;
}
```

Use any hexadecimal color needed to match your design. In addition to the text color, you can also modify the text decoration (the type of underline attribute the link has), background color (behind the text), font weight (bold), and other style attributes in the CSS Styles panel.

The second most common usage for the Compound selector type is for creating styles that are either combinations of tags or tags that are nested inside of other tags. Tag combinations are for times when you need to create a style that you'll apply to multiple tags, such as the <body>, <th>, and <td> tags:

```
body,th,td {
    margin: 0px;
    padding: 0px;
    font-family: Verdana, Arial, Helvetica, sans-serif;
    font-size: 10px;
    color: #99ffff;
    font-weight: bold;
}
```

Nested compound tag styles are used when you want to apply a style to a very specific part of a page. For example, in the following code, the selector name applies to all <td> elements that are within any <tr> elements that are within any <html> elements with id "showerheads". In other words, this style is only applied to content inside of cells inside of a table with the id="showerheads":

```
#showerheads tr td {
    font-family: Georgia, "Times New Roman", Times, serif;
    font-weight: bold;
    color: #393;
}
```

Book III
Chapter 1

Looking Good with
Cascading Style
Sheets (CSS)

Other great resources for finding more about CSS and compound selectors include the following:

```
www.w3schools.com/css/
http://reference.sitepoint.com/css
www.csszengarden.com/
www.meyerweb.com/eric/css/
www.htmlhelp.com/reference/css/
```

Adding a Style to a New or Existing Style Sheet

To create an internal or external style sheet, you start by defining a style. You can create a custom style, tag redefine, or compound style (all of which are described in the preceding section) using the CSS Styles panel.

Open your HTML document and follow these steps to add a style to a new or existing style sheet:

1. **Click the New CSS Rule button at the bottom of the CSS Styles panel.**

You can also choose Format⇨CSS Styles⇨New.

The New CSS Rule dialog box opens, as shown in Figure 1-7.

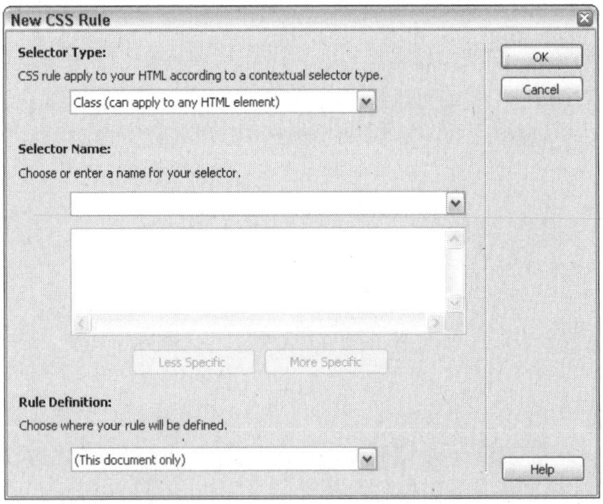

Figure 1-7:
Create a
new CSS
rule (style).

2. **Choose a selector type from the following options:**

- **Class** creates a custom style that can be applied to any content such as a word, phrase, sentence, graphic, or layer.

- **ID** creates a style for tags with specific ID attributes.

- **Tag** redefines the look of an existing tag, such as <p> and <h1>.

- **Compound** selectors style links, combinations of tags, and nested tags. They can also be used to create styles using combinators, attribute selectors, pseudoclasses, and pseudoelements.

3. **For the Selector Name, depending on the selector type you choose in Step 3, do one of the following:**

- **Class (can apply to any HTML element):** Enter a name for your new style in the Selector Name text box with a period (.) before the style name, as in **.discount**.

Class names must begin with a period and can have any combination of numbers and letters, but no spaces or other special characters. Fortunately, if you forget to enter the period before the style name, Dreamweaver automatically enters it for you. This, however, is not foolproof; if your style doesn't display in a browser, check the CSS to see if the period is missing before the class name.

- **ID (applies to only one HTML element):** Enter the ID of the element you'd like to style in the Name text box, as in `#showerheads`.

   After you enter an ID, any object with the same ID is automatically styled with this CSS rule.

- **Tag (redefines and HTML element):** Enter an HTML tag in the Tag text box or select the tag that your style redefines from the Tag drop-down list, such as `<h1>`, `<table>`, or `<p>`.

- **Compound (based on your selection):** Select a pseudoclass selector from the drop-down menu for redefining the different link styles from the Selector drop-down list, or type the HTML tag, the combination of tags separated by commas, or the nested tag sequence of the new style in the Selector Name text box.

   For example, typing **#showerheads tr td** creates a style that would automatically apply to any content inside of a table cell inside an element with the ID `"showerheads"`, typing **body,th,td** creates a style that automatically applies to multiple tags, and typing or selecting **a:link**, **a:visited**, **a:active**, or **a:hover** creates a style that redefines one of four link state styles. If you know how to create the more advanced compound selector styles, type the proper syntax for that compound selector style into the Style text box.

   After you've typed in a name for your selector, a description appears in the description box below the Selector Name field.

   This selector name applies your rule to all `<td>` elements that are within any `<tr>` elements that are within any HTML elements with the ID `"showerheads"`.

   To understand these style descriptions more readily, be sure to click the More Specific button below the description area.

4. **Under Rule Definition, choose one of the following options to specify the location of the new style information:**

   - Choose **(New Style Sheet File)** to create a new external style sheet.

   - Choose **(This Document Only)** to create an internal style sheet.

   - Choose the filename of any existing external CSS file, if available, from the drop-down list.

5. **If you chose to add the new style to a new style sheet in Step 4, the Save Style Sheet File As dialog box appears. Enter a name for your new CSS and click OK to save it to the specified directory. Then skip ahead to Step 7.**

   Be sure to name your new CSS with the .css file extension and save it to the root level of your currently managed site. Upon closing this dialog box, Dreamweaver automatically opens the CSS Rule Definition dialog box for defining the new style.

6. **Click OK to close the New CSS Rule dialog box.**

   The CSS Rule Definition dialog box appears, as shown in Figure 1-8.

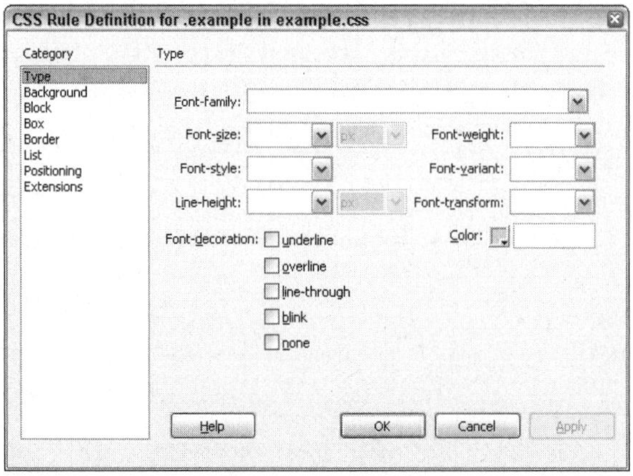

Figure 1-8: Choose style attributes when creating a new style.

[Screenshot: CSS Rule Definition for .example in example.css dialog box, showing Category list (Type, Background, Block, Box, Border, List, Positioning, Extensions) and Type options including Font-family, Font-size, Font-weight, Font-style, Font-variant, Line-height, Font-transform, Font-decoration (underline, overline, line-through, blink, none), and Color, with Help, OK, Cancel, and Apply buttons.]

Depending on your selection in Step 3, the title bar in the CSS Rule Definition dialog box may display slightly different text. For instance, if adding a style to an existing CSS, the title bar reads CSS Rule Definition for *.example* in *example.css*.

7. **Enter the style information for the new style, in any combination of categories.**

   When you select a category from the listing on the left, the right side of the panel changes to support that category's options. The upcoming section "Exploring the CSS Rule Definition Dialog Box" covers all the category options in this dialog box.

To preview before committing to the style settings, click the Apply button. Don't feel pressured to get the style to look exactly right during the creation process, as you can easily edit the styles at any time (see the "Editing a CSS Style" section, later in this chapter).

8. Click OK.

The new style is added to the style sheet and displays in the CSS Styles panel. To cancel out of the New CSS Rule dialog box without adding a style, click the Cancel button.

9. Repeat Steps 1 through 8 to create additional styles in the same internal or external CSS.

You can add as many styles as you want to the CSS, and you can create both internal and external styles at any time. For greatest ease of use, we recommend that you create a single external CSS file and place all of your style rules there. That way, you can use a single style sheet for an entire Web site!

Attaching a Style Sheet to Your Document

You can attach an existing style sheet to your document at any stage of development. It can be a fully realized style sheet or a blank one that you build as you style your document; for the purposes of attaching the style sheet, its contents don't matter so long as the file is created and saved in advance with the .css file extension.

If you have an existing external style sheet (perhaps a copy of one used on another project or one provided by another member of your team) or want to use one of Dreamweaver's sample style sheets, save it to the local root folder of your currently managed site or in a folder at the root level of that site. Then follow these steps:

1. Open the CSS Styles panel and click the Attach Style Sheet button at the bottom of the panel (refer to Figure 1-4).

The Attach External Style Sheet dialog box opens, as shown in Figure 1-9.

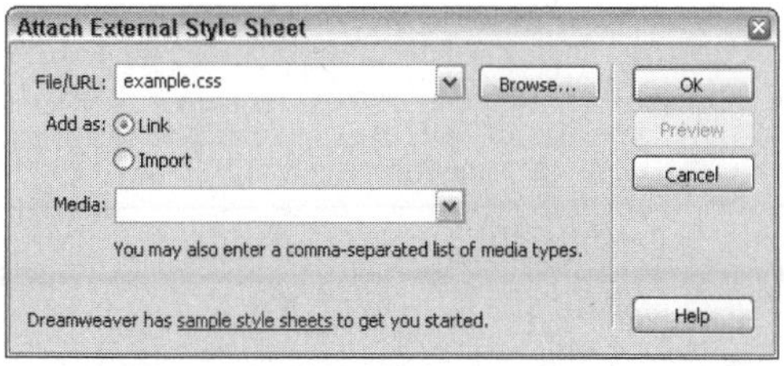

Book III
Chapter 1

Looking Good with
Cascading Style
Sheets (CSS)

Figure 1-9:
Attach an
external
CSS to a
page.

2. **In the File/URL field, enter the name of the existing style sheet or click the Browse button to navigate to and select the existing style sheet.**

Dreamweaver has several sample style sheets you can use either as-is or as a starting point for customizing your own style sheet. To use one of the existing style sheets, click the Sample Style Sheets link inside the dialog box. The Sample Style Sheets dialog box opens from which you can preview and select a style sheet from the listing. Click OK and Dreamweaver instantly attaches that selected style sheet to your page.

3. **In the Add As field, choose the Link or Import radio button.**

Link: Choose the Link option to add the CSS as an external file, where a line of link code containing the CSS file you specified is inserted into the head of the page:

```
<link href="example.css" rel="stylesheet" type="text/css">
```

Import: Choose the Import option to add a special @import link to the CSS internally, in the head area of the page:

```
<style type="text/css">
<!--
@import url("example.css");
-->
</style>
```

Both options link to external CSS files; however, the second method is less reliable with older browsers than the first, so when linking, choose the Link radio button, or simply include both methods in the code.

4. **In the Media field, either select an option from the drop-down list or leave this field blank.**

Media types refer to the different types of devices or media a user can view your page with — such as a screen device (like a browser), a hand-held device (like a BlackBerry), or a printer. Choose a media type from the drop-down list to identify the linked CSS as being the one to use when that device is used to view the page.

To enter multiple media types at once, separate each type with a comma, as in **screen, printer, handheld.**

To find out more about CSS for media, visit the World Wide Web Consortium at www.w3.org/TR/CSS21/media.html.

5. **Click the Preview button to see how the CSS will change the appearance of your document.**

6. **Click OK to attach the CSS to your document.**

The CSS Styles panel displays the newly attached external style sheet. To tell the difference between internal and external styles, look for the word <style> or the name of the external CSS; Internal styles display in a list below a <style> tag, whereas external style sheets display below the CSS filename.

Applying a Custom Class Style

You can apply custom styles you've created in your internal or external style sheets to any selected asset in an open document. For example, you may want certain words in a sentence to stand out from the rest of the text or style graphics with uniform styling attributes. Before applying a custom style, create the style with the CSS Styles panel (see the preceding section).

To apply a custom style to your document, follow these steps:

1. **Select the content to be styled in either Design or Code view.**

   To assist in selecting an exact tag, select the tag in the tag selector bar at the bottom left edge of the Document window.

2. **Using the Properties inspector, select the custom style from the Targeted Rule or Class drop-down list.**

   The Targeted Rule and Class menus both list the custom styles by name, but the Class menu also shows a preview of style names (as shown in Figure 1-10), making them easier to recognize.

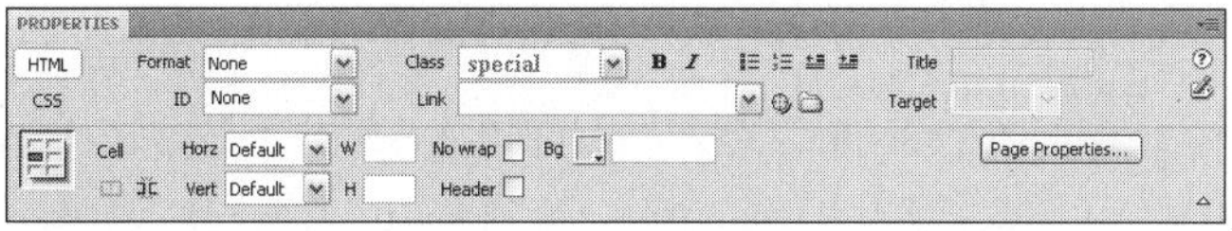

Figure 1-10:
Apply custom styles with the Class menu.

Book III
Chapter 1

Looking Good with Cascading Style Sheets (CSS)

Dreamweaver styles your selection by either adding the <span> tag with your custom class around your selection, or by appending an existing tag with the new custom class:

```
<p>Applying <span class="special">custom</span> styles is easy!</p>
<p class="special">Applying custom styles is easy!</p>
```

To remove a custom style from a selection, select the text or object in Design view and choose None from the top of the Class drop-down list in the HTML tab of the Properties inspector. In the CSS tab of the Properties inspector, you can remove a custom style from a selection by choosing <remove class> from the Targeted Rule drop-down list. (See Figure 1-2.)

Editing a CSS Style

Editing styles in the CSS Styles panel is as easy as creating a new style. Essentially you're changing the style attributes in the same dialog box you used to initially create the style in. You can use either Current or All mode to enter the style changes.

Editing in All mode

To edit a CSS style with the CSS Styles panel in All mode, open your HTML document and follow these steps:

1. Click the All button at the top of the panel.

A list of style rules used on the entire document displays in the All Rules pane, whether internal or external.

2. Select the style that needs editing.

Now you have two options: You can edit that style's properties directly in the Properties pane at the bottom of the panel, or you can reopen the Rule Definition dialog box, inside which you can make adjustments to the selected style. To use the dialog box, proceed to Step 3.

3. Click the Edit Rule button at the bottom of the panel (refer to Figure 1-4).

The CSS Rule Definition dialog box opens, identifying the style and location by name, such as CSS Rule Definition for *.example* in *example.css*.

You can also reopen the CSS Rule Definition dialog box by

- Double-clicking the style name in the CSS Styles panel.

- Right-clicking (Windows) or Control+clicking (Mac) the style name and selecting Edit from the context menu.

- Clicking the Edit Rule button on the CSS Properties inspector.

4. Edit the style information as needed in any of the style categories.

The upcoming section "Exploring the CSS Rule Definition Dialog Box" covers the different options in this dialog box.

To preview before committing to the edited style settings, click the Apply button.

5. Click OK.

The edited style with its new style attributes displays in the CSS Styles panel. To cancel out of the New CSS Rule Definition dialog box without modifying the style, click the Cancel button.

Editing in Current mode

To edit a CSS style with the CSS Styles panel in Current mode, follow these steps:

1. **Click the Current button at the top of the panel.**

A summary of style properties for any currently selected style displays.

2. **Select a text element or other asset on the page to view its style properties.**

The CSS Styles panel shows the summary for the current selection including detailed information about the style location and editable style properties.

3. **To edit any of the style's properties, select a rule in the Summary pane and edit those properties directly in the Properties pane at the bottom of the panel.**

Or you can double-click the rule in the Summary pane to enter changes in the CSS Rule Definition dialog box. This option is only available if you've enabled the Edit Using CSS Dialog setting in the CSS Styles category of Dreamweaver's Preferences.

The upcoming section "Exploring the CSS Rule Definition Dialog Box" covers the different options in this dialog box.

To preview before committing to the settings, click the Apply button.

4. **Click OK.**

The edited style with its new style attributes displays in the CSS Styles panel. To cancel out of the New CSS Rule Definition dialog box without modifying the style, click the Cancel button.

You can also edit your styles by hand in Code view.

Adding properties to a CSS style

Add properties to any existing CSS style at any time by following these steps:

1. **Choose a rule in the All Rules pane in All mode or pick a property in the Summary section of Current mode.**

2. **Do one of the following:**

- Click the Show Only Set Properties button and then click the Add Properties link in the Properties pane.

- Click either the Show Category View or Show List View button, and fill in the new property value next to the property you want to add.

**Book III
Chapter 1**

Looking Good with
Cascading Style
Sheets (CSS)

You can also add properties to an existing style at any time by hand coding in Code view, or by selecting the rule in All mode and reopening the CSS Rule Definition dialog box by double-clicking the Edit Rule button at the bottom of the CSS Styles panel.

Deleting a CSS Style

Sometimes you create a style and then never use it. To help clear the CSS file of unnecessary style information — which also keeps the overall file size low — delete any unused styles from your style sheet before publishing your site.

To delete a style from a style sheet listed in the CSS Styles panel, follow these steps:

1. **Click the All button at the top of the panel.**

A list of style rules used on the entire document displays, whether internal or external.

2. **Select the style you want to delete.**

3. **Click the Delete CSS Rule button at the bottom of the panel (refer to Figure 1-4).**

You can also right-click (Windows) or Control+click (Mac) the style name and choose Delete from the context menu.

If you feel comfortable doing so, you can also delete internal styles from your document or external styles from an external CSS file in Code view.

Removing styles by either method only removes the style from the CSS, not from within the HTML code. To remove the application of a removed style from HTML, use the Find and Replace dialog box to search the entire site for that style attribute. For details about using the Find and Replace dialog box to remove specified content, see Book II, Chapter 2.

Exploring the CSS Rule Definition Dialog Box

With the CSS Rule Definition dialog box, Adobe has created a simple user interface to create, test, and apply styles. The dialog box includes several categories of style rules that you can add in any combination, including style rules for type, background, block, box, border, list, positioning, and extensions.

To use the dialog box, first select a category from the left side of the panel. Then choose styling options from the right side of the panel. The right side of the panel's options are determined by the category you select on the left.

As a general rule, when entering individual values to rules with Top, Bottom, Left, and Right fields, enter **0** or **None** for sides that should not contain values. Doing so improves the chances of different browsers rendering your styles consistently.

Type properties

Use the Type category (shown in Figure 1-11) to create specific font attributes and type styles. In addition to the font face, you can customize the font size, line height, style, decoration, and weight, among other settings.

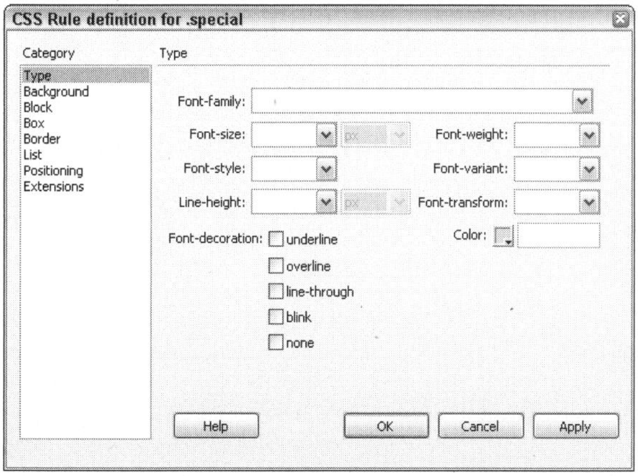

Figure 1-11: Create text styles with the Type category settings.

Not all browsers support all the type properties, and some elements appear differently on a Mac than they do on a PC, so be sure to test the CSS styles in all your target browsers on both platforms before publishing your site. This gives you the opportunity to select different style attributes for your styles if needed.

The following rules are available in the Type category:

✦ **Font-family:** Select a Web-safe font family from the drop-down list or type the name of the Web-safe font or font set you want to use. Default sets include cross-platform–compatible fonts such as "Verdana, Arial, Helvetica, Sans-serif".

   To create your own custom font sets, select the Edit Font List option from the bottom of the drop-down list. The Edit Font List dialog box opens, wherein you create new lists from available system fonts. (For more of a discussion on font sets, see Book II, Chapter 2.)

✦ **Font-size:** Choose from preset font sizes ranging from 9 to 36 from the drop-down list or type a number in the size field. Specify font size in px (pixels), pc (picas), pt (points), in (inches), mm (millimeters), cm (centimeters), (ems), (exs), or % (percentage). Although using pixels is generally recommended over points (the primary unit for print design) to ensure uniform display on both Macs and PCs, due to a resizing issue in Internet Explorer, many CSS tutorials now suggest you use ems for font sizes instead. Additionally, when font sizes are set to ems, they resize correctly if the browser's default text size setting is changed. Resizing will not occur if the fonts are set to pixels.

✦ **Font-style:** Select normal (the default), italic, or oblique as the font style. The oblique style is similar to italic, only it typically refers to a sans-serif font that's tilted about 12 degrees before being adjusted to improve the font's appearance.

✦ **Line-height:** This setting, also called *leading,* sets the text line height from baseline to baseline. Choose Normal to use the automatically calculated standard ratio of font size to line height, or enter a number value in pixels, points, in, cm, mm, picas, ems, exs, or %.

✦ **Font-decoration:** The following options are available for text decoration:

  • **underline:** Adds an underline to the selected text. This setting is the default for links.

  • **overline:** Adds an overline to the selected text. The overline looks just like an underline, only it's above the characters rather than below them. It's a strange-looking style, to be sure, so try not to use it for styling links unless you know your audience is sharp enough to figure it out.

  • **line-through:** Adds a line-through, or *strikethrough,* effect to the selected text.

  • **blink:** Makes the text blink, or *flash*, in the browser window. (This setting is not a recommended practice and happens to be very annoying to site visitors, so don't use it.)

  • **none:** Removes all decorative formatting, including underlines on links. This setting is the default for normal text.

✦ **Font-weight:** The default font weight is normal, but you may specify the amount of boldness using other font weight options including bold, bolder, lighter, and bold settings in increments of 100 from 100 to 900, where normal is equal to 400 and bold is equal to 700.

✦ **Font-variant:** Select normal or small caps. Normal refers to the default font variance of upper and lowercase figures. A small caps setting converts text to display in small caps.

✦ **Font-transform:** Options include capitalize, uppercase, lowercase, and none. For example, selecting uppercase changes the display from normal upper and lowercase lettering to all uppercase letters.

✦ **Color:** Select a color from the Web-safe palette or system color picker (the circle at the top right edge of the popup palette). You can also type the hexadecimal code into this field; just remember to include the number symbol (#) before the hex number, as in **#990033 or #903** (which is shorthand when the characters in each pair match: 99 becomes 9, 00 becomes 0, and 33 becomes 3), so the color renders properly in the browser.

Background properties

The Background category's rules (see Figure 1-12) define the background settings of various elements on a document. For example, you can add a background color to a page, a table cell, a layer, or selected text.

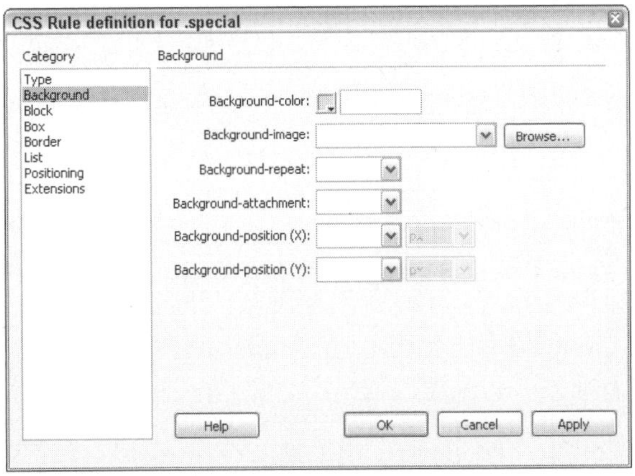

Figure 1-12:
Add custom background properties to your styles.

The following rules are available in the Background category:

✦ **Background-color:** Apply a background color to the body of the page, text, tables, table cells, layers, and more. Select a background color from the Web-safe palette or system color picker, or type the hexadecimal code along with the number symbol (#) before the hex number (as in **#990033**), so the color renders properly in the browser.

✦ **Background-image:** Type a filename or browse to and select the location and filename of an image. You can apply background images to the body of the page, text, a table, table cell, or layer.

✦ **Background-repeat:** Instruct the browser how to display the background image. By default, background images automatically repeat, or *tile*, both vertically and horizontally unless otherwise specified:

• **no-repeat:** Displays the background image once, without any horizontal or vertical repeating.

- **repeat:** Mirrors the default setting of continuous horizontal and vertical repeating of a normal background image.

- **repeat-x:** Forces the specified background image to tile horizontally only. Images are cut off at the borders to fit the element's dimensions.

- **repeat-y:** Forces the specified background image to tile vertically only. Images are cut off at the borders to fit the element's dimensions.

✦ **Background-attachment:** Choose how the background image interacts with content above it:

- **fixed:** Treats the background image as if it is immovably fixed to the background of the browser, while text and other assets on the page scroll past or over it.

- **scroll:** Adds the background image to the page so that text and other assets on the page scroll along with it.

- **inherit:** Inherits the fixed or scroll rule from a parent asset, such as a table cell inside a table. This option doesn't display in the attachment field in Dreamweaver, but you can type it in the text box. (In fact, the inherit option can be ascribed to every property, including the repeat and font-size properties.)

Browsers inconsistently support these features, so use them with caution.

✦ **Background-position (X):** Determine where in the browser window the background image begins its **horizontal** display or repeat. Enter positioning settings for Left, Center, or Right, or type your own value in pixels, points, in, cm, mm, picas, ems, exs, or %.

✦ **Background-position (Y):** Determine where in the browser window the background image begins its **vertical** display or repeat. Add positioning settings for Top, Center, or Bottom, or type your own value in pixels, points, in, cm, mm, picas, ems, exs, or %.

To center a single image inside the browser window, create a style for the <body> tag and set the Horizontal and Vertical alignment to center in conjunction with a fixed, non-repeating, background attachment. In the following example, a file called logo.gif is used as the single, centered background image:

```
<style type="text/css">
<!--
body {
    background-attachment: fixed;
    background-image: url(images/logo.gif);
    background-repeat: no-repeat;
    background-position: center;
}
-->
</style>
```

Block properties

The Block rules (shown in Figure 1-13) control the space and alignment of styled tags and attributes. Elements that Dreamweaver treats as CSS layout blocks include

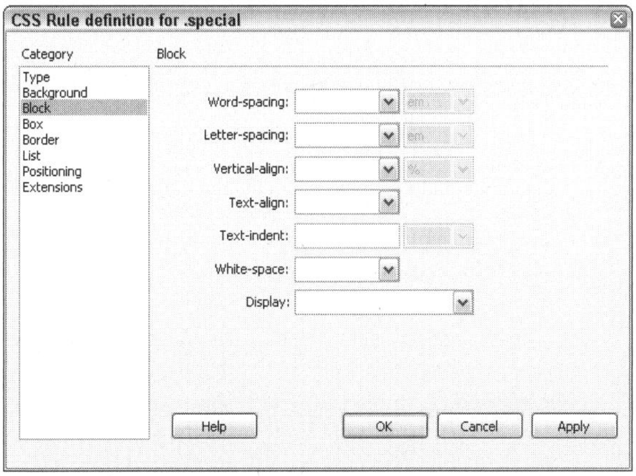

CSS Rule definition for .special

Category   Block

Type
Background
Block
Box
Border
List
Positioning
Extensions

Word-spacing:

Letter-spacing:

Vertical-align:

Text-align:

Text-indent:

White-space:

Display:

Help   OK   Cancel   Apply

Figure 1-13:
Add style
properties
to set
spacing and
alignment.

✦ `<div>` tags assigned with absolute or relative positions

✦ `<form>` and `<table>` tags

✦ Images assigned with absolute or relative positions

✦ Tags using the `display:block` style

✦ Paragraphs assigned with absolute or relative positions

Book III
Chapter 1

Looking Good with
Cascading Style
Sheets (CSS)

You can view CSS layout block properties such as layout outlines, backgrounds, and box models with Dreamweaver's Visual Aids. To toggle the visibility of these properties on and off, choose View➪Visual Aids and then pick the visual aid you want from the submenu.

The following rules are available in the Block category:

✦ **Wordspacing:** Select or enter a numerical value in pixels, points, in, cm, mm, picas, ems, exs, or % to evenly control the space between individual words. Both positive and negative values are acceptable.

✦ **Letterspacing:** Evenly increase or decrease space between letters and characters by adding positive or negative numerical values in pixels, points, in, cm, mm, picas, ems, exs, or %. Be aware that these settings override text justification. Internet Explorer 4 and up and Netscape Navigator 6 and up support this rule.

✦ **Vertical-align:** Choose Baseline, Sub, Super, Top, Text-top, Middle, Bottom, Text-bottom, or Value to enter a value in pixels, points, in, cm, mm, picas, ems, exs, or %. Preview these alignments in a browser window (except for any in an `<img>` tag) to see their effect (press F12 in Windows or Shift-F12 on a Mac).

✦ **Text-align:** Choose Left, Right, Center, or Justify.

✦ **Text-indent:** Enter a text indent numerical value in pixels, points, in, cm, mm, picas, ems, exs, or % to set the rule for indenting the first line of text. Indent sizes may be positive or negative values.

✦ **White-space:** Determine how white space inside a block element displays:

   • **Normal:** Collapses any white space.

   • **Pre:** Leaves the white space as it was coded.

   • **Nowrap:** Wraps text only when the code contains the line break `<br>` tags. Netscape Navigator and Internet Explorer 5.5 and later support this rule.

✦ **Display:** Determines whether the element displays in the browser at all, and if so, how. You may, for instance, want to use one of these settings to turn off a style attribute in a CSS for print media:

   • **none:** Completely turns off, or hides, the display of the styled element.

   • **inline:** Displays the element inline with other elements, typically inside the current block.

   • **block:** Forces an element to display as a block.

   • **list-item:** Displays elements as a list item with bullets, similar to the `<ul>` and `<ol>` tags.

   • **run-in:** Forces a block box following a run-in box to become an inline box of the block box. Only Opera 5 and later and Internet Explorer 5 for Macs currently support this feature.

   • **compact:** Styles a box of content in such a way that subsequent block boxes display to its left side when room permits. Though a bit buggy, this feature is currently supported by Opera 5 and 7. (For a visual illustration of this feature, see `www.quirksmode.org/css/display.html#compact`.)

   • **marker:** Add a marker setting to format content inside a marker box, such as adding numbers or graphics to a list or special notations to styled content.

   • **table:** Displays elements as a table. Nested elements display as table-row and table-cell, as they appear if contained in typical `<tr>` and `<td>` tags. Other table display settings include inline-table, table-row-group, table-header-group, table-footer-group, table-row, table-column-group, table-column, table-cell, and table-caption.

For more details regarding block display properties, visit the W3C Web site at

```
www.w3.org/TR/REC-CSS2/visuren.html#display-prop
www.w3.org/TR/REC-CSS2/generate.html#markers
www.w3.org/TR/REC-CSS2/tables.html#value-def-table-column
```

Box properties

The Box rules (shown in Figure 1-14) define tags and attributes that control the position of assets in the document. Box rules apply to individual sides of the styled asset when adding margin and padding values.

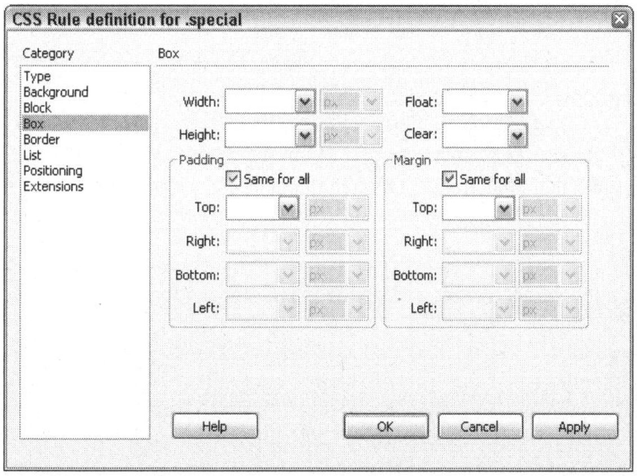

Figure 1-14:
Create
styles to set
the position
of page
content.

Check the Same for All check box to have uniform (four-sided) box settings.

Unless you have other rules for other sides of an asset, when entering individual values to rules with Top, Bottom, Left, and Right fields, enter **0** or **None** for sides that don't contain values.

The following rules are available in the Box category:

✦ **Width/Height:** Select Auto or enter a value in pixels, points, in, cm, mm, picas, ems, exs, or %. Auto adjusts the layer's size to fit the area of the layer's contents, while a fixed value expands the layer to a fixed size. Note that the width refers to the space inside the padding, except in Internet Explorer, which is buggy.

✦ **Float:** When you float an object (like an image, paragraph, div, or list), it is turned into a block-level element that can then be positioned left or right, relative to the current line. Choose Left, Right, or None to control the position of the element that in turn controls the direction in which other objects float or flow around an object.

✦ **Clear:** Choose Left, Right, Both, or None to control the side of an asset that does not allow AP Elements to sit next to them. When an AP Element appears on the side specified with a clear setting, the asset with the clear setting gets bumped to the area below it.

✦ **Padding:** Adds space between the content of an element and its border or inner margin, such as a word inside of a table cell. Enter individual padding values in pixels, points, in, cm, mm, picas, ems, exs, or % to the Top, Right, Bottom, and Left sides of the styled element. Deselect the Same for All box to adjust sides individually.

✦ **Margin:** Adds space between the border of an asset and other nearby assets, as with the area surrounding a sentence or the margin space on the outer edge of the browser window. Add individual margin values in pixels, points, in, cm, mm, picas, ems, exs, or % to the Top, Right, Bottom, and Left sides of the styled asset. Deselect the Same for All box to adjust sides individually.

Border properties

Use the Border rules (shown in Figure 1-15) to define the style, width, and color for border features around styled content.

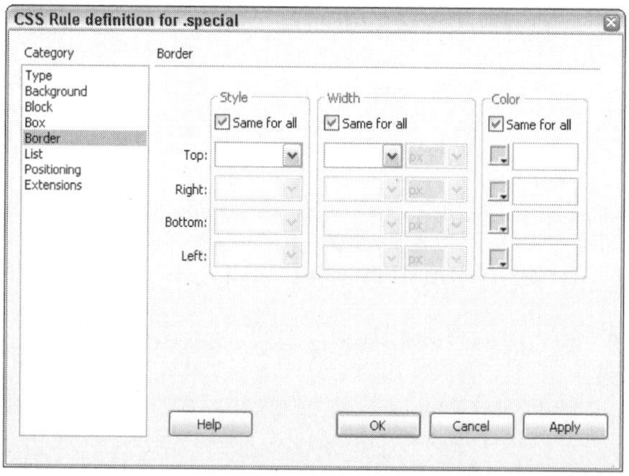

Figure 1-15: Create custom border styles with the Border category.

Check the Same for All check box to create uniform border settings, or uncheck it to adjust the sides individually.

The following rules are available in the Border category:

✦ **Style:** Add border styles to your assets using the following settings: None, Dotted, Dashed, Solid, Double, Groove, Ridge, Inset, or Outset. Preview the styles in Live View, or in a browser window (press F12 or Shift+F12) as Dreamweaver does not display this attribute in the Document window.

✦ **Width:** Enter border thickness as Thin, Medium, or Thick, or enter a value in pixels, points, in, cm, mm, picas, ems, exs, or % to the Top, Right, Bottom, and Left fields.

✦ **Color:** Select a border color from the Web-safe palette or system color picker, or type the hexadecimal code along with the number symbol (#) before the hex number, as in **#990033**, so the color renders properly in the browser.

List properties

Lists in HTML can be numbered or bulleted, and when styling lists with CSS, both list types can have different style options than HTML alone provides for. With CSS, for instance, you can use a custom designed image in place of the default bullet types. Figure 1-16 shows the List category. You can also set the position of the bullet image relative to the list item text.

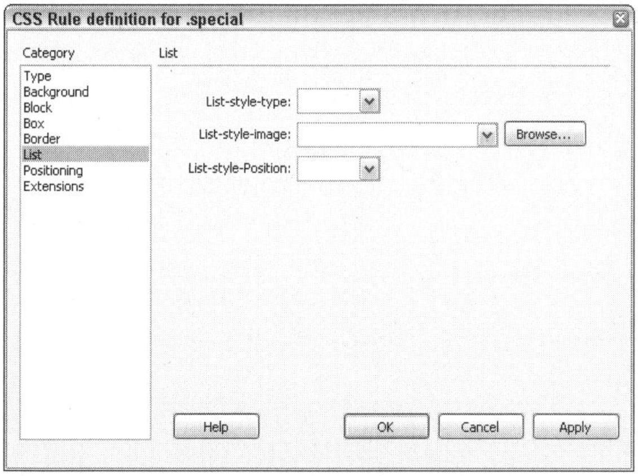

Figure 1-16:
Create custom list styles with the List category.

The following rules are available in the List category:

✦ **List-style-type:** If creating bulleted lists, select from Disc, Circle, or Square as the list type. If creating numbered lists, choose from Decimal, Lower-roman, Upper-roman, Lower-alpha, Upper, Alpha, or None.

✦ **List-style-image:** Type the filename and location of the graphic, or browse to and select the graphic to be used as the bullet image.

✦ **List-style-Position:** Determine how the list item text interacts with the list item's bullet or number.

  • **Outside:** Forces the text to indent and wrap around the bullet/ number.

  • **Inside:** Wraps the text along the left margin.

Positioning properties

Use the Positioning rules (shown in Figure 1-17) to modify the tag or selected text into a layer. For example, you can control an AP Element layer or an image's position within the browser window using positioning rules.

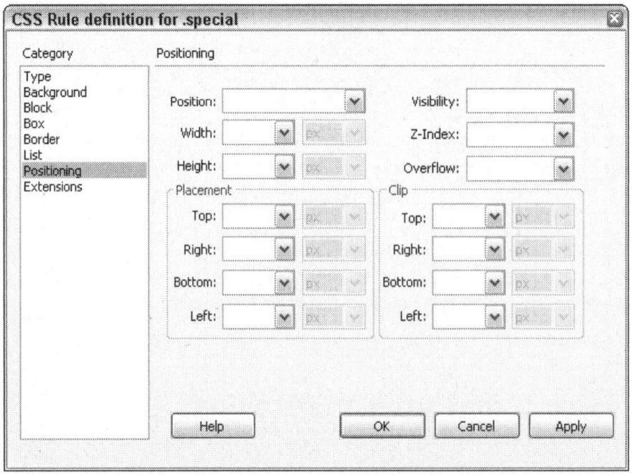

Figure 1-17: Choose options for setting the position of a AP Element or image.

The following rules are available in the Positioning category:

✦ **Position:** Using the coordinates entered in the Placement boxes, determine positioning of the layer or tag relative to the browser window:

  • **Absolute:** Positioning is relative to the top-left corner of the browser.

  • **Fixed:** Positioning is fixed to the top-left corner of the browser.

  • **Relative:** Positioning is relative to the styled object's position in the text flow of the file. You must preview this effect in a browser (press F12 or Shift-F12).

  • **Static:** Similar to Relative, Static positioning puts the styled object at its location in the text flow, causing elements to stack vertically. This option is the default position of elements when no type is selected.

✦ **Width:** Select Auto or enter a width value in pixels, points, in, cm, mm, picas, ems, exs, or %. Auto sets the layer's size to fit the width of the layer's contents, whereas a fixed value holds the width open to a fixed size.

✦ **Height:** Select Auto or enter a height value in pixels, points, in, cm, mm, picas, ems, exs, or %. Auto sets the layer's size to fit the height of the layer's contents, whereas a fixed value holds the height open to a fixed size.

✦ **Visibility:** Choose Inherit, Visible, or Hidden to set the initial display settings of the layer:

• **Inherit:** Forces the layer to inherit the visibility property of the layer's parent. If no parent exists, the layer is visible.

• **Visible:** Displays the layer's contents, regardless of a parent's visibility value.

• **Hidden:** Hides the layer's contents, regardless of a parent's visibility value.

✦ **Z-Index:** Determine the styled layer's stacking order relative to the browser window:

• **Auto:** Gets the next available z-index number

• **Inherit:** Inherits a parent's z-index

You can also manually enter a specific number. The lower the number, the closer to the background; the higher the number, the closer to the viewer. Layers can have both positive and negative values.

You can also change the z-index number of AP Elements quickly through the AP Elements panel.

**Book III
Chapter 1**

✦ **Overflow:** Specify how the browser handles the content in a CSS layer or AP Element that exceed the boundaries of the box the layer sits in:

• **Visible:** Increase the layer's size (usually its height attribute first, then its width) so that all the layer's contents are visible.

• **Hidden:** Maintain the width and height settings of the layer's original size and cuts off, or clips from view, any content that exceeds this size.

• **Scroll:** Add scroll bars to the layer regardless of whether the content fits or exceeds the layer's size. You must preview this option in Live View or in a browser window (press F12 or Shift+F12), as it doesn't display in the Dreamweaver workspace. Furthermore, this feature only works in browsers that support the feature, such as Internet Explorer and Netscape Navigator 6.0 and up.

• **Auto:** Add scroll bars automatically if the contents of the layer exceed the layer's width and height. You must also preview this option in Live View or in a browser window (press F12 or Shift+F12) because it doesn't display in the Dreamweaver workspace.

✦ **Placement:** Set the exact size and position of the block element. Browsers then rely on the Type setting for interpreting the location. Be aware that sizes may be overridden if content exceeds the block element's size. The default units for size and position are pixels, but for CSS layers, you can also use points, in, cm, mm, picas, ems, exs, or % to the Top, Right, Bottom, and Left sides of the layer.

✦ **Clip:** Set the visible area of the layer relative to the layer's top-left edge. Besides clipping content, the clipped area can be accessed with JavaScript to manipulate the values and thereby create special effects like *wipes* that hide or reveal content on absolutely positioned layers. Enter clip region dimensions in pixels, points, in, cm, mm, picas, ems, exs, or % to the Top, Right, Bottom, and Left sides of the layer.

Extensions properties

Extensions apply forced page breaks and unusual visual effects including pointer styles to your documents. Most browsers don't yet support many of these extensions, but support may be forthcoming in the next few years, so be sure to test extensively before publishing them on your site. In fact, there are many more options in this category than display inside the CSS Rule Definition dialog box. To view all of the options in the Extensions category, click the Show Category View button at the bottom of the CSS Styles panel and expand the Extensions category in the Properties pane. Figure 1-18 shows the Extensions category.

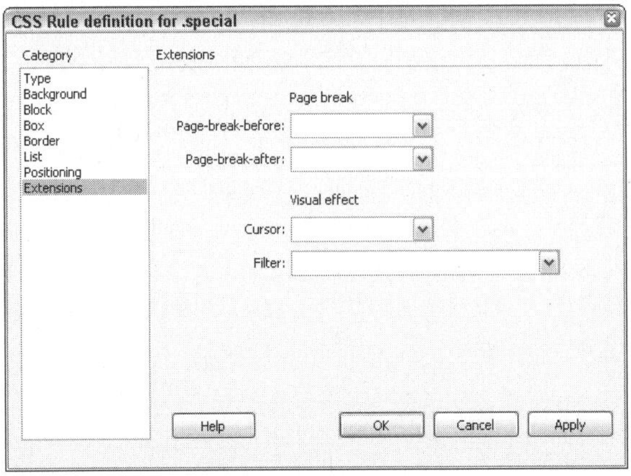

Figure 1-18: Add visual effects and page breaks to your files.

The following style attributes are available in the Extensions category of the CSS Rule Definition dialog box:

✦ **Page-break-before/Page-break-after:** Forces a page break during the printing process before or after an asset styled with this option. For instance, you may want to force a page break after every instance of a particular image on the Web page styled with this feature. Enter **auto**, **always**, **left**, or **right** in the Before and After fields. Though this feature is not supported by any 4.0 browser, most 6.0 and 8.0 browsers do support this feature.

✦ **Cursor:** Select a different cursor that displays when the pointer mouses over an object controlled by the style. Cool effects include crosshair, text, wait, default, help, e-resize, ne-resize, n-resize, nw-resize, w-resize, sw-resize, s-resize, se-resize, and auto. Internet Explorer 4.0 and up and Netscape Navigator 6 and up support these effects.

✦ **Filter:** Apply several special-effect filters, such as drop shadow and glow, to styled asset. Remember to test the setting in multiple browsers before publishing (press F12 or Shift+F12).

Renaming CSS Styles

Dreamweaver CS4 streamlines the process of renaming custom styles. In the past, you'd have to change the name in the style sheet and update all the instances of the style name on all the pages of the site for the name change to be complete. Now, you can edit the name in one location and Dreamweaver handles all the sitewide updates.

To rename a custom (class) CSS style, follow these steps:

1. **From the Properties inspector, choose Rename from the Style drop-down list.**

Or, in the CSS Styles panel, select the style name and choose Rename from the panel Options menu.

The Rename Style dialog box opens, as shown in Figure 1-19.

**Book III
Chapter 1**

Looking Good with
Cascading Style
Sheets (CSS)

Figure 1-19:
Rename
custom
styles.

2. **Select the style you want to rename from the list of available styles in the Rename Style drop-down list and enter the new name in the New Name field.**

Be sure not to use any spaces or special characters in the new filename.

3. **Click OK.**

When the style is on an internal CSS, the change takes place automatically and the Results panel opens showing you all instances of the edited style name. When the style is on an external CSS, however, Dreamweaver alerts you of this and offers to fix the name change in all documents sitewide using the Find & Replace dialog box.

4. **Click the Yes button to change the style name in all documents, the No button to change the name on the style sheet only without updating the site, or the Cancel button to stop the name change process.**

   When you click Yes, the Find and Replace dialog box appears.

5. **If you clicked Yes in Step 4, the Find and Replace dialog box opens, ready to make the global update.**

   Dreamweaver auto-populates the Find and Replace dialog box with the appropriate settings to fix the name change, but you must decide where the updates should occur. Select Current Document, Open Documents, Folder, Selected Files in Site, or Entire Current Local Site.

6. **Click the Replace All button.**

   The Results panel opens to display the results.

Exporting Internal Styles to an External Style Sheet

You can export internal styles to an external style sheet in Dreamweaver in a couple of ways. For example, you may have started a new project using one of the provided Dreamweaver HTML/CSS Layouts, which places CSS styling and positioning rules in the head of the page, and are ready to relocate the CSS to an external file. The first way is to cut the styles from the internal style sheet in Code view, and then paste them into an external style sheet. The second way uses the CSS Styles panel, requires no hand coding, and is as fast as clicking a few buttons!

To export internal styles to an external style sheet, follow these steps:

1. **Click the All button at the top of the CSS Styles panel.**

   A list of all the style rules used on the entire document displays, including internal and external styles.

2. **Below the All button, select all the styles under the <style> tag in the All Rules section.**

   To select them all, click on the top style first, and then Shift+Click on the bottom style. All the contents of the internal style sheet are selected.

3. **Select the option to Move CSS Rules from the CSS Styles panel options menu.**

   The Move To External Style Sheet dialog box appears.

   You can also select the Move CSS Rules option from the CSS Styles panel Context menu by right-clicking or Control-clicking on one of the selected styles.

4. **Move the selected styles to an existing or new style sheet:**

Move to existing: Select an existing CSS file from the drop-down menu or by clicking the Browse button.

Move to new style sheet: Enter a filename for the new, exported CSS file, or select an existing CSS file from the drop-down menu or by clicking the Browser button.

5. **Click OK to save the exported file.**

   Name the file and save it into the existing managed site or navigate to and select another folder to save the new CSS file into.

6. **Remove the internal style tags from the page.**

   With the `<style>` tag still selected in the CSS Styles panel, click the Delete Embedded Style Sheet (trash) button at the bottom of the panel (refer to Figure 1-4).

7. **If you moved the internal styles to a new external style sheet, you need to attach the new CSS to your HTML file. Click the Attach Style Sheet button at the bottom of the panel to add a link to the new external CSS.**

   Enter the File/URL of the new CSS, click the Add as Link or Import radio button, enter a media type, and click OK. Dreamweaver adds the link or @import code to attach the selected CSS to the open document.

The CSS Styles panel now lists the name of the newly linked external CSS. Continue using the new external CSS by adding new styles and editing existing styles as needed.

To move styles from within Code view, select the style(s) you'd like to move to an external CSS file and click the Move or Convert CSS button on the Coding toolbar. This opens the Move to External Style Sheet dialog box as described previously.

**Book III
Chapter 1**

Looking Good with
Cascading Style
Sheets (CSS)

Converting Inline Styles to CSS Rules

From time to time, you may want or need to convert an inline style into a normal CSS rule and place that new rule into an internal or external CSS file. For example, an inline style like this:

```
<p>Life is <span style="font-family: Georgia, 'Times New Roman', Times, serif;
    font-size: 16px; font-weight: bold; color: #F63;">sweet!</span></p>
```

can be converted into a regular CSS rule with the custom class name, .sweet, like this:

```
.sweet {
    font-family: Georgia, 'Times New Roman', Times, serif;
    font-size: 16px;
    font-weight: bold;
    color: #F63;
}
```

The sentence above could then be simply written as

```
<p>Life is <span class="sweet">sweet!</span></p>
```

To convert an inline style to a CSS rule, follow these steps:

1. **Select or place your cursor inside of the code of the object styled with an inline style, and select Format⇨CSS Styles⇨Convert Inline Style to CSS Rule.**

The Convert Inline CSS dialog box appears, as shown in Figure 1-20.

You can also access this dialog box by selecting the same option from the context menu when right-clicking (Windows) or Control-clicking on the object in Design view. In Code view, access the dialog box by clicking the Move or Convert CSS button on the Coding toolbar.

Figure 1-20:
Convert
inline CSS to
CSS Rules.

2. **Select one of the following options from the Convert to drop-down menu:**

- **A new CSS class:** Creates a new custom class style. Be sure to use the syntax `.stylename` with a period before the name of the style.

- **All span tags:** Creates a new style that redefines the `<span>` tag. As this method redefines a tag that has many uses besides selectively applying custom styles and inline styles, this is NOT a recommended option.

- **A new CSS selector:** Creates a style that is automatically applied to any object with a matching ID attribute. Be sure to use the syntax `#stylename` with a number symbol (#) before the name of the style.

3. **Enter a name for your converted CSS style in the field to the right of your Convert to selection.**

4. **In the Create rule in area, select a new location for the converted style:**

Style sheet: Select an existing CSS file from the drop-down menu or by clicking the Browse button.

The head of this document: Select this option to move the converted inline style to the internal style sheet in the head of the document.

5. **Click OK to complete the conversion.**

   The newly converted inline style is now applied to the same selection but as a CSS rule on an internal or external CSS file.

Using Design Time Style Sheets

Design Time Style Sheets allow you to view, edit, and hide multiple style sheets while working on a document in Design view. Though most sites use only one external CSS file, you may need multiple style sheets if you're developing two different versions of the same Web site — one for Windows and one for Macintosh-only site visitors, or you might want to develop two different CSS files, — one for on screen and one for the print.

This multiple style sheet option is only enabled within Dreamweaver's Design view to assist you with editing style sheets. In a browser window, however, only the style sheet that is actually attached inside the document appears to style the page.

Follow these steps to set up Design Time Style Sheets:

1. **Choose Format⇨CSS Styles⇨Design-time from the main menu.**

   The Design Time Style Sheets dialog box appears, as shown in Figure 1-21.

**Book III
Chapter 1**

**Looking Good with
Cascading Style
Sheets (CSS)**

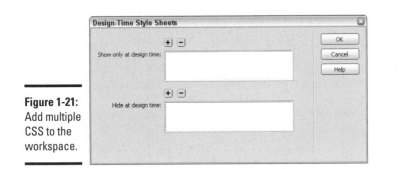

Figure 1-21:
Add multiple
CSS to the
workspace.

2. **In the dialog box, add the settings to hide or show selected style sheets:**

   - **Show a style sheet:** Click the plus (+) button above the Show Only at Design Time field. Browse to and select the style sheet from the Select File dialog box. Repeat to add additional style sheets as needed.

   - **Hide a style sheet:** Click the plus (+) button above the Hide at Design Time field. Browse to and select the style sheet from the Select File dialog box. Repeat to add additional style sheets as you need.

- **Remove a style sheet:** Select the style sheet you want to remove in either category and click the minus (–) button above that category.

3. **Click OK to close the dialog box.**

The CSS Styles panel updates to reflect the new style sheet settings, with hidden or design indicators to show each style sheet's design-time status.

Using the Code Navigator

New in Dreamweaver CS4 is a feature called the Code Navigator which, when put into action, opens a popup window, like the one shown in Figure 1-22, that lets you view and access the CSS code related to a selection or the area surrounding your cursor.

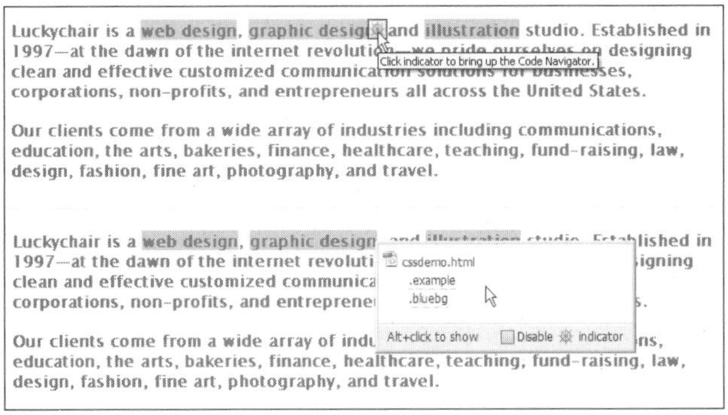

Figure 1-22:
The Code
Navigator
popup
window.

Luckychair is a web design, graphic design, and illustration studio. Established in 1997—at the dawn of the internet revolution—we pride ourselves on designing clean and effective customized communication solutions for businesses, corporations, non-profits, and entrepreneurs all across the United States.

Our clients come from a wide array of industries including communications, education, the arts, bakeries, finance, healthcare, teaching, fund-raising, law, design, fashion, fine art, photography, and travel.

Luckychair is a web design, graphic design, and illustration studio. Established in 1997—at the dawn of the internet revolution—we pride ourselves on designing clean and effective customized communica... corporations, non-profits, and entreprene...

cssdemo.html
.example
.bluebg

Alt+click to show   □ Disable ☼ indicator

Our clients come from a wide array of indu... education, the arts, bakeries, finance, healthcare, teaching, fund-raising, law, design, fashion, fine art, photography, and travel.

You can access the Code Navigator in any of the following ways:

+ **Alt-click (Windows) or Option-click (Mac) on an element:** This method is the default method for opening the Code Navigator popup window.

+ **Click the Code Navigator icon in Design View:** When you select an object, or let your cursor rest for a moment somewhere on the page, the Code Navigator icon appears. Click the icon to open the popup window.

+ **Click the Code Navigator button in Code View:** To access the Code Navigator icon in Code view, click the Show Code Navigator button on the Coding toolbar.

+ **Select View⇨Code Navigator:** This option (near the bottom of the View menu) opens the Code Navigator popup window.

The Navigator icon can be turned on and off by clicking the Disable button inside the popup window.

After the popup window appears, you can hover your mouse over any of the CSS styles listed to view the complete style, with all its selectors and declarations. This can be helpful if you're trying to find the hex value of a color or a font used on a particular word or sentence.

To edit a style listed in the popup window, click it and the corresponding CSS code appears both in code view and inside the CSS Styles panel, so you can quickly view and edit it if desired. All changes to the CSS are live, so adjusting the style in code view is the same as adjusting the style in the CSS Styles panel and (nearly) all changes appear immediately on your page in Design view.

To test any changes you make to the CSS, click the Live View button or launch a browser window by clicking the Preview/Debug in Browser button on the Document toolbar.

Use the Code Navigator in conjunction with Live View or Live Code view to quickly view and edit related relevant code and files.

In addition to displaying CSS code, the Code Navigator also displays related documents when launching the Code Navigator on objects using JavaScript and Server-Side Includes. Related files might include a Dreamweaver template (DWT files), a library file (LBI files), a CSS file, an external JavaScript file, an iframe source file, or an external SSI (SHTML, CFML, PHP, ASP, ASPX, and so on).

**Book III
Chapter 1**

**Looking Good with
Cascading Style
Sheets (CSS)**

Chapter 2: Building Sites with Templates

In This Chapter

✔ Creating a template

✔ Creating editable template regions

✔ Nesting templates

✔ Creating a template-based document

✔ Editing templates and the pages that use them

*D*reamweaver has created a quick and easy way to manage the look of your Web site with a master file process called Templates. You can unify the overall design of your Web site into one file, called a *template,* and then use that file as the basis for creating all the other pages on your site.

Templates enable you to control which parts of the template-based pages on your site can be edited and which parts remain fixed across all the pages on a site:

✦ The *editable regions* on a template are defined areas for specific parts of a Web document that have different content on each page of the site, such as the page header, the body of the page, or a subnavigation element. You need to define and name each editable region in the template. This helps you keep track of the content that should be placed inside it when you create template-based documents.

For example, the body editable region on the template-based Contact page would display detailed contact information and the body editable region on the template-based About page would display detailed information about the company.

✦ The *uneditable areas* of a template, by contrast, are the parts of the layout and design that are constant throughout the Web site. You don't need to define uneditable areas in the template as you do with editable regions; only editable regions in template-based pages are editable.

For example, your navigation and company logo placement should be in the same location from page to page throughout the site; these areas would be uneditable on any template-based pages. Uneditable areas are a particularly useful tool when you work in a team with other designers, writers, and Web developers.

You discover the true beauty and power of Dreamweaver templates when you need to update part of your master layout or design (that means changing any of the uneditable areas of the template). Instead of having to individually modify those elements on each of the pages on your managed site, you need to update only the template, and Dreamweaver automatically updates those elements on all the pages that utilize that template!

You can apply templates to blank or existing documents, and if you change your mind after applying a template to a page, you can simply detach it.

You can also remove template markup or export a page without template markup. After editing a template, Dreamweaver can selectively update pages that use the template or update code inside the entire managed site. Furthermore, from within a page created from a template, you can modify editable tag attributes such as image source or width. One of the most amazing functions of templates, however, is that you can completely modify the entire look of a Web site without having to redo the content, just by attaching a different template to the page!

When you publish your site, you don't need to upload templates to the remote server because they do not affect site functionality. Rather, Dreamweaver uses them as a local tool to help you control the code for common areas on all the pages that use the template file. What you do need to upload to the remote server are all the pages created from the template.

This chapter gives you the lowdown on templates and why they're such a powerful tool, especially for small-to-medium–sized Web sites. You also find detailed instructions for creating, using, editing, and deleting templates.

If you are building a larger site or a site that uses dynamic functionality, other solutions may work better, such as server-side includes (see Book III, Chapter 3) or building a dynamic site using a database and a programming language such as ASP, JSP, PHP, or ColdFusion.

Creating a Template

You can create a template from an existing HTML, Adobe ColdFusion, or Microsoft ASP document, or you can build a template from scratch with a new, untitled, blank template file. After creating the file, you can add editable regions to the template, as described in the later section "Working with Editable Regions." You can also add Design Notes to the file (see Book VI, Chapter 1 for details), as well as modify the default highlighting and code colors in the Preferences dialog box (skip ahead to the "Creating editable regions" section).

In the process of creating a template, Dreamweaver marks up the document code with special Dreamweaver template comment tags that identify the document as a template and define the various areas of the template. The first template comment tag is inserted right after the opening HTML tag, as in the following example:

```
<!-- InstanceBegin template=î/Templates/mytemplate.dwtî -->
```

Additional template comment tags, such as the ones that mark the beginning and ending of editable regions, are inserted throughout the file to assist Dreamweaver with sitewide editing.

Dreamweaver templates use a series of comment tag markup code to define areas of the template as editable or uneditable. Although it's not necessary that you know what these tags mean or even how they work to use templates, you can learn more about these on Adobe's Web site at `help.adobe.com/en_US/Dreamweaver/10.0_Using/WScbb6b82af5544594822510a94ae8d65-7a79a.html`.

Converting an HTML page into a template

You can convert any existing HTML page into a template. However, we suggest taking the time to create a page with the design layout you want to use for the entire Web site. Design a master HTML page: Add the text and graphics, enter alternate text tags to images, create hyperlinks where needed, assign JavaScript rollover button behaviors, add text formatting with Cascading Style Sheets, check for spelling mistakes, and include any other media and dynamic settings necessary on the page.

Test this master HTML page in multiple browsers for link accuracy, layout consistency, and dynamic functionality to ensure the new template you create from this master page doesn't contain any errors.

After you're sure the master HTML page is fully functional, open the page in the Dreamweaver workspace window and follow these steps to convert the file into a Dreamweaver template:

1. **Choose File⇨Save as Template.**

Be sure to choose *Save as Template* rather than *Save* from the File menu.

You can also click the Templates button on the Common category of the Insert panel and select Make Template from the Templates drop-down list to begin the conversion process.

The Save as Template dialog box appears (see Figure 2-1).

Book III
Chapter 2

Building Sites with Templates

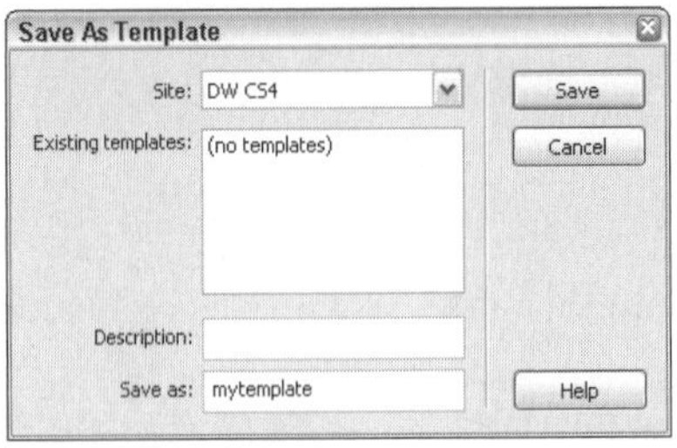

Figure 2-1:
Save your
template
file with
a unique
name.

(Save As Template dialog box)

Save As Template

Site: DW CS4

Existing templates: (no templates)

Description:

Save as: mytemplate

Save
Cancel
Help

2. **From the Site drop-down menu, select a site from the list of all your managed sites into which the new template will be saved.**

   When creating a template in a managed site, that site's name should automatically be selected.

3. **In the Description field, enter a short description.**

   The description displays in the Description field of the New from Template dialog box when creating a new template-based page.

4. **In the Save As field, enter a name for the template.**

   For simplicity, name the template after the project or client and use all lowercase letters with no spaces or special characters, as in xyzcompany.

5. **Click the Save button. When prompted to update links, click the Yes button.**

   If you click the No button, the links and paths no longer function properly.

   Dreamweaver creates a Templates folder in the Files panel and places the newly created template file inside that folder, which means the template's location relative to the other files on the site has changed; it's now inside a folder at the root level.

   Leave the template files inside the Templates folder and do not store any non-template files there. This helps you avoid causing errors to template paths.

6. **To create an editable region, select the content on the template and choose Insert⇨Template Objects⇨Editable Region. Enter a name for the editable region and click OK.**

   Each editable region can contain any asset or combination of items such as a word or block of text, a graphic, a table cell, or even an entire table. Dreamweaver prompts you to name each editable area. Name them using a descriptive term to define their purpose, such as *header*, *bodytext*, or *storephoto*. When naming editable regions, use single or conjoined words written in all lowercase letters without spaces or any special characters.

   For a more in-depth discussion of editable regions, see "Working with Editable Regions," later in this chapter.

TECHNICAL STUFF

Using server scripts in templates

Of necessity, some server scripts must be added to the document code above and below the opening and closing `<html>` tags. When server scripts are placed inside templates, however, Dreamweaver may not always copy the script code — or subsequent changes made to it — to pages generated using a particular template, and that could cause significant server errors when scripts in the body of a template-based document depend on these "outside HTML" scripts.

Though Dreamweaver warns you about changing outside HTML scripts, you can avoid the problem altogether by adding the following code to the `<head>` area of the template:

```
<!-- TemplateInfo
        codeOutsideHTMLIsLocked="true"
    -->
```

The addition of this line of code to the head of the template forces Dreamweaver to copy any changes to scripts outside the `<html>` tags to documents based on that template.

Keep in mind that adding this code removes the ability to edit these scripts in the template-based documents. Therefore, you can either edit the scripts in the template or edit them individually in the template-based documents, but not both.

7. **Save and close the template.**

   Template files automatically are saved in the Templates folder with the .dwt file extension; when opened in the Dreamweaver workspace, they display the word `<<Template>>` in the title bar.

Creating a new template from scratch

To create a new, blank template into which you add all the necessary content, follow these steps:

1. **Choose File⇨New to open the New Document window, which is shown in Figure 2-2.**

2. **To create a new, untitled template page, select Blank Template from the Category list and a template type, such as HTML Template, from the Template Type list.**

3. **Click the Create button.**

   The new template page opens as an untitled, unsaved template file inside the Dreamweaver workspace.

4. **Add content to the new template.**

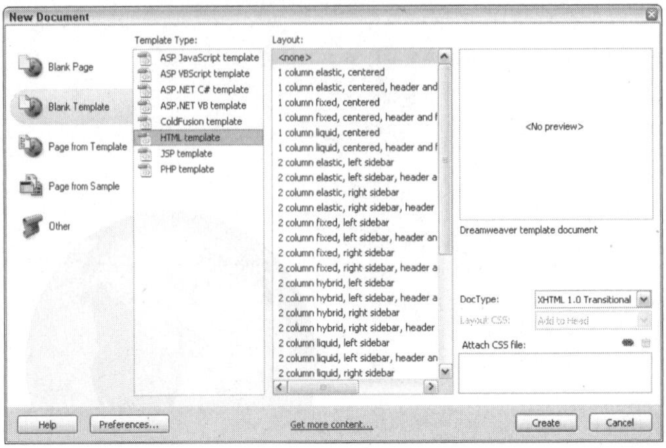

Figure 2-2:
Create
a new
template
using the
Blank
Template
category.

When adding content to the template, pay attention to the document-relative links and paths in the Properties inspector (see Book I, Chapter 3 for details). A correct path includes code that points from the Templates folder to the linked document and appends the link with the appropriate document-relative code, such as `../contact.html` instead of `contact.html`. For best results, use the Point to File or Folder buttons in the Properties inspector to ensure the links are correct.

5. **To create an editable region, select the content in the template and then choose Insert⇨Template Objects⇨Editable Region. Enter a name for the editable region and click OK.**

   Read the upcoming section "Working with Editable Regions" for instructions on all the editable template region types.

6. **Choose File⇨Save As Template.**

   The Save As Template dialog box opens (see Figure 2-3).

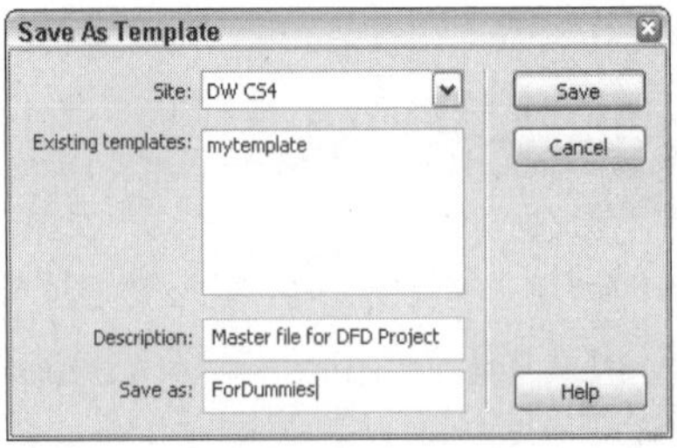

Figure 2-3:
Enter
template
details in
this dialog
box.

7. **From the Site drop-down list, select a managed site to save the new file into.**

8. **(Optional) Add a description for the template.**

   The description displays in the Preview area of the New Document window.

9. **In the Save As field, provide the template with an appropriate file-name. Then click Save.**

   Use all lowercase letters with no spaces or special characters for the template name, as in abcwidgets.

   Template files automatically are saved in the Templates folder with the .dwt file extension; when opened in the Dreamweaver workspace window, they display the word <<Template>> in the title bar.

Working with Editable Regions

The editable regions are the parts of a template that are unlocked, or edit-able, in a template-based page. These editable regions are perfect for areas that are specific to the page's purpose. For instance, each page may have its own header graphic, text, and subnavigation areas.

Each editable region can contain any element or combination of elements such as a block of text, a graphic, and a table. Although you may create as many editable regions as you want, each template should have at least one editable region.

Editable regions are the most basic form of editable areas on a template. In addition to these, you can also create optional editable regions, repeating regions and repeating tables, and editable tag attributes, as described later in this chapter.

Creating editable regions

To create an editable region on a template, follow these steps:

1. **Select the contents in the template file that you want to set as an edit-able region.**

   For example, select a header graphic that displays the name of the page in a special font (as shown in Figure 2-4). Or, rather than selecting con-tent, place the insertion point at the point on the page where you want to insert an editable area.

Turn this header graphic into an editable region.

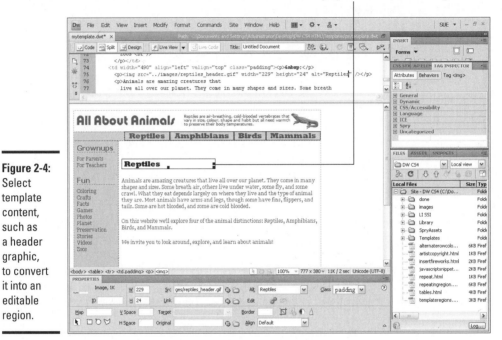

Figure 2-4:
Select
template
content,
such as
a header
graphic,
to convert
it into an
editable
region.

When creating editable regions that include tables and layers (AP Elements), pay attention to the source code of your selection. For example, when you select the `<td>` tag and convert it into an editable region, that editable region includes both the table cell and its contents. By contrast, when you make only the contents of a cell into an editable region, only the contents of the cell become editable and any formatting associated with the table cell itself remains uneditable. Likewise, when creating editable areas with layers, when you select a `<div>` tag along with the layer's contents, the layer's positioning and contents are editable. But if you select and convert only the contents of a layer into an editable region, only the contents are editable and the layer's position remains fixed.

2. **Choose Insert⊷Template Objects⊷Editable Region.**

   You can also click the Templates button on the Common category of the Insert panel and choose Editable Region from the drop-down list.

   The New Editable Region dialog box opens, as shown in Figure 2-5.

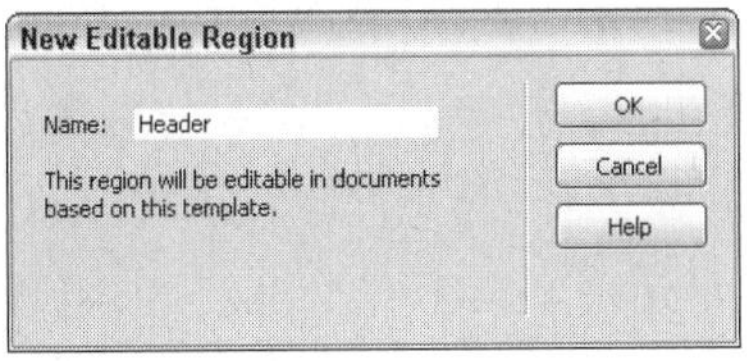

Figure 2-5:
Name
editable
template
regions.

New Editable Region

Name: Header

This region will be editable in documents
based on this template.

OK

Cancel

Help

3. **Enter a name for the new editable region.**

Name editable areas using a descriptive term such as header, phone, or
headshot, using single or conjoined words written in all lowercase letters without any spaces or other special characters.

4. **Click OK.**

Dreamweaver converts your selection into an editable region by adding template markup comment tags in Code view. These editable content regions
begin and end with the following code:

```
<!-- TemplateBeginEditable> ... <!-- TemplateEndEditable -->
```

The space between the template markup indicates areas that remain editable in template-based documents. Take care, however, not to modify the
template markup when working in Code view, as Dreamweaver uses this
markup to manage template updates.

In Design view, editable regions on a template are defined by a blue rectangular outline, topped by a tab labeled with the name you just provided,
surrounding the selection for the new editable region (see Figure 2-6). The
blue color is Dreamweaver's preset editable region color, which you can
change in the Highlighting category of the Preferences dialog box. Choose
Edit➪Preferences (Windows) or Dreamweaver➪Preferences (Mac).

Editable regions in pages created from templates are shown with the same
blue label and outline, clearly marking where content can be edited.

Removing editable regions

From time to time, you may need to remove an editable region from your
template. For example, because nested editable regions are not allowed in
Dreamweaver, you may decide to enlarge or reduce the size of an existing
editable region to better define the editable areas on the template, which
requires you to delete an existing region before defining a new area.

**Book III
Chapter 2**

**Building Sites with
Templates**

Editable region

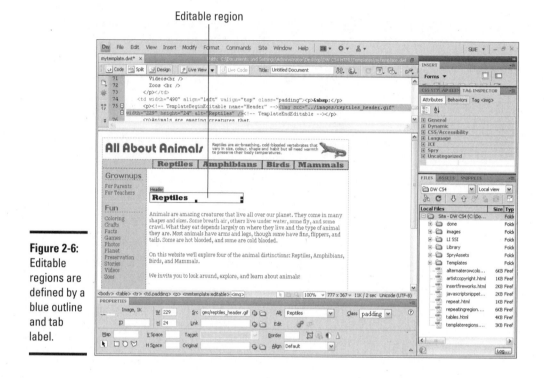

Figure 2-6:
Editable
regions are
defined by a
blue outline
and tab
label.

To remove an editable region from a template, follow these steps:

1. **Open the template in the Dreamweaver workspace window.**

2. **Select the region by clicking the blue tab in the upper-left corner of the editable region.**

   Or place your cursor inside the editable region you want to delete so that Dreamweaver knows which code you want to remove.

3. **Choose Modify⇨Templates⇨Remove Template Markup.**

   Dreamweaver instantly removes the template markup for that editable region, including the code in Code view and the blue outlines in Design view. The content in that region isn't deleted on the template. However, for template-based files, you need to resolve the issue of where to place any content that used to be in the removed region, which we talk about in the next section.

Renaming editable regions

If you accidentally misspell an editable region label, you can remove and then reapply the editable region with the correct spelling. But for simple name changes to an editable region, Dreamweaver has an even better solution:

1. **Open the template in the Dreamweaver workspace window.**

2. **Select the region you want to rename by clicking the blue tab in the upper-left corner of the editable region.**

For example, suppose you have an editable region called *email* that you want to rename as *address*.

3. **Choose Modify➪Quick Tag Editor.**

The Quick Tag Editor opens, shown in Figure 2-7, where you adjust the code.

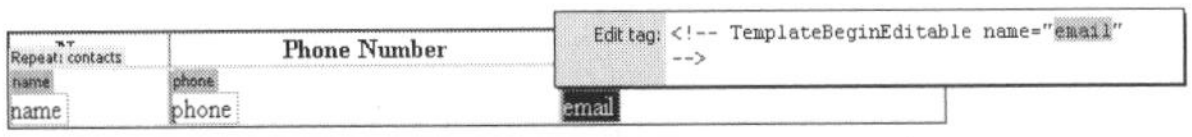

Figure 2-7:
Use the
Quick Tag
Editor to edit
code.

If you prefer, you can also modify the code directly in Code view.

The code in the Quick Tag Editor looks something like this:

```
<!-- TemplateBeginEditable name="email" -->
```

4. **Type the new editable region name in the area in quotes.**

Using the same example, change email to address:

```
<!-- TemplateBeginEditable name="address" -->
```

An even quicker method for renaming the editable template region on a template is to select the editable region by clicking the editable region's blue tab and changing the name in the Properties inspector.

5. **Choose File➪Save to save the template.**

Dreamweaver opens the Update Template Files dialog box.

6. **Click the Update button to update all the template-based files in the managed site.**

We don't recommend clicking the Don't Update button as it updates only the template file, but not any of the template-based files.

Dreamweaver launches the Inconsistent Region Names dialog box, shown in Figure 2-8, to map any new region names to any old region locations. If you fail to map the regions, content in the old region name area may be discarded on pages using the template.

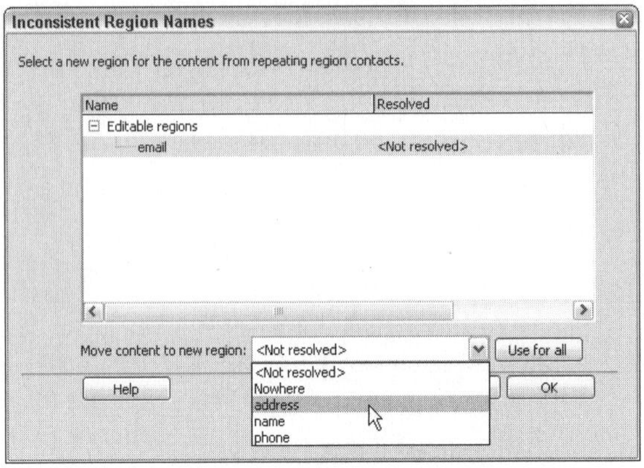

Figure 2-8:
Use the
Inconsistent
Regions
Names
dialog box
to map old
editable
region
names
to new
editable
regions.

7. **In the Name column under Editable Regions, select the old editable region name. Then choose the new region name from the Move Content to New Region drop-down list.**

   After selecting the new region name, you see the new region name listed under the Resolved column of the dialog box.

8. **Continue mapping remaining regions, if you need.**

9. **Click OK.**

   Dreamweaver automatically closes the Inconsistent Region Names dialog box and finishes the region renaming process by updating all the pages on the site that use the template you just modified.

10. **Click the Close button on the Update Pages dialog box.**

    The process of changing the region name is complete. If you have any files open that use the template you just modified, save the files before closing them to accept the most recent changes.

Exporting a site without any template markup

In addition to removing or renaming editable regions, Dreamweaver can export an entire Web site full of template-based files to another folder without any template markup. The exported file can even be in XML format if you like. One benefit of removing the markup is that the file sizes may be slightly smaller. Furthermore, when you export an XML version, the XML file is transportable as well as easily importable back into Dreamweaver and other applications.

To export a site without any template code, follow these steps:

1. **Choose Modify➪Templates➪Export without Markup.**

   The Export Site without Template Markup dialog box opens, as shown in Figure 2-9.

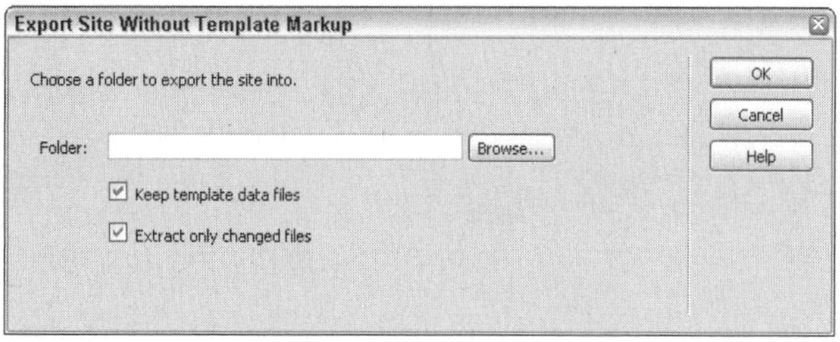

**Book III
Chapter 2**

Building Sites with Templates

Figure 2-9:
Export template-based Web files without template markup.

2. **In the Folder field, choose a destination folder outside of the current managed site.**

3. **To save an XML version of exported template-based documents, check the Keep Template Data Files check box. To update changes to files that have already been exported, check the Extract Only Changed Files check box.**

   XML (eXtensible Markup Language) is a simple text format that is used to describe data for electronic publishing and exchanging data on the Web. Visit the W3.org (`www.w3.org/XML`) and W3Schools (`www.w3schools.com/xml/xml_whatis.asp`) Web sites to discover more about XML.

4. **Click OK.**

Creating Optional and Optional Editable Regions

Use optional regions on a template for content such as graphics or text that may or may not be needed on every template-based page. For example, you can create an optional region for a Back to Top link that can be either visible or hidden, depending on the length of the text placed on the page above it. By using optional regions, you let the users of template-based files decide whether they want to include the optional region in the pages they're adding content to.

Within optional regions, you can also set values for template parameters (such as true/false operations) and make conditional statements (such as if . . . else statements) that can later be edited in the template-based file. Dreamweaver adds template comment tags to the page code for the new optional region in two locations. In the head, you see something like this:

```
<!-- TemplateParam name="saleImage" type="boolean" value="true" -->
```

Then in the code, where the optional region appears, you see additional comment tags like this:

```
<!-- TemplateBeginIf cond="saleImage" -->
<p><img src="/images/onsale.gif" width="100" height="23"> </p>
<!-- TemplateEndIf -->
```

Similar to regular optional regions, *optional editable regions* are also controlled by the template user from within the template-based page, but have the added feature of allowing the template user to edit the optional region's contents.

Creating optional regions

To create an optional region, follow these steps:

1. **Open the template in the Dreamweaver workspace window.**

2. **Select the content that you want to set as the optional region.**

3. **Choose Insert⇨Template Objects⇨Optional Region.**

   You can also click the Templates button on the Common category of the Insert panel and choose Optional Region from the drop-down list.

   The New Optional Region dialog box opens, as shown in Figure 2-10.

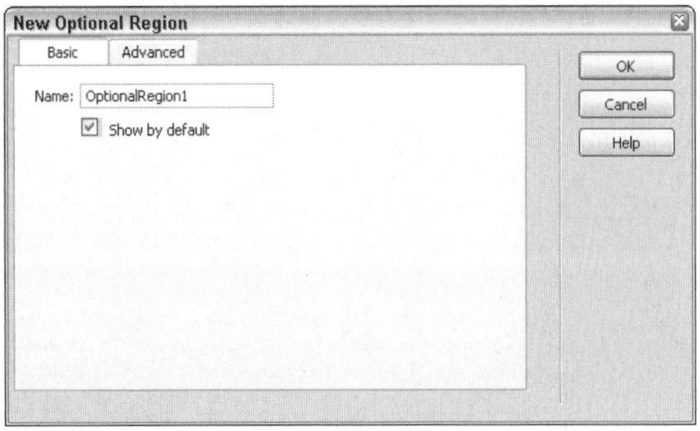

Figure 2-10: Use this dialog box to specify optional regions within a template.

4. **On the Basic tab, enter a name for the new optional region and enable or disable the Show by Default option.**

   When Show by Default is enabled, the new optional region appears on the template-based page; when disabled, the optional region is hidden on the template-based page.

5. **(Optional) On the Advanced tab, enter additional parameters or expressions for the region:**

   • **Use Parameter:** Select this option to choose an existing parameter from the drop-down list that the selected content should be linked to.

   • **Enter Expression:** Choose this option to write your own template expressions for controlling whether the region is visible or hidden by default, such as the expression COUNTRY=='United States'.

   Use parameters to control the display of the optional region or expressions to define conditional statements, such as if . . . else statements or true/false operations. Regions can have a default setting of either show or hide.

6. **Click OK.**

The new optional region is inserted onto the template.

Creating optional editable regions

To create an optional editable region, follow these steps:

1. **Open the template in the Dreamweaver workspace window.**

2. **Click your cursor inside the template file where you want to insert the optional editable region.**

Insert the optional editable region before inserting the content into the region: You can't wrap an editable region around a selection.

3. **Choose Insert⇨Template Objects⇨Editable Optional Region.**

You can also click the Templates button on the Common category of the Insert panel and choose Editable Optional Region from the drop-down list.

The New Optional Editable Region dialog box opens.

4. **On the Basic tab, enter a name for the new optional editable region.**

5. **(Optional) Click the Advanced tab (shown in Figure 2-11) to add other options such as parameters for conditional statements or expressions.**

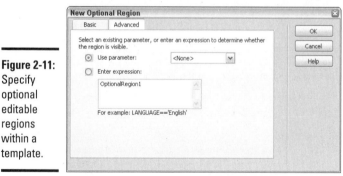

Figure 2-11: Specify optional editable regions within a template.

**Book III
Chapter 2**

Building Sites with Templates

See Step 5 in the preceding section for details on setting parameters and entering expressions.

6. **Click OK.**

Modifying optional regions

After you add an optional editable region to a template, you can modify its settings, including whether the region is hidden or showing.

To modify an optional region, follow these steps:

1. **Open a template-based document in the workspace window.**

2. **Inside the Document window, do one of the following to open the Optional Region dialog box:**

   • **Design view:** Click the template tab of the optional region you want to edit.

   • **Code view:** Click the comment tag of the optional region you want to edit.

3. **Click the Edit button in the Properties inspector.**

   The New Optional Region dialog box opens (refer to Figure 2-10).

4. **Make any desired changes to the optional region.**

5. **Click OK when you finish making changes.**

Creating Repeating Regions

Repeating regions in a template are wonderful to use when you have consistent content areas that repeat, such as rows in a table, but are unsure as to how many sections any particular page may need. With a repeating region, the number of sections can be controlled from within the template-based page, whereas the overall layout and design is still controlled by the template.

For example, Figure 2-12 shows a repeating table that lists all of ABC Company's store locations by name, phone number, and address. From inside the template-based page, the template user can add, delete, and reorder table rows by clicking the repeating region buttons.

Add new row   Move row down

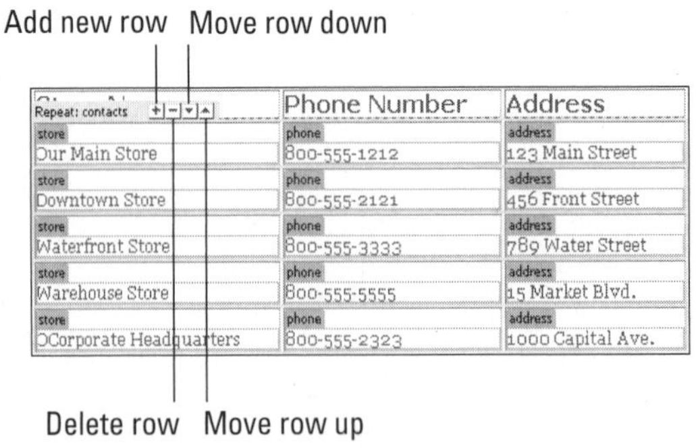

Figure 2-12:
Click these
buttons to
manage
the content
inside the
repeating
region.

	Phone Number	Address
Repeat: contacts		
store	phone	address
Our Main Store	800-555-1212	123 Main Street
store	phone	address
Downtown Store	800-555-2121	456 Front Street
store	phone	address
Waterfront Store	800-555-3333	789 Water Street
store	phone	address
Warehouse Store	800-555-5555	15 Market Blvd.
store	phone	address
Corporate Headquarters	800-555-2323	1000 Capital Ave.

Delete row   Move row up

Adjust table rows with the repeating region buttons:

✦ **Add a new row:** Click the plus (+) button.

✦ **Delete a row:** Place your cursor inside an editable area in the row you want to remove and click the minus (–) button at the top of the table.

✦ **Move an entry up or down:** Place your cursor inside an editable area on the row you want to adjust and click the Up or Down arrow buttons at the top of the table.

You can also choose Modify➪Templates and choose a repeating entry or move position option from the submenu.

You can add two kinds of repeating regions to a template file: *repeating regions* and *repeating tables*. Although repeating regions are mostly used for tables, you can use them for other things as well, such as a product detail layout including text and graphics. If you need a region's contents to be editable, create a regular editable region from that content: The repeating regions themselves are not editable.

Creating repeating regions

To create a repeating region, follow these steps:

1. **Open the template in the Dreamweaver workspace window.**

2. **Place the cursor where you want to insert the new repeating region.**

3. **To add the repeating region, choose Insert➪Template Objects➪ Repeating Region.**

You can also click the Templates button on the Common category of the Insert panel and choose Repeating Region from the drop-down list.

The New Repeating Region dialog box opens.

4. **Enter a name for the new repeating template region.**

When naming repeating template regions, use single or conjoined words written in all lowercase letters without spaces or any special characters.

5. **Click OK.**

Dreamweaver inserts the new repeating region into the template.

Creating repeating tables

Use a repeating table for making editable areas with repeating rows. You can also set table attributes and pick which consecutive rows within the table repeat.

Follow these steps to create a repeating table:

1. **Open the template in the Dreamweaver workspace window.**

2. **Place your cursor inside the file where you want to insert the table.**

3. **Choose Insert➪Template Objects➪Repeating Table.**

   You can also click the Templates button on the Common category of the Insert panel and choose Repeating Table from the drop-down list to open the dialog box.

   The Insert Repeating Table dialog box opens, shown in Figure 2-13.

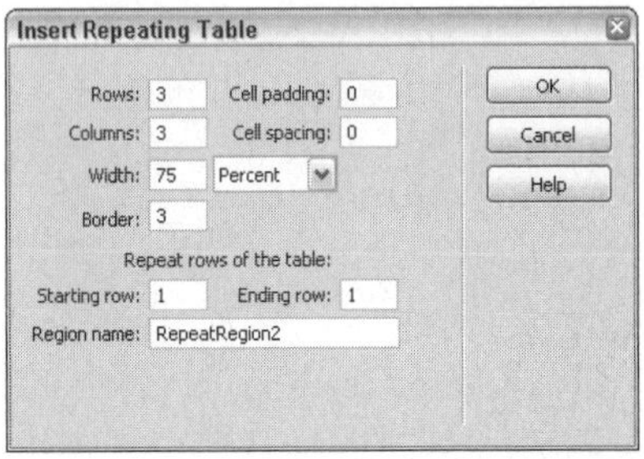

Figure 2-13:
Add a
repeating
table to your
template.

4. **Specify the following attributes for the new repeating table:**

   • **Rows** and **Columns:** Enter the number of rows and columns for the repeating table.

   • **Cell Padding:** Enter a number in pixels to increase the space between the cell's walls and its contents. If left blank, the cell padding displays as if it were set to 1 pixel. To remove cell padding completely, set the size to 0.

   • **Cell Spacing:** Enter a number in pixels to increase the walls of the repeating table between the cells. If left blank, the cell spacing displays as if it were set to 2 pixels. To remove cell spacing completely, set the size to 0.

   • **Width:** Enter a number to set the fixed width of the repeating table in pixels or enter a percentage width between 1 and 100 percent.

   • **Border:** Enter the number in pixels for the table border. If left blank, the border displays as if it were set to 1 pixel. To remove a border completely, set the border size to 0.

   • **Starting Row:** Enter the row number that begins the repeating region within the repeating table.

   • **Ending Row:** Enter the row number that marks the end of the repeating region within the repeating table.

   • **Region Name:** Specify a name for the repeating region within the repeating table.

5. **Click OK.**

   The repeating table is inserted into your template.

Add alternating row background colors

After (and only after) you insert a repeating table in your template, you can add some template markup to create alternate table row background colors in your template-based pages. The markup is added to the first repeating region `<tr>` tag in the template, inside Code view:

```
<tr bgcolor="@@(_index & 1 ? '#FFFFFF' :
        '#FFFFCC')@@">
```

You can change the #FFFFFF (white) and #FFFFCC (pale yellow) hexadecimal values of the alternating rows in the sample code to any other colors to match your particular Web design color scheme. The main thing is that the syntax is correct and the code is placed in the right part of your template.

The following example shows the template's repeating table code with repeating regions and alternating background row colors (see the figure):

```
<table width="600" border="1"
        cellpadding="3" cellspacing="0"
        bordercolor="#666666">
```

```
<tr><th>First Name</th><th>Last Name</
        th><th>Telephone</th></tr>
<!-- TemplateBeginRepeat name="contacts"
        -->
<tr bgcolor="@@(_index & 1 ? '#FFFFFF' :
        '#FFFFCC')@@">
<td> <!-- TemplateBeginEditable
        name="firstname" --> firstname
        <!-- TemplateEndEditable -->
</td>
<td> <!-- TemplateBeginEditable
        name="lastname" --> lastname
        <!-- TemplateEndEditable -->
</td>
<td> <!-- TemplateBeginEditable
        name="telephone" --> telephone
        <!-- TemplateEndEditable -->
</td>
</tr>
  <!-- TemplateEndRepeat -->
</table>
```

After you add this line of code to the repeating table on your template, any new rows added to the repeating region on the table in the template-based page use the alternating row colors you specified in the code.

**Book III
Chapter 2**

Building Sites with Templates

Creating Editable Tag Attributes

Editable tag attributes let you create unlocked tag attributes in a template, which can be modified from within the template-based page. For instance, a table may be locked into the page design, but with editable tag attributes, its width or border thickness may be set by the template user. Set as many editable tag attributes in the template as you want. Attributes can include text, Boolean (true/false), URL, and color data types.

To create an editable tag attribute, follow these steps:

1. **Open the template in the Dreamweaver workspace window.**

2. **Select the tag of the object you want to add an editable tag attribute to.**

3. **Choose Modify⇨Templates⇨Make Attribute Editable.**

   The Editable Tag Attributes dialog box opens, as shown in Figure 2-14.

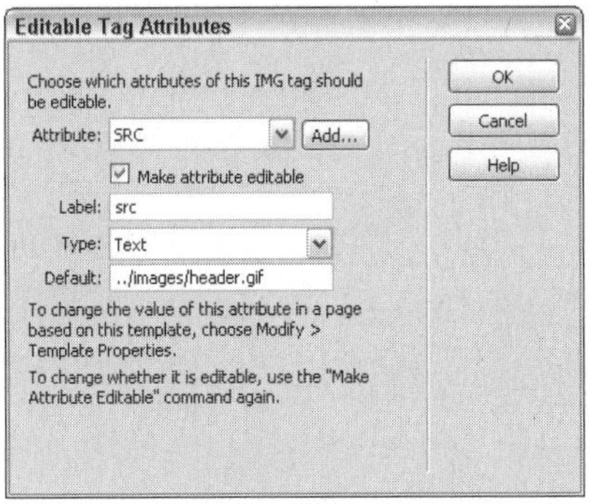

Figure 2-14: Specify editable tag attributes in your templates.

4. **Enter details for the attribute you want to make editable:**

   • **Attribute:** If the attribute you want to make editable is listed in the drop-down list, select it. If the attribute is not listed, click the Add button to enter the name of the new attribute.

   • **Make Attribute Editable:** Enable this feature to make the attribute editable. After you enable this field, the remaining fields in the dialog box become active.

   • **Label:** Type a unique name for the attribute to help identify its purpose, such as **tableBorder** or **buttonSrc.**

   • **Type:** Choose a value from the drop-down list that helps set the attribute's editability. Your options include the following:

   • **Text:** Text values allow you to type a text value to edit the tag attribute. For example, you can use text to define the value (*left*, *right*, or *center*) of the align attribute.

   • **URL:** Select this option to add a link to an object, such as the path to the source file of a graphic.

   • **Color:** Choose this option to select a color from the color palette.

   • **True/False:** Select this option to change the value of an attribute from true to false, or vice versa.

- **Number:** Select this option if you want to type a number for the value of an attribute, such as when you want to change the border attribute of an image.

- **Default:** This field shows the value of the selected object's current attribute. Type a new initial value for the parameter in the template-based file.

5. **If creating multiple editable tag attributes for the selected tag, repeat Steps 2 through 4 until you've set all the editable tag attributes.**

6. **Click OK to accept the settings.**

   Each editable tag attribute adds template parameters to the code whereby the initial value of the attribute is set in the template and the parameter can be changed from within the template-based document.

Changing editable tag attributes in template-based files

To modify an editable tag attribute from within a template-based document, open the file in the Dreamweaver workspace window and do the following:

1. **Choose Modify⇨Template Properties.**

   The Template Properties dialog box opens, as shown in Figure 2-15.

Book III
Chapter 2

Building Sites with Templates

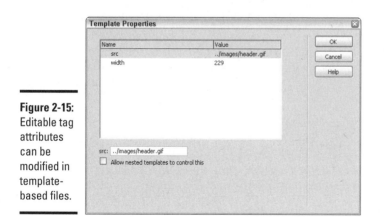

Figure 2-15: Editable tag attributes can be modified in template-based files.

2. **Select the editable tag attribute to modify from the Name column.**

   The bottom half of the dialog box updates to display the corresponding attribute editing options.

3. **Modify the selected editable tag attribute.**

For instance, if one of the attributes allowed the value of the background color of the page to be modified, the bottom of the dialog box displays a Background Color Picker field for selecting a new background color.

4. **If modifying multiple editable tag attributes at once, repeat Steps 2 and 3.**

5. **Click OK.**

Resetting an editable tag attribute to uneditable

To change an editable tag attribute to an uneditable one, open the template and follow these steps:

1. **Select the editable tag in Code view.**

   Selecting the tag makes the editable attribute for this tag automatically display in the Attribute field of the Editable Tag Attributes dialog box.

2. **Choose Modify➪Templates➪Make Attribute Editable.**

   The Editable Tag Attributes dialog box opens (refer to Figure 2-14).

3. **Deselect the Make Attribute Editable check box next to the attributes you want to disable and click OK.**

4. **Save the template and update all the template-based files.**

Building Nested Templates

Nested templates are templates whose design layouts and editable areas are based on another template file. A nested template is created when a template-based file is modified and then resaved as a new template file with new editable regions. For example, you can create a nested template that contains specific layout elements, such as a real-estate listing Web site where the detail information for each listing shares the same layout yet the overall page layout and design instructions come from the original template.

To make nested templates quickly, begin the creation process with a new template-based document that uses the base template you intend to modify.

Creating nested templates

To create a nested template, follow these steps:

1. **Create a template-based document from the base (original) template.**

   Choose File➪New and click the Page from Template button in the New Document dialog box. Select the managed site from the Site listing, then select the template that you want to use, and click the Create button in the dialog box. A new template-based document opens in the workspace window.

The nesting feature doesn't work if you attempt to create a new template from an existing template file. You must create the nested template from a template-based document.

2. **Choose File➪Save as Template.**

   You can also click the Templates button on the Common category of the Insert panel and choose Make Nested Template from the drop-down list.

   The Save As Template dialog box opens.

3. **Name the new nested template and click OK.**

4. **Add content and new editable regions to the nested template.**

   For example, a new nested area can contain a table layout with an image, a header graphic, and a nested table for displaying content. For details on creating an editable region, see "Working with Editable Regions," earlier in the chapter.

5. **When you finish making changes, save the file before creating template-based pages from the new nested template.**

Modifying nested templates

By default, the base template passes along any editable regions to the nested template. To convert an editable region passed through from a base template to a nested template into an uneditable region, you need to add some markup to the nested template.

To prevent an editable region from being passed to the nested template, follow these steps:

1. **Open the nested template in the Dreamweaver workspace.**

2. **In Code view, add the following code to the editable region code:**

```
@@(" ")@@
```

   Add this code anywhere between the template markup tags: `<!-- InstanceBeginEditable --> <!-- InstanceEndEditable -->`

   For example, code would change from

```
<td><!-- InstanceBeginEditable name="Address" -->
Address 1
<!-- InstanceEndEditable --></td>
```

   to this:

```
<td><!-- InstanceBeginEditable name="Address" -->
@@(" ")@@ Address 1
<!-- InstanceEndEditable --></td>
```

**Book III
Chapter 2**

Building Sites with Templates

Blocked editable regions inside nested templates display with a little expression marker inside their boundaries, as shown in Figure 2-16. In Design view, they also display with an orange highlighting color around the region, compared to the blue used to identify regular editable regions.

Expression icon

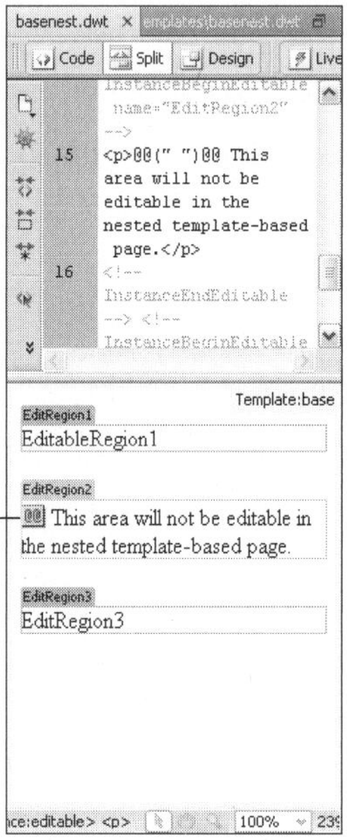

Figure 2-16:
In Design
view,
uneditable
regions
in nested
templates
display
a small
expression
icon.

Although nested templates look nearly identical to base templates, they do not necessarily share common areas when edits are made to the base template. For example, if you add a sentence to a noneditable region on the base template, that content doesn't pass through or appear on the nested template.

Creating a New Document from a Template

After you create a template and set all the editable regions needed inside it, you can begin building the Web site with pages generated from the template.

Create a new template-based page by following these steps:

1. **Choose File⇨New to open the New Document dialog box.**

2. **Click the Page from Template button to select the template by site and template name.**

Be sure that the Update Page When Template Changes check box is checked. Then click the Create button. The new template-based page opens in the Document window.

3. **Choose File⇨Save to save the new template-based file to the local root folder of the managed site.**

   The file is saved as a regular HTML file based on a Dreamweaver template. As shown in Figure 2-17, template-based pages are quickly identifiable by the yellow highlighted rectangle displaying around the inside of the entire document, topped by a yellow Template: *filename* tab at the top right edge of the page.

Figure 2-17: The Template tab in Design view.

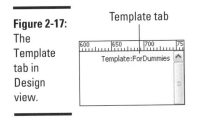

4. **Add page-specific content to the editable areas of the page.**

   Add text, graphics, tables, and other elements as you need.

   Locked uneditable regions are easily identifiable by the mouse pointer changing into the locked region pointer (see Figure 2-18).

Figure 2-18: The locked symbol.

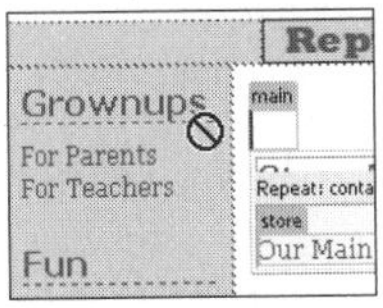

Book III
Chapter 2

Building Sites with Templates

Continue building all the pages for the Web site in a similar fashion until your site is complete, fully tested, and ready for uploading.

Editing Templates and Updating Pages

Whenever you modify and save a template, Dreamweaver not only recognizes that the template has changed, but also gives you the option to automatically update all the documents on the local managed site that were created with that template. If you'd rather selectively update template-based documents, Dreamweaver provides a method for that as well.

Modifying a template and updating all the pages that use it

You can update a template in Dreamweaver whenever you want and then apply the changes to all the files based on that template. For example, suppose that you want to change the name of one of the main navigation links (for example, changing "Buy" to "Order") on all the template-based pages on your site. To make the change, open the template that you used to create the template-based pages and modify the link and any other content that may need changing. When you save the template with these changes, Dreamweaver then updates all the pages created with that template.

To edit a template and update all the pages that use the template, follow these steps:

1. **Open an existing template by double-clicking the template file listed inside the Templates folder in the Files panel.**

   You can also select the template from the Templates folder in the Files panel and choose File⇨Open from the Files panel Options menu.

2. **Make any changes to the template.**

   As long as the template file is open in the Dreamweaver workspace, you can perform multiple undos from the History panel or choose Edit⇨Undo.

3. **Choose File⇨Save.**

   Dreamweaver recognizes any changes made to a template and opens the Update Template Files dialog box (shown in Figure 2-19), which prompts you to let the program automatically update all pages that use the template.

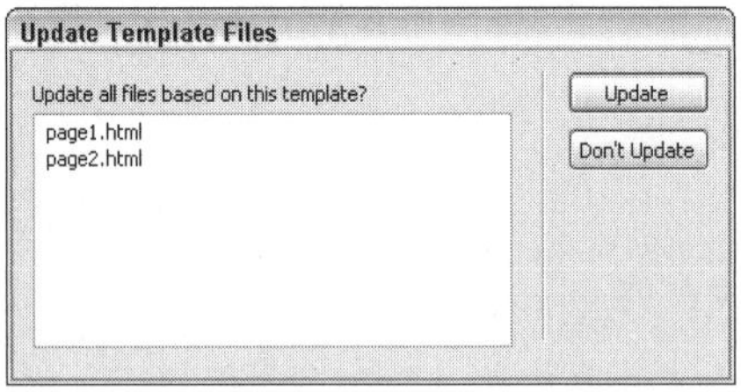

Figure 2-19:
Dream-
weaver
automates
the
template-
based page
updating
process.

> **Update Template Files**
>
> Update all files based on this template?
>
> page1.html
> page2.html
>
> [Update]
> [Don't Update]

4. **To update any pages that use this template, click the Update button.**

   When the update is complete, the Update Template Files dialog box displays a status log to confirm how many files were examined and updated. Dreamweaver actually hard-codes the changes into all the files that use the template. You can now confidently upload all the changed documents to the remote server.

Another automatic feature Dreamweaver performs when saving changes to templates is syntax checking to ensure that any expression or template parameter added in Code view is accurate. If the syntax is bad, Dreamweaver displays an error message with a reference to the line of code containing the error. You can manually check template syntax at any time by choosing Modify⇨Templates⇨Check Template Syntax.

Although you can edit regular pages in Contribute, you must edit templates in Dreamweaver. For more information about working with Contribute sites, turn to Book VI.

Selectively updating pages with the most recent version of the template

If you make edits to a template but don't want to apply them to all the pages based on it, such as when you add a template to your site from an external source or edit the template in another program, you can manually update the pages. This is also how you can make modifications to a template before committing to updating all the pages on the site, as long as you click No to the Dreamweaver prompt that asks if you want to update all the files that use that template. You can use two methods to selectively update template-based pages.

To update a single template-based document, follow these steps:

1. **Open the template-based document in the workspace window.**

2. **Choose Modify⇨Templates⇨Update Current Page.**

   The current page updates to reflect the most recent version of the template file upon which it is based.

3. **Choose File⇨Save to save the open page.**

   You must save the page to save the updates.

You can update multiple template-based documents — an entire site or just the files that are attached to the specified template — at once by following these steps:

1. **Choose Modify⇨Templates⇨Update Pages.**

   The Update Pages dialog box opens.

2. **Choose one of the following options:**

   • **Update the entire site:** Select Entire Site from the Look In drop-down list; select your site from the second drop-down list.

   • **Update pages with a specific template:** Select Files that Use from the Look In drop-down list; select the Dreamweaver template .dwt file that you want to use to perform the update.

3. **Click the Start button to begin the update.**

   The Update Pages dialog box performs the update. To see the status log, click the Show Log check box. Updates are immediate.

4. **When you finish your update, click Close to close the dialog box.**

Applying Templates to Pages

You can selectively apply templates to pages open in the Document window with the Assets panel, regardless of whether you previously applied the template.

To apply a template to a new, open document from the Assets panel:

✦ Click the Templates button along the left margin of the Assets panel, select the template from the list, and click the Apply button at the bottom of the panel.

✦ Click the Templates button along the left margin of the Assets panel, then drag and drop the template file into the open Document window.

If you want to apply a template to a document that currently uses a different template, follow these steps:

1. **Open the document in the Dreamweaver workspace.**

2. **Choose Modify⇨Templates⇨Apply Template to Page.**

   The Select Template dialog box opens.

3. **Choose a site from the list of managed sites and a template from the list of available templates in that site.**

4. **Click the Select button in the dialog box.**

   The Inconsistent Region Names dialog box opens.

5. **Map the editable regions from the old template to the new template. In the Name column under Editable Regions, select the old editable region name. Then choose the new region name from the Move Content to New Region drop-down list.**

   This tells Dreamweaver which editable regions in the new template the content from the old template's editable areas should go into. For instance, the old template may have two editable regions called `body` and `head`, whereas the new template has two regions called `main` and `header`. Select and match those regions from the old template to the regions on the new template so the content on the existing page moves to the specified region of the new template.

If you do not properly map the regions from the old template to the new one when prompted, the information in those regions will not be copied as the new template is applied.

When regions in the old and new templates have the same names, content in those editable regions are automatically matched up. If all regions match up, the mapping process happens automatically.

6. **Choose File⇨Save to save the updated page.**

For an alternate method, create a new template-based page, and transfer content (by copying and pasting) from the editable regions on the original file to the editable regions on the new template-based page.

Detaching Templates from Pages

Why would you want to detach a template? You may need a page that looks like the rest of the site but is not controlled by the template, or perhaps a particular page needs to be significantly different from the rest of the site, and modifying a template-based page is easier than building the new page from scratch. Or maybe you want to quickly remove all the editable regions and other template markup on a page rather than having to selectively remove the restrictive code. Whatever your reason, the detachment process is fairly simple.

To detach a template from a page, follow these steps:

1. **Open the document in the Dreamweaver workspace.**

2. **Choose Modify⇨Templates⇨Detach from Template.**

   All the template-specific markup is removed from the file, making any formerly uneditable areas in the code fully editable again.

3. **Save the file.**

After you detach the template from the page, you can reattach it by choosing Modify⇨Templates⇨Apply Template to Page. Additionally, you can reattach the template by undoing the detachment through the History panel as long as you keep the document open (see Book III, Chapter 4 for more on the History panel). However, after you save and close the file, you have to reattach the template manually.

Managing Templates

Use the Assets panel for renaming and deleting any of your existing templates. To display the list of templates, click the Templates button along the left margin of the Assets panel (see Figure 2-20).

Book III
Chapter 2

Building Sites with Templates

Templates

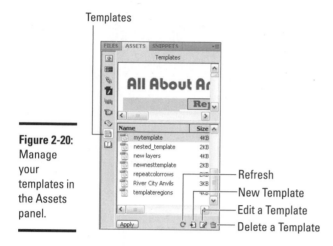

Figure 2-20:
Manage
your
templates in
the Assets
panel.

Refresh
New Template
Edit a Template
Delete a Template

Renaming a template

Should you ever need to rename a template, Dreamweaver can automate the name change across all the files in the managed site.

To rename a template in the Assets panel, follow these steps:

1. **From the Templates listing in the Assets panel, click to select the template name that you want to change.**

Make sure that the template file you're renaming is not open. You can also rename the template from the Files panel.

2. **Click the filename again so the text becomes selectable; type a new filename.**

If you accidentally double-click and open the template for editing, try the single-click, pause, single-click method again on the template filename.

3. **Press Enter (Windows) or Return (Mac) to complete the name change.**

Dreamweaver prompts you to update all the template-based documents that use this file.

4. **Click the Update button to update all the template-based files.**

Deleting a template file

At the end of a project, you may need to delete a template file that wasn't used on the site:

1. **From the templates listing in the Assets panel, click to select the template that you want to delete.**

2. Click the Delete button at the bottom of the Assets panel.

After clicking the button, you're prompted to confirm the deletion.

When deleting files, remember that after they're gone, your files are gone for good. If you think you may need the file in the future, make a backup of the entire managed site before making the deletion.

Documents based on a deleted template are not automatically detached from it; rather, they keep their existing format, including editable regions. If you need to, you can convert template-based files into regular HTML files by choosing Modify➪Templates➪Detach from Template.

Chapter 3: Using Library Items and Server-Side Includes

In This Chapter

✔ **Creating library items**

✔ **Managing and editing library items**

✔ **Creating server-side includes (SSIs)**

✔ **Inserting and editing SSIs**

Dreamweaver provides you with two different ways of creating reusable assets for your Web pages: *library items* and *server-side includes*. You can add both to documents, templates, and template-based pages, and both can contain any content that normally goes in the body of the page. Here's a closer look at the two options:

✦ **Library items:** These special files contain content of your choice that you can insert onto multiple Web pages, yet manage the contents of in one location. After it is inserted on a page, the library item content gets hard-coded into the HTML surrounded by special Dreamweaver library item comment tags. Any time you edit the library item's contents, all the pages that contain the library files are automatically updated. Library items are great for subnavigation, data tables, copyright notices, and other common page elements that need frequent editing.

✦ **Server-side include (SSI) files:** Like library items, SSIs are special files containing specific content that you can add to multiple Web pages and update in one centralized location. The main difference from library items, however, is that SSI content isn't hard-coded into the HTML file it's inserted into; instead, SSI files are saved as external HTML files and are then linked — similar to CSS — to a file. When the page is viewed in a browser, the browser finds the external SSI file and displays that content as if it were naturally coded into the page. Use SSIs for sections of Web pages that need frequent or constant editing on larger Web sites, such as a navigation item, daily menu, or class schedule.

This chapter shows you how to create, use, and edit library items and server-side includes.

Introducing Library Items

If you're familiar with Dreamweaver's templates (discussed in Book III, Chapter 2), library items work in a similar way. Whereas templates are the master documents from which you create new documents, *library items* are simply master page elements (such as navigation menus, tables, and images) containing whatever content you desire. You can use them as many times as you want without the need for rewriting the code each time. Library items are typically placed inside templates or used as stand-alone master elements in regular or template-based pages.

To understand more plainly how library items work, think of the original/ duplicate relationship of a rubber stamp. Your rubber stamp has the original design, and when you ink it up, you can stamp it to make as many copies of that stamp's design as you like. Similarly, with library items you create the original library item, save it, and then insert a copy of it when and where you need it on your Web pages.

Creating Library Items

Create library items from any selected content in the body of your page, including text, graphics, forms, tables, media, and JavaScript. If the selected content has images or other linked items, those items must stay in their original locations for the library item to work properly.

When your library items include Dreamweaver JavaScript *behaviors* (which let visitors interact in some way with your Web page), Dreamweaver also copies the element and its *event handler* (an action that specifies when the event occurs, such as onMouseOver) to the library item file. Then, when you insert that library item into another document, Dreamweaver automatically adds the necessary JavaScript functions into the <head> area of the file so the copied library item containing the behavior works in the new file. By contrast, when hand-coding JavaScript behaviors, be sure to use the Call JavaScript behavior as part of the library item to execute the code; the behavior allows you to set a function or line of script to execute when a particular event happens in the browser. (See Book IV, Chapter 2 for more on behaviors.)

Here are some general guidelines of when to use library items:

✦ Your Web site is small (less than 30 pages).

✦ You manage the site yourself.

✦ You expect to make periodic changes to the library items or you anticipate the library item content may need altering in the future.

✦ You understand that making edits to the library items requires a rewriting of all the pages on your site that use those library items, which therefore means you must upload all the updated files to your server before site visitors can view those changes.

✦ Your Web host doesn't support server-side includes.

✦ Every bit of processor speed is important to you (pages with SSIs take a little longer to load in a browser than pages containing library items).

Here are some good uses for library items:

✦ Footers

✦ Navigation elements

✦ Parts of your page/site that may require periodic updating and appear on multiple pages, such as product tag lines, sponsorship listings, and contact information.

✦ Copyright notices

One great use for a library item is a copyright notice at the foot of a page, such as: *Copyright 2008. All rights reserved.* It uses the current year now, but come January 1st, you need to update the year. Fortunately, when you're ready to make the date change, you need to update only the original library item while Dreamweaver updates all the pages that use the library item with the new code.

Creating a selection-based library item

Follow these steps to create a library item based on content you've created:

1. **In the Files panel, click the Assets tab and then click the Library button in the left margin of the Assets panel.**

The Library options appear in the Assets panel (see Figure 3-1).

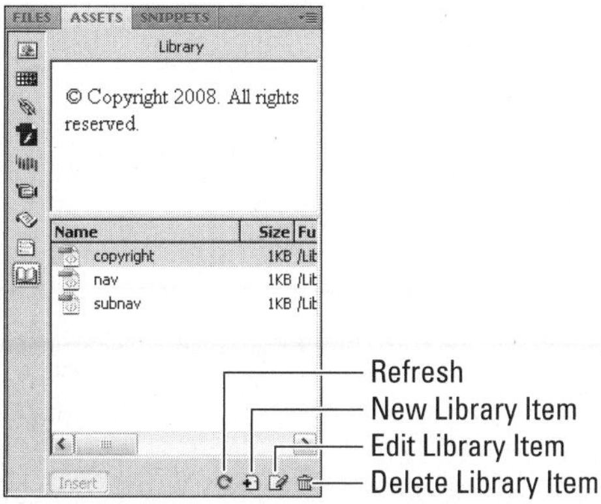

Figure 3-1:
The Library Items view in the Assets panel.

— Refresh
— New Library Item
— Edit Library Item
— Delete Library Item

**Book III
Chapter 3**

Using Library Items and Server-Side Includes

2. **In Code or Design view of an open document, select the content you want to convert into a library item.**

   Library items can contain text, graphics, links, tables, JavaScript, Flash movies, and other HTML code elements.

   In the copyright example, select the copyright sentence in your document such as: *Copyright 2008. All rights reserved.*

3. **Click the New Library Item button in the Assets panel.**

   You can also choose Modify⇨Library⇨Add Object to Library to create a new library item.

   Dreamweaver converts your selected code into a library item with the .lbi file extension, and then creates a Library folder and puts your newly created library item there.

   You know your code converted properly to a library item because it displays in your page, in Design and Code views, as a block of code with pale yellow highlighting.

4. **Give your new library item a descriptive name, such as copyright, and press Enter (Windows) or Return (Mac).**

   By default, new library items are called untitled.lbi until you rename them in the Assets panel. See the later section, "Renaming library items" for more on this.

Creating an empty library item

For times when you know you need a library item on your site but don't have the content for it yet — such as when a client still needs to send you approved text — you can create and use an empty library item. You can edit the library item when the content becomes available.

You can create an empty library item for editing at a later time by following these steps:

1. **In the Files panel, click the Assets tab and then click the Library button in the left margin of the Assets panel.**

2. **Click the New Library Item button at the bottom of the panel.**

   A new untitled library item is added to the Library folder. Make sure nothing is selected in the Document window before doing so; otherwise, the selected content is converted into a library item. That means if you have a library item selected on the page, it becomes duplicated.

3. **Give your new library item a descriptive name and press Enter (Windows) or Return (Mac).**

   You can now add the library item to your pages and edit the content at any time.

Changing library highlighting preferences

You can change the highlighting color and the visibility of the highlighting of library items in the Preferences dialog box.

To alter the highlight color, follow these steps:

1. Choose Edit➪Preferences (Windows) or Dreamweaver➪Preferences (Mac) to open the Preferences dialog box.

2. Choose the Highlighting category on the left side of the dialog box.

3. On the right side of the panel, click the Library Items color box to choose a new highlight color with the color picker or type the hexadecimal value in the text box.

4. Click Show to see the highlighted library color in your documents or deselect the Show option to hide the highlighting.

5. Click OK.

To see library item highlight colors in your documents, choose View➪Visual Aids➪Invisible Elements. Toggle on and off the display of library item highlighting.

Inserting a Library Item in Your Document

When you insert a library item in a document, the entire contents of that library item are added to the page along with library item markup tags, as shown in the following example:

```
<!-- #BeginLibraryItem "/Library/copyright.lbi" -->&copy; Copyright 2008. All
     rights reserved.<!-- #EndLibraryItem -->
```

Follow these steps to insert a library item on a page:

1. **Place your cursor inside the open document where you want to insert the library item.**

Setting the insertion point determines the location of the library item. For example, if you want to insert a library item that's a copyright notice, place your cursor at the foot of a page.

2. **Open the Library area of the Assets panel by clicking the Assets tab in the Files panel and clicking the Library button at the left edge of the panel.**

The Library button looks like an open book.

3. **Select the library item that you want to insert.**

The Library area of the Assets panel contains a list of all available library items for the currently managed site. If you have created library items but do not see them in this listing, click the blue Refresh button at the bottom of the Assets panel.

Book III
Chapter 3

Using Library Items and Server-Side Includes

4. **Click the Insert button in the Library area of the Assets panel.**

   You can also drag and drop the library item from the Library area of the Assets panel into your open document.

Notice that when you insert your library item, Dreamweaver writes opening and closing comment tags along with your library item contents, as shown in Figure 3-2.

Figure 3-2:
Highlighting and comment tags appear when inserting library items.

If you want to insert the contents of a library item onto a page without the library item markup, press Ctrl (Windows) or Option (Mac) while dragging the item onto the document from the Assets panel. The content becomes disconnected from the library source so the library item doesn't control the content.

Using library items sounds so easy that you may be wondering why you wouldn't use them. The main complaint about library items is this: Because the library items are hard-coded into your pages, when you edit them, any pages on your site that contain them must be updated with the new code and subsequently uploaded to your server before site visitors can see those changes. When your site has a lot of pages, the time the uploading process takes to complete is a major consideration. This is especially an issue when your site uses the Check In/Check Out system. Furthermore, updating library items alters the Last Modified time of each file, making it more difficult for you to track when a file's unique content was actually last changed.

Editing and Managing Library Items

After you successfully create a library item, you can edit it any time. You can then apply those changes to a single page, the entire site, or all the files that use the library item.

In addition to regular content updates, you may occasionally need to perform other management tasks such as renaming, deleting, detaching, duplicating, or re-creating a library item.

Editing library items

Follow these steps to edit a library item:

1. **In the Files panel, click the Assets tab and click the Library button in the left margin of the Assets panel.**

2. **Select the library item that you want to edit.**

   If you're unsure what the library item is named, look in the preview pane of the Library area of the Assets panel to see a thumbnail of the library item.

3. **Click the Edit button on the bottom of the Library area of the Assets panel to open the library item in the Dreamweaver workspace window.**

   You can also open the library item into its own Document window by selecting the library item in Design or Code view and clicking the Edit button in the Properties inspector.

4. **Edit the library item and save the changes by choosing File⇨Save.**

   Because library items are hard-coded into your pages, Dreamweaver prompts you to update all the pages that contain that item.

5. **Click OK if you want Dreamweaver to find all the instances of the original library item code on any pages on your site and update it to match the changes you just made.**

   If you happen to skip this updating prompt, manually perform updates by choosing Modify⇨Library and the item you want to update.

Updating documents and sites that use library items

After editing a library item, you may want to manually update the files that use it. You can update a single page from within that document, your entire site, or all the files that use a particular library item.

To update a library item in the open document, choose Modify⇨Library⇨ Update Current Page.

To update an entire site or all files using a specific library item, follow these steps after you edit the library item:

1. **Choose Modify⇨Library⇨Update Pages.**

The Update Pages dialog box opens, as shown in Figure 3-3.

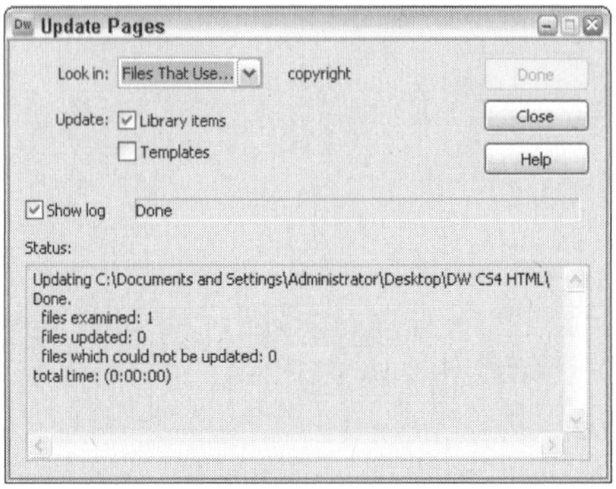

Figure 3-3: Update library items on an entire site.

The dialog box shows the following interface:

Update Pages

Look in: Files That Use... ▾   copyright   Done

Update: ☑ Library items   Close
☐ Templates   Help

☑ Show log   Done

Status:

Updating C:\Documents and Settings\Administrator\Desktop\DW CS4 HTML\
Done.
 files examined: 1
 files updated: 0
 files which could not be updated: 0
total time: (0:00:00)

2. **Select an option from the Look In drop-down list, depending on what you want to do:**

- **Update the library item sitewide:** Select Entire Site, and in the right drop-down list, select the name of the site.

- **Update the library item in all files:** Select Files That Use, and in the right drop-down list, select the library item name.

3. **Check to see that Library Items is checked as an Update option.**

4. **Click the Start button to begin the update process.**

Select the Show Log check box to view a status log of the update process. There you find a record of the number of files on the site that were examined and updated, plus any files that Dreamweaver was unable to update.

5. **When you finish, click Close.**

Renaming library items

You can easily rename library items in the Library area of the Assets panel of a managed site, and it's recommended you perform your library name changes from within Dreamweaver.

Renaming a library item outside of Dreamweaver breaks the library links to the documents that use them.

To rename a library item, follow these steps:

1. **In the Files panel, click the Assets tab and click the Library button in the left margin of the Assets panel.**

2. **Select the library item you want to rename.**

If you're unsure of the library item's current name, look in the preview pane of the Library area of the Assets panel to see a thumbnail of the library item.

3. **Click the library item name again, so that the text becomes editable, and type the new name.**

If you accidentally double-click and open the library item for editing, try the single-click, pause, single-click method again on the library item filename.

4. **After entering the new name, press Enter (Windows) or Return (Mac) to complete the name change.**

Dreamweaver opens the Update Files dialog box.

5. **Click the Update button.**

Dreamweaver automatically updates all the documents in the managed site that use this library item. To prevent Dreamweaver from performing the automatic update, click the Don't Update button. For example, you may want to delay if you intend on changing multiple library files on a site.

Deleting library items

To help keep your library items organized while developing your site, delete any unused or unnecessary library items from the Library area of the Assets panel by following these steps:

1. **In the Files panel, click the Assets tab and click the Library button in the left margin of the Assets panel.**

2. **Select the library item that you want to delete.**

If you're unsure of the name of the library item you want to delete, select an item from the list and look in the preview pane to see a thumbnail of the selected item.

3. **To permanently delete the library item from the library, press the Delete key on your keyboard and confirm the deletion.**

You can also click the Delete button at the bottom of the Assets panel and confirm the deletion.

This deletion process permanently removes the library item from the library, although it doesn't delete instances of that item from the contents of any documents that used it. Therefore, delete your library items with care.

Detaching library items

After you insert a library item into a document, you can't edit an individual instance of it unless you break the link between the library item and the document by detaching it and converting the library item into editable text. Then, when you update the original library item after an instance is detached, the detached instance doesn't update along with the other instances of the library item.

You may want to detach an instance of a library item from its source for many reasons:

✦ You need to modify a significant portion of the library item on a single page.

✦ You've only used the library item on a single page.

✦ You want to insert a library item created for another site. You insert it on a page, detach it to break the links to that other site, and then re-create the link within the currently managed site.

To detach a library item and convert it into editable text, follow these steps:

1. **Select the library item in the document that you want to convert.**

2. **Click the Detach from Original button in the Properties inspector.**

Dreamweaver alerts you that making the item editable prevents it from receiving updates from the original library item.

3. **Click OK.**

The selected library item then loses its library item highlighting and markup to become normal, editable text.

To modify library items that contain Dreamweaver behaviors, you must detach the library item from its source to make the behavior editable. After editing the behavior, use the updated content to create a new library item or use it as a replacement for its previous version.

Copying a library item from one site to another

To use an existing library item on one Web site in another managed site, follow these steps:

1. **In the Files panel, click the Assets tab and click the Library button.**

2. **From the list of Library items that appears, select the library item that you want to duplicate.**

3. **To make a copy inside another managed site, choose Copy to Site from the Options menu in the Assets panel and select the desired managed site by name from the submenu.**

   Dreamweaver copies the duplicate into the selected managed site. If the new site does not already have a Library folder, Dreamweaver creates one and places the copied library item into it.

Re-creating library items

Occasionally, you delete a library item from the Library area of the Assets panel even though instances of it still remain throughout the site. If you want the library item back to control modifications made to all the instances, you must re-create it.

Here's how to re-create a library item:

1. **In an open document, select the instance of the library item that you need to re-create.**

2. **Click the Recreate button in the Properties inspector.**

   A new library item is added to the Library area of the Assets panel. If a library item already exists there with the same name, Dreamweaver asks if you want to overwrite the existing file. Click OK to proceed.

   A master copy of the re-created library item is inserted into the Library folder.

Understanding Server-Side Includes

If you understand how to create and use library items (as described earlier in the chapter), you can quickly grasp the concept behind server-side includes (SSIs). Like library items, SSIs can be composed of HTML, JavaScript, or graphics. But unlike library items, they have no opening and closing comment tags surrounding the code and the content of the SSI is not hard-coded into your Web page. Rather, a simple line of code is added to your page that points to the external SSI file on your server, like this:

```
<!--#include file="serversideinclude.html" -->
```

Only the reference to, and not the contents of, the SSI file are part of the include instructions.

An SSI is an external HTML file that a server adds to the page it's inserted on when a browser requests that page from the server. The server then processes the include instructions and delivers a document that replaces the SSI statement code with the content of the SSI file.

When making the decision to use SSI, keep these points in mind:

✦ Servers process, or *parse,* pages with SSIs differently than regular HTML documents, and that may put more demand on a server's processor, which in turn could lead to slower page serving for all the pages on your entire site.

✦ When you preview the file with the include instructions in a browser locally (before testing it on a live server), your browser doesn't *parse* the SSI, in which case you may not see the include content on the page.

To solve this issue, Dreamweaver lets you preview documents in Design view exactly as they'll appear on a server. Furthermore, by checking the Preview Using Temporary File option in the Preview in Browser category of Dreamweaver's Preferences dialog box, you can create a temporary copy of the file for preview and testing that displays the SSI in your local browser by mimicking how the file would behave on a server.

✦ The SSI markup syntax must match the type of Web server the files are being displayed on. Some servers are configured to examine all files to see if they have server-side includes, whereas other servers examine only files with the .shtml, .shtm, or .inc file extension.

Your particular server may require that you rename all files containing SSIs with the .shtml, .shtm, or .inc file extension. For example, you may need to rename a file with an SSI named menu.html to menu.shtml to manifest the include properly. Check with your system administrator or host provider to see whether you're required to change the file extension for documents with SSIs.

The bottom line is that you should test files containing SSIs on a server before publishing them on the Internet, just in case the host server isn't configured to display them properly or you need to modify your code to support them.

Creating and Inserting Server-Side Includes

Like a regular HTML file, a server-side include file (an example of which is shown in Figure 3-4) is composed of the content you want to include on another page, and should be saved with the .html or .htm file extension. What it shouldn't contain, however, are any <doctype>, <meta>, or opening or closing <html>, <head>, <title>, or <body> tags in the code. This is because the SSI is *included* on another page that already has those HTML tags. Figure 3-5 demonstrates how an SSI file is included in the code of another document.

Figure 3-4:
A server-side include file.

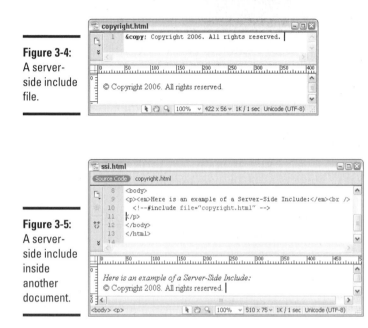

Figure 3-5:
A server-side include inside another document.

If any one or more of the following general guidelines apply, you may want to use server-side includes:

✦ Your Web site is large (more than 30 pages).

✦ Two or more people manage the site from different locations.

✦ You have site content that needs frequent editing.

✦ You are confident your host provider supports SSIs.

✦ Your clients want to update part of the site regularly, and they understand and can write the SSI content in HTML themselves.

✦ You have a client who doesn't have Dreamweaver and can't take advantage of library items.

✦ You love the fact that you only have to upload the SSI files to the server when their content changes, rather than uploading all the files that contain them, as you must do for library items.

✦ Your site is database driven (ASP, JSP, PHP, CFML). Although your site does not need to have a database to use SSIs, if it does, that alone is a big enough reason to consider using SSIs.

✦ You've tested your server and are confident that the SSIs work.

Here are some good uses for SSIs:

✦ Footers

✦ Copyright notices

✦ Navigation elements

✦ Jump menus

✦ Parts of your page/site that may require periodic updating, such as class schedules, course descriptions, news items, and so on

✦ Parts of your site that require regular updates, such as a menu or event listing

If you're uncertain whether a library item or server-side include is best for your projects, consider this general rule: If the site is small, use library items. If the site is large and needs regular updates to certain parts of the content, your server supports them, and you don't mind the ever-so-slightly slower page opening times, use SSIs.

Creating a server-side include

One fast way to create an SSI file is to first build the content in a normal Dreamweaver HTML file, and then copy the content from that file and paste it into an empty document that doesn't contain any HTML markup.

Presuming you've already created a document with the content for the SSI, follow these instructions to convert that content into a server-side include file:

1. **Open the document that has the content for the SSI file.**

2. **Select the content and choose Edit⇨Copy.**

The copied content is temporarily placed in your computer's Clipboard. Close that file without saving the changes.

3. **Choose File⇨New to open a new Blank Page HTML document in the Dreamweaver workspace window.**

4. **In Code view, choose Edit⇨Select All to select all the code in the file, and press the Delete or Backspace key on your keyboard.**

Be sure the entire document is empty of all code before proceeding.

5. **With your cursor still in Code view of the empty file, choose Edit⇨ Paste to paste the copied content from the original file.**

6. **Save the new SSI file with an appropriate filename and the .html or .htm file extension.**

If you plan on having several SSI files on the same Web site, consider saving all the SSI files into one folder at the site's root level for better organization of the SSI files.

You can now insert the SSI file into another file, as described in the next section.

Inserting a server-side include

Dreamweaver writes the appropriate syntax into your code when you use the built-in SSI command. Insert your server-side include files into regular documents, dynamic documents, templates, or template-based files.

To insert an SSI into a page, follow these steps:

1. **Open the document that you want to add the SSI to.**

2. **Click the cursor where you want the SSI to display.**

   Use either Design or Code view.

3. **Choose Insert⇨Server-Side Include.**

   The Select File dialog box opens.

4. **Browse to and select the SSI .html file.**

   If you've saved your SSI files into a separate folder, navigate to that folder and select the appropriate SSI file.

5. **Click OK.**

   Dreamweaver adds the appropriate SSI code to your document, as shown in the following example where the SSI file, called copyright.html, is located in a folder called ssi:

   ```
   <!--#include file="/ssi/copyright.html" -->
   ```

6. **Select the newly inserted SSI in Design view, and then choose File or Virtual as the include type in the Properties inspector.**

   You can choose from two SSI types: File or Virtual. Depending on the type of server you have, you may need to replace the word *file* with *virtual* in the include instructions. Apache servers typically use the Virtual setting (this is the Dreamweaver default), whereas File is the standard for Microsoft Internet Information Server (IIS). If you're not sure which one to choose, try the first one, and if that doesn't work, try the second, or better yet, ask your host provider or system administrator for guidance.

   When the server runs IIS software, ask your host provider or system administrator about installing special software if you include a file in a folder above the current folder in the site root folder hierarchy.

   If your server uses another kind of software besides Apache or IIS, check with your host provider or system administrator for which SSI type to use.

   Dreamweaver immediately displays the include file's content in Design view, such as while showing include instruction markup in Code view, such as

```
<!--#include file="/ssi/copyright.html" -->
```

7. **Save the file that contains the newly inserted SSI with the .html or .shtml file extension as instructed by your system administrator or host provider.**

   The include file itself doesn't need any particular extension. However, if you want the include file to also include another sub-file, you need to save the include file as an .shtml file (or whatever extension type enables server-side includes on your server).

8. **Upload the SSI files and any documents containing SSI to your remote host server.**

   If you saved the SSI files into a local folder, be sure to upload the same folder structure to the server so the links to the SSI files match.

To change to a different SSI file after inserting one on a page, select the server-side include in the open file and click the folder button next to the Filename field in the Properties inspector to browse for and choose a new SSI file.

The SSIs now render seamlessly in the browser window. If the SSI files do not display in the browser, you need to convert your Web site linking system to use site root-relative linking, as the next section describes.

Document versus root-relative links

When working with SSIs, their mere existence on some Web servers may require site root-relative linking rather than document-relative linking. In other words, you may need to add a forward slash before the SSI filename such as the following:

Document-Relative:

```
<!--#include file="ssi/serversideinclude.
       html" -->
```

Site Root-Relative:

```
<!--#include file="/ssi/
       serversideinclude.html" -->
```

The forward slash at the start of the path, before the folder or filename, tells the browser viewing the site to use the root level as the starting point for locating files on the server.

Speak with your system administrator or host provider to find out if and how they support SSIs before building your pages with them. If you do ultimately choose to use server-side includes, test them on your server to ensure they'll display properly before publishing the entire site.

For further information about relative links and site organization, see Book I, Chapter 2.

Editing Server-Side Includes

Edit a server-side include file just as you would any other HTML document by opening the file in the Dreamweaver workspace, making changes, saving it, and uploading the changed SSI file to the host server.

To open the file for editing in the Dreamweaver workspace window, double-click the SSI file from its location in the Files panel. You can also select the SSI content in Design or Code view of the page it's inserted on and click the Edit button in the Properties inspector, or simply double-click the SSI content in Design view.

Within Dreamweaver's Design view, edits to the SSI file appear immediately in the files containing them, but for site visitors to see the changes in a browser window, you must upload the updated SSI file to the host server.

Chapter 4: Creating Code Snippets and History Panel Commands

In This Chapter

✔ Understanding snippets

✔ Using Dreamweaver's snippets

✔ Making your own snippets

✔ Editing, deleting, and managing snippets

✔ Working with the History panel

✔ Creating History panel commands

*I*f you build a lot of Web sites, you know that you'll use certain elements over and over again, but each time you need them, you either have to recall a particular command or, more likely, copy and paste the code containing the content you want to reuse. Knowing that is not the most efficient way to work, Dreamweaver created a solution called Code Snippets that, after they're created, become available to you across all of your managed sites. Snippets are valuable timesavers that every Dreamweaver user should discover and take advantage of.

Don't confuse snippets with library items or SSIs (which we cover in Book III, Chapter 3). Snippets are intended to be used as either shortcuts for inserting a single instance of content on a page or as a way of quickly modifying selected content in a file.

Similar in theory to Microsoft's macros or Adobe's Actions, Code Snippets are a fantastic way to automate some of your repetitive tasks and make your job easier. They are composed of bits of code or content that you can save, edit, use, and reuse as often as you want on any Web site you happen to be working on. Dreamweaver even comes with a great set of prewritten, logically categorized, ready-to-use snippets. You can find them sitting in the Snippets panel (which you open by choosing Window➪Snippets).

Other terrific timesaving tools are the temporary and permanent custom commands you can create with the Dreamweaver History panel (which you open by choosing Window➪History). Record and save any series of steps — such as select, bold, deselect — to play again and again at a later time.

In this chapter, you find out how to create, insert, edit, and delete Snippets, as well as organize them in folders to share with your workmates. This chapter also covers how to record and play History panel commands.

Understanding What Snippets Do

The best snippets are the ones that save you time or at least limit the work you need to perform so you don't have to retype anything, such as the following:

✦ Code including HTML, JavaScript, ASP, JSP, PHP, and even CFML (ColdFusion Markup Language).

✦ Text that you use often. For instance, you may like to add a copyright notice such as © *2008 All rights reserved* at the foot of your pages.

✦ Navigation tables with bullets and text that have temporary links already applied to each navigation word so all you need to do after inserting the snippet on your page is type the real navigation names and links.

✦ JavaScript information, such as the Set Text of Status Bar JavaScript behavior, or perhaps opening and closing comment tags.

There are two basic types of snippets:

✦ **Wrap snippets** insert code before and after any selected content on the page, such as adding `<span>` tags around a selected line of text, as in

```
<span>This sentence is wrapped with span tags .</span>
```

✦ **Block snippets** simply drop in the snippet content after the insertion point on the page, such as a line of code with JavaScript to display the current date.

Using Dreamweaver's Snippets

Dreamweaver comes with a great set of preset snippets already categorized into files for Comments, Footers, Form Elements, JavaScript, Meta, Navigation, Text, and ~Legacy. Open the Snippets panel by choosing Window➪Snippets to review Dreamweaver's snippets folders, as shown in Figure 4-1.

Each folder includes a list of snippets organized alphabetically by name. To preview each snippet for how it will appear on the page, select it and look in the preview pane of the Snippets panel. To read a description of the snippet and review the code that it uses, click the Edit Snippet button at the bottom of the panel to open the Snippet dialog box.

To use a block snippet, place an insertion point inside an open document, select the snippet from the Snippets panel, and click the Insert button at the bottom of the panel. You can also drag and drop the snippet from the panel into an open document, as you would an image or any other media file.

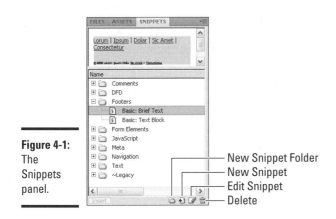

Figure 4-1:
The
Snippets
panel.

New Snippet Folder
New Snippet
Edit Snippet
Delete

To use a wrap snippet, select the content in Design view that the snippet will wrap around, select the snippet in the Snippets panel, and click the Insert button at the bottom of the panel.

You can find several good Web sites — including the Adobe Web site — to exchange snippets with other designers and programmers. Search for **Dreamweaver snippets** or **Snippets exchange.** Then, when you download new snippets or create your own, you can file them in any of the existing Dreamweaver snippets folders or create new folders and file them there.

Creating Code Snippets

To create a Code Snippet, you must first begin by knowing what you want to turn into a snippet. Think about what can save you time, such as a snippet to create a time/date stamp, or the types of content you frequently use, such as copyright notices or meta tag information.

Snippets can be as simple or as complex as you need them to be. The following sections show you how to create four types of snippets from scratch: text, JavaScript, wrap, and graphic.

To download copies of the snippets described in this chapter, visit www. luckychair.com/downloads.html.

Creating a text snippet

Say you work with lots of artists and have a standard copyright notice you want to use regarding their work being displayed online. By creating a code snippet, you never have to type that copyright notice again, save for adding the correct artist name and company information after inserting the snippet into your page.

Follow these steps to insert a text snippet on your Web page:

1. **Choose Window⇨Snippets to open the Snippets panel.**

2. **Click the New Snippet button (refer to Figure 4-1).**

The Snippet dialog box opens.

3. **Type a name for the snippet in the Name text box.**

Snippet names can't contain characters that are invalid in filenames, such as slashes (/ or \), special characters, or double quotes (").

In Figure 4-2, the snippet is named Artist Copyright Notice.

Snippet	☒
Name: Artist Copyright Statement	OK
Description: Inserts standard copyright statement for artists.	Cancel
	Help
Snippet type: ○ Wrap selection ⊙ Insert block	
Insert code: All artwork featured on THIS WEBSITE is copyrighted material and may not be reproduced, downloaded, or used in any other format, on any other product, without permission from THIS COMPANY and the artist.	
Preview type: ○ Design ⊙ Code	

Figure 4-2:
Enter your
snippet
details.

4. **Write a text description for the snippet in the Description text box.**

For a copyright notice, your description may look like this: Inserts standard copyright statement for artists.

5. **Select Insert Block as the snippet type.**

The Insert Block type is best for snippets containing content only. By contrast, the Wrap Selection type surrounds or wraps around your selected content, which is especially helpful for applying links, scripts, special formatting, and navigation.

6. **Add the code in the Insert Code text box.**

Here's what to type for the Copyright example:

```
All artwork featured on THIS WEBSITE is copyrighted material and may not
    be reproduced, downloaded, or used in any other format, on any other
    product, without permission from THIS COMPANY and the artist.
```

7. **Pick a preview type: Design or Code.**

   The Code preview type shows the code in the preview pane of the Snippets panel. To see how graphics contained in your snippet may appear, choose Design view.

8. **Click OK when you're done.**

   Your new snippet appears in the Snippets panel.

To use your new snippet, open an HTML page and, in either Design or Code view, click anywhere on the page to create an insertion point with your cursor.

Select the new snippet from the Snippets panel and click the Insert button or double-click the Snippet name to quickly insert the snippet onto your page. The snippet appears on your page, as shown in Figure 4-3.

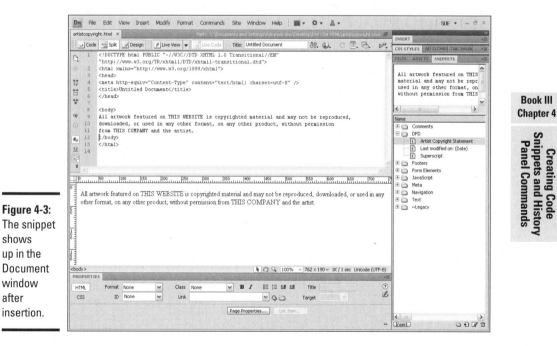

Figure 4-3:
The snippet shows up in the Document window after insertion.

Book III Chapter 4

Creating Code
Snippets and History
Panel Commands

Creating a JavaScript snippet

A lot of great free JavaScripts snippets are available on the Internet for use on a Web page that aren't built into the Dreamweaver interface (turn to Book IV, Chapter 2 to find out about JavaScript). You can find many useful free JavaScripts on the following sites:

```
www.dynamicdrive.com/
www.javascript.com/
javascript.internet.com/
www.javascriptkit.com/cutpastejava.shtml
www.java-scripts.net/
www.javafile.com/
webdeveloper.earthweb.com/webjs/
www.javascriptsearch.com/
```

Regularly used JavaScripts make great Code Snippets. Besides saving you valuable time, one of the greatest advantages to using JavaScript snippets is that you needn't understand the JavaScript code to use them. The following are some great examples of JavaScript that you can easily convert into reusable Code Snippets:

✦ Time/date stamps and clock scripts

✦ Customizable menu navigation scripts

✦ Game scripts

✦ Password-protection scripts

✦ Text and status bar effects scripts

✦ Image effects and slide show scripts

Follow these steps to make a JavaScript snippet:

1. **Open the Snippets panel by choosing Window➪Snippets.**

2. **Click the New Snippet button at the bottom of the Snippets panel (refer to Figure 4-1).**

The Snippet dialog box opens.

3. **Type a name for the snippet in the Name text box.**

Suppose, for example, you want to create a snippet with JavaScript that displays the document's last modified date starting with the words, `This document was last modified on:`. In the Name text box, type something like **This document was last modified on: (Date)** for the name.

4. **Write a text description for the snippet in the Description text box.**

You may also want to include instructions about how to use the snippet. For example, you can note to insert the snippet in the `<head>`, not the `<body>` tag and that the snippet is only supported by particular browser versions.

5. **Choose Insert Block for the snippet type.**

JavaScript is code that modifies the behavior of your content, so you always choose Insert Block as the type rather than Wrap.

6. **Insert the code in the Insert Code text box.**

The following JavaScript example inserts the current date into your Web page. If using CSS for styling your page, disregard the <b> and <font> tags. You can also customize the script to display something else besides This document was last modified on: before the date by modifying the line of code that says document.write("This document was last modified on: ");. Type this data:

```
<p><font face="arial, helvetica" size="1"><b>
<SCRIPT LANGUAGE="JavaScript">
function initArray() {
this.length = initArray.arguments.length
for (var i = 0; i < this.length; i++)
this[i+1] = initArray.arguments[i] }
var DOWArray = new initArray("Sunday","Monday","Tuesday","Wednesday","Thu
    rsday","Friday","Saturday");
var MOYArray = new initArray("January","February","March","April","May","
    June","July","August","September","October","November","December");
var LastModDate = new Date(document.lastModified);
document.write("This document was last modified on: ");
document.write(DOWArray[(LastModDate.getDay()+1)], ", ");
document.write(MOYArray[(LastModDate.getMonth()+1)]," ");
document.write(LastModDate.getDate(),", ",2008);
document.write(".");
</SCRIPT></b></font></p>
```

The final output looks something like this:

```
This document was last modified on: Monday, September 8, 2008
```

7. Pick Code as the Preview Type.

The Code preview type shows you the code in the preview pane of the Snippet panel.

8. Click OK when you're done.

To test your new snippet, click anywhere on any open page in Design view to create an insertion point with your cursor and double-click the snippet in the Snippets panel.

When snippets containing JavaScript are inserted on a page, Dreamweaver's Design view may either indicate you have JavaScript code on your page by displaying an invisible element icon, or you may see nothing at all in Design view, though you see the newly inserted code in Code view in both cases. Browsers, by contrast, display the JavaScript as it's meant to display and function. Therefore, for testing purposes, be sure to press F12 (or Shift+F12) to launch your primary browser to see how the JavaScript snippet looks.

To turn on the yellow script invisible element, choose Edit➪Preferences (Windows) or Dreamweaver➪Preferences (Mac) to launch Dreamweaver's Preferences dialog box. Select Invisible Elements from the Category list on the left and then select the Scripts option. Upon clicking OK, Dreamweaver indicates with the invisible element icon in Design view that you have JavaScript on your page.

Figure 4-4 shows how the icon looks as well as how the snippet actually appears in a browser.

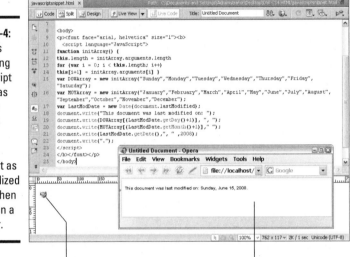

Figure 4-4: Snippets containing JavaScript appear as invisible element icons in Design view, but as fully realized script when viewed in a browser.

Invisible Element

Snippets preview in browser

Creating a snippet with the wrap option

The wrap option allows you to write opening and closing tags that surround whatever code or content is selected on your page. Wrap snippets are especially helpful for applying links, scripts, special formatting, and navigation. For instance, you may want to create a snippet that quickly adds a link around selected text, such as `<a href="#">link</a>`. To create a snippet with the wrap option, follow these steps:

1. **Open the Snippets panel by choosing Window⇨Snippets.**

The Snippets panel appears.

2. **Click the New Snippets button (refer to Figure 4-1).**

The Snippets dialog box appears.

3. **Type a name for the snippet in the Name text box.**

Say, for example, that you want to generate a snippet that superscripts text, such as on 42nd Street. In the Name text box, type **Superscript.**

4. **Write a text description for the snippet in the Description text box.**

In this example, type something like this for the description: This snippet will Superscript any selected content using the `<sup></sup>` tags.

5. **Choose Wrap Selection as the Snippet type.**

Use this type because the code in your snippet will surround or wrap around your selected content. When selecting the Wrap Selection type, notice that the dialog box changes from displaying one box for code input to displaying two boxes, as shown in Figure 4-5.

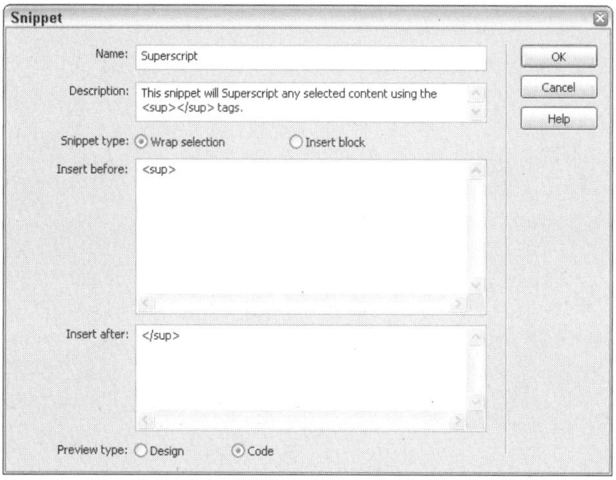

Book III
Chapter 4

Creating Code
Snippets and History
Panel Commands

Figure 4-5:
Enter your snippet in the Insert Before and Insert After boxes.

6. **Add the appropriate code to the Insert Before box.**

To create a superscript snippet, type the following:

```
<sup>
```

7. **Add the appropriate code to the Insert After box.**

To continue creating the superscript snippet, type the following:

```
</sup>
```

8. **Pick Code as the Preview Type.**

Because wrap snippets typically have no graphics, select Code as the preview type to see code in the preview pane of the Snippet panel.

9. **Click OK when you're done.**

The wrap snippet is inserted in your Web page (see Figure 4-6).

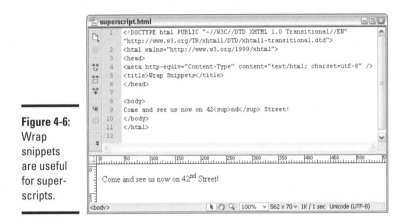

Figure 4-6:
Wrap
snippets
are useful
for super-
scripts.

Applying wrap snippets is a little different than block type snippets because if you want the code to wrap around the content, you must select the copy on your page that you want to apply the snippet to *before* you insert the snippet code. Using the 42nd Street example, highlight the nd in Design view first, and then insert the snippet. Because this snippet contains simple HTML tags, Dreamweaver's Design view renders and displays the superscript code for you, without the need to launch a browser to see it. Alternately, you don't have to apply wrap tags to existing text; you could insert the wrap snippet on the page first and then add content between the tags at a later time.

Creating a snippet with graphics

Good uses for graphic snippets include

+ **Special symbol graphics:** Create a graphic with a stylized ™ or other symbol in a particular font.

+ **Animated GIFs:** Design an animated graphic, such as a flashing NEW graphic, to add next to special entries on your site.

+ **Reusable page elements:** Build reusable elements with For Placement Only (FPO) text and graphics, such as a sidebar subnavigation area.

Snippets with graphics work the same as snippets with text and JavaScript, but with one added benefit when you choose Design as the Preview Type in the Snippet dialog box. Like the Design or Code views you see when editing a page in Dreamweaver, the Snippets panel has a little preview pane above the named list of snippets. Selecting Design as the preview type in the Snippet dialog box makes Dreamweaver render the code in the preview pane as it would in Design view (see Figure 4-7). By contrast, if you select Code as the preview type, Dreamweaver shows the code of the snippet in the preview pane.

Figure 4-7:
The snippet displays in the preview pane of the Snippets panel.

Adding keyboard shortcuts to play snippets

You can easily and quickly customize keyboard shortcuts to run any of your snippets with key commands using Dreamweaver's Keyboard Shortcut Editor. You can also create, remove, and edit shortcuts at any time.

To create custom keyboard shortcuts for your snippets, follow these steps:

1. **Choose Edit➪Keyboard Shortcuts (Windows) or Dreamweaver➪Keyboard Shortcuts (Mac).**

   The Keyboard Shortcuts dialog box appears.

2. **Create a duplicate of the default Macromedia Standard shortcut set by clicking the Duplicate button. Name your duplicate set.**

   Making a duplicate set ensures that you can always go back to the factory default settings in the future if you need to.

3. **Select Snippets from the Commands drop-down list to see a list of your custom snippets along with the standard snippets.**

4. **Navigate through the list to find the snippet you want to assign a keyboard shortcut to.**

5. **Click the plus (+) button to add a shortcut.**

6. **Place your cursor in the Press Key field and press the combination of shortcut keys.**

   Be careful not to use a key combination reserved for programs other than Dreamweaver, such as F11, F12, or ⌘+H on a Mac, or Option+R on Windows.

   Be sure to press all the keys at once, such as Ctrl+Alt+Shift+9 (Windows) or ⌘+Opt+Shift+9 (Mac). Dreamweaver displays alerts for any shortcut key combos that are already assigned to another function within the program so you won't accidentally overwrite one of the presets. Feel free, though, to overwrite a preset if you find it useful.

7. **Click OK when done.**

   Your new shortcut works immediately.

To see all the existing keyboard shortcuts at a glance, export a copy by clicking the Export Set As HTML button inside the dialog box.

If you do not see your image rendered in the preview pane in the Snippets panel, you may need to edit your snippet code to use site root-relative linking for the graphic instead of the default document-relative link.

Here's an example of a document-relative image link:

```
<p><img src="images/trademark.gif" width="87" height="87" border="1"></p>
```

To make the image link site-root relative, you must add a forward slash (/) before the graphic source folder, like this:

```
<p><img src="/images/trademark.gif" width="87" height="87" border="1"></p>
```

You may also need to add the forward slash (/) to any HREF links in your graphic snippets, as in this site root-relative link example:

```
<a href="/about.html">about</a>
```

For a thorough discussion about site root-relative versus document-relative linking, see Book I, Chapter 3 on root level organization.

Working with Snippets

Snippets are easy to edit and delete and easy to file and manage. You can even share snippets with your coworkers.

Sharing snippets

If you want to share your custom snippets with other members of your work team, you can easily copy them from one computer to another. Here's how to share Code Snippets:

1. **Find and copy them from the Configuration/Snippets folder inside of the Dreamweaver application folder.**

   You can find and copy the snippet files (.CSN format) outside of the Dreamweaver application using the Windows File Manager or Mac Finder.

2. **Paste them into a shared folder on your computer/network or e-mail them to your co-workers.**

3. **Have the other team members copy the snippet files to their Configuration/Snippets folders in their Dreamweaver application folders.**

   After they're in place, the snippets are ready to use.

You should be able to find your custom snippets in the Adobe Dreamweaver Configuration folder, but that folder can actually be in a few different places on your computer, depending on your platform. See Danilo Celic's blog entry at www.communitymx.com/blog/index.cfm?newsid=27 for possible locations on both a Mac and a PC. To see your custom snippets, you may need to try adjusting the Application Data (Windows) or Application Support (Mac) folder properties to view both hidden and read-only files.

If you're interested in a faster method for sharing your custom snippets with others, visit Massimo Foti's Web site at www.massimocorner.com, where you can download his free Dreamweaver Snippets Import/Export 1.0 Extension (click the Utilities link under Dreamweaver Extensions). Install the extension with Adobe's Extension Manager (see Book IV, Chapter 2 for instructions on using the Manager). After they're installed, the tool lets you import and export snippets straight from the Snippets panel.

Editing snippets

After you create a snippet, you'll probably rarely need to edit it. However, some snippets may contain specific dates or graphics that need occasional updating or editing. Additionally, you may want to create a new version of an existing snippet. In any case, editing a code snippet is simple and straightforward.

To edit a snippet, follow these steps:

1. **Select the snippet from the Snippets panel and click the Edit Snippet button at the bottom of the panel.**

   The Snippet dialog box appears.

2. **Make any desired changes to the snippet.**

3. **When finished, click OK and the new changes are ready to use.**

Deleting snippets

To delete a Code Snippet quickly and permanently, select the snippet from the Snippets panel and then either click the Remove button (refer to Figure 4-1) or press the Delete key.

Dreamweaver always displays an alert dialog box asking if you're sure you want to delete that particular snippet, giving you a chance to cancel the command if you change your mind about deleting it.

Managing snippets

One of the cool things about the Snippets panel is that you can create folders to manage your snippets into logical categories. Moving snippets around the Snippets panel, from folder to folder, is as easy as dragging and dropping.

If you want to create a new folder for your snippets, follow these steps:

1. **Click the New Snippet Folder button at the bottom of the Snippets panel.**

2. **Type a name for the new folder and then press Enter (Windows) or Return (Mac).**

   If you don't name it, the folder is called "untitled" by default, but you can always change the name later.

Rename and delete folders as needed. To delete a folder, select it and click the Delete button at the bottom of the Snippets panel.

Creating History Panel Commands

The History panel is one of those panels that many Dreamweaver users don't take full advantage of. When a document is open in the Dreamweaver workspace, the History panel records all the actions you make in the file up to a certain number of steps (specified in the General category of the Preferences dialog box). Keep in mind that after you save and close the document, the history steps associated with the file go away; when you reopen the file, a new history is created.

Through the History panel, you can take multiple steps backwards with the use of the panel's slider as well as copy and paste steps to use on the current or other open documents. In addition to using the History panel to undo and redo steps, you can also record your own custom actions and save them as reusable, playable commands to automate repetitive actions.

Working with the History Panel

To view the panel, choose Window➪History or press Shift+F10. As you work, notice how the panel records each step you make. For example, when you type text, a typing layer displays the copy you just entered. When you apply bold to your text, an Apply Bold layer appears in the panel. Each action creates a new action layer in the panel, as shown in Figure 4-8.

To undo a single step in your document, drag the slider in the History panel up a layer in the list (or choose Edit➪Undo). To undo multiple steps, simply drag the slider to the desired step in the History panel or click to the left of the path next to the slider to scroll automatically to that step. After undoing a single step or multiple steps, any subsequent new actions erase and overwrite previous actions.

Although it's not advised, you can erase the history list for a document by right-clicking (Windows) or Control+clicking (Mac) the History panel and choosing Clear History. After clearing the history in this manner, you can't undo any steps in your document.

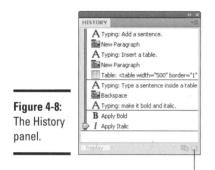

Figure 4-8:
The History
panel.

Record

Recording commands

To record and save a command, be sure the panel is open before you perform the actions you want to save. After you perform the actions, you can
record and save them.

Keep these points in mind when recording actions:

✦ Use the arrow keys instead of the mouse to move the insertion point in
the document. You can also use the arrow keys plus Shift to make or
extend a selection. Mouse movements aren't saved and are identified in
the History panel with a black divider line between the steps.

✦ Other actions are also unrepeatable, such as dragging an asset from one
place on the page to another. These types of steps display a small red X
next to the action layer in the History panel.

Follow these steps to record and save a command:

1. **Open the History panel by choosing Window⇨History.**

Press Shift+F10 to quickly open the panel.

2. **Edit your document.**

The History panel records all your actions as individual steps.

3. **In the History panel, select the step you want to record.**

To select multiple steps, Shift+click to select consecutive steps;
Ctrl+click (Windows) or ⌘+click (Mac) to select or deselect non-
consecutive steps.

4. **Click the Save Selected Steps as a Command button at the bottom of
the panel.**

The Save As Command dialog box appears, prompting you to enter a
name for the new command.

5. **Name the new command.**

   Name your commands using simple descriptive titles, such as Bold & Italic.

6. **Click OK.**

   The new command appears by name at the bottom of the Commands menu.

You can also make a temporary command by clicking the Copy Selected Steps to the Clipboard button at the bottom of the panel after selecting a series of steps. The steps are temporarily stored on the Clipboard for easy pasting into any open document in Design view.

New commands are saved as JavaScript or HTML files in the Dreamweaver/Configuration/Commands folder.

Playing commands

Playing a saved command is as easy as choosing it by name from the Commands menu. For example, if you create a Bold and Italic command that bolds and italicizes a selection, select some text on your document and then choose Commands➪Bold and Italic to play the command, as shown in Figure 4-9.

Figure 4-9: Select the command you created from the Commands menu.

Commands	Site	Window	Help
Start Recording			Ctrl+Shift+X
Play Recorded Command			
Edit Command List...			
Get More Commands...			
Get AIR Extension...			
Manage Extensions...			
Check Spelling			Shift+F7
Apply Source Formatting			
Apply Source Formatting to Selection			
Clean Up XHTML...			
Clean Up Word HTML...			
Externalize JavaScript...			
Remove FLV Detection			
Optimize Image...			
Create Web Photo Album...			
Sort Table...			
Insert Mark of the Web			
Bold and Italic			

More options are available when playing commands with the History panel. You may repeat the last step, repeat a series of consecutive or touching steps, or repeat a series of nonconsecutive steps:

✦ **Repeat a single step:** Select a step in the History panel and click the Replay button. Or choose Edit➪Redo (Action).

✦ **Repeat a series of consecutive steps:** Select the steps in the History panel and click the Replay button.

To select multiple steps, either drag from one step to another or click the first step and Shift+click the last step. Whichever steps are highlighted are the ones that play.

✦ **Repeat a series of non-consecutive steps:** Select a step in the History panel and Ctrl+click (Windows) or ⌘+click (Mac) to select other steps; then click the Replay button. Steps replay in the order they appear in the History panel.

✦ **Deselect a selected step:** Ctrl+click (Windows) or ⌘+click (Mac) the step.

You can also copy and paste steps from one open document to another, as each file has its own history of steps. Simply select the steps and click the Copy Steps button in the History panel. Then choose Edit➪Paste in the new document to paste the steps.

If you paste selected steps into a text editor (like Notepad or TextEdit), Code view, or the Code inspector, you may notice that the pasted information appears as JavaScript, which can be really useful for learning to write your own Dreamweaver scripts. For example, the copied command to insert and resize an image is this:

```
<img src="image23.gif" width="100" height="46" />
```

This line appears in a text editor as a bit of JavaScript like this:

```
dw.getDocumentDOM().insertHTML('<img src=\"image23.gif\">', false);
dw.getDocumentDOM().resizeSelection('100', '46');
```

Renaming and deleting commands

After saving a new command, you can rename or delete it.

To rename a command:

1. **Choose Commands➪Edit Command List.**

2. **Select the command in the list and enter a new name.**

3. **Click the Close button.**

To delete a command:

1. **Choose Commands➪Edit Command List.**

**Book III
Chapter 4**

**Creating Code
Snippets and History
Panel Commands**

2. **Select the command in the list and click the Delete button.**

Clicking the Delete button permanently removes the command from the Commands menu.

3. **Click the Close button.**

Recording commands with the Commands menu

Another way to record temporary commands is to use the Commands menu instead of the History panel. Temporary commands stay on the Commands menu and you can play them on any open document as long as you have Dreamweaver open. Temporary commands disappear when you do one of the following:

- You close Dreamweaver. The temporary command is erased.

- You record a new temporary command. The new command takes the place of the old command.

To record a temporary command:

1. **Choose Commands⇨Start Recording before performing the steps you want to copy.**

   You can also begin the recording process by pressing Ctrl+Shift+X (Windows) or ⌘+Shift+X (Mac).

2. **Perform the steps.**

   Whenever possible, press the arrow keys instead of moving the mouse to reposition the cursor during the recording process.

3. **When finished, choose Commands⇨Stop Recording.**

To play back a temporary command, choose Commands⇨Play Recorded Command.

You can also begin the playback process by pressing Ctrl+Shift+R (Windows) or ⌘+Shift+R (Mac).

To save a temporary command into a permanent command with the History panel:

1. **Choose Commands⇨Play Recorded Command.**

   The command plays and displays a new Run Command step at the bottom of the History panel.

2. **Select the new Run Command step in the History panel and click the Save As Command button.**

   The Save As Command dialog box opens.

3. **Name the command and click OK to save it.**

   The command now appears at the bottom of the Commands menu.

Click the Get More Commands link on the Command menu to launch Adobe's Dreamweaver Exchange to browse for and download additional commands.

Chapter 5: Integrating Dreamweaver with Fireworks

In This Chapter

✔ **Working with Fireworks**

✔ **Setting launch-and-edit preferences**

✔ **Inserting Fireworks images**

✔ **Making changes to your Fireworks images and tables**

✔ **Image optimizing in Fireworks**

✔ **Inserting, pasting, and updating Fireworks HTML**

Dreamweaver is tightly integrated with Adobe Fireworks, a Web image creation, editing, and optimization program. Fireworks lets you create animations, pop-up menus, and *rollover buttons* (buttons that change in appearance when you mouse over them); *optimize* your graphics (reduce the file size while preserving image quality to improve download times in a browser); and export graphics, HTML, and JavaScript code to an HTML editor like Dreamweaver — all without needing to know a lick of code.

When used together, Fireworks and Dreamweaver provide you with a smooth process for editing, optimizing, and exporting graphics into HTML pages. This process, called *roundtrip editing,* enables you to make seamless updates to your Fireworks graphic and HTML files while working in Dreamweaver. The code stays accurate to preserve links and other functionality such as rollover behaviors.

During the roundtrip editing process, Fireworks creates special *Design Notes* about all the graphics and HTML exported to Dreamweaver. The Notes, which are generated during the graphic export process, are sent from Fireworks into Dreamweaver, store references to the Web-ready images (GIF, JPEG, HTML), and enable Dreamweaver to quickly locate them and the Fireworks source files (PNG) they were created from. In addition, the Design Notes often include information about the export process itself, such as the location of JavaScript data within the HTML files and details such as rollover capabilities and hotspots about the graphics inside of table cells.

To be fair, Fireworks is not a prerequisite for creating or designing Web sites, so please don't feel that you must run out and buy Fireworks to successfully build a Web site; it's entirely possible to build an entire Web site without using Fireworks or any of its features. Many designers actually prefer to use other design, illustration, and Web graphic optimization programs, such as Photoshop, Illustrator, or an old copy of ImageReady CS2 to create their Web graphics. What Fireworks is required for, however, are all the features described in this chapter.

To download a free 30-day trial version of Fireworks, go to www.adobe.com/products/fireworks/.

This chapter presumes that you already own and know how to use Fireworks but need help using it together with Dreamweaver. Here you find out how to insert Fireworks images, edit images and tables, optimize your images in Fireworks, and add and edit Fireworks HTML in Dreamweaver.

Preparing to Work with Dreamweaver and Fireworks

Before you begin a roundtrip editing process, you must enable a few settings within Fireworks and Dreamweaver to ensure the smoothest possible integration between the programs. Specifically, you must configure your launch-and-edit preferences in Fireworks, and optimize Dreamweaver for working with Fireworks by adding Fireworks as a primary image editor.

Setting Fireworks launch-and-edit preferences

If you use Fireworks to create and edit images, by default Fireworks exports those images from a source PNG (Portable Network Graphics) file. PNG is an image compression file format that allows for the exporting of Web graphics with the highest image quality and a relatively small file size. A source PNG file is a master file that Fireworks uses to generate Web-ready graphics.

When creating graphics in Fireworks, be sure to store the PNG source files in a different place on your computer than the Web graphics generated from them so you don't accidentally alter them.

By default, when you edit a Fireworks image within Dreamweaver, Fireworks launches and automatically reopens the source PNG file. This is the Fireworks default launch-and-edit preference. You can also set the preferences in Fireworks to either have Dreamweaver open and directly edit the inserted graphics (which is not a good choice because Dreamweaver is not an image editing or optimization application) or have Fireworks open and use the inserted Web-ready image for editing instead of the image's source PNG file (which is not good either because the original source PNG always generates better quality Web graphics than an already optimized Web graphic).

You should note that Dreamweaver only recognizes these launch-and-edit preferences when certain conditions apply:

✦ You must specifically open and optimize images that include the right Design Notes path to the source PNG file. You can ensure you're using the right Design Notes path to the source PNG by selecting the Always Use Source PNG option for the launch-and-edit preference (see the next section).

✦ The image can't be a part of a Fireworks table. Fireworks tables use a series of images with the HTML code. You must always open the source PNG file inside Fireworks to edit any of the graphics from within Dreamweaver.

To set Fireworks' launch-and-edit preferences, follow these steps:

1. **Choose Edit➪Preferences (Windows) or Fireworks➪Preferences (Mac) to open the Fireworks Preferences dialog box.**

2. **Click the Launch and Edit option in the Category listing on the left side of the dialog box.**

   After this option is selected, the Launch and Edit options appear on the right side of the panel, as shown in Figure 5-1.

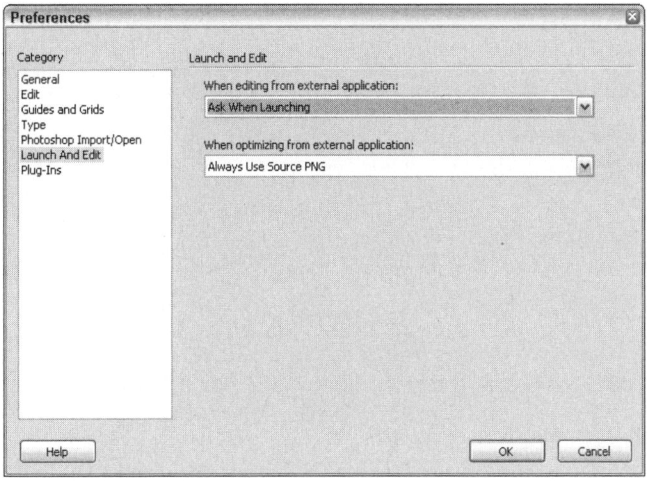

Figure 5-1:
Choose
launch-
and-edit
preferences
in Fireworks.

3. **Set the Launch and Edit preference options for editing and optimizing Fireworks images to be exported to external applications such as Dreamweaver. Select one of the following options in each of the drop-down lists:**

   • **Always Use Source PNG:** (Recommended) This setting enables Fireworks to open the PNG file defined in Design Notes as the source for the externally placed graphics. When edits are made to the source PNG, all those changes are automatically updated in the exported or placed Web graphic.

- **Never Use Source PNG:** This option tells Fireworks to open the placed graphic for editing, even if a source PNG file is available. Changes to the graphic are permanent and appear in the placed graphic. The source PNG file stays the same.

- **Ask When Launching:** If you want to use both methods intermittently, select this option to choose the PNG file or the placed graphic on a case-by-case basis.

4. **When you finish, click OK to save your changes.**

Optimizing Dreamweaver for use with Fireworks

Make the following changes to optimize Dreamweaver for use with Fireworks.

Enable Design Notes

Verify that the managed site you're creating or using has Design Notes enabled. This is the default site setting in Dreamweaver.

1. **Choose Site⊃Manage Sites.**

2. **Select your site and click the Edit button in the Manage Sites dialog box.**

3. **Click the Advanced tab in the Site Definition dialog box.**

4. **Choose Design Notes from the Category list and verify that the Maintain Design Notes option is enabled.**

   If you want to share Design Notes with others on your team, also enable the Upload Design Notes for Sharing option.

Add Fireworks as an image editor

In the Dreamweaver Preferences dialog box, set Fireworks as the primary external image editor for selected graphics files. This enables Fireworks to be the editor that automatically launches for editing your placed graphics files. For example, you may want to launch Fireworks as the primary editor for GIF and PNG files, and another application for editing JPEG files.

To add Fireworks as an image editor, follow these steps:

1. **Choose Edit⊃Preferences (Windows) or Dreamweaver⊃Preferences (Mac).**

   The Dreamweaver Preferences dialog box appears.

2. **In the File Types/Editors category, as shown in Figure 5-2, click the plus (+) button to add Fireworks (and any other applications you want to include) as an editor for any of the graphic extensions.**

Dreamweaver doesn't automatically detect that you have Fireworks installed so you must enter the path to the Fireworks application in the Fireworks text box.

3. **To make Fireworks the primary editor for any selected extension on the left, select Fireworks from the list of editors on the right and click the Make Primary button.**

   For example, after adding Fireworks to the list in Step 2, select it and click the Make Primary button. The Fireworks application name has (Primary) appended to it.

4. **Click OK when you're finished.**

Save all your Fireworks files in the same site folder

Save all your Fireworks PNG source and Web-ready files in the same Dreamweaver site folder. This ensures that everyone in a workgroup can easily find and edit all the source files for the site.

Export Fireworks image files to the same site folder

Exporting Web graphics from Fireworks into a Dreamweaver site folder ensures that Design Notes are integrated and up-to-date. Fireworks creates a Notes folder for the Design Notes, which Dreamweaver uses to update code and graphics.

Using Fireworks Images in Dreamweaver

When you're ready to insert Fireworks images into your Dreamweaver document, you can do so two ways. The first way is to place exported Fireworks graphics directly into a file by choosing Insert⇨Image in Dreamweaver. The other way is to design images in Fireworks to replace Dreamweaver image placeholders.

Inserting a Fireworks image in a Dreamweaver document

When you've designed, saved, and exported your graphics from Fireworks, you're ready to import those exported graphics into a Dreamweaver document. If you need help creating, saving, and exporting Fireworks graphics, refer to the Fireworks Help files or download a copy of the Fireworks manual from Adobe at www.adobe.com/support/documentation/en/fireworks/.

Follow these steps to insert an exported Fireworks image into a Dreamweaver file:

1. **In Dreamweaver, click inside the document where you want the image to go and choose Insert⇨Image.**

Or, on the Common category of the Insert panel, click and drag the Image button into the open document.

The Select Image Source dialog box opens.

2. **Browse to and select the exported Fireworks image and click OK (Windows) or Open (Mac) to complete the insertion.**

If you select an image from outside the Dreamweaver local managed site folder, a message appears asking if you want Dreamweaver to copy the file into the root folder of the managed Dreamweaver site. Click Yes.

Now you can easily edit your images in Fireworks using the roundtrip editing feature, as described in "Editing Images in Fireworks Tables," later in the chapter.

Replacing an image placeholder with a Fireworks graphic

In Dreamweaver, you can create *image placeholders* that set aside space for graphics that haven't been created yet. (See Book II, Chapter 3 for details on creating image placeholders.) With roundtrip editing, you can select an individual image placeholder in Dreamweaver and use Fireworks to create a graphic to replace it.

Before beginning the roundtrip editing process, be sure that you specify Fireworks as the image editor for .png files (as described in "Optimizing Dreamweaver for Use with Fireworks," earlier in the chapter) and create all the image placeholders in a Dreamweaver document.

Follow these steps to replace a Dreamweaver image placeholder with a Fireworks image:

1. **In your Dreamweaver document, select the image placeholder (see Figure 5-3) that you want to replace.**

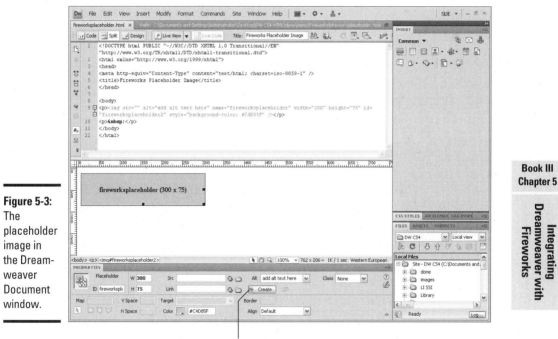

Figure 5-3:
The placeholder image in the Dreamweaver Document window.

The Create button

Book III
Chapter 5

Integrating Dreamweaver with Fireworks

2. **Click the Create button in the Properties inspector to launch Fireworks.**

Fireworks opens the selected image placeholder in Editing from Dreamweaver mode.

3. **In Fireworks, design the replacement image.**

Fireworks detects image placeholder settings from Dreamweaver, such as image width and height, alternate text, and image ID, as well as links, text alignment settings, and JavaScript behaviors, and uses these settings as the basis for the replacement graphic. Therefore, you may just see an empty white canvas instead of an exact replica of the placeholder image.

Links assigned to image placeholders in Dreamweaver are maintained but are not visible inside Fireworks. Therefore, if you add a new link or hotspot from within Fireworks, the original Dreamweaver link is still there. However, if you cut a slice from the image in Fireworks, the Dreamweaver link is deleted when the image gets updated.

4. **In the Fireworks Optimize panel, select an image optimization setting, such as JPG, PNG, or GIF.**

   Select JPG for photographs or images with lots of gradient blends, and select GIF or PNG for images with large flat areas of color.

5. **Select File⇨Export to export a copy of the optimized graphic into the Dreamweaver managed site.**

   If you haven't managed a site in Dreamweaver yet, quickly transfer over to Dreamweaver and create a managed site before proceeding.

6. **When you finish designing the image (see Figure 5-4), click the Done button at the top of the image document window to save the original PNG file for future editing.**

The Done button

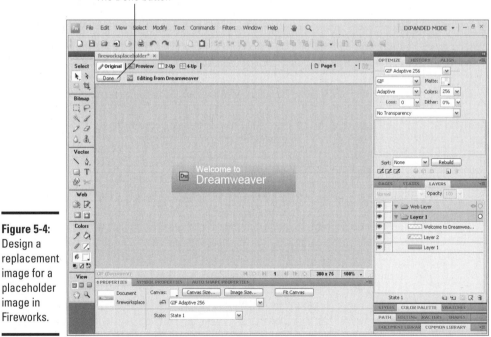

Figure 5-4:
Design a replacement image for a placeholder image in Fireworks.

Fireworks launches the Save As dialog box, prompting you to save the PNG file.

7. Browse to and select the root folder of your managed Dreamweaver site as the location to save the PNG file.

Or, better yet, save the PNG file into a different location so that you can keep track of the original file separate from the optimized graphics you create from it.

8. Enter a name in the File Name text box.

If you previously named the image in Dreamweaver when creating the image placeholder, the File Name text box is already filled in with that name.

9. Click the Save button to save the PNG file.

The Export dialog box opens.

10. From the Export dialog box, select the Dreamweaver site folder for the Save In option.

You'll be saving an optimized version of the file here.

11. Enter a name in the Name text box.

Again, the PNG filename is in the Name text box.

12. Choose a graphic type from the Save as Type drop-down list.

Select the file type (GIF or JPEG) or the type of file you're exporting, such as HTML and Images, Images Only, or HTML Only.

13. Click the Save or Export button to save the optimized file.

The replacement image PNG file is saved, Fireworks gets minimized, and you return to Dreamweaver, where the exported Web-ready file (or Fireworks table) has replaced the image placeholder, as shown in Figure 5-5.

Repeat these steps for each Dreamweaver image placeholder you want to replace. If a replacement graphic file needs further editing, select the image in Dreamweaver and click the Edit button in the Properties inspector, as described in the next section, "Editing Images in Fireworks Tables."

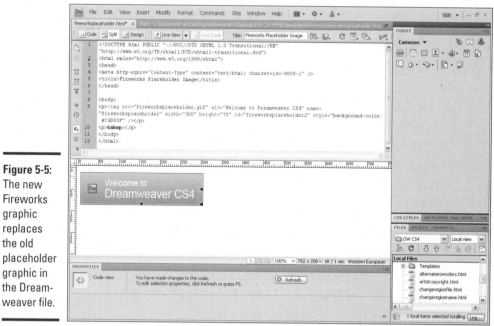

Figure 5-5:
The new
Fireworks
graphic
replaces
the old
placeholder
graphic in
the Dream-
weaver file.

Editing Images in Fireworks Tables

Fireworks *tables* are Fireworks-generated navigation bars, pop-up menus, and sliced images, which have nothing to do with traditional HTML tables.

Before editing any images containing Fireworks tables, be sure you've set up Fireworks launch-and-edit preferences and optimized Dreamweaver for use with Fireworks (refer to the "Preparing to Work with Dreamweaver and Fireworks" section, earlier in this chapter).

Then, if you want to edit a Fireworks image in your Dreamweaver document, you can either have Dreamweaver launch Fireworks to edit it there or use the limited image editing tools (crop, resample, brightness and contrast, and sharpen) to edit your image within Dreamweaver.

When editing images or image *slices* (graphics that are cut into smaller pieces) that are part of a Fireworks table, Dreamweaver opens Fireworks automatically, which in turn opens the source PNG file for the entire Fireworks table.

When editing images that are part of a Fireworks table, you can edit the entire table as long as the `<!--fw table-->` comment tag is visible in the HTML code. That comment gets automatically inserted whenever the source PNG gets exported from Fireworks to a Dreamweaver site using the Dreamweaver Style HTML and Images setting.

To edit Fireworks images placed in Dreamweaver files, follow these steps:

1. **In Dreamweaver, select the image or image slice in the open document that you want to edit.**

   The Properties inspector identifies the selected graphic as a Fireworks image or Fireworks table right below the Properties inspector tab, along with the name of the source PNG file.

2. **Click the Edit button in the Properties inspector to launch Fireworks.**

   Fireworks opens the source PNG file for editing (see Figure 5-6). If Fireworks can't find the source PNG file, it prompts you to find it. If the source file is missing, you can use the inserted image as the source for the edits.

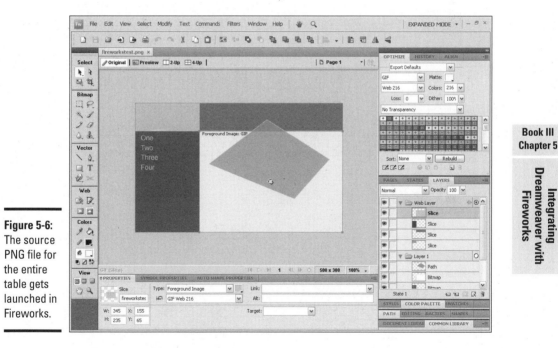

Figure 5-6:
The source PNG file for the entire table gets launched in Fireworks.

3. **In Fireworks, edit the source PNG file.**

4. **When finished, click the Done button.**

   Fireworks saves the changes to the PNG file, exports the updated graphic (or HTML with images), and returns to Dreamweaver, where the updated image or table appears in the open document.

Optimizing Your Images in Fireworks

Before you add Fireworks images to your Dreamweaver document, you should *optimize* those images for use on the Web. By optimizing your images, you reduce the amount of time the user's browser takes to download and display the images. By optimizing images in Fireworks, you can

✦ Reduce the image file size while maintaining image quality

✦ Change the file format of the Web-ready image

✦ Adjust color depth and other format-specific options to control file size

After inserting your images into a Dreamweaver document, you can still make changes to those images using a special Image Preview dialog box.

To change settings for Fireworks images placed in Dreamweaver, follow these steps:

1. **In Dreamweaver, select the image you want to optimize from an open document and choose Commands⇨Optimize Image.**

If the placed image in the document has a source PNG file, Fireworks uses that file. However, if that source file cannot be found, Fireworks may prompt you to locate the source PNG file.

The Image Preview dialog box opens, as shown in Figure 5-7.

Figure 5-7:
Use the Image Preview optimization dialog box to change optimization settings of Fireworks images placed in Dreamweaver files.

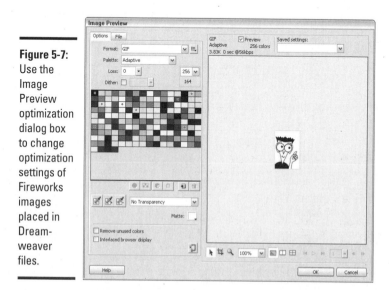

2. **On the Options tab, change the optimization settings to support the selected file format:**

   - **Format:** Select a file format for the optimized graphic. Choose from GIF, JPEG, PNG-8, PNG-24, or PNG-32.

   - **Palette:** (GIFs and PNGs only) Choose a color palette for the graphic. Options include Adaptive, Web Adaptive, Web 216, Exact, Windows and Macintosh, Grayscale, Black and White, Uniform, and Custom.

   - **Loss:** (GIFs only) Add a loss setting to compress GIF files for smaller file sizes. The higher the number, the smaller the file, but the greater the potential loss of image quality.

   - **Dither:** (GIFs and PNGs only) Enable the dithering option to control how colors not in the selected palette are approximated using colors within the palette.

   - **Transparency:** (GIFs and PNGs only) Choose a transparency setting.

   - **Quality:** (JPEGs only) Adjust the quality setting to control the loss of image quality during compression. Higher numbers produce better quality images with larger file sizes.

   - **Smoothing:** (JPEGs only) Enable a smoothing setting to blur hard edges in the graphic and reduce file size. Higher numbers reduce file size but can distort the quality of the image.

   - **Matte:** Select a matte color for graphic to match the color of the page the graphic or object will be on top of.

3. **On the File tab, edit the scale and export area of the graphic file.**

   To modify the size of the image, adjust the Scale field in percentages or type the exact pixels in the Width and Height fields.

   To optimize and export only part of the selected graphic, enter X and Y coordinates relative to the original graphic dimensions as well as W and H sizes.

4. **Click the Update button when finished.**

   The updated image exports with any new settings. Exporting includes updating the placed GIF or JPEG file in Dreamweaver, as well as the source PNG file.

   If the image format has changed, Dreamweaver's link checker prompts you to verify the graphic's link references. For instance, if you changed the format of a graphic called submit.jpg from JPEG to GIF, click OK and all references to submit.jpg are converted to submit.gif.

Using Fireworks HTML in Dreamweaver

You can quickly insert Fireworks-generated HTML (including all graphics, formatting, and JavaScript behaviors) into a Dreamweaver document. This roundtrip feature lets you design Web elements in Fireworks and add them to new or existing Dreamweaver files. Or as an alternative, you can simply copy and paste your HTML code from Fireworks to Dreamweaver. Either method allows you to design in Fireworks. For example, you can create a navigation bar with a series of buttons, each of which has JavaScript rollover functionality including a hyperlink to another page.

Inserting Fireworks HTML in a Dreamweaver document

After you design your Web elements in Fireworks, inserting the element into your Web page is a two-step process: You must export the HTML into a managed Dreamweaver site and then insert it on your Dreamweaver page.

Follow these steps to export the Fireworks HTML into Dreamweaver:

1. **Select File⇨Export.**

The Export dialog box opens.

2. **Enter a filename for the exported HTML file, choose the Dreamweaver site folder as the Save in destination for the file, and select other options relative to the Export command.**

Select the desired export, HTML, and slices settings, such as HTML and Images, Export HTML File, and Export Slices.

3. **Click the Export button to complete the export process.**

After you export the Fireworks HTML into a Dreamweaver site folder, follow these steps to insert the exported HTML into a Dreamweaver document:

1. **In Dreamweaver, click your cursor inside the document where you want to insert the Fireworks HTML code.**

2. **Choose Insert⇨Image Objects⇨Fireworks HTML.**

You can also click the Insert Fireworks HTML button on the Common category of the Insert panel.

The Insert Fireworks HTML dialog box appears.

3. **Browse to and select the exported Fireworks HTML file.**

4. **(Optional) Check the Delete File After Insertion option if you want to delete the original files after the Fireworks HTML is inserted into the Dreamweaver file.**

If the original Fireworks HTML is on a network drive, however, it's immediately deleted. This setting does not affect source PNG files associated with the HTML.

5. Click OK.

Dreamweaver inserts the Fireworks HTML into the Dreamweaver file (see Figure 5-8). This insertion process includes HTML code, graphic images, slices, and JavaScript.

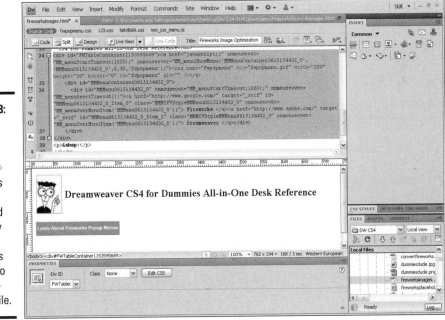

Figure 5-8:
Use the
Insert⇨
Image
Objects⇨
Fireworks
HTML
command
to quickly
insert
Fireworks
HTML into
a Dream-
weaver file.

Pasting Fireworks HTML in a Dreamweaver document

As an alternative to using the Insert Fireworks HTML command from the previous section, you can also copy and paste the Fireworks-generated HTML code directly inside a Dreamweaver file.

To copy and paste Fireworks HTML into a Dreamweaver document, follow these steps:

1. In Fireworks, choose Edit⇨Copy HTML Code.

Fireworks presumes you intend to copy the entire file, so unless you want to copy only a part of the graphic, you don't need to select anything.

The Copy HTML Code Wizard dialog box opens.

2. **Use the wizard to walk through the process of exporting Fireworks HTML and images. Click the Next button to proceed through each step in the wizard.**

   - **Screen 1:** Select an HTML or XHTML style for the copied HTML, such as Dreamweaver XHTML.

   - **Screen 2:** Enter a base filename for the copied graphic slices. For example, if the graphic is for a logo for ABC company, the base file-name might be abclogo. Click the Optional HTML settings button to specify additional settings for HTML output.

   - **Screen 3:** Click the Browse button to select a destination for the copied HTML code. Typically this is the root folder of your managed Dreamweaver site.

   - **Screen 4:** Click the Finish button. Web-ready images export to the destination folder, and the HTML code copies to your computer's Clipboard.

3. **In Dreamweaver, click your cursor inside the document where you want to paste the HTML code and choose Edit⇨Paste Fireworks HTML.**

   The copied Fireworks HTML and any associated JavaScript code are pasted into the Dreamweaver file. At the same time, links to the images inside the pasted code are updated to match the freshly exported Fireworks images in the Dreamweaver site folder.

Updating Fireworks HTML in a Dreamweaver Document

To edit Fireworks HTML files inserted in Dreamweaver documents from within Fireworks and without launching Dreamweaver, try the Fireworks Update HTML command. This command lets you make changes to source PNG files in Fireworks and automatically update exported HTML and image files placed in Dreamweaver, even if Dreamweaver isn't running.

Follow these steps to update any Fireworks HTML you have in your Dreamweaver document:

1. **In Fireworks, open the source PNG file for the Fireworks HTML that you want to edit.**

   Make any edits to the source PNG file that you need.

2. **Choose File⇨Save.**

   You must save your changes before moving on to the next step.

3. **Choose File⇨Update HTML.**

   In the Locate HTML File dialog box that opens, browse to and select the Dreamweaver folder containing the HTML file that needs updating.

4. **Select the file to be updated and click the Open button.**

   The Update HTML dialog box opens, where you can choose whether to replace images and associated HTML or only update images. Make your selection and click OK.

5. **In the Select Images Folder dialog box, select the folder in the Dreamweaver site where you want to place the updated image files, and click Select (Windows) or Choose (Mac).**

   The updated Fireworks HTML and images, including any associated JavaScript code, are saved into the Dreamweaver file.

Should Fireworks be unable to find a matching HTML file to update, you have the option of inserting new HTML into the chosen Dreamweaver file. Any JavaScript associated with the HTML is added into the document code appropriately.

Editing Fireworks Pop-Up Menus

A pop-up menu is a navigation menu that temporarily appears in a browser window when the user makes a specific mouse action. If you've created any pop-up menus in Fireworks 8 or later, you can now edit them either directly in Dreamweaver or use Fireworks roundtrip editing. If you created your pop-up menu in earlier versions of Fireworks, you have to edit it in Dreamweaver.

 If you make changes to your Fireworks pop-up menus directly in Dreamweaver and then subsequently make changes to them in Fireworks, you lose all your previous edits to the menus except for text changes. To avoid this, always create your menus in Fireworks first and then use Dreamweaver exclusively to customize the menus. However, if you prefer to do the menu editing in Fireworks, do not edit them in Dreamweaver at all and instead exclusively use the roundtrip editing feature.

Roundtrip pop-up menu editing (Fireworks 8 and later)

If you want to edit a pop-up menu that you created with Fireworks 8 or later, you can do roundtrip editing of the pop-up menu:

1. **In Dreamweaver, select the graphic in the Fireworks table that contains the Fireworks pop-up menu, and click the Edit button in the Properties inspector.**

Fireworks launches and opens the source PNG file for the pop-up menu.

2. **In Fireworks, select the slice in the table that has the pop-up menu you want to edit and choose Modify⇨Pop-up Menu⇨Edit Pop-up Menu.**

   The Fireworks Pop-up Menu Editor opens.

3. **Adjust the menu content, appearance, and position.**

4. **When you finish, click the Done button in the Pop-up Menu Editor to close the dialog box, and click the Done button on the Fireworks toolbar to save the changes to the menu.**

   The edited menu is updated in Dreamweaver.

Pop-up menu editing (Fireworks MX 2004 and earlier)

If you want to edit a pop-up menu you built with Fireworks MX 2004 or earlier, you can't use Fireworks' roundtrip editing. Instead, you must use Dreamweaver to edit the menu.

To edit pop-up menus created with Fireworks MX 2004 or earlier, follow these steps:

1. **In Dreamweaver, select the image or hotspot that triggers the pop-up menu.**

2. **In the Behaviors panel (choose Window⇨Behaviors), double-click the Show Pop-up Menu icon from the Actions list.**

   The Show Pop-up Menu dialog box opens where you can edit the menu. Note: The Show Pop-up Menu is a deprecated JavaScript behavior for Dreamweaver CS4, which means it is supported but no longer recommended as a method for creating popup menus.

3. **If needed, add, change, or rearrange menu items.**

4. **Click OK to save the changes.**

Chapter 6: Dreamweaver Cross-Application Integration

In This Chapter

✔ Working with Flash

✔ Inserting Photoshop images

✔ Accessing and using the Bridge

✔ Integrating with Device Central

✔ Getting the most out of Dreamweaver and AIR

*B*esides enabling you to add Fireworks images with JavaScript and HTML to your Dreamweaver pages, Dreamweaver provides cross-application integration with several other software programs as well, including Flash, Photoshop, Bridge, Device Central, and AIR. Whether you currently use these applications or have never even heard of some of them, this chapter provides you with a general overview of how each of them work with Dreamweaver.

In this chapter, you find out how to work with Flash to launch and edit source FLA files from any inserted SWF; insert and optimize Photoshop graphics into Dreamweaver using the Copy/Paste and Smart Object work-flows; edit both the optimized graphics as well as the original source PSD file; access and use Bridge to browse, find, organize, preview, and insert images into Dreamweaver; preview your Web content for mobile devices in Device Central; find tips on creating mobile Web content; and discover how to set up Dreamweaver to use Adobe AIR.

Working with Adobe Flash

Similar to the Fireworks workflow, Dreamweaver allows you to easily launch and edit the source FLA files for any SWF files inserted onto your Web pages and then return the updated file back to Dreamweaver. To do this, all you need to do is have Flash installed on your computer and configure Dreamweaver to be the primary editor of SWF files.

To make Flash the primary editor of FLA and SWF files, follow these steps:

1. **Choose Edit➪Preferences (Windows) or Fireworks➪Preferences (Mac) to open Dreamweaver's Preferences dialog box.**

2. **In the File Types/Editors category, as shown in Figure 6-1, select the .swf, .swt, .spl extension group under the Extensions listing. Under the Editors heading, select Flash, and then click the Make Primary button.**

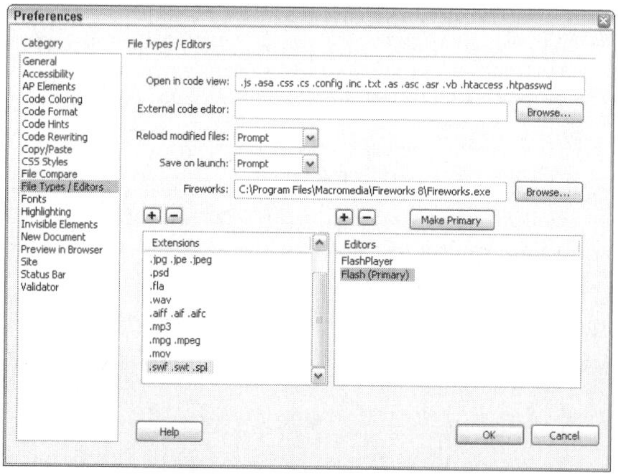

Figure 6-1:
Set Flash as
the Primary
editor for
.swf, .swt,
and .spl file
extensions.

By default, the FlashPlayer is set to be the primary editor associated with these files. By setting Flash as the primary editor, you can launch Flash from the Properties inspector to edit the FLA files associated with the SWF files inserted on your pages.

3. **Repeat Step 2 for any additional Flash file extensions you want Flash be the primary editor for.**

For example, you may want to add the .flv extension to the list and set Flash as the primary editor for those.

4. **Click OK when you're finished.**

To launch Flash as the editor for the original source FLA files associated with the SWF files inserted on your file, make sure the SWF file is saved somewhere inside your managed site, open the file containing the SWF, and then select the SWF file in your document window. After you've selected it, input the path to the source FLA file in the Flash SRC field on the Properties inspector and click the Flash Edit button. If Flash can't find the source file, you are prompted to find it. Additionally, if you're using the Check In/Check Out feature in the Files panel and the SWF or FLA files are locked, you may need to check out the SWF file before the file can be edited.

After you save the updated FLA file in Flash, the edited version of the SWF is re-exported to your document and Flash closes. You can also send the updated SWF file back to Dreamweaver without closing Flash by selecting File⇨Update for Dreamweaver.

Inserting and Optimizing Photoshop Graphics

If you don't own Fireworks but do have Photoshop, you'll be amazed at how well Photoshop integrates with Dreamweaver. You can use two different workflows when working with Photoshop and Dreamweaver, depending on your specific needs.

First, you can now use Dreamweaver to optimize your PSD files into Web graphics (GIF, PNG, and JPEG). When you insert the PSD file, Dreamweaver adds a Smart Object to the file, which links directly back to the original file if you need to make any edits to the optimized graphic.

Both Fireworks and Photoshop can be installed on the same computer and used for different Dreamweaver image editing tasks. To have Photoshop be the primary image editing program for particular file types, open Dreamweaver's Preferences and, in the File Types/Editors category, add Photoshop as the image editor for the desired file types.

Second, you can paste parts of or all of a layered or sliced Photoshop file into any Web page in Dreamweaver. Technically, the pasted graphics are not connected to the originals for round trip (from Photoshop to Dreamweaver, and back again) editing like you can do in Fireworks, nor are they connected to the original PSD file like Smart Objects are, but if you need to modify any graphics pasted into Dreamweaver in this way, you can easily go back into Photoshop to do your edits and then re-copy and paste the graphics back into Dreamweaver.

The Smart Objects workflow

A Smart Object is an image that has been placed from one Adobe application to another, retaining all of its original application's qualities. Smart Objects are linked to the original file in case they need to be altered. With Photoshop and Dreamweaver, the Smart Object workflow is the preferred method of using Dreamweaver to add optimized graphics to your Dreamweaver files.

In Dreamweaver, you can easily tell that a particular graphic is a Smart Object by the Smart Object icon that appears in the top left corner of the Smart Object image, as illustrated in Figure 6-2.

Smart Object icon

Figure 6-2:
Smart
Objects
display an
icon, making
them easy
to identify.

If at any time the original PSD file is edited after a Smart Object linked to it has been placed into your Dreamweaver file, Dreamweaver detects the change and makes one of the green arrows of the Smart Object icon turn red. You can then select the Smart Object graphic in Dreamweaver and easily update the graphic by pressing the Update from Original button in the Properties inspector. You can also update one or more Smart Objects at once through the Assets panel by selecting the image and choosing Update from Original from the Asset panel options menu.

Smart Objects can also be resized, cropped, resampled, sharpened, and have their brightness and contrast adjusted using the buttons on the Properties inspector. For details about using these tools, see Book II, Chapter 3.

To keep their design files separate from their Web files, most designers save the Photoshop PSD files that are used to create the SmartObjects outside of the managed Dreamweaver site. To make the editing process go more smoothly, you could put a copy of the PSD file at the root level of your managed site. However, if you do, be sure to cloak the PSD file so that the graphics are not uploaded to the server when publishing your site. (See Book V, Chapter III to learn more about cloaking.)

To place a Photoshop Smart Object into Dreamweaver, follow these steps:

1. **You can insert your Smart Object in either of the following two ways:**

- Drag and drop the desired Photoshop PSD file from the Files panel into the Design view area of your open Dreamweaver document.

- Select Insert⇨Image and select the Photoshop PSD file.

Either of these actions launches Dreamweaver's Image Preview dialog box, seen in Figure 6-3.

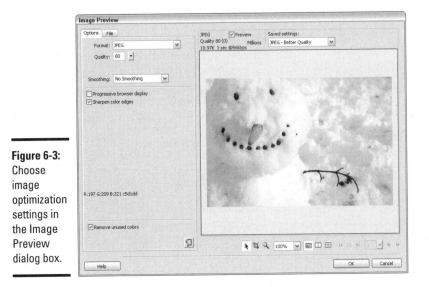

Figure 6-3:
Choose image optimization settings in the Image Preview dialog box.

2. **Select the desired file format and optimization settings in the Options tab.**

Format: Select a file format for the optimized graphic. Choose from GIF, JPEG, PNG-8, PNG-24, or PNG-32.

The file format you select determines how the rest of the dialog box looks. For instance, the JPG format offers different optimization settings than the PNG and GIF formats.

GIF and PNG settings:

- **Palette:** Choose a color palette for the graphic. Options include Adaptive, Web Adaptive, Web 216, Exact, Windows and Macintosh, Grayscale, Black and White, Uniform, and Custom.

- **Loss:** Add a loss setting to compress GIF files for smaller file sizes. The higher the number, the smaller the file, but the greater the potential loss of image quality.

- **Number of Colors:** Select the number of colors in your image from 2 to 256.

- **Dither:** Enable the dithering option to control how colors not in the selected palette are approximated using colors within the palette. Adjust the amount of dithering from 0-100% using the dithering menu.

- **Transparency:** Choose a transparency setting of either No, Index (for GIF), or Alpha (for PNG-8).

- **Matte:** Select a matte color for graphic to match the color of the page the graphic or object will be sitting on top of.

- **Remove Unused Colors:** Removes unused colors from the graphic, thereby making the file size smaller.

- **Interlaced Browser Display:** (GIFs and PNG-8 only) Makes the image load in multiple passes in the browser window, showing a low resolution image first and progressively improving the image until it is fully cached in the browser.

- **Optimize to Size:** Launches a wizard that allows you to optimize the graphic based on a desired file size in kilobytes (Kb). File size is reduced by making adjustments to the number of colors and dithering setting.

JPEG settings:

- **Quality:** Adjust the quality setting to control the loss of image quality during compression. Higher numbers produce better quality images with larger file sizes.

- **Smoothing:** Enable a smoothing setting to blur hard edges in the graphic and reduce file size. Higher numbers reduce file size but can distort the quality of the image.

- **Progressive Browser Display:** Makes the image load in multiple passes in the browser window, showing a low resolution image first and progressively improving the image until it is fully cached in the browser.

- **Sharpen Color Edges:** (JPEGs only) When enabled, this option provides a sharper image quality. Sharpen Color Edges is on by default.

- **Matte:** Select a matte color for graphic to match the color of the page the graphic or object will be sitting on top of.

- **Remove Unused Colors:** Removes unused colors from the graphic, thereby making the file size smaller.

- **Optimize to Size:** Launches a wizard that allows you to optimize the graphic based on a desired file size in kilobytes (Kb). File size is reduced by making adjustments to the number of colors and dithering setting.

3. **(Optional) On the File tab, edit the scale and export area of the pasted graphic.**

   To modify the size of the image, adjust the Scale field in percentages or type the exact pixels in the Width and Height fields.

   To optimize and export only part of the selected graphic, enter X and Y coordinates relative to the original graphic dimensions as well as W and H sizes.

4. **Click the OK button to save the optimized graphic.**

   Dreamweaver opens the Save Web Image dialog box.

5. **In the Save Web Image dialog box, select a destination and filename for your optimized graphic, and click the Save button.**

   For example, when working in a managed site in Dreamweaver, you might select the images folder sitting at the root level of your managed site as the location to save your images into. The name of the file is totally up to you, although you should try to name your graphics after their purpose so that they'll be easy to identify as you use them, such as nav_01.gif, onsalenow.jpg, or closeup.png.

   When Accessibility options are enabled for images, you'll be prompted to add Alt text for your Smart Object image in the Image Tag Accessibility Attributes dialog box. Either add the information and click the OK button, or click the Cancel button to add the image without Alt text.

Editing the Smart Object's Optimization Settings

To edit the optimization settings of a placed Smart Object image, select the image and click the Edit Image Settings button on the Properties inspector. This relaunches the Image Preview dialog box, inside which you can non-destructively adjust the optimization settings based on the original source PSD file. When you're finished adjusting these settings, save the updated optimized graphic and Dreamweaver overwrites the original optimized graphic with the new one.

Editing the Smart Object's Original PSD

To edit the original Photoshop PSD file linked to your Smart Object from within Dreamweaver, select the Smart Object in Design view of your open document and click the Edit button on the Properties inspector. When you are finished making changes to the Photoshop file, save the file in Photoshop. Upon returning to Dreamweaver, reselect the Smart Object and click the Update from Original button on the Properties inspector.

To watch a video tutorial about using Photoshop to create Smart Objects when inserting PSD files into Dreamweaver, go to www.adobe.com/go/vid0200.

The Copy/Paste workflow

To create an optimized graphic without inserting a Smart Object, you can use the Copy/Paste workflow. As mentioned previously, with this method, no Smart Object is created, which means there is no link to the original source Photoshop file. Therefore, to edit an image on your page that has been optimized in this fashion, you must reopen the original file in Photoshop and repeat the following steps to replace the current optimized graphic with a new one.

Any time you use the Copy/Paste workflow, Dreamweaver automatically adds Design Notes to your file that include image information such as the location of the source Photoshop file. To find out more about Design Notes, turn to Book VI, Chapter 1.

When you're ready to copy and paste your work from Photoshop into Dreamweaver, follow these steps:

1. **In Photoshop, select the slices or layers (or make a selection with any of the selection tools) and copy them by selecting Edit⇨Copy (for slices or a selection on a single layer) or Edit⇨Copy Merged (for selected layers or multi-layer selections).**

   If you're selecting slices, use the Edit Slice tool; when selecting layers, use the layers panel to Shift+Ctrl+click (Windows) or Shift+⌘+click (Mac) the thumbnails of the desired layers; for selections, use any of the marquee or magic wand selection tools.

2. **Switch over to Dreamweaver and select Edit⇨Paste.**

   Dreamweaver's Image Preview dialog box opens (see Figure 6-3).

3. **Select the desired optimization, scale, and export settings in the Options and File tabs of the dialog box.**

   Refer to the previous section "The Smart Object Workflow" for details on these settings.

4. **Click the OK button to save the optimized graphic.**

   Dreamweaver opens the Save Web Image dialog box.

5. **In the Save Web Image dialog box, select a destination and filename for your optimized graphic and click the Save button.**

   If you are prompted to do so, enter in an Image description to add the `alt` attribute to your optimized image when Dreamweaver inserts it onto your Web page. Otherwise, the image is inserted onto your page without it; you can always add or edit the Alt attribute to the selected image on the Properties inspector.

Editing the pasted optimized graphic's original PSD

If you need to make changes to a pasted optimized graphic after it has been added to your Dreamweaver page, repeat the preceding steps, making sure to save the updated graphic with the same filename into the same location in your managed site so that the new version overwrites the old version.

You can launch the original source PSD file in Photoshop from the pasted image in Dreamweaver if you first set Photoshop to be the default editor for that file extension in Dreamweaver's File/Types category of the Preferences dialog box, and then select the graphic and enter the path to the original Photoshop file in the Properties inspector. After you've done that, you can select the graphic in Design view and then click the Edit button on the Properties inspector, which in turn opens the original file in Photoshop. When you are finished making changes to the Photoshop file, save the file in Photoshop, and then repeat the Copy/Paste workflow steps above to create a new optimized graphic for Dreamweaver. If you save the new graphic with the same name as the old file, the new graphic replaces the old one.

Reoptimizing the pasted optimized graphic

To edit the optimization settings of an optimized image that you've added to your page using the Copy/Paste workflow, select the image and click the Edit Image Settings button on the Properties inspector. This relaunches the Image Preview dialog box, inside which you can non-destructively adjust the optimization settings based on the original source PSD file. When you're finished, save the updated optimized graphic and Dreamweaver overwrites the original optimized graphic with the new one.

To watch a video about the Copy/Paste workflow between different Adobe programs like Photoshop and Dreamweaver, go to `www.adobe.com/go/vid0193`.

Accessing and Using Adobe's Bridge

Adobe Bridge is simply one of the best cross-platform file browsing programs for finding, organizing, and previewing your files — both Adobe and non-Adobe — for all your Web, print, video, and audio projects. As an Adobe application, Bridge can be launched from any Creative Suite program (except Acrobat 8) or as a standalone application from where you can select a file and launch any Adobe Creative Suite program that supports the selected file's format.

Use Bridge, as seen here in Figure 6-4, with Dreamweaver to preview, sort, and search for files, add meta data, and insert selected files into your documents. You can also do automated tasks like batch renaming, as well as manage your digital photographs and stock art.

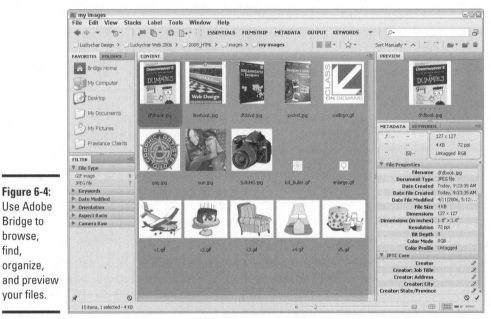

Figure 6-4:
Use Adobe
Bridge to
browse,
find,
organize,
and preview
your files.

To watch an Adobe video on the Adobe Bridge Web workflow, go to www. adobe.com/designcenter/video_workshop/?id=vid0192.

Launching Bridge from Dreamweaver

Launch Bridge from within Dreamweaver in any of the following ways:

✦ Select File➪Browse in Bridge.

✦ Launch Bridge using the keyboard shortcut, Ctrl+Alt+O (Windows) or ⌘+Option+O (Macintosh).

✦ Click the Bridge icon on the Standard Document toolbar. If hidden, select View➪Toolbars➪Standard to make the Standard toolbar visible.

Launching Dreamweaver from Bridge

To launch Dreamweaver from within Bridge, select File➪Open With➪Adobe Dreamweaver, or select a file and then right-click (Windows) or Control+ click (Macintosh) it to open the context menu, from which you may select Open With➪Adobe Dreamweaver.

Inserting a file from Bridge

After you've launched Bridge, you can select and insert a file into the location of your cursor in Dreamweaver's Design view by one of two methods:

✦ Drag and drop the selected file(s) from Bridge into your open Web document.

✦ Select a single file and choose File➪Place In Dreamweaver.

If the selected file is not already in your managed site's root folder or images folder, Dreamweaver prompts you to put a copy of the selected file in there. When inserting Web-ready graphics like GIF, PNG, and JPG files, you may also be prompted to add image tag accessibility attributes for your newly inserted file.

Integrating Your Files with Device Central

With Device Central, Dreamweaver users can now preview how their files will appear in a selection of different mobile devices. Within Device Central, which uses the Opera browser's Small Screen Rendering system, you can see how your mobile content looks on a small screen and test whether CSS and other Web page markup is coded correctly.

To begin previewing your Web content for mobile devices, open the file in Dreamweaver and select File➪Preview in Browser➪Device Central, or click the Preview/Debug in Browser button on the Document toolbar and select the option to Preview in Device Central.

After Device Central launches, as shown in Figure 6-5, your Web page displays inside the Emulator tab, where you can review your file as well as choose other devices listed in the Device Sets or Online Library panes.

One popular device, the Apple iphone, is unfortunately not available within Device Central, but you can test for that online at www.iphonetester.com.

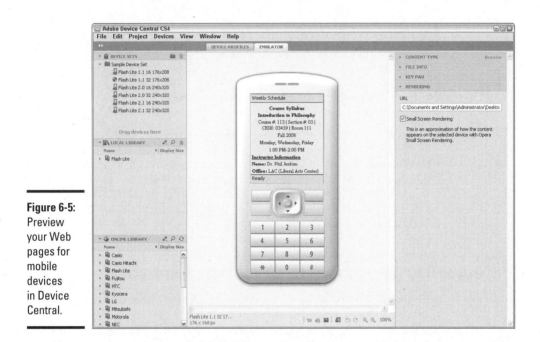

Figure 6-5:
Preview your Web pages for mobile devices in Device Central.

Tips for creating mobile content

Creating and designing mobile content is a bit different than creating content for normal Web pages. For example, although individual mobile devices may support certain HTML features, the Opera Small-Screen Rendering does not support certain elements including frames, pop-up browser windows, and certain font styles such as underlines, overlines, strikethroughs, blinking, and marquees. Also, images must be made smaller than normal to render without skewing in the smaller device window. Try, too, to keep fonts, colors, and styles to a minimum, while making sure to use CSS or HTML to set width and height attributes for images as well as adding `alt` attributes for all your images. Lastly, when using Spry elements on your mobile content pages, be sure to insert the following two lines of code into your pages for accurate CSS and JavaScript rendering:

```
<link href="SpryAccordion.
    css" media="screen"
    rel="stylesheet"
    type="text/css"/>
<link href="SpryAccordion2.
    css" media="handheld"
    rel="stylesheet"
    type="text/css"/>
```

For even more design tips and information about creating mobile content, see `www.adobe.com/go/learn_cs_mobilewiki_en`.

For instruction and details about using Device Central, visit `http://live docs.adobe.com/en_US/DeviceCentral/1.1/index.html`.

Setting Up Dreamweaver to Use Adobe AIR

Adobe AIR is a relatively new cross-operating system software application that lets users develop and deploy multiplatform Rich Internet Applications (RIAs) to the desktop using Flash, Flex, HTML, JavaScript, and Ajax. What makes AIR so powerful is that you can create these RIAs in a familiar environment. So in Dreamweaver, for instance, you could build an application using HTML, JavaScript, CSS, and Spry Widgets (Ajax).

To use an AIR application, you simply run it and interact with it on their desktop like your other native desktop applications. Even better, these applications work on Mac, PC, and Linux platforms, providing consistent and predictable performance to users. In essence, AIR helps you deliver desktop applications to end users without worrying about cross-platform development requirements or performance issues.

Using Adobe AIR requires two things: First, you have to download and install the Adobe AIR authoring application. Second, you have to download and install the Adobe AIR extension for Dreamweaver, which lets you package and preview your AIR applications from within Dreamweaver.

You can download the latest version of the free AIR application and the Adobe AIR SDK at `www.adobe.com/products/air/tools/ajax/`, which gives you the tools you need to build and deploy the AIR applications.

After that, you must install the Adobe AIR extension for Dreamweaver to begin using Dreamweaver to package and preview your Adobe AIR applications within Dreamweaver.

Follow these steps to download and install the Adobe AIR Extension for Dreamweaver:

1. **Download the Adobe AIR extension for Dreamweaver to your desktop.**

   The link to download the extension can be found on Adobe's Tools for AIR and Ajax Web page at `www.adobe.com/products/air/tools/ajax/`.

   The extension is provided in MXP format for easy installation using Adobe's Extension Manager software. Make sure you select the AIR and not the AIR SDK file.

2. **Double-click the MXP file to launch the Extension Manager.**

This both opens the Extension Manager and begins the installation process of the MXP file. Follow the on-screen prompts to accept the terms of the extension installation disclaimer. When finished, the Extension Manager notifies you that the extension has been successfully installed.

3. **Exit and then restart Dreamweaver CS4.**

The extension is fully functional only after you restart Dreamweaver.

After the AIR application and extension have been installed, you can begin using Dreamweaver to package and preview AIR applications by selecting Site⇨Create AIR File.

For instructions on using the Dreamweaver AIR extension, see `http://livedocs.adobe.com/air/1/devappshtml/help.html?content=AIR_extension_1.html`.

To find out more about Developing Adobe AIR applications with HTML and Ajax, try the following Web sites:

```
www.adobe.com/go/learn_air_html_en
www.adobe.com/products/air/tools/ajax/
www.adobe.com/support/documentation/en/air/#html-ajax
http://livedocs.adobe.com/air/1/devappshtml/help.
    html?content=splash.html
http://help.adobe.com/en_US/AIR/1.1/devappshtml/
```

To date, nearly 200 Adobe AIR applications are available to download and use for free. Applications include such tools as the BrandGopher (a domain name research tool), Shrink O'Matic (an image batch resizer), and Timeloc (a desktop tool that tracks your time on various projects). You can find these applications and more on the Adobe AIR Marketplace Web site at `www.adobe.com/cfusion/exchange/index.cfm?event=productHome&exc=24&loc=en_us`.

Book IV

Energizing Your Site

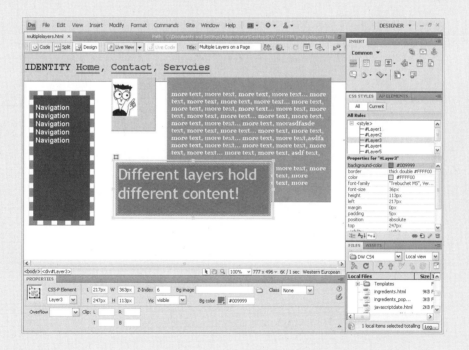

Contents at a Glance

Chapter 1: Working with Layers

In This Chapter

✔ **Understanding how layers work**

✔ **Using the AP Elements panel**

✔ **Setting layer preferences**

✔ **Creating, editing, and managing layers**

✔ **Using CSS with layers**

✔ **Converting AP Divs to tables (and tables to AP Divs)**

*L*ayers are containers for HTML page elements that you can place anywhere on your Web page. Typically coded with the `<div>` tag, *layers*
can hold any kind of content you'd place elsewhere in the body of a document, such as text, graphics, JavaScript, Flash movies, and more.

Also referred to as *layout objects*, layers can be positioned anywhere on a
page, including on top of and inside of each other, allowing you to create
interesting page layouts. In addition, you can make layers visible or hidden,
styled and positioned with CSS, animated across the browser window,
nested inside one another, and stacked in any order. Combined with
JavaScript behaviors, you can manipulate layers in a browser window and
provide engaging opportunities for visitor interaction.

Because of their flexibility, layers have become the new solution for many
complex Web layouts. Although many new browsers support layers, some
of the older versions do not (that's not too much of an issue because these
days the ratio of browsers that don't support layers is extremely low). Still,
if you need to ensure compatibility with an isolated pool of older browsers, or if you want to cover all eventualities, you could convert your layers
into a table-based layout using the Convert command (as described in the
"Converting AP Divs to Tables and Tables to AP Divs" section at the end of
this chapter), so that any browser — even the oldest one — can interpret
the content.

This chapter explores all the aspects of using layers in Dreamweaver. It
starts with an introduction to inserting layout objects with the Layout category of the Insert panel and layers management with the AP Elements panel,
plus other things like showing you how to set layer attributes. The chapter
also covers how to use CSS to style and position layers and how to convert
layers into a table-based layout, and vice versa.

Understanding Layers

Layers are what the W3C refers to as a *block-level element*. Block-level elements are containers that can hold content (such as images, text, and Flash movies), be any size, and be positioned anywhere on a page when styled with CSS. Unlike tables, you can align and position blocks together on a page to create fairly sophisticated layouts, including layers that overlap!

Figure 1-1 shows how you can have multiple layers on a page, each with unique content, positioning, and styles.

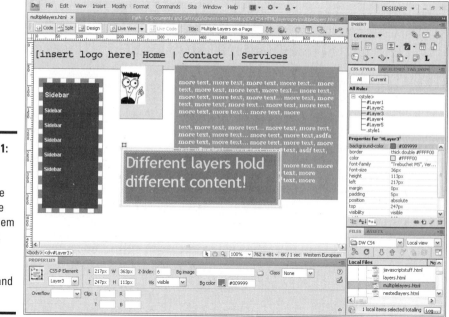

Figure 1-1:
Position layers anywhere on a page and fill them with text, images, Flash movies, and more.

Traditionally, Web designers have used table-based page layouts to build their pages, placing graphics and content inside tables. With tables, the cells are side by side and the content can't overlap. One of the drawbacks of a table-based layout is that content and form are meshed together in one document, which doesn't quite harness the full power of formatting and styling with layers and CSS. The full power of CSS comes when you begin laying out pages with layers and using styles to position and style objects on the page. Tables, by contrast, tend to be more static than layers and offer fewer opportunities for CSS formatting and styling. With layers, when you strip some of the formatting instructions from the HTML and hand them off to a Cascading Style Sheet, not only is the HTML code much cleaner, but the formatting capabilities of CSS enable you to lay out pages without the use of (or with significantly less reliance upon) tables. Tables aren't necessarily a bad thing; they're just being relied on less for formatting than they used to be.

In Dreamweaver, there are two kinds of layers that can be drawn or inserted into your pages: the regular `<div>` tag (which is a container tag that can hold any elements that appear elsewhere on the page) and the AP Div (which is controlled by the AP Elements panel, is automatically labeled with an `id`, as in `<div id="apDiv1"></div>`, and adds an ID CSS rule, as in `#apDiv1`, to the page's CSS) both of which are accessible through the Insert⇨Layout Objects submenu and on the Layout category of the Insert panel.

When you insert the `<div>` tag, the Insert Div Tag dialog box opens, as shown in Figure 1-2, prompting you to set the insertion, class, or ID for the tag:

✦ **Insert:** Choose at Insertion Point, After Start of Tag, or Before End of Tag as the location where the `<div>` tag should be placed in the code relative to the tag you select from the tag menu beside it.

✦ **Class:** Apply a CSS custom class style to the `<div>` as you're inserting the tag onto the page.

✦ **ID:** Apply a CSS ID style to the `<div>` as you're inserting the tag onto the page.

✦ **New CSS Rule:** Click this button to create a new class or ID style in your CSS on the fly and apply it to the `<div>` as you insert the tag onto the page.

You can also insert `<div>` tag layers by clicking the Insert Div Tag button in the Layout category of the Insert panel.

After the `<div>` tag layer is inserted on the page, you add content to it, style it, and reposition it; however, it is not tied into the AP Elements panel. In other words, with `<div>` tag layers, you can't manage the layer's visibility, ID, and z-index through the AP Elements panel; only AP Div layers can be managed by the AP Elements panel. The visibility, ID, and z-index of `<div>` tag layers must be managed with CSS through the CSS Styles panel.

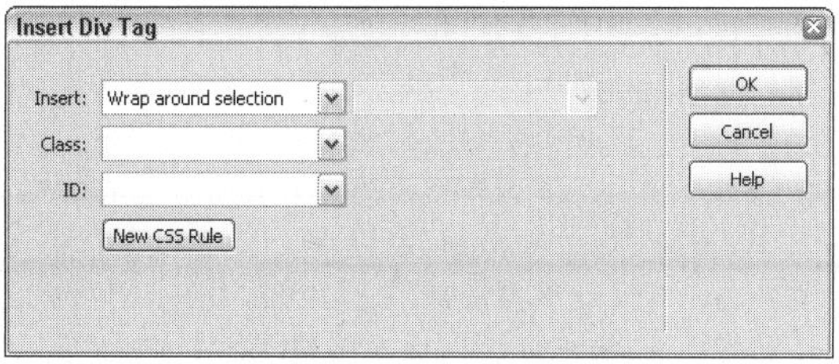

Figure 1-2:
Adding a
`<div>` tag
prompts you
to select
options from
the Insert
Div Tag
dialog box.

Insert Div Tag

Insert: Wrap around selection

Class:

ID:

New CSS Rule

OK

Cancel

Help

By contrast, when you draw or insert an AP Div layer in Dreamweaver (as described in the next section), CSS style data for the layer's size and positioning is automatically inserted into an internal style sheet in the head of the open document, the <div> tag is inserted in the code at the insertion point with the layer id value of apDiv1, and a marker for the layer appears in the AP Elements panel. Subsequent layers added to the page are given id values of apDiv2, apDiv3, apDiv4, and so forth. To better identify each AP Div layer by its contents, however, you can change the id names in the Properties inspector or in the AP Elements panel after inserting them on the page.

AP Div tags are a good tool to enable beginners to find out about layers and CSS without having to set all the technical CSS positioning and style attributes (id, positions, width, height, z-index) in the CSS panel, which can be somewhat intimidating when you first start out coding by hand. Later on, as you get familiar with how the AP Div tags work, you can use the regular <div> tags and give them an id or class with more ease.

Here's an example of the HTML code after inserting an AP Div layer on a page:

```
<!DOCTYPE HTML PUBLIC "-//W3C//DTD HTML 4.01 Transitional//EN"
"http://www.w3.org/TR/html4/loose.dtd">
<html>
<head>
<meta http-equiv="Content-Type" content="text/html; charset=iso-8859-1">
<title>Working with Layers</title>
<style type="text/css">
<!--
#apDiv1 {
    position:absolute;
    width:200px;
    height:115px;
    z-index:1;
}
-->
</style>
</head>
<body>
  <div id="apDiv1"></div>
</body>
</html>
```

Don't confuse <div> tags and AP Div layers with the old <layer> and <ilayer> tags used for positioning, which arrived as a blip on the Netscape 4 radar but quickly went away by Netscape 6. These tags are no longer supported by any browsers nor contained in any W3C standards. Rather, the layers used in Dreamweaver refer to the <div> tag being paired with the id attribute and used as a block-level container for HTML content.

Creating Layers

Whether you insert a `<div>` tag or an AP Div, you can place these layers anywhere on the page, nest them inside one another, place content in them, style and position them with CSS, and size them to any rectangular shape. You can add layers to a page by three simple methods: drawing, inserting, and dropping. Use any and all of the methods interchangeably to suit your particular Web design needs.

Drawing an AP Div layer

The most effective way to add a layer to your page is to draw it because it can be drawn anywhere on the page. Plus, drawing a layer automatically makes it an AP Div layer, giving you more control over it through the AP Elements panel.

To draw a single AP Div layer on a page, follow these steps:

1. **In the Layout category of the Insert panel, click the Draw AP Div button.**

2. **In Design view of your open document window, click and drag a rectangular shape where the new AP Div layer should appear.**

   The drag can flow in any direction from the insertion point. Remember that the layer size and placement is approximate at this phase (see Figure 1-3).

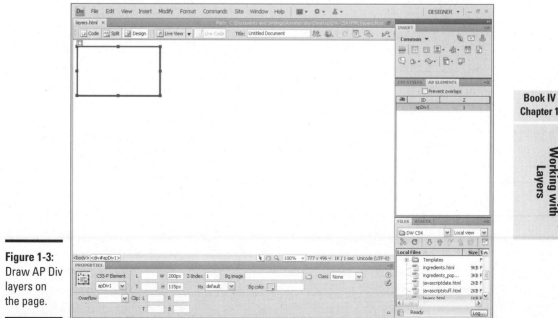

Figure 1-3: Draw AP Div layers on the page.

To draw multiple layers at the same time without having to click the Draw Layer button each time, press and hold Ctrl (Windows) or ⌘ (Mac) as you drag and draw your layers; as long as you keep it pressed, you can continue drawing new layers.

3. **When the size and placement of the drawn layer is acceptable, release the mouse.**

4. **To add more layers to the page, repeat Steps 1 through 3.**

   New layers added to the page are stacked directly on top of one another, each with a unique layer id and z-index number for identification and stacking order.

Dreamweaver provides two other ways to add AP Div layers to your page:

✦ **Insert a layer:** Place the cursor in your document where you want to insert the new layer. Choose Insert⇨Layout Objects⇨AP Div. The new layer is automatically inserted at the insertion point.

   New layers added to the page stack directly on top of one another (unless you've repositioned the insertion point), each with a unique layer id and z-index number for identification and stacking order.

✦ **Drop a layer:** In the Layout category of the Insert panel, click the Draw AP Div button, and then drag and drop it into the open Document window.

   The new blank AP Div layer is automatically inserted at the default position in the top-left corner of the Document window. Repeat the process to add more layers to the page.

 For more precise layout and placement of layers, some people find it helpful to enable the Grid and Snap to Grid features when drawing layers on the page. To find out more about using and customizing the grid, see Book I, Chapter 1.

Adding content to layers

Layers can hold most of the kinds of content you'd place in the body of a document, such as text, graphics, JavaScript, Flash movies, and more. When you're ready to add content to a layer, place the insertion point inside the layer and either paste information, begin typing, or insert content using any of the options on the Insert menu, Insert panel, or Assets panel.

Creating nested layers

A *nested layer* is a layer that's controlled by, but not necessarily inside of, another layer. More simply, think of nested layers as having an interesting parent-child relationship where the child layer can move or function independently of the parent layer, but when the parent layer moves or hides, the child does too. The HTML code of a nested layer is inside the code of the parent layer, which you can see when you view the source code, even though the nested layer may appear elsewhere on the screen due to absolute positioning. Nested layers can be useful, for example, when creating custom navigation menus or when using layers that need to hide and show at the same time.

Figure 1-4 shows an example of how a nested layer appears in Design view, Code view, and the Layers panel.

Figure 1-4:
Nested layers are easy to identify in Code view and the AP Elements panel, but may be difficult to spot in Design view.

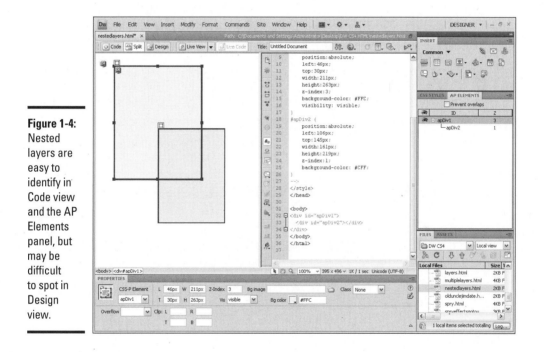

Before you can create nested layers, make sure that the Nesting preference is enabled in the Preferences dialog box (as described in the next section). Then follow these steps to create a nested AP Div layer:

1. **Choose Insert⇨Layout Objects⇨AP Div.**

The new blank layer is automatically inserted at the top of the page. If you'd prefer, you can draw your AP Div instead of inserting it (see "Drawing an AP Div layer" above).

2. **Place the cursor inside the new layer, and then choose Insert⇨Layout Objects⇨AP Div to create a second layer.**

The second layer is nested inside the first layer.

3. **To reposition the nested layer (the second layer), select the nested layer in the AP Elements panel to make it active, and do one of the following:**

   • Press the arrow keys to move the layer.

   • Click the AP Div layer's selection handle (on the top-left corner) and drag the layer to its new location.

Setting layer preferences

When you insert AP Div layers onto a page, the layers are added using the default dimensions and other attributes as specified in the Layers category of the Preferences dialog box. For example, if Dreamweaver's default layer width and height is set to 200 x 115 pixels, all new AP Div layers are added to the page at that default size unless you add a layer to the page by drawing it (see the "Drawing an AP Div layer" section earlier in this chapter). By comparison, regular Div Tag layers have no dimensions unless or until you set them with CSS.

You can edit the default AP Div layer size settings at any time by following these steps:

1. **Choose Edit⇨Preferences (Windows) or Dreamweaver⇨Preferences (Mac).**

   The Preferences dialog box appears.

2. **Select the AP Elements category in the left column of the panel to display the AP Elements default attributes, as shown in Figure 1-5.**

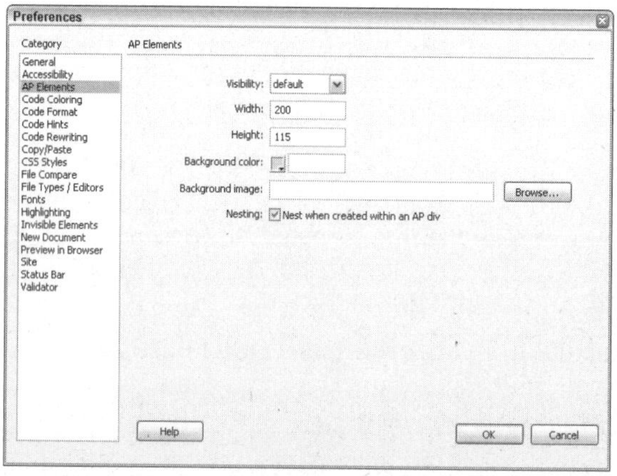

Figure 1-5:
These settings determine the default properties of all new AP Div layers.

3. **To set the default visibility of the layer (whether the layer will be seen or hidden from view when the page loads in the browser), select an option from the Visibility drop-down list.**

   Options include Default (visible), Visible, Hidden, and Inherit.

4. **To set the default pixel width and height for new layers, fill in the Width and Height text boxes.**

5. **To specify a color for the default background color for all new layers, select a color from the Background Color palette or enter a hexadecimal value.**

   By default, there is no background color set. If you do enter a color, be sure to enter the number symbol before the hexadecimal value, as in #FF0000.

6. **To add a default background image for all new layers, click the Browse button to find and select the graphic.**

7. **If you want to create nested AP Div layers, select the Nesting check box.**

   The nesting option enables you to draw a layer inside the bounds of another layer.

8. **While still in the Preferences dialog box, select the Invisible Elements category and enable the Anchor Points for AP Elements option.**

   When you enable this option, each AP Div layer has its own yellow anchor point marker, which can assist greatly in the selection of specific layers in Design view, especially when several layers overlap or have visibility set to hidden.

9. **Click OK to close the Preferences dialog box.**

Managing AP Div Layers with the AP Elements Panel

The AP Elements panel is the place to go to select AP Div layers, name them, change their *z-index* (stacking order), modify nesting placement, enable overlapping, and edit visibility settings. The AP Elements panel is in a panel group with the CSS Styles panel and Tag Inspector panel. To open the AP Elements panel, choose Window➪AP Elements or click on the AP Elements panel tab within its panel group.

The AP Elements panel lists the AP Div layers on a page by visibility setting, name, and z-index number, as shown in Figure 1-6. The sorting order of the list is determined by the z-index. High z-index numbered layers appear at the top of the list, whereas lower z-index numbered layers appear at the bottom of the list.

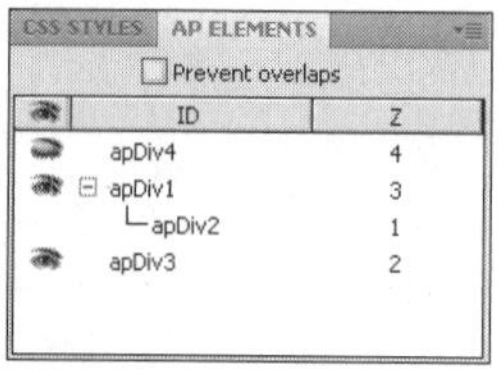

Figure 1-6:
The AP
Elements
panel
displays
information
about all of
the AP Div
layers on
the page.

Try not to be confused by the default layer names and the z-index numbers. The default layer names are arbitrarily assigned when you create the layers (you can rename them to reflect their purpose) and are only meant to assist with identifying layers and applying CSS styles to them. The z-index, however, is used for the ordering or stacking of the layers between the browser and the site visitor. For example, on a page with 12 regular, non-nested layers, each named `apDiv1`, `apDiv2`, `apDiv3`, and so on, where you want `apDiv7` to appear on top of the other layers, assign `apDiv7` a higher stacking order than 12. When you have nested layers on the page, nested layers often appear on top of parent layers, regardless of the stacking number of the parent. Within a nested group, though, normal z-index ordering applies.

If you rename your layers through the AP Elements panel, you may have an easier time arranging them into the desired stacking order. Plus, when you use the AP Elements to rearrange, the z-index numbers self-adjust as you rearrange the layers.

Preventing layer overlap

To prevent layers from overlapping each other as you draw, move, or resize them, enable the Prevent Overlap option at the top of the AP Elements panel. This feature is handy if you plan on using layers for page layout or converting the layers into tables (as described in the "Converting AP Divs to Tables and Tables to AP Divs," section later in this chapter), or if you want to add layers to your page that fit right up against one another without any gaps.

Although the Prevent Overlap option doesn't modify existing layer overlaps until you change them manually, it prevents you from drawing new layers on top of or inside another layer. It also prevents existing layers from being moved onto or resized over another layer, and instead helps layers snap into position next to each other.

To prevent layer overlaps, do one of the following:

✦ In the AP Elements panel, enable the Prevent Overlaps option.

✦ In Design view, choose Modify➪Arrange➪Prevent AP Element Overlaps.

For most layer creation, layer movement, and layer resizing on a page, the Prevent Overlaps feature works wonderfully. However, some layer actions still allow you to add new layers that do overlap existing layers even with this option selected. For instance, layers inserted with the Insert menu and positioned with data in the Properties inspector can overlap existing layers in Design view. You can achieve the same effect when editing layer HTML source code directly in Code view.

If you like the way the new overlapping layers look in Design view and in your target browsers, the overlapping layers can be left as they are. However, to remove layer overlaps from a page, enable the Prevent Overlaps option first, and then drag the layers to a new position in Design view. The new layers snap into position next to, and not on top of, adjoining layers.

Naming layers

A layer's name refers to the layer's `id`. The `id` is then used to attach CSS and positioning information to the layer. By default, Dreamweaver names layers `apDiv1`, `apDiv2`, and so on, but you can rename them with unique names through the AP Elements panel.

Though this may seem a bit confusing, layers can have a class and/or an id name. For instance, you can also reference a div class by creating a style and assigning it to a layer, as in `<div class="sidebar">`, and you could have an AP Div layer that also used the same class, as in `<div id="apDiv2" class="sidebar">`. (For a refresher on working with CSS, turn to Book III, Chapter 1.)

To edit the name of an AP Div layer with the AP Elements panel, follow these steps:

1. **In the ID column of the AP Elements panel, double-click the layer name you want to edit.**

   The current name of the layer is highlighted.

2. **Type the new name for the layer. Then press Enter (Windows) or Return (Mac).**

   The new layer name is reflected in the code's `<div>` tag `id` attribute as well as in the layer's CSS style info embedded in the head of the document, in the AP Elements panel, and in the Properties inspector.

Changing the z-index (stacking order)

You can modify the *z-index*, or stacking order, of an AP Div layer with either the AP Elements panel or the Properties inspector. The higher the z-index number, the closer to the top of the list and the closer the layer appears to the visitor in the browser window relative to the other visible layers on the page.

To edit the z-index of a layer on the Layers panel, select a layer by its name and drag it up or down in the list to the new desired position. When moving a layer, a dark line appears between existing layers to assist with layer placement, indicating a safe spot to release the layer. Be alert when moving layers: The repositioning can affect a layer's nesting and visibility as well as its z-index.

Editing layer visibility

Using the AP Elements panel with Design view, you can show or hide layers to get an idea of how the page displays in a browser window under different conditions. The default visibility status for all layers is to display layers both in Design view and in a browser window.

To set or change an AP Div layer's visibility in the AP Elements panel, click in the eye (visibility) column next to the layer name that you want to alter visibility for:

✦ **Open eye:** Indicates the layer is visible when the page initially displays in a browser.

✦ **Closed eye:** Indicates the layer is hidden, or invisible, when the page initially displays in a browser.

✦ **No eye:** When no eye icon is next to a layer, no visibility is set for the layer and it inherits the parent layer's visibility status or the default visibility setting, which is visible. Nested layers inherit parent visibility settings, and non-nested layers inherit the document body's visibility settings (which is visible, unless you have hidden the body with CSS).

Figure 1-7 shows the AP Elements panel with sample layers set to on (show), off (hide), and none (default).

Figure 1-7:
Use the AP
Elements
panel to
specify
each layer's
visibility
setting.

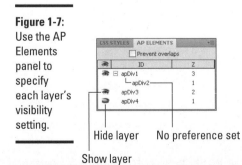

Hide layer   No preference set

Show layer

To change all the layers on the page to Visible or Hidden at once, click the eye header icon at the top of the visibility column. The eye header icon works as a toggle button to switch between visible and hidden for all layers. Click once to make all layers visible. Click again to make all layers hidden.

Selecting and Adjusting AP Div Layers

Before moving, aligning, resizing, or editing the contents of a layer, you must first select the layer. A selected AP Div layer is identifiable by its bold blue outline, corner and mid-section border anchor points, and the visibility of the selection handle on the layer's top-left corner, as shown in Figure 1-8.

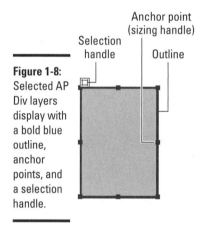

Figure 1-8:
Selected AP Div layers display with a bold blue outline, anchor points, and a selection handle.

Anchor point
(sizing handle)

Selection
handle

Outline

Selecting layers

To assist you with selecting the layer, hover your mouse over the layer's edge and a highlight border appears. When you see the highlight border, click the layer's edge to select the entire layer.

You can change the color of the layer highlighting — or turn the feature off — by modifying the Mouse-Over option in the Highlighting category of the Preferences dialog box. Choose Edit⇨Preferences (Windows) or Dreamweaver⇨Edit (Mac).

You can also select a layer in any of these other ways:

✦ In the AP Elements panel, click the name of the layer you want to select.

✦ In Design view, do any of the following:

• Click anywhere inside the layer to make the layer active; then click the layer's border or selection handle.

• Ctrl+Shift+click (Windows) or ⌘+Shift+click (Mac) inside a layer.

If you want to select multiple AP Div layers, do either of the following:

✦ In Design view, Shift+click the border, selection handle, or inside area of any two or more layers.

✦ In the AP Elements panel, Shift+click two or more layer names.

With multiple layer selection, the corner and mid-section layer border anchor points turn hollow and the layers are highlighted in blue in the AP Elements panel.

Resizing and moving AP Div layers

Select the layer or layers using any of the selection methods in the previous section before making any adjustments such as resizing, moving, or aligning:

✦ **Resize a layer:** Drag the selected layer's resize handles to the new desired size. You can also adjust the layer's Width and Height sizes in the Properties inspector, or, if using CSS, adjust the size in the layer's CSS through the CSS panel.

✦ **Resize multiple layers at once:** Select two or more layers and enter Width and Height values in the Multiple Layers W and H fields in the Properties inspector.

✦ **Move a selected layer or layers in Design view:** Drag the selection handle. With multiple layers, drag the selection handle of the last selected layer.

You can reposition layers on the page just like graphics and other objects; however, if you've enabled the Prevent Overlaps option, you can't reposition the layer on top of another layer. (See "Preventing layer overlap," earlier in the chapter, for more on this option.)

✦ **Align two or more selected layers:** Choose Modify➪Arrange and choose an alignment option. Align layers to the left, right, top, or bottom edge of the last selected layer. When aligning nested layers, any child layer moves along with the parent layer, but isn't included in the alignment unless explicitly selected first.

Setting Layer Properties

Layers have properties that, among other things, define their size, position, name, z-index (stacking order), background color, and visibility. Although you can also set a layer's name, visibility status, and z-index in the AP Elements panel, you can easily adjust all the layer's properties in one go around using the Properties inspector.

Properties are real-time attributes that immediately reflect on the page in Design view when you press Tab or Enter (Windows), or Return (Mac). Therefore, any time you adjust an AP Div layer property in the Properties inspector, the AP Elements panel updates to reflect the new layer settings. This also works in the reverse direction; when you make modifications in the AP Elements panel, the Properties inspector also instantly updates.

The Properties inspector (shown in Figure 1-9) includes the following layer properties:

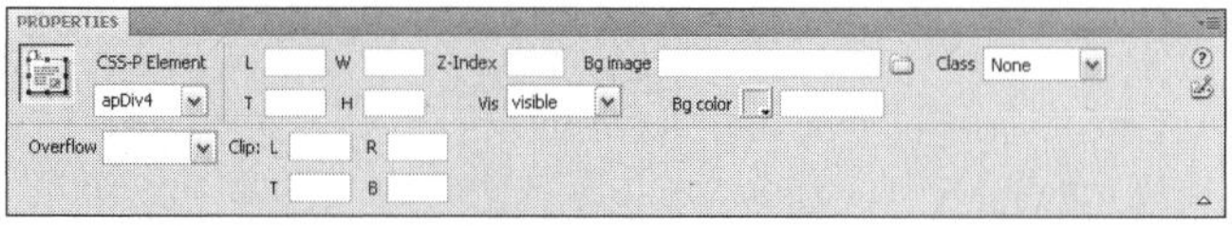

Figure 1-9:
Set
properties
for selected
layers.

+ **Layer ID** identifies each layer using a unique name or ID. The name you enter is used to attach CSS styles and JavaScript behaviors to the layer. Make sure each layer id is a single word using letters or numbers but without any funky characters, dashes, hyphens, periods, or spaces.

+ **L** and **T** (left and top) are the coordinates or absolute position of the layer relative to the top-left corner of the containing box, which is usually the body of the page, but can sometimes be a parent layer. For example, a setting of left:100px and top:300px places the layer exactly 100 pixels from the left and 300 pixels from the top of the browser window. Nested layers use these coordinates for absolute positioning relative to the parent layer. If you switch to Code view, you see that whenever the left and top are specified, the position attribute in the CSS is always set to position:absolute.

+ **W** and **H** (width and height) are the size of the layer. By default, layer sizes are specified in pixels, such as 100px. To enter another unit, add the appropriate abbreviation after the number without a space, such as **1in, 10pt,** or **80%.** Acceptable units include (px) pixels, in (inches), pc (picas), pt (points), mm (millimeters), cm (centimeters), or % (percentage of a parent layer's size).

When the contents of a layer exceed the specified size of the layer and the Overflow setting is set to Visible, the bottom of the layer grows to display all the layer's contents in both Design view and in a browser window. To use the specified width and height instead, adjust the Overflow setting.

**Book IV
Chapter 1**

**Working with
Layers**

✦ **Z-Index** sets the stacking order of the layer. Enter positive or negative numbers. In a browser, the lower numbered layers appear behind the higher numbered layers.

Note: If you select a `<layer>` or `<ilayer>` tag in the code instead of the `<div>` tag, additional options appear in the Properties inspector:

- **Left, Top** specifies the layer's position relative to the layer's parent top, left coordinates.

- **PageX, PageY** uses X and Y coordinates for positioning relative to the page.

- **A/B** (**Above/Below**) sets the stacking order of the selected layer relative from the first A/B menu to the layer name selected in the second A/B menu.

- **Src** selects another HTML file to display inside the layer. (This feature does not render in Design view, but displays in LiveView or in a browser.)

✦ **Vis (Visibility)** determines whether you can see the selected layer on the Web page when the page initially loads in a browser:

- **Default** uses a browser's default layer visibility status, which in most cases is Inherit.

- **Visible** displays the layer and its contents in a browser.

- **Hidden** hides the layer and its contents from view in a browser.

- **Inherit** uses the same visibility setting as a parent layer's visibility. Nested layers inherit parent visibility settings, and non-nested layers inherit the document body's visibility settings, which is always visible.

You can manipulate the visibility feature with JavaScript to hide and show layers when certain events occur, such as an `onMouseOver` event. See Book IV, Chapter 2 to find out more about how to manipulate layers with JavaScript.

✦ **Background Image** adds a background image for the layer. When specified, a background image tiles both vertically and horizontally to fill the entire visible area of the layer.

✦ **Background Color** adds a background color to the layer. Be sure to enter the number symbol before the hexadecimal value, as in `#FF0000`. When both a background color and background image are set, the background image sits on top of the background color.

✦ **Class** applies a custom CSS style to the layer from an internal or externally linked cascading style sheet.

✦ **Overflow** determines how content that exceeds the specified size of the layer gets handled. This option currently has inconsistent browser support, so be sure to test this feature in all your target browsers to see if it works properly or fails acceptably (in other words, maybe it doesn't work, but it also doesn't look that terrible and can function fine without it):

- **Default** displays the layer and its contents in a browser.

- **Visible** expands the layer to fit the size of the contents and display the full layer's contents.

- **Hidden** hides contents that exceed the layer's size from view in a browser.

- **Scroll** adds scroll bars to the specified size of the layer, regardless of whether the contents exceed the specified size.

- **Auto** adds scroll bars to the specified size of the layer only when the contents exceed that size.

✦ **Clip (L/R/T/B)** determines the visible area of a visible layer. Set Left, Right, Top, and Bottom coordinates for the visible clipping area on the layer. Numbers are measured in pixels relative to the top-left corner of the layer. You must set the Overflow option to Hidden, Scroll, or Auto for this feature to work properly. Figure 1-10 shows an example of a selected layer with a specified clipping area.

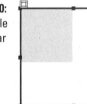

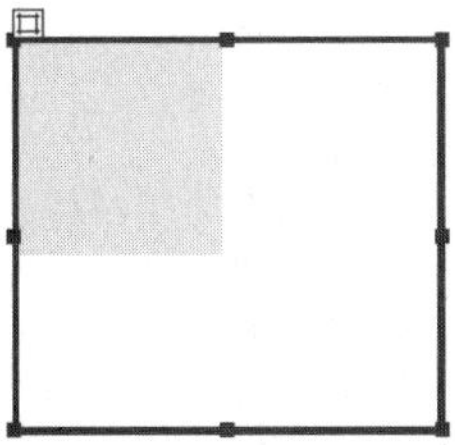

Figure 1-10: Set a visible rectangular clip area within the AP Div layer.

For example, to make a clipping area of 50 x 50 pixels at the top, left edge of the layer, set L to **0**, T to **0**, R to **50**, and B to **50.**

Controlling Layer Style and Positioning with CSS

Dreamweaver CS4 is configured to create individual layer ID styles in an internal style sheet for all the new AP Div layers added to your page. These layer styles control all the AP Div layer style attributes — for example, the layer's background color and font preferences — as well as the layer's size and position on the page.

The benefit of using CSS with your layers — both AP Divs and Div Tags — is that you can

✦ Utilize all the capabilities of CSS with your layers.

✦ Move the CSS information to an external style sheet and link that CSS to all the pages on your site.

✦ Use these individual layer styles to control the look and placement of layers of the same name across multiple pages.

For instance, you may have a layer called `navigation` that contains navigation links that go on every page of your site. If you need to modify any of the properties of the layer (not the layer's content, just its position and style), you could modify the properties for that style through the CSS panel, and all the pages on the site that contain a layer called `navigation` are updated with those new properties.

Changing a CSS property should not be confused with changing a template or SSI, which was covered in Book III, Chapters 2 and 3.

When you're creating an AP Div layer in Dreamweaver CS4, two things happen in the code simultaneously:

✦ The layer is added to the code at the insertion point using the `<div>` tag, which gets assigned with a temporary layer `id` value of something like `apDiv1` or `apDiv1` (rename layers at any time using the AP Elements panel or Properties inspector).

✦ The layer's size and positioning information gets translated into CSS syntax and is automatically inserted between `<style>` tags into the head of the open document.

Here's an example:

```
<!DOCTYPE HTML PUBLIC "-//W3C//DTD HTML 4.01 Transitional//EN"
"http://www.w3.org/TR/html4/loose.dtd">
<html>
<head>
<meta http-equiv="Content-Type" content="text/html; charset=iso-8859-1">
<title>Working with Layers</title>
<style type="text/css">
<!--
#navigation {
    position:absolute;
    left:0px;
    top:0px;
    width:760px;
    height:150px;
    z-index:1;
}
-->
</style>
</head>
<body>
  <div id="navigation"></div>
</body>
</html>
```

Notice that the layer's CSS style name inside the `<style>` tags displays a number symbol (#) before the layer's `id`, in this case, `#navigation`. Whenever the number symbol is paired with a layer's `id` as a style name in a style sheet, the style data gets automatically applied (much like a tag redefine style) to the layer with the same `id`. To illustrate, a set of style definitions using the style name `#header` is automatically applied to a layer with the `id="header"` and a set of style definitions using the style name `#closeup` is automatically applied to a layer with the `id="closeup"`.

Ideally, all the style and positioning information for all the content on all the pages on a Web site are in one centralized location, preferably a single external style sheet. Therefore, you need to export the internal CSS style data for layers entered automatically on the page by Dreamweaver to an external style sheet. You can export internal styles two ways:

✦ Cut and paste the internal styles to an external style sheet.

✦ Use the Move CSS Rules options from the CSS Styles panel options menu to move internal CSS to an external CSS file. (See Book III, Chapter 1 to use the export command.)

After transferring the style sheet positioning data to an external style sheet, continue adding additional styling information, such as the layer's background color, font face, font size, and font color, to the layer style.

To add style information to a layer style, follow these steps:

1. **In the CSS Styles panel, select the layer style name and click the Edit Style button (which looks like a pencil) at the bottom of the panel.**

The CSS Rule Definition dialog box for the selected layer style opens.

2. **Edit or add new layer style definitions in any of the categories in the dialog box.**

When you select a category from the listing on the left, the right side of the panel changes to support that category's options. For example, to add a background color, select the Background category and click the Background Color color picker icon to select a hexadecimal value for the background color. See Book III, Chapter 1 for more guidance on picking the appropriate settings in the CSS Rule Definition dialog box.

3. **To preview before committing to the style settings, click the Apply button.**

4. **When you finish making changes, click OK.**

The updated style information is added to the style sheet and is displayed in the CSS Styles panel.

**Book IV
Chapter 1**

Working with Layers

In the following style example, part of the style data (from `position` to `visibility`) is used for the layer's positioning and the rest (from `background-color` to `border`) is for layer styling:

```
#sidebar {
    position:absolute;
    left:157px;
    top:38px;
    width:229px;
    height:279px;
    z-index:1;
    visibility: visible;
    background-color: #FF3366;
    font-family: Arial, Helvetica, sans-serif;
    font-size: 14px;
    font-weight: bold;
    color: #FFFFFF;
    margin: 0px;
    padding-top: 10px;
    padding-right: 0px;
    padding-bottom: 0px;
    padding-left: 10px;
    border: 10px solid #99CC00;
}
```

Controlling Layers with Behaviors

Dreamweaver comes with nearly 20 pre-written JavaScript behaviors that allow a designer to create interactive sites by controlling or manipulating objects on a Web page. Here are three behaviors that apply directly to layers:

✦ **Drag AP Element:** This behavior allows you to provide a visitor with the ability of dragging or moving a layer inside a browser window. Often used for interactive games and puzzles, the behavior allows the following things:

  • **Snap-to capability:** Visitors can drag layers in any direction and they snap to a target destination within a specified number of pixels.

  • **Handles:** You can define a drag handle somewhere on the layer.

  • **Event handlers:** You can assign an event handler to the layer as the trigger for the layer's mobility, such as when a visitor moves the mouse over or clicks the layer.

✦ **Set Text of Container:** This behavior allows you to replace the contents of an entire layer with new HTML content and formatting, including any JavaScript property, global variable, function call, or other valid expression embedded in the code, when an event is triggered by a visitor's action, such as mousing over the layer.

✦ **Show-Hide Elements:** Use the Show-Hide Elements behavior when you want to control a layer's visibility with user interactivity. For example, you can have a rollover button that, when clicked, reveals a hidden layer. Then, on that layer you can include a link or graphic that, when clicked, hides the layer.

Book IV, Chapter 2 describes each of these behaviors, including how to insert, modify, and remove them.

Converting AP Divs to Tables and Tables to AP Divs

Layers, due to their flexibility, have become the new solution for many Web designers who need to create complex page layouts. A tables-based layout is still great when you have a lot of images that need to fit together tightly within a specified area of the page, such as a navigation table or other menu-type item. But a layers-based layout can look like a tables-based layout, plus you have the added control of positioning the layer and styling the layer's content using CSS. Alternatively, you may find it useful to combine the use of tables and layers for your layout.

Although now considered less contemporary and standards-compliant than a layout that relies almost exclusively on layers, tables are still a supported method for page layout (or partial page layout) because most browsers support tables, whereas layers are not supported by older browsers. If you want the flexibility of layers but need to use tables for your code, consider using layers to design page layouts and then converting the layers into tables before adding content to the page.

For future compatibility, accessibility, vaildatability, and standards-compliancy, try to do all your layout using layers and limit table usage to holding data.

The conversion process is very simple and you can toggle an entire page layout from AP Div layers to tables and tables to AP Div layers. Although you can't use the conversion to convert a single layer or table, keep experimenting until you get your layout perfect.

Be forewarned that the conversion process has two major shortcomings:

✦ The conversion from layers to a table may create a table with a bunch of empty cells, which you then need to manually merge to simplify the table.

✦ You can't apply the conversion process to templates or template-based pages; you must create the table in a normal file and then convert it into a template. If the layout is simply a component of a template-based page, build the table in a new, blank document first and then paste the finished layout into the template-based page.

When creating a layout using layers, be sure to enable the Prevent Overlaps option to constrain layers from nesting or overlapping (see "Preventing layer overlap," earlier in the chapter). Because table cells can't overlap, the layers that are converted into tables can't overlap either.

Converting AP Div layers to a table

To convert a layout using AP Div layers to table-based layout, follow these steps:

1. **Create the layers-based layout in a new, blank HTML document and save the file.**

2. **Choose Modify➪Convert➪AP Divs to Table.**

The Convert AP Divs to Table dialog box opens, shown in Figure 1-11.

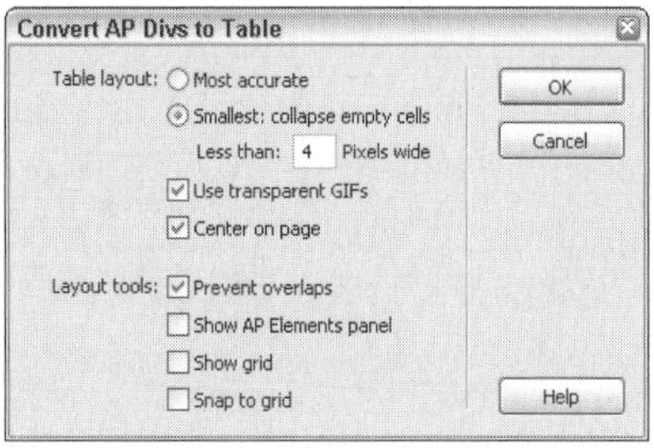

Figure 1-11:
Convert
a layers-
based
layout to
tables.

3. **Specify Table Layout and Layout Tool options:**

- **Most Accurate:** This default option makes a table cell for each layer as well as creates additional cells when needed to ensure that spacing between the old layers is maintained in the new table layout.

- **Smallest: Collapse Empty Cells:** Select this option to align the edges of layers into columns or rows of table cells when within a specified number of pixels. Although this feature creates tables with less empty rows and tables, the layout may not be as precise as the original.

- **Use Transparent GIFs:** Choose this feature to have Dreamweaver add presized transparent GIFs to the bottom row of the table, which forces browsers to display the table using the same column widths. The drawback to this feature is that the table is not easily resized by simply dragging columns. When disabled, the columns are easily resizable, but the table itself may not display the same in all browsers.

- **Center on Page:** By default, the table displays aligned to the left of the browser. Select this option to center the new table on the page using the `align="center"` attribute inside the opening `<table>` tag.

- **Prevent Layer Overlaps:** Pick this option to prevent layers from being drawn, resized, or moved on top of one another.

- **Show AP Elements Panel:** Select this option to open the AP Elements panel.

- **Show Grid:** Choose this option to see the grid in Design view. The grid can assist you with the placement of layers on the page.

- **Snap to Grid:** Select this feature to make the layers snap to the grid when placing, sizing, and moving layers on the page.

4. **Click OK to complete the conversion.**

   If the layout contains overlapping or nested layers, an alert message may appear stating that the file isn't compatible with 3.0 browsers and the conversion is cancelled. If that happens, make adjustments to the layers and try the conversion process again.

Converting tables to AP Div layers

To convert a layout using tables to a layers-based layout, follow these steps:

1. **Create the tables-based layout in a new, blank HTML document and save the file.**

   Only table cells with content convert into layers; table cells without content or background color disappear from the page layout during the conversion process. If you don't want this to happen, be sure to add some kind of content to the cells you do want to convert into layers.

   Any content on the page that wasn't in a table before is put into its own layer during the conversion.

2. **Choose Modify⇨Convert⇨Tables to AP Divs.**

   The Convert Tables to AP Divs dialog box opens, as shown in Figure 1-12.

Figure 1-12:
The Convert Tables to AP Divs dialog box.

```
Convert Tables to AP Divs                    [x]
Layout tools:  [ ] Prevent overlaps          [  OK  ]
               [✓] Show AP Elements panel
               [ ] Show grid                 [ Cancel ]
               [✓] Snap to grid              [  Help  ]
```

3. **Enable the desired Layout Tools options:**

   - **Prevent Layer Overlaps:** This option prevents layers from being drawn, resized, or moved on top of one another.

   - **Show Layers Panel:** Choose this option to open the Layers panel.

   - **Show Grid:** Select this option to see the grid in Design view. The grid can assist you with the placement of layers on the page.

   - **Snap to Grid:** Select this option to make the layers snap to the grid when placing, sizing, and moving layers on the page.

4. **Click OK to complete the conversion.**

Chapter 2: Jazzing Up Pages with JavaScript Behaviors and Spry Widgets

In This Chapter

✔ **Understanding JavaScript behaviors**

✔ **Using Dreamweaver's default behaviors**

✔ **Changing and deleting behaviors**

✔ **Using the Extension Manager to install third-party behaviors**

✔ **Using Spry Widgets to add visitor interactivity**

*J*avaScript is a scripting language created by Netscape that enables you to create interactive sites when you embed the scripts in your HTML pages. All the newest versions of the major browsers support JavaScript because it is an open-source language, which means anyone can write and use it without having to buy a license.

JavaScript is fairly easy to learn and use, and even easier to copy and paste from free sources online. It does have a downside, however, in that roughly 10 percent of all Web visitors will have their JavaScript disabled, either by choice or by necessity. For example, people who like to surf faster sometimes keep their JavaScript disabled. Also, visitors who are visually impaired may be accessing the Web with an assistive device, like a Screen Reader, that requires that JavaScript be turned off.

JavaScript can enhance your Web site and provide many kinds of interactivity for the visitor. For example, with JavaScript, you can create rollover buttons and navigation menus; display dates, times, and slide shows; add cookies to a visitor's computer; play games; process forms; and even control browser windows. Likewise, Dreamweaver's Spry Widgets (a combination of HTML, CSS, and JavaScript) can provide interesting ways of displaying interactive content to visitors that would otherwise not be possible.

Dreamweaver CS4 comes with the following commonly used JavaScripts, which it refers to as *behaviors*, ready to insert onto your pages from the Behaviors panel:

Call JavaScript	Change Property
Check Plug-in	Drag AP Element
(Spry) Effects	Go to URL
Jump Menu	Jump Menu Go
Open Browser Window	Popup Message
Preload Images	Set Nav Bar Image
Set Text of Container	Set Text of Frame
Set Text of Status Bar	Set Text of Text Field
Show-Hide Elements	Swap Image
Swap Image Restore	Validate Form

At the very bottom of the Behaviors listing is an option called ~Deprecated, which lists a few other behaviors in its submenu. These behaviors are no longer recommended for use, although they are still supported in case you inherit a Web site that uses them and need to modify them. For documentation about using these deprecated behaviors, see the "Adding built-in Dreamweaver behaviors" help page on Dreamweaver's LiveDocs Web site: `http://help.adobe.com/en_US/Dreamweaver/10.0_Using/WSc78c5 058ca073340dcda9110b1f693f21-7b14a.html`.

Dreamweaver also comes with the following Spry Widgets, which are easily inserted onto you pages through the Layout category of the Insert panel:

Spry Menu Bar	Spry Tabbed Panels
Spry Accordion	Spry Collapsible Panel
Spry Tooltip	

This chapter shows you what JavaScript behaviors do and how you can insert, modify, or delete them. You also find information about downloading third-party behaviors from Adobe's Dreamweaver Exchange and installing them using the Adobe's Extension Manager. At the end of the chapter, you get a brief introduction to working with Spry Widgets.

Understanding JavaScript Behaviors

JavaScript is a scripting language, not a programming language. Unlike programming languages such as C or VisualBasic, JavaScript is not that difficult to learn. You also shouldn't confuse JavaScript with Java, the object-oriented programming language used for writing applets. Unlike Java and other programming languages, JavaScript doesn't require compilation to run and it's much, much easier to write.

JavaScript includes three main types: client-side JavaScript (CSJS), server-side JavaScript (SSJS), and core JavaScript (CJS). Because server-side and core are more complex, this chapter deals exclusively with Dreamweaver's client-side JavaScript Behaviors. Client-side JavaScript builds on the core JavaScript commands by adding common functionality useful in a browser situation. For a comprehensive look at JavaScript, check out WebTeacher's entry at www.webteacher.com/javascript/. If you'd like to try your hand at some JavaScript tutorials, a fine place to begin is at the W3Schools Web site at www.w3schools.com/js/default.asp.

Client-side JavaScripts, or *behaviors* as Dreamweaver calls them, run in browsers (not on servers) and are the combination of an *event* and an *action* triggered by that event:

✦ **Events** are things that a visitor does to interact with a page (or things that happen to a page without visitor interaction, such as when the page loads in a browser) that trigger an action script that causes something on the page to change. Different events are associated with each page element. For instance, the onMouseOver event occurs when visitors move their mouse over a particular element on the page (for example, a graphic) that contains a JavaScript. That event then *triggers,* or tells, the browser to check the page's code to *call,* or put into action, any additional JavaScript based on the event.

✦ **Actions** are the parts of a script that perform specific tasks such as opening another browser window, displaying a message in the browser's status bar, swapping an image in a rollover button, or hiding and showing layers. A great example of a script that uses the onMouseOver event to call an action is a rollover button. When you visit a site, you typically see the button graphic in its normal state. However, when you move your cursor over the button, you see a replacement image (called an *over state* image) appear instead of the normal state. In most cases, when you move your mouse off or away from the over state graphic, the normal state graphic reappears.

Although you don't need to master JavaScript to use it, you would certainly benefit from any time spent learning more about it. If you're interested in reading more about this scripting language, check out *JavaScript For Dummies,* by Emily A. Vander Veer (Wiley).

Adding JavaScript to Your Page

Using the Dreamweaver Behaviors panel and some of the other tools that support JavaScript interactivity, you can add JavaScript to HTML pages in four different ways:

✦ As an internal script in the head of a page between the `<script></script>` tags, with event functions specified in the body tag when necessary, such as `onLoad="preloadImages();"`.

✦ As an external script file using the `<script src="...">` tag inside the head of an HTML page, similar to linked external Cascading Style Sheets.

✦ As an *event handler* (the event that triggers the JavaScript) inside HTML elements on forms to perform certain functions, such as validating form field entries by visitors before the form gets processed, returning the results of a Celsius to Fahrenheit temperature conversion, or calling a JavaScript alert window to pop open.

✦ With the `javascript:` URL protocol to add functionality to a page for actions such as reloading a page in the browser window, as in this example of a text link:

```
<a href="javascript:history.go(0)">Reload This Page</a>
```

Besides using the Behaviors panel, Dreamweaver also supports the addition of JavaScript behaviors to your pages in a handful of other ways, although you may need to alter scripts obtained from outside Dreamweaver to get them to work specifically with your Web site:

✦ Write your own JavaScripts and hand-code them in the Code editor.

✦ Copy and paste JavaScripts into your pages from another source, such as a script you used on another site or copied from a free scripts Web site.

✦ Insert them into your pages as JavaScript snippets. (Book III, Chapter 4 discusses snippets.)

✦ Download, install, and use third-party behaviors (scripts for use in a Dreamweaver site that were developed by anyone other than Adobe), as described at the end of this chapter.

When hand-coding or copying JavaScript behaviors, be sure you add the code in Code view rather than Design view. You also need to pay close attention to where you place the behavior script, as JavaScript often contains one to three parts: a script that goes into the head of the page, an event handler that goes into the `<body>` tag of the page, and some inline script that goes somewhere inside the body area of your page to call and display the script.

For example, take a look at Listing 2-1, which is a mouse cursor effect by Marcin Wojtowicz from the JavaScriptKit Web site (`www.javascriptkit.com`). This example requires script between the `<head>` tags and between the opening and closing `<body>` tags. You also need to copy and upload a cursor graphic to your managed site and to the server for this effect to function properly.

Listing 2-1:   Cut and Paste Cursor Trail

```
<!DOCTYPE html PUBLIC "-//W3C//DTD XHTML 1.0 Transitional//EN" "http://www.
    w3.org/TR/xhtml1/DTD/xhtml1-transitional.dtd">
<html xmlns="http://www.w3.org/1999/xhtml">
<head>
<meta http-equiv="Content-Type" content="text/html; charset=utf-8" />
<title>Cut and Paste Cursor Trail</title>
</head>
<body>
<script language="JavaScript1.2">
<!--
var trailLength = 8 // The length of trail (8 by default; put more for longer
    "tail")
var path = "cursor.gif" // URL of your image
var standardbody=(document.compatMode=="CSS1Compat")? document.documentElement :
    document.body //create reference to common "body" across doctypes
var i,d = 0
function initTrail() { // prepares the script
    images = new Array() // prepare the image array
    for (i = 0; i < parseInt(trailLength); i++) {
    images[i] = new Image()
    images[i].src = path
    }
    storage = new Array() // prepare the storage for the coordinates
    for (i = 0; i < images.length*3; i++) {
    storage[i] = 0
    }
    for (i = 0; i < images.length; i++) { // make divs for IE and layers for
    Navigator
        document.write('<div id="obj' + i + '" style="position: absolute;
    z-Index: 100; height: 0; width: 0"><img src="' + images[i].src + '"></div>')
    }
    trail()
}
function trail() { // trailing function
    for (i = 0; i < images.length; i++) { // for every div/layer
        document.getElementById("obj" + i).style.top = storage[d]+'px' // the
    Y-coordinate
```

(continued)

Listing 2-1 *(continued)*

```
        document.getElementById("obj" + i).style.left = + storage[d+1]+'px' //
    the X-coordinate
    d = d+2
    }
    for (i = storage.length; i >= 2; i--) { // save the coordinate for the div/
    layer that's behind
    storage[i] = storage[i-2]
    }
    d = 0 // reset for future use
    var timer = setTimeout("trail()",10) // call recursively
}
function processEvent(e) { // catches and processes the mousemove event
    if (window.event) { // for IE
    storage[0] = window.event.y+standardbody.scrollTop+10
    storage[1] = window.event.x+standardbody.scrollLeft+10
    } else {
    storage[0] = e.pageY+12
    storage[1] = e.pageX+12
    }
}
    initTrail()
    document.onmousemove = processEvent // start capturing
//-->
</script>
</body>
</html>
```

When inserted on a page, this script makes cursor trails. It's pretty basic stuff, but neat.

Another thing you may want to consider whenever you add JavaScript behaviors to your pages is to add content between `<noscript>` tags for visitors who view sites with old versions of browsers or with browsers that have the JavaScript turned off, as in the following example:

```
<noscript>
This page includes code that requires a browser that can interpret JavaScript,
    such as Internet Explorer 4.0 and above, Netscape Navigator 4.0 and above,
    Safari 1.0 and above, and Firefox 1.0 and above. If you see this message you
    may not have full access to this page's content.
</noscript>
```

Place the `<noscript>` tags and contents inside the body of the page where you want the message to display when conditions warrant it. You can find a free snippet of this `<noscript>` tag with text at www.luckychair.com.

Using Dreamweaver's Default Behaviors

When you're first starting to work with JavaScript, trying to remember what goes where and when can be complicated. To ease the learning curve, try inserting a behavior with Dreamweaver's Behaviors panel.

Dreamweaver comes with nearly 20 preinstalled behaviors you can use to embed client-side JavaScript code in your documents. Many of these scripts let visitors interact with content on your pages. The behaviors are typically made up of events combined with actions that trigger those events.

Behaviors can do all kinds of things. For example, the Open Browser Window behavior can open a page and force the browser window to resize automatically to a predetermined pixel width and height, and the Check Plug-in behavior can detect whether the visitor's browser has a particular plug-in installed and, when missing, can redirect visitors to another page with instructions for finding and downloading the required plug-in. (Both of these behaviors are described in detail later in this chapter.)

Using Dreamweaver's Behaviors panel, you can quickly add these scripts to your page. All the behaviors have dialog boxes to guide you through the process of entering in required data for customizing and inserting them. You can even choose the appropriate event handler to trigger the behavior's action, as well as specify that a certain event triggers several actions at once and set the order of those actions.

All of Dreamweaver's behaviors have been written to work in IE 4.0 and later and Netscape 4.0 and later. Many of them also work fine in Netscape 3.0 and later, but most of them don't work properly in IE 3.0. To maintain the best possible cross-browser compatibility, take care when removing or editing the JavaScript code by hand.

Using the Behaviors panel

To open the Behaviors panel, choose Window⇨Behaviors. In Dreamweaver CS4, the Behaviors panel is nested with the Attributes panel inside the Tag Inspector panel, as shown in Figure 2-1.

Click to open
Actions menu

Figure 2-1:
The
Behaviors
panel shows
behaviors
and events.

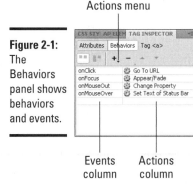

Events
column

Actions
column

The Behaviors panel becomes active when you have a document open in the Dreamweaver workspace window. To find out more about any previously applied behaviors, select the object or tag with the behavior on the page and any behaviors associated with the object or tag appear in the Behaviors panel listing. When an event includes multiple actions, the actions are triggered in the order they appear in the list.

Behaviors are typically attached to tags for text and graphics, but you can also apply them to the <body> element, to links, and to form fields.

The Behavior panel's Actions menu (which you open by clicking the Actions [+] button) lists Dreamweaver's preset behaviors. Which behaviors are available or disabled on this menu depends on two factors:

✦ Which object or asset on the page you select prior to clicking the Actions (+) button.

✦ Which browser is selected in the Show Events For submenu at the bottom of the Actions menu (see Figure 2-2). The browser you select determines which events are supported and thus which Actions display, as every browser provides different sets of events that can be associated with the actions in this list.

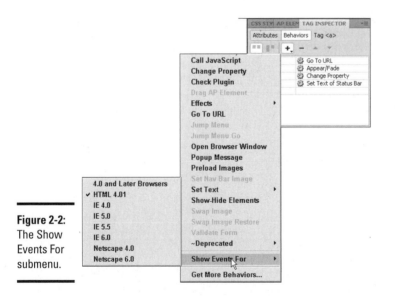

Figure 2-2:
The Show Events For submenu.

You can use the Show Events For submenu to help figure out whether certain browsers support selected behaviors for certain page assets. Try inserting the object on your page and attaching a behavior to it. When events are *grayed out,* or disabled, the specified browser doesn't support them.

Attaching a behavior

Attaching behaviors to objects on your page is fairly easy and requires only a few simple steps. Typically, you select an object or linked text on the page, choose a behavior from the Behaviors panel, complete the dialog box that appears associated with the behavior, and verify that the *event handler* (the event that triggers the action) matches your needs.

To attach a behavior, follow these steps:

1. **Select an object or element on the page, such as a graphic or a text link.**

When attaching a behavior to the entire page, select the opening <body> tag from the Tag selector at the bottom-left corner of the open Document window.

2. **If you're attaching a behavior to text, you need to add a null link. To do so, type the JavaScript null link (`javascript:;`) in the Link text box in the Properties inspector.**

You can't attach a behavior to plain text, but you can attach it to a link. For this reason, if you're attaching a behavior to text, you must add a *null link* (a link that doesn't go anywhere) to the selected text before you can attach the behavior.

Remember, the null link must contain both the colon and semicolon.

If you want to remove the underline from linked text but add some other property (for example, a color) so that the behavior is available but the text that triggers the behavior to occur doesn't look like a traditional link, you could add some inline CSS to the link's `<a href>` tag to disable the default link underline and convert the text to another color, like this:

```
<a href="javascript:;" style="text-decoration:none;
    color:#000000;">Example 1</a>
```

Better still would be to create and use a non-underlining class in an external CSS, as many CSS purists frown upon inline styles.

3. **Open the Behaviors panel by choosing Window➪Behaviors.**

4. **Click the Actions (+) button in the Behaviors panel and select an action from the list.**

The actions that are active in the list support the selected element; any actions that are grayed out are unusable for that selection. Either the asset doesn't exist in the document or the target browser specified in the Show Events For submenu doesn't support that action. For example, you can't use the Drag AP Element action if no layers are present on the page. All the actions in this list work in 4.0 and later browsers, but some don't work in browsers older than that.

After selecting an action, a dialog box opens with parameters to set and options to select that support the behavior.

5. **Fill in the action's dialog box to specify how you want the behavior to work.**

   Some dialog boxes have multiple tabs with several fields for data entry.

6. **When you finish, click OK.**

   The behavior is inserted into the page, and the default event handler for that behavior (such as onClick) automatically appears in the Behavior panel's Events column (the first column in the panel).

7. **If you want to change the event handler to something else, such as onLoad or onMouseDown, select the current event handler from the Behaviors panel. Then select a different event handler from the Events drop-down menu.**

   If the event handler you want to use is not on the list, try changing the target browser in the Show Events For menu at the bottom of the Behaviors panel Actions menu.

Changing and deleting behaviors

You can modify or delete a behavior at any time. For instance, you can change the event handler, add and remove actions, edit action parameters, and delete attached behaviors.

To change a behavior in Dreamweaver, follow these steps:

1. **Select the asset on the page that has the behavior attached to it.**

2. **In the Behaviors panel, select the associated action you want to change.**

3. **Do any of the following to change the behavior:**

   • **Change the order of the actions:** When two or more actions are listed in the Behaviors panel, you can rearrange the order of the actions by selecting an action and clicking the up or down arrows.

   • **Edit an action's parameters:** Double-click the action name to launch the action's dialog box and change the action's parameters. You can also launch the dialog box by selecting the behavior's name and pressing Enter (Windows) or Return (Mac).

   • **Delete a behavior:** Delete a behavior by selecting it by name and clicking the minus (–) button in the Behaviors panel or pressing the Delete key on your keyboard.

In your code, some behaviors' events may appear in parentheses to indicate links, for example, when you attach some behaviors to an image. In those cases, Dreamweaver automatically wraps the <a> tag around images and defines a null link using the `javascript:;` syntax in the Properties inspector's Link text field, as with this example:

```
<a href="javascript:;" onClick="MM_openBrWindow('welcome.html','','width=300,hei
  ght=300')"><img src="images/logo.gif" width="195" height="200" border="0"></
  a>
```

In these cases, you can still edit the behavior in the Behaviors panel if you like, or edit the JavaScript behavior in Code view.

Updating old behaviors

For pages with behaviors created in Dreamweaver versions 1-4, you have to manually update the behaviors in the current version of Dreamweaver. Fortunately, this process takes a little less time because of help provided by Dreamweaver. When you manually update one instance of a behavior, Dreamweaver automatically updates all other instances of the same behavior. Granted, you still need to update all the old behaviors on every other page on your site, but at least the process goes a little faster with this helpful feature.

Follow these steps to update an old behavior:

1. **Select the asset on the page that has the old behavior attached to it.**

2. **Open the Behaviors panel by choosing Window⇨Behaviors.**

3. **Double-click the action in the Behaviors panel. In the behavior's dialog box, verify or modify any of the settings.**

   Opening the behavior's dialog box in the newer version of Dreamweaver updates the behavior code.

4. **Click OK in the behavior's dialog box.**

   Dreamweaver automatically updates any other instances of that behavior on the same page.

Call JavaScript

With the Call JavaScript behavior, you can add your own JavaScript to your page as a custom function or a line of code that is triggered by a specified event. For example, you could add JavaScript that makes the browser window close when the user clicks a specified button. If you know JavaScript, you can write these JavaScript behaviors yourself, or if you're not familiar with JavaScript syntax, you can usually find free source code on the large number of JavaScript tutorial and library Web sites, including these:

```
www.w3schools.com/js/default.asp
www.dynamicdrive.com/
www.javascriptkit.com/javatutors/
javascript.internet.com/
```

To add the Call JavaScript behavior to a document, follow these steps:

1. **Select an object or text link on your page.**

2. **Click the Actions (+) button in the Behaviors panel, and choose Call JavaScript.**

   The Call JavaScript dialog box opens, as shown in Figure 2-3.

Call JavaScript	
JavaScript:	OK
	Cancel
	Help

3. **In the JavaScript box, type your JavaScript or function:**

   For example, to make a Close button, enter in either one of the following scripts, including the parentheses and semicolon:

   ```
   javascript:window.close();
   ```

   or

   ```
   window.close();
   ```

   Dreamweaver writes the JavaScript function to the head of the page for you, which means technically all you really need to type is the function name, such as `closepopup()`.

4. **Click OK to close the dialog box.**

5. **Verify that the event handler listed in the Events column of the Behaviors panel is the one you want to use.**

   You can use the Behaviors panel to change the event handler. If the event handler you want to use is not on the list, try changing the target browser in the Show Events For menu at the bottom of the Behaviors panel Actions menu.

Change Property

You can use the Change Property behavior to change an object's properties, such as the background color of a layer, the text contained inside a `<div>` tag, or the source file of an image. The properties that you can change depend largely on the browser type and version your visitors use when viewing the page. For example, IE 4.0 and up supports many more properties than do IE 3.0, NN 3.0, and NN 4.0.

Because this behavior requires you to type some code in the dialog box it uses, be sure you know HTML and understand JavaScript a little before using it, and test the actions in your target browsers before publishing them.

To use the Change Property behavior on a page, follow these steps:

1. **Select an object on your page.**

   You can modify these objects or tags with this behavior: `layer`, `div`, `span`, `img`, `form`, `input/checkbox`, `input/radio`, `input/text`, `text area`, `input/password`, and `select`.

2. **Click the Actions (+) button in the Behaviors panel and select Change Property.**

   The Change Property dialog box opens, as shown in Figure 2-4.

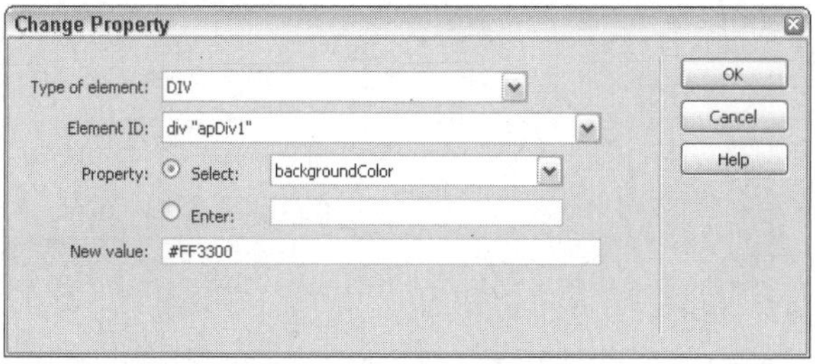

Figure 2-4:
Select the object type and specify the property to change.

Change Property	☒
Type of element: DIV ▾	OK
Element ID: div "apDiv1" ▾	Cancel
Property: ⊙ Select: backgroundColor ▾	Help
○ Enter:	
New value: #FF3300	

3. **From the Type of Element menu, choose the object type that matches your selection.**

   For example, to change the background color of a layer, select DIV.

   The Element ID drop-down list changes to support that selection.

4. **From the Element ID list, choose the object whose properties you want to change.**

   When the Type of Element selected is not found on the page, you see an Element Not Found message on the Element ID menu, such as `*** no FORMs found ***`.

5. **In the Property section, select a property that you want to change from the Select drop-down list, or select the Enter Property radio button and type the property name in the Enter text field.**

   Pay close attention to spelling and letter case when typing the JavaScript property name.

6. **In the New Value text field, type the new value for the property.**

For example, if you're changing the background color of a layer, type a hexadecimal value preceded by a number symbol (#), like #FF3300.

7. **Click OK to close the dialog box.**

8. **Verify that the event handler listed in the Events column of the Behaviors panel is the one you want to use.**

   Because the property of the object changes when the event occurs, you need to check that the right event is listed with the action in the Behaviors panel. If necessary, change the event handler in the Behaviors panel; if the event handler you want to use is not on the list, try changing the target browser on the Show Events For menu at the bottom of the Behaviors panel Actions menu.

Check Plug-In

The Check Plug-in behavior checks to see if the user's computer has the necessary plug-ins installed to successfully view your page. If the user has the necessary plug-ins, the Check Plug-in behavior displays the current page; if the user doesn't have the required plug-in, it can send the visitor to an alternate page. For example, you may have created a Shockwave movie for your site that requires the latest free Shockwave player. Use the Check Plug-in behavior to detect whether the right Flash player is installed and, if it is not, send visitors to a page telling them how to find and install the required plug-in.

Internet Explorer can't interpret JavaScript for plug-in detection. As a workaround in Windows, when you select Flash or Director, Dreamweaver writes the VBScript to your page that auto-detects those plug-ins in IE. Unfortunately, IE on the Mac has no workaround. By contrast, Netscape Navigator always detects plug-ins on both Mac and Win.

To add the Check Plug-in behavior to your page, follow these steps:

1. **Select an object on your page.**

2. **Click the Actions (+) button in the Behaviors panel, and select Check Plugin.**

   The Check Plugin dialog box opens, as shown in Figure 2-5.

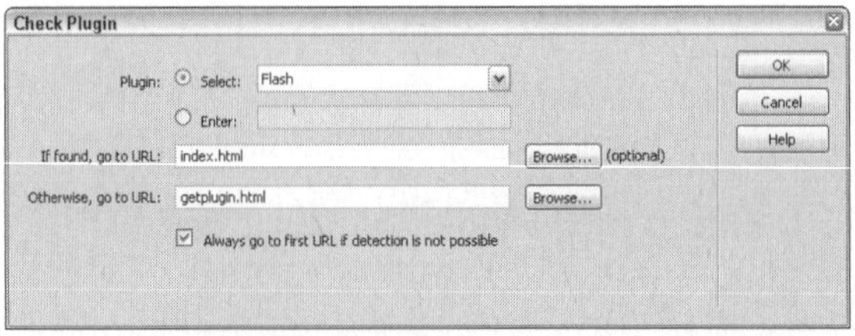

Figure 2-5: The Check Browser behavior can send a visitor to a page you specify.

3. **Select a plug-in type from the Select drop-down list, or type the plug-in name in the Enter text field.**

Plug-in options include Flash, Shockwave, LiveAudio, QuickTime, and Windows Media Player. When typing the plug-in name in the text field, the spelling and letter case must be accurate for this behavior to work.

To find out more about plug-ins, see the Netscape About Plug-ins page: On Windows, open Netscape and choose Help⇨About Plug-ins. On a Mac, open Netscape and choose About Plug-ins from the Apple menu.

4. **Enter a URL in both the If Found, Go To URL and Otherwise, Go To URL fields.**

Typically, the If Found URL is the page to go to when the plug-in is installed on the visitor's computer, and the Otherwise URL is the page to go to if the plug-in is not installed. When you want visitors without the plug-in to stay on the current page, leave the Otherwise URL field blank.

When either of the URLs are remote (not on your Web site), be sure to type the **http://** prefix before the www in the Web address, as in `http://www.adobe.com`.

5. **Enable the Always Go to First URL if Detection Is Not Possible option for visitors using Internet Explorer.**

When you enable this option, the visitor is sent to the URL in the If Found text field; when you leave this option disabled, the visitor is sent to the Otherwise URL.

If you're not sure whether to enable or disable this option, I recommend enabling this feature so that IE visitors lacking the plug-in are prompted by their browsers to download and install it before viewing the page.

6. **Click OK to close the dialog box.**

7. **Verify that the event handler listed in the Events column of the Behaviors panel is the one you want to use.**

The default event handler for this behavior is `onFocus`. If desired, change the event handler in the Behaviors panel.

Drag AP Element

If you're using AP Div layers on your site and want to add some interesting viewer interactivity, consider adding the Drag AP Element behavior to allow site visitors to move and reposition these layers in the browser window. This is a great behavior for creating interactive games, puzzles, movable navigation layers, and other user interface controls.

The Drag AP Element behavior enables visitors to drag layers up, down, left, right, and diagonally in their browsers. Among other things, you can also set a target destination for the layer (think puzzles) and whether to snap the layer to the target within a specified number of pixels.

**Book IV
Chapter 2**

Jazzing Up Pages with JavaScript Behaviors and Spry Widgets

Like all behaviors, the action must be called before the behavior can be used, so you need to choose the right event handler. For this reason, you must attach this behavior to the `<body>` tag and use the `onLoad` event handler to trigger the event. This ensures the layer is ready for dragging the second the page finishes loading in the browser.

Alternatively, you could attach the behavior to a link inside the layer that takes up the entire layer size (such as a linked image) paired with the `on MouseOver` event handler. You have to first apply the behavior to the `<body>` tag so that Dreamweaver can add all the JavaScript to the page that defines the drag layer function. Then you move by hand the `onload` script line from the `<body>` tag to the new link location in the code. The last thing you do is change the event handler in the Behaviors panel, as in the following code:

From this:

```
<body onload="MM_dragLayer('apDiv1','',0,0,0,0,true,false,-1,-1,-1,-
    1,false,false,0,'',false,'')">
<div id="apDiv1">
  <p><a href="http://www.dummies.com"><img src="images/dummies.gif"
    name="dummies" width="50" height="80" border="0" id="dummies"/></a></p>
</div>
</body>
```

To this:

```
<body>
<div id="apDiv1">
  <p><a href="http://www.dummies.com"><img src="images/dummies.gif"
    name="dummies" width=""50" height="80" border="0" id="dummies"
    onmouseover="MM_dragLayer('apDiv1','',0,0,0,0,true,false,-1,-1,-1,-
    1,false,false,0,'',false,'') "/></a></p>
</div>
</body>
```

To attach the Drag AP Element behavior to an AP Div layer on your page, follow these steps:

1. **Draw an AP Div layer on the page.**

   Choose Insert⇨Layout Object⇨AP Div, or click the Draw AP Div button on the Layout category of the Insert panel and draw a layer in an open document in Design view.

   See Book IV, Chapter 1 for the skinny on layers.

2. **Select the opening `<body>` tag with the Tag selector (which is located in the bottom-left corner of the Document window).**

   You must select the `<body>` tag to apply this behavior.

3. **Click the Actions (+) button in the Behaviors panel, and select Drag AP Element.**

The Drag AP Element dialog box opens, as shown in Figure 2-6. The dialog box has two tabs: Basic and Advanced. Each tab allows you to enter specific parameters for this behavior.

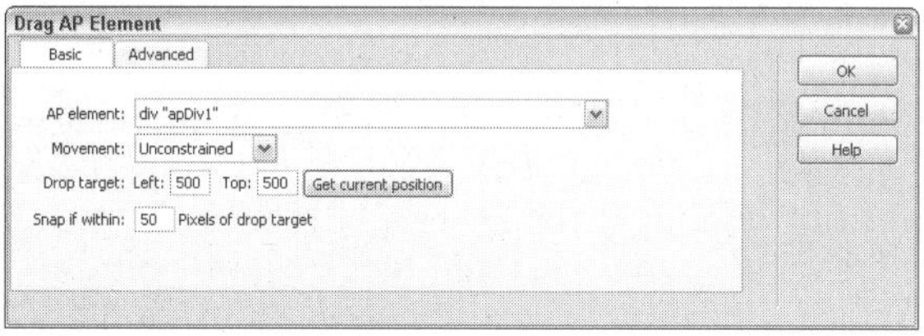

Figure 2-6:
Specify a drop target position and whether to constrain the layer's movement.

4. **On the Basic tab, select the layer to be dragged from the AP Element menu.**

   Layers are listed alphabetically by name (`div "apDiv1"`) to help you identify them quickly. If you forgot to rename your layers to something more meaningful, cancel out of the dialog box, select and name the layer(s) in the AP Elements panel, and then reopen the Drag AP Element dialog box.

5. **From the Movement menu, choose Unconstrained or Constrained.**

   Select Unconstrained for free-form movement, as with puzzles and games, or choose Constrained for movements that need to be controlled, as with sliders or other movable elements.

6. **For constrained movements, type pixel values for the Up, Down, Left, and Right parameters.**

   The pixel coordinates are relative to the layer's original position, and you can enter positive, negative, and 0 values in any of the fields. For example, if you want to constrain movement of the layer to the left and right only, enter positive pixel values in the Left and Right boxes and 0s in the Up and Down boxes.

7. **In the Drop Target fields, type Left and Top pixel values for the desired finish position of the layer, relative to the top-left corner of the browser window.**

   The target is considered reached when the layer's top and left positioning values match the drop target's top and left coordinates.

   To get the selected layer's current top and left coordinates, click the **Get Current Position** button. This sometimes helps when you're trying to guesstimate pixel values for the drop target position relative to the current position.

**Book IV
Chapter 2**

**Jazzing Up Pages with
JavaScript Behaviors
and Spry Widgets**

8. **(Optional) If you want the layer to snap to the drop target coordinates when the visitor drags it within a specified range, enter a pixel value for the range in the Snap if Within text box.**

The bigger the number, the easier the visitor can drag the layer to the drop target.

9. **Select the Advanced tab to enter additional parameters and call JavaScript for the dragged layer:**

   - **Drag Handle:** By default the Entire Element option is selected, which means the whole layer acts as a drag handle. If you want only a specific part of the layer to be used as a drag handle, select the Area Within Element option and enter the Top and Left coordinate values and a Width and Height in pixels for the drag handle.

   - **While Dragging:** When the Bring Element to Front option is enabled, you can select Leave on Top or Restore Z-Index to alter the stacking order of the layer while dragging it.

   - **Call JavaScript:** Type JavaScript code or a function name in the Call JavaScript text field. This feature requires an understanding of JavaScript and how to collect data about the layer as it's being dragged. The JavaScript code repeats while the layer is being dragged.

   - **When Dropped:** Type additional JavaScript code or a function name in this Call JavaScript field to call actions when the layer is dropped or reaches its target destination.

   - **Only if Snapped:** When enabled, the When Dropped Call JavaScript executes only when the dragged layer reaches the drop target.

10. **Click OK to close the dialog box.**

11. **Verify that the event handler listed in the Events column of the Behaviors panel is the one you want to use.**

The default event handler for this behavior is onLoad. If desired, change the event handler in the Behaviors panel. Note: The onClick and onMouseDown event handlers don't work well with this behavior.

Spry Effects

Spry effects are special visual JavaScript effects that you can apply to almost any object or element on a Web page without having to apply any extra code or tags. To apply the effects, you must either select the object or make sure it has an ID assigned to it. However, for ease of use, you really should give the element a unique ID before applying the effect.

Each effect has three parts to it:

✦ The JavaScript effect object (which is the script)

✦ The trigger element that the visitor interacts with (like a button) to start the effect

✦ The element that is being changed by the effect (like a layer that shakes from side to side)

Spry effects can modify any combination of an element's opacity, visibility, size, position, and CSS style properties. What makes these effects unique is that the visitor's interaction with the element only causes the element to be updated, rather than having to refresh the entire HTML Web page.

Here's a listing of all the Spry effects you can choose from:

✦ **Appear/Fade:** Makes a hidden element visible or makes a visible element fade away to invisible.

✦ **Blind:** Hides or reveals an element using a simulated window blind effect that goes up or down.

✦ **Grow/Shrink:** Grows or shrinks the element in size.

✦ **Highlight:** Changes the background color style of an element. Can be applied to any element on the page except `body`, `frame`, `frameset`, `noframes`, or `applet`.

✦ **Shake:** Shakes the element back and forth from left to right.

✦ **Slide:** Moves the element up or down from it's current position.

✦ **Squish:** Shrinks the element until it disappears into the top left corner of the browser window.

As you add any of these Spry effects to your page, Dreamweaver automatically adds an extra line of code to the HTML markup between the `<head>` tags of your page that links to an external JavaScript called SpryEffects.js:

```
<head>
. . .
<script type="text/javascript" src="SpryEffects.js"></script>
<head>
```

This external file, which contains the scripts for all the Spry effects, is then added to the root level of your local managed site. The file can be moved into a subfolder (such as `js/` or `includes/`) if you like, as long as you ensure the link path to the file is correct. In addition, the file must be uploaded to the host server along with your other files for the effect(s) on your page(s) to work properly.

To add a Spry effect to an element your page, follow these steps:

1. **Insert the element or type in the text that will become the trigger for the event.**

   For example, the trigger can be a button graphic, a line, or word of text with a null link applied to it, or a layer with a unique ID attribute.

2. **Insert the element or type in the text that will become the object of the event.**

   This can also be a graphic, text with a null link, a layer, or nearly any other element in HTML. (See the effects listing above for exceptions to each of the effect types.)

3. **Select the element or object you'd like the Spry effect applied to.**

   Selecting it helps Dreamweaver identify where to apply the Spry effect in the markup.

4. **From the Behaviors panel, select the desired effect from the Effects submenu.**

   The dialog box of the selected effect opens. Figure 2-7 shows an example of the Appear/Fade dialog box.

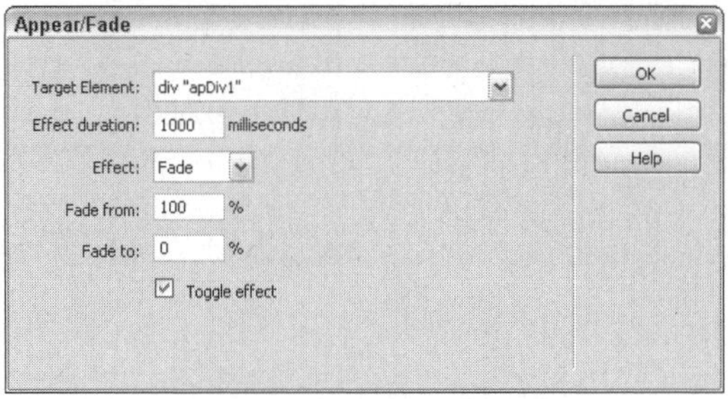

Figure 2-7:
Customize your Spry effect.

5. **Complete the dialog box with the desired settings.**

   • **Target Element:** Select the target element from the drop-down menu. If you don't see the name of the object you'd like to target in the listing, close the dialog box, select that object, and add an ID to it with the Properties inspector before returning to these steps.

   • **Effect Duration:** The Spry effect takes place over the number of milliseconds you set here. (One thousand milliseconds is equal to 1 second.)

   • **Effect:** Select the desired effect from the drop-down menu. Most Spry effects have two options to choose from, such as fade in or fade out.

- **Effect From/To:** Select the percentage or pixel distance of the effect, such as 100% to 0% or 1 pixel to 500 pixels. Each Spry effect has different options here.

- **Toggle Effect:** Enable this option to have the trigger be a toggle for the effect. For example, with the Grow/Shrink effect, clicking once makes the target object shrink and clicking again makes the target object grow.

6. **Click OK to close the dialog box and add the Spry effect JavaScript to your page.**

   Dreamweaver automatically adds the necessary JavaScript to the <head> of the page, to the trigger element, and to the target object, along with adding the SpryEffects.js file to the root level of your managed site.

7. **If desired, repeat Steps 4-6 to add additional Spry effects to your target object.**

   Many of the effects can be combined to create effect clusters where effects run concurrently or sequentially. For ideas and examples, check out `http://labs.adobe.com/technologies/spry/demos/effects/index.html`.

Spry effects are listed in the Behaviors panel along with the event handler, such as `onClick`. If desired, you can change the event handler by clicking it once to reveal the drop-down menu arrow, and then clicking the drop-down menu to select another event handler. You can also reopen the Spry Effect dialog box to modify the event settings by double-clicking the event name.

For a full description and overview of the Spry effects available in Dreamweaver, go to `www.adobe.com/go/learn_dw_spryeffects`.

You can also find samples and documentation for Spry on Adobe Labs at `http://labs.adobe.com/technologies/spry/`.

Go to URL

Add the Go to URL behavior to insert JavaScript that opens a new page in the same browser window or in a specified frame. Use this behavior in combination with other behaviors so that the link information is placed inside the JavaScript rather than in the Properties inspector (for instance, when you add a link to a graphic that has multiple rollover behaviors). When working with frames, this action is particularly useful because you can set the action to change the contents of multiple frames with one click. (For more on frames, see Book IV, Chapter 3.)

When using the "Go To URL" behavior, the traditional mouse effect that changes the arrow into a hand when you mouse over a link.

To add the Go to URL action to your page, follow these steps:

1. Select an image, object, or text link on your page.

This image, object, or text becomes the link that triggers the action.

2. Click the Actions (+) button in the Behaviors panel, and select Go to URL.

The Go to URL dialog box, shown in Figure 2-8, opens, displaying a list of windows or frame names.

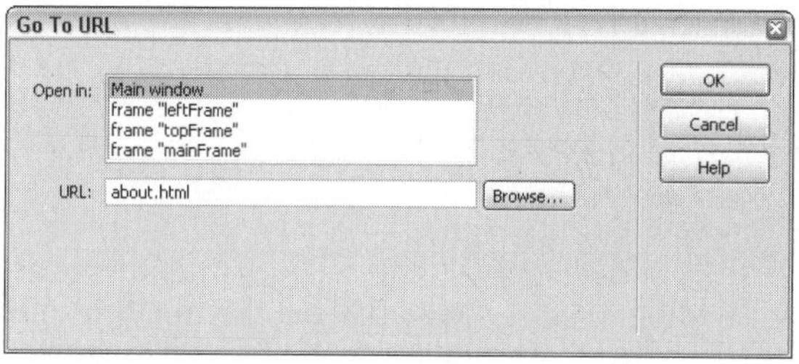

Figure 2-8:
Select
the main
window or
individual
frames.

Go To URL	
Open in:	Main window
	frame "leftFrame"
	frame "topFrame"
	frame "mainFrame"
URL:	about.html

OK   Cancel   Help

Browse...

3. In the Open In field, select a window or frame as the target destination for the URL.

For example, if you're using the behavior to open a page in the same window, the Open In field lists only Main Window as the target destination. When working with framesets, the frame names are listed, such as `topFrame`, `mainFrame`, and `leftFrame`, along with Main Window.

Try not to name your frames `top`, `blank`, `self`, or `parent`, as these filenames may conflict with the reserved frame target names (`_top`, `_blank`, `_self`, or `_parent`) and create strange results in different browsers.

4. In the URL field, type the path and filename of the document to be opened, or click the Browse button to find and select the file.

If the page you want to open is not on your site, be sure to include the **http://** prefix before the www in the Web address.

5. If changing URLs in multiple frames, repeat Steps 3 and 4 to select frames and URLs.

For example, to open two URLs with one event using frames, you can select `mainFrame` and type **welcome.html** in the URL field to open welcome.html in the `mainFrame`, and select `leftFrame` and type **navigation.html** in the URL field to open navigation.html in the `leftFrame`.

6. **Click OK to close the dialog box.**

7. **Verify that the event handler listed in the Events column of the Behaviors panel is the one you want to use.**

The default event handler for the Go to URL behavior is `onClick`. If desired, you can change the event handler in the Behaviors panel.

Jump Menu/Jump Menu Go

A jump menu is a pop-up menu of links that automatically opens another page in the browser when an item on the menu is selected. The Jump Menu behavior simply controls the structure and content of the menu links. The links on the menu can be to files on your Web site, pages on other Web sites, links to graphics, e-mail addresses, PDFs, Word documents, PowerPoint files, or any other kind of file that a browser can open.

Creating a jump menu

To add a jump menu to your page, follow these steps:

1. **Insert a jump menu by choosing Insert⊃Form Objects⊃Jump Menu.**

You can also click the Jump Menu button in the Forms category of the Insert panel. The Insert Jump Menu dialog box opens, shown in Figure 2-9.

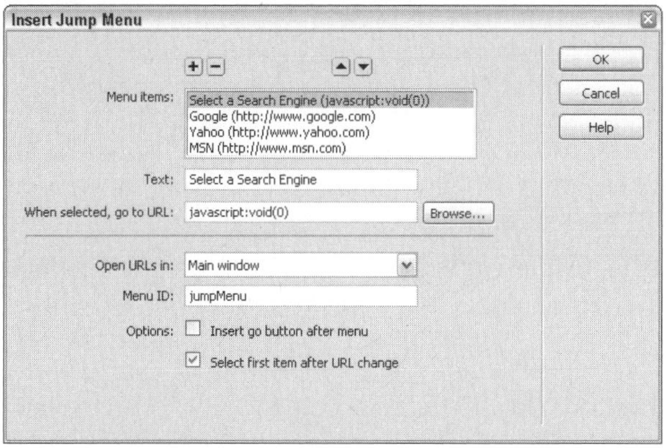

Figure 2-9: Create jump menus quickly with the Insert Jump Menu dialog box.

Book IV Chapter 2

Jazzing Up Pages with JavaScript Behaviors and Spry Widgets

2. **Click the plus (+) button above the Menu Items area to add an item to the menu and complete the fields:**

- **Text:** Type a name for the menu item.

- **When selected, go to URL:** Type the path and filename that identifies the jump to URL destination.

When creating a menu *header* for the first entry in the jump menu, such as *Select a State* or *Choose One,* add a null JavaScript link to the URL field, like this: `javascript:void(0)`. This null link prevents the page containing the jump menu from doing anything to the page if that option is selected. If you don't specify a destination, the script uses the menu text as the filename and tries to jump to a Web page with that name.

3. **Repeat Step 2 for each additional item on the list. Click the up and down arrows to sort and reposition list items.**

   For example, you may want to reposition the menu items to be listed alphabetically. To sort, select an item and click the up or down button.

4. **In the lower half of the dialog box, complete the remaining fields and enable or disable the other menu options:**

   • **Open URLs In:** Select Main Window, or when working with framesets or multiple windows, select any of the other window or frame names from the list.

   • **Menu ID:** When the page has only one menu, the default menu name available for selection is called `jumpMenu`.

   • **Insert Go Button After Menu:** Enable this option to add a Go button after the jump menu, which means the visitor must select an item from the menu and click the Go button to jump to the destination URL. Leave this option disabled to have the jump menu control the automatic jump to the target destination.

   • **Select First Item After URL Change:** Enable this option to have the menu revert to the first item in the list after every selection. This is particularly useful if you have created a menu header at the top of the list, such as *Choose a Country* or *Quantity*.

5. **Click OK to close the dialog box.**

6. **Verify that the event handler listed in the Events column of the Behaviors panel is the one you want to use.**

   The default event handler for the Jump Menu behavior is `onChange` and the default event handler for the Jump Menu Go behavior is `onClick`. If desired, you can change the event handlers in the Behaviors panel.

Dreamweaver adds the jump menu form field and form tags to your page along with the proper JavaScript to control the behavior. If you add the Go button to your menu, the jump menu is included in the Behaviors panel with the Jump Menu behavior and button and Jump Menu Go behavior.

Editing the Jump Menu behavior

If you need to edit the menu after adding it to a page, you can reopen the Insert Jump Menu dialog box through the Behaviors panel. Follow these steps:

1. **Select the jump menu in the open document and make sure the Behaviors panel is open.**

2. **Double-click the Jump Menu icon in the Actions column in the Behaviors panel.**

The Insert Jump Menu dialog box reopens (refer to Figure 2-9).

3. **Make changes to the menu as you need to.**

You can add new entries to the menu listing, rearrange entries, edit or remove existing entries, and specify target windows for the target URLs in any of the entries.

4. **Click OK to close the dialog box.**

Adding and removing a Go button

You can do two other things with the Jump Menu or Jump Menu Go behavior:

✦ **Add a Go button** if you originally created the jump menu without it. Adding a Go button to a jump menu is a good idea when working in framesets, as it allows visitors to reselect menu options that they already have selected.

✦ **Remove the Go button** if you've added it originally and no longer want it there.

Follow these steps to add a Go button to your jump menu:

1. **Place your cursor to the right of the jump menu in the open document and add a button to the page by clicking the Button icon in the Forms category of the Insert panel.**

You can also insert a button by choosing Insert⇨Form⇨Button.

2. **With the button still selected, select the None radio button in the Action area of the Properties inspector.**

The button value and label changes from Submit to Button.

3. **In the Value field in the Properties inspector, type Go.**

The button's value (label) changes from Button to Go. If desired, you can also edit the button's ID from button to Go.

4. **With the button still selected, click the Actions (+) button in the Behaviors panel, and select Jump Menu Go.**

5. **Select the jump menu that you want the new Go button associated with.**

If the page has only one jump menu, the drop-down menu says jump-Menu.

6. **Click OK to close the dialog box.**

   The Jump Menu Go button now has the Jump Menu Go behavior attached to it with the `onClick` event handler.

Follow these steps to remove the Go button from your jump menu:

1. **Select the Jump Menu Go button on the open document.**

2. **In the Behaviors panel, select the Jump Menu Go behavior and click the minus (–) Actions button.**

   Dreamweaver removes any JavaScript from the code on your page associated with this behavior.

3. **With the Go button still selected, press the Delete key to delete the button from the page.**

   The jump menu now needs a behavior so it can work properly.

4. **Select the jump menu and, from the Behaviors panel, choose the Jump Menu behavior.**

   The behavior picks up all the existing items in the list and reassigns the correct event handler (`onChange`) to the menu.

Open Browser Window

The Open Browser Window behavior lets you open any URL in a new browser window on top of the current browser window. You can also set some of the new window's properties, such as its name (`id`), width, and height, and whether certain features appear on the new window, such as the status bar, menu bar, and scroll bars.

For instance, if you sell energy bars, you may want to have the product's nutritional information open in a new browser window when a visitor clicks a text link. With the Open Browser Window behavior, you can have the new browser window open to a specific size with no resize handles, scroll bars, menu bar, status bar, navigation bar, or location bar, such as the example in Figure 2-10.

By default, none of the new window attributes are enabled in the Open Browser Window dialog box, which means you must enter the URL to display and enable any features that you want for your new window. As long as you enter at least one attribute, the new window won't resemble the parent window's attributes and instead has only the attributes you specify. However, if you don't enter any window attributes other than the URL, the new window opens at the same size and with the same attributes as the parent window.

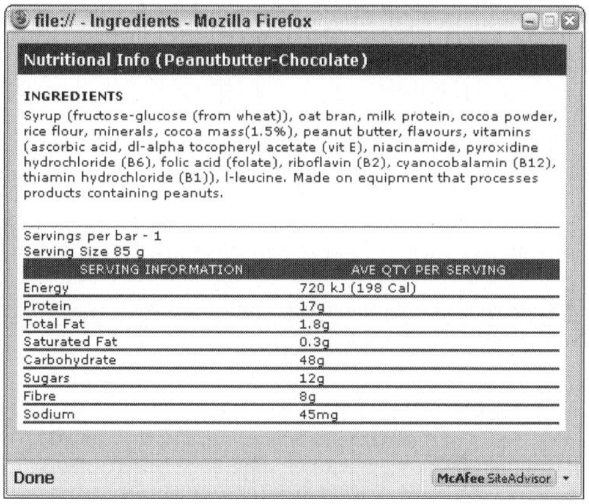

Figure 2-10:
The Open
Browser
Window
behavior
opens
another
page in
a new
browser
window.

Before you find out how to use this behavior, keep in mind that pop-up windows are often over- and improperly used and abused. Some people even consider new browser windows a form of Internet pollution! Also, some of the newer browsers, third-party browser plug-ins, and firewalls out there automatically prevent popups from occurring. For these reason, try to use this feature sparingly for specific purposes, such as showing a detailed image of a product you're selling or to display another document in a separate window from the rest of your site. In fact, you may want to add a warning message near the link that clicking the link opens a new window.

To add the Open Browser Window action to your page, follow these steps:

1. **Select an image or text on your page that will become the link to the pop-up window.**

This object or text becomes the link that triggers the action to open a new browser window.

When using text to open the new window, be sure to add a *null link* (a link that doesn't go anywhere) to the selected text before assigning the behavior. To create a null link, select the text and type `javascript:;` in the Link text box in the Properties inspector. Type carefully; the null link must contain both the colon and semicolon as shown in the previous sentence.

2. **Click the Actions (+) button in the Behaviors panel and select Open Browser Window.**

The Open Browser Window dialog box opens (see Figure 2-11), displaying a text field to add the URL of the page to be opened and a set of new window attribute options.

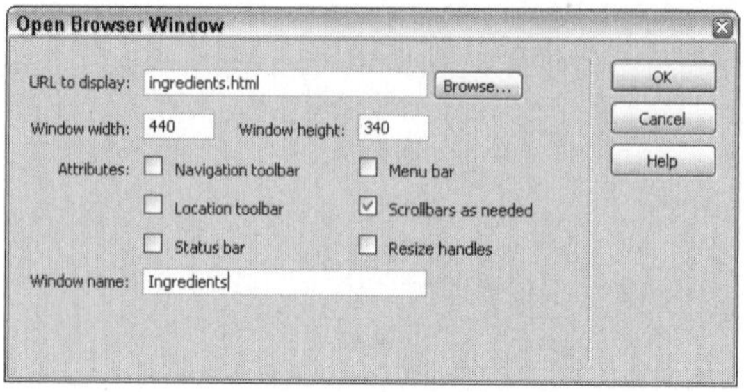

Figure 2-11:
Set target
URL and
browser
window
attributes.

3. **Next to URL to Display, click the Browse button to select a local file or type the URL that you want to open in the new browser window.**

    When entering a remote URL, you need to type the **http://** prefix before the www address, as in `http://www.adobe.com`.

4. **Specify new window attributes:**

    • **Window Width** and **Window Height:** Enter a number in pixels to set the size of the new window.

    • **Navigation Toolbar:** This window toolbar has browser navigation buttons including the Back, Home, and Reload buttons.

    • **Location Toolbar:** This toolbar shows browser options including the current URL or location of the visitor.

    • **Status Bar:** The status bar is located at the bottom-left edge of the browser window and displays such information as the URL, special messages, and page loading times.

    • **Menu Bar:** This part of the browser window (Windows) or desktop (Mac) has menu options for your applications such as File, Edit, View, and so on. When you disable this option in Windows, the visitor can only close or minimize the new window. On a Mac, the menu bar stays at the top of the desktop regardless of the Menu Bar setting.

    • **Scrollbars As Needed:** Enable this option to view scroll bars on the new browser window when the content in that window exceeds the visible size of the window. When you disable this option, any content that extends beyond the size of the window is hidden.

    • **Resize Handles:** This option enables or disables resize handles from appearing in the bottom-right corner of the window. When enabled, the visitor can click and drag the handles to resize the window. If disabled, the window size is fixed and cannot be changed.

    • **Window Name:** Enter a name or `id` for the new window in this field. Names help target the new window with links, apply CSS styles to the window contents, and control the window using other JavaScript behaviors. Make sure the window name doesn't include any special characters, spaces, or punctuation, and is written in lowercase letters.

5. **Click OK to close the dialog box.**

6. **Verify that the event handler listed in the Events column of the Behaviors panel is the one you want to use.**

   The default event handler for the Open Browser Window behavior is `onClick`. If desired, you can change the event handler in the Behaviors panel.

Although it's not part of the Dreamweaver dialog box for this behavior, you can hand-code additional information to specify the location of the new window when it opens, relative to the top-left corner of the parent browser window. In the code directly after the width and height dimensions, add top and left pixel coordinates separated by commas and no spaces, as in this example:

```
<a href="javascript:;" onclick="MM_openBrWindow('index.html','Details','width=300
   ,height=300,top=500,left=300')">View Details</a>
```

Popup Message

The Popup Message behavior opens a JavaScript alert window with your specific text message. Because it's a text-only script, the look of the alert window is totally controlled by the site visitor's browser, which means you can't format the text message in any way. The only thing in common as a layout feature between the different browsers, in fact, is that along with your message, they all display an OK button for the user to click to acknowledge seeing the message.

For this reason, this type of alert message is best used when you don't care how the message is formatted and rather want to communicate something to the visitor instead of needing the visitor to interact with the site in some way. If you really need to control how the message looks, use the Open Browser Window behavior (described previously in the chapter) to display your message instead.

On the plus side, these JavaScript alert messages can have any JavaScript property, global variable, function call, or other valid expression embedded inside the text as long as it's embedded inside braces ({}). For example, to have visitors open a box that displays the current date, type the following script into the behavior dialog box: `Today is {new Date()}.`

After it's been added to the page, the behavior's JavaScript in the code takes on the following syntax:

```
<p onclick="MM_popupMsg('Today is de'+(new Date())+'') ">Click here for today's
   date.</p>
```

When a viewer clicks the link, the script returns an alert box that looks like the example in Figure 2-12.

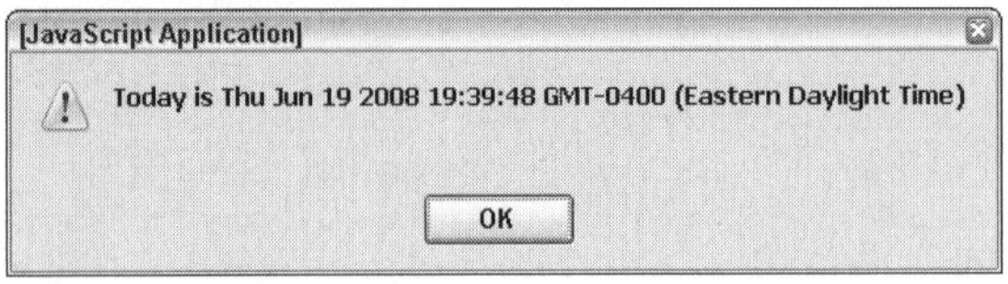

Figure 2-12:
An alert
window.

[JavaScript Application]

⚠ Today is Thu Jun 19 2008 19:39:48 GMT-0400 (Eastern Daylight Time)

OK

To add a pop-up message to your page, follow these steps:

1. **Select a word, phrase, image, or other object on your page as the trigger for the alert box behavior.**

2. **Click the Actions (+) button in the Behaviors panel and select Popup Message.**

   The Popup Message dialog box appears, shown in Figure 2-13.

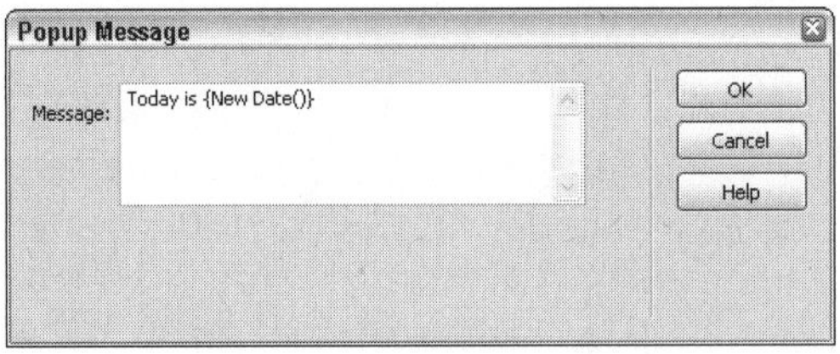

Figure 2-13:
Create
JavaScript
alert
messages.

Popup Message

Message: Today is {New Date()}

OK
Cancel
Help

3. **Type your text message, including any additional JavaScript expressions.**

   Using the same example, which gives the visitor the option of viewing the current date by clicking a text link, type the following into the Popup Message dialog box:

   ```
   Today is {new Date()}.
   ```

   To have a brace display as part of the alert, type it with a backslash before the brace, like this (\ {).

4. **Click OK to close the Popup Message dialog box.**

5. **Verify that the event handler listed in the Events column of the Behaviors panel is the one you want to use.**

   The default event handler for the Popup Message is `onClick`. You can change the event handler in the Behaviors panel, if desired.

Preload Images

The Preload Images behavior preloads specified images into the browser's cache so that they're ready for viewing when called by the browser. The preload process is invisible to the site visitor and helps ensure a seamless visitor experience with the Web site. Use this behavior when you want to preload images that are not on the page when the page initially loads in the browser or for images on the page that are not associated with the Swap Image behavior.

Follow these steps to add the Preload Images action to your page:

1. **Select an object or text link on your page as the trigger for the event behavior.**

2. **Click the Actions (+) button in the Behaviors panel and select Preload Images.**

   The Preload Images dialog box opens (see Figure 2-14).

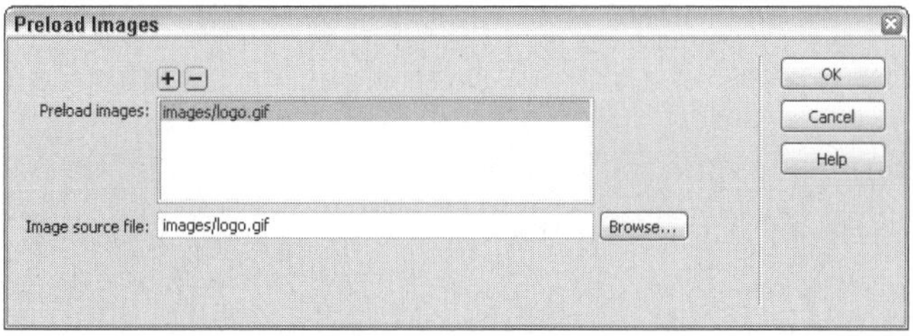

Figure 2-14:
Preload
as many
images as
you like.

3. **In the Image Source field, type the path and filename of the image you want to preload or click the Browse button to find and select an image.**

4. **Click the plus (+) button to add the image name to the Preload Images listing.**

   The image and its path are added to the Preload Images listing, as in `images/more.gif`.

5. **Repeat Steps 3 and 4 to add more images to the Preload list.**

   To remove an image from the listing, select the image from the list and click the minus (–) button.

6. **Click OK to close the Preload Images dialog box.**

7. **Verify that the event handler listed in the Events column of the Behaviors panel is the one you want to use.**

   The default event handler for the Preload Images behavior is `onLoad`. You can change the event handler in the Behaviors panel.

Book IV
Chapter 2

Jazzing Up Pages with JavaScript Behaviors and Spry Widgets

Set Nav Bar Image

The Set Nav Bar Image behavior lets you convert any graphic into a navigation bar image or alter the way existing navigation bar images display on the page. Keep in mind that each Web page can only have one navigation bar. If you attempt to add an additional nav bar to a page, Dreamweaver warns you that you can't do that, but it does allow edits to the existing bar. If you haven't created a navigation bar with images yet, check out Book II, Chapter 3 before proceeding. To edit an image with the Set Nav Bar Image behavior, follow these steps:

1. Select an image on an existing navigation bar for editing.

To use the Set Nav Bar Image behavior to convert a plain image into a navigation bar image, select that image, select the Set Nav Bar Image behavior from the Actions menu in the Behaviors panel, and complete the Set Nav Bar Image dialog box.

2. In the Actions column in the Behaviors panel, double-click the Set Nav Bar Image action connected with the selected image.

The Set Nav Bar Image dialog box opens (shown in Figure 2-15).

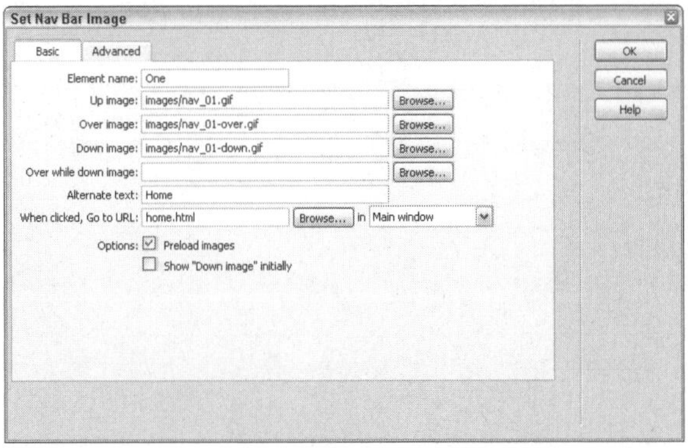

Figure 2-15:
Use this behavior to convert any graphic into a nav bar image.

3. Edit the Basic tab dialog box options as needed.

You can add or change the Up, Over, Down, and Over While Down state images, as well as their URLs and window destination targets.

4. Click OK when you finish making changes.

To edit several images at once for a navigation bar button, follow these steps:

1. **Select an image in the navigation bar that you need to edit.**

2. **In the Actions column in the Behaviors panel, double-click the Set Nav Bar Image action related with the image.**

   The Set Nav Bar Image dialog box opens.

3. **Select the Advanced tab.**

   Figure 2-16 shows the Advanced tab.

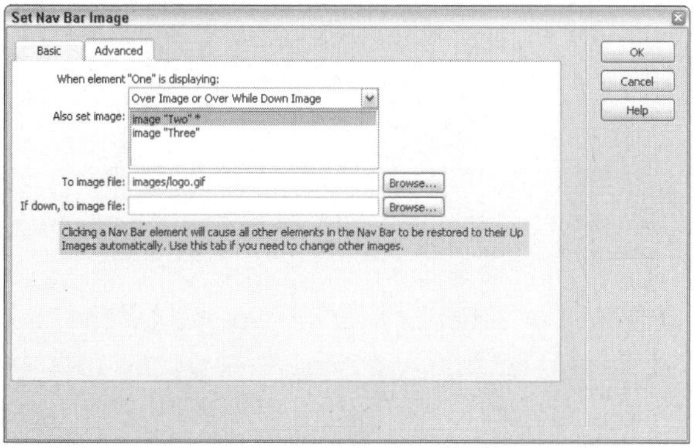

Figure 2-16: Create an action to change multiple images.

4. **From the When Element "*name*" Is Displaying menu, choose an image state:**

   • **Over Image or Over While Down Image:** Pick this option to change how another image displays when the user clicks the selected image.

   • **Down Image:** Pick this option to change how another image displays when the user moves the mouse over the selected image.

5. **From the Also Set Image box, select the graphic that changes when the user moves the mouse over or clicks the selected image.**

6. **In the To Image File field, browse for or type the path and filename of the image to be displayed.**

7. **If applicable, in the If Down, To Image File field, browse for or type the path and filename of the image to be displayed.**

   This option is presented only when you select the Over Image or Over While Down Image option for the When Element Is Displaying choice in Step 3.

8. **Click OK to close the dialog box.**

**Book IV
Chapter 2**

Jazzing Up Pages with JavaScript Behaviors and Spry Widgets

Set Text of Container

The Set Text of Container behavior replaces existing text content and for-matting of a layer with new text content and formatting in any container element, such as a table cell, layer, or even a `<span>` tag. The new text content can have any JavaScript property, global variable, function call, or other valid expression embedded inside the text as long as it's embedded inside braces ({ }). You can even have a brace display in the content by adding a backslash before it, like this (\ {).

By allowing you to change the content inside a container, this behavior is an alternative to hiding the current layer and showing another layer with different content. For example, you could change the text inside the current layer from a message that tells visitors to click for details to a message containing those details.

To begin using this behavior, you must start with at least one container with an ID on the page. For instance, you may want to apply this behavior to an AP Div layer. (See Book IV, Chapter 1 to learn more about working with layers).

To attach the Set Text of Container action to a page, follow these steps:

1. **Select a container on your page.**

2. **Click the Actions (+) button in the Behaviors panel and choose Set Text⇨Set Text of Container.**

   The Set Text of Container dialog box opens (see Figure 2-17).

Figure 2-17:
Change the text inside a container.

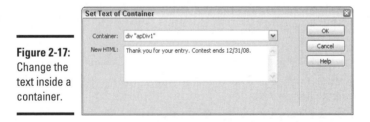

3. **From the Container menu, select the target container.**

   The target container is the container where the new content is displayed. If the container you want to target isn't listed, your target doesn't yet have an ID attribute. Close the dialog box, give your container an ID with the Properties inspector, and start over at Step 1.

4. **In the New HTML text box, type or paste the replacement HTML content for the targeted container.**

Enter any HTML including valid JavaScript and formatting code. When no formatting is entered with the New HTML text, the original text color and background color of the container is applied to the new text content.

5. **Click OK to close the dialog box.**

6. **Verify that the event handler listed in the Events column of the Behaviors panel is the one you want to use.**

   The default event handler for this behavior is `onClick`.

Set Text of Frame

The Set Text of Frame behavior works exclusively with framesets and allows you to replace text or HTML content in a frame with a specified action. The HTML replacement content can include any JavaScript property, global variable, function call, or other valid expression embedded inside the text as long as it's embedded inside braces ({ }). To have a brace display, type it with a backslash, like this (\ {).

By allowing you to change the content on a page inside a frame, this behavior is an alternative to opening another page in a frame. For example, you may want to change the text inside a frame containing a graphic that, when moused over, changes to display a special message to the visitor or identifies the URL of the page inside the frame.

With this behavior, most of the frame's formatting is lost, but you can retain the background and text colors if you want. If you need to control more than text content, you may want to open a new page in the frame instead.

To begin using this behavior, you must start with a frameset (see Book IV, Chapter 3). You can use any of Dreamweaver's preset framesets when you're creating a new document: Choose File➪New, and then in the New Document window, select a sample Frameset from the Sample Folder inside the Page from Sample category. Or choose Modify➪Frameset➪Split Frame and select any option to create a quick and simple frameset on an existing open document.

To add the Set Text of Frame action to your page, follow these steps:

1. **Select an object or text link on your page to attach the behavior to.**

   The object can be inside any of the frames in the frameset.

2. **Click the Actions (+) button in the Behaviors panel and choose Set Text➪Set Text of Frame.**

   The Set Text of Frame dialog box opens, shown in Figure 2-18, where you can enter in the new HTML content for the page.

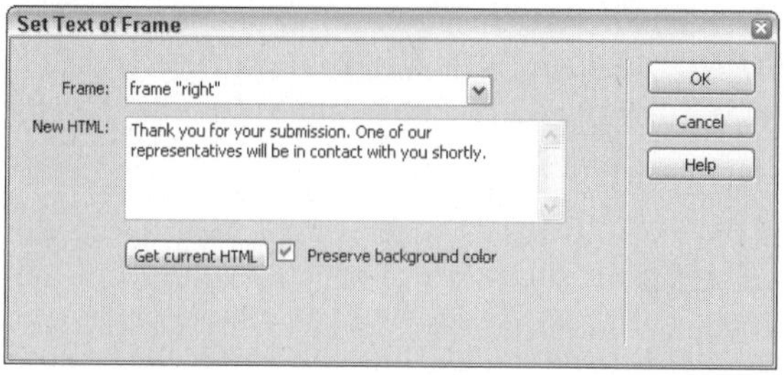

Figure 2-18:
Enter
replacement
HTML
content for
a targeted
frame.

Set Text of Frame

Frame: | frame "right" |

New HTML: | Thank you for your submission. One of our representatives will be in contact with you shortly. |

OK
Cancel
Help

Get current HTML ☑ Preserve background color

---

3. **From the Frame menu, select the target frame.**

The target frame is the frame that displays the replacement content.

4. **In the New HTML text box, type or paste the replacement HTML content for the targeted frame.**

To copy the existing `<body>` content of the selected target frame into the text box, click the Get Current HTML button.

To use the same background color of the current frame's page with the new text, enable the Preserve Background Color check box.

5. **Click OK to close the dialog box.**

6. **Verify that the event handler listed in the Events column of the Behaviors panel is the one you want to use.**

If desired, you can change the event handler in the Behaviors panel.

Set Text of Status Bar

Use the Set Text of Status Bar action to add a text message to the browser window's status bar (at the bottom-left corner of the window) when the visitor interacts with the page in a specified way. For example, you can have the status bar display a message about a particular link or image on the page when the visitor mouses over that link or graphic (On Sale through July 31st, 2009!) or list the title of the given page (Contact Us Today for a Free Consultation!) rather than its URL, which appears by default.

Although adding a message to the browser status bar can be an interesting way to enhance a site visitor's experience of a page, many visitors don't know to look in this area for messages or may even have the status bar disabled. Also, because the status bar displays useful information from the browser, replacing it with your own text can be seen as rude to some visitors.

For these reasons, using this behavior for optional information messages rather than important ones is for the best. Therefore, for the important messages, consider using the Popup Message, Open Browser Window, or Show-Hide Layers behaviors, all of which are described in this chapter.

Also, just like the Popup Message behavior, you can have any JavaScript property, global variable, function call, or other valid expression embedded inside the status bar text as long as it's embedded inside braces ({ }).

To add the Set Text of Status Bar action to your page, follow these steps:

1. **Select an object or text link on your page.**

   This is the object or text link that triggers the action.

2. **Click the Actions (+) button in the Behaviors panel and choose Set Text⇨Set Text of Status Bar.**

   The Set Text of Status Bar dialog box opens (see Figure 2-19).

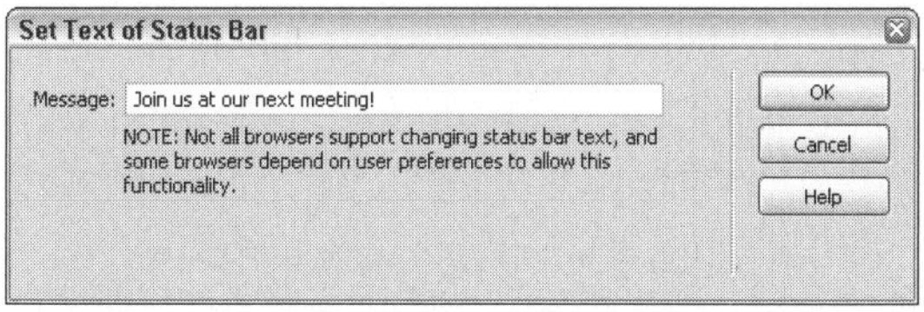

Figure 2-19:
Add a custom message to the browser status bar.

Set Text of Status Bar	
Message: Join us at our next meeting!	OK
NOTE: Not all browsers support changing status bar text, and some browsers depend on user preferences to allow this functionality.	Cancel
	Help

3. **Type your text message including any additional JavaScript expressions.**

   For example, to display the URL for the visited page when mousing over a target object or text link using a JavaScript function, type the following code:

   ```
   The URL for this page is {window.location}.
   ```

   Try to keep your message short because many browsers that support this behavior may truncate longer messages.

4. **Click OK to close the dialog box.**

5. **Verify that the event handler listed in the Events column of the Behaviors panel is the one you want to use.**

   The default event handler for the Set Text of Status Bar behavior is onMouseOver, but you can change it, if needed, in the Behaviors panel.

Book IV
Chapter 2

Jazzing Up Pages with
JavaScript Behaviors
and Spry Widgets

Set Text of Text Field

This handy behavior replaces the existing content of a text field on a form with specified new content. For example, you may want to enter sample text so a visitor knows the type of content they're expected to type into the field. The new HTML content can have any JavaScript property, global variable, function call, or other valid expression embedded inside the text as long as it's embedded inside braces ({ }). You can even have a brace display by adding a backslash before it, like this (\ {).

To begin using this behavior, you must start with at least one text field in a form on the page. To add a text field to your page, choose Insert⇨Form⇨Text Field, or click the Text Field button in the Forms category of the Insert panel to insert a text field at the insertion point on an open document. If prompted to add the Form Tag, click Yes. When the page has multiple text fields, it's also helpful to name all the form fields to better identify them before attaching this behavior.

Follow these steps to use the Set Text of Text Field behavior:

1. **Select a text field in a form on the open document.**

2. **Click the Actions (+) button in the Behaviors panel and choose Set Text⇨Set Text of Text Field.**

The Set Text of Text Field dialog box opens, as shown in Figure 2-20.

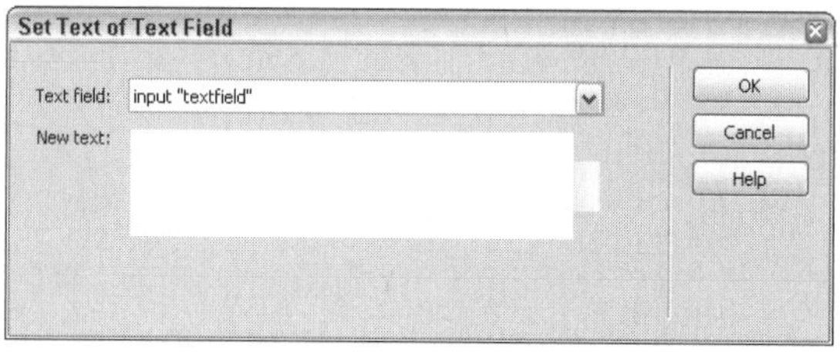

Figure 2-20: Add example text into a form field.

3. **From the Text Field menu, select the target text field.**

The target text field is where the new content displays.

4. **In the New Text text box, type or paste the replacement text.**

5. **Click OK to close the dialog box.**

6. **Verify that the event handler listed in the Events column of the Behaviors panel is the one you want to use.**

The default event handler is onMouseOver. If you don't like the event handler, you can change it in the Behaviors panel. If the event handler you want to use is not on the list, try changing the target browser in the Show Events For menu at the bottom of the Behaviors panel Actions menu.

Show-Hide Elements

When one or more AP Div layers are present on your page, you can control a layer's *visibility* (whether it's shown or hidden) with the Show-Hide Elements behavior. You can also use this behavior to restore an AP Div layer's visibility to its default setting.

The Show-Hide Elements behavior is great for hiding and showing information as a visitor interacts with objects on your Web page. For example, you may have an online photo gallery page with a series of thumbnail images and an area to display close-up images. With the Show-Hide Elements behavior, when the visitor slides the mouse over one of the thumbnail images, an AP Div layer with a close-up image is shown, and when the visitor's mouse moves off the thumbnail, the close-up AP Div layer is hidden.

Before using this behavior, you must have at least one AP Div layer on the page. To add an AP Div layer to your page, choose Insert⇨Layout Objects⇨AP Div, or click the AP Div button in the Layout category of the Insert panel and draw an AP Div layer anywhere in an open document. You may also want to rename all your AP Div layers with the Properties inspector or inside the AP Elements panel before attaching this behavior to objects on your page to help identify them easier. (Book IV, Chapter 1 describes layers in detail.)

Follow these steps to use the Show-Hide Elements behavior on your page:

1. **Select any object on your page (except a layer) such as a text link, image, or any object with an `id` attribute.**

2. **Click the Actions (+) button in the Behaviors panel and select Show-Hide Elements.**

   The Show-Hide Elements dialog box opens (see Figure 2-21). If the behavior is not available in the list of actions, you may need to select a different object on your page, like the `<body>` tag or a link (`<a>` tag).

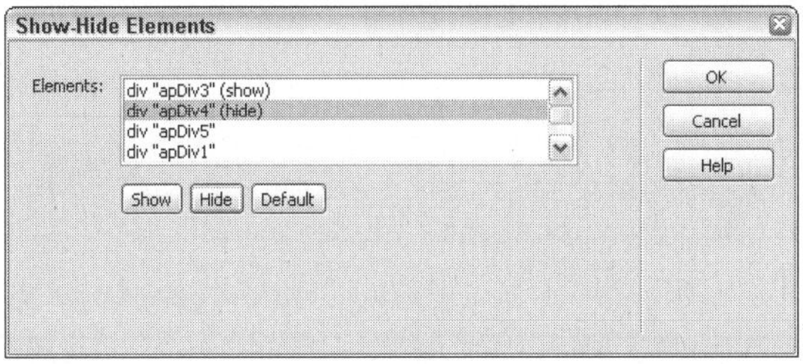

**Book IV
Chapter 2**

Jazzing Up Pages with JavaScript Behaviors and Spry Widgets

Figure 2-21: Alter a layer's visibility in the browser.

3. **From the Elements menu, select the element that you want to change the visibility for.**

4. **Edit the element's visibility status by clicking any of the following buttons:**

   • **Show:** Shows the selected element.

   • **Hide:** Hides the selected element.

   • **Default:** Restores an element's default visibility.

5. **Repeat Steps 3 and 4 for each additional element that you want to modify.**

   A single event handler controls all the elements selected here.

6. **Click OK to close the dialog box.**

7. **Verify that the event handler listed in the Events column of the Behaviors panel is the one you want to use.**

   You can always change the event handler in the Behaviors panel.

Be aware that some browsers support layers differently than others. Netscape, for instance, often collapses layers to fit the content of the layer. To stop browsers from altering layers, try setting layer clip parameters or adding images or text to the layer to hold the layer open to the size you want it to be (see Book IV, Chapter 1 for more information on setting layer clip parameters).

Another cool use for this behavior is to make a preload layer by creating a layer that covers the rest of the page as the page loads. Your visitors are engaged with other content, such as a Flash move, while the main content loads. Then, when the content finishes loading, the "preload layer" is hidden.

Follow these steps to make a preload layer with the Show-Hide Layers behavior:

1. **Create an AP Div layer on your page in the size you need that will cover the page's main content while it loads.**

   To add an AP Div layer to your page, click the AP Div button in the Layout category of the Insert panel and draw an AP Div layer anywhere in an open document.

2. **Name the new AP Div layer "preload" or something similar in the Properties inspector or in the AP Elements panel to help easily identify the layer when attaching the behavior.**

3. **In the AP Elements panel, select the preload layer and drag it to the top of the list of layers.**

   The preload layer needs to be at the top of the z-index (stacking order) for the behavior to work properly.

4. **With the preload layer selected, edit the layer's background color to match the rest of the page.**

Use the color picker in the Properties inspector to set the layer background color.

5. **To add HTML content inside of the preload layer, click inside the layer and type or paste the content.**

As an example, on the preload layer you may want to play a flash SWF file, display an animated GIF, or show a `Please wait. . .page loading` type of message.

6. **On the Tag selector at the bottom of the open document window, select the `<body>` tag, click the Actions (+) button in the Behaviors panel, and select Show-Hide Elements.**

The Show-Hide Layers dialog box opens.

7. **Select the preload layer from the Named Elements listing and click the Hide button.**

8. **Click OK to close the dialog box.**

9. **Verify that the event handler next to the Show-Hide Layers behavior says `onLoad`.**

If not, change the event handler to `onLoad` in the Properties inspector.

Swap Image

With the Swap Image behavior, you can assign a rollover button script to any graphic on the page. When the user moves the cursor over the graphic, the JavaScript tells the user's browser to display a new graphic (the *over state* graphic) in its place. You also have the option to preload images and restore the graphic to its original state with the `onMouseOut` event. You can even assign rollover graphics to several graphics on the page with one event handler, such as changing a button graphic and an image graphic at the same time when the visitor places the mouse over the button graphic.

The script for this behavior calls an action that changes the image listed in the `src` attribute of the `<img>` tag. The two things you need to do in advance of using this behavior are to name the normal state image in the Name field in the Properties inspector and to ensure that the over state image has the same width and height dimensions as the normal state graphic for a smooth mouseover effect.

**Book IV
Chapter 2**

Jazzing Up Pages with JavaScript Behaviors and Spry Widgets

To add the Swap Image behavior to your page, follow these steps:

1. **Select an image on your page.**

If you need to insert an image, click the Image button in the Common category of the Insert panel or choose Insert➪Image.

2. **In the Properties inspector, type a name (ID) for the image in the Name field.**

If you forget to name your images, you can still use the Swap Image action, but it may be hard to assign the behavior to the correct image when your page has multiple unnamed images.

3. **If assigning the same rollover action to multiple graphics on your page, repeat Steps 1 and 2 until all the graphics on your page are in place and named.**

In other words, if you know you want images 2 and 3 to change when image 1 is moused over, insert and name images 2 and 3.

4. **Select the image on the page you want to attach the behavior to, click the Actions (+) button in the Behaviors panel and select Swap Image.**

The Swap Image dialog box appears displaying a list of named (and unnamed) images on the page (see Figure 2-22).

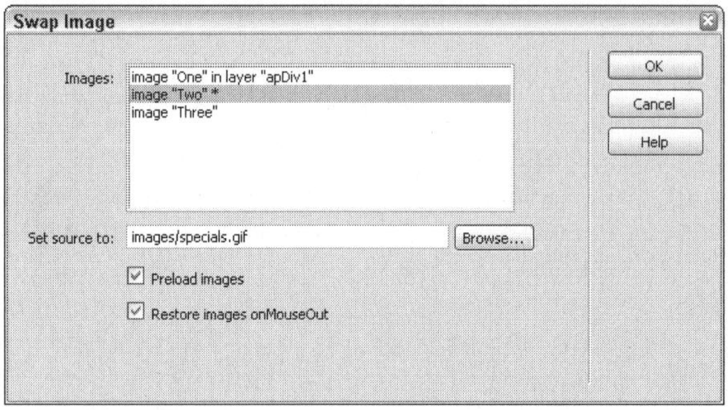

Figure 2-22:
Add the
Swap Image
behavior
to named
images on
your page.

5. **Select a named image from the list that you want to assign a rollover graphic to and click the Browse button to select the over state graphic for that image.**

If you know the path and filename, you can type it in the Set Source To text field rather than browsing for it.

6. **Repeat Steps 4 and 5 to create multiple rollover actions at once.**

This would be, say, if you want to change both a photo and a button graphic with one mouseover event.

7. **Select the Preload Images and Swap Image Restore options.**

By default both options are enabled, which are recommended settings:

- **Preload Images:** This setting adds JavaScript to the head area of the page that tells the visitor's browser to preload the rollover graphics when the page loads so that the user experiences no delay in viewing the rollover effect. Leave this option enabled, as images that aren't preloaded could create problems for displaying the page in a browser.

- **Swap Image Restore:** This option adds JavaScript to the page that tells the browser to restore the over state image to the normal state image when the site visitor moves the mouse cursor away from the rollover image graphic.

Figure 2-23 shows an example of how you can use the Swap Image behavior to create multiple over states for a single mouse event. When a visitor mouses over a main navigation button, like the one for reptiles, the navigation button over state graphic appears, along with a graphic of a lizard and a graphic containing text about reptiles.

Graphic containing text   Graphic

Figure 2-23:
Create
dynamic
rollover
graphic
effects.

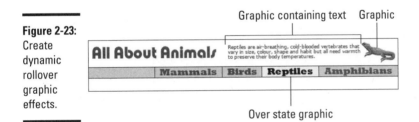

Over state graphic

Swap Image Restore

The Swap Image Restore action restores a swapped image to its original state. Because the Swap Image Restore action is added automatically when you use the Swap Image behavior and leaves the Restore option enabled, you'll probably never need to manually add the Swap Image Restore action.

On the blue moon occasion when you need to use it, simply select the behavior from the Actions menu in the Behavior panel and click OK in the Swap Image Restore dialog box. Dreamweaver adds the appropriate JavaScript to your page to restore the last set of swapped images to their original source graphics.

**Book IV
Chapter 2**

**Jazzing Up Pages with
JavaScript Behaviors
and Spry Widgets**

Validate Form

The Validate Form action verifies whether the visitor has accurately completed a form, and, when inaccurate, displays a JavaScript alert window with an error message. To use this behavior, turn to Book II, Chapter 7, which is entirely devoted to creating forms.

Using Third-Party Behaviors

Dreamweaver is an *extensible* program, which means that you can enhance its functionality by installing object, command, behavior, and other extensions that perform various functions. You can find a ton of these third-party extensions at the Adobe Exchange Web site and by searching for the term *Dreamweaver Extensions* in your favorite search engine.

When you find extensions you want to try, you can download them and use the Adobe Extension Manager to install them on your computer. The Extension Manager is a standalone application that installs, manages, and uninstalls extensions in Dreamweaver and other Adobe programs. Dreamweaver installs the Extension Manager as part of the Dreamweaver software installation process.

Visiting the Adobe Exchange Web site

More than a thousand extensions are available in the Dreamweaver Exchange section of Adobe's Exchange Web site. Among them, you'll find extensions to insert form fields, format tables, create navigation menus, and e-commerce shopping carts. Many of the extensions are offered for free to registered Adobe members. Others are available as either shareware requiring small fees or as fully supported software extensions for those willing to pay full price.

Adobe has its Dreamweaver extensions grouped into several categories, including Accessibility, App Servers, Browsers, DHTML/Layers, Extension Development, Fireworks, Flash Media, Learning, Navigation, Productivity, Rich Media, Scripting, Security, Style/Format, Tables, Text, Commerce, Content, and Web Analysis.

In addition to listing the platform availability (Windows, Mac, or both) for each of the extensions on the Web site, you can also find such helpful statistics as the number of recorded downloads, a user rating based on 5-star rating system, the Dreamweaver product version compatibility (8, MX, MX 2004, CS3, CS4), and the date the extension was released. You can also find links to a variety of discussion groups and user reviews on the site to help you make the best decision about which extensions to download.

To download and install extensions from the Adobe Dreamweaver Exchange Web site, follow these steps:

1. **Open the Dreamweaver Exchange Web site by choosing Help⇨ Dreamweaver Exchange.**

The Adobe Exchange opens in your primary Web browser, presuming you have a live Internet connection.

2. **Click the Dreamweaver link in the Exchanges by Product list.**

3. **Look around the various categories or search for extensions related to specific functions you're interested in.**

To find out more about an extension before downloading or purchasing it, click the extension name.

4. **When you find a behavior you want, download or save it.**

When accessing extensions on the exchange, browsers often give you the option of downloading and installing the extension directly from the source or saving the extension file to your local computer.

When you opt to save the file to your computer, Adobe recommends that you save the extensions to a Downloaded Extensions folder within the Dreamweaver application folder on your computer so you can manage all the extensions in one location. Another option is to download them to your desktop, and then move them to another folder after installation for archiving purposes.

Using the Extension Manager

Using the Extension Manager to install your third-party extensions is really easy. To launch the application, choose Help⇨Manage Extensions. If for some reason you do not have the application installed on your computer, visit the Adobe Web site at `www.adobe.com/exchange/em_download/` to download a free copy of the latest version of the application.

To install, manage, and uninstall extensions with the Extension Manager, follow these steps:

1. **From the Extension Manager's main menu, choose File⇨Install Extension to install the new extension.**

Some extensions install immediately, whereas others launch the Extension Manager application panel and display the Adobe disclaimer. If this happens, skip to Step 4. Otherwise, continue to Step 2.

2. **In the Extension Manager, select the Adobe application under the Products listing into which you want to install the extension (for example, Dreamweaver or Fireworks).**

This step is especially important when you have multiple Adobe products or multiple versions of the same product installed on the computer. When you upgrade your application, the extensions are either installed into the newest or currently running version or you are prompted to update them.

3. **Choose File⇨Install Extension.**

   The Select Extension to Install dialog box opens. Browse to and select an extension file with the .mxp file extension and click the Open or Install button.

4. **Read the Adobe Extension Manager disclaimer that appears, including any extension license information.**

   You must accept the terms of the disclaimer and license to complete the installation.

5. **If prompted to replace any existing files, click Yes (or Yes to All) to accept the version of the extension being installed.**

   If you click No, the current version of that file is kept. If you click Cancel, the installation stops without replacing or installing any new files.

   Note: Some extensions require you to close and restart Dreamweaver before taking effect.

Figure 2-24 shows how newly installed extensions appear in the list of Installed and Enabled Extensions in the Extension Manager.

For online help with Adobe's Extension Manager, visit `http://help.adobe.com/en_US/ExtensionManager/2.0/index.html`.

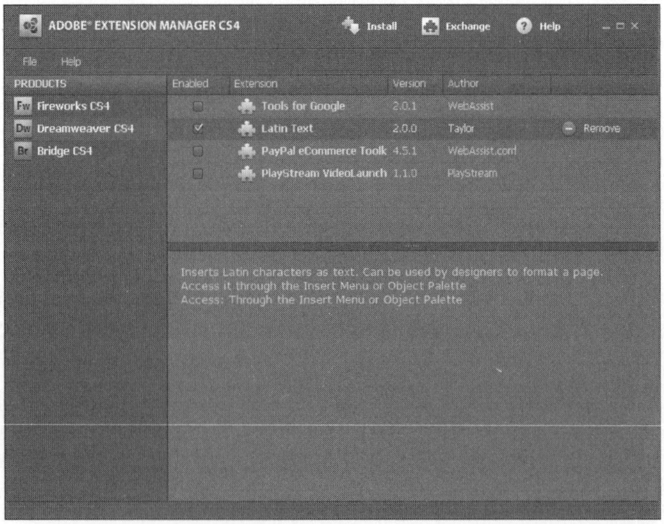

Figure 2-24: The Extension Manage lists all installed extensions as well as extension details including version, type, and author.

Working with Spry Widgets

Spry Widgets are part of the Spry framework for Ajax that was introduced in Dreamweaver CS3. They are a special library of JavaScript *widgets* that help Web designers, coders, and programmers who have a basic understanding of HTML, CSS, and JavaScript build XLM-rich Web pages that offer unique and interesting interactive experiences for site visitors.

In addition to Spry Widgets, there are also Spry Validation Form Fields (which you can find out more about in Book II, Chapter 7), Spry Effects, which can be applied to elements on your pages through the Behaviors panel (see the "Spry Effects" section earlier in this chapter), and Spry Data Sets, which let you build dynamic pages by loading and manipulating data from a specified data source, and are documented in detail online at `http://livedocs.adobe.com/en_US/Spry/SDG/index.html`.

What makes these Spry assets so powerful is that they're easy to use and customize after you understand how to work with them. However, to get the most use out of the Spry Widgets, you need a firm understanding of HTML, CSS, and JavaScript. Spry Widgets are more advanced Dreamweaver tools intended for the experienced Dreamweaver user.

To view all of the currently available Spry Widgets in CS4, open the Spry category of the Insert panel, as shown in Figure 2-25. The first four widgets (Spry Data Set, Spry Region, Spry Repeat, and Spry Repeat List) are tools to use when creating dynamic pages. The Spry Validation widgets (from Spry Validation Text Field to Spry Validation Radio Group) are for adding dynamic interactivity and validation functionality to forms, and the remaining widgets are for adding general interactivity to your pages, such as creating a Spry Menu Bar, Spry Tabbed Panels, Spry Accordion, Spry Collapsible Panel, and Spry Tooltip.

Here is a description of the general Spry Widgets you can add to your pages:

+ **Spry Menu Bar:** A fully customizable set of navigation buttons with unlimited submenu capabilities based on the List Item HTML tags (`<ul>`, `<li>`, and `<a>`) and CSS styling. Buttons have both normal and hover states styled with CSS, allowing for relatively easy customizable colors and fonts.

+ **Spry Tabbed Panel:** A set of tabbed panels that can contain a large amount of content in a smaller defined space. Panels can be opened and closed by visitors by clicking on the individual panel tabs, and only one panel is revealed at a time.

+ **Spry Accordion Panel:** A set of collapsible panels that can contain a large amount of content in a smaller defined space. Panels can be opened and closed by visitors by clicking on the individual panel tabs, and only one panel is revealed at a time.

Figure 2-25:
Use the
Spry menu
in the Insert
panel to
insert Spry
widgets.

+ **Spry Collapsible Panel:** A single collapsible panel that can contain a large amount of content in a small defined space. Visitors can expand and collapse the panel by clicking on the panel's tab.

+ **Spry Tooltip:** Provides tool tips to visitors when they hover their mouse over a particular object or bit of text on the Web page. Tips disappear when the visitors move their mouse away from the object that triggered the tooltip.

To use these widgets, start by inserting a Spry widget into your page, like the ones shown in Figure 2-26. After the widget is inserted, you can modify how it works by adding customized content, and, if you like, by editing the look and feel of how the widget appears in the browser, as all of the Spry widgets are styled with an external CSS file.

Each time you insert a Spry widget into your page, a corresponding CSS file (such as SpryAssets/SpryTabbedPanels.css) and JavaScript file (such as SpryAssets/SpryTabbedPanels.js) is added to the root level of your managed site inside a folder called SpryAssets. Sometimes, the widget may include graphics too, and those are also automatically added to the SpryAssets folder. You must upload this folder and its contents along with the page containing the Spry widget to the host server for the widget to function properly.

All of the general Spry Widgets listed in the preceding section can be inserted on to your pages in the same way. After insertion, you can customize them with your own data and modify their styles through the CSS Styles panel.

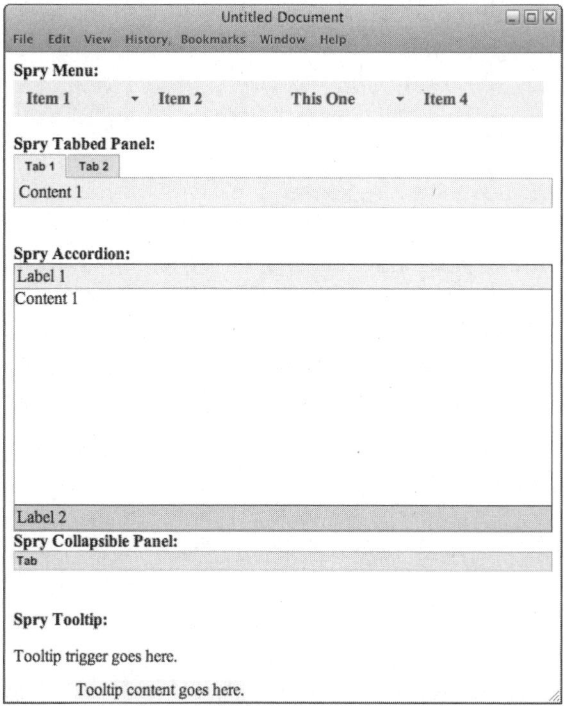

Figure 2-26:
Spry
widgets
offer visitors
customized
interactive
content.

To insert a Spry Menu Bar, Spry Tabbed Panel, Spry Accordion panel, Spry Collapsible Panel, or Spry Tooltip onto your page, follow these steps:

1. **Place your cursor inside the area on your page where you want to insert the Spry Widget.**

2. **Click the desired Spry Widget button on the Spry category of the Insert panel.**

   When inserting the Spry Menu Bar, you are prompted to select either a Horizontal or Vertical layout before Dreamweaver adds the code to the page. For all other widgets, the code is automatically inserted onto the page.

3. **With the Widget still selected (with the blue widget tab visible in Design view), use the Properties inspector to customize the widget.**

   By default, the widget is generically named (such as `sprytooltip1` or `Accordion2`); however, you can change the name, which appears as the widget's `id` attribute, on the Properties inspector, and Dreamweaver updates all instances of the widget on the linked JavaScript and CSS files.

**Book IV
Chapter 2**

**Jazzing Up Pages with
JavaScript Behaviors
and Spry Widgets**

- **Spry Menu Bar:** Add, remove, label, and reorder menu and submenu items, and add links, link title, and link targets.

- **Spry Tabbed Panel:** Add, remove, label, and reorder tabs, set the default panel that is opened when the page loads, and add content to each of the tab panels.

- **Spry Accordion:** Add, remove, label, and reorder tabs on the accordion and add content to each of the tab panels.

- **Spry Collapsible Panel:** Label and add content to the panel, set the panel display and default state to open or closed, and enable or disable panel animation.

- **Spry Tooltip:** Customize trigger and tooltip content, specify the trigger from a menu of all elements on the page with `id` attributes, set the horizontal and vertical offset, hide and show delay, special effect (none, blind, fade), and whether the tip should follow the mouse or hide on mouse out.

4. **When applicable, add customized content to the Widget in Design view.**

   For example, the labels and content of most widgets can be adjusted in Design view.

5. **Customize the Widget style through the CSS Styles panel.**

   The CSS files for each of the widgets are listed in the CSS Styles panel. Finding the right one to edit, however, may be a bit difficult without Dreamweaver's Help File documentation. Here's a listing of all the links for customizing each of the widgets:

   ```
   www.adobe.com/go/learn_dw_sprymenubar_custom
   www.adobe.com/go/learn_dw_sprytabbedpanels_custom
   www.adobe.com/go/learn_dw_spryaccordion_custom
   www.adobe.com/go/learn_dw_sprycollapsiblepanel_custom
   ```

   To customize the style of the Spry Tooltip widget, expand the SpryTooltip.css listed in the CSS Styles panel and make adjustments, as desired, to the `.iframeTooltip` and `.tooltipContent` styles.

For more information about Spry Framework for Ajax, see Adobe's Online Developers Guide at `http://livedocs.adobe.com/en_US/Spry/SDG/index.html`, where you can discover more about Spry widgets and effects, Spry data sets, and building dynamic pages with Spry. You can also find helpful tutorials on the Spry Framework for Ajax Technology Center at `www.adobe.com/devnet/spry/` and informative video tutorials at `www.adobe.com/designcenter/video_workshop/`.

Chapter 3: Designing Pages with Frames

In This Chapter

✓ **Understanding frames**

✓ **Creating frames and framesets**

✓ **Modifying frame and frameset properties**

✓ **Targeting frames with links**

✓ **Adding noframes content**

✓ **Creating floating frames**

*B*ack in the early days of the Internet, the most common use of frames was to ease navigation and reduce page loading wait times for site visitors using dialup modem connections. The idea behind frames is this: The browser window is divided into several panes, or *frames,* that each display different HTML pages, independent of the content in the other frames. Furthermore, by specifying the target frame within your hyperlinks, you can control which frame a new page opens in when a user clicks a link.

Suppose, for instance, a user visits a Web site comprised of a three part frameset with company information in the top frame, some navigation buttons in the left frame, and information pertinent to the Web site's products or services, such as contact information, in the main frame. With this type of frameset, a visitor can click a link in the navigation frame, and the linked page opens in the main frame of the frameset.

Today many people visiting Web sites have high-speed connections, such as DSL, cable, T-1, or broadband. With these faster types of Internet access, frames are no longer necessary as a navigation or layout tool. Today, the recommended practice is to create page layouts using layers (see Book IV, Chapter 1) and CSS (see Book III, Chapter 1). In addition, frames have coding, printer, browser, and SEO issues, including problems with bookmarking pages and effective search engine optimization.

Nevertheless, they're still used every once in a long while, so you should know how to use them, especially in the event that you inherit a site that was built with them.

This chapter provides you with an overview of frames, including how to create and modify framesets, set attributes for frames and framesets, set the target attribute of links to display pages in specific frames, add noframes content for visitors using browsers without frame support, and insert floating frames on a page.

Understanding Frames

Frames enable you to divide a browser window into multiple panes, which are called *frames*. Each frame contains a unique Web page that displays independently of the pages in the other frames in the browser window. Then, with regular HTML, you can control the contents of each framed area separately. For example, when a visitor clicks a link, you can have some frames on the page remain static while the content in another frame changes.

In the code, a page that defines the frame divisions or layout is called a *frameset*. The frameset itself doesn't display any content in the browser window (except when you use the `<noframes>` tag, as described at the end of this chapter). Rather, the frameset provides formatting and layout instructions to the browser on how to display the pages *inside* the frames. In other words, the frameset is merely a container in which other documents display.

You can use frames to format your entire Web site or just a particular section or page of a site. When using frames as the layout format for your entire Web site, you typically save the frameset file as index.html so the page loads in the browser window when people visit the URL. When the frameset page loads, the browser collects and displays the pages inside the individual frames.

You can divide frames vertically and horizontally into as many frame rows and columns as you need to achieve your layout. For example, in Figure 3-1, the browser window is divided into three frames with static company information in the top frame, static navigation links in the left frame, and general information in the main frame. When a visitor clicks a link in the navigation area, a new page displays in the main frame.

In the code, `<frameset>` tags replace the `<body>` tags, and the `<frame>` tags further define divisions in the frameset, as in the following sample code:

```
<frameset rows="80,*" cols="*" frameborder="NO" border="0" framespacing="0">
  <frame src="top.html" name="topFrame" scrolling="NO" noresize title="topFrame">
  <frameset cols="80,*" frameborder="NO" border="0" framespacing="0">
    <frame src="left.html" name="leftFrame" scrolling="NO" noresize
    title="leftFrame">
    <frame src="main.html" name="mainFrame" title="mainFrame">
  </frameset>
</frameset>
```

Top frame

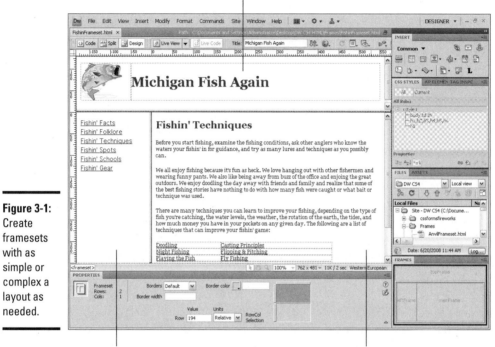

Figure 3-1:
Create
framesets
with as
simple or
complex a
layout as
needed.

Left frame   Main frame

When you create new frames, rows are created top to bottom, and columns are created left to right. The smallest frameset division can contain either two rows or two columns. However, you can nest a frameset within a frame of another frameset, to any level of nesting, for some highly complex page display effects.

After you divide your page into a frameset, specify the frameset and the frame parameters and attributes in the Properties inspector, just as you do with text and graphics. For instance, you can set the width and height of frames, the number of rows and columns in the frameset, the source page for a frame along with the source page margin width and height, a name or ID of a frame for targeting purposes, a border width and border color, whether the frame has scroll bars, and whether a visitor can resize it.

There are both good and bad things about framesets; frames are great because

✦ You can display multiple pages in one browser window.

✦ You can use them for displaying Web gallery images, including thumbnails and close-up images.

Book IV
Chapter 3

Designing Pages
with Frames

✦ The browser does not need to reload graphics for each page, which speeds up page display.

✦ Each page in a frame can have its own set of scroll bars, which means a visitor can scroll in one frame of the browser while referring to the unmoving area of another frame of the browser.

✦ You can use several JavaScript behaviors with frames, such as the Set Text of Frame, Go to URL, and Insert Jump Menu options. These behaviors allow you to modify content of a page in a frame without opening a new page in the frame, create a link to another page in particular frame, and open a new page in a particular frame of the frameset using a jump menu. For details on each of these and other scripts, check out Book IV, Chapter 2.

Frames are not so good because

✦ Visitors can't bookmark individual pages within framesets. The URL of the frameset page (usually `index.html`) doesn't change at all as the visitor navigates through the site. Also, visitors can't save individual configurations of pages in frames.

✦ Search engines have trouble indexing pages making search engine optimization nearly impossible.

✦ You need to define the `target` attribute of link tags so new pages open in the correct frame.

✦ Visitors with disabilities may have difficulty navigating the frames.

✦ Designing framesets can get very confusing.

✦ Precisely aligning elements between frames is more difficult than aligning elements on regular unframed pages.

✦ You're likely to create errors with links and targets.

✦ Most site visitors don't like frames, especially badly crafted framesets.

Creating Frames and Framesets

Before creating framesets in Dreamweaver, you need to do two things to customize your work environment and improve the display of the frameset document in Design view:

✦ **Open the Frames panel.** The Frames panel, shown in Figure 3-2, displays all the frames in a frameset document and can assist you with selecting the frame elements during the frameset building process. To open the Frames panel, choose Window➪Frames.

✦ **Enable the Frame Borders visual aids.** When you have this feature enabled, the open document displays frame borders and divider bars, as shown in Figure 3-3. To enable Frame Borders visual aids, choose View➪Visual Aids➪Frame Borders.

Figure 3-2:
Open the
Frames
panel before
working
with frames.

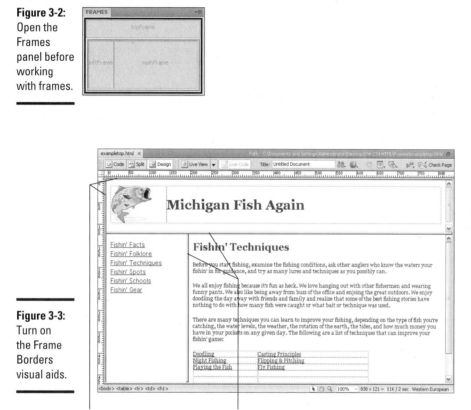

Figure 3-3:
Turn on
the Frame
Borders
visual aids.

Frame borders   Divider bars

The W3C recognized frames as of the HTML 4.0 doctype, and because browsers need to know what they're looking at, Dreamweaver automatically inserts the appropriate doctype when creating frames. This ensures that the browsers interpret the file accurately. However, if you're hand-coding or inheriting a frameset from another source (as with a Web site redesign project, for instance), be sure to add the following doctype to the master frameset file above the opening `<html>` tag:

```
<!DOCTYPE HTML PUBLIC "-//W3C//DTD HTML 4.01 Frameset//EN" "http://www.w3.org/TR/
    html4/frameset.dtd">
```

When working in XHTML, use the XHTML Frameset DTD instead:

```
<!DOCTYPE html PUBLIC "-//W3C//DTD XHTML 1.0 Frameset//EN" "http://www.w3.org/TR/
    xhtml1/DTD/xhtml1-frameset.dtd">
```

Building framesets is a somewhat complex process and you need to set them up carefully to display correctly in browsers. For that reason, try following these general steps whenever building framesets:

1. **Create the frameset and select the files that you want to appear in each frame.**

See the following section for details.

2. **Save the frameset and all the files in each frame, and name each of the frames for later targeting with links.**

See "Saving Frames and Framesets," later in the chapter.

3. **Set the properties for the frameset and the individual frames in the Properties inspector to achieve the look you want.**

See the later section "Setting Frame Properties with the Properties Inspector."

4. **Set the target attribute for all the links on all the pages to display in the frames of the frameset so they'll accurately display where you intend them to.**

For details, see "Targeting Frames with Links."

In the next few sections, you find out how to create a frameset and select files for the frames.

Using predefined framesets to create a new file

When you need a simple frameset with two to three frames, consider using one of Dreamweaver's predefined framesets. To create a new document with one of the predefined framesets, follow these steps:

1. **Choose File⇨New to open the New Document dialog box, shown in Figure 3-4.**

2. **Select the Page from Sample category and choose a predefined frameset from the Frameset Sample Folder.**

If you're not sure which frameset to choose, select any frameset in the Sample Page list; a preview and description of that preset appears on the right.

3. **Click the Create button.**

The new frameset appears in the Document window.

Note: If the Frame Tag Accessibility Attributes dialog box opens, select a frame in the frameset from the Frame menu and add a title for that frame. Repeat this process until all the frames in the frameset have titles and then click OK. To bypass accessibility tags and just insert the frames without frame titles, click the Cancel button.

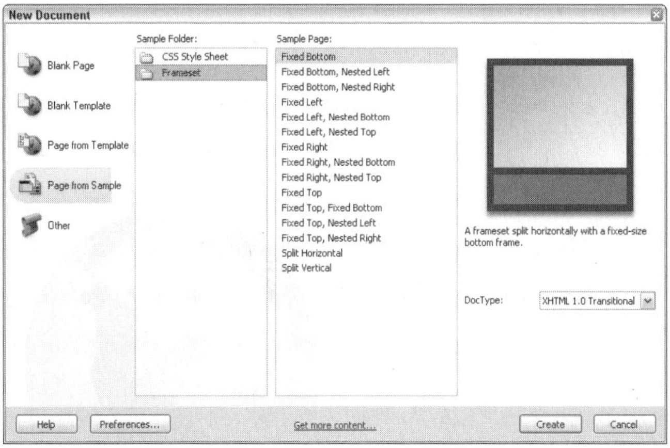

Figure 3-4:
Choose a
predefined
frameset
from the
Frameset
Sample
Folder in
the Page
from Sample
category
of the New
Document
dialog box.

Displaying a file in a predefined frameset

Another way of using the predefined framesets is to convert an existing open document into a file displaying inside a frameset. To display a file inside a predefined frameset, follow these steps:

1. **Open the file you want to display inside a frame in a frameset.**

2. **Place an insertion point somewhere inside the file.**

3. **Choose a predefined frameset from the Frames button drop-down menu on the Layout category of the Insert panel.**

When you're trying to decide which frameset to choose, look at the thumbnail images that appear next to the predefined frameset options, as shown in Figure 3-5. The frame in blue indicates where your document appears if you select the predefined frameset. The white areas represent the frames that open in the frameset, where you can display other documents.

Note: If you've enabled the Frame Accessibility features in the Preferences dialog box, the Frame Tag Accessibility Attributes dialog box, shown in Figure 3-6, opens.

Select a frame in the frameset from the Frame menu and add a title for that frame. Repeat this process until all the frames in the frameset have titles.

To bypass this feature, click the Cancel button and Dreamweaver creates the frameset without the associated accessibility tags and attributes in the code.

Figure 3-5:
Use the
Frames
menu on
the Layout
category of
the Insert
panel to
convert an
existing
page into
a page
inside of a
predefined
frameset.

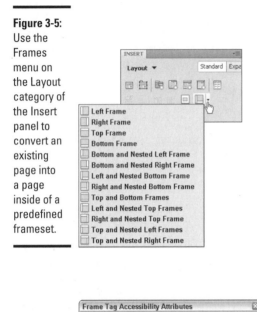

Figure 3-6:
The Frame
Tag
Accessibility
Attributes
dialog box.

Creating custom framesets

You can create a custom frameset in Dreamweaver by splitting an existing Document window into frames. To design a custom frameset from a blank, open document, do either of the following:

✦ Choose Modify⇨Frameset and choose a splitting option from the submenu, such as Split Frame Left or Split Frame Down.

✦ Enable the Frame Borders visual aids, and then manually drag a frame border into the open document in Design view to split the frame into a frameset. The frame borders are the thin gray bars located on the top and left edges of the Document window between the ruler (select View⇨Rulers⇨Show) and the content area of the page.

To further customize and refine the frameset with additional frames, continue splitting frames by these methods or the other techniques available in Dreamweaver, as described in the next section.

Adding, Removing, and Resizing Frames

Before adding, removing, or resizing frames, enable the Frame Borders visual aids and open the Frames panel, as described in "Creating Frames and Framesets," earlier in the chapter. Visual aids enable you to see the frame borders and frame divisions so that you can modify divisions on a frameset, and the Frames panel assists you with selecting and naming the frames.

Adding frames

To add frame divisions, do any of the following:

✦ **Divide a frame or set of frames vertically or horizontally:** In Design view, drag a frame border from the top or left edge of the window (near the ruler) to the middle of the page.

✦ **Divide a frame vertically or horizontally but do not split any existing frames:** Ctrl+drag (Windows) or ⌘+drag (Mac) when dragging a new frame border.

✦ **Split a frame into four parts:** In Design view, drag a frame border from a corner to the middle of the frame. Begin dragging when the cursor turns into a four-sided arrow.

✦ **Split a frame with a border that doesn't touch the edge of the master frameset:** In Design view, Alt+drag (Windows) or Option+drag (Mac) to drag a new frame border from an existing frame border.

✦ **Divide the frame that contains the insertion point:** Choose Modify⇨Frameset and then select a split option.

Although they're super easy to split, you can't easily merge frames the way you can with table cells. Try, therefore, to have a clear idea of the frameset layout you need before building it. For instance, when you need a frameset with three frames, split the page into two frames first, and then split one of the two frames into a third frame.

Removing frames

To remove a frame division, do either of the following in Design view:

✦ Drag a frame border off the side of the page onto the ruler bar.

✦ Drag a frame border onto the border of a parent frame or frameset.

Because you can't completely remove framesets by dragging, you must delete the file or modify the code. For instance, after you remove all the frame borders from a page, the code still displays a frame `doctype`, `<frame>`, and `<noframes>` tags, as in the following:

```
<!DOCTYPE HTML PUBLIC "-//W3C//DTD HTML 4.01 Frameset//EN" "http://www.w3.org/TR/
    html4/frameset.dtd">
<html xmlns="http://www.w3.org/1999/xhtml">
<head>
<meta http-equiv="Content-Type" content="text/html; charset=utf-8">
<title>Untitled Document</title>
</head>
<frame src="file:///C/Project Files/ProjectName/Untitled-1">
<noframes><body>
</body></noframes>
</html>
```

As you can see, the doctype still identifies the file as a page using framesets, and the `<frame>` and `<noframes>` tags identify the content as sitting inside a frame structure. If you want to use the page as a regular HTML file, you could modify the code to reflect the doctype and tags of a normal HTML or XHTML document, but creating a new document by choosing File⇨New is much faster.

Resizing a frame

To resize a frame, do either of the following:

✦ In Design view, drag the frame borders inside the Document window to the size you want.

✦ Select a frame or frameset in the Frames panel and in the Properties inspector set the exact sizes for the frames in pixels or percentages, or choose the Relative size setting.

Nested Framesets

Nested framesets occur when a frameset sits inside another frameset. Nesting is very common, found in even the simplest of framesets. You can nest as many framesets as you need to achieve your layout. The three-part Web site shown in Figure 3-7 is an example of a frameset containing two nested framesets. The main window is divided into two rows, top and bottom, and the bottom row is further split into two columns, left and right. The entire bottom row is the first nested frameset inside of the master frameset. In the right column of the bottom row, another nested frameset is split into two columns.

You can create nested framesets two ways:

✦ Define the inner frameset in the same file as the outer frameset or in a separate file of its own. In other words, you can use Dreamweaver's frame-splitting tools to create the complex structure of the frameset all in the same master frameset file.

✦ Open a separate, external frameset page inside one of the frames of the frameset using the Open in Frame command (as described in the next section).

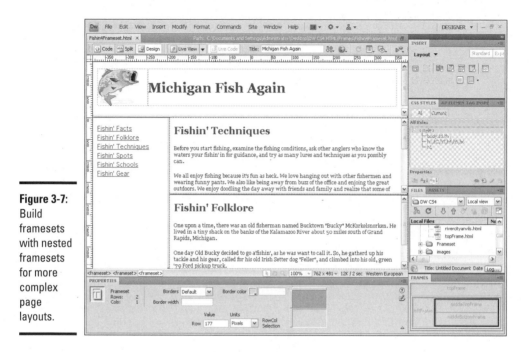

Figure 3-7:
Build
framesets
with nested
framesets
for more
complex
page
layouts.

Because framesets can get very complicated very fast — especially when
you start targeted linking — you may do better nesting with the first method.

Fortunately, when you use the frame-splitting tools Dreamweaver provides,
you can virtually forget about having to oversee the complexity of nesting
details because Dreamweaver handles the coding for you.

Opening Pages in a Frame

After creating the layout for your frameset, you can add new page content to
any blank untitled documents in the frameset, or even better, open an existing page within an empty frame.

To open an existing page in a frame, follow these steps:

1. **In a saved frameset, place your cursor anywhere inside the frame
where you want to open your page (see Figure 3-8).**

If you haven't saved and titled the master frameset yet, do so before proceeding by selecting the outer frameset in the Frames panel and choosing File⇨Save Frameset or File⇨Save Frameset As. After you've saved
it, give the frameset a title by typing one into the Title field on the document toolbar.

Figure 3-8:
Place your cursor inside the empty frame.

2. **Choose File⇨Open in Frame.**

   Do *not* select the File⇨Open option! You want the fifth option down in the list, Open in Frame, which comes after New, Open, Browse in Bridge, and Open Recent, as shown in Figure 3-9.

Figure 3-9:
Select the Open in Frame option.

New...	Ctrl+N
Open...	Ctrl+O
Browse in Bridge...	Ctrl+Alt+O
Open Recent	▶
Open in Frame...	Ctrl+Shift+O
Close	Ctrl+W
Close All	Ctrl+Shift+W

The Select HTML File dialog box opens.

3. **Browse to and select the HTML file you want to open in that frame or type the path and filename of the page you want to open. Click OK (Windows) or Choose (Mac).**

   The selected page appears inside the frame on the frameset, as shown in Figure 3-10.

Figure 3-10:
The selected page appears inside the frame of the frameset.

If at any time you want to change the page that is currently open in the frameset, select the frame in the Frames panel and edit the Src field in the Properties inspector to select another document.

Saving Frames and Framesets

When you save them properly, all the files inside a frameset display accurately in a browser. Therefore, after creating a frameset, you must save both the frameset document and all the individual files in each of the frames. You can save all the frames and framesets at once by using the Save All command. Or, if you prefer, save the frameset and individual frame documents one at a time.

Saving all the files in the frameset

To save a frameset and all files opened in each of the frames at once, follow these steps:

1. **Choose File⇨Save All.**

All the files associated with the frameset are saved including the frameset document and all the files opened in each of the frames.

The Save As dialog box appears, as shown in Figure 3-11.

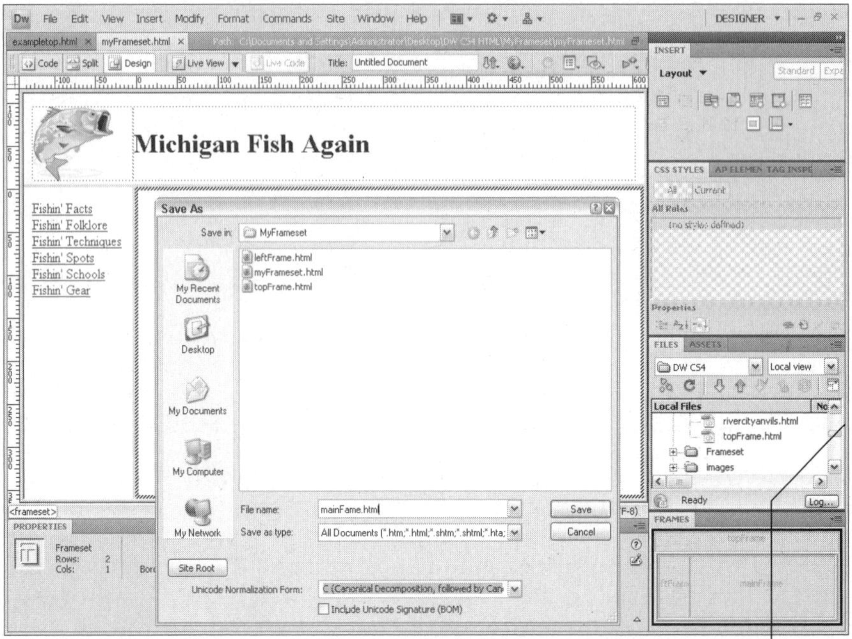

Figure 3-11:
In Design view, a dark border appears around the frame being saved when you're saving the frameset and its files.

This border designates which frame you are saving.

2. **Dreamweaver prompts you to save and name each file. Each time the Save As dialog box appears, look at the document in Design view to identify the frame you're saving, and then enter a filename and click Save.**

   The frame with a dark border surrounding it is the frame you're saving. Figure 3-11 shows an example of how the border surrounds the frame.

   If you choose File⇨Open in Frame to open existing files inside all your frames, you only need to name and save the frameset file.

Saving only the frameset file

To save only the frameset, follow these steps:

1. **In the Frames panel or in the Document window, select the frameset.**

   You can select the frameset with either of the following methods:

   • In the Document window, click in the border between any two frames in the frameset.

   • In the Frames panel, click the master frameset border that surrounds the entire frameset. You can tell you've selected the frameset when the Frames panel displays a black border around the outermost frameset.

2. **To save the selected frameset, choose File⇨Save Frameset.**

Saving an individual file in a frame

To save a file opened inside a frame:

1. **Click inside the frame that contains the file you want to save.**

2. **To save the selected file, choose File⇨Save Frame.**

Titling a Frameset

One of the most often overlooked parts of a frameset is the frameset title. The title for the frameset page appears in the title bar at the top of an open browser window. If left unaltered, the title bar reads Untitled Document, which is not helpful to site visitors and may be perceived as unprofessional, so be sure to title the frameset file!

It can sometimes be tricky to select the correct piece of a frameset to add the title, so be sure you're selecting the frameset and not one of the individual frames within it: Titles on those pages don't appear in the browser window.

Follow these steps to name your frameset file:

1. **Select the frameset by any of the following methods:**

   - In the Document window, click in the border between any two frames in the frameset.

   - In the Frames panel, click the master frameset border that surrounds the entire frameset. You can tell it's selected when the Frames panel displays a black border around the outermost frameset.

2. **Type a title for the file in the Title text box on the Document toolbar, as shown in Figure 3-12.**

   To ensure that you've entered in the title correctly, preview your frameset in a browser window. If the title bar of the browser matches your input, consider it a success!

Figure 3-12:
Add a title to
the frameset
document.

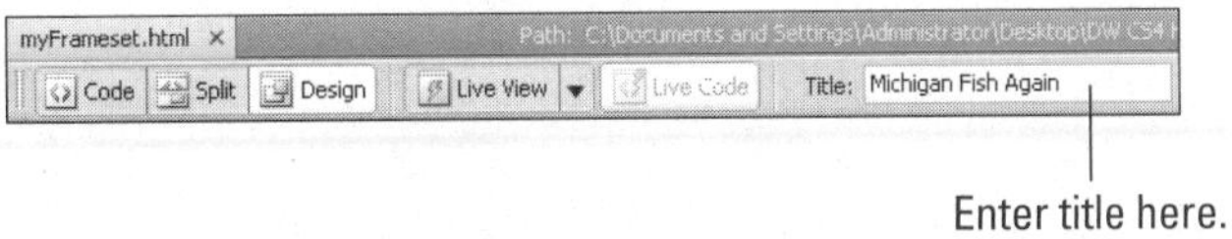

Enter title here.

Setting the Background Color of a File in a Frame

You can easily set the background color of a page displaying in a frame by applying internal CSS through the Page Properties dialog box. For more complex layouts and styling, however, use external Cascading Style Sheets through the CSS Styles panel to set the background color of a page along with other styling options (see Book III, Chapter 1).

Follow these steps to change the background color of a file in a frame:

1. **In Design view, click inside the frame where you want to change the background color of the page.**

2. **Choose Modify⇨Page Properties.**

   You can also click the Page Properties button in the Properties inspector.

   The Page Properties dialog box opens.

3. **Click the Background Color color picker icon to choose a color for the page background, or type the hexadecimal value including the number symbol (#) in the Background color text box, such as** #003300**.**

   The color is applied to your page and Dreamweaver writes the internal CSS code in the head area of the page.

4. **Click OK to close the dialog box.**

Setting Frame Properties with the Properties Inspector

The settings in the Properties inspector control different viewable parts of the frame or frameset that display in a browser window, such as adding a frame border in a particular size and color or setting row and column values. Tables 3-1 and 3-2 show the attributes for framesets and frames.

Table 3-1	Frameset Attributes
Frameset Attributes	*Used For*
cols="50,25%,*"	Sets the number and size of columns (each column separated with a comma). An asterisk (*) represents a value equal to the remaining space in a browser window after frames with pixel or percentage space are allocated.
rows="23,23,23,23"	Sets the number and size of rows.
border="1"	Sets the frame border in pixels for IE.
frameborder="5"	Sets the frame border in pixels for Netscape.
framespacing="5"	Sets the frame spacing in pixels for Netscape.

Table 3-2		Frame Attributes
Frame Attributes	*Value*	*Used For*
`framebor-der="0"`	0 or 1	Enter **0** or **No** to hide, **1** or **Yes** to show a border between frames.
`framespac-ing="5"`	0 – 100	Sets the frames spacing in pixels for Netscape.
`margin-width=""`	0 – 100	When set to 0, the frame displays flush with the left and right edge of the frame.
`margin-height=""`	0 – 100	If set to 5, a 5-pixel-wide space is between the window and the top of the frame.
`name=""`	Any name	Assign a name to your frames so you can use them as targets with the `<a>` tag.
`noresize`	None	Disallow the user to resize the frame.
`scrolling=""`	Auto/on/off	Decide whether to include the scroll bars on the right side of each frame. The auto setting displays scroll bars only when content in the frame exceeds the frame size.
`src=""`	Filename. html	Set the filename and its location on your hard drive (or the server hard drive) to display in the frame. Remember that servers use UNIX, which makes file-names case sensitive.

The next two sections show you how to specify properties for frames and framesets.

Setting frameset properties

Follow these steps to set frameset properties with the Properties inspector:

1. **Select a frameset by either of the following methods:**

   - In the Document window, click in the border between any two frames in the frameset.

   - In the Frames panel, click the frameset border. You can tell you've selected the frameset by the thick black border surrounding it.

2. **In the Properties inspector, check to see if the expander arrow (in the lower-right corner) is pointing up or down. If the arrow points down, click it to reveal all the properties, as shown in Figure 3-13.**

3. **In the Properties inspector, enter information to set the attributes for the frameset.**

Figure 3-13:
The
Properties
inspector
showing
all of the
frameset
properties.

Here's a rundown of the options in the Properties inspector:

✦ **Borders:** Determine if borders display around the frames in a browser window. Choose Yes to display the borders, No to hide borders, or Default to use a browser's default border setting.

✦ **Border Width:** Set the width of the border to any size in pixels. If you've selected No from the Borders drop-down list, leave this field blank.

✦ **Border Color:** Use the color picker icon or type a hexadecimal value including the number symbol (**#**) before it, such as **#999999,** to set the color of the border for the selected frameset.

✦ **Row/Col Selection:** To set the frame size of any particular frame in a selected frameset, select a frameset in the Frames panel. Click one of the tabs (left or right for columns, top or bottom for rows) on the Row/Col Selection area of the Properties inspector and enter a height or width value in the adjoining Row/Col Value text box.

✦ **Units:** Determine the size of the selected Row/Col:

• **Pixels:** Sets the size of the selected row or column to a fixed pixel width or height. Choose this option for frames you want to remain a fixed size, as with a navigation frame. Frames with pixel values are allocated space before frames using percents and relative sizes.

• **Percent:** Sets the selected row or column to a percentage of the total width and height of the frameset. Percentages are allocated space after frames set with pixels but before frames set with relative values.

• **Relative:** Sets the row or column to be as large or small as the remaining space available in a browser window after frames sized with pixels and percentages. Any number you've entered in the Value field is replaced with an asterisk (*) in the code to represent the relative value. You can also enter a number in the Value field with the Relative setting, such as 3*, which displays in the code as `<frameset rows="23,3*,*">`. In this example, the 3* is 200 percent bigger than 1*.

Setting frame properties

To set frame properties with the Properties inspector, follow these steps:

1. **Select a frame in a frameset document by clicking anywhere inside the desired frame's border.**

You can tell a frame is selected when a thin black line outlines it.

2. **In the Properties inspector, check to see if the expander arrow is pointing up or down. If the arrow is pointing down, click it to reveal all the frame properties.**

Figure 3-14 shows all the properties of a frame.

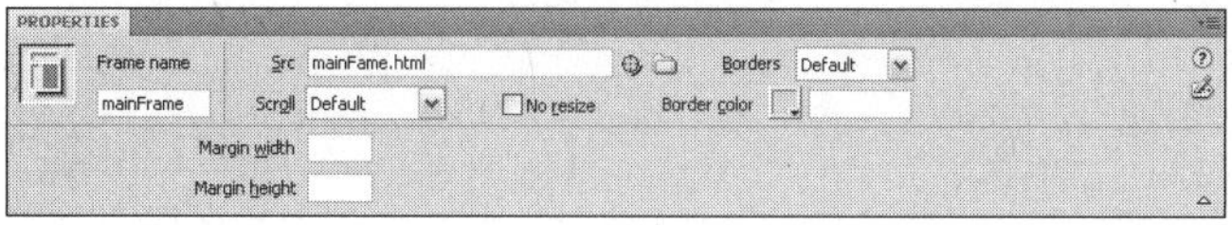

Figure 3-14:
The
Properties
inspector
showing all
the frame
properties.

3. **In the Properties inspector, enter information to set the options for the frame.**

You can change the following properties for a frame:

✦ **Frame Name:** Get in the habit of naming all your frames as you create them. The name of the frame is absolutely necessary if you want to target a frame and open a new page inside it. Name your frames with a single word that starts with a letter and does not contain any funky characters, dashes, periods, or spaces (though you can use an underscore, as in `left_frame`). Try not to use words that are common in HTML and JavaScript such as `top` or `parent`, but instead use descriptive terms such as `left`, `main`, or `nav`.

✦ **Src:** This path and filename of the document displays inside the selected frame. Click the folder icon to browse for and select the file, or if you know the path and filename, type it directly into the Src text box.

✦ **Scroll:** Decide whether scroll bars appear on the frame. The Default value does not turn the scroll bars on or off, but instead tells the page to adopt the default scroll bar settings of the browser displaying it. Most browsers use the Auto setting as the default, meaning the frame displays scroll bars when the contents of a frame exceed the display area in the browser. You can also select No for never, or Yes for always.

**Book IV
Chapter 3**

**Designing Pages
with Frames**

✦ **No Resize:** Stops users from dragging any visible frame borders and changing the size of the frame in the browser window. It does not affect your ability to modify frame sizes in Dreamweaver.

✦ **Borders:** To view or hide borders around the selected frame in a browser window, select Yes, No, or Default. The Default setting for most browsers is to show the borders unless the parent frameset has borders set to No. To truly hide all borders from displaying, choose No for the frameset and all the frames that share the border. If you have doubts about the visibility or invisibility of the border, test the page in several browsers and alter the settings until you get the effect you want.

✦ **Border Color:** Use the color picker or type a hexadecimal value in this field to set the color of the borders for the frame. The color you specify overrides the color of the parent frameset border. Be warned that the logic of frame borders is very complex and may not make immediate sense. One simple solution is to use the same border color throughout the frameset. Remember to add the number symbol before the hexadecimal value, as in **#FF0033.**

✦ **Margin Width:** Set the width of the space between the frame borders and the content by entering pixels here. This setting is a frame, not a page, attribute.

✦ **Margin Height:** Set the height of the space between the frame borders and the content by entering pixels here. This setting is a frame, not a page, attribute.

Frame Accessibility Settings

To work with Frame Accessibility settings in Dreamweaver, you can either enable the settings in the Accessibility category of the Preferences dialog box so that you always add accessibility tags as you create the frameset, or set accessibility values for frames and framesets after you create the frames.

Setting accessibility preferences

To enable (or disable) Frame Accessibility settings in Preferences, follow these steps:

1. **Open the Preferences dialog box by choosing Edit⇨Preferences (Windows) or Dreamweaver⇨Preferences (Mac).**

2. **Select the Accessibility category on the left side of the dialog box.**

3. **The Frames option, as shown in Figure 3-15, should be enabled by default.**

    To disable it, deselect the Frames check box.

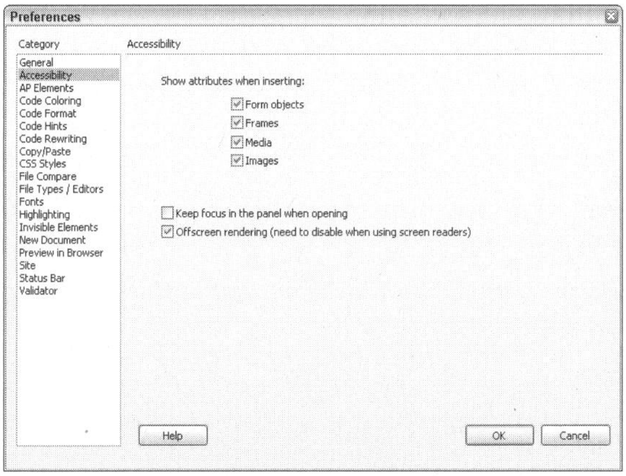

Book IV
Chapter 3

Figure 3-15:
Alter the
Dream-
weaver
Accessibility
preferences.

Adding or editing accessibility settings to a frame with the Tag Editor

To set accessibility values for an individual frame, follow these steps:

1. **In the Frames panel, click a frame to select it.**

2. **Choose Modify⇨Edit Tag to open the Tag Editor.**

3. **Select Style Sheet/Accessibility from the Category list to display a set of frame accessibility options.**

4. **Enter accessibility values and click OK to close the dialog box.**

   The values are added to the document code.

Targeting Frames with Links

How do you specify which frame should display the linked page when a visitor clicks a link? With the target attribute of the link (`<a>`) tag, of course. With framesets, you can use the default `_top` or `_parent` target attribute, or if you happen to name the frames when building the frameset, you can also use the frame names as target destinations for your linked files. Setting the target frame is exactly like setting the target on an ordinary link, but with an expanded set of options to address the different areas where a link could be opened.

To illustrate, suppose you have a frameset that has the standard two rows with the bottom row split into two columns (see Figure 3-16). Logically, you can name the top frame `topFrame`, the left frame `leftFrame`, and the right frame `mainFrame` (because that's where the bulk of your new content is). When you place navigation links in the left frame, you can add the target attribute equal to `mainFrame` so that the linked page opens in the main frame of the frameset, as in this line of code:

```
<a href="techniques.html" target="mainFrame">Fishin' Techniques</a>
```

Designing Pages
with Frames

So, for example, in Figure 3-16, if the user clicks any of the navigation links in the left frame (Fishin' Facts, Fishin' Folklore, and so on), a new page opens in the main frame.

Figure 3-16: Select the target of the frame you want the linked page to load in.

Target a specific frame when setting links with these steps:

1. **In Design view, select the text or object that you want to convert into a targeted link.**

2. **In the Link text box in the Properties inspector, select the file to link to.**

   Type the path and filename, click the folder icon to browse and select the file, or drag the Point-to-File icon onto the file in the Files panel.

3. **In the Target menu in the Properties inspector, choose the frame or window where you want the linked file to display:**

   - **_blank:** Opens the linked file in a brand new browser window above, or on top of, the existing parent window.

   - **_parent:** Opens the linked file inside the parent frameset of the frame where the link appears, replacing the frameset with the content of the linked file.

   - **_self:** Opens the linked file inside the same frame the link exists in and replaces the previous content. This option is the default for all links unless another setting overrides it.

- **_top:** Removes any and all framesets and opens the linked file inside the main browser window.

- **(Frame_Name):** When you name all the frames, the frame names appear in this list and you can select one as the target frame. You must be editing the document within the frameset structure to view the frame names. Otherwise, when editing files in their own windows, type the target frame name in the Target field in the Properties inspector.

When linking to a page outside of your Web site while using frames, use the `target="_blank"` or `target="_top"` option. This forces the page to open in a new window or remove the master frameset while making it clear to visitors that the link is a separate entity from your site.

Adding Noframes Content

In HTML, elements that are not understood by a browser are ignored. This means, for example, that if the user's browser doesn't support frames, nothing displays on the page unless you add content inside `<noframes>` tags. Place these tags after the closing `<frameset>` tag on the master frameset and nest them with the `<body>` tags so the content displays in the body area of the page when the frames content doesn't display.

In Listing 3-1, if the frames content doesn't display in the user's browser window, a message displays explaining that the visitor's browser doesn't support frames.

Listing 3-1   Using the Noframes Tag to Display a Message

```
<frameset rows="80,*" cols="*" frameborder="NO" border="0" framespacing="0">
  <frame src="top.html" name="topFrame" scrolling="NO"
  noresize title="topFrame">
  <frameset rows="*" cols="150,*" frameborder="NO" border="0"
  framespacing="0">
    <frame src="left.html" name="leftFrame" scrolling="NO"
    noresize title="leftFrame">
    <frame src="main.html" name="mainFrame"
    title="mainFrame">
  </frameset>
</frameset>
<noframes><body>
Your browser does not support frames. We encourage you to upgrade your browser
    to a version that provides frame support so you can fully experience the
    content provided here:
For Windows:  Internet Explorer 5 or greater | Firefox | Opera
For Macintosh:  Safari | Firefox | Opera
For Unix/Linux:  Firefox | Opera
You might also find it helpful to view the <a href="noFramesIndex.
    html">frameless</a>version of our site. </body></noframes>
```

The noframes content is coded as part of the frameset syntax and only displays in browsers that either don't support frames or have frames disabled.

To add or edit noframes content, follow these steps:

1. **Choose Modify⇨Frameset⇨Edit NoFrames Content.**

   The document window and the words NoFrames Content temporarily replaces any content previously displaying in Design view (see Figure 3-17).

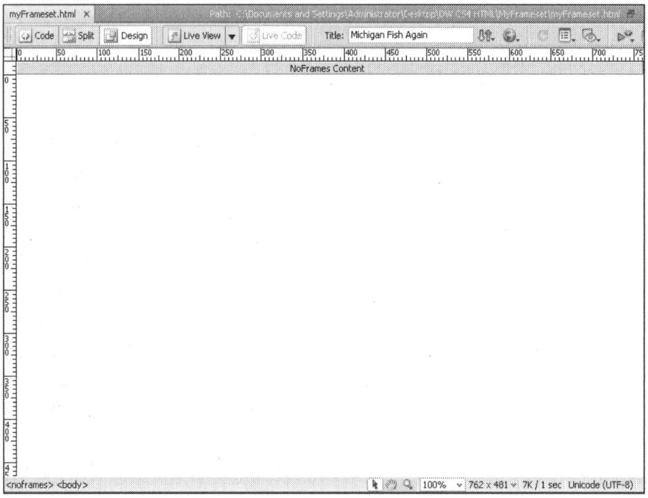

Figure 3-17: Use the Edit NoFrames Content command to edit noframes content.

2. **In the noframes area of the Document window, type or paste the noframes content, the same way you would for a regular HTML page.**

   Or enter code by choosing Window⇨Code Inspector. When the Code inspector opens, add the HTML content between the `<body>` tags nested inside of the `<noframes>` tags.

3. **Choose Modify⇨Frameset⇨Edit NoFrames Content to return to Design view of the frameset file.**

Whatever you write for your specific noframes content, try to include both a message about upgrading to a browser that supports framesets (with links to those download pages!) and some kind of acknowledgement of the visitor's use of an old browser or a browser with disabled frames, or better yet, because nearly all browsers do support frames, consider including content and links for search engine optimization in the noframes area. Because the main point of a Web site is to provide information to all site visitors, treat the noframes content as another opportunity to communicate positively with site visitors.

Creating Floating Frames

Floating frames, or *inline frames,* are framesets or pages embedded inside the body of another page using the `<iframe>` tag. Normally, frames have to stick to the sides of the browser window. However, floating frames can sit anywhere inside a browser window.

When would you want to use floating frames? To display multiple pages in a bookmarkable page, such as a Web photo gallery with clickable thumbnail graphics and close-up images. Or perhaps for those times you want to display a lot of content in a small, scrollable area within another page — for example, a long user agreement — rather than having the visitor scroll down a long page of content.

Floating frame structure is fairly simple. Unlike the `<frameset>` tags that require `<frame>` tags to identify the source of the content in each frame, the floating frame code uses the single opening and closing `<iframe>` tags that include the size of the floating frame and the source file that displays inside it:

```
<iframe width="300" height="150" src="iframefile.html" align="left"></iframe>
```

To add a floating frame to your page you could, of course, hand-code it. If you want to use Dreamweaver's interface, however, follow these steps:

1. **Place your cursor inside the file where you want the floating frame to appear.**

2. **Choose Insert⇨Tag.**

   The Tag Chooser dialog box opens.

3. **Click to expand the HTML Tags folder and select Page Elements on the left side of the dialog box; then select iframe from the list on the right, as Figure 3-18 shows.**

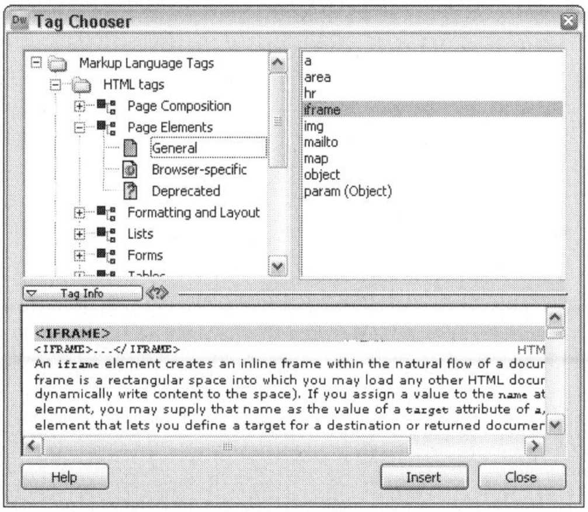

Figure 3-18: Dreamweaver's Tag Chooser lets you select and insert specific tags.

4. **Click the Insert button.**

   The Tag Editor–iframe dialog box opens.

5. **Complete the dialog box with the attributes you want.**

   Floating frames have attributes similar to framesets and frames that you need to specify if you want to override the default browser settings. Use these attribute settings to visually differentiate (or not) the floating frame content from the rest of the content on the page.

   Figure 3-19 shows the fields completed with sample content. Here's a rundown of the options in the dialog box:

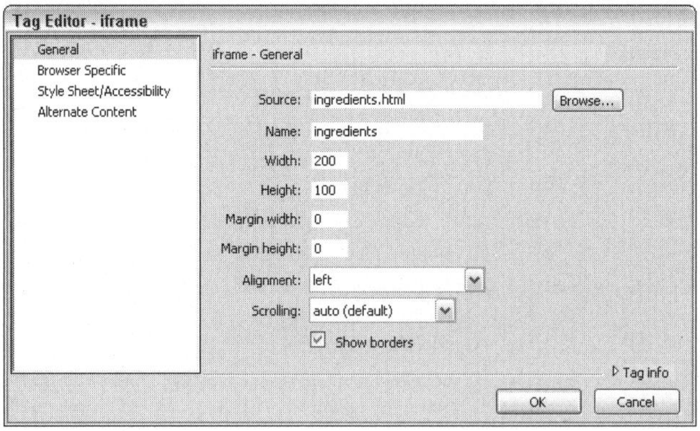

Figure 3-19: Set `<iframe>` tag attributes easily using Dreamweaver's Tag Editor.

- **Source:** Type the URL or path and filename of the file to display in the floating frame.

- **Name:** Give the frame a name so you can use it for targeting. As long as you name the iframe in the code, you can target the iframe just like a frame within the frameset. For example, if you name an iframe `contactlist`, you can specify that name as a target for a link:

  ```
  <iframe src="iframefile.html" name="contactlist" width="300" height="150"
      align="left" frameborder="2" marginwidth="0" marginheight="0"
      scrolling="auto"></iframe>
  <a href="contactlist.html" target="contactlist">See our Contact List</a>
  ```

- **Width and Height**: Set the width and height of the iframe using fixed pixels or percentages relative to the visitor's browser and monitor resolution settings.

  ```
  Margin Width and Height: To adjust the margin space surrounding the
      floating frame, set the width and height in pixels.
  ```

- **Alignment:** Align the iframe relative to the horizontal sides of the browser with the align attributes of top, bottom, middle, left, or right.

- **Scrolling:** To add or remove scroll bars on the iframe, include the scrolling attribute in your iframe code. Use `scrolling ="no"` to remove scroll bars, `scrolling="yes"` to always include scroll bars, and `scrolling="auto"` to add scroll bars as needed:

```
<iframe width="300" height="150" src="iframefile.html" align="left"
    frameborder="2" hspace="5" vspace="5" scrolling="auto"></iframe>
```

- **Show Borders:** Decide whether to include frame borders on the floating frame, which by default displays if you don't change this setting. When you enable the Show Borders option, the frameborder attribute is absent and the browser displays a simple border. By contrast, when you disable the Show Borders option, the frameborder attribute is set to 0 and the floating frame appears borderless.

6. **(Optional) Complete the fields in the Browser Specific, Style Sheet/Accessibility, and Alternate Content categories of the Tag Editor.**

   For example, you may want to add alternate content between the opening and closing `<iframe>` tags for older browsers:

   ```
   <iframe width="300" height="150" src="iframefile.html" align="left"
       frameborder="2" hspace="5" vspace="5" scrolling="auto">Alternate
       content for older browsers.</iframe>
   ```

   Additionally, though it's not part of the Tag Editor, you can add (by hand-coding) the `long description` attribute with a URL of a page containing a long description of the contents inside the floating frame:

   ```
   <iframe width="300" height="150" src="iframefile.html" align="left"
       frameborder="2" hspace="5" vspace="5" scrolling="auto"
       name="contactlist" longdesc="iframefiledescription.html"> </iframe>
   ```

7. **Click OK to close the Tag Editor.**

   The iframe code is added to your page.

8. **Click the Close button to close the Tag Chooser.**

   For even more precise placement of the floating frame on your page, you can envelope the `<iframe>` tags with floating `<div>` layer tags and use Cascading Style Sheets to create a style that absolutely positions the div, and therefore, also the iframe. Here's an example:

   ```
   <div id="floatingframe"><iframe width="300" height="150" src="iframefile.html"
       align="left"></iframe></div>
   ```

   Your CSS could look something like this:

   ```
   <style type="text/css">
   <!--
   #floatingframe {
   position:absolute;
   left: 100px;
   top: 100px;
   width: 300px;
   height: 150px;
   z-index: 5;
   }
   -->
   </style>
   ```

Although Dreamweaver can't display the iframe content in Design view, it shows an appropriately sized gray iframe placeholder box on the page, as shown in Figure 3-20. The placeholder box represents the width and height of the iframe embedded in the source code. To view the iframe content as you intend it to appear to visitors, open the page in a browser window.

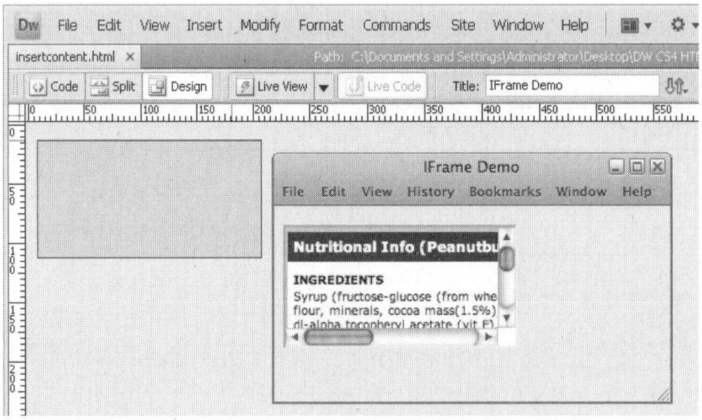

Figure 3-20:
Although the actual iframe displays in a browser, Dreamweaver displays the iframe only as a placeholder box in Design view.

Floating frames in older browsers

Originally recognized only by IE 3.0, floating frames are now widely supported by IE 3.0 and up, Netscape 6.0 and up, Opera, Firefox, Safari, and other popular browsers. For older browsers, the contents inside the iframes don't display on the page. Some tutorials on iframes may instruct you to add a `<frame>` tag with the same document source as your iframe in between the `<iframe>` tags to account for older browsers, like this:

```
<iframe width="300" height="150"
     src="iframefile.html"
     align="left" frameborder="2"
     scrolling="auto"
     name="contactlist"><frame
     src="iframefile.html"> </
     iframe>
```

Although not a perfect solution, it may improve the display of your iframe content on the page in older browsers.

Another option worth considering is to add a browser detection script to the page with the iframe where older browsers are redirected to another page that includes the content of the iframe source file.

Chapter 4: Making Your Pages XHTML-Compliant

X HTML *(eXtensible HyperText Markup Language)* is a form of HTML coding that extends document functionality by conforming to more strict *eXtensible Markup Language* (XML) rules. XML, a markup language used to represent complex object relationships, is used by many Web applications and services.

XHTML is not just a cleaner and stricter version of HTML; you can also view, edit, and validate XHTML pages with standard XML tools. Plus, XHTML works wonderfully in combination with Cascading Style Sheets (CSS) and is fully supported by Dreamweaver. (For an introductory tutorial about XML, visit www.w3schools.com/xml/default.asp.)

In 2000, the W3C proposed that XHTML be the new language for building Web pages, and in 2002, XHTML became an accepted standard, whereby all new browsers should contain built-in XHTML support. Using XHTML also ensures the forward and backward compatibility of your Web files. In other words, XHTML is the future of Web development. This chapter gives you the basics you need to get started.

Understanding the Benefits of Using XHTML with Dreamweaver

The biggest benefit of using XHTML with Dreamweaver is that Dreamweaver makes the transition from HTML to XHTML virtually painless. Dreamweaver provides you with the option of choosing XHTML as the primary markup language. When you select this option, the program automatically inserts the appropriate doctype tag on the page and writes XHTML-compliant code. Furthermore, you can easily convert a page from HTML to XHTML (and XHTML to HTML, if needed) using Dreamweaver's Convert command, and have Dreamweaver perform code validation to ensure the code is XHTML-compliant prior to publishing your pages online.

Creating XHTML-compliant documents in Dreamweaver is easy to do and provides both immediate and long-term benefits, including the following:

✦ **Simple transition to advanced technology:** Because the Web is moving toward XML, the simple transition to XHTML enables you to take advantage of this new technology for your Web sites.

✦ **Cleaner code:** With its strict guidelines, XHTML provides for cleaner and more uniform coding. Cleaner code means more accurate rendering in browsers.

✦ **Improved accessibility:** Users can view XHTML files on many different media types, including Braille displays, screen readers, wireless devices, and other specialized Web environments, in addition to Web browsers that provide wider access of information and improved accessibility for people with disabilities.

The key to XHTML is the concept of *extensibility*. XHTML combines HTML's ability to define the way content displays with XML's ability to describe how content functions. Because XHTML is an application of XML, any language with an XML parser can parse XHTML. For programmers, this means you can reuse any content you write in XHTML. *That's* extensibility.

Getting the Basics of XHTML Syntax

Before you can fully appreciate the benefits of XHTML, you have to know some important regulations. Check out the following sections for more information.

Discovering the strict rules you can't live without

XHTML is written with a very strict set of rules. You must adhere to all of the following rules:

✦ Specify a doctype tag before the opening `<html>` tag.

✦ Write all tags and attributes in lowercase.

✦ Surround all attribute values with double quotes (`"like this"`), as in `<p align="center">`.

✦ Assign a value to all attributes, as with `<input checked="checked">`.

✦ Replace attribute values containing special HTML characters such as &, <, and >, with entity representations; for example, "&", ">", and "<".

✦ Replace the `id` attribute with the name attribute when attaching attri-butes to elements in all circumstances, with the exception of form input elements such as `<select>` or `<input>`.

✦ Close all tags without inner content with `/>`, including non-container tags such as `br`, `hr`, and `img`. For instance, the XHTML shorthand ver-sion of `<br></br>` is `<br />`.

✦ Remove all special coding, such as inline style sheets and inline JavaScript, from the XHTML document and store it in separate `.css` and `.js` files, with references in the head to those external files:

```
<link rel="stylesheet" type="text/css" ref="my_style.css" />
<script language="JavaScript" src="my_javascript.js"></script>
```

✦ Use CSS for text formatting in XHTML documents. XHTML doesn't sup-port the `<font>` tag.

Taking advantage of strict and transitional rules

One key feature that sets XHTML apart from HTML is its use of markup that conforms to and takes advantage of XML rules used in Web applications and services. These rules, specified in the `doctype`, as shown in the following example, can be *strict* or *transitional*. Strict rules are better at automating data processing than transitional rules are, but both work great on plain static Web pages.

```
<!DOCTYPE html PUBLIC "-//W3C//DTD XHTML 1.0 Transitional//EN" "http://www.
    w3.org/TR/xhtml1/DTD/xhtml1-transitional.dtd">
```

XHTML files have three parts: the `doctype`, which states the *DTD* (docu-ment type definition); the `<head>`; and the `<body>`. The `<doctype>` tag defines the syntactic constraints allowed the code as well as the usage and meaning of those constraints. The `<head>` and `<body>` areas are just like regular HTML files, with a few additional syntax rule changes in the code, such as properly closing and nesting tags (see the previous section for more information).

You can set the DTD definition to *strict, transitional,* or *frameset.* Here are some sample DTD definitions for each type, along with descriptions:

✦ **Strict:** Use this DTD with Cascading Style Sheets:

```
<!DOCTYPE html PUBLIC "-//W3C//DTD XHTML 1.0 Transitional//EN" "http://
    www.w3.org/TR/xhtml1/DTD/xhtml1-transitional.dtd">
```

✦ **Transitional:** Choose the Transitional DTD with HTML and CSS. For example, you can add the `bgcolor` attribute to the `<body>` tag when you want to ensure your pages render accurately in older browsers that don't support CSS:

```
<!DOCTYPE html PUBLIC "-//W3C//DTD XHTML 1.0 Transitional//EN" "http://
    www.w3.org/TR/xhtml1/DTD/xhtml1-transitional.dtd">
```

✦ **Frameset:** Use this DTD with frames:

```
<!DOCTYPE html PUBLIC "-//W3C//DTD XHTML 1.0 Frameset//EN" "http://www.
    w3.org/TR/xhtml1/DTD/xhtml1-frameset.dtd">
```

To find out more about XHTML 1.0, visit the World Wide Web Consortium (W3C) Web site, where you find information about XHTML 1.0 specification (`www.w3c.org/TR/xhtml1/`), DTD definitions (`www.w3.org/TR/xhtml1/dtds.html`), and free online tools for markup validation of published Web sites (`http://validator.w3.org/`) and unpublished local files (`http://validator.w3.org/file-upload.html`).

Handling Dreamweaver's Automatic XHTML Code Compliance Tools

Inside the New Document window, seen here in Figure 4-1, Dreamweaver gives you the option of selecting an XHTML Document Type (DTD) for generating and cleaning up your XHTML code:

✦ XHTML 1.0 Transitional.

✦ XHTML 1.0 Strict.

✦ XHTML 1.1.

✦ XHTML Mobile 1.0.

✦ XHTML 1.0 Frameset. (This option is not selectable when creating new HTML pages. Instead, the DTD automatically gets added to your code when creating pages using frames when you choose either the XHTML 1.0 Transitional or Strict DTD.)

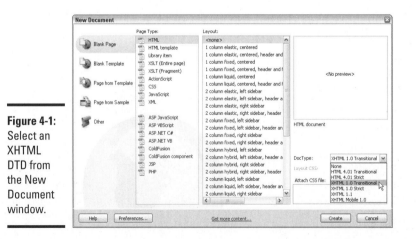

Figure 4-1:
Select an
XHTML
DTD from
the New
Document
window.

Each of these DTDs renders XHTML-compliant code. If you're unsure which DTD to use, select XHTML 1.0 Transitional.

After you select a DTD, Dreamweaver writes code that automatically meets XHTML requirements. Table 4-1 provides an overview of those requirements.

Table 4-1	Dreamweaver XHTML Compliance
XHTML Code Requirements	*Dreamweaver Automatically Writes XHTML Compliant Code*
The page must contain a doctype declaration above the opening HTML or XHTML tag and must include one of the three document type definition (DTD) files for XHTML (strict, transitional, or frameset).	For regular, noframe XHTML documents, the doctype gets added to the file: `<!DOCTYPE html PUBLIC "-//W3C//DTD XHTML 1.0 Transitional//EN" "http://www.w3.org/TR/xhtml1/DTD/xhtml1-transitional.dtd">`
	For XHTML files with framesets: `<!DOCTYPE html PUBLIC "-//W3C//DTD XHTML 1.0 Frameset//EN" "http://www.w3.org/TR/xhtml1/DTD/xhtml1-frameset.dtd">`
The page's root element must be HTML and it must designate the XHTML namespace. The namespace is an attribute of the HTML tag that defines the document as XML.	Dreamweaver adds the `html` root element and namespace attribute to the file: `<html xmlns="http://www.w3.org/1999/xhtml">`
All XHTML files must have `head`, `title`, and `body` elements, and all framesets must have `head`, `title`, and `frameset` elements.	All XHTML files include the `head`, `title`, and `body` elements, and all frameset XHTML files include the `head`, `title`, and `frameset` elements.
Any included script or style element in the code must have a `type` attribute. For example, the `type` attribute of the `stylesheet element` is `text/css`.	Dreamweaver automatically adds the `type` and `language` attributes in `script` elements, and the `type` attribute in `style` elements for all newly generated code, and adds them, if missing, when cleaning up XHTML.
All element and attribute names must be coded in lowercase.	Dreamweaver makes sure that all element and attribute names are in lowercase for all newly generated XHTML code and converts text to lowercase when cleaning up XHTML with the Clean Up XHTML command.

(continued)

Table 4-1 *(continued)*

XHTML Code Requirements	*Dreamweaver Automatically Writes XHTML Compliant Code*
All `area` and `img` elements must have the `alt` attribute.	Dreamweaver automatically adds these attributes to newly generated code and inserts them if missing when cleaning up XHTML. Missing `alt` attributes are also part of validation reports.
Elements must use proper nesting: `<p><b>This is incorrect.</p></b>` `<p><b>This is correct.</b></p>`	Dreamweaver automatically writes properly nested code and can fix bad nesting from code generated outside Dreamweaver with the Clean Up XHTML command.
All elements must have closing tags, unless specifically declared in the DTD as empty.	Dreamweaver adds closing tags to all newly generated code and adds missing closing tags when cleaning up XHTML.
All empty elements must have closing tags or have opening tags ending with `/>`. This includes non-container tags such as ` `, `<hr>`, and `<img>`. For instance, ` ` would no longer be valid, but ` </br>` and ` ` are both valid and acceptable formats. This requirement applies to the following empty elements: `area`, `base`, `basefont`, `br`, `col`, `frame`, `hr`, `img`, `input`, `isindex`, `link`, `meta`, and `param`. The preferred method for backward-compatibility in non-XML-enabled browsers is to add a space before the `/>` when closing non-container tags, as in `<hr />`, not `<hr/>`.	Dreamweaver adds the appropriate space before the closing slash (" /") to all empty elements and noncontainer tags both when generating new code and cleaning up XHTML.

XHTML Code Requirements	Dreamweaver Automatically Writes XHTML Compliant Code
All attributes with no value must be assigned a value, as with `<input checked="checked">`. The old minimized format, `<input checked>`, is not valid. This requirement applies to the following attributes: `checked`, `compact`, `declare`, `defer`, `disabled`, `ismap`, `multiple`, `noresize`, `noshade`, `nowrap`, `readonly`, and `selected`.	Dreamweaver adds quotation marks around all attribute-value pairs in newly generated code and corrects them when cleaning up XHTML. ***Note:*** This feature is for browsers that support HTML 4 and above. For older browsers, these Boolean attributes may not display accurately.
All attribute values must be surrounded by double (`" "`) quotes: `<p align="center">`.	Dreamweaver adds quotation marks around all attribute values for newly generated code, and adds missing quote marks as needed when cleaning up XHTML.
The `id` attribute must replace or be included, in addition to the name attribute, when attaching attributes to elements in all circumstances, with the exception of form input elements like `<select>` or `<input>`. This requirement applies to the following: `a`, `applet`, `form`, `frame`, `iframe`, `img`, and `map`. For example, `<a name="FAQ1">FAQ Answer 1</a>` is not valid because it lacks the id attribute. The correct form includes both id and name attributes: `<a name="FAQ1" id="FAQ1">FAQ Answer 1</a>`.	Dreamweaver automatically adds both the `name` and `id` attributes to the same value, when the name attribute is entered in the Properties Inspector, when generating new code, and when cleaning up XHTML.
Attributes with enumerated type values must be coded in lowercase. The enumerated type value is a value that can be chosen from a list of possible values, as with the `OL` attribute, which allows values for type equal to Number, Roman Small, Roman Larger, Alphabet Small, and Alphabet Larger (1, I, i, A, and a).	Dreamweaver automatically writes these enumerated type values in lowercase for new code and adjusts the case when cleaning up XHTML.

Making Sure Your Documents Follow XHTML Syntax

Dreamweaver's preferences allow you to set the default DTD for your files. If you set the default DTD to XHTML 1.0 Transitional, for example, every time you create a new Dreamweaver document, it's XHTML-compliant (see the upcoming section). Furthermore, if you're working with existing HTML files, you can tell Dreamweaver to convert the HTML code to XHTML-compliant markup using Dreamweaver's Convert XHTML command.

Creating a new XHTML document with Dreamweaver

Each time you create a new document, you can choose to have Dreamweaver write XHTML code instead of HTML code. Here's what you need to do:

1. **Choose File⇨New.**

The New Document window opens.

2. **Choose a page category and type.**

For XHTML files, select the Blank Page, Blank Template, or Page from Sample page category and choose a Page, Template, or Sample Type from the center pane. For example, you could select the Blank Page category and the HTML Page Type.

3. **Select an XHTML document type from the Document Type (DTD) drop-down list.**

Choose XHTML 1.0 Transitional, XHTML 1.0 Strict, XHTML 1.1, or XHTML 1.0 Mobile as the DTD. If you're creating a frameset, the appropriate XHTML Frameset DTD is automatically inserted into your frameset page when you select any of the XHTML DTD types.

4. **Click the Create button.**

The new document opens in the Dreamweaver workspace window and any content you add to your page automatically conforms to XHTML rules.

Telling Dreamweaver to create XHTML-compliant files all the time

You can set up Dreamweaver to create XHTML-compliant files by default in the Preferences dialog box. Follow these steps:

1. **Choose Edit⇨Preferences (Windows) or Dreamweaver⇨Preferences (Mac).**

The Preferences dialog box appears.

2. **Select the New Document category (shown in Figure 4-2) and choose one of the XHTML DTDs from the Default Document Type (DTD) drop-down list.**

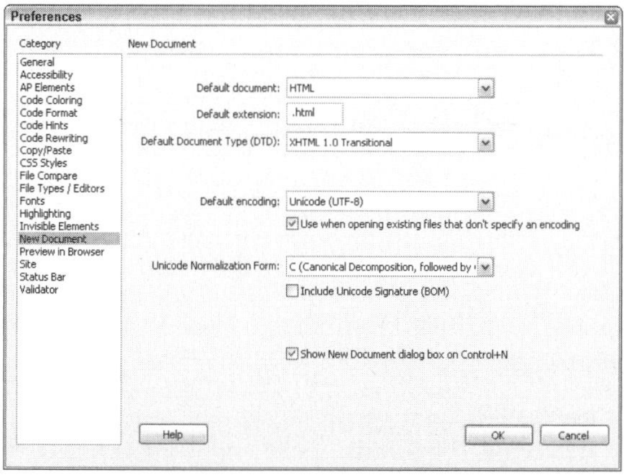

Figure 4-2:
Set the default document type definition to XHTML.

Choose from XHTML 1.0 Transitional, XHTML 1.0 Strict, XHTML 1.1, or XHTML Mobile 1.0. If you're creating a frameset, the appropriate XHTML Frameset DTD automatically is inserted into your frameset page when you select any of the XHTML DTD types.

If you're unsure of which option to select, choose XHTML 1.0 Transitional, which allows for both HTML and CSS markup and is a little less strict than XHTML 1.0 Strict.

3. **Click OK.**

Dreamweaver is now set up to write XHTML-compliant code for all new documents.

Transforming HTML document code into XHTML

Choose Commands➪Clean Up XHTML to have Dreamweaver get rid of HTML inconsistencies and make sure your documents are XHTML-ready. Dreamweaver does everything it needs to do — automatically — to instantly convert tag attributes to all lowercase, fix syntax errors, and add or report missing required tag attributes, such as images with missing `alt` attributes. For more detailed information on cleaning up your code with the Clean Up HTML/XHTML command, see Book V, Chapter 2.

Converting existing HTML files to XHTML

If you want to turn your existing HTML documents into XHTML documents, we could give you a set of complicated steps, but why should we? The reality is that Dreamweaver makes this task so painfully simple that you may actually wonder if you've missed something. Simply open an HTML document in the Dreamweaver workspace window and perform one of the following tasks:

✦ If your HTML file doesn't use frames, choose File➪Convert and select an XHTML DTD type.

✦ If your HTML file uses frames, select the frameset, choose File➪Convert, and choose XHTML 1.0 Frameset. Then place your cursor inside a document in any of the frames in the frameset, choose File➪Convert, and select an XHTML DTD type. The HTML code inside the frameset converts from HTML to XHTML. Repeat this process for each document that appears inside a frame in the frameset.

Note: Although it doesn't really matter if you mix and match DTDs, you should probably pick one type and stick with it for the entire frameset. If you're unsure which DTD to choose for the pages that are displayed inside the frames of your frameset, use XHTML 1.0 Transitional.

Making sure your HTML file can be converted to XHTML

Although we wish it weren't true, some HTML files can't be converted to XHTML and not all files can be made XHTML-compliant. For example, some template-based files written in HTML can't be converted to XHTML because the converted file must be in the same language as the template file.

The best way to determine whether you can convert one of your HTML files to XHTML is to test it. After converting the file, try entering a few line breaks to the code. If the code looks like <br />, the conversion was a success. To ensure that your code is fully compliant after the conversion, however, choose Commands➪Clean Up XHTML to perform XHTML validation on all your documents. Check out Book V, Chapter 2 for more information about this useful tool.

Validating Your XHTML

Dreamweaver has a built-in tool for validating your XHTML code. The tool looks for any and all tag or syntax code errors and lets you know what it thinks you should do by displaying a convenient report. In addition to XHTML, this tool also validates HTML, XML, JavaServer Pages (JSP), ColdFusion Markup Language (CFML), and Wireless Markup Language (WML). For step-by-step instructions on validating your XHTML, as well as other tips on using Reports to test your site before publishing, Book V, Chapter 1 covers everything you need to know about validating XHTML.

Book V
Publishing Your Site

The 5th Wave   By Rich Tennant

"This is a 'dot—com' company, Stacey. Risk taking is a given. If you're not comfortable running with scissors, cleaning your ear with a darning needle, or swimming right after a big meal, this might not be the place for you."

Contents at a Glance

Chapter 1: Using Reports to Test Your Site before Publishing

In This Chapter

✔ Previewing your site before you publish it

✔ Validating your code

✔ Testing your pages with the Results panel

✔ Checking and fixing broken links

*B*efore you launch your Web site on the Internet, you need to spend some time reviewing your site content to address accessibility issues, spelling errors, broken links, orphaned files, and code syntax problems. The benefits of following some general testing guidelines are endless. Nothing is worse than a site that doesn't work as it should. That's why this chapter gives you expert advice on performing browser compatibility checks, shows you how to test your pages with browser page previews, and helps you adjust download times.

Even when taking extreme care during the site building process within Dreamweaver, only very rarely will a created Web site be absolutely perfect. No matter what you do, it's hard not to create a site that has browser compatibility issues, spelling errors, and an occasional broken links. Making testing a priority helps catch these issues so you can present a professional quality product on the Web, which is something that will set your site apart.

Happily, Dreamweaver comes with several tools that help you tinker with your site until everything's perfect. First of all, you can use the powerful HTML and Workflow reports. These tools enable you to review your page content and make important improvements before publishing. In addition, the Results panel has several site evaluation tools that you can run to streamline testing and fixing problems on your pages. This chapter shows you how to use the Results panel to search code, validate tags, test pages for potential problems in specified target browsers, fix links, use the FTP log, and run a Server Debug report. You can also use the Preferences dialog box to determine page-loading times for the best viewing experience.

Testing Your Site

You've put all the work into getting your site together, and now all you want to do is publish the darn thing. Well, not so fast. You have to go through the essential testing phase before the site goes live.

In fact, you should test your site and fix problems throughout the entire Web site building process, but if you've waited until now, that's okay too.

All your site's pages should look good and function as you intend them to in all the browsers you're targeting. That means you have to verify the accuracy of your links and check download times for your larger files. Running reports can be a crucial part of this process; you can run several built-in reports from Dreamweaver's Results panel to make sure that all the code is right on the money.

Following general testing guidelines

Your main goal, ultimately, is to try to build a Web site that users enjoy viewing and navigating. If you follow these few simple guidelines, you're well on your way:

✦ **Preview your pages in as many browsers and browser versions as possible, on both Macs and PCs, to ensure browser compatibility.** You need to verify that the pages work the way you intend them to — or fail in a way that's acceptable to you — so make sure that you really spend some time previewing just about every combination of browser version and operating system you can think of. Your Web pages should look good in browsers that both support and don't support JavaScript, layers, CSS, and plug-ins. For assistance, check out www.browsershots.org.

✦ **Check your links — both internal and external — and fix any that are broken or don't work as you intended.** The Link Check report tests internal links and identifies any that are broken, external, and orphaned. See the "Checking and Fixing Links" section later in this chapter for more details.

✦ **Check the file sizes of all your Web pages and pay attention to their download times.** When pages have a lot of content, especially when they include large graphic files, some or all the page content may not load until all the data finishes loading.

✦ **Run reports on your site.** Always test for potential errors and common coding omissions or mistakes such as missing Alt attributes on images, untitled files, and redundant or improperly nested tags. (See the "Searching Your Code for Tags and Attributes" section, later in this chapter).

✦ **Validate all your tags.** Validating tags is the best way to ensure that your code syntax meets compliance standards. If you find any broken or missing information, fix it now. (See the "Validating Your Code" section later in this chapter.)

After you publish the site and begin to maintain it, continue to check the site regularly for possible errors, such as broken links, problematic HTML, JavaScript, and CSS, and browser incompatibilities. For specific issues, visit the Dreamweaver discussion forums on the Adobe Web site at `www.adobe.com/cfusion/webforums/forum/`. There you can find discussion strings related to common browser and platform issues as well as technical notes and helpful tips from other Dreamweaver users.

Previewing your pages in a browser

Dreamweaver CS4 writes code that supports industry standards and best practices, such as the use of advanced CSS, RSS, and XML feeds, and accessibility requirements. The main graphical browsers — Internet Explorer, Safari, Firefox, Opera, and Netscape — support Cascading Style Sheets. Of course, just because the main browsers should support these features doesn't mean that they automatically will. The only way to know for sure is to check for compatibility issues.

When fashioning a Web site, determining your target audience for the site in advance is very helpful. If you know your target, you can figure out what browsers users are likely to have. For example, if you're building an intranet site for employees who all use new PCs running the latest version of Internet Explorer, the need to test the site on other browsers isn't as critical. On the other hand, if you're building a site selling widgets on the Internet, it's essential to test a variety of operating systems and as many browsers and browser versions as possible.

You should also use the Target Browser Check report to assist you with the testing of your site in multiple browsers. This test checks the code in your files and reports tags, attributes, and CSS values and properties that are unsupported by your target browsers without altering any of the code. You can find out how to run the Target Browser Check report and use all the report features in the section, "Testing Your Pages with Browser Compatibility," later in this chapter.

Setting the primary and secondary browsers

Dreamweaver enables you to specify two different browsers as the primary and secondary browsers that launch for page previews using Dreamweaver's Preview in Browser keyboard shortcuts. To specify the primary and secondary preview browsers, follow these steps:

1. **Choose File⇨Preview in Browser⇨Edit Browser List.**

   You can also launch the preferences by choosing Edit⇨Preferences (Windows) or Dreamweaver⇨Preferences (Mac).

   The Preferences dialog box opens, as shown in Figure 1-1.

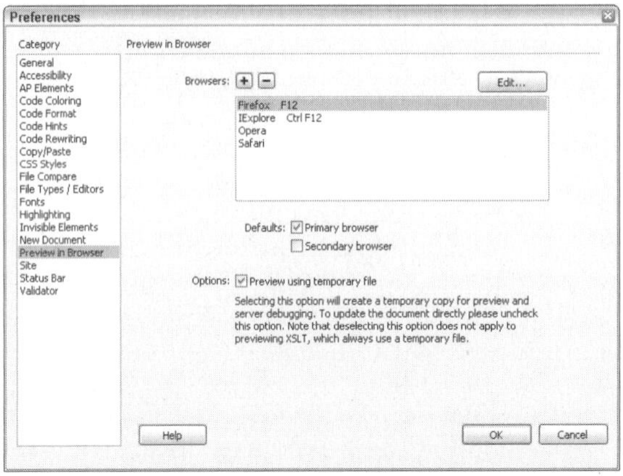

Figure 1-1:
Add browsers and set primary and secondary browser options.

2. **Select the Preview in Browser category from the Category list on the left side of the Preferences dialog box and choose a browser from the browser list on the right.**

   To add or remove browsers from the list, see Step 3 and 4 below. Otherwise, skip to Step 5.

3. **To add a browser to the list of browsers, click the plus (+) button and enter information about the browser in the Add Browser dialog box that appears.**

   Type the browser name and version in the Name field, such as IE 7.0. In the Application field, browse to and select the browser's application file. Click OK when you finish. The new browser appears in the browser listing.

   Add as many browsers as you like to this list. Although you can only select two browsers as the primary and secondary browsers for launching with a keyboard shortcut, you can preview your page with any of the browsers installed on your computer, as described in the next section.

4. **To delete a browser from the list of browsers, select the browser you want to delete and click the minus (–) button.**

   Deleted browser names immediately disappear from the list.

5. **Select a browser from the list and click to add a check mark next to Primary Browser to set the primary browser.**

6. **Select another browser from the list and add a check mark next to Secondary Browser to set the secondary browser.**

   Now you can press F12 (Windows) or Option+F12 (Mac) and your open document launches in the primary browser; pressing Ctrl+F12 (Windows) and ⌘+F12 (Mac) launches your open file in the secondary browser.

7. **Enable or disable the Preview Using Temporary File option.**

When enabled, this option tells your computer to create a temporary copy of the file in the browser window for previewing and server debugging. When this option is disabled, the document may not display accurately in the browser; however, you can make updates and changes directly to the file.

Previewing pages in multiple browsers

When you design pages in Dreamweaver, Design view provides you with a general idea of how your page looks in a browser window, but it can sometimes display items differently than it will in a browser window. What Design view can't do, however, is display every part of CSS and some dynamic features, such as JavaScript, or the very subtle HTML display differences between browsers. Likewise, clicking the Live View button on the Document toolbar can show you roughly how your page looks in a generic browser, but it is not capable of rendering all of a Web page's features as a real browser would. Therefore, the only way to truly see exactly how a page looks to visitors is to preview pages in individual browsers. In fact, you should test all the pages on your site on as many browsers as possible and on both the Mac and Windows platforms.

Fortunately, with Dreamweaver, you can preview and test your pages in more than one browser at a time. To set which browsers you want Dreamweaver to test, check out the previous section, "Setting the primary and secondary browsers." Then follow these simple steps:

1. **To preview your page in your primary browser, press F12 (Windows) or Option+F12 (Mac).**

   The document launches in the specified primary browser.

2. **To preview your page in your secondary browser, press Ctrl+F12 (Windows) or ⌘+F12 (Mac).**

   The document launches in the specified secondary browser.

3. **To preview the file in a third (or fourth or fifth, and so on) browser, choose File⇨Preview in Browser to select any of the browsers from the Preview list.**

4. **Verify the links, dynamic content, and layout of the page.**

   Check all your JavaScript behaviors, links, plug-ins, ActiveX controls, and any other media files installed on the page.

   If some content on your page doesn't display accurately in one or more of your target browsers, you have more work ahead of you. For example, your page may need adjustments to some JavaScript behaviors, CSS, or some other features on the page.

If you're testing your page with Internet Explorer on a computer running Windows XP with Server Pack 2, the browser may display a message that some content on the page has been restricted. You can fix this problem by inserting the Mark of the Web code as described in the aptly named sidebar, "Inserting the Mark of the Web."

Setting download times and size

Dreamweaver provides you with important download times and size data to help you control the way visitors with varying connection speeds experience your pages.

Dreamweaver calculates the file size of an open document by counting the K (kilobytes) of all text and linked objects, such as images and Flash movies, and then provides a download time estimate based on the default connection speed (kilobits per second, or Kbps) you've entered in the Status Bar preferences. You can use this information to determine whether to modify the page to improve its load time.

Inserting the Mark of the Web

If you have Windows XP Service Pack 2 installed on your PC, you may have problems previewing local Dreamweaver files with active content and scripts (such as Flash movies or client-side JavaScript behaviors) in Internet Explorer. You can easily determine whether Internet Explorer is having problems with your content if a pale-yellow security message bar at the top of the browser window appears saying the file's active content has been restricted, as shown in the following figure.

> **Dreamweaver – Microsoft Internet Explorer**
>
> File   Edit   View   Favorites   Tools   Help
>
> Back   ×   Search   Favorites
>
> Address
>
> To help protect your security, Internet Explorer has restricted this file from showing active content that could access your computer. Click here for options…
>
> My Computer

Right-click the security message bar and choose Allow Blocked Content to run the content or scripts in the Local Machine zone. For better protection, add the Mark of the Web code to your pages for testing purposes, and then remove it before publishing.

One of the reasons Internet Explorer added this feature was to protect local machines from hackers and attackers that use the Local Machine zone. The Mark of the Web instructs the browser to run the active content on the page in the Internet zone instead of in the Local Machine zone.

To insert the Mark of the Web to view active content in Internet Explorer running Windows XP Service Pack 2, follow these steps:

1. **Open your document in the Dreamweaver workspace.**

2. **Choose Commands⇨Insert Mark of the Web.**

The following line of generic code is automatically inserted into the head of your code:

```
<!-- saved from url=(0014)about:internet
   -->
```

If you want to include the code in your published projects, you should customize the URL by having it point to your domain name. You also need to modify the number, such as (0028), to match the number of characters in your domain name starting with the h in http and ending with the last letter of your domain name, as with the m of .com in the following example:

```
<!-- saved from url=(0028)http://www.
       yourdomainURL.com -->
```

If you don't want to include the code in your published projects, you can easily remove the code through Dreamweaver.

To remove the Mark of the Web code, do one of the following:

✔ Select and delete the code directly from Code view

✔ Choose Commands⇨Remove Mark of the Web

Note: This command is compatible with the Windows versions of Dreamweaver MX, MX 2004, 8, CS2, CS3, and CS4.

To find out more about this feature, see the TeachNote 19578 on the Adobe Web site at www.adobe.com/go/19578.

 The average time visitors connecting at 56Kbps are willing to wait for a page to display without feedback is eight seconds. Thus, your goal should be to get all your pages up and working in less than eight seconds. If your page weighs in at higher than 30K, you may want to consider reducing the number of objects or assets on the page (for example, using CSS rollovers instead of graphic rollovers).

By default, the connection speed in the Status Bar preferences is set to 56K, but you can change this setting to another speed. For example, when designing a site for an intranet on a T-1 (1500Kbps speed) circuit, you can change the preference to 1500 kilobits per second. To set the download time and size preferences, follow these steps:

1. **Choose Edit⇨Preferences (Windows) or Dreamweaver⇨Preferences (Mac).**

The Preferences dialog box opens.

2. **Click the Status Bar category on the left side of the dialog box.**

   Status Bar preference options appear on the right side of the dialog box, as shown in Figure 1-2.

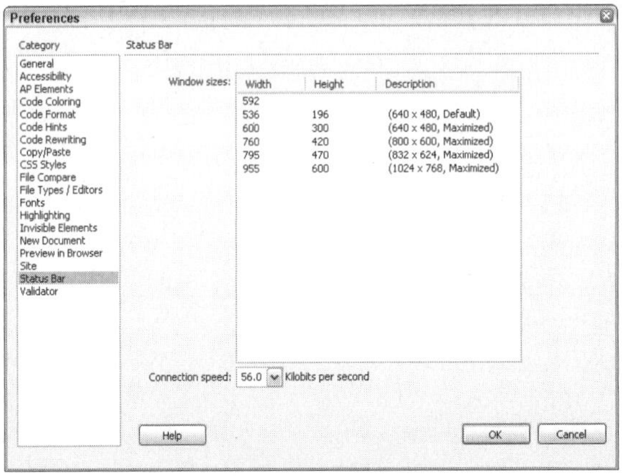

Figure 1-2:
Choose a
connection
speed in the
Status Bar
preferences.

3. **Select a connection speed from the Connection Speed drop-down list at the bottom of the dialog box.**

   Dreamweaver uses the speed you select to estimate the download time of your page. Although it's important to think about dial-up users, the majority of Web users are on some sort of higher speed connection, so changing the default connection speed may give you a more accurate representation of website visitors. (See Book I, Chapter 2 for more information on building a site for a target audience.)

Examining the Results Panel

Dreamweaver reports enable you to quickly find, test, and fix the content on your Web pages from one convenient location: the Results panel. To view the Results panel, choose Window➪Results or press F7.

The Results panel, shown in Figure 1-3, has several tabs that provide access to the following report types:

✦ **Search:** Search your code for your tags and attributes.

✦ **Reference:** Find reference information about HTML, XHTML, CSS, JavaScript, Accessibility, and programming languages.

✦ **Validation:** Validate your code.

✦ **Browser Compatibility:** Test your page with a targeted browser.

✦ **Link Checker:** Check and fix links.

✦ **Site Reports:** Run Workflow and HTML reports.

✦ **FTP Log:** View file transfer activity.

✦ **Server Debug:** Debug a ColdFusion application.

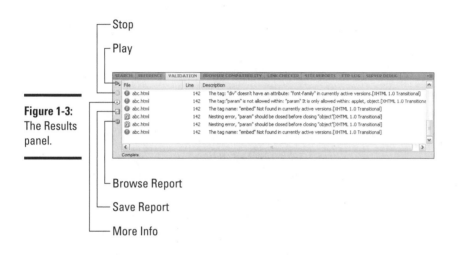

— Stop

— Play

Figure 1-3:
The Results
panel.

— Browse Report

— Save Report

— More Info

A green Play icon (a triangular icon reminiscent of a Play button in a media player) appears in every tab view except the Reference and FTP Log tabs. Clicking the Play icon launches the reports related to the active tab.

The following sections discuss how you can use the Results panel to view reports and fix problems throughout your site.

Searching Your Code for Tags and Attributes

If any of the reports identify problems in your code, you may want to globally change those problems throughout your entire Web site. You can use the Search tab of the Results panel to open Dreamweaver's Find and Replace dialog box. The Find and Replace tool enables you to search for specific text, tags, and attributes in text or source code on a document, selected files, a specific folder, or all the files inside a defined site. After it is found, you can replace that text, tag, code, or content with new information.

Turn to Book II, Chapter 2 to find out how to search for specific tags and attributes, search for text in specific tags, save and reuse search strings, and search using regular expressions.

Validating Your Code

The Validation panel checks HTML or XHTML code in the current document, entire current local site, or selected files in the site for tag, syntax, and other common formatting errors. It checks in many languages such as HTML, XHTML, JavaServer Pages (JSP), ColdFusion Markup Language (CFML), XML, and Wireless Markup Language (WML). It then displays the results in the Validation panel (see Figure 1-4).

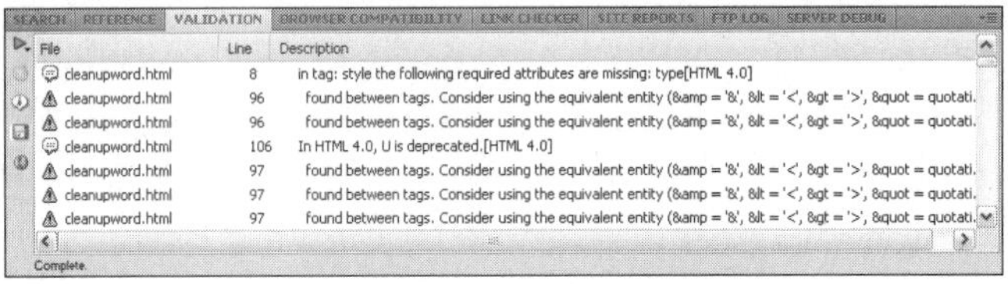

Figure 1-4: The Validation panel.

Running the Validation panel

To validate your HTML/XHTML code, follow these steps:

1. **On the Validation tab of the Results panel, click the green Validate button (looks like a play button) and select a validation option from the menu.**

   You can choose to validate the current page only, the entire local site, or selected files (from the Files panel) on the site.

   You can also validate code for a single page by choosing File⇨Validate⇨Markup. If your page uses XHTML or XML, however, choose File⇨Validate⇨As XML instead.

   The validation results display on the Validation tab of the Results panel and includes messages about errors and warnings as well as a list of all the syntax and tag errors Dreamweaver detected (see Figure 1-4).

   Results display as errors, warnings, or messages. See the "Testing Your Pages with Browser Compatibility" section later in this chapter for details about each of these result types.

   If the report finds no code errors, Dreamweaver displays a `No errors or warning` message. Congratulations!

2. **To fix an error, warning, or message in the results listing, double-click the error, warning, or message in the Validation panel list.**

   The document with the error opens in the Document window and the error is highlighted, ready for you to fix it. If you want, you can correct these changes directly in the document code, and then rerun the validation report to ensure the changes are compliant.

To find out more about any of the errors in the list, right-click (Windows) or Control+click (Mac) the error message in the list and select More Info from the context menu. The complete error message appears in its own pop-up window. This feature works for all results listed in the Validation, Browser Compatibility, and Site Reports tabs of the Results panel.

3. **(Optional) Click the Save Report button to save the report as an XML file.**

   The Save Report button looks like a disk and can be found on the left edge of the Results panel (refer to Figure 1-4).

   It's easy to open an XML file in Microsoft Excel and then create a spreadsheet from it for tracking purposes such as marking off files, errors, and status.

4. **Click the Browse Report button to see and print the report from a browser window.**

   The Browse Report button looks like a tiny picture of the earth and can be found on the left edge of the Results panel (refer to Figure 1-4).

Setting Validator preferences

The Validator not only quickly finds syntax problems in your code, but you can also customize it in Dreamweaver's Preferences to check for specific tag-based languages or problems in the code. Remember, however, that these preferences settings are ignored if your file contains a specific doctype.

To set Dreamweaver's Validator preferences, follow these steps:

1. **Choose Edit⇨Preferences (Windows) or Dreamweaver⇨Preferences (Mac) to open the Preferences dialog box.**

2. **Choose the Validator category to view the Validator preferences (see Figure 1-5).**

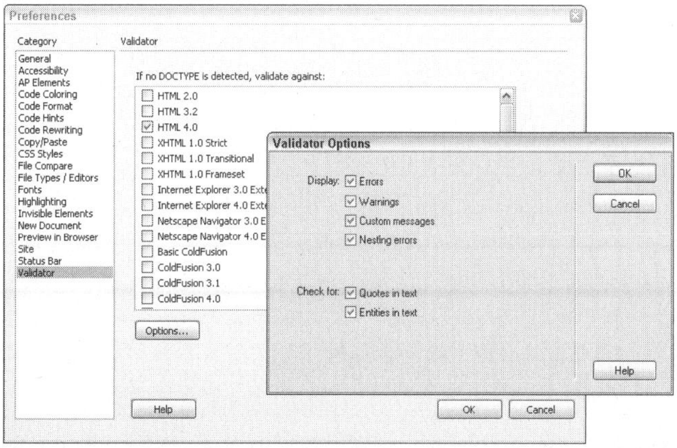

Figure 1-5:
Customize the Validator preferences.

3. **Select a doctype for Dreamweaver to validate against when no doctype is specified in the file.**

   You can select only one doctype at a time. For example, you can select XHTML 1.0 Transitional, but not HTML 4.0 too.

4. **Click the Options button to set specific validator options.**

   The Display options enable you to set the type of errors or warnings included in the Results panel. By default, all options are selected and are universal for all doctypes.

   You can also have the Validator check for quotes or entries in text. Both options are selected by default. Leaving the Quotes in Text option enabled tells Dreamweaver to include warnings about quotation marks in the document text. You should use the `&quot;` entity instead. Leaving the Entities in Text option enabled tells Dreamweaver to find certain characters in the text and convert them to their entity equivalents, such as `&amp;` instead of `&`.

5. **Click OK to close the Validator Options box and click OK again to close the Preferences dialog box.**

   Changes to the Validator Preferences go into effect immediately, but you can modify them at any time.

Testing Your Pages with Browser Compatibility

The Browser Compatibility report tests your HTML files for any tags or attributes that are deprecated (such as `<b>`, `<i>`, `<center>`, or `<font>`) or are unsupported by the target browsers on your computer (such as the height attribute of the `<table>` tag in Firefox 1.0, Netscape Navigator 7.0 & 8.0, and Safari 1.0 and 2.0). This is much different than simply previewing your page in a browser, as described earlier in this chapter, which only shows you how the page would look in a particular browser.

You can run the Browser Compatibility report on the current document, the entire local site, or selected files (from the Files panel) of a site. After making corrections to the files on your site, you can run the report again to ensure your changes haven't caused any other browser issues.

Before you run the Browser Compatibility report, set the target browsers for the report, as described in the next section, so error results are returned for the browsers you want.

Setting the target browsers for Browser Compatibility

You can target several browsers for the Browser Compatibility report to test code against, regardless of whether you have all the browsers installed on your computer. For example, if you're working on a PC platform, you can still test for Internet Explorer 5.2 on a Mac.

To set the target browsers for the Browser Compatibility report, follow these steps:

1. **Open the Results panel, click the Browser Compatibility tab, press the green Check Browser Compatibility button, and select Settings.**

The Target Browsers dialog box appears, as shown in Figure 1-6.

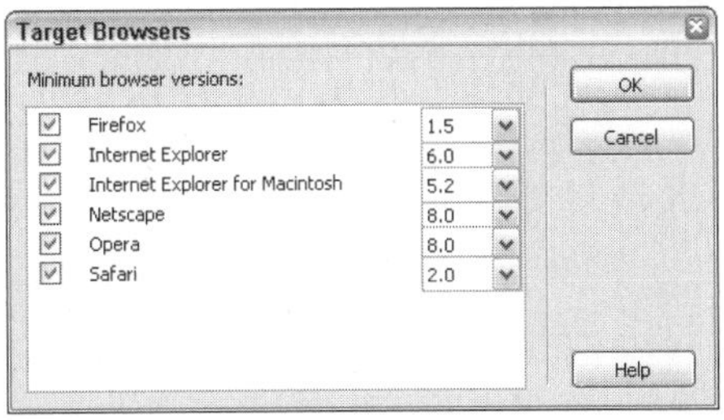

Figure 1-6:
Choose several browsers and browser version in the Target Browsers dialog box.

Target Browsers		
Minimum browser versions:		OK
☑ Firefox	1.5	Cancel
☑ Internet Explorer	6.0	
☑ Internet Explorer for Macintosh	5.2	
☑ Netscape	8.0	
☑ Opera	8.0	
☑ Safari	2.0	Help

2. **If they're not already checked, add a check mark next to each browser against which you want to verify code in the Target Browser Check report.**

3. **Next to each selected browser, choose a minimum browser version against which you want to verify the code.**

For example, to verify code against Safari, put a check mark next to Safari and choose either 1.0 or 2.0 as the browser version.

At a minimum, you should consider checking Internet Explorer 6.0, Netscape 8.0, Safari 2.0, Opera 8.0, and Firefox 1.5.

For the latest information about trends in browser usage, operating systems, and screen resolution, visit the w3schools.com Web site at www. w3schools.com/browsers/browsers_stats.asp.

4. **When you finish, click OK to close the dialog box and save your changes.**

After they're set, these browsers are included in the Browser Compatibility report results.

Using the Browser Compatibility panel

To run a Browser Compatibility report, follow these steps:

1. **Open the Results panel, click the Browser Compatibility tab, and click the green Check Target Browsers button to select the Check Browser Compatibility for this report.**

You can run this report against the code in the current document, the entire local site, or selected files in the site.

2. **The report runs and returns the results in the Results panel.**

If the report takes a long time to generate and you want to stop it before it's complete, click the Cancel icon, which appears on the left edge of the Target Browser Check panel.

The Browser Compatibility report defines three levels of problems: *errors, warnings,* and *informational messages,* each easily identifiable by an icon next to the filename that contains the potential problem, as shown in Figure 1-7:

Informational messages

Figure 1-7:
The
Browser
Compatibility
report.

Errors

Warnings

✦ **Errors:** These messages, displayed with a red polygon and a white exclamation mark, identify code problems that may cause display issues in a particular browser or issues with unsupported tags that may potentially cause an unknown problem. A typical error alert about the `id` attribute looks like this: `The id attribute of the Object tag is not supported. [Netscape Navigator 6.0]`.

✦ **Warnings:** Code identified with a yellow triangle and a white exclamation mark is a warning. This code won't display correctly in a specified browser, but it probably won't cause additional or serious display issues. The following message about the `<object>` tag is a typical warning:

```
The title attribute of the OBJECT tag is not supported.
[Safari 1.0, Safari 2.0].
```

✦ **Messages:** A particular browser doesn't support code identified with an informational message (a white word balloon). But it probably doesn't have any visible effect altering the display of the page in the browser. The message is an FYI and not anything you have to worry about or respond to. For example, ignored tag attributes such as this `<html xmlns="http://www.w3.org/1999/xhtml">` HTML tag give rise to a benign `The xmlns attribute of the HTML tag is not supported, but it has no detrimental effect. [Netscape Navigator 6.0, Netscape Navigator 7.0]` informational message.

You can perform other tasks in the Browser Compatibility panel, including the following:

✦ **View long error messages:** Longer error messages may be truncated in the Results panel. To see the complete long error messages, click the More Info button on the left side of the panel. A Description dialog box appears showing the full error message and the browsers and browser versions that don't support the code.

✦ **Jump to code:** Double-click the error message in the Results panel. Problematic code is highlighted in the open file in Code view. This trick helps speed up the correction process!

✦ **Jump to next or previous error:** Click Next Error or Previous Error from the Browser Compatibility menu on the Document toolbar. This is just another useful way to jump directly to any code that may be problematic and speeds up the process of fixing any errors in the code by hand.

✦ **Fix errors:** Make changes directly in Code view or in the Browser Compatibility panel. You can find out how to fix errors in the next section, "Viewing and fixing errors."

✦ **Save a Report:** Click the Save Report button on the left edge of the panel and save the report in the location of your choice with the .doc, .txt. or .html file extension.

✦ **View a report in a browser:** To see a copy of the report in a browser, click the Browse Report button on the left edge of the panel.

✦ **Ignore specific errors:** Right-click (Windows) or Control+click (Mac) any of the red underlined tags or attributes in Code view and select Ignore Error from the context menu. The errors you ignore are converted into warnings. From then on, Dreamweaver stops displaying that error type with the red wavy underline in Code view for all documents.

✦ **Edit the Ignored Errors list:** Choose Edit Ignored Errors List from the context menu in the Browser Compatibility panel. The Exceptions.xml file opens, and you can manually make changes to the exceptions listing.

Viewing and fixing errors

You can easily see the errors in the code of a document identified in the results of a Browser Compatibility. Double-click any of the errors in the results listing to open that document in the Dreamweaver workspace in Code or Split view; anywhere you see a wavy red underline in the code is where Dreamweaver has identified potentially problematic code that may cause an error in one or more of your specified target browsers. If Dreamweaver doesn't identify any errors, you don't see any wavy red underlines in the code; instead, you see the No Errors button on the Document toolbar to the right of the Title text box where the Browser Compatibility button displayed before.

You need to analyze errors in Code view to find out the best way to resolve them. Here are some tips:

✦ **Hover the cursor over red-underlined code:** To find out which target browsers don't support a particular red underlined tag or attribute in the code, hover the cursor over any of the red underlined code in Code view. An error tip appears, displaying relevant error information, including browser and version types.

✦ **Right-click (Windows) or Control+click (Mac) red-underlined code:** In Code view, you can access other target browser check commands by right-clicking (Windows) or Control+clicking (Mac) any of the red underlined tags or attributes in the code. Select an option from the context-sensitive menu that appears. For example, to see a report for the entire open document, select Show All Errors from the context-sensitive menu. The Results panel displays errors, warnings, and messages.

Only target browser errors, and not warnings and messages, display in Code view of an open file. Therefore, if you want to see all potential code issues, including the warnings and information messages, run a manual check on the entire document or site and review the results in the Results panel.

The Browser Compatibility report doesn't check the accuracy of any scripts contained in the code or validate your syntax. It evaluates any markup that specified target browsers may not support by using an editable text file called `browser profiles` that specifies which tags particular browsers support. For information about editing the text file, to change the existing browser profile, or add a new profile, visit the Adobe Support Center and look for a "Customizing Dreamweaver" heading. You can find the Support Center at `www.adobe.com/support/dreamweaver/`.

Checking and Fixing Links

The Link Checker panel identifies broken internal, external, and broken links on your pages. *Broken links* are often associated with the wrong filename or contain typos, and *orphaned files* are files on a defined site that are not being linked to on the site and can be safely removed from the site listing. However, because Dreamweaver only verifies local files within a defined site, it displays — but can't verify — *external links*.

The Link Checker panel is accessible from the Results panel. To view it, select the Link Checker tab in the Results panel.

By identifying and listing all the links in one location, you can quickly verify them and make manual corrections as needed. In fact, you can fix all these links right in the Link Checker panel by selecting and editing the links listed by the report or by opening the files in question and fixing the errors on the page in Code view or with the Properties inspector.

To run a report to identify broken links, orphaned files, and external links, follow these steps:

1. **Open the Results panel, click the Link Checker tab, and press the green Check Links button to select a Check Links option for this report.**

   You can run this report against the code in the current document, the entire local site, or selected files in the site.

   The Results panel lists the results.

2. **Select a report results type from the Show menu to view the results of each report in the Link Checker panel.**

   Your options include Broken Links, External Links, or Orphaned Files.

   To fix broken links, follow Steps 3 through 7.

   External links are listed for your information, but you can't test them through the panel. To test these links for accuracy, you must launch the page in a browser and click each link by hand. You can, however, modify spelling errors in external links in the Link Checker panel.

   You can safely delete orphaned files from the Link Checker panel or by selecting and deleting files from the Files panel. Deleting an orphaned file permanently removes the file from your computer. If you think you may need the orphaned file sometime in the future, however, make a backup of the site before deleting the orphans or simply move the orphaned files to a location outside the managed site.

3. **To fix a broken link, select Broken Links from the Show menu in the Link Checker panel and select a broken link from the results list under the Broken Links column (see Figure 1-8).**

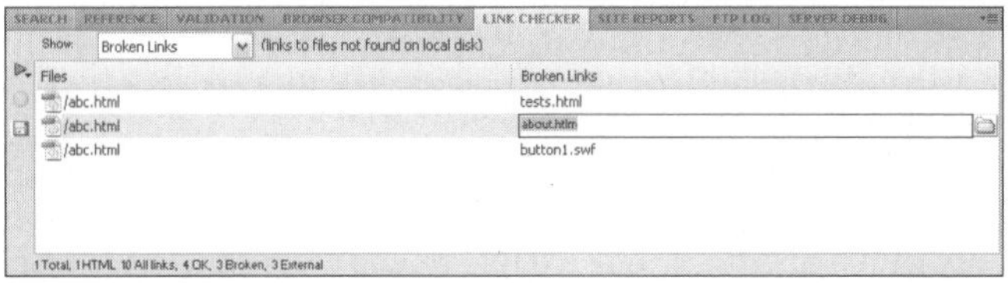

Figure 1-8:
Select a
broken link
to correct
in the Link
Checker
panel.

SEARCH	REFERENCE	VALIDATION	BROWSER COMPATIBILITY	LINK CHECKER	SITE REPORTS	FTP LOG	SERVER DEBUG	

Show   Broken Links   ▾   (links to files not found on local disk)

Files	Broken Links
/abc.html	tests.html
/abc.html	about.htm
/abc.html	button1.swf

1 Total, 1 HTML 10 All links, 4 OK, 3 Broken, 3 External

A folder button appears to the right of the selected link.

4. **Click the folder button to browse to and select a new file to update the link, or type the correct URL or filename over the existing broken link information.**

To correct a broken link with the Properties inspector, open the file by double-clicking the link's source page from the Files column of the Results listing. The broken link in the opened file is highlighted in Design view and Code view, and the broken link displays in the Link field in the Properties inspector. Correct the link in the Properties inspector, and save and close the file. To verify the broken link is now correct, rerun the Link Check report.

When fixing a broken link to an image from within the document the image is contained in, be sure to click the Refresh button next to the image W and H labels in the Properties inspector so the corrected image uses its actual size, rather than the old image width and height dimensions. The W and H labels are displayed as bold characters when the new image dimensions need refreshing and as normal type when the W and H dimensions match the selected image.

5. **Press Enter (Windows) or Return (Mac) to accept the new link.**

When multiple instances of the same broken link appear throughout the list, Dreamweaver asks whether you want to apply the same change to the other instances. Click Yes to update all instances or No to update only the current instance.

If you've enabled the Check In/Check Out system, you need to check out the files before modifying them. If Dreamweaver can't locate any particular file associated with a broken link, a warning message indicates that the file was not found. Any broken links associated with the missing file remain broken.

6. **Repeat Steps 3 through 5 for each broken link.**

7. **Click the Save Report button on the left side of the panel to save a copy of the report.**

   You can also choose Options⇨Save Results. Save your reports with the .doc, .txt, or .html file extension.

When you fix links by following these steps, the links are automatically removed from the Results list on the Link Checker panel. If you fix a link but it still appears in the list, Dreamweaver didn't recognize your corrections. Perhaps the new filename you've added is wrong. Try fixing the link from the Reports panel, saving the open file, and rerunning the Link Check report.

After running a report, a Web site might not show any "Browser support issues" in the results panel, but this doesn't mean that the page is going to display exactly the same in all browsers. There is a big difference between a page being compatible and the page displaying the desired visual effect you are trying to achieve for a Web site. For example, a Web page might not have any issues when you run the browser compatibility check, but CSS elements on the page (height, position, fonts, margin, and so on) can have wide ranging differences across many browsers that need to be checked. To be safe, run the browser compatibility check to fix obvious coding errors, best practices, and so on, and then view the Web site in the specified target browsers and platforms to check if the desired layout and look and feel are consistent.

Handling Workflow and HTML Reports

The Site Reports panel provides quick access to the Reports dialog box, from which you can select and run a variety of Workflow and HTML reports. Consider using these reports to begin your site clean up prior to site launch.

Launching reports

The Workflow reports are great if you're working on a major site with a group of people. The main function of the reports is to help team members work together more effectively. As long as you've defined a remote site connection in the managed site, these reports can provide important statistics on Design Notes, file modification dates, and file checkout status. For example, you can run a report to see which team members have files checked out or which files contain Design Notes. The Design Notes report can even contain specific name and value parameters, such as `Author=Sue`, for more specific search results. (Design Notes are described in detail in Book VI, Chapter 1.)

The HTML reports are a must for all Web sites, big and small. These reports identify problems in your code that could bloat file sizes, cause slower page viewing times, and even prevent your pages from displaying properly. HTML reports include data about missing `Alt` attributes on images, removable empty tags, untitled documents, nested font tags that can be combined, redundant nested tags, and accessibility issues.

You can run both Workflow and HTML reports simultaneously through the Reports dialog box; follow these steps:

1. **Choose Site⇨Reports.**

   The Reports dialog box opens, as shown in Figure 1-9, where you'll see several different report options awaiting your selection.

Figure 1-9: Select individual Workflow and HTML Reports from the Reports dialog box.

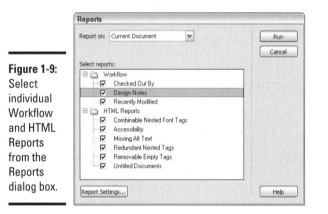

To run an accessibility-only report, choose File⇨Check Page⇨Check Accessibility. The accessibility report results appear on the Site Reports tab of the Results panel.

2. **Choose an option from the Report On drop-down list.**

   Choose the option that matches your specific needs. For example, if you want to check just the current page, select Current Document; to check the whole site, choose Entire Current Local Site; if you want to check some, but not all, of the pages on the site, choose Selected Files in Site or Folder.

3. **Select categories from the Workflow options:**

   - **Checked Out By:** This option generates a report of all files checked out by a specific person.

   - **Design Notes:** This report creates a list of Design Notes for either a set of selected files or the entire Web site.

   - **Recently Modified:** This option makes a list of files that have been created or modified within a specific number of days or within a chosen range of dates.

4. **Click the Report Settings button.**

When you enable any of the Workflow reports, you should also select each report and click the Report Settings button at the bottom of the dialog box to choose customized options for each specific report. For example, to search for all the files checked out by Lee, select the Checked Out By category, click the Report Settings button, and type the name **Lee** in the Checked Out By dialog box.

- **Checked Out By:** Enter the name of the team member this report searches for, such as **Jane Smith.**

- **Design Notes:** Enter names and value pairs and choose comparison values from the corresponding menus, such as **status is draft.**

- **Recently Modified:** Enter data for the report to search for files that were created or modified within a specific number of days or a range of dates, as in **Files Created or Modified in the Last 7 Days**.

5. **Select categories from the HTML Reports options:**

- **Combinable Nested Font Tags:** This report option shows a list of any nested font tags that could be combined to make the code cleaner. For example, `<font size="5"><font color="#CC0000">big red text</font></font>` would be cleaned up as `<font size="5" color="#CC0000">big red text</font>`.

- **Accessibility:** This option creates a report listing any code that does not comply with the Section 508 accessibility guidelines of the 1998 Rehabilitation Act.

- **Missing Alt Text:** Select this option to show a list of all `<img>` tags missing alternate text attributes. This attribute displays in browsers that are set to download image files manually or in place of images in text-only browsers, and to be read by screen reader software.

- **Redundant Nested Tags:** This setting lists any redundant tags that could be removed for cleaner code. For example, in the sentence `<b>Monkeys like to eat <b>bananas</b> and cake.</b>`, the `<b>` tags surrounding the word `bananas` are redundant.

- **Removable Empty Tags:** Choose this option to see a list of tags without content inside of them, as in `<span></span>` or `<font size="1"></font>`, but not `<i>kitten</i>`.

- **Untitled Documents:** Choose this option to find any untitled documents on your site as well as files with default, missing, or duplicate title tags.

6. **Click the Run button to generate the report.**

Some report options may require that you save any unsaved open files or choose a specific folder or site prior to displaying report results. The results themselves display on the Site Reports tab of the Results panel (see Figure 1-10).

Figure 1-10:
Site reports results are listed in the Site Reports area of the Results panel.

SEARCH	REFERENCE	VALIDATION	BROWSER COMPATIBILITY	LINE CHECKER	SITE REPORTS	FTP LOG	SERVER DEBUG	

File	Line	Description
services.html		Design Note info:Modified=Sept 8, 2008
services.html	10	Warning: Combinable nested tag: <FONT>
services.html	14	Non spacer IMG with valid ALT [S508 a/WCAG 1.1 P1] -- FAILED -- No ALT defined for image.
services.html	14	Non spacer IMG needs LONGDESC [S508 a/WCAG 1.1 P1] -- MANUAL -- Non-spacer image may need a ...
services.html	2	Color is not essential [S508 c/WCAG 2.1 P1] -- MANUAL --
services.html	2	Colors are visible [S508 c/WCAG 2.2 P1] -- MANUAL --
services.html	8	Skip repetitive links [S508 o/WCAG 13.6 P1] -- MANUAL -- Check if a textual link is present for skipping ...
services.html	8	GIFs do not cause the screen to flicker [S508 j/WCAG 7.1 P1] -- MANUAL -- The page contains GIF imag...

Complete.

Saving reports as XML files

You can save your report results as an XML file for later importing to a database, spreadsheet, or template instance for printing or for display in a browser window. Because report data is essentially temporary information that reflects the current state of a document, folder, site, or selected files, saving report results may be very useful if your company or client's company likes to archive the report data.

To save and use a report, follow these steps:

1. **Run your report.**

2. **Before saving the report, you can view code, sort, or review report data by any of the following methods:**

- **View Code:** To view and edit any code in a document listed in the report, double-click a line in the report to open the document in the Document window. The document opens in either Code or Split view.

- **Sort:** To sort report data, click the column heading above the category. You can sort by filename, description, or line number.

- **Review:** To review a description of any of the problems listed on the report, select a line in the report and click the More Info button, which appears on the left edge of the panel. The description information displays in the Reference panel.

3. **Click the Save Report button.**

The Save As dialog box appears. The default filename for your saved report is ResultsReport.xml. You can change the filename to anything you like, as long as you keep the file type as XML.

When you finish reviewing report data, choose Commands⇨Clean Up HTML/XHTML to automatically fix the HTML errors.

Viewing File Transfer Activity with the FTP Log

The FTP Log panel displays FTP file transfer activity for all the times you use the Get, Put, Check In, and Check Out commands in the Files panel. This log activity is very helpful when you're troubleshooting connection errors or documenting transfer process information.

To save FTP log information, select all the content in the FTP Log panel; right-click (Windows) or Control+click (Mac) and choose the Select All option. Then copy and paste the data into another file, such as a Microsoft Word document, a text file, or HTML file.

Debugging a ColdFusion Application (Windows)

Choose the Server Debug panel to see helpful information that can assist you with debugging a ColdFusion application in Windows without having to exit Dreamweaver.

If you don't see any data in this panel, you must first assign a testing server to the site definition to specify where to process dynamic pages. The testing server can be your local machine, or a staging, development, or production server. To set the testing server, open the Site Definition dialog box for the defined site, click the Advanced tab, and choose the Testing Server category. From there, you can enter the necessary information to identify the testing server. For more information on setting up a testing server, see Book VII, Chapter 1.

If you work on a Mac, press ⌘+F12 to open any ColdFusion pages in a separate browser window. From there, you can find errors at the bottom of the page.

Before beginning the debugging process, you may need to enable certain features in ColdFusion Administrator. For example, when using ColdFusion MX 7.0 and above, Dreamweaver automatically enables debugging, but if you're running ColdFusion MX 6.1 or earlier, you must enable debugging settings manually. See Dreamweaver's ColdFusion documentation for assistance with these settings by choosing Help⇨ColdFusion Help.

If you're testing your pages in Internet Explorer, consider enabling Internet Explorer to refresh page data each time the page displays so that the browser displays the most recent data available. In Internet Explorer, choose Tools⇨Internet Options and click the General tab. Click the Settings button in the Temporary Internet Files area. The Settings dialog box appears, where you select the Every Visit to Page option.

To run the Server Debug report on a ColdFusion page, follow these steps:

1. **Open the ColdFusion page in the Document window.**

2. **Click the Preview/Server Debug in Browser button on the Document toolbar.**

   The page is requested from the ColdFusion server and appears on an internal Internet Explorer browser. Any errors and their possible causes appear at the bottom of the page.

   At the same time, the Server Debug panel also displays information to assist with the debugging process. For example, the report may list SQL queries, server variables, and an execution time summary.

3. **To expand the Exceptions category on the Server Debug panel, if one appears, click the plus (+) button.**

   The Exceptions category appears only when the server finds problems with the page. Expanding the category reveals a more detailed list of information about each problem.

4. **To fix any problems listed in the Location column of the Server Debug panel, click the page URL to open the page.**

   The page opens and the code in question is highlighted in Code view so that you can edit it. You may be prompted to locate the document on your own if Dreamweaver can't automatically locate it for you.

5. **Fix errors and save the files to the server; click the Preview/Server Debug in Browser button again.**

   The browser gathers the latest information from your page and the server and renders the page again in an internal browser. The Server Debug panel also updates to show you any remaining or new potential problems. After all the problems are addressed, the Exceptions category disappears from the panel.

6. **Exit the debugging mode by choosing View⇨Design or View⇨Code.**

Chapter 2: Keeping Your Code Clean

In This Chapter

✔ **Changing code preferences**

✔ **Removing irrelevant code with the Clean Up Word HTML/XHTML command**

✔ **Applying source formatting to your pages**

✔ **Running a spell check**

✔ **Updating links sitewide**

*W*henever you build and edit Web pages in Dreamweaver — especially if you're hand-coding or pasting content — some of the markup may get crowded with redundant elements and unnecessary or unwanted code. You need to remove those extra bits of code from all the pages on the site whether you do that in advance (by setting preferences), during page creation (by selecting paste and import options), or as a final code clean-up (with Dreamweaver's HTML/XHTML Clean Up, spell check, and other code reporting tools) when the site is complete.

Why? Actually, for a few reasons. For one thing, that extra code adds to the overall file size that can impact page-loading times in a browser. For another thing, badly formatted code may confuse some browsers, causing the information on your pages to display less accurately than you intended. Even more important perhaps is the fact that some code errors can prevent browsers from displaying the HTML or XHTML entirely. If these issues aren't enough to convince you to clean up your code before publishing, you've been warned. At least think about keeping your code as clean and error free as possible as a reflection of your professionalism. After all, anyone can look at your Web site code by simply doing a View Source.

So how do you go about cleaning up your Web site code without having to review the code in each file, line by line? Fortunately, the answer can be as simple as running a few quick commands in Dreamweaver. First, set up some of Dreamweaver's preferences to avoid some of the issues in advance. If you've already created your site, you should still set up Dreamweaver's preferences so any new documents you create use these settings.

After Dreamweaver's preferences are set, you should perform the following tasks, in roughly the following order, to make sure that your code is error free and clear of miscellaneous junk: Run Dreamweaver's spell checker, use the appropriate commands to remove unnecessary code pasted from other programs, apply source formatting to your pages if it's missing, and, finally fix or change links across the site.

Eliminating Formatting Issues Before They Occur

The developers at Dreamweaver understand that previously applied formatting can be a killer to your code. Imagine this scenario: You're designing a new site. Your client, who is very eager to "help" you, sends you a bunch of content for the Web as text documents created with a program like Microsoft Word. (Alternatively, the file could come from other word processor software or as Microsoft HTML files.) No matter how the files start out, if they're filled with a lot of fancy formatting (from italics to complicated styles) and structural additions (such as automatic bullet lists and tables), you need to transform them *before* you put them into Dreamweaver.

Although the text may start out well formatted and well organized in the original client-provided file, the second you copy and paste the content into Dreamweaver without first setting Dreamweaver's Copy/Paste preferences, some of the formatting data may get translated into inline HTML formatting tags and be included with the text along the way. For example, a styled sentence pasted from Microsoft Word might look something like this:

```
<p class=MsoNormal><strong><span style="font-family:'Comic Sans MS'; font-
    size:20pt; color:#3366FF; ">Let's all do the Scrambled-Egg Dance</span></
    strong></p>
```

You can — and probably should — replace most of that Word-generated HTML formatting code with your own CSS formatting markup. In addition to creating and applying a style sheet, you need to remove the HTML formatting code from the page, either by hand or using the Find and Replace tool. When you remove everything that could end up being a problem (like the Word-generated HTML formatting), your sentence looks more like this:

```
<p><strong>Let's all do the Scrambled-Egg Dance</strong></p>
```

Ultimately, the best defense against bad code is a good offensive strategy. The following sections list some preferences and settings that you can put into place before you even start building a site. If you use these tools now, getting your pages cleaned up before publishing is that much easier.

Setting Copy and Paste preferences

To help solve some of this transfer of undesired code, Dreamweaver CS4 allows you to set Copy/Paste preferences for pasted data from Microsoft Word and other word processing programs. To change the Copy/Paste preferences, follow these steps:

1. **Choose Edit⇨Preferences (Windows) or Dreamweaver⇨Preferences (Mac).**

The Preferences dialog box opens.

2. **Select the Copy/Paste category on the left.**

On the right side of the dialog box you see some Copy/Paste options (see Figure 2-1):

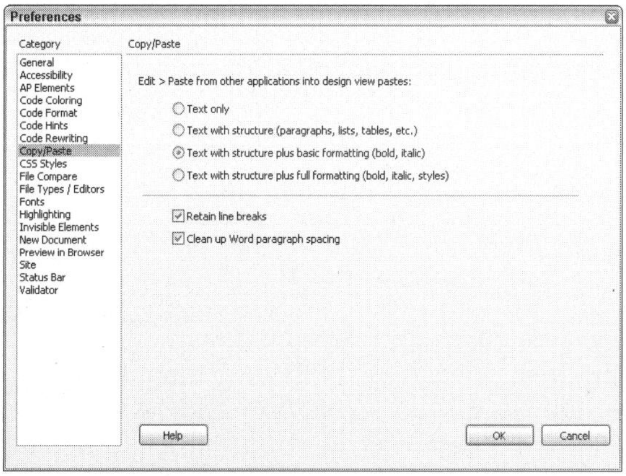

Figure 2-1: Set your Copy/Paste preferences to automatically remove unwanted markup from copied text.

- **Text only:** Not surprisingly, this option is the simplest and gives you the greatest control.

- **Text with Structure:** Dreamweaver's definition of *structure* is any formatting that affects the overall appearance of paragraphs, lists, or tables. It's not concerned with individual font formatting.

- **Text with Structure Plus Basic Formatting:** Dreamweaver's definition of *basic formatting* is stuff like **boldface,** *italics,* and underlining.

- **Text with Structure Plus Full Formatting:** Dreamweaver defines *full formatting* as formatting that affects not just the basics but also individual styles.

- **Retain Line Breaks:** This option keeps any line breaks from the source when the content is pasted.

- **Clean Up Word Paragraph Spacing:** Use this option to remove extra space between paragraphs when content copied from Microsoft Word is pasted into a Dreamweaver file.

If you're unsure which options to select, choose Text with Structure Plus Basic Formatting with both Retain Line Breaks and Clean Up Word Paragraph Spacing enabled. Basic formatting tags like `<strong>` and `<em>` are more effective markup for accessibility than creating styles that use bold and italic, as screen readers modify intonation for content inside these tags.

3. **Click OK to close the Preferences dialog box.**

New preference settings take effect immediately. You can always come back and modify these preferences later if the need arises.

Using the Paste Special command

The Paste Special command enables you to control how much (and what kind of) formatting is moved from the original file to your Dreamweaver file each time you perform a paste.

When you use the regular Paste option for copied content, your paste includes all the formatting contained in the source content. However, when you copy information from a Word document that's been formatted with a special font, font color, font size, bold and italics, and alignment and want to paste it into your Dreamweaver file *without* the font formatting while retaining the list structure, bold, and italic settings, use the Paste Special option.

When you use Edit➪Paste Special instead of the regular Paste command, the Paste Special dialog box, shown in Figure 2-2, opens so you can select a Paste preference for the copied content you're about to paste. The options in the dialog box are the same choices in the Copy/Paste category of the Preferences dialog box (refer to the previous section, "Setting Copy and Paste preferences," for information about your options). The default setting in the Paste Special dialog box matches the setting you choose in the Copy/ Paste preferences, but you can override that default option on a case-by-case basis using the Paste Special command.

Figure 2-2: Select Paste Preferences from the Paste Special dialog box.

Paste Special

Paste as:

- Text only
- Text with structure (paragraphs, lists, tables, etc.)
- Text with structure plus basic formatting (bold, italic)
- Text with structure plus full formatting (bold, italic, styles)

☐ Retain line breaks

☐ Clean up Word paragraph spacing

Paste Preferences...

OK   Cancel   Help

Cleaning Up Word HTML

Microsoft Word has a feature that enables users to convert documents into Microsoft HTML files that are viewable in a browser window. Not a bad option, really. Unfortunately, in versions of Word 97 and later, Microsoft adds extra markup for the purpose of displaying the content in a browser window and leaves in extra formatting data only necessary for the display of the page as a document. All this extra code adds to the overall file size and may affect the speed with which the page loads in a browser.

You can easily remove the extra markup (such as redundant or unnecessary nested tags, as well as Word-specific markup) with the Clean Up Word HTML command. Using this handy tool is a good way to keep file sizes as small as possible, and cleaning up the code is essential if you plan on using style sheets.

As a precaution, always try to retain a backup copy of the original Word (.doc) and especially Word HTML (.html) files before performing the clean up, because the Word HTML file may not reopen in Word after the clean-up.

Follow these steps to clean up an HTML file generated by Word 97 or later:

1. **Open the Microsoft HTML file in the Dreamweaver workspace window.**

   To see the Microsoft markup in the code before it gets removed, switch to Code or Split view by choosing View⇨Code or View⇨Code and Design.

2. **Choose Commands⇨Clean Up Word HTML.**

   The Clean Up Word HTML dialog box, shown in Figure 2-3, appears.

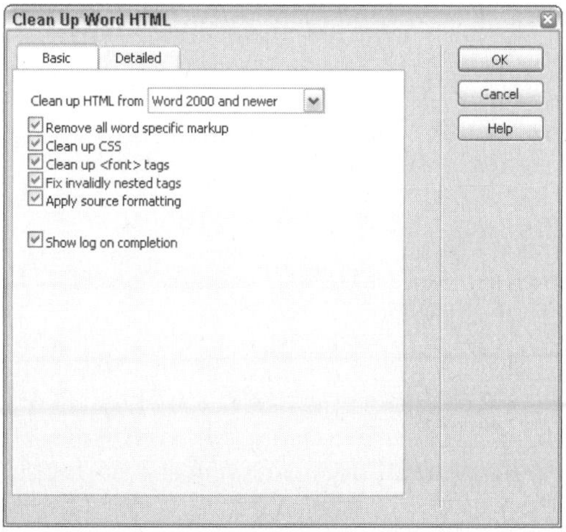

Figure 2-3:
Use the default settings in the Clean Up Word HTML dialog box for the best Word HTML clean-up results.

Dreamweaver attempts to auto-detect the version of Word the file was generated in. If the file version is undetectable, you can choose the proper version from the Clean Up HTML From drop-down list.

3. **Select any clean-up options that you want.**

The default settings are to have Dreamweaver check for and fix everything it possibly can.

We recommend that you keep the default settings on the Basic tab intact. These options are pretty crucial to stripping all the Microsoft markup from the document. If anything, you may want to tinker with the options even more (you can do so by clicking the Detailed tab):

- **Remove All Word Specific Markup:** This setting removes all Microsoft Word-specific HTML, metadata, and link tags, XML markup, and other style markup.

- **Clean Up CSS:** Use this setting to remove all Word-specific CSS, especially any inline styles that match parent styles in the markup. The options here also zap style attributes that start with Mso, styles applied to table rows and cells, and any declarations that are not CSS.

- **Clean Up <font> Tags:** Choose this setting to remove HTML font tags and convert the entire body text to size 2 HTML text.

- **Fix Invalidly Nested Tags:** This option deletes font markup tags that Word inserted outside heading and paragraph (block-level) tags.

- **Apply Source Formatting:** This option applies the source formatting options you chose in the SourceFormat.txt file and the Code Format category of Dreamweaver's Preferences to the page. For more on this feature, see the "Introducing your Code Category preferences" and "Applying Source Formatting" sections later in this chapter.

- **Show Log On Completion:** Select this option to view a log of changes performed during the clean-up. Definitely turn this feature on so you can see how much Dreamweaver has improved the file!

4. **Click OK.**

Dreamweaver performs the clean-up with the selected settings. Depending on the size of your site, this process may take a minute or two.

Checking Your Spelling, Grammar, and Readability

When it comes time to proofread your copy for spelling and grammatical errors, much of the responsibility sits with you. Although Dreamweaver offers a spell checking feature, it's not automatic, so you have to remember to run the spell check prior to publishing your Web site. And, although the spell checker may catch some of your spelling errors, it won't alert you to poorly chosen words, *homophones* (words that sound the same but have vastly different meanings, such as *sight* and *site*), words used out of context, or other common grammatical errors that can have an impact on meaning (such as *it's* instead of *its*).

The best way to make sure that everything makes sense is to use your eyes. No mechanical tool can substitute for taking the time to read (and reread) your site content. In fact, you should have at least two other people assist you in checking your site for spelling, grammar, and readability. Even better, consider setting up a temporary Web site in a folder on your Web server to share with your proofreaders to help streamline the process. This can also server as a perfect opportunity to review the site in different browser and operating system combinations as part of your real life, pre-launch browser compatibility testing.

Before you recruit your coworkers, friends, clients, and family members to join in on the spell checking fun, use the Dreamweaver Check Spelling command, which isolates common spelling errors in text while ignoring HTML tags and attribute values in the code.

Follow these steps to check and correct spelling:

1. **In Dreamweaver, open the document to be spell checked.**

2. **Choose Commands⇨Check Spelling or press Shift+F7.**

The Check Spelling dialog box, shown in Figure 2-4, appears if Dreamweaver finds a word or words that are not recognized. If Dreamweaver finds no errors, you may see a recommendation that you begin a new spell check from the start of the document. Otherwise, you're presented with a Spelling Check Completed alert box.

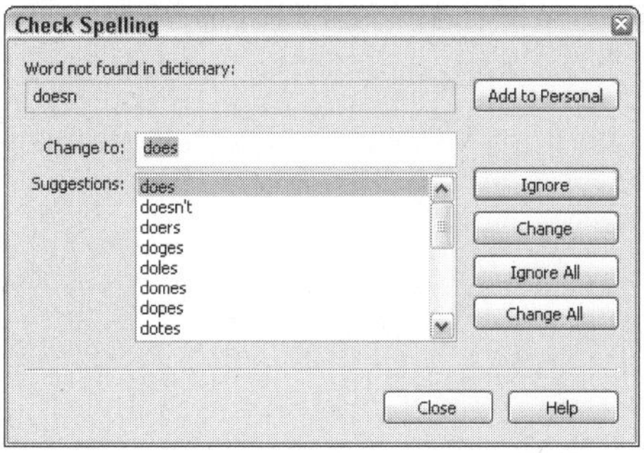

Figure 2-4:
Use the
Check
Spelling
dialog box
to ignore or
change un-
recognized
words.

> **Check Spelling**
>
> Word not found in dictionary:
> doesn   [Add to Personal]
>
> Change to: [does]
>
> Suggestions: | does | [Ignore]
> | | doesn't | [Change]
> | | doers |
> | | doges | [Ignore All]
> | | doles |
> | | domes | [Change All]
> | | dopes |
> | | dotes |
>
> [Close]   [Help]

3. **Choose an option to handle each unrecognized word:**

- **Add to Personal** adds the unrecognized word to the personal dictionary, which appends the default or substitute language dictionary. This is particularly helpful when working on sites that reuse particular words or often used made-up terms that fall outside the traditional vernacular, like *knowledgeability* and *truthiness*.

- **Ignore** ignores the current instance of an unrecognized word.

- **Change** replaces the unrecognized word with a selected suggestion or text typed in the Change To text box.

- **Ignore All** ignores all instances of an unrecognized word.
- **Change All** replaces all instances of the unrecognized word with the selected suggestion or text typed in the Change To text box.

If you accidentally click Ignore All or Select All for the wrong thing, errors can occur where previously there were none. Checking each found item on an individual basis is always a good idea.

The Dreamweaver spell checker uses the U.S. English spelling dictionary by default, but you can choose other dictionaries from the Spelling Dictionary drop-down list in the General category of Dreamweaver's Preferences.

Getting Your HTML and XHTML Code Consistent

Most Web designers speak a few markup dialects, such as XHTML and HTML. Like most multilingual individuals, you may lapse into a hybrid language that (unfortunately) only you understand (we figure it's the markup equivalent of *Spanglish*). Or maybe you're translating something from HTML to XHTML. In either case, winding up with some inconsistent tags, unneeded comments, and redundant or unnecessary tags in your code sometimes happens to the best of us. To do general HTML cleanup work on your files, such as removing empty container or redundant nested tags, run the Clean Up HTML/XHTML command on any open document.

Dreamweaver auto-detects the doctype of the document open in the workspace window and displays the HTML or XHTML Clean Up command on the Commands menu to match the doctype it detects. For example, if the doctype is HTML, the Clean Up HTML command appears on the Commands menu; if the doctype is XHTML, the Clean Up XHTML command appears instead.

When your file uses XHTML markup instead of HTML, this command performs all the XHTML clean-up tasks, plus it instantly converts all the tag attributes to lowercase, fixes XHTML syntax errors, and adds or reports any required tag attributes that are missing, such as images with missing `<alt>` text.

To clean up HTML/XHTML code, follow these steps:

1. **Open the document. For HTML documents, choose Commands⇨Clean Up HTML. For XHTML documents, choose Commands⇨Clean Up XHTML.**

The Clean Up HTML/XHTML dialog box opens, as shown in Figure 2-5.

Figure 2-5:
Choose
options to
clean up
your text
from the
Clean Up
HTML/
XHTML
dialog box.

Clean Up HTML / XHTML

Remove: ☑ Empty container tags (<b></b>, <h1></h1>, ...)
☑ Redundant nested tags
☐ Non-Dreamweaver HTML comments
☐ Dreamweaver special markup
☐ Specific tag(s):

Options: ☑ Combine nested <font> Tags when possible
☑ Show log on completion

OK
Cancel
Help

2. **Choose any combination of clean up options:**

- **Empty Container Tags:** This option removes tags without content inside of them, as in `<i></i>` or `<font size="2"></font>`, but not `<i>hello</i>`.

- **Redundant Nested Tags:** Clean up any redundant tags with this setting. For example, in the sentence `<b>Blue frogs hop on <b>green</b> lily pads.</b>`, the `<b>` tags surrounding the word `green` are redundant.

- **Non-Dreamweaver HTML Comments:** This option removes any comments in the code that Dreamweaver didn't automatically insert. For instance, a comment tag to define the beginning of image slices in the code like `<!-- ImageReady Slices (filename.psd) -->` or a comment tag from you to another member of your work group, like `<!-- Phil, insert the Peanut Data table here -->` would be removed, but code to identify a Dreamweaver-editable area like this `<!-- #BeginEditable "doctitle" -->` would not.

- **Dreamweaver Special Markup:** Use this option to remove the special markup tags that Dreamweaver uses to automatically update templates and library items. Removing this special markup detaches the document from its original source, as with a template-based file and its source template file.

- **Specific Tag(s):** To remove specific markup from the code, type the tag in the Specific Tag text box. To remove multiple tags at the same time, separate tags with commas, as in `span`, `font`.

- **Combine Nested <font> Tags When Possible:** This option combines any nested font tags when they could be joined to do the same task. For example, `<font size="2"><font color="#006699"> little blue Thomas train</font></font>` would be cleaned up as `<font size="2" color="#006699"> little blue Thomas train</font>`.

- **Show Log On Completion:** Check this box to have an alert box with details about the clean-up display at the end of the clean-up process. Leave this option enabled to see how much your file is improved.

3. **Click OK to start the cleanup process.**

   If you left the Show Log On Completion check box enabled, a Clean Up Summary alert window opens when the clean-up process is finished, listing details about the clean-up. You may see messages such as XHTML syntax fixed or 12 comment(s) removed.

Reviewing Source Formatting and Making Changes

Dreamweaver has done a wonderful job coloring and organizing the coding environment to assist you with reviewing and editing your code. For instance with CSS markup, style information is color coded to differentiate between the style or selector name, the style property, value, and separators between them in the declaration, and the opening and closing style tags. And take a look at the code for any table on a page; the <table>, <tr>, and <td> tags are in one color (teal), the values (like a color value of #99CCFF) for any properties in the table are in another color (royal blue), and any content placed inside a table cell is yet another color (black).

Dreamweaver provides the flexibility of allowing you to customize the coding color preferences if you ever want to change them. That means, for example, if you're trying to isolate specific tags in the code, you could change the color of those tags.

In fact, you can set Dreamweaver preferences to specify code formatting, editing, coloring, viewing, and hinting options. All coding preferences apply to both new documents and new content on existing documents created in Dreamweaver.

Setting code formatting preferences

To customize your Dreamweaver coding environment, follow these steps:

1. **Choose Edit➪Preferences (Windows) or Dreamweaver➪Preferences.**

   The Dreamweaver Preferences dialog box appears.

2. **Choose one of the code categories on the left and edit the preferences for that category as needed.**

   A description of each code category and its preferences settings is listed in the following section.

3. **Click OK to save the new settings.**

Introducing your Code Category preferences

Though it may appear you have more preferences than you know what to do with, take a quick look at the following options to see if you want to adjust anything to improve your coding environment:

✦ **Code Coloring:** Change the default code colors for different document types, which means you can use one set of colors for HTML code and another set of colors for PHP code. After you select a document type, click the Edit Coloring Scheme button. You can modify the code text and background colors, along with Bold, Italic, or Underline styles, for specific code elements such as form tags, JavaScript elements, CSS elements, and library items (see Figure 2-6). For example, if you wanted your image tags to stand out, you'd select the HTML Image Tags style and change the text color, background color, and perhaps apply bold and underline, too.

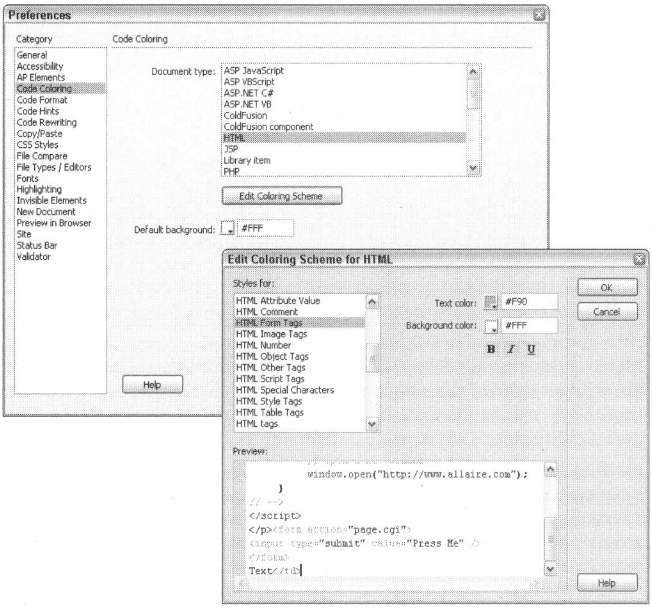

Figure 2-6:
Edit the coloring scheme for different document types.

✦ **Code Format:** Set code formatting preferences such as default indent and tab size, default attribute and tag case, and other options, as shown in Figure 2-7:

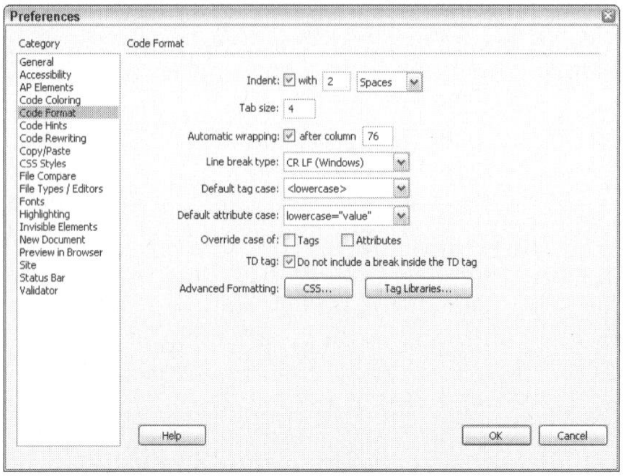

Figure 2-7:
Set Code
Format
preferences
for normal
coding and
use with
the Apply
Source
Formatting
command.

- **Indent:** This option indents Dreamweaver-generated code (though not for any code you hand-code) according to the number of spaces or tabs set in the With field and drop-down list.

- **Tab Size:** This option sets the character width of each tab character in Code view. For instance, if set to 5, each tab displays as a blank space equal to five characters wide. This measure also affects the indent size when you've selected Tabs from the With drop-down list.

- **Automatic Wrapping:** Enable this option to have the code automatically wrap in Code view, with the insertion of a line break character, when it reaches the number of characters set in the After Column field. This is different than the Wrap option, which virtually wraps the code when it reaches the edge of the window in Code view but doesn't actually add line break characters.

- **Line Break Type:** This preference identifies the type of remote server hosting your site. Choose Windows, Macintosh, or Unix to ensure the line breaks in your code appear correctly when viewed on the remote server. This option only applies to binary transfer mode when connected with FTP; the ASCII transfer mode is ignored. However, when downloading files in ASCII mode, the line breaks are automatically set to match the computer's OS, and when uploading in ASCII mode, the line breaks are automatically set to CR LF (Windows).

- **Default Tag Case/Default Attribute Case:** These two settings control whether your code uses uppercase or lowercase for tags and attributes in Design view. These settings have no control over editing in Code view or over existing document attributes, unless you select one or both of the Override Case Of options.

- **Override Case Of: Tags and Attributes:** Turn on one or both of these options to have Dreamweaver enforce the case rules set for the Default Tag Case and Default Attribute Case at all times. This automatically converts code in existing files as well as enforces case rules for content added to new files.

Because the Web is moving more toward XHTML compliance and XHTML requires lowercase letters for the coding of tags and attributes, it's best to set Default Tag Case and Default Attribute Case to lowercase and enable Override Case of settings for both tags and attributes.

- **Advanced Formatting:** Click the CSS button to open the CSS Source Format Options dialog box, inside which you can adjust CSS format settings for indents, properties, selectors, and blank line rules. Click the Tag Library button to open the Tag Library Editor, where, if you had some specific need, you could adjust the format for specified HTML and programming language tags.

✦ **Code Hints:** Decide how Dreamweaver's code hint preferences display in Code view and in the Quick Tag Editor. Here are your options:

- **Close Tags:** Choose to have Dreamweaver automatically insert closing tags after typing "</", add closing tags after entering the opening tag's angle bracket (>), or never insert closing tags.

- **Enable Code Hints:** Choose to see code hints when typing in Code view. Use the code hint delay slider to adjust the number of seconds to wait before the hints are shown.

- **Menus:** Choose this option to select from a list of menus which kinds of code hints display.

✦ **Code Rewriting:** Select how Dreamweaver rewrites or fixes invalid code. These settings can rewrite code when opening files, copying and pasting form data, and entering link URLs and attributes in Dreamweaver. They won't, however, change code when you're editing HTML or scripts in Code view. When you have these features disabled, Dreamweaver shows the invalid markup for HTML that it would have rewritten in the Document window.

- **Fix Invalidly Nested and Unclosed Tags:** This setting reorders improperly nested tags as well as inserting any missing quote marks or closing brackets. For example, `<strong><em>Monkey!</strong></em>` would be rewritten as `<strong><em>Monkey!</em></strong>`, and `<div <img src="images/logo.gif"></div>` would be rewritten as `<div><img src="images/logo.gif"></div>`.

- **Rename Form Items When Pasting:** When pasting elements from other documents, this default setting makes sure that the page has no form objects with the same name. For example, if one text field is named `textfield`, the next would be named `textfield2`, and so on.

- **Remove Extra Closing Tags:** This setting deletes any extra closing tags that don't have opening tag mates.

- **Warn When Fixing or Removing Tags: (Only available when Remove Extra Closing Tags is enabled)** Enable this setting to see a summary of invalid HTML markup that Dreamweaver couldn't fix. The summary identifies the source of the problem by using line and column numbers so that you can easily find and fix the error.

- **Never Rewrite Code: In Files with Extensions: (Only available when Remove Extra Closing Tags is enabled)** Enable or disable Dreamweaver from rewriting code in files with particular filename extensions, like .css or .shtml. This setting is particularly handy when adding third-party tags to your code.

The next four options do not apply to existing code or new URLs typed in Code view but do apply to all new coding added to documents in Design view and through the Properties inspector:

- **Encode <, >, &, and " in Attribute Values Using &:** Because attribute values entered or edited in Dreamweaver must have legal characters, the default setting makes sure that entered data conforms to those standards.

- **Do Not Encode Special Characters:** Stop Dreamweaver from adjusting URLs that use nonlegal characters.

- **Encode Special Characters in URL Using &#:** This setting makes sure that URLs use only legal characters by using special encoding.

- **Encode Special Characters in URL Using %:** Like the previous setting, this option makes sure that URLs have only legal characters, but uses a different encoding method for special characters. This option works well with older browsers, but doesn't work so well with some characters in other languages.

Applying Source Formatting

You can use the Code Format coding preferences listed in the previous section for the creation of new Dreamweaver files and additions to existing documents. You can't, however, use them on HTML files that you created *before* these preferences were set. To do that, you'd essentially be reformatting the old code. If you want to change the original code, therefore, you must *apply source formatting.* Applying source formatting means using the Code Format settings you customized in the previous section to reformat the code in an existing HTML file.

You can apply source formatting to an entire document or to a particular selection on a page.

Applying source formatting to a complete file

To apply source formatting to an existing file, follow these steps:

1. **Open the file in Dreamweaver.**

2. **Choose Commands⇨Apply Source Formatting.**

   Dreamweaver immediately applies all existing and any new coding preferences to the page code.

3. **Save the file by choosing File⇨Save.**

Applying source formatting to a selection of a file

To apply source formatting to a selection of an existing file, follow these steps:

1. **Open the file in Dreamweaver and select the content in Design view that you want to modify with the new coding preferences.**

   Selected content must be *contiguous* (touching). There is no option for selecting multiple, non-touching areas of your document. If you need to apply source formatting to several sections of a page, repeat these steps for each section.

2. **Choose Commands⇨Apply Source Formatting to Selection.**

   Dreamweaver immediately applies any new coding preferences to the selected page code.

3. **Save the updated file by choosing File⇨Save.**

Changing Links Sitewide

In a managed site, whenever you rename or move a file, Dreamweaver offers to automatically update those links for you. You can also manually change links throughout your site at any time. (To discover more about links in general, see Book II, Chapter 4. To find out how to check and fix links with Dreamweaver's Check Links report, see Book V, Chapter 1.)

The Change Link Sitewide feature enables you to change individual text, e-mail, FTP, null, and script links from one setting to another. For example, you may have a text link, such as "This Month's Newsletter," that needs to point to a new HTML file each month, such as /newsletters/september. html this month and /newsletters/october.html next month. Likewise, if you need to change an e-mail address across all the pages on a Web site (such as changing mailto:info@dummies.com to mailto:orders@ dummies.com), you can use this command to do it.

Follow these steps to change a link throughout your site:

1. **In the Files panel, select a file from the Local view listing.**

   If you're changing an e-mail address, FTP, script, or null link, you can skip this step.

2. **Choose Site⇨Change Link Sitewide.**

   Or choose Site⇨Change Link Sitewide from the Files panel Options menu.

   The Change Link Sitewide dialog box appears, as shown in Figure 2-8.

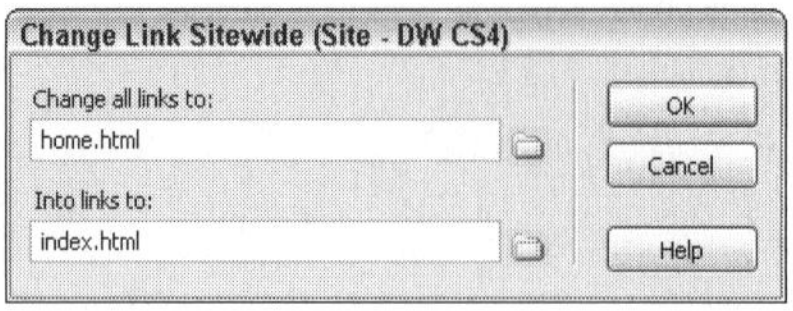

Figure 2-8:
Change
individual
links
sitewide.

Change Link Sitewide (Site - DW CS4)

Change all links to:
home.html

Into links to:
index.html

OK

Cancel

Help

3. **Enter the current and new link information in the Change All Links To and Into Links To text fields, respectively.**

For changing filenames, enter the old filename and new filename in the appropriate text fields. For any other type of link, enter the complete old and new text of the link you want to change. For instance, to replace one e-mail address with another, type **mailto:info@example.com** for the old address and **mailto:contact@example.com** for the new address.

4. **Click OK.**

Dreamweaver updates all instances of that link with the new link information. Any path associated with the former link remains intact, regardless of whether the path is site root-relative or document-relative.

After the change is made, the file with the old filename becomes an orphan with no files on the managed site pointing to it. You can safely delete it from the local site folder without any fear of creating broken links. When uploading the updated pages to the remote server, don't forget to manually delete the same orphaned file from the remote server so that site visitors see the changed links.

Chapter 3: Preparing to Publish Your Files Online

In This Chapter

✔ Setting up a remote connection

✔ Choosing a remote access type

✔ Cloaking files and folders

*I*n Book V, Chapter 1, you discover how to run Workflow and HTML reports to check for coding errors on your pages. Then, in Book V, Chapter 2, you find out how easy cleaning up your code is when you use the Clean Up and Spell Checking commands. The next step to take before you publish your site is to set up a remote connection for your site. (We cover the final step, actually transferring your files, in Book V, Chapter 4.)

The *remote connection* defines the folder or destination where you're publishing your files. The remote folder can be on a testing server or production server, or any other type of server for storing your published files.

In this chapter, we show you how to create a remote connection for uploading and downloading files. You also find out how to cloak file types and folders to make sure that specified files aren't included in sitewide operations like uploading, report generation, and changing links.

Creating a Remote Connection

Before you set up a remote connection, you need to create a managed site. If you still need to set up a proper structure for your site, turn to Book I, Chapter 3 to find out about general Web site structure, document-relative, and site root-relative paths, and how to create a managed site in Dreamweaver.

Setting up a remote connection requires you to specify a *remote folder*. This folder is the server location where you store a copy of the Web site's files, separate from the local version on your own computer. You need this copy in place (and in a remote location) so that you can test, produce, deploy, and collaborate on the site.

If you plan on running the Web server on your local computer, you don't need to specify a remote folder; as long as the local folder points to the system running your Web server, Dreamweaver automatically uses the local folder (specified in the Local Info category) as the remote folder.

Setting up a remote folder

You can connect and access the remote folder using any of several methods. This section focuses on using the Advanced tab of the Site Definition dialog box to enter all your remote folder information.

To set up a remote folder, follow these steps:

1. **Choose Site⇨Manage Sites.**

   Or choose Sites⇨Manage Sites from the Files panel Options menu.

   The Manage Sites dialog box appears.

2. **Select a managed site from the Dreamweaver site listing.**

   If you don't see any sites listed, you must create a new *managed site* before proceeding (see Book I, Chapter 3).

3. **Click the Edit button.**

   The Site Definition dialog box appears.

4. **Click the Advanced tab, if it's not already showing.**

   The Advanced site definition options enable you to enter specific information about your managed site.

5. **Click the Remote Info category, and then from the Access menu, select one of the access types for uploading and downloading files to and from the remote site folder on the Web server.**

   A *remote access type* is simply the means to transfer files from your local computer to a remote location.

   The option that's best for you depends on how large the team of Web developers working on the site is, as well as the existing technology you already have in place:

   - **None:** Select this option if you won't be uploading the site to a server using Dreamweaver. You can also select this option to remove prior access settings.

   - **FTP:** Choose this option if you'll be using File Transfer Protocol (FTP) to connect to your Web server. Where prompted, enter FTP host, Host directory (if any), Login, and Password information, as well as firewall, server compatibility, or secure/passive FTP settings. The FTP access method presumes you've already registered your domain name (with a company like Network Solutions) and secured a hosting plan for your domain with a reputable host provider (check out the top 10 list at www.webhostinginspector.com).

     To connect and disconnect to a remote folder with FTP, all you need to do is click the Connect to Remote Host button in the Files panel.

- **Local/Network:** Select this option if you'll be running a Web server on your local computer or accessing a local area network (LAN) folder. Click the folder icon next to the Remote Folder text field to browse for and select the folder to which you want to send the remote site files. You don't need to manually connect and disconnect to a remote folder with network access because you're always connected if you choose this type of access method. You may, however, want to click the Refresh button in the Files panel often so that you can see the latest version of your remote files.

- **WebDAV (Web-based Distributed Authoring and Versioning):** Use this access method if you connect to a server that supports the WebDAV protocol, such as a Microsoft Internet Information Server (IIS) 5.0 or an Apache Web server with the right configuration settings. Enter the URL for the WebDAV server, username, and password before testing the connection.

- **RDS (Rapid Development Services):** Use this setting to connect to your Web server using RDS. The remote folder must be on a computer running ColdFusion. Click the Settings button to enter the host name for the server, the port number, and the remote root folder's full host directory, username, and password.

- **Microsoft Visual SourceSafe:** This is a Windows-only setting. Select this access method if you connect to your Web server using Microsoft Visual SourceSafe for Windows and have Microsoft Visual SourceSafe client Version 6 installed on the local computer. Click the Settings button to specify the Microsoft Visual SourceSafe database path, project, username, and password.

After you make your selection, the appropriate options for that access type appear below the Access menu. For instance, if you select FTP, you see text fields for inputting FTP access information, such as host URL, username, and password.

To find out how to set each of the access types, see the following section, "Configuring a remote access type."

6. **Click OK to save the entered information.**

Dreamweaver saves remote information settings and closes the Site Definition dialog box. You may then click the Done button in the Manage Sites dialog box to close it. Dreamweaver is now set up to make a connection to the specified remote server.

Configuring a remote access type

Your development environment determines which remote access type you choose, as well as where the remote folder resides. The following sections show you how to select and set category options for each of the remote access types available.

For each of these remote access types, these options also appear:

✦ **Maintain Synchronization Information:** Choose to synchronize local and remote files automatically. This option is enabled by default, so you must deselect it if you don't want Dreamweaver to synchronize your files. (We recommend keeping the option enabled if you want Dreamweaver to automate the synchronization process — Dreamweaver's synchronization tools are very useful. For details on the entire synchronization process, read Book V, Chapter 4.)

✦ **Automatically Upload Files to Server on Save:** Most developers leave this option disabled so they can test locally before publishing the updated files to the remote server. When enabled, Dreamweaver uploads files to the remote site whenever files are saved locally.

✦ **Enable File Check In and Check Out:** When enabled, three additional fields appear. These fields are the Check Out Files When Opening check box, the Check Out Name field, and E-mail Address field of the main person using the current workstation. Unless you work in a group setting (see Book VI, Chapter 1), leave this option disabled.

FTP

One of the most common methods of accessing a Web server is by using File Transfer Protocol (FTP). This is a good catchall remote access option, and the most common protocol used for transferring files. This section covers how to use Dreamweaver's built-in FTP client for transferring files, but you could also transfer your files using any of the more common stand-alone FTP client applications (see Book VII, Chapter 2).

Access the Site Definition dialog box and follow these steps to enter information in the Remote Info category (see Figure 3-1):

1. **Enter the FTP host name where you will upload your files in the FTP Host field.**

The FTP host name is the full Internet name of the server, such as `ftp.adobe.com` or `www.mysampleURL.com`. Don't enter any additional text such as the protocol name before the host name. You can also enter the IP address if you have it. If you do not know this information, contact your host provider or system administrator.

2. **In the Host Directory field, enter the address of the host directory provided by your service provider.**

The host directory is the location on the remote site where the files that will be visible to the Internet public are stored.

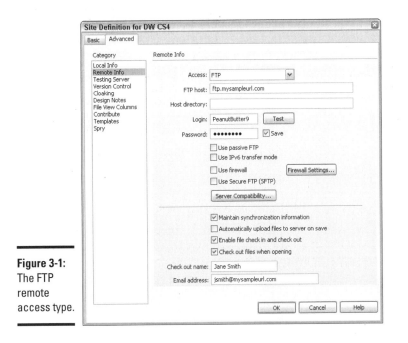

Figure 3-1:
The FTP
remote
access type.

Not all servers require this information, so if you don't know it, leave this text field empty or speak with your host provider or system administrator before continuing. Some servers use a directory called `public_html` or `www`, or use your host account username. To see if you have a directory as part of your hosting plan, establish an FTP connection without one to see whether the Remote view lists any host directory folders, such as `public_html`. If you see a directory folder, make a note of it and complete this step later.

3. **Enter the login (or username) and password you're using to connect to the FTP server in the Login and Password fields.**

When you order your Web hosting plan, your host provider gives you this information for your account. If you don't know your login/username and password, contact your host provider or system administrator.

Keep your login/username and password confidential.

4. **Click the Test button to test your FTP connection.**

If your FTP host name, host directory, login/username, and password information are valid, Dreamweaver displays an alert message that says the connection was a success. If the connection fails, an error message appears telling you that a connection could not be established. If that happens, check the spelling and accuracy of all the information you've entered, paying special attention to character case and spelling, and try again.

By default, Dreamweaver saves your FTP login information and password.

5. **If you prefer to enter your password each time you log in to your remote folder using FTP, deselect the Save check box to the right of the Password text box.**

6. **(Optional) Enable the Use Passive FTP and/or the IPv6 transfer mode options if your firewall configuration requires it.**

   Passive FTP uses the local software to set up the connection, rather than relying on the remote server to create the connection. For more information about whether you should use this option, contact your host provider or system administrator, and see the Adobe TechNote 15220 at www.adobe.com/go/tn_15220.

   IPv6 transfer mode is an Extended Data Connection Type that must be set when using an IPv6-enabled FTP server. For more information about this connection option, visit www.ipv6.org.

7. **Enable the Use Firewall option when connecting to a remote server from behind a firewall.**

   If you're unsure whether you need to enable this option, speak with your company's system administrator.

   If you need to edit the firewall host or port information, click the Firewall Settings button. This opens the Preferences dialog box with the Site category options showing (see Figure 3-2), where you can modify, among other things, the FTP connection, transfer, and hosting preferences:

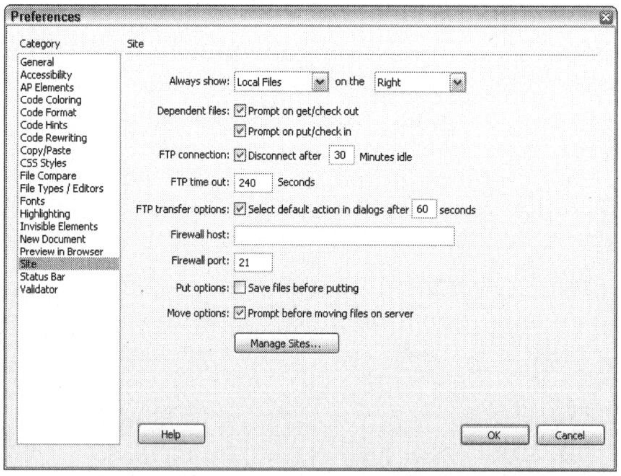

Figure 3-2:
Modify
the FTP
connection
settings.

- **Always Show:** When using Dreamweaver for FTP, adjust these settings to determine which site (local or remote) is shown by default in the Files panel. You can also choose which pane in the expanded Files panel (left or right) displays local and remote files. Dreamweaver's default is to always show local files on the right, which happens to be the opposite of most stand-alone FTP client applications.

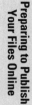

- **Dependent Files:** Enable one or both of these options to have Dreamweaver display a prompt when transferring dependent files (such as images, PDFs, CSS, and so on) that the browser needs when displaying the pages being uploaded. Both options are enabled by default, so we recommend you leave these settings as they are.

- **FTP Connection:** Set the disconnect time after a period of idleness, such as 30 minutes.

- **FTP Time Out:** Set the number of seconds it takes for Dreamweaver to attempt making a connection with the server. If there's no response after the time specified, a warning alert displays. The default is 240 seconds.

- **FTP Transfer Options:** Use this setting to have Dreamweaver use a default option after the number of seconds specified to display a dialog box during the file transfer when there's no user response.

- **Firewall Host:** Enter the address of the proxy servers through which you connect to remote servers when using a firewall. Leave this field blank if you don't use a firewall.

- **Firewall Port:** If you do use a firewall host to connect to a remote server, enter the port number here. Otherwise, leave this field set to 21, the default number for FTP.

- **Put Options:** Enable the Save Files Before Putting feature to have unsaved files automatically save before you upload them to the server.

- **Move Options:** Enable the Prompt Before Moving Files on Server option to have Dreamweaver prompt you before you move files on the server.

After making a selection, click OK or Cancel to close the Preferences and return to the Remote Info category of the Site Definition dialog box.

8. **(Optional) Enable the Use Secure FTP (SFTP) option if you need to connect with SFTP for secure authentication.**

SFTP uses public keys and encryption to create a secure connection with the testing server running an SFTP server. SFTP is a more secure option than regular FTP, however very few Web hosts currently support it.

9. **(Optional) Click the Server Compatibility button if you're having difficulty making a successful connection with the server:**

- **Use FTP Performance Optimization:** Deselect this option if you're having trouble connecting to the server with Dreamweaver.

- **Use Alternative FTP Move Method:** Enable this option if you're getting errors when rollbacks are enabled or when moving files.

10. **Click OK to save these settings and exit the Site Definition dialog box.**

Local/Network

Use the Local/Network access type when you're running a Web server on your local computer or accessing a network folder.

One of the benefits of this configuration is that you're always online. Access the Site Definition dialog box, and then in the Remote Info category, follow these steps to complete the always-connected Local/Network access configuration:

1. **Next to the Remote Folder text field, click the folder button to browse to and select the remote folder that contains your remote site files.**

On a local machine running a Web server, this folder is probably located on the Web server, as shown in Figure 3-3. If your computer is running on a network, the folder is the one on the network that stores the remote site files.

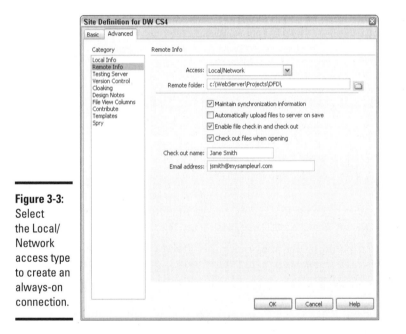

Figure 3-3:
Select the Local/ Network access type to create an always-on connection.

2. **Click OK to save these settings and exit the Site Definition dialog box.**

WebDAV

Use WebDAV, or Web-based Distributed Authoring and Versioning, as your access method if you're connecting to a server that supports the WebDAV protocol. For documentation, specifications, software, and other information, visit www.webdav.org. Microsoft Internet Information Server (IIS) 5.0 and Apache Web servers with the right configuration settings are the only servers that should use this remote access setup. If you're not sure whether your server falls into this category, it probably doesn't.

To set up your configuration, first access the Site Definition dialog box. In the Remote Info category, follow these steps:

1. **Type the full URL that points to the directory on the WebDAV server you want to connect to, as shown in Figure 3-4.**

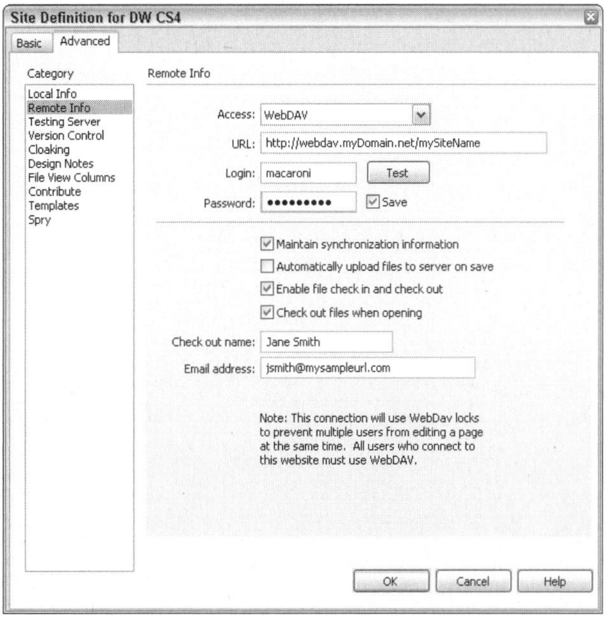

Figure 3-4:
Enter the connected server's URL including protocol, port, and directory for WebDAV access.

The URL includes protocol, port, and directory, like this: `http://webdav.mydomain.net/mySiteName`.

2. **Type your login and password in the text fields provided.**

The login and password are used only for server authentication.

3. **Click the Test button to test the connection.**

If the full URL, username, and password information are valid, Dreamweaver displays an alert message that the connection was a success. If the connection fails, an error message appears. Check the spelling, pay attention to character case, and review the accuracy of the URL before you try again.

4. **Click the Save option to store your password for future sessions.**

5. **Click OK to save these settings and exit the Site Definition dialog box.**

RDS

Use the RDS remote access setting to connect to a Web server running ColdFusion with Rapid Development Services (RDS). To learn more about working with ColdFusion, visit the ColdFusion Resources Support site at www.adobe.com/support/documentation/en/coldfusion/. If you're not sure whether your server is running ColdFusion with RDS, it probably isn't. To set up your configuration, first access the Site Definition dialog box. In the Remote Info category, follow these steps:

1. **Select RDS as the access type and click the Settings button.**

The Configure RDS Server dialog box appears, as shown in Figure 3-5.

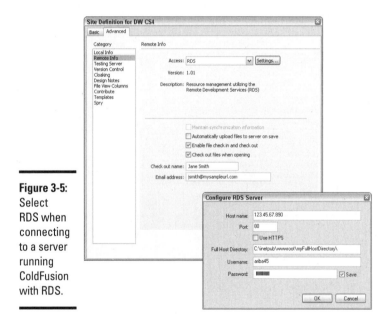

Figure 3-5: Select RDS when connecting to a server running ColdFusion with RDS.

2. **In the Configure RDS Server dialog box, complete all the fields:**

- **Host Name:** Type the name of the host computer where the Web server is installed. Often, the host name appears as an IP address or URL.

- **Port:** Enter the port number you want to use to connect to the remote location. By default, Dreamweaver enters port 80. If you have no reason to change this setting, don't.

- **Full Host Directory:** Enter the local path of the root remote folder, as in C:\inetpub\wwwroot\myFullHostDirectory\.

- **Username** and **Password:** Enter a username and password for the RDS. If you don't see these fields, you've already set the username and password in the ColdFusion Administrator.

- **Save:** By default, these settings are automatically saved. To enter these settings manually each time you connect, deselect the Save option.

3. **Click OK to close this dialog box.**

   You return to the Site Definition dialog box.

4. **Click OK to save these settings and exit the Site Definition dialog box.**

Microsoft Visual SourceSafe

Use the Microsoft Visual SourceSafe option (which is a Windows-only access method) when you're connecting to a Web server using Microsoft Visual SourceSafe for Windows and have Microsoft Visual SourceSafe Client Version 6 installed on the local computer. Visual SourceSafe is a team oriented source control software program that aids programmers with software development projects through the use of a check in/check out file system. For more information about this Microsoft software, visit http://msdn. microsoft.com/en-us/vs2005/aa718670.aspx

If you're not sure whether your server is running this application, it probably isn't. To set up your configuration, first access the Site Definition dialog box. In the Remote Info category, follow these steps:

1. **Select Microsoft Visual SourceSafe as the access type and click the Settings button.**

   The Open Microsoft Visual SourceSafe Database dialog box appears, as shown in Figure 3-6.

2. **In the Open Microsoft Visual SourceSafe Database dialog box, complete all the fields to configure the database:**

   - **Database Path:** Type the full file path to the Microsoft Visual SourceSafe database or click the Browse button to browse for and select the database. The selected file becomes the srcsafe.ini file that launches Microsoft Visual SourceSafe.

   - **Project:** Type the project within the Microsoft Visual SourceSafe database to be used as the remote site's root directory.

   - **Username** and **Password:** Enter a username and password for the database.

   - **Save:** By default these settings are automatically saved. To enter these settings manually each time you connect, deselect the Save option.

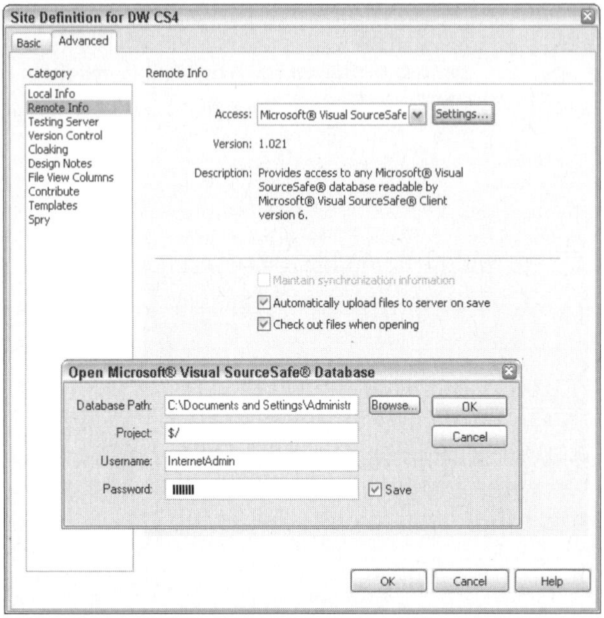

Figure 3-6:
Select
Microsoft
Visual
SourceSafe
when
connecting
to a
Microsoft
Visual
SourceSafe
database.

[Site Definition for DW CS4 dialog box shown with Basic and Advanced tabs. Category list includes Local Info, Remote Info, Testing Server, Version Control, Cloaking, Design Notes, File View Columns, Contribute, Templates, Spry. Remote Info panel shows Access: Microsoft® Visual SourceSafe, Settings button, Version: 1.021, Description: Provides access to any Microsoft® Visual SourceSafe® database readable by Microsoft® Visual SourceSafe® Client version 6. Checkboxes: Maintain synchronization information, Automatically upload files to server on save, Check out files when opening. Open Microsoft® Visual SourceSafe® Database dialog: Database Path: C:\Documents and Settings\Administr, Browse, OK; Project: $/; Username: InternetAdmin; Password: ||||||, Save; Cancel. Bottom buttons: OK, Cancel, Help.]

3. **Click OK to close this dialog box and return to the Site Definition dialog box.**

4. **Click OK to save these settings and exit the Site Definition dialog box.**

Cloaking Your Files and Folders

Cloaking is a Dreamweaver feature that enables you to exclude specified folders and file types from sitewide operations such as uploading to a server through Dreamweaver, report generation, and changing links. For example, if you transfer files to a remote server using Dreamweaver's Get and Put or Check In/Check Out systems, cloaking shields some of those files from being uploaded to or checked out from the remote server.

When else does cloaking come in handy? Well, it definitely helps if you have some files on your local site that you don't want to transfer to the server. If some files aren't being changed or updated (like graphics or PDFs), or if some files really don't need to be on the server (like templates and library items), you have no real reason to keep transferring them, right? Say you're running a busy design services Web site that requires weekly and some-times daily updates. If you don't want to upload the same white papers and graphic files every day, you can cloak .pdf, .gif, and .jpg file types in the Cloaking category of the Site Definition dialog box. Those files on that site would then be excluded from the file transfer process until such time as you changed the cloaking information again.

You need to know a few things about cloaking:

✦ **Dreamweaver, by default, enables cloaking for each managed site.** This means you can cloak and/or uncloak individual files and folders through the Files panel. You can disable the setting if you need to with the Cloaking category of the Site Definition dialog box.

✦ **When cloaking is enabled, you can further set Dreamweaver to automatically exclude files with specific file suffixes.** For example, if you wanted to exclude all .png and .fla files from sitewide operations, you could.

✦ **Dreamweaver saves and uses the cloaking settings entered in the Cloaking category of the Site Definition dialog box for each managed site.** You don't need to reenter these settings every time you view a particular site.

You can cloak folders, files, and file types when conducting the following sitewide procedures:

✦ Transferring files with the Get/Put or Check In/Check Out system

✦ Synchronizing a local site with a remote site

✦ Creating sitewide reports

✦ Updating templates and library items

Although Dreamweaver excludes cloaked templates and library items from Get/Put operations, don't exclude them from batch operations, as that might cause synchronization issues between them and their instances.

✦ Changing the contents in the Asset panel

✦ Finding newer local and remote files

✦ Changing or checking links

Enabling and disabling cloaking options

To disable or enable cloaking and specify file types to exclude for any managed site, follow these steps:

1. **Choose Site⇨Manage Sites to open the Manage Sites dialog box.**

2. **Select a site from the site listing and click the Edit button.**

The Site Definition dialog box opens with the Advanced tab showing (click the Advanced tab if the Basic tab is showing).

3. **Select the Cloaking category from the left side of the Advanced tab.**

The Cloaking settings appear, and the Enable Cloaking option is set by default. To disable this feature, deselect this check box.

If you disable the cloaking feature, all previously cloaked files become uncloaked. When you enable the feature again, all prior cloaking settings are restored.

4. **(Optional) Select the Cloak Files Ending With check box.**

   If you want to cloak files that end with certain suffixes, continue with Step 5. Otherwise skip to Step 6.

5. **In the text box below the Cloak Files Ending With check box, enter the file types you want excluded from site operations.**

   The file types can be any pattern at the end of a filename; you're not limited to merely entering file extensions. For example, you can cloak all files with the .txt extension or all files and folders that end with _bak.

   As you can see in Figure 3-7, you can even specify multiple file patterns by separating each pattern with a single space. Do not use colons, commas, or semicolons to separate your parameters, as doing so causes errors.

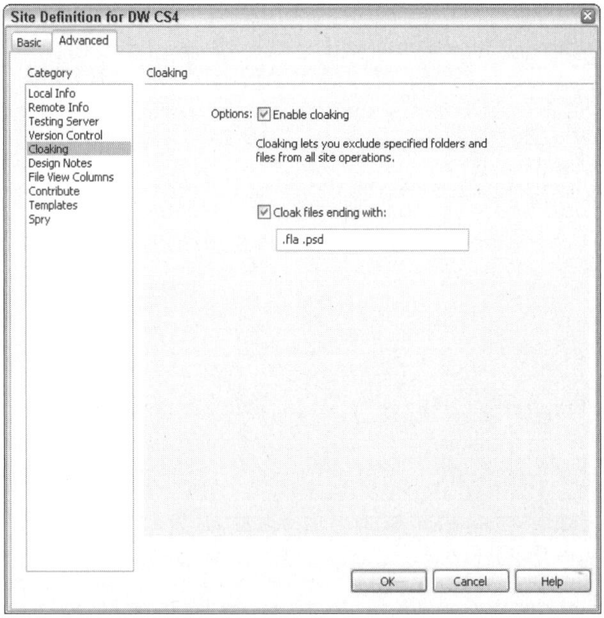

Figure 3-7:
Enter
cloaking file
extensions
to exclude
certain files
and folders
during site
operations.

In the Files panel, you can easily identify cloaked files because a red diagonal line appears through the icon associated with the cloaked file. When you disable or otherwise change the cloaking setting so that the file is no longer cloaked, the red line disappears.

6. **Click OK to exit the Site Definition dialog box.**

Cloaking individual folders

Although you can't cloak the root folder of a managed site (because that would mean the entire site would be excluded from sitewide operations), you can cloak any of the site's other folders, such as a folder for external CSS or JavaScript files.

To cloak individual folders on a site, follow these steps:

1. **Select a folder, or multiple folders, in the Files panel.**

The selected folders can be cloaked or uncloaked, and when multiple folders have been selected, you may uncloak them all at the same time.

2. **Right-click (Windows) or Control+click (Mac) one of the selected folders, choose Cloaking from the context menu, and select Cloak, Uncloak, or Uncloak All.**

You can also access these Cloaking options from the Options menu in the Files panel. Because the default setting for all sites is to have cloaking enabled, depending on which folder(s) you have selected, you can choose to uncloak individual folders, to cloak specified folders, or to uncloak all selected folders at the same time.

In the Files panel, folders that are cloaked have a diagonal red line through the folder icon next to the folder name. Folders that aren't cloaked appear without a red line through them.

Take caution when using the Uncloak All feature. Although enabling this option uncloaks folders, it doesn't really disable the cloaking system itself. What's worse, there is no efficient way to re-cloak previously cloaked files and folders other than selecting the files and folders by hand to recloak them.

Uncloaking previously cloaked file types

If you change your mind after cloaking specified file types, you can easily uncloak them. Follow these steps to do so:

1. **Right-click (Windows) or Control+click (Mac) in the Files panel and choose Cloaking⇨Settings from the context menu.**

The Site Definition dialog box opens to the Advanced tab with the Cloaking category selected.

2. **To uncloak previously cloaked files, do any of the following:**

- Delete the file patterns in the text box below the Cloak Files Ending check box.

- Disable the Cloak Files Ending With check box. This action leaves the file patterns previously entered into the text field, but temporarily disables the cloaking action.

3. **Click OK to exit the Site Definition dialog box.**

   After you exit the Site Definition dialog box, any red diagonal lines appearing through the file icons of any previously cloaked files in the Files panel disappear, leaving the files uncloaked.

You can also right-click (Windows) or Control+click (Mac) any file or folder in the Files panel and choose Cloaking⊏>Uncloak or Cloaking⊏>Uncloak All. The first option removes cloaking from the selected file, while the second option removes all prior cloaking settings, including any file endings entered in the Cloaking category of the Site Definition dialog box. You *can't* undo this action, so be sure you really want to uncloak.

Chapter 4: Publishing Your Web Pages Online

*T*he final step of publishing your site is getting your files online. Luckily, with Dreamweaver's built-in FTP features, you can quickly transfer your Web site files to a remote server.

During the transfer process, Dreamweaver can verify that both your local and remote file and folder structures match one another and even identify which files are newer on either the local or remote site to help you streamline the publishing process. You can also use the handy Synchronize Files command to copy updated files between local and remote sites, if necessary, and to decide whether to delete any files on the destination site that don't have corresponding files on the starting site.

You can always manually transfer individual files and folders at any time, but having Dreamweaver synchronize your files totally ensures that both locations have the most recent versions of all the files at all times.

This chapter walks you through the file transfer process as well as explains *background transfers.* We show you how to use the Files panel for *uploading* files (putting them online) and *downloading* files (getting them from the Internet to your computer), and how to use the Synchronize Files command to synchronize your local and remote files.

Understanding File Transfer Basics

A typical work process involves designing, building, and testing a local version of your Web site before publishing it on the Internet. After you finish all those tasks, you need to establish a connection with the remote server (as described in Book V, Chapter 3) and send an exact copy of the local files to the server location so that anyone on the Internet can see them.

If, after putting your files online, you need to make changes to your site, you can make your modifications to the local version of the files, and then upload the changed files to the server to overwrite the older versions of those files.

File transfers go in one direction: You either *put,* or upload, local files to the remote server, or you *get* (download) files from the remote server to your local computer. For instance, while you may normally only *put* files from your local computer up onto the remote server, you may occasionally need to *get* a copy of the remote site for your local archive or a new workstation, or to restore an old or corrupted version of a file.

When you transfer your files from local to remote, all the default read and write privileges of the original file are maintained with the transfer. However, when you get files with the Check In/Check Out feature turned on, the copies sent to your local site are marked with read-only privileges so you can't alter them and other team members can still access those files for check out. See Book VI, Chapter 1 for more about the Check In/Check Out feature.

Transferring dependent files

When you transfer files, you upload *copies* of the files rather than the original files themselves. The process may only take a matter of seconds, depending on the file size and the number of extra things that appear on the page or are linked to it, such as graphics, PDFs, style sheets, library items, server-side includes, and JavaScript files, which may or may not need to be uploaded with the file.

By default, Dreamweaver asks whether you want to include any *dependent files* — the page's graphics, movies, style sheets, for example — during a transfer, to which you can choose Yes or No. If the prompt doesn't appear, you can force it by holding Alt (Windows) or Option (Mac) when you click the Get, Put, Check In, and Check Out buttons in the Files panel.

Also, because Dreamweaver treats library items as dependents, which could cause report errors when those files are *put* on some servers, consider cloaking the library items to prevent them from transferring automatically. To find out how to cloak library items, see Book V, Chapter 3.

Working during file transfers

During your file transfers (no matter your transfer method), Dreamweaver enables you to continue doing any non-server-related work, such as editing text, adding images, creating style sheets, attaching JavaScript behaviors, and running reports. Dreamweaver calls these *background file transfers*.

We discuss the technology you use for file transfers in Book V, Chapter 3, so if you're curious about using your LAN versus an FTP connection to upload files, skip back to that chapter and get reading.

You do have a few file transfer limitations, however, which means Dreamweaver can't perform some server-related tasks simultaneously. Server-related work that you *can't* do during file transfers includes the following:

✦ Additional file transfers, checking files in and out, and undoing checkouts

✦ Creating database connections and bindings

✦ Previewing live data or inserting a Web service

✦ Deleting or saving files and folders on a remote server

✦ Opening, dragging, or inserting images on files on a remote server

✦ Copying, cutting, and pasting files on a remote server

✦ Refreshing Dreamweaver's Remote view in the Files panel

✦ Previewing files in a browser on a testing server

✦ Automatically putting (uploading) files to the remote server when saving

Putting Files on and Getting Files from the Remote Server

The *Get* and *Put* commands are fantastic collaboration tools, although you can put them to good use even if you fly solo in your Dreamweaver endeavors. The Get and Put commands enable you to transfer files from your local computer to your remote host location without checking files in and out of the site. That means you can even put a version of a file you're editing onto the server as you continue working on that file.

If you use Dreamweaver as part of a team, you should enable Design Notes and use the Check In/Check Out feature. Even if you work alone, you can still enable the Check In/Check Out system. For instance, though you're one person, you may work at two locations and choose to check in files to help keep track of their location and check out status. Turn to Book VI, Chapter 1 to find out more about these features.

The Get and Put commands are accessible through the Files panel, where you can upload and download files from your local machine to the remote server:

✦ **Get** copies files from the remote site to your local machine.

✦ **Put** places local files onto the remote site.

Examining the Files panel transfer options

You can transfer files to and from your local machine and a remote server with the Files panel in either the collapsed or expanded view, although you may prefer to use the expanded view to see a list of all the files on both the local and remote sites at the same time.

In collapsed mode, the top of the Files panel has a simple row of buttons to assist you with transferring files to and from a remote server, as shown in Figure 4-1:

Connect/
Disconnect   Check Out Files

Put Files   Check In Files

Get Files   Expand/Collapse

Refresh   Site View

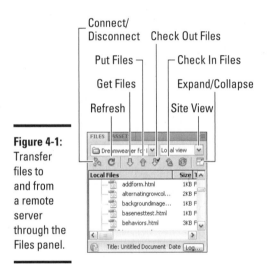

Figure 4-1:
Transfer
files to
and from
a remote
server
through the
Files panel.

♦ **Site Management Menu:** Choose the site you need to transfer files for from this list. This menu appears in both the collapsed and expanded views and lists all the *managed sites* you've created in Dreamweaver. For more details on creating a managed site, see Book I, Chapter 3.

♦ **Site View Menu:** When the Files panel is collapsed, use this menu to toggle between the four site views (Local, Remote, Testing Server, and Repository). In the expanded view, this menu disappears and three other buttons (Site Files, Testing Server, Repository Files) are shown in its place:

- **Local:** Select this view to see the file structure of the local site in the Files panel. You can also use this view to see both local and remote sites with the Files panel split into two panes. In the expanded view, this option is presented as a button.

- **Remote:** Select this view to see the file structure of the remote site. You must set up a remote site in advance for you to see the remote site files. For details on setting up a remote site, see Book V, Chapter 3.

- **Testing Server:** This view shows a directory listing of the testing server only in normal view, or both the testing server and local site files in the expanded view. You must set up a testing server in advance for you to see the testing server site. In the expanded view, this option is presented as a button. For details on setting up a testing server, see Book VII, Chapter 1.

- **Repository:** This view shows a listing of all the files in your repository when working with Subversion (SVN), a versioning control system. For more on working with Subversion software visit `http://subversion.tigris.org/`.

✦ **Connect/Disconnect:** Connect/disconnect to the remote site with FTP, SFTP, RDS, WebDAV, and Microsoft Visual SourceSafe. With FTP connections, Dreamweaver disconnects from a remote site if it has no activity for over 30 minutes. To increase or decrease the idle time, choose Edit➪Preferences (Windows) or Dreamweaver➪Preferences (Mac) and enter a new number in the Site category of the Preferences dialog box. If after adjusting the idle time it appears like you're still getting disconnected for no reason, it could be the Web server, some Web hosts disconnect after only a few minutes of inactivity.

✦ **Refresh:** Manually refresh both the local and the remote file listings.

✦ **View Site FTP Log:** This button (which only bears the letters "FTP" and should not be confused with the Log button at the bottom of the Files panel) only appears in the *expanded* Files panel after the initial FTP transfer. Click this button to launch the Results panel where you can view the FTP log that contains a record of the site's FTP file transfer activity. See the "Viewing the FTP and background file activity logs" section later in this chapter for more information about FTP logs.

✦ **Get File(s):** Get copies of files and folders selected in the Files panel from the remote server to your local site. Any existing files on the local site become overwritten during the Get process.

✦ **Put Files(s):** Put copies of files and folders selected in the Files panel from the local site to the remote or testing server. Files with the same name on the server are overwritten with the newer versions from the local site.

✦ **Check Out Files:** This option is only available when you're using the Check In/Check Out system (which is described in Book VI, Chapter 1). Click this button to get a copy of a selected file from the remote server to your local site. If the file already exists on the local site, this process overwrites the local version of the file. After the file copies over to the local site, the file on the server is marked as checked out and a small green check mark icon appears next to the filename in the Files panel.

✦ **Check In Files:** This option is only available when you're using the Check In/Check Out system. Click this button to put a copy of a selected file from the local site to the remote server. After the file copies, the server version file is marked as Checked In and the local site file has a small lock icon next to the filename as an indication of the local file's read-only status.

✦ **Synchronize:** This button allows you to launch the synchronization command. For details about the synchronization process, read the section, "Keeping Your Local and Remote Site Files Up to Date" later in this chapter.

✦ **Expand/Collapse:** This button toggles the Files panel between the collapsed view and the expanded view. In the collapsed view, the Files panel displays the Local, Remote, Repository, or Testing Server views. In the expanded view, you can view a directory listing of files in both the local and remote or testing server sites. By default, the local site appears in the right pane, but you can modify this setting in the Site category of Dreamweaver's Preferences.

In expanded mode, the Files panel expands into two panes for displaying both local and remote files and a complete row of buttons appear at the top of the panel to assist you with transferring files to and from a remote server, as shown in Figure 4-2.

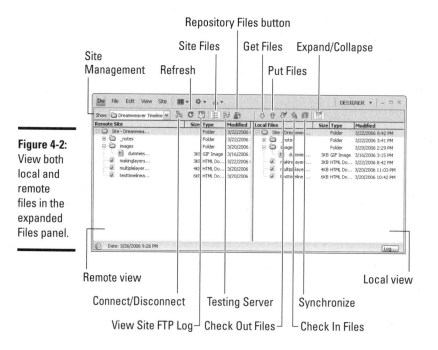

Figure 4-2:
View both local and remote files in the expanded Files panel.

Putting files on a remote server

To put files on the remote server, follow these steps:

1. **In the Files panel, select the files you want to upload.**

Use either Local view or Remote view to select your files. If you're attempting to upload only local files that are more recent than their remote counterparts, see the "Keeping Your Local and Remote Site Files Up to Date" section later in this chapter.

2. **Click the Put Files button (which looks like an upward facing blue arrow) at the top of the Files panel.**

   You can also right-click (Windows) or Control+click (Mac) the file in the Files panel and choose Put from the context menu.

   If you attempt to transfer a file (or multiple files, for that matter) that you've edited but haven't yet saved, a dialog box may appear (depending on your settings), prompting you to save the files prior to copying them to the remote destination. See Book V, Chapter 3 for more information on setting these preferences.

3. **If prompted to save unsaved open files, click the Yes button to save the files or the No button to put the most recent version of the files on the remote server while leaving the unsaved files open in the Dreamweaver workspace.**

   The Dependent Files dialog box opens if the transferred files contain any dependents.

4. **Click the Yes button to upload dependent files, or No to bypass this upload feature.**

   For example, if the remote site already contains most or all the dependent files (such as images and style sheets), you don't need to upload them again unless they have been updated.

   The file transfer begins immediately — too fast, perhaps, for you to even review the Transfer Status dialog box. If you do see the status dialog box, however, and you need to cancel the transfer, you can click the Cancel button if you're quick enough.

Getting files from a remote server

To get files from the remote or testing server onto your local site using the Files panel, follow these steps:

1. **In the Files panel, select the files to download.**

   Although you're more likely to select files from the Remote view, you can also select the files from Local view.

   If you want to get only remote files that have been recently changed, you're better off with the Synchronize command as described in the section, "Keeping Your Local and Remote Site Files Up to Date" later in this chapter.

2. **Click the Get Files button at the top of the Files panel.**

   Or right-click (Windows) or Control+click (Mac) the file in the Files panel and choose Get from the context menu.

   The Dependent Files dialog box opens if you've enabled this setting in the Site category of the Preferences dialog box (see Book V, Chapter 3).

3. **Click the Yes button to download any dependent files, or click No to bypass this feature, or Cancel to stop the transfer.**

   If the local site already contains most or all the dependent files, don't bother downloading them again.

   The file transfer begins immediately. When using Check In/Check Out in a collaborative situation, Dreamweaver transfers a copy of each file to the local site, and then marks it as read-only until you check it in again. When you have Check In/Check Out disabled, copies to the local site have the default read and write privileges.

When you get files from the server, you're not actually removing them from the server. The files are copied, and those copies are transferred to your local computer.

Viewing the FTP and background file activity logs

When you transfer files in either direction — whether you're getting or putting files — Dreamweaver keeps two logs of the file and transfer activity. The logs include operations and outcomes such as whether the transfer was a success or failure, in case you need to troubleshoot connection errors or want to keep a record of the transfer process.

Each log records and stores data in different ways and in different locations:

✦ **Background File Activity Log:** This log only appears during a background file transfer but you can access it at any time subsequent to the first transfer. This log records details about the transfer, including start and finish times, the name of the files being transferred, and the number of files successfully updated. To view this log, click the Log button at the bottom of the Files panel. The Background File Activity dialog box opens, as shown in Figure 4-3. You can save this log as a text file by clicking the Save Log button in the dialog box.

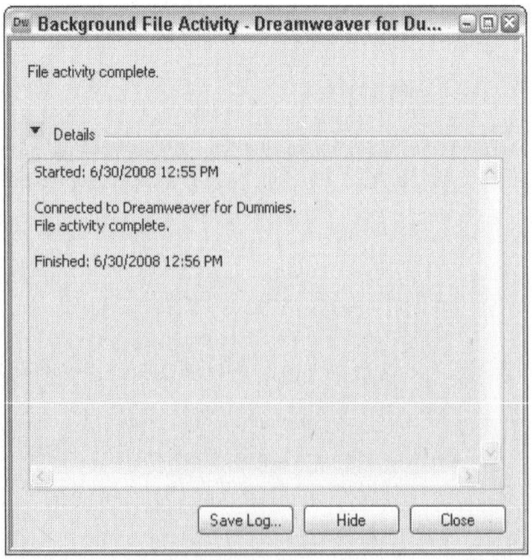

Figure 4-3:
The Background File Activity dialog box.

> **Background File Activity - Dreamweaver for Du...**
>
> File activity complete.
>
> ▼ Details
>
> Started: 6/30/2008 12:55 PM
>
> Connected to Dreamweaver for Dummies.
> File activity complete.
>
> Finished: 6/30/2008 12:56 PM
>
> [Save Log...] [Hide] [Close]

✦ **FTP Log:** This log keeps a running record of all file FTP transfer activity. You can access it through the expanded Files panel after the initial file transfer, or through the Results panel at any time subsequent to the first transfer. To view the FTP log, open the Results panel (choose Window⇨Results) and click the FTP Log tab, as shown in the example in Figure 4-4. You can save the content on this log by selecting all the content and right-clicking (Windows) or Control+clicking (Mac) to copy it, and then pasting it into any text editor or other application before saving the file with the appropriate file extension.

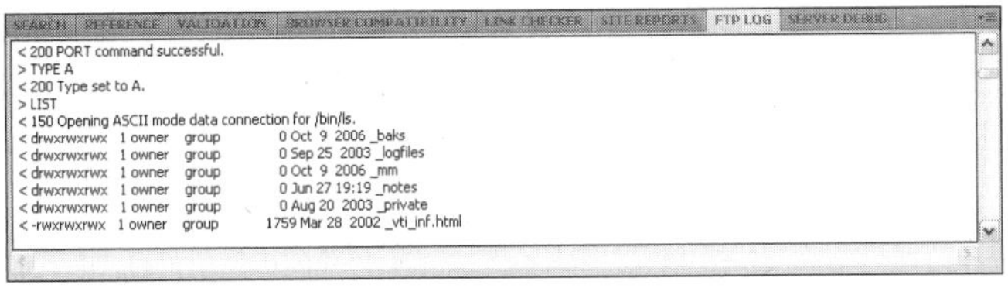

Figure 4-4:
The FTP
Log in the
Results
panel.

Keeping Your Local and Remote Site Files Up to Date

After you establish a remote connection and create a mirror copy of your local site on the remote server, you can use Dreamweaver's Synchronize Files command to synchronize the files between the two locations. Synchronization isn't exactly the same thing as transferring files; it's mainly a cleanup/housekeeping feature, useful mostly for making sure that existing (not new) files on both your local and remote sites are up to date.

You can set the synchronization settings a variety of ways. Specify, if you like, that the entire site gets synchronized, or override that option by selecting individual files to ignore, put, get, or delete during the synchronization. At the end of the synchronization process, Dreamweaver provides confirmation of the updated files.

Viewing the newest files without synchronization

Before you begin synching files, you may find viewing all your Web site files by date helpful. The idea is to see which files are newer in both locations *before* you synchronize.

To select the newest files that haven't been synchronized, do one of the following:

✦ In the Files panel, right-click (Windows) or Control+click (Mac) anywhere in the listing area and choose Select⇨Newer Local or Select⇨Newer Remote.

✦ Choose Edit➪Select Newer Local or Edit➪Select Newer Remote from the Files panel Options menu.

You can also search for recently modified files without synchronization by choosing Edit➪Select Recently Modified. When you make this selection, the Select Recently Modified dialog box shown in Figure 4-5 appears, where you can choose to view files created or modified within a specified number of days or view files created within a specified range of dates.

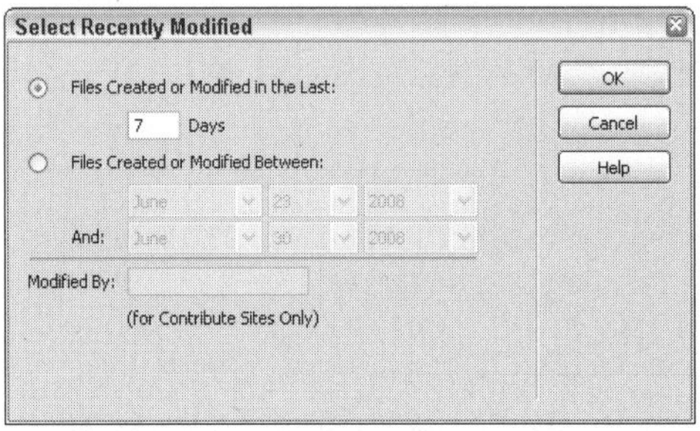

Figure 4-5: View files in Local or Remote view that were created or modified recently.

The new or recently modified files are selected and appear with gray high-lighting behind them (as shown in Figure 4-6) in the Files panel for easy identification, making them easy to update with the synchronization command, which is explained in the following section.

Figure 4-6: Recently modified files highlighted in the Files panel.

Synchronizing your files

When you're ready to synchronize your files, follow these steps:

1. **From the Files panel, choose a site from the Managed Site drop-down list.**

If you haven't managed a site in Dreamweaver yet, see Book I, Chapter 3.

If you want to synchronize specific files or folders in the site, select them in the Files panel before proceeding.

2. **Choose Site⇨Synchronize Sitewide from the main menu.**

The Synchronize Files dialog box, shown in Figure 4-7, appears.

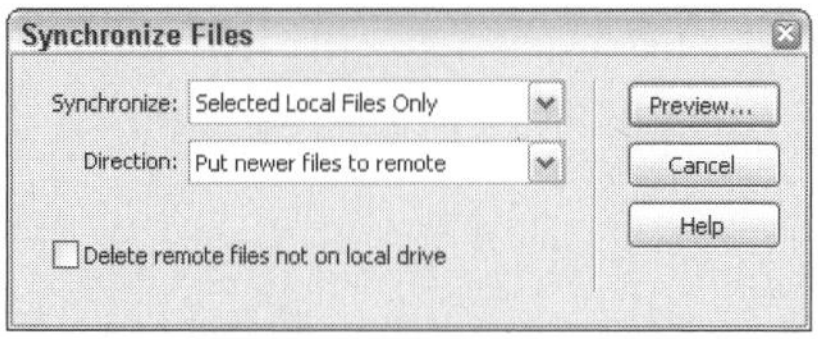

Figure 4-7:
The
Synchronize
Files dialog
box.

3. **Choose an option from the Synchronize drop-down list:**

- **Entire Managed Site:** Select this option to synchronize all the files on the selected managed site.

- **Selected Local Files Only:** Use this option when you need to synchronize selected files from a managed site (the option says Selected Remote Files Only when your most recent file selection was done in the Remote view of the Files panel).

4. **Choose an option from the Direction drop-down list:**

- **Put Newer Files to Remote:** Upload any files from the local site that have been updated since the last upload, plus any new files that don't appear on the remote server yet.

- **Get Newer Files from Remote:** Download remote files that have been updated since the last download, plus any new files that don't appear on the local site yet.

- **Get and Put Newer Files:** Put the most recent versions of all the files, including any missing files, on both local and remote sites.

5. **Select or deselect the Delete Remote Files Not on Local Drive option.**

Select this option to have Dreamweaver remove files on the destination site when originals don't exist. For example, if you delete a local file prior to transferring, this option also deletes the deleted file's counterpart from the remote site.

6. **Click the Preview button.**

Before committing to the synchronization process, you must review a list of all the files that are updating in the Synchronize dialog box shown in Figure 4-8.

Figure 4-8:
The Synchronize dialog box shows the files being synchronized.

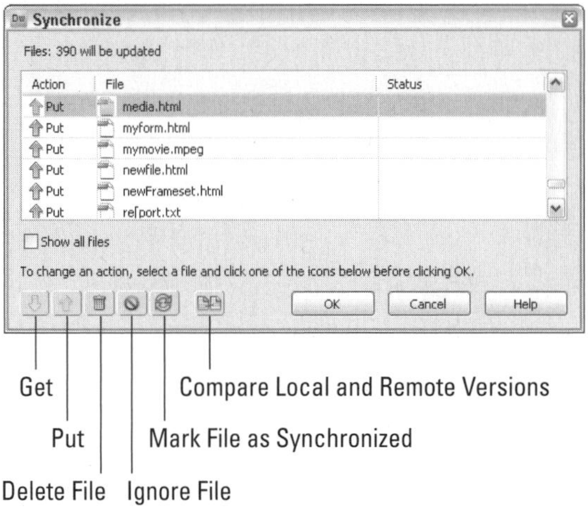

> **Synchronize**
>
> Files: 390 will be updated
>
> | Action | File | Status |
> |--------|------|--------|
> | ⬆ Put | media.html | |
> | ⬆ Put | myform.html | |
> | ⬆ Put | mymovie.mpeg | |
> | ⬆ Put | newfile.html | |
> | ⬆ Put | newFrameset.html | |
> | ⬆ Put | refport.txt | |
>
> ☐ Show all files
>
> To change an action, select a file and click one of the icons below before clicking OK.
>
> [OK] [Cancel] [Help]

Get
Put
Delete File   Ignore File
Compare Local and Remote Versions
Mark File as Synchronized

If you want, you can change the action associated with each file (Get, Put, Delete, and Ignore). To change any of the actions associated with the files, select a file and click the appropriate button at the bottom of the dialog box.

7. **Click OK to begin the synchronization.**

   If all the files are already in sync, Dreamweaver displays a message that politely notifies you that the synchronization isn't necessary. Otherwise, the synchronization process runs. When it's done, Dreamweaver returns to the Files panel.

This option requires the installation of a third-party comparison/merging application and the specification of that application in the File Compare category of the Preferences dialog box. For details about Adobe recommended file comparison tools and how to use them, visit the Adobe Web site at `http://help.adobe.com/en_US/Dreamweaver/10.0_Using/WSc78c5 058ca073340dcda9110b1f693f21-7edca.html`.

TECHNICAL STUFF

Using diff tools (if you have 'em)

One of the actions in the Synchronization dialog box is to compare local and remote versions of the files with a third-party tool *before* the synchronization process. These tools, also called *diff tools,* can compare code between two versions of the same file so that you can merge changes between the files before the transfer process.

Book VI
Working Collaboratively

The 5th Wave   By Rich Tennant

©RICHTENNANT

"Ooo-wait! That's perfect for the clinic's home page. Just stretch it out a little further... little more..."

Contents at a Glance

Chapter 1: Working Efficiently with a Team

In This Chapter

✔ **Enabling and using Design Notes**

✔ **Using the Check In/Check Out feature**

✔ **Customizing File View Columns**

Most likely, you're not working alone. The larger the Web site, the greater the odds that you're getting help from other people. Most Web sites these days require a team — someone who works on the dynamic aspect, a JavaScript expert, and yet more people who work on the HTML and the graphics. And of course, you, who pulls all these aspects together into one cohesive Web site.

How do you keep track of who is working on what at a certain time? Team members overwriting files or two members working simultaneously on the same file are what work nightmares are made of.

Dreamweaver comes to your rescue. It includes several features to keep you in tune with your other team members, such as Design Notes and the Check In/Check Out feature. And if you customize the columns in the Files panel, you can see at a glance the status of each page in the Web site. We discuss all these features — and how you can use all of them to work efficiently with your team — in this chapter.

Attaching Design Notes to Your Files

Dreamweaver's Design Notes are reminder notes, like the one in Figure 1-1, that you can create and attach to individual files on a site to help you and your team with site file management. You can attach Design Notes to documents, templates, images, Flash content, ActiveX controls, and applets. The Design Notes data itself is stored in a separate linked file that allows for shared access and retrieval. This tool is a must if you're working collaboratively on site design and management.

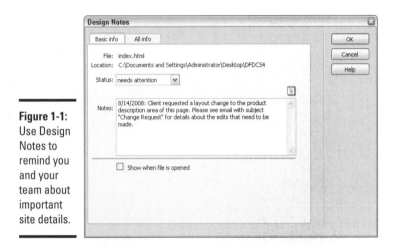

Figure 1-1:
Use Design
Notes to
remind you
and your
team about
important
site details.

Design Notes come in two flavors:

✦ **Notes you create:** The Design Notes feature is especially helpful if you're exchanging files within a design team or workgroup. For example, you may have a monthly newsletter that gets updated to a site on the first day of each month. With Design Notes, you can add comments about file transfer data, archived file locations, and other information related to the uploading of the newest newsletter. You may also want to use Design Notes for storing sensitive data such as marketing strategy guidelines or pricing arrangements.

✦ **Notes that are created for you automatically:** Adobe's Fireworks and Flash programs integrate and update Design Notes all on their own (whether you want them or not) so that you can use them later in Dreamweaver sites with the same site-root path. When you open files in either of those programs and export them to another file format, the Design Notes feature launches (behind the scenes) to store data about the original source file, such as filename, type, and location. For instance, when opening the fatcat.png file in Fireworks and exporting it as fatcat.gif, Fireworks creates a Design Note called fatcat.gif.mno that includes the name of the original .png file and the absolute location where it is stored:

```
fw_source="file:///LocalDisk/sites/assets/orig/fatcat.png"
```

In Dreamweaver, when the graphic is imported from Fireworks, the Design Notes automatically copy to the site. Then, if you need to edit the graphic in Fireworks, Fireworks can use those Design Notes to quickly locate the original .png file and open it for editing, all the while adding any new data to the Design Notes.

Enabling and disabling Design Notes

By default, Design Notes are enabled for each managed site, but you can change them in the Design Notes category of the Site Definition dialog box. Follow these steps:

1. **Choose Site⇨Manage Sites to open the Manage Sites dialog box.**

2. **Select a site from the site listing and click the Edit button.**

The Site Definition dialog box opens. Click the Advanced tab if it's not showing.

3. **Select the Design Notes category.**

The Design Notes category options appear, as shown in Figure 1-2. The Maintain Design Notes option is enabled by default; however, the Upload Design Notes for Sharing options is disabled. To toggle these features on and off, check or uncheck the options as needed.

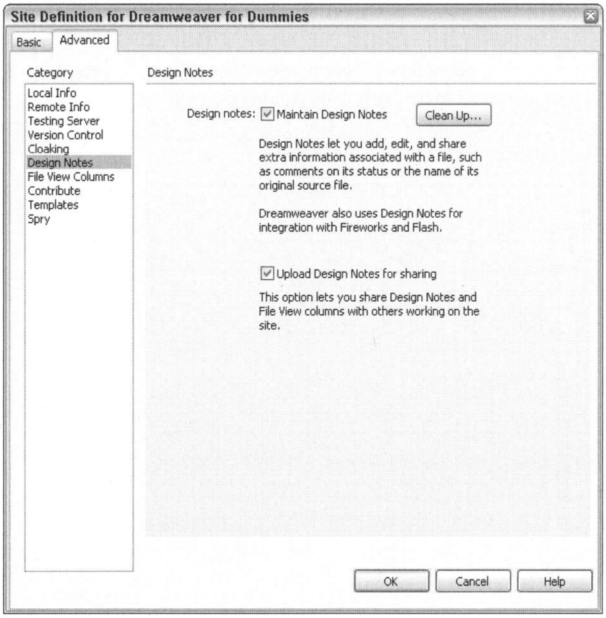

Site Definition for Dreamweaver for Dummies

Basic | Advanced

Category | Design Notes

Local Info
Remote Info
Testing Server
Version Control
Cloaking
Design Notes
File View Columns
Contribute
Templates
Spry

Design notes: ☑ Maintain Design Notes   [Clean Up...]

Design Notes let you add, edit, and share
extra information associated with a file, such
as comments on its status or the name of its
original source file.

Dreamweaver also uses Design Notes for
integration with Fireworks and Flash.

☑ Upload Design Notes for sharing

This option lets you share Design Notes and
File View columns with others working on the
site.

[OK] [Cancel] [Help]

Figure 1-2:
Enable or
disable
Design
Notes for
your site.

4. **Enable or disable the Upload Design Notes for Sharing option.**

• **Enable:** If you want Dreamweaver to upload the Design Notes associated with files on the site along with the rest of your files when it transfers files to the remote server, leave the Upload Design Notes for Sharing option enabled.

- **Disable:** To keep Design Notes locally and not have Dreamweaver upload them to the remote site when files are transferred, disable this option.

Enabling Design Notes for sharing online creates security risks, especially when Design Notes are used for storing sensitive data such as marketing strategy guidelines or pricing arrangements, as described in the previous section.

5. **Click OK to exit the Site Definition dialog box.**

Removing Design Notes

Design Notes, when enabled, do increase the file transfer time slightly, so if you're working alone and do not use this feature, you may want to disable and remove them completely.

To disable and permanently remove Design Notes, follow these steps:

1. **Deselect the Maintain Design Notes option in the Design Notes category of the Site Definition dialog box (see the previous section).**

2. **Click the Clean Up button to delete all the Design Notes from your local computer.**

3. **To proceed, click the Yes button.**

   Dreamweaver deletes all the Design Notes on the local computer.

   You can't undo this step, so be sure this is something you really want to do before clicking the Yes button!

   Click the No button if you have a change of heart and want to leave Design Notes as they are.

4. **Click OK to exit the Site Definition dialog box.**

Adding Design Notes to a file

Add your own Design Notes to individual files, folders, or templates on your site every time you modify the content and want to communicate with other members of the team about it. When you add Design Notes to a template, they attach only to the template and aren't copied to any template-based documents. That way, individual template-based files can each have their own individual Design Notes! You can also attach Design Notes to graphics, Flash movies, ActiveX controls, applets, and Shockwave objects.

To add Design Notes to a file, follow these steps:

1. **Open the file you want to add the Design Notes to and choose File➪Design Notes.**

   Or right-click (Windows) or Control+click (Mac) a closed file in the Files panel and choose Design Notes from the context menu.

   If you want to add Design Notes to a file that's located on a remote site, you must check out the file first (see the next section "Checking Files In and Out," to find out more about using the Check In/Check Out feature). Then you can add the Design Notes to the local version of the file.

   The Design Notes dialog box opens.

2. **On the Basic Info tab, fill in the following fields to create your Design Notes:**

   - **Status:** Select a status for the file from the Status menu. The status reflects the document's current condition, relative to it being finalized and ready for publication. Dreamweaver presents you with eight status settings to choose from: Draft, Revision1, Revision2, Revision3, Alpha, Beta, Final, and Needs Attention. To create your own custom status setting (such as "Pending approval"), move on to Step 3.

   - **Date:** To insert the current date in your Design Notes, click the Date icon above the right corner of the Notes field.

   - **Notes:** Type your Design Notes in the text field.

   - **Show When File Is Opened:** Select this check box to have the Design Notes appear automatically when the file is opened.

3. **On the All Info tab, click the plus (+) button to add new *key/value pairs*, which you can use as custom status settings and search criteria for Design Notes reports:**

   - **Keys:** Enter a word in the Name field to identify the first part of the note information, such as **Author** or **Status**.

   - **Values:** Enter a word or two in the Value field to represent the attribute for the associated key, such as **Sue** or **Draft6**.

   Each *key* must have a *value* and can be composed of any words — as customized as you need — to assist you. For example, create custom status definitions, such as *Status=Draft6* or a key/value pair to refine a Design Note report, such as *Author=Sue, V=2.b,* or *Revision=4/15/06,* as shown in Figure 1-3.

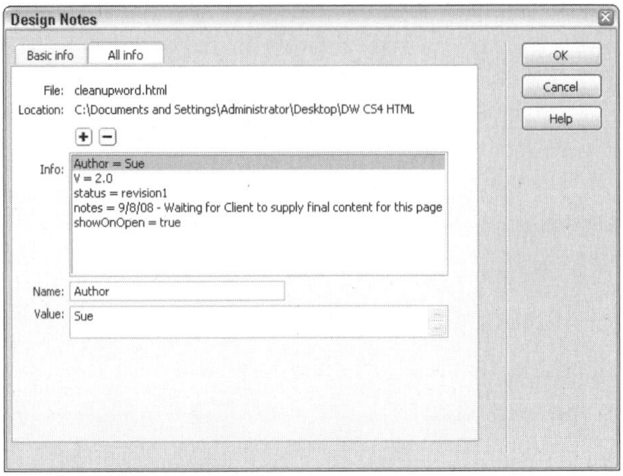

Figure 1-3:
Enter key/
value pairs
in the All
Info tab of
the Design
Notes
dialog box.

To delete an existing key/value pair, select it from the list and click the minus (–) button.

4. **Click OK to close the Design Notes dialog box.**

   Design Notes for each file are saved in a _notes folder on your site. The individual Design Notes files are named after the document they're attached to and have the .mno file extension. For instance, if the main filename is contact.html, the corresponding Design Notes file is _notes/contact.html.mno.

Viewing and editing Design Notes

After you add Design Notes to a file, you can view, edit, and add additional information to them at any time. To see which files have Design Notes attached to them, view the Files panel in expanded mode by clicking the expand/collapse button at the top of the Files panel. Look for a Design Notes icon (it looks like a little yellow cartoon speech bubble) next to the filename in the Notes column, as shown in Figure 1-4.

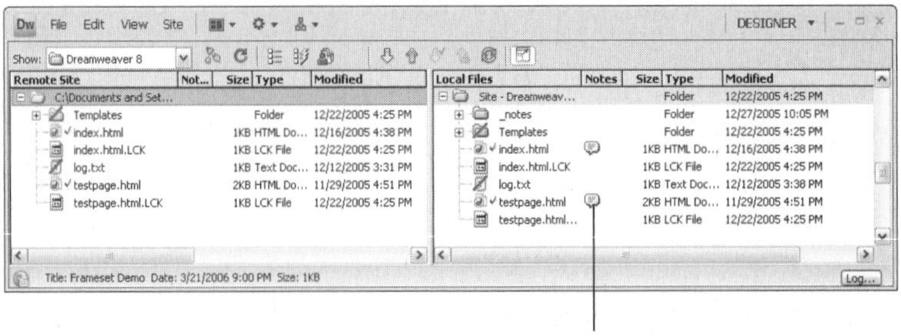

Figure 1-4:
Files with
Design
Notes
display
a Design
Notes icon
next to the
filename.

Design Notes icon

By default, the Design Notes icons aren't enabled in the expanded Files panel. To see them, you must enable the visibility of the Notes column in the File View Columns category of the Site Definition dialog box. Turn to the "Defining File View Columns" section for details.

Checking Files In and Out

When you're working as a member of a collaborative team, using the Check In/Check Out Files feature is a must. The beauty of the system is that you must check in and check out files not only from the remote site but from the shared local site as well — so no two people can work on the same file at the same time. This single innovation goes a long way toward maintaining the integrity of a Web site.

Dreamweaver uses a simple icon system next to filenames within the Files panel to help keep track of all the files and their check in/check out status. When a file is checked out, Dreamweaver shows the person's name and a red check mark next to the checked out file. When a file is checked back in, a green check mark appears. After checking a file back in, the local copy of the file becomes read-only and a little lock icon appears next to the filename. The remote files, however, can't be turned into read-only versions after checkout. That means that if anyone transfers files to the remote server with a program other than Dreamweaver, the remote files can be overwritten. To help prevent this from accidentally happening when using other programs, a .lck file usually appears next to the checked out file as a sort of visual indication of the file's checked out status.

To enable the Check In/Check Out system, do the following:

1. **Choose Site⇨Manage Sites to launch the Manage Sites dialog box.**

2. **Select the site and click the Edit button to open the Site Definition dialog box.**

3. **Click the Advanced Tab.**

4. **Select Remote Info from the Category list. The Check In/Check Out information (see Figure 1-5) is located at the bottom of the Remote Info information.**

   Note: If the Check In/Check Out options aren't displaying, check to see that you've selected an access type and configured it. (Turn to Book V, Chapter 3 if you still need to do this.) You must enter remote information before enabling Check In/Check Out.

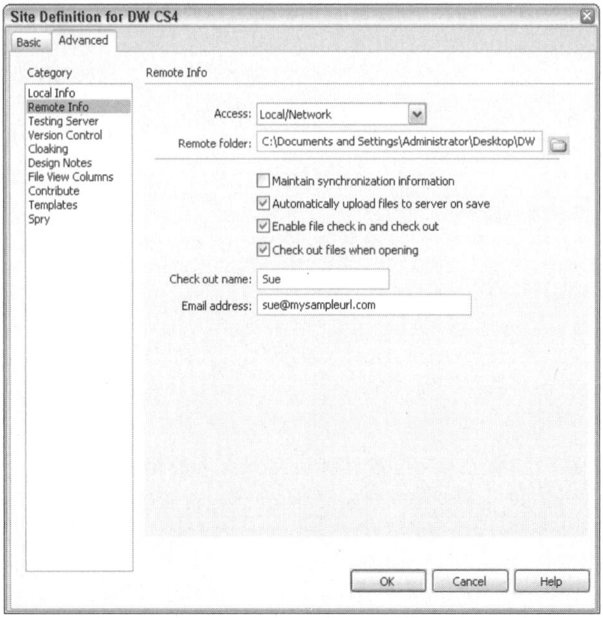

Figure 1-5:
Enable the
Check In/
Out feature.

5. **Select the Enable File Check In and Check Out box.**

If you're using FTP, enter a checkout name and e-mail address. The
e-mail address you enter here becomes a clickable link in the Files panel
when the file is checked out. If you want, you can place check marks
next to the other options so that files can be automatically checked out
and uploaded when they're saved.

6. **Click OK to save your settings and close the Site Definition dialog box.**

The Check In/Check Out settings work immediately and can be modified or
disabled at any time. To begin checking files into and out of a remote folder
in the Files panel, follow these steps:

1. **Select the files you want to check in or out.**

2. **Click the Check In or Check Out buttons at the top of the Files panel
toolbar.**

Expand the Files panel for a view of both local and remote files.

3. **Click Yes or No as appropriate when prompted to include dependent
files, such as graphics or CSS files.**

When a remote file is checked out, its counterpart in the local file listing in
the Files panel appears with a little lock icon next to it, as shown in Figure
1-6. The lock is virtual, however, and you can remove its locked status if
needed.

Check In ─┐ ┌─ Check Out

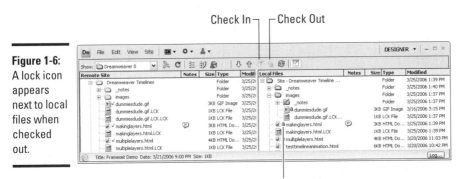

Figure 1-6:
A lock icon appears next to local files when checked out.

Locked file

Book VI
Chapter 1

Working Efficiently
with a Team

To manually unlock a file, select the file in the Files panel and right-click (Windows) or Control+click (Mac) to select Turn Off Read Only for a regular site, or Undo Check Out for a Contribute site. If prompted, click Yes to confirm that you want to unlock the file.

Using Version Control with Subversion

If you happen to use Subversion (SVN), the free, open source version control system software, you can easily integrate Subversion into Dreamweaver, which gives you even more control over file versioning, rollbacks, and editing of your files during the Check In/Check Out process.

Although it's not a full SVN client, Dreamweaver does allow users to collaboratively manage and edit files on a remote Web server, as well as get the latest versions of files, edit them, and commit the files when finished — all without having to set up a command-line interface or install any third-party utilities.

To define Subversion as your version control system, follow these steps:

1. **Choose Site⇨Manage Sites to launch the Manage Sites dialog box.**

2. **Select the site and click the Edit button to open the Site Definition dialog box.**

3. **Click the Advanced Tab.**

4. **Select Version Control from the Category list and select the Subversion option from the Access menu, as shown in Figure 1-7.**

    Once the Subversion option is selected, the rest of the Subversion settings become visible in the dialog box.

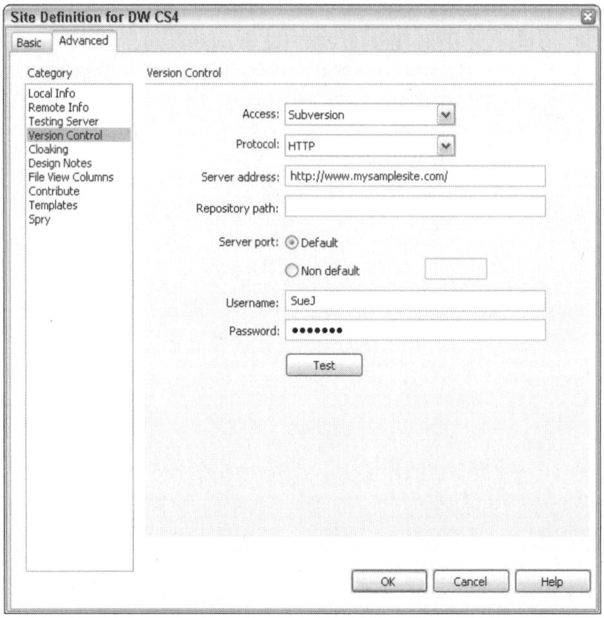

Figure 1-7:
Set version control settings for Subversion.

5. **Fill in the fields in the dialog box:**

   • **Protocol:** Select HTTP, HTTPS, SVN, or SVN+ SSH, which determines how clients authenticate themselves to the server.

   • **Server Address:** Enter in the server address.

   • **Repository Path:** Enter in the path to the repository.

   • **Server Port:** Leave the server port set to default unless you need to set it to another port number. In that case, select Non-default and enter in the alternate server port number in the field next to the Non-default option.

   • **Username:** Enter your username.

   • **Password:** Enter your password.

6. **Click the Test button to verify the connection.**

   If the connection is working, Dreamweaver alerts you that the connection was successful. If the connection was not made, you see an error alert. Check the spelling of the server address, username, and password and try again. If you continue to have difficulty establishing a connection, speak with your system administrator for assistance.

For more information about working with Subversion software and to download your free copy of the Subversion *software*, visit `http://subversion.tigris.org/`.

Defining File View Columns

In the expanded Files panel, Dreamweaver displays all the file and folder details in columns next to each of the filenames. Using the File View Columns category of the Site Definition dialog box, you can tailor which file and folder details display by modifying the default column settings and adding customized columns. Here are a few of the things you can do to change the File View Columns:

+ Add new custom columns (up to ten custom columns).

+ Delete custom columns.

+ Rename custom columns.

+ Show and Hide columns.

   You can't hide the filename column.

+ Realign and reorder columns.

+ Set column sharing options with users connected to a site.

+ Attach Design Notes to custom columns.

Customizing File View Columns

Each member of your team can customize their computer to view the contents of the expanded Files panel to suit their specific needs. You can add, edit, remove, hide, and show Dreamweaver's built-in columns, as well as add personal customized columns associated with your Design Notes on your own computer or to be shared with the entire work team!

To add, edit, or delete File View Columns in the Files panel, follow these steps:

1. **Choose Site⇨Manage Sites to open the Manage Sites dialog box.**

2. **Select a site from the site listing and click the Edit button.**

   The Site Definition dialog box appears. If the Advanced tab isn't showing, click the Advanced tab.

3. **Select the File View Columns category.**

   The File View Columns category options display, as shown in Figure 1-8.

4. **To hide any of the built-in categories, select the category and deselect the Options: Show check box.**

   Categories marked with Hide in the Show column are hidden from view in the Files panel.

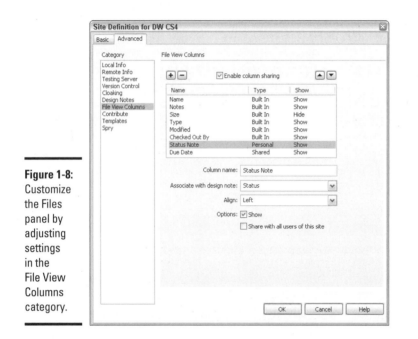

Figure 1-8:
Customize
the Files
panel by
adjusting
settings
in the
File View
Columns
category.

5. **To add a new custom column, click the plus (+) button.**

   Enter the name of the new column in the Column Name text box, select a Design Notes value from the Associate with Design Note drop-down menu or type your own, select an alignment option for the custom column, and decide to make the custom column visible (Show) or hidden (Hide). Custom columns are marked as Personal in the Type column.

6. **To remove a custom column, select the column from the list and click the minus (–) button.**

   Deletion is immediate and undoable, and does not come with a confirmation message, so take special care when deleting columns.

7. **To share a custom column, select the column from the list, click the Enable Column Sharing check box above the column listing, and select both the Show and the Share with All Users of This Site check boxes.**

   These options enable all users connected to the site to view and share the column. Shared columns are marked as Shared in the Type column.

8. **Click the up and down arrows to reorder any of the columns (except for the Name column, which is always first).**

   For example, if you want the Size column to be next to the Name column, select the Size column and click the up arrow button once to reposition the Size column next to the Name column.

9. **Click OK to exit the Site Definition dialog box.**

Sorting columns

After customizing columns, return to the expanded Files panel to sort column data by any of the column headings. Click a heading once to sort all the file data by that column. Click the same heading a second time to reverse the order of the sort from ascending to descending, or vice-versa.

Chapter 2: Setting Up and Connecting to a Contribute Site

In This Chapter

✔ **Building a site for Contribute users**

✔ **Connecting to a Contribute site**

✔ **Transferring files to and from a Contribute site**

✔ **Setting server file and folder permissions**

✔ **Understanding and using Contribute special files**

*I*n 2003, before Macromedia was purchased by Adobe, Macromedia developed a great little software program called Contribute (the current version is Contribute CS4) that, for under $200 per user, enables nontechnical people to edit some of the content on their Dreamweaver-created Web sites. With Contribute, even your least technical clients or office mates can edit and update pages on the site without any fear of breaking or ruining the site.

The program is as easy to use as Microsoft Word and comes with a fantastic instructional tutorial. Contribute has its own built-in Web browser with FTP access that enables you to navigate and download a copy of any existing page on your Web site to your local computer. From there, you can make any edits you want and publish them back to the remote server.

For example, from Contribute, users can download a local copy of a Web page from their site, modify it locally, and upload the changed page to the Web site, thereby overwriting what was previously online. If you're working with several people in a workgroup, all members can use Contribute to edit pages on a Web site as long as they have copies of Contribute installed on their computers. Of course, one person has to act as the *site administrator.* Typically that person is either the Web designer who builds the site in Dreamweaver or the Contribute workgroup manager. And because you have to have one Big Cheese, Contribute comes with tools that enable you to create and administer Web sites that are optimized for seamless editing and updating. We explain some of these tools in this chapter and in Book VI, Chapter 3.

To find out more about the differences between Dreamweaver and Contribute, and to find out how to manage a Dreamweaver site for Contribute users, be sure to read Book VI, Chapter 3.

In this chapter, you also discover the important differences between building a site in Dreamweaver for Contribute users and building regular Dreamweaver sites. Then you make a Contribute-compatible site connection, use Dreamweaver to administer the site to do things like set file and folder permissions for users, and transfer the Contribute site files to the remote server.

Understanding Contribute Best Practices

A Contribute site really isn't much different from other Web sites you build in Dreamweaver, but you do have to keep a few considerations in mind when you plan and build a site for Contribute users. For example, Contribute is intended to bring the technical elite and the technical novice together so that they can build and maintain an excellent site. That means laying out a logical yet simple site plan that multiple users can understand and use, just as you would when designing a non-Contribute site.

The Contribute software was very appropriately named. The program not only empowers users to contribute to the Web site in meaningful ways, but it also prevents users from making catastrophic changes that could cripple the site's essential functions (or worse).

Setting up Dreamweaver to work with Contribute is essential. You need to make sure that Contribute users can get in, do what they need to do, and get out — without mucking up the site infrastructure and processes. Here are a few things you should remember to do:

✦ **When you create a new managed site, don't forget to enable Contribute settings.** To access Contribute settings, click the Advanced tab in the Site Definition dialog box.

✦ **Build a Dreamweaver template-driven Web site with specified editable content areas.** Although you don't have to do this, doing so makes the site easier for novices to use when editing and creating new pages in Contribute. For example, you may want to specify one editable area on the template for the main text area of the page, another area for page headers, and another for graphics.

✦ **Make site navigation as simple as possible.** See the section "Leaving a Trail of Bread Crumbs for Contribute Users," later in this chapter.

✦ **Use Dreamweaver to create a style sheet and apply styles to the pages on the Contribute site.** Although you can apply styles (but not create them) with Contribute, it's often faster and easier to do CSS stuff in Dreamweaver.

If Contribute users are using Microsoft Word to write and format site content, consider naming styles after Word style names so Contribute can map the styles when a user copies and pastes data from a Word file into a Contribute file.

✦ **Hide some styles to prevent Contribute users from changing them.** To hide a particular style from Contribute users, edit the style name in Code view so that it starts with `mmhide_`. For instance, if you have a style that makes text bold and 36 pixels called `Bold36`, rename the style to `mmhide_Bold36`.

✦ **Set up read and write file and folder permissions on the server for Contribute users.** Setting up permissions designates what Contribute users can and cannot access and edit on the site after it's published.

✦ **Group similar items together, don't go crazy with folder nesting, and include index pages to each folder that contain links to all the other pages within the folder.** To modify or create new pages, Contribute users must be able to navigate to existing site files through Contribute's browser interface. After your folders are set up, be sure to encourage users to save new pages they create on the site into the appropriate folders.

✦ **Create a Contribute-compatible site connection and test it in preparation for uploading the files to the remote server.** That way, you know in advance that everything is functioning when you hand off the basic site maintenance tasks to Contribute users later.

Making a Dreamweaver Site Connection Compatible with Contribute

Before building a Contribute site, you need to create a managed site in Dreamweaver so the program knows where on your local machine you're housing all the files you create for the new Contribute site.

You also need to enable Contribute compatibility within Dreamweaver through the Manage Sites dialog box. One of the great benefits of enabling Contribute compatibility is that Dreamweaver automatically saves a version of each file when it's opened. That way, if a user ever needs to revert to a previous version of that file, he can *roll back* to that version easily. See Book VI, Chapter 3 for more details about the rollback process.

Before you can use Contribute, you need to create a new managed site in Dreamweaver. See Book I, Chapter 3 for details.

After you've defined your site, follow these steps in Dreamweaver to enable site compatibility with Contribute:

1. **From the main menu or from the Options menu in the Files panel, choose Site➪Manage Sites.**

The Manage Sites dialog box opens.

2. **Select the site you want to make compatible with Contribute and click the Edit button.**

3. **Choose the Advanced tab in the Site Definition dialog box.**

4. **Click the Contribute category near the bottom of the Category list.**

   The dialog box displays the Enable Contribute Compatibility option, as shown in Figure 2-1.

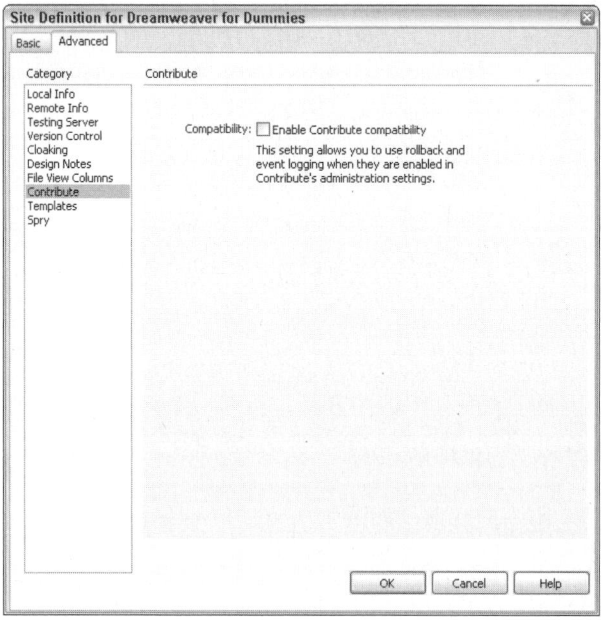

Figure 2-1:
Enable your site for Contribute compatibility.

Site Definition for Dreamweaver for Dummies

Basic | Advanced

Category | Contribute

Local Info
Remote Info
Testing Server
Version Control
Cloaking
Design Notes
File View Columns
Contribute
Templates
Spry

Compatibility: ☐ Enable Contribute compatibility

This setting allows you to use rollback and event logging when they are enabled in Contribute's administration settings.

OK | Cancel | Help

5. **Select the Enable Contribute Compatibility check box.**

   Dreamweaver may alert you that you need to select a remote access method (see Book V, Chapter 3), or enable Check In/Out and Design Notes (see Book VI, Chapter 1) prior to enabling the Enable Contribute Compatibility option.

6. **Click OK to accept all the settings in the Site Definition box.**

7. **Click the Done button to close the Manage Sites dialog box.**

After you enable site compatibility with Contribute, you can successfully administer the site with Dreamweaver. You can set up and test the server connection, set server and folder permissions for Contribute users, and transfer files to the remote server, all from within Dreamweaver.

You create the Contribute site just as you do any other site, including having a local and remote copy of all the files. The main difference between a regular site and a Contribute site is that you set up the Contribute site in Dreamweaver so that users can log into the remote site, download pages, modify pages, and upload those pages back to the remote server with Contribute.

Using Dreamweaver to Administer a Contribute Site

Before you can administer a Contribute site from Dreamweaver, you must also have a copy of Contribute software installed on your computer. After you have both software programs installed on the same computer, you can use Dreamweaver to launch Contribute for site administration tasks such as

✦ Changing the administrative settings for the Contribute site

✦ Setting up Contribute users with individual *connection keys* (the electronic version of a password that enables them to access the remote server to download, modify, and upload edited pages on the Web site)

✦ Setting and changing permissions to Contribute roles, which determine the level of access any one Contribute user has on a Web site

One of the great benefits to being a Contribute administrator is that you can assign user roles for each Contribute user and set file and folder permissions for each one. None of these roles and permissions settings affect the Dreamweaver Administrator, however. The Dreamweaver administrator (that's you) is the master of all.

Follow these steps to administer a Contribute site in Dreamweaver:

1. **Select the Contribute category in the Site Definition dialog box.**

If you're not sure how to do this, follow Steps 1 through 4 in the preceding section.

2. **Click the Administer Site in Contribute button (shown in Figure 2-2).**

This button appears only after you enable Contribute compatibility as outlined in the preceding section.

3. **In the dialog box that appears (shown in Figure 2-3), select a method for editing and click the Yes button to become the Web site's Contribute Administrator.**

Your computer launches Contribute (if it's not already open), and the Administer Website dialog box appears (see Figure 2-4).

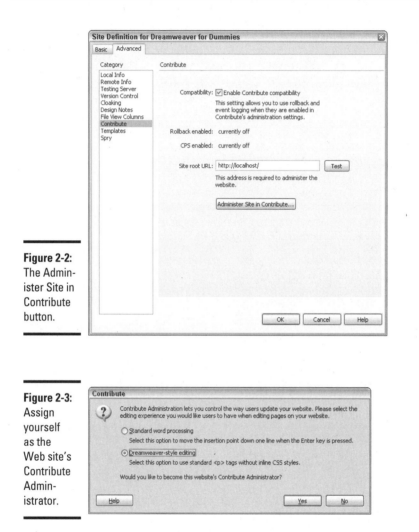

Figure 2-2:
The Administer Site in Contribute button.

Figure 2-3:
Assign yourself as the Web site's Contribute Administrator.

4. **In the Administer Website dialog box, you can perform the following tasks:**

   • To change administrative settings, select the Administration category to enter a contact e-mail address, set the Administrator password, or remove administrative settings for this site.

   • To edit role settings, select the Users and Roles category and edit or remove existing roles and create new roles.

   • To send connection keys (Contribute site access information) to users, select the Contribute user's name from the list of connected users and click the Send Connection Key button.

   You should, at minimum, set the Administrator password. Additional settings in the Administer Website dialog box are entirely up to you.

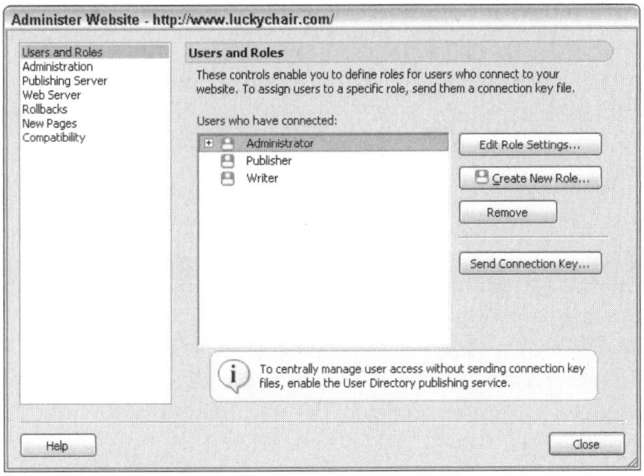

Figure 2-4:
Configure
settings
for the
Contribute
site.

Note: This book focuses on using Dreamweaver. If you need more detailed support on Contribute, such as setting up administrative settings, connection keys, and user roles, read the Contribute Help files on Adobe's LiveDocs Web site at

http://www.adobe.com/support/documentation/en/contribute/

5. **Click OK to accept all the settings in the Administer Website dialog box.**

6. **Click OK to close the Site Definition dialog box.**

7. **Click Done to close the Manage Sites dialog box.**

Making the Most of Templates

Remember when you were just starting out in your career as a Web designer? If not, start reflecting. When you conceive of a Web site for Contribute users, the design can be as elaborate as your imagination can fathom, but you need to ensure that the design has content areas that are easy to edit from the Contribute user's (read novice's) perspective.

Although using templates is by no means required, building a Web site from a Dreamweaver template is one of the best ways to create and manage a site for Contribute users. We recommend that you use a master template in Dreamweaver to build all the pages on the site. That way, you can create editable areas within the template to define what content (including text, graphics, tables, and more) Contribute users can edit. You (as Administrator) still maintain the look and feel of the site, which means you can easily update the layout at a later time, should you need to. See Book III, Chapter 2 to find more about templates.

After you create the templates and build the site in Dreamweaver, you can upload the templates, along with the site files, to the server to make them available to Contribute users. As long as the site root folder for each user's profile matches the site root folder you define for the site in Dreamweaver, the templates appear in Contribute's New Page dialog box when users create a new page.

If you choose not to build the Contribute site using Dreamweaver templates, you could instead designate any page on the site as a Contribute template, from which users can create new pages. For simplicity's sake, we refer to these Contribute-Administrator-designated-template pages as *Contribute templates.*

The main difference between the two template types is that Dreamweaver templates can have editable areas and locked areas, whereas Contribute templates are completely editable. We recommend you use Dreamweaver templates because you have much more control over the integrity of any new template-based pages that are created.

To create a (fully editable) Contribute template, follow these steps:

1. **In Dreamweaver, select the Contribute category in the Site Definition dialog box.**

   If you're not sure how to do this, follow Steps 1 through 4 in the earlier section "Making a Dreamweaver Site Connection Compatible with Contribute."

2. **Click the Administer Site in Contribute button.**

   This button appears only after you enable Contribute compatibility (as described in the earlier section "Making a Dreamweaver Site Connection Compatible with Contribute").

   If you created an Administrator password when configuring Dreamweaver to administer a Contribute site, the Administrator Password dialog box opens.

3. **Enter an Administrator password if prompted and click OK.**

   Your computer launches Contribute (if it's not already open), and the Administer Website dialog box appears (refer to Figure 2-4).

4. **Select the Administrator role in the Users and Roles category and click the Edit Role Settings button.**

   The Edit Administrator Settings dialog box opens.

5. **Choose the New Pages category (shown in Figure 2-5).**

6. **Select the Create a New Page by Copying a Page from This List check box, click the Add button, and select a page on the site to use as a Contribute template.**

7. **Click OK to close the Edit Administrator Settings dialog box.**

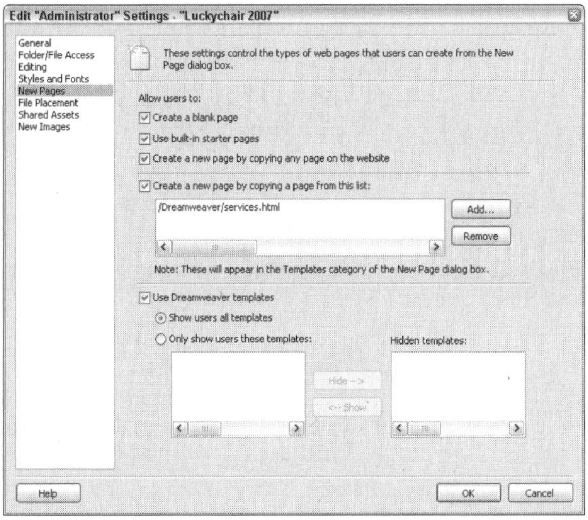

Figure 2-5:
Create new
Contribute
templates
from any
existing
page.

8. **Click Close to close the Administer Website dialog box.**

Now Contribute users can use pages in this list as a starting point for creat-ing new pages.

Leaving a Trail of Bread Crumbs for Contribute Users

When you build a site for Contribute users, try to create a site structure that is easy to navigate. Here are some basic site-organization tips:

✦ **If you're building a small site, organize content in a logical manner by having all the files reside at the root level.** To keep things simple, don't go too crazy with nested folders. You want Contribute users to be able to easily find what they need and not feel flustered because they can't seem to open the page they need to edit. For consistency, also remem-ber to keep your file names short with no spaces or no funky characters.

✦ **If you're building a larger site, or if your small site necessitates a folder structure, use folders to organize similar Web pages.** When using sub-folders to organize content, make sure that each folder has a main page with the filename index.html that contains links to all the other pages within that folder. Then the main page opens automatically in a browser when the URL specifies that folder name, and Contribute users can easily navigate to and open any of the pages in that folder for editing.

For example, if a company provides ten services and needs a separate Web page for each service, organizing all ten services' HTML files inside a Services folder is a logical file management solution. Then the URL, when displayed in a browser, would look something like `http://www.mysamplesite.com/services/`.

Using folders may make Contribute editing go faster than when you use a flat document structure, especially when a lot of editing is going on. With folders, the different versions of files are contained in separate directories, making editing go a little faster.

✦ **If you have server-side includes for HTML content, such as footers or navigation tables, create a simple HTML page with links to all the include files on the site.** Contribute users can then use that HTML page to navigate to and edit the include files.

Connecting to a Contribute Site

In Dreamweaver, you can treat a Contribute site just like any other site by connecting to a remote server and editing pages as needed.

That being said, although you can connect to a remote site in several different ways, not all of them are compatible with Contribute. Specifically, the following connections have restrictions:

✦ **Your local computer acts as the Web server:** To share your connection with Contribute users, you need to set up the site with FTP or a network connection instead of using the local folder path.

✦ **You're using WebDAV or Microsoft Visual SourceSafe:** You're out of luck. These connection options aren't compatible with Contribute.

✦ **You're using an RDS (Rapid Development Services) connection:** You can achieve Contribute compatibility, but you need to customize your connection prior to sharing with Contribute users.

When you enable the site for use with Contribute, Dreamweaver creates a site root URL for the Contribute site based on other information about the site. Unfortunately, this information is not always accurate, so you may need to test the connection manually. To see whether your connection is accurate, open the Dreamweaver Site Definition dialog box, and in the Contribute category, click the Test button. Dreamweaver notifies you if the connection is good or lets you know if the connection needs troubleshooting. If it's good, you're ready to transfer files. For troubleshooting help, see "Troubleshooting a Contribute Site in Dreamweaver," later in the chapter.

Transferring files to and from a Contribute site from within Dreamweaver

Just as Dreamweaver has its Check In/Out system, Contribute uses its own method of file transfer to help prevent multiple users from accessing and editing the same file at the same time. In Contribute, users download and open a *draft* of a page, edit it, and then publish it to the remote server. (Your Contribute users can learn how to do that by taking the cool Contribute tutorial that comes with Contribute.)

As Contribute Administrator, you can use Dreamweaver to transfer files to the remote server instead of uploading and downloading files from within Contribute. Just be sure to always use the Check In/Check Out commands as discussed in Book VI, Chapter 1 when transferring files to a Contribute site from within Dreamweaver.

If you accidentally use Dreamweaver's Get/Put commands instead of Check In/Check Out when transferring files to the remote server, they may accidentally overwrite changes another Contribute user has made to a file. As a fail-safe, Dreamweaver gives you a warning if someone else checks out a file.

To aid with the Check In/Out process, Dreamweaver makes automatic backups of all Contribute site files upon check in and puts them in the _baks folder along with your name and a date stamp in a Design Notes file.

Turn to Book V, Chapter 4 to find out how to transfer files from a local site to the remote server.

Setting Contribute file and folder permissions

As the Contribute Administrator, you can set unique file and folder permissions for every Contribute user in a group. These permissions are attached to each user's role rather than to the files and folders. While enforced on Contribute users, these permissions don't affect the files when edited from within Dreamweaver.

For example, a Contribute user with read-only permission to a folder can't write to that folder. The same goes for read access to dependent files.

If a Contribute user doesn't have permission to access an images folder, those images appear as broken image icons when viewing the file for editing purposes in Contribute. Because templates reside in a Templates subfolder at the root level of the site, you need to be aware of read and write permissions so that Contribute users can create new files from templates as needed.

Additionally, Contribute doesn't have any way to manage read-write privileges assigned to files and folders; those must be managed directly on the remote server through Dreamweaver.

Understanding Contribute Special Files

Contribute creates a bunch of special files to assist with the administration and editing process of your Contribute Web site. These special files are not viewable by site visitors, and they don't need to be edited or updated by you. They just exist in the background on the remote server to help Dreamweaver manage Contribute files for all the users making changes to pages on the site. These files include

Book VI Chapter 2

Setting Up and Connecting to a Contribute Site

✦ Backup files for old or rollback versions of files in the Contribute-generated _baks folder

✦ Contribute site management files with the .csi file extension that are saved in the Contribute-generated _mm folder

✦ Design Notes files with metadata about the files (see Book VI, Chapter 1 to find more about Design Notes)

✦ Temporary files with the .tmp extension created for previewing purposes within Contribute

✦ Temporary locked (read-only) files to show Contribute users when those files are opened elsewhere

When Contribute creates all these special administrative files, they are automatically updated and uploaded to the publicly accessible remote server for the Web site. If you don't want to see these Contribute files on your server (specifically the _mm and _baks folders), you can create what's called a *staging server* (or *production server*) as a place for Contribute users to work on the site before publishing them to the remote server. After users complete any changes to their pages, those site files can be copied from the staging server to the production server without the special files. To discover how to add another level of security that blocks folders beginning with an underscore from being copied to the production server, search for *Web site security* and *Staging Servers and Contribute* in Contribute Help.

Troubleshooting a Contribute Site in Dreamweaver

If you have a problem with a Contribute site in Dreamweaver, most likely it has something to do with the connection or the administration tools. Fortunately, both are fairly easy to troubleshoot. Of course, this book gives only a large-scale view of Contribute, so if your problem falls beyond the information offered here, you should search the Contribute Help files for more information.

Fixing connection problems

You can figure out whether you have a connection problem fairly easily because Dreamweaver enables you to test the remote connection with the root URL any time. All you need to do is click a button related to site administration for Contribute. If the URL is incorrect, Dreamweaver displays an error message.

You can manually check the connection at any time by following these steps in Dreamweaver:

1. **Open the Contribute category on the Advanced tab of the Site Definition dialog box.**

If you're not sure how to do this, follow Steps 1 through 4 in the earlier section "Making a Dreamweaver Site Connection Compatible with Contribute."

2. **Copy and paste the Site Root URL from the dialog box into a browser to see whether the URL is valid.**

   If it's not, check the spelling and syntax to correct the URL.

3. **Select Remote Info from the Category list.**

   The right side of the dialog box now displays the Remote Info details.

4. **Click the Test button to test the connection.**

   When the connection is good, Dreamweaver displays an alert message that says it successfully connected with the remote server. When the connection is bad, you see an error message indicating what may be wrong with the connection, such as `Your login or password is incorrect`.

   If you're sure the URL is right but you still get an error message, speak to your system administrator or host provider; the problem is probably server-related.

Checking the _mm folder

If the Contribute administration tools aren't working right, the problem may lie in the _mm folder, which should contain a shared settings site-management file with a long funny name and the .csi file extension.

The first thing you need to do is to verify that the read and write permissions are enabled on the server. If they aren't, enable them and try using the administration tools again. If they are enabled, you may need to re-establish a connection as administrator, which re-creates or replaces a missing or corrupted shared-settings file in the _mm folder.

If you're still having problems, follow these steps:

1. **Check the _mm folder in the Contribute site from within Dreamweaver to make sure that it contains a shared-settings file with the .csi extension.**

   The file has an odd filename like cthubff3ce10d8490f3d1.csi.

   This folder and this file are necessary for proper site administration.

2. **If the file is missing or possibly corrupted, you may need to create a new site connection within Dreamweaver and attempt to become the Site Administrator again.**

   The _mm folder and shared settings file are automatically created when you become the Contribute Administrator. If they are missing or corrupted, re-establishing yourself as the site administrator creates new files.

If the problem persists, search for *Troubleshooting* in Contribute's Help files for more information.

Chapter 3: Managing a Contribute Site

In This Chapter

✔ **Using the rollback feature**

✔ **Editing remote files**

✔ **Making templates available to Contribute users**

✔ **Gaining access to files that are checked out**

✔ **Using Dreamweaver to update templates and CSS**

Managing a Contribute site using Dreamweaver is easy and is not much different from creating and managing a non-Contribute site. A key benefit of managing the site using Dreamweaver instead of Contribute, however, is that Dreamweaver automatically does some file management tasks for you that Contribute simply can't do.

Contribute users can, for example, browse to a page on their site, download a copy of it; edit the text, images, links, and tables on it (if they have been granted permission to do so by the Administrator); save the file; and then send it back to the server, which instantly displays the updated page.

Contribute users can't, however, do some of the more complex site-management and page-editing tasks, such as editing or creating new styles in a CSS, renaming and moving files, or making global changes to the site's layout by editing a Dreamweaver template. The Contribute Site Administrator in Dreamweaver must do these things.

In the previous chapter, we show you how to create and set up a Contribute site. This chapter deals with file management. If you're ready to manage a Contribute site, we presume that you have already done the following things:

✦ Installed Contribute and Dreamweaver on the same local computer.

✦ Connected to the Contribute site with Dreamweaver. In the Dreamweaver Site Definition dialog box, you have to enter the Contribute site's Local Site and Remote Site information. You must include a local root folder and a site root URL on the server.

✦ Tested the site's connectivity by making sure that the root URL works.

✦ Enabled Contribute compatibility in Dreamweaver. You should also turn on Design Notes and the Check In/Check Out feature (as described in Book VI, Chapter 1).

✦ Clicked the Administer Site in Contribute button in the Dreamweaver Site Definition dialog box to provide administration details for the site and for Contribute users as required.

✦ Designed, built, and uploaded a Contribute site to the remote server.

If you haven't done all these things, flip back to Book VI, Chapter 2 before continuing.

Managing Contribute Files Using Dreamweaver

As the Dreamweaver Administrator, you can perform certain high-level tasks that Contribute users can't. Table 3-1 contains a list of general tasks that can be performed in one or both programs. These management tasks include *rolling back* to older versions of files; editing, deleting, moving, and renaming files; giving Contribute users access to templates even though they don't have root folder access; and unlocking locked files on the remote server.

Table 3-1	Web Site Management Tasks	
Contribute Site Management Tasks	*Dreamweaver Administrator*	*Contribute User*
Connect to the Web site on the remote server	Yes	Yes
Set up Contribute users and define user roles	Yes	No
Check in/check out files	Yes	Yes, as part of the Edit/Publish process
Edit files	Yes	Yes
Move and rename files	Yes	No
Delete files	Yes	Yes, but only if Administrator has enabled this option for the user
Create new pages	Yes	Yes
Create new Dreamweaver template-based pages	Yes	Yes, but only if Administrator has granted permission to the Templates folder on the server
Convert files with FlashPaper	Yes	Yes

Contribute Site Management Tasks	Dreamweaver Administrator	Contribute User
Roll back files	Yes	Yes, but only if Administrator has enabled this option for the user
Administer a Web site	Yes	Yes, but only if Administrator has enabled this option for the site
Create Contribute templates	Yes	Yes, but this is typically allowed for only one person
Create Dreamweaver templates	Yes	No
Access Dreamweaver templates	Yes	No
Modify Dreamweaver templates	Yes	No
Create, edit, delete external CSS linked to pages	Yes	No
Enable event log in	Yes	No
Unlock locked files on the remote server	Yes	No
Create Design Notes	Yes	No

Book VI
Chapter 3

Managing a
Contribute Site

Be benevolent with your power. Give your Contribute users the right access to the right tools, and you may be surprised to discover that you create less work for yourself.

Rolling back your files

You have probably enabled compatibility between Dreamweaver and Contribute by now. If you haven't, open the Site Definition dialog box in Dreamweaver, as explained in Book VI, Chapter 2.

The next step is to log in to the Contribute site through Dreamweaver as the Administrator. When the Administer Website dialog box opens, select the Rollbacks category and select the Enable Rollbacks feature, as shown in Figure 3-1. The default number of file versions to keep for rollback purposes is three, but you can increase or decrease the number if you like.

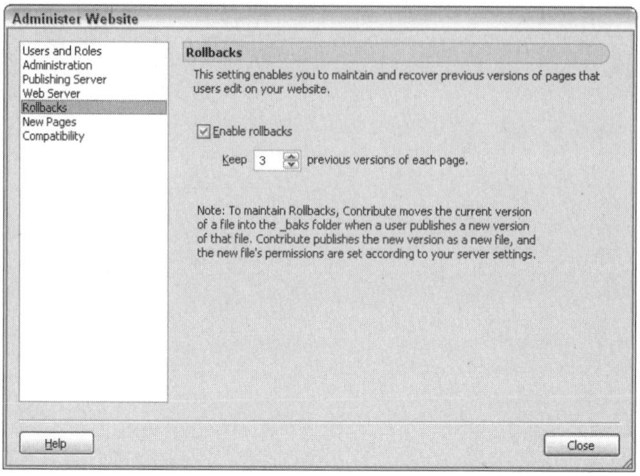

Administer Website

Users and Roles
Administration
Publishing Server
Web Server
Rollbacks
New Pages
Compatibility

Rollbacks

This setting enables you to maintain and recover previous versions of pages that users edit on your website.

☑ Enable rollbacks

Keep 3 ▢ previous versions of each page.

Note: To maintain Rollbacks, Contribute moves the current version of a file into the _baks folder when a user publishes a new version of that file. Contribute publishes the new version as a new file, and the new file's permissions are set according to your server settings.

Help   Close

Figure 3-1:
Enable the
Rollbacks
feature.

After that, you need to enable the rollback feature within Contribute. To do so, choose Edit⇨Administer Website and select the name of the Contribute site. The Administer Website dialog box opens, which looks exactly like the dialog box that opens from within Dreamweaver. Select the Rollbacks category and select the Enable Rollbacks feature and then click the Close button to close the dialog box.

With rollback turned on, Dreamweaver automatically saves every version of a file (up to the number specified in the Rollbacks category, which is typically three versions) as it is edited. If you need to revert to a previous version of a file, no problem; each version is stored with the date and editor's name for easy retrieval. You can use a previous version to roll back to and overwrite any mistakes that were made on the most recent version.

Be sure to cloak the backup folder so that it isn't copied to the live Web site upon transferring files to the Web server. (See Book V, Chapter 3 for more information on cloaking.)

You may think that the Rollbacks feature is a function you'd never need, but trust us when we tell you it can come in handy some day. The more Contribute users working on a site, the greater the likelihood of the need to roll back files.

To roll back a file in Dreamweaver, follow these steps:

1. **In the Files panel, right-click (Windows) or Control+click (Mac) the filename that you want to roll back.**

2. **From the context menu that appears, choose Roll Back Page.**

The Roll Back Page dialog box appears displaying a list of versions of the file you can select and roll back to, as shown in Figure 3-2.

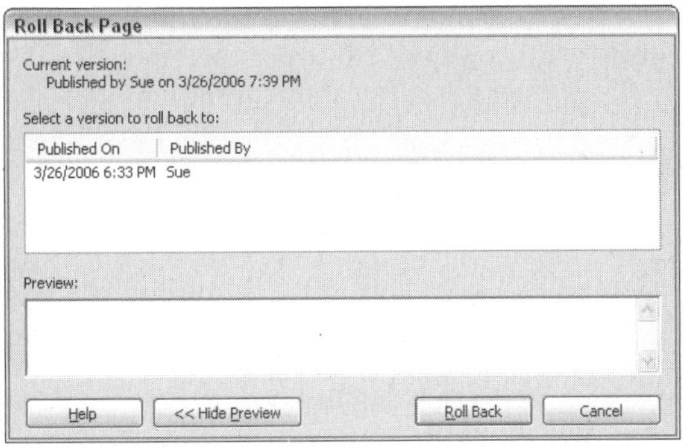

Roll Back Page

Current version:
Published by Sue on 3/26/2006 7:39 PM

Select a version to roll back to:

Published On	Published By
3/26/2006 6:33 PM	Sue

Preview:

| Help | << Hide Preview | Roll Back | Cancel |

Figure 3-2:
Select a
version of
a file to roll
back.

3. **Select the version of the file you want to roll back to.**

When there are no prior versions, the dialog box displays a message that you can't roll back to a previous version of the selected file.

4. **Click the Roll Back button to roll back to the selected version, or the Cancel button to exit the dialog box.**

The rollback version replaces the newest version of the file.

Making changes to Contribute files

Contribute users can do some tasks, such as edit and republish existing files, create new pages based on existing pages, and create brand-new pages to add to a Contribute site. They can't, however, delete, move, and rename files, or do certain file editing tasks on a remote Contribute site. The site Administrator must perform these tasks through Dreamweaver.

Keep in mind the following points when making changes to Contribute files:

✦ **Editing files:** Use the Check In/Check Out feature (instead of Get and Put) to check out the file to which you want to make changes, make the changes, save the file, and check it back in.

We discuss editing templates and style sheets later in this chapter, in the section, "Using Dreamweaver to Edit a Contribute Site."

✦ **Moving and renaming files:** On the surface, moving a file from one location on the remote server to another, or even renaming a file, works the same in a Contribute site as it does in a Dreamweaver site. But Dreamweaver tracks and saves these changes in the _baks folder, and modifies the filename or location in all the previous versions of the file. That way, if you need to roll back to a previous version, the file location or name change stays intact. Pretty smart, huh?

We strongly recommend that if you have to move or rename a file, you do so from within Dreamweaver.

✦ **Deleting files:** If you're using Dreamweaver to delete a file, Dreamweaver asks whether you want to fully delete all previous versions of that file at the same time. If you say yes, they all disappear forever. If you say no, Dreamweaver saves a copy of the current version as a new version of the file in the _baks folder on the remote server for future restoration using the Roll Back Page command.

To delete a file on a remote Contribute site using Dreamweaver, follow these steps:

1. **In the Remote pane of the Files panel, select the file you want to delete and press the Delete key on your keyboard.**

A Confirmation dialog box opens for you to confirm the deletion.

2. **If you want to also delete any rollback versions of the selected file, enable the Delete Rollback Versions option.**

Deselect the Delete Rollback Versions option to keep previous versions of the selected file online, including a copy of the version you're deleting.

3. **Click Yes to delete the selected file.**

You can't undo this action! Deleted files are permanently removed from the server and are irretrievable.

Enabling Contribute users to use templates

When you set up folder and file permissions for users on the Contribute site through Dreamweaver's Administer Website dialog box, be sure to give Contribute users read access to any files and folders on the remote server. Such folders include root-level files, images subfolders, and perhaps read access to the Templates folder if you want Contribute users to create template-based files from Dreamweaver-generated templates. You can grant file and folder permissions by selecting a user and clicking the Edit Role Settings button. When the Edit "Role" Settings dialog box opens, select the Folder/File Access category from the left side of the panel, shown in Figure 3-3, and set user folder access and file deletion settings on the right.

If you're weary of granting users permission to the Templates folder, you could allow them to use Dreamweaver templates by copying the entire Template folder from the main site's root folder to the Contribute site's remote root folder through the Files panel.

Thereafter, whenever the Dreamweaver templates are updated on the main site through Dreamweaver, you must remember to copy the updated templates to the Template folder on the remote Contribute site. Copying the updated templates to the Contribute site is the only way to overwrite the older files so that users can access them.

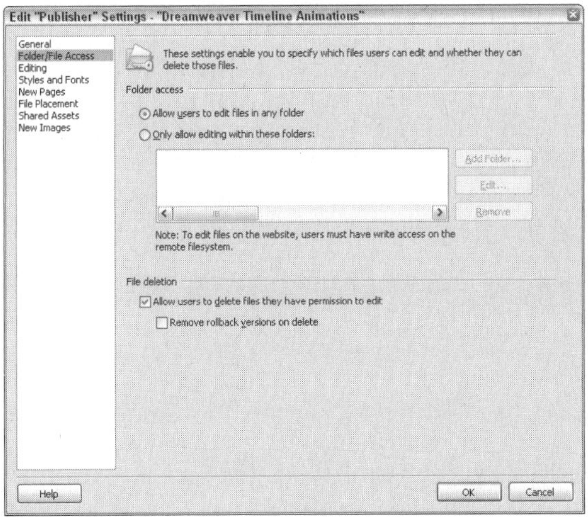

Book VI
Chapter 3

Managing a
Contribute Site

Figure 3-3:
Set file
and folder
permissions
for Contri-
bute users.

Unlocking a checked out file

When you enable the Check In/Check Out feature, it may sometimes appear (by the presence of a lock next to the file on the user's computer) that a remote file is checked out when it really isn't. That means the file isn't really locked, but in order for any users to access the file, the lock needs to be removed. As Administrator, you have that power.

Before you unlock the file through Dreamweaver, be sure the file's not really checked out by a Contribute user. If the file is unlocked when it really is checked out, that would grant file access to multiple users with the potential of creating multiple versions of the file at once!

To manually unlock a file in a Contribute site that appears to be checked out when it really isn't, select the file in Dreamweaver's Files panel, right-click (Windows) or Control+click (Mac) it, and select Undo Check Out. If prompted, click Yes to confirm that you indeed want to unlock the file. To find out more about the Check In/Check Out feature, see Book VI, Chapter 1.

Using Dreamweaver to Edit a Contribute Site

Some things, *you* — as Administrator — can do in both Dreamweaver and Contribute. Some tasks, you should perform only in Dreamweaver. Make any robust changes to a Contribute site, such as modifying a template or CSS, in Dreamweaver to maintain the integrity of the site's design.

Updating templates in a Contribute site

Contribute users can't change Dreamweaver templates, and that's a good thing because they're typically not Web designers. If a template needs editing, you need to do it in Dreamweaver. What part of a template might you need to edit? Perhaps you need to remove a navigation button from the layout or edit some text that appears on every page. Or maybe you need to overhaul the site design, with all new graphics, while keeping the overall content intact.

If you remove or rename an editable region from a template, Contribute users may not know what to do with the content from the old editable region. To avoid confusion, try to make changes to the templates before or after normal business hours and be sure to have Contribute users close down and relaunch their Contribute programs prior to making any new changes to the site. Contribute users can only get new remote server information to their local computers by closing and relaunching Contribute.

To edit a Dreamweaver template used in a Contribute site, follow these steps:

1. **In Dreamweaver, open, edit, and save the Contribute site template.**

   Find out more about templates in Book III, Chapter 2.

2. **Tell the Contribute users about the change so that they can close and restart their Contribute programs.**

   Restarting Contribute enables Contribute users to access the site with the most recent documents and templates.

Editing style sheets in a Contribute site

Making sure that the look and feel of a site stays under tight control is important in any Web design scenario. Contribute users aren't allowed to change the contents of style sheets, which means that you don't have to worry about style sheets being messed up by anyone but you and any other Dreamweaver users on the team.

As with any site using style sheets, when you delete a style, the tag to apply that style to a particular word, sentence, or paragraph still resides in the code of the Web pages. The discrepancy may confuse your Contribute users. To quickly remove or rename style tags from an entire site, use Dreamweaver's Find and Replace tool (see Book II, Chapter 2).

Also, let the Contribute users know about any changes you make to the CSS during work hours because they can't see changes to any pages they're currently editing until they publish the page back to the site.

Follow these steps to edit a style in a Contribute site through Dreamweaver:

1. **Use Dreamweaver's style-sheet editing tools.**

You have a variety of options. You can use the CSS Styles panel, the Attributes panel, or edit the CSS code by hand. See Book III, Chapter 1 for everything you wanted to know about using CSS in Dreamweaver but were afraid to ask.

2. **Tell the Contribute users about the change so that they can publish and re-edit pages with the newest version of the style sheet.**

Better yet, tell users to restart Contribute so they can access all the site pages and assets with the most recent versions of everything.

Book VII
Building Web Applications

The 5th Wave   By Rich Tennant

FREELANCER NED WILLIS CONSULTS WITH A MEMBER OF HIS TECHNICAL STAFF

"...and that's pretty much all there is to converting a document to an HTML file."

Contents at a Glance

Chapter 1: Preparing to Build Web Applications

In This Chapter

✔ Selecting a Web application platform

✔ Installing an application server

✔ Analyzing your choices for Web and application servers

✔ Defining the Testing Server settings in Dreamweaver

✔ Choosing a database

From Web site to Web app: That's the transformation that many Web developers find themselves dealing with as the needs of their Web sites expand over time. A typical scenario goes something like this: At the start, a company is content to create a static site presenting its products and services. However, over time, it realizes that their Web site could be far more useful to their customers if they offered more interactive and dynamic content. So, they transform their static, made-beforehand site into a full-scale Web application.

The first challenge when planning how to build applications from Web pages is picking a set of tools to use. This chapter explores various Web application platforms and application servers and how to choose the right ones for your needs. We also touch on various languages, such as PHP, ASP, Java Server Pages (JSP), and ColdFusion, that work hand-in-hand with the application server when generating your dynamic Web pages. Finally, this chapter gives you the lowdown on designing your database and choosing the right database application.

Understanding Web Applications

A basic Web site consists of HTML pages and related assets (such as images, CSS style sheets, and so on). After this set of files are placed onto a Web server, each file can be accessed by a browser through a unique URL. Because the content that the user sees is already contained in the HTML files, no further processing is necessary beyond sending the page to the browser for display (see Figure 1-1).

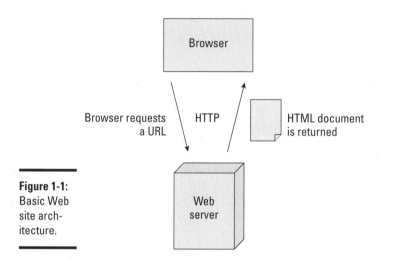

Figure 1-1:
Basic Web
site arch-
itecture.

In contrast, Web applications don't have a set number of pre-made HTML files. Instead, its HTML content is generated on-the-fly by a layer on the server — often called an *application layer* or *logic layer* — based on programming code.

Consider this example. Take PHP, one of the most popular Web application languages. When you work with it, you store the programming code in text-based .php files. When a .php file is requested by the browser, the Web server in turn calls the PHP application server to process the .php file. When the app server is done doing its magic, it sends a dynamically generated document to the browser for display (see Figure 1-2). To the user, it still looks like a normal Web page — but the way in which it goes to the browser is altogether different.

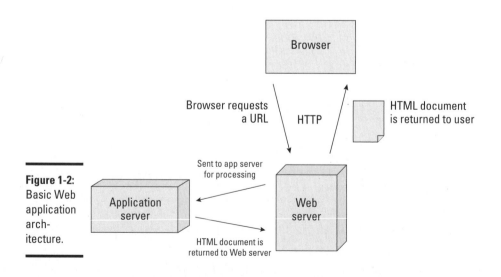

Figure 1-2:
Basic Web
application
arch-
itecture.

Choosing a Web Application Platform

Web application platforms (or application servers) run behind the scenes on the Web server. The application server supports the processing of your Web pages, acting as a helper to the Web server for processing the code that's part of the requested pages.

Dreamweaver CS4 allows you to create pages and sites that can be integrated in a variety of Web application platforms, including PHP, ASP, ASP.NET, and JSP. Each of these languages corresponds to a Dreamweaver document type (such as .php, .asp, or .jsp).

If you're already familiar with one of these languages, choose that one. If they're all new to you, PHP and ASP are very popular choices. You can find plenty of help and sample code on the Web for both of them.

Choosing a Web Server

Before you can develop Web services, you need to choose the underlying server technology. The two popular choices are Microsoft Internet Information Services (IIS) and Apache. As discussed below, your decision will often be based on where you plan to host the server.

**Book VII
Chapter 1**

Hosted sites

If your Web site is hosted by a Web hosting provider, you are already using one of these two servers even if you don't realize it. Many ISPs even allow you to choose between Unix/Apache or Microsoft IIS server plans.

If you're still in the process of selecting a hosting company for your Web sites, or if you want to test your Web application pages on your computer without uploading them to a remote server, compare the pros and cons of using the IIS Web platform versus the Apache Web platform.

For Web designers and developers, the major platform decision usually boils down to programming language and database support. Microsoft platform is the best choice for ASP and ASP.NET, whereas Apache is ideal for PHP and JSP.

When working with hosting sites, Dreamweaver allows you to generate a Web service proxy that allows the Web page to communicate with the Web service publisher. The *proxy,* also known as an *abstraction class,* contains the fields, methods, and properties of the Web service and makes them available to the locally hosted page. When you generate a proxy for your page, Dreamweaver lets you view it in the Components panel (choose Window⇨Components to open the panel).

Preparing to Build
Web Applications

Hosting your own site

If you are hosting the server on your own machine (either for testing or live purposes), you'll want to want to explore two options.

Apache

Apache server is the most popular Web server available. It's an *open-source* product, so it's free to download and use. Apache works well with PHP and JSP, which we talk about later in the chapter.

If you are running Windows, you can download the latest Apache version at `http://httpd.apache.org`.

If you're using Mac OS X and you want to run your Web application files locally, you already have Apache installed. To enable it, you simply pop over to your System Preferences tool, as described in the following steps:

1. **From the Apple menu, choose System Preferences.**

The System Preferences application in Mac OS X controls the configuration of your system, including optional components such as Apache.

2. **Click the Sharing icon.**

The Sharing panel tells OS X which services your computer provides, including Apache and file sharing.

3. **Select the On check box beside Web Sharing in the services list.**

Web Sharing is turned on, as shown in Figure 1-3.

You're all set to start using Apache.

Figure 1-3:
Turning on
the Apache
server.

A special host

A *localhost address* points to a special IP address, 127.0.0.1. It always points to the local computer. Typically, computers have two IP addresses: the public one, such as 128.34.34.34, and the localhost host address, 127.0.0.1. In order for Web users at large to access your Web pages, they must reference the external address.

Microsoft IIS

Microsoft IIS is a good choice for hosting your Web site if you're planning to develop pages with ASP or ASP.NET programming languages because IIS has built-in support for handling those development languages.

Windows Vista does not install IIS 7.0 by default, but it can be selected among the list of optionally installed components. However, note that Vista Basic does not support ASP and ASP.NET.

When you run IIS 7.0 on Vista, it restricts performance based on active concurrent requests, but does not limit the number of connections allowed. In contrast, for older systems, Windows XP restricted version of IIS 5.1 allows you to host one Web site and supports only 10 simultaneous connections.

In general, the version of Windows you're running determines which version of IIS you can run.

To install or verify that IIS is installed on your Vista computer, follow these steps:

1. **Choose Start⇨Control Panel⇨Programs.**

2. **Click the Turn Windows Features On or Off link.**

    You'll need to confirm this step.

    The Windows Features dialog box is displayed.

3. **If the check box beside Internet Information Services is not selected, do so now.**

    If it is already selected, you are all set and can cancel out of the process.

4. **Click OK to install IIS.**

To install or verify that IIS is installed on your Windows XP computer, follow these steps:

1. **Choose Start⇨Control Panel⇨Add/Remove Programs or choose Start⇨Control Panel and double-click the Add/Remove Programs icon.**

The same dialog box that you've probably used to remove software opens.

2. **In the Add or Remove Programs window, click the Add/Remove Windows Components button.**

   This step tells Windows that you want to change which Microsoft components (including IIS) are installed.

   The Windows Components Wizard opens.

3. **Click the Internet Information Services check box.**

   Windows tells you approximately how much space you need to install IIS. If the check box was already checked, that means IIS is already installed and you can stop.

4. **Click Next.**

   You may need your Windows Installer CD-ROM to install IIS, so make sure it's somewhere handy.

5. **Follow the onscreen prompts to finish installing IIS and then click OK.**

When IIS installs, it will create a default directory for storing Web pages at `c:\Inetpub\wwwroot`. This is often called the *Web root folder.*

Choosing an Application Server

Perhaps the most critical decision you make as you begin developing Web applications is choosing the application server, because the actual programming you do is based on your choice. Here are your major options to consider.

PHP

PHP is an open-source programming language and application server that is built for creating Web applications. It works well with many databases, including the popular open-source database MySQL.

It supports all major operating systems, including Windows, Mac OS X, and Linux. It integrates with either IIS or Apache to form a PHP Application Server. For Apache, it's loaded as an Apache Module. For IIS, it's loaded as an ISAPI add-on.

Many ISPs come with pre-installed support for PHP, whereas others require you to configure it manually on your server.

If you are installing it on your own computer, follow these instructions for Windows and Mac OS X.

Windows setup

Installing PHP for use with IIS is fairly easy with the automatic installation available from the PHP site. Download PHP from www.php.net. Get the automatic installation package under Windows Binaries; it's an executable (.exe) file. Be sure to use a download mirror that's close to where you live.

After you download the file, follow these steps to install PHP:

1. **Double-click the .exe file.**

2. **Click Next to install.**

3. **Agree to the license terms by clicking I Agree.**

4. **Select the Standard Install radio button and click Next.**

   The standard install uses default values for many of the settings. You can use the defaults without problems.

5. **Click Next to accept the default installation directory of C:\PHP.**

6. **(Optional) Enter values for the Mail Configuration.**

   You can also leave the default values.

   These are the same settings you selected when you configured your e-mail client.

7. **Select Microsoft IIS 4 or higher from the list of HTTP servers if you installed IIS, or select Apache if you installed the Apache Web server.**

8. **Click Next.**

9. **To begin the installation, click Next again.**

10. **Click OK in the IIS Has Been Configured dialog box.**

    This dialog box only appears if you didn't select IIS as your HTTP server.

11. **Click OK in the Installation Complete dialog box.**

    If you're using Windows NT, follow the directions in the dialog box; otherwise, the installation is complete.

Mac OS X setup

Mac OS X includes the files necessary to run PHP, but those files require manual editing that's quite tedious for most users. To enable PHP support for Mac OS X without messing around with your system files, visit www.entropy.ch/software/macosx/php and then follow these steps:

1. **Download an installer file for Mac OS X based on the version of Mac OS X you're running.**

2. **The Mac installer file is a .dmg disk image. Double-click the .dmg file.**

   The Mac mounts the disk image and displays a drive icon with the files.

3. **When you see the installer package, double-click it and follow the directions.**

That was pretty simple, huh? Congratulations: You've successfully installed the PHP application server for your Mac.

Active Server Pages (ASP)

Active Server Pages (ASP) is designed to work with the IIS Web platform. Dreamweaver CS4 supports building ASP code that can stand alone or be modified outside of Dreamweaver.

ASP aims to make Web application development as easy as possible by grouping common tasks together into objects. These objects include Application, ASPError, Request, Response, Server, and Session objects. The ASPError, for example, provides functions for handling errors.

ASP pages use either JavaScript or VBScript as the programming language. Dreamweaver knows what code to put in regardless of which one you choose.

ASP.NET

ASP.NET, despite its name being similar to ASP, is really a complete rewrite of the ASP development platform to conform to the Microsoft .NET platform.

You can download ASP.NET and related toolkits at `http://asp.net`.

Java Server Pages (JSP)

JSP uses the Java language and processor to deliver Web-based applications. JSP pages are different from other pages because they're compiled into byte code by the JSP compiler. These compiled JSP pages are called *servlets*.

Apache Jakarta Tomcat is the servlet container that's used for both the Java Servlet and JSP technologies. Apache Jakarta Tomcat is an open-source application that helps develop large-scale, high-traffic Web applications.

Jakarta Tomcat is available from `http://tomcat.apache.org`. If you're using Windows, download the core Windows Executable installer. For Mac OS X, visit `http://developer.apple.com/internet/java/tomcat1.html` for instructions on installing the Mac OS X binaries of Tomcat.

Other commercial JSP Application Severs include the following:

✦ Macromedia JRun

✦ Sun ONE Application Server

✦ IBM WebSphere

✦ BEA WebLogic

Most commercial distributions include a 30-day trial period to allow you to test-drive it before buying.

ColdFusion

ColdFusion is a Web application programming language that has markup syntax resembling HTML. ColdFusion allows people familiar with tag-based languages such as HTML to easily learn how to program Web apps.

Considering Web/Application Server Combinations

Although each of the Web platforms and application servers described in this chapter offer similar capabilities, processing Web application pages that have code in them differs slightly because of where all additional files are located and the URL to access these files.

The Web root folder for your application varies depending on the Web platform you choose and what your ISP dictates as the Web root. You want to create a directory in your Web root folder for each Web application you build.

Table 1-1 lists the default Web root folder and base URLs for each combination of Web platforms and application servers.

Table 1-1	Default Web Root and Base URLs	
Web Server	*Default Web Root*	*Default Base URL*
Apache on Windows	`c:\apache\htdocs`	`http://localhost/`
Apache on Mac OS X	`/Users/UserName/Sites`	`http://localhost/~UserName/`
IIS	`c:\inetpub\wwwroot`	`http://localhost/`
ColdFusion	`c:\cfusionMX7\wwwroot`	`http://localhost:8500/`
Jakarta Tomcat on Windows	`c:\jakarta-tomcat-4.x.x\webapps\ROOT\`	`http://localhost:8080/`

For Apache on Mac OS X, the username is the short Macintosh username (which you define when you create a user account).

You can verify that you have the correct Web root setup by placing a sample file in the Web root directory and then navigating your browser to the base URL. An example of a test file is a file called `index.html` that contains the following:

```
<html>
<body>
Hello!
</body>
</html>
```

If you're running IIS and place the file in `c:\inetpub\wwwroot`, for example, you can access it from your Web browser at `http://localhost/index.html`.

Setting Up the Testing Server in Dreamweaver

The Testing Server category in the Advanced Site Definition dialog box tells Dreamweaver how to process the Web application pages locally while you're developing them. Often, you simply use a local directory if you're using a server technology that your local Web platform can process, such as IIS/ASP on Windows or Apache/PHP on Mac OSX.

Here's how to set up the Testing Server category:

1. **Choose Site⇨Manage Site.**

   The Manage Site dialog box appears.

2. **Select your site from the list and click the Edit button.**

   If you need to create a site from scratch, see Book I, Chapter 3.

3. **Click the Advanced tab at the top of the dialog box.**

4. **Click the Testing Server category on the left side of the Site Definition dialog box.**

   This screen starts out with only two drop-down lists, for the server model and the remote access type, as shown in Figure 1-4.

5. **Pick the server technology from the Server Model drop-down list.**

   Your choices are

   • ASP JavaScript

   • ASP VBScript

   • ASP.NET C#

   • ASP.NET VB

- ColdFusion
- JSP
- PHP MySQL

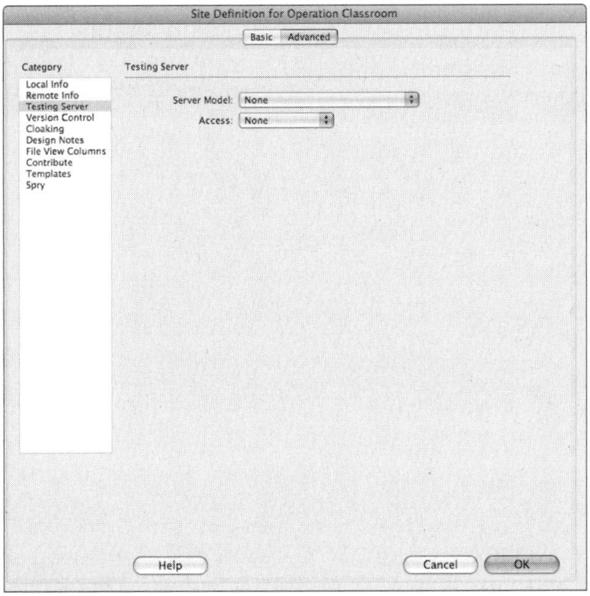

Figure 1-4:
Fill in the
Testing
Server
category for
your site.

6. **Select how to get your files from your local computer to your remote site from the Access drop-down list.**

   Your selections include

   - None
   - FTP
   - Local/Network
   - WebDAV

   In most testing cases, you'll want to use Local/Network (see Figure 1-5).

7. **In the URL Prefix field, enter the URL path that your testing server uses to publish the pages.**

   If this is on your local machine, it looks like `http://localhost/myapp` (where `myapp` is the specific directory for your app. If it's on a remote server, the URL path includes the full domain name, such as `http://www.example.com/myapp`.

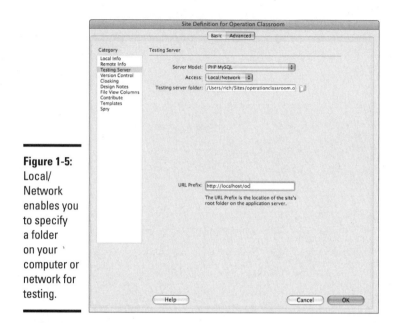

Site Definition for Operation Classroom

Basic | Advanced

Category	Testing Server
Local Info	
Remote Info	Server Model: PHP MySQL
Testing Server	Access: Local/Network
Version Control	Testing server folder: /Users/rich/Sites/operationclassroom.o
Cloaking	
Design Notes	
File View Columns	
Contribute	
Templates	
Spry	

URL Prefix: http://localhost/oc

The URL Prefix is the location of the site's
root folder on the application server.

Help   Cancel   OK

Figure 1-5:
Local/
Network
enables you
to specify
a folder
on your
computer or
network for
testing.

Dreamweaver assumes, by default, that both the Web server and application server are running on the same system. Therefore, if you specify a remote location (see Book V, Chapter 3), Dreamweaver assumes that the testing server is the same URL. If you don't enter a remote category, Dreamweaver makes sure that the default testing server matches the local folder.

8. **Click OK to save your changes and begin using the new site.**

Introducing Databases

Perhaps the most common reason that many Web designers and developers have for using a Web application server is in order to dynamically pull data from a database and display it in a Web document.

A *database* (or *relational database*) is a collection of data organized in such a way that you can quickly add, retrieve, or modify the information. For example, Amazon.com and Facebook use enormous databases that enable users to search and navigate the immense amounts of data on their sites. Creating your own database is nothing more than putting data into a logical system that stores and retrieves related information.

The information in a database is organized into grid-like tables. Each table has multiple *fields* (or *columns*) and individual records in *rows.* For example, take a look at Table 1-2, the Employees table.

Table 1-2		Employees	
EmployeeID	*FirstName*	*LastName*	*Department*
697882	Max	Smart	Accounting
598066	Joe	Fox	Sales
596072	Kosmo	Kramer	Sales

At the top of the Employees table are the column (field) names: EmployeeID, FirstName, LastName, and Department. The three subsequent rows contain the individual records.

To extract your data correctly, you need to set up the relationships between pieces of data properly. Data has three kinds of relationships:

+ **One-to-one:** In a one-to-one relationship, each item is related to one and only one other item. In the Employees table, the Employee ID and the name of the employee have a one-to-one relationship. Each employee has one and only one ID number, and each ID number can belong to one and only one employee.

+ **One-to-many:** A one-to-many relationship has *keys* (unique identifiers) from one table that appear multiple times in another table. Say you have a Department table along with an Employees table. The Employees table has a one-to-many relationship with the Department table. A department (such as Accounting) can have many employees, but each employee can work in only one department.

+ **Many-to-many:** A many-to-many relationship means that two tables each have multiple keys from another table.

Your data should also conform to *normalization* rules (a series of progressively strict rules to help you build a well-designed database):

+ **First normal form:** For your database to be in first normal form, it must satisfy two requirements. First, every table must not have repeating columns that contain the same kind of data, and secondly, all columns must contain only one value.

+ **Second normal form:** Stricter than the first normal form, the second normal form requires that each field be based specifically on the key.

+ **Third normal form:** The third normal form expands on the second normal form by allowing no other column in the table except for the key column to define any other column.

If you're interested in delving deeper into the subject of databases, we recommend that you check out *Database Development For Dummies* by Allen G. Taylor (Wiley).

Choosing a Database

You have many relational database choices. Any of these databases work well with Dreamweaver:

+ **MySQL** (www.mysql.com): The open source MySQL is one of the most popular databases for Web apps. Many Web hosting providers provide support for it. You can also download it for free and run it on a Windows, Mac OS X, or Linux machine.

 Unless you want to go with a Microsoft-centric solution, MySQL is recommended for its quality, ease of use, and scalability.

+ **Microsoft Office Access** (www.microsoft.com/access): If you're just getting started and used to working with Microsoft Office apps, you may wish to consider using Access. It's good for establishing a small, simple database when you're not overly concerned about performance. It's also bundled with Microsoft Office, so it isn't very expensive (you may even already have it installed).

 Some Web hosting providers provide support for Microsoft Access databases.

+ **Microsoft SQL Server** (www.microsoft.com/sql): The popular Microsoft offering is SQL Server. Although it is more complex than other database choices, it has the power to handle a large quantity of requests from users of your Web site.

+ **PostgreSQL** (www.postgresql.org) is an open-source "object-relational" database that many Web hosts support. You can also download it to run on all major platforms, including Windows and Mac OS X.

After you choose the right database for your needs, consult your database system's documentation for details on how to create the database. Book VII, Chapters 2 through 6, gives you the details on setting up PHP, ASP, ASP.NET, JSP, and ColdFusion database connections in Dreamweaver.

Chapter 2: Configuring MySQL Database Connections for PHP

In This Chapter

✓ **Connecting to a MySQL database**

✓ **Adding a database connection**

✓ **Editing or deleting a database connection**

*I*f you've decided to go the open-source route and use PHP as your application server platform and MySQL for your database, this chapter is for you. (If you haven't set up PHP, see Book VII, Chapter 1 for details.) You'll find the discussion helpful whether you're working with a Web-hosted remote server or running PHP and MySQL on your local machine.

In this chapter, we show you how to connect to it and create a dynamic Web page with PHP in Dreamweaver CS4. Additionally, you find out how to set up a MySQL database connection and add, edit, or delete a connection.

However, before you begin, make sure that you have a Dreamweaver site created or opened that has the Remote Info and Testing Server settings filled in and operational. Dreamweaver needs this info to connect to the database.

Adding a PHP Database Connection

To create a database connection in PHP to access a MySQL database, you need to create a new dynamic PHP page. The database connection enables Dreamweaver to interact with the database using database connections through PHP. Dreamweaver automatically adds code specific to your dynamic page type to your new dynamic page when creating a database connection.

Creating a new dynamic PHP page

To create a new dynamic PHP page in Dreamweaver, follow these steps:

1. **Choose File⇨New.**

   The New Document window opens, as shown in Figure 2-1.

2. **Click the PHP icon in the Page Type list.**

3. **Optionally, choose a Layout from the list.**

   For now, feel free to leave <none> selected in the Layout column.

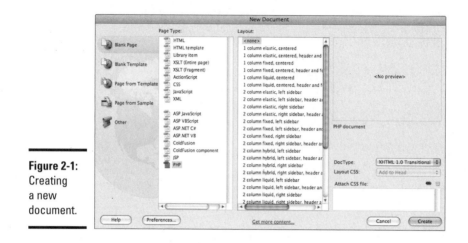

Figure 2-1:
Creating
a new
document.

4. **Select a Document Type (DTD) from the DocType drop-down list.**

   This setting makes your page XHTML-compliant. Select the default, XHTML 1.0 Transitional.

5. **Click Create.**

   A new dynamic PHP page is created, as seen in Figure 2-2.

Figure 2-2:
A new PHP
document is
ready to go.

Creating the database connection for PHP

After you create a new dynamic PHP page (as described in the preceding steps), you can connect to the database. I'll show you how to connect to an existing MySQL database in this section. However, if you'd like info on how to get started with MySQL databases, check out www.mysql.com.

Connect to an existing MySQL database by following these steps:

1. **Choose Window⇨Databases to open the Databases panel.**

The Databases panel opens. If you have a site open and a testing server configured, each of the steps is checked, as shown in Figure 2-3.

Figure 2-3:
The Databases panel before defining a database connection.

2. **Click the plus (+) button, and, from the drop-down list that appears, select MySQL Connection.**

The MySQL Connection dialog box opens, as shown in Figure 2-4.

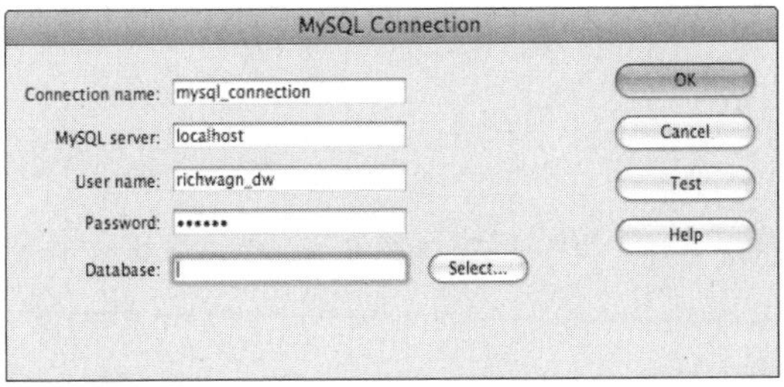

Figure 2-4:
The MySQL Connection dialog box.

3. **Enter a name for the database connection in the Connection Name field.**

Dreamweaver uses this name to reference your database connection. The name can contain only letters, numbers, and underscores.

4. **Enter the host name or IP address of the database server in the MySQL Server field.**

   This may be a host name or IP address.

   If the MySQL server resides on the same system as the Web or application server, reference it locally with the host name `localhost`. This value applies even if you are connecting to a remote server.

5. **Enter the username for the database in the User Name field.**

   MySQL enables you to create users and assign permissions in its Web-based control panel. See your MySQL control panel if you need to set up a user.

6. **Enter the corresponding password in the Password field.**

7. **Click the Select button.**

   If your settings are correct to this point, the Select Database dialog box opens with available databases, as shown in Figure 2-5.

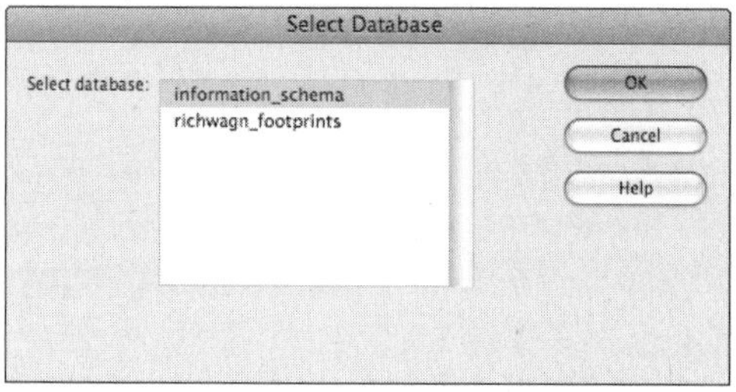

Figure 2-5:
The Select
Database
dialog box.

If you are using a Web hosting provider and receive an error, check to make sure that MySQL is configured to allow external IP connections. The exact instructions will depend on your particular Web host.

8. **Select your database from the list and then click OK.**

   The Select Database dialog box closes, and the name of the database you selected appears in the Database field of the MySQL Connection dialog box.

9. **Click the Test button to confirm that your connection is set up properly.**

   An alert box tells you whether the connection was successful.

10. **Click OK to close the alert box.**

11. **Click OK to close the MySQL Connection dialog box.**

    Dreamweaver creates the database connection (see Figure 2-6).

You can then click down on the outline structure to display Stored Procedures, Tables, and Views (see Figure 2-7).

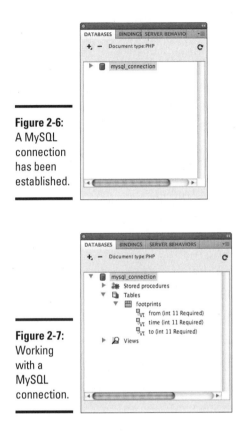

Figure 2-6:
A MySQL
connection
has been
established.

Figure 2-7:
Working
with a
MySQL
connection.

Editing a PHP Database Connection

Just in case you change the password for your database connection or the address of your database server changes, you need to know how to update your MySQL database connection settings.

To edit a MySQL database connection in PHP, follow these steps:

1. **Click the Databases tab of the Application panel.**

2. **Right-click the database connection you want to edit.**

3. **Select Edit Connection.**

   The MySQL Connection dialog box opens.

4. **Edit the connection properties as necessary.**

5. **Click the Test button to confirm that your connection is properly set up.**

   An alert box tells you whether the connection was successful.

6. **Click OK to close the alert box.**

7. **Click OK to close the MySQL Connection dialog box.**

   Dreamweaver saves your changes to the database connection.

Deleting a PHP Database Connection

To delete a MySQL database connection in PHP, follow these steps:

1. **Open the Databases tab of the Application panel.**

2. **Right-click the database connection you want to delete.**

   A list of options appears.

3. **Choose Delete Connection.**

   An alert box appears to confirm your deletion.

4. **Click Yes.**

   The database connection is deleted and removed from the list of connections on the Databases tab in the Application panel.

Deleting the database connection deletes a PHP file that Dreamweaver created in a Connections directory in your local directory. The directory itself remains. You can delete this directory if you want to keep your directory uncluttered.

Chapter 3: Configuring ASP Database Connections

In This Chapter

✔ Gathering database connection information

✔ Adding a database connection

✔ Connecting to a remote database

✔ Editing or deleting a database connection

*I*n this chapter, we show you how to set up a database connection in ASP (Active Server Pages) using Dreamweaver. You find out how to add, edit, and delete a database connection and connect to a remote database.

However, before you begin, make sure you have the details on connecting to your database. To make a connection in ASP to a database, here is what you need to know:

✦ The type of database you're connecting to (for example, SQL Server or Oracle)

✦ The host name of the database server, or the IP address if no host name is available

✦ The username and password to access your database

✦ The name of the database to which you are trying to connect, or the Data Source Name (DSN)

Before starting, you need to have a site opened with a valid testing server setup, either on your local computer or a remote server. See Book I, Chapter 3 for more information.

Understanding ASP Database Connections

Dreamweaver offers two ways to connect to a database when using ASP:

✦ **Data Source Name (DSN):** The DSN is a setting configured on your application server that contains the information needed to connect to your database. ASP then connects through the DSN instead of connecting directly from ASP. The advantage of using a DSN is that it's simpler than setting up the OLE DB (Object Linking and Embedding, Database) driver, described next.

✦ **Custom connection string:** To set up a custom connection string, you enter information about your database server, and ASP uses that information to connect directly to your database. Connecting directly to a database requires ASP to run a small program called a *driver,* which enables ASP to speak directly with your database. Because this *OLE DB* driver talks directly to the database, it's faster than other drivers but requires a few extra steps (such as downloading and installing the driver).

OLE DB drivers are available for download from the provider of the database. For example, Microsoft supplies Access and SQL Server OLE DB drivers as part of its MDAC download at www.microsoft.com/down loads/details.aspx?FamilyID=6c050fe3-c795-4b7d-b037-185d0506396c&displaylang=en.

To download OLE DB drivers for Oracle databases, visit www.oracle. com/technology/software/tech/windows/ole_db/index.html. These packages come with installers that guide you through the process of installing the OLE DB driver on your computer.

If your Web hosting provider supports ASP, you can connect to an ODBC DSN provided on their server.

Before you can create an ASP database connection, you have to create a new dynamic ASP page. Creating a new dynamic ASP page enables Dreamweaver to interact with the database using database connections through ASP.

Creating a New ASP Page

To create a new dynamic ASP page, follow these steps:

1. **Choose File⇨New.**

The New Document window appears, as shown in Figure 3-1.

2. **Select ASP JavaScript or ASP VBScript from the Page Type list.**

This selection is based on the type of scripting enabled on your server. For this example, we select ASP JavaScript.

3. **Optionally, select a layout style from the Layout list.**

We leave <none> selected in this example.

4. **Select a document type definition (DTD) from the DocType drop-down list.**

This setting makes your page XHTML-compliant. Select the default option, which is XHTML 1.0 Transitional.

5. **Click Create.**

A new dynamic ASP page is created.

After you create a new dynamic ASP page, you can establish the database connection.

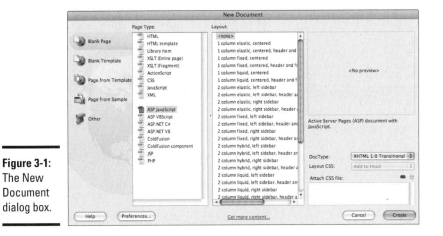

Figure 3-1:
The New
Document
dialog box.

Connecting to a Database with a Data Source Name (DSN)

To create a database connection in ASP through a DSN, follow these steps:

1. **Choose Window⇨Database to open the Databases panel, as shown in Figure 3-2.**

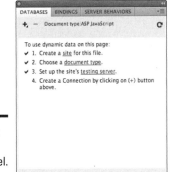

Figure 3-2:
The Data-
bases panel.

2. **Click the plus (+) button; in the drop-down list that appears, select Data Source Name (DSN).**

The Data Source Name (DSN) dialog box opens, as shown in Figure 3-3.

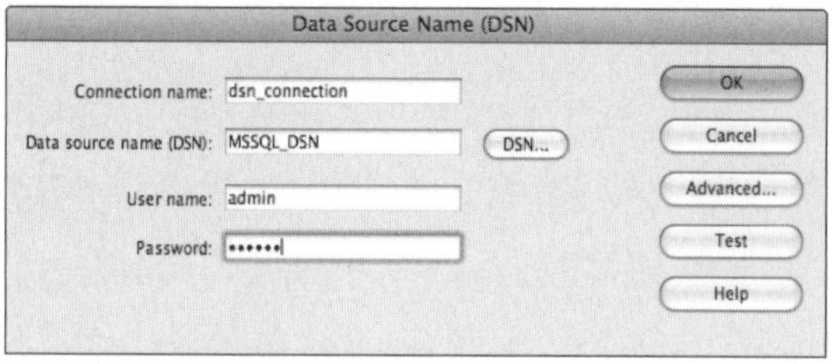

Figure 3-3:
The Data
Source
Name (DSN)
dialog box.

Data Source Name (DSN)

Connection name:	dsn_connection	OK
Data source name (DSN):	MSSQL_DSN	DSN... Cancel
User name:	admin	Advanced...
Password:	••••••	Test
		Help

3. **Enter a name for the new database connection in the Connection Name field.**

   Dreamweaver uses this name to reference your database connection. The name can contain only letters, numbers, and the underscore character: No other characters are permitted.

4. **Enter the username for the database in the User Name field.**

   The server's administrator should provide this information.

5. **Enter the corresponding password in the Password field.**

   The password goes with the username from the previous step.

6. **Click the DSN button.**

   The Select ODBC DSN dialog box appears.

7. **Select the Data Source Name (DSN) of your database from the Select ODBC DSN list, and then click OK.**

   The Select ODBC DSN dialog box closes, and the name of the selected DSN appears in the Data Source Name (DSN) field of the Data Source Name (DSN) dialog box.

8. **Click the Test button to confirm your settings.**

   An alert box tells you whether the connection was made successfully. The two most common causes of an error are an incorrect username and password. Try connecting to the database using the client that's supplied with the database. This verifies that you have the correct user, password, and database names.

9. **Click OK to close the alert box, and then click OK once more to close the Data Source Name (DSN) dialog box.**

   The database connection is created, and it's listed on the Databases panel (see Figure 3-4).

Figure 3-4:
The Data-
bases
panel with
the newly
created
database
connection.

Connecting to a Database with a Custom Connection String

To create a database connection in ASP through a custom connection string, follow these steps:

1. **Open the Databases panel by choosing Window⇨Databases.**

2. **Click the plus (+) button and then select Custom Connection String from the drop-down list that appears.**

   The Custom Connection String dialog box opens, as shown in Figure 3-5.

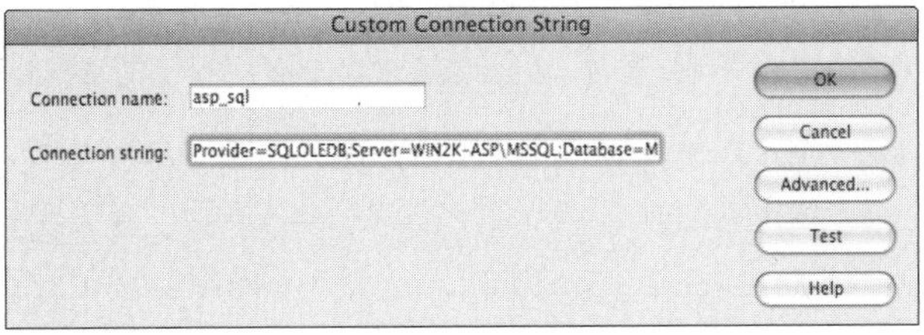

Book VII
Chapter 3

Configuring
ASP Database
Connections

Figure 3-5:
Custom
Connection
String
dialog box.

3. **Enter a name for the database connection in the Connection Name field.**

   Dreamweaver uses this name to reference your database connection. The name can only contain letters, numbers, and the underscore character: No other characters are permitted.

4. **Enter a connection string for your database in the Connection String field.**

For example, suppose that you want to connect to a database named Thor on an SQL server named Poseidon, with the username dbadmin and a password of pass. The connection string would look like this:

```
Provider=SQLOLEDB;Server=Poseidon;Database=Thor;UID=dbadmin;PWD=pass
```

To connect to Oracle, you use the same connection string as in the previous example, except you use the following Provider value:

```
Provider=OraOLEDB;
```

To connect to an Access database file, the connection string looks something like this, depending on the location of the file:

```
Driver={Microsoft Access Driver (*.mdb)};DBQ=d:\inetpub\wwwroot\data\
    myaccessdb.mdb
```

DBQ= specifies the path to the Access database file on the hosting server where it resides. Although this connection string lacks some of the fields, it's still a complete, valid connection string. Because we didn't specify the provider, Dreamweaver defaults to the ODBC driver.

5. **Click the Test button to confirm your settings.**

   An alert box tells you whether the connection was successful.

6. **Click OK in the alert box.**

   The alert box closes, and the Custom Connection String dialog box appears.

7. **Click OK to close the Custom Connection String dialog box.**

   Dreamweaver creates the new database connection and lists it on the Databases panel.

Connecting to a Remote Database without a DSN

More than likely, you're planning to host your site with a commercial ISP or hosting provider. If your ISP provides a DSN, connecting to the database works the same as in the preceding steps. However, many hosting providers don't provide a DSN to connect to a remote ODBC database, so you may have to specify the ODBC connection details without a DSN.

To set up a custom connection string to access a remote database, you need to know the *physical path* to your database file.

Understanding physical paths and virtual paths

When you upload your pages to a Web server using Dreamweaver, they're placed in a folder on the Web server just like when you copy files from one place to another on your own computer. For example, if you upload your pages to a Web server running Microsoft IIS, your files may be placed in the following directory:

```
d:\inetpub\wwwroot\
```

If your home page file was named `index.htm`, the *physical path* to your home page would be

```
d:\inetpub\wwwroot\index.htm
```

When you use your Web browser to visit a Web site, however, you don't type the physical path. Instead, you enter the URL:

```
http://example.com/index.htm
```

This URL helps you access the `index.htm` page. The piece of the URL that follows the Web site name is the *virtual path.* In this example, the virtual path is `index.htm`.

When a Web site is configured on a Web server, the server is instructed to point all requests for a particular virtual path to a corresponding physical path. In the preceding example, all requests for pages located at `http://example.com/rich` are transparently fulfilled with the files in the physical path: `d:\inetpub\wwwroot\rich`.

Finding the database's physical path when you know the virtual path

If you need to know the physical path to your database, but only have the virtual path, you're in luck. The ASP method `MapPath()` allows you to feed a virtual path and get back the corresponding physical path. Follow these steps to use `MapPath()` to retrieve a physical path:

1. **Create a new ASP document based on the instructions in the "Creating a New ASP Page" section previously in this chapter.**

2. **Click the Code button on the Document toolbar to switch to Code view.**

The Document window displays the code for your page.

3. **Enter the following ASP code inside the document body:**

```
<% Response.Write(Server.MapPath("/virtualpath/fileinpath")) %>
```

Replace `virtualpath` with the site's virtual path, and replace `filein path` with the name of a file in the directory. If you're just looking for the physical path of the site's root directory, simply enter a forward slash (/) in the quotes.

4. **Click the Design button to switch to Design view.**

The Document window displays your page with the ASP code hidden.

5. **Click the Live Data button.**

Dreamweaver displays the physical path, which corresponds with the virtual path you entered in the ASP code snippet.

Connecting to a remote database with a virtual path

Using a virtual path to connect to your file-based database actually calls a command on your remote server to look up the physical path. The command string used is determined by your ASP server's scripting language, either JavaScript or VBScript. You need to create a custom connection string to connect to the remote database without using a DSN.

For JavaScript, your custom connection string looks like this:

```
"Driver={Microsoft Access Driver (*.mdb)};DBQ=" + Server.MapPath("/virtualpath/
    databasefile.mdb")
```

For VBScript, your custom connection string looks like this:

```
"Driver={Microsoft Access Driver (*.mdb)};DBQ=" & Server.MapPath("/virtualpath/
    databasefile.mdb")
```

In either case, replace `virtualpath` with the site's virtual path and replace `databasefile.mdb` with the name of the database file in the directory.

To prevent a user from downloading your entire database, always place your .mdb database files in a directory that isn't in your Web root.

To set up a database connection using the custom connection string, follow the steps in "Connecting to a Database with a Custom Connection String," earlier in this chapter. In Step 4, use the custom connection string you just created.

Editing an ASP Database Connection

Sometimes after you set up a database connection, some of the connection details may change. For example, the server that hosts the database could change, or you might select a new password for the database. To edit an ASP database connection in Dreamweaver to reflect these changes, follow these steps:

1. **In the Databases panel, right-click the database connection you want to edit and choose Edit Connection from the drop-down list that appears.**

   The Custom Connection String or Data Source Name dialog box opens, depending on which type of connection you're editing.

2. **Edit the connection properties as necessary.**

3. **Click the Test button to confirm your settings.**

   An alert box tells you whether the connection was made successfully.

4. **Click OK to close the alert box, and click OK once more to close the connection dialog box.**

   Dreamweaver saves your changes to the database connection.

Deleting an ASP Database Connection

To delete an ASP database connection in Dreamweaver, follow these steps:

1. **On the Databases panel, right-click the database connection you want to delete and choose Delete Connection from the drop-down list that appears.**

   An alert box appears to confirm the deletion.

2. **Click Yes to confirm the deletion.**

   The database connection is deleted and removed from the list of connections on the Databases panel.

Chapter 4: Configuring ASP.NET Database Connections

In This Chapter

✔ **Gathering database connection information**

✔ **Adding a database connection**

✔ **Editing or deleting a database connection**

A SP.NET is another application server platform that you can use inside Dreamweaver to connect to your remote or local database. In this chapter, we show you how to set up a database connection in ASP.NET using Dreamweaver CS4.

To make a connection in ASP.NET to a database, you need to gather the necessary information about your database, including

+ Type of database you are connecting to (for example, SQL Server, Access, or Oracle)

+ Host name of the database server, or the IP address if no host name is available

+ Username and password to access your database

+ Name of the database to which you are trying to connect: in the case of a file-based database such as Access, the location of the database file

Make sure you have a site open and the test server configured before continuing. (See Book VII, Chapter 1 for details.)

Exploring ASP.NET Database Connections

Dreamweaver offers two ways to connect to a database using ASP.NET:

+ **OLE DB connection:** With this method, you enter the information about your database server, and ASP.NET uses that information to connect directly to your database. Connecting directly to a database requires ASP.NET to run a driver program to be able to speak directly with your specific type of database. Because the *OLE DB* driver talks directly to the database, it's fast.

OLE DB drivers are available for download from the provider of the database. For example, Microsoft supplies Access and SQL Server OLE DB drivers as part of its MDAC download at `www.microsoft.com/down loads/details.aspx?FamilyID=6c050fe3-c795-4b7d-b037-185d0506396c&displaylang=en`.

To download OLE DB drivers for Oracle databases, visit `www.oracle.com/technology/software/tech/windows/ole_db/index.html`. These packages come with installers that guide you through the process of installing the OLE DB driver on your computer.

If your ISP supports ASP.NET, you may be able to connect to an ODBC DSN provided on their server.

✦ **SQL Server connection:** This setting is specific to connecting with MS SQL Server databases. The SQL Server connection option is nearly identical to the OLE DB connection option for MS SQL Server, except that you don't have to give Dreamweaver a Provider value in the SQL Server connection option.

Go ahead and create an SQL Server connection if using SQL Server; otherwise, create an OLE DB database connection. Before you create an ASP.NET database connection, you must first create a new dynamic ASP.NET page. Creating a new dynamic ASP.NET page enables Dreamweaver to interact with the database using database connections through ASP.NET.

Creating a New ASP.NET Page

To create a new dynamic ASP.NET page, follow these steps:

1. **Choose File⇨New.**

   The New Document window opens.

2. **Select ASP.NET C# or ASP.NET VBScript from the Page Type list.**

   This selection is based on your preference or the type of scripting available on your server.

3. **Select a document type definition (DTD) from the DocType drop-down list.**

   This setting makes your page XHTML-compliant. Select the default option, which is XHTML 1.0 Transitional.

4. **Click Create.**

   A new ASP.NET page is created and ready for scripting.

After you create a new dynamic ASP.NET page, you can establish the database connection. You can create an OLE DB connection using either the templates or data link properties, which we cover in the next section. An alternative to connect to an SQL Server database is through the method provided in the Microsoft .NET Framework, which we discuss later in the chapter in the section titled, "Building an SQL Server connection."

Building an OLE DB Connection

OLE DB serves as a good all-around choice for ASP.NET developers, regardless of the database you are connecting to.

If you are using SQL Server, you can use either OLE DB or the dedicated connection discussed in the following section.

Using templates

To use a template to create an OLE DB connection in ASP.NET, follow these steps:

1. **Open the Databases panel by choosing Window⇨Databases.**

2. **Click the plus (+) button and select OLE DB Connection from the drop-down list.**

The OLE DB Connection dialog box opens.

3. **Enter a name for the database connection in the Connection Name field.**

Dreamweaver uses this name to reference your database connection. The name can only contain letters, numbers, or an underscore: No other characters are permitted.

4. **Click the Templates button.**

The Connection String Template dialog box appears.

5. **Select your database type from the Select Template list and then click OK.**

The Connection String Template dialog box closes, and the template for the database type you selected appears in the Connection String text box in the OLE DB Connection dialog box.

You can skip Steps 6 and 7 if you selected the UDL file template.

6. **Enter the user ID for the database by replacing the [*username*] text with the username provided to access your database.**

Do not include the square brackets when entering the username. Remember to end the line with a semicolon.

Book VII
Chapter 4

Configuring ASP.
NET Database
Connections

Most ISPs with hosted databases provide a page for you to view your database username and password. If not, contact the person who supports the database for the username and password.

7. **Enter the password for the database by replacing the text [*password*] with the password provided to access your database.**

   Do not include the square brackets when entering the password, and be sure the line ends with a semicolon.

   The UDL file template doesn't require this step.

8. **Modify the remainder of the template values using the settings detailed in Table 4-1.**

   Table 4-1 provides you with details on the values to enter for each connection string template.

Table 4-1	OLE DB Connection Settings	
Template Name	**Database Type**	**Properties**

Oracle (Microsoft Provider)	Oracle	`Provider=MSDAORA;`
		`Data`
		`Source=[OracleInstanceName];`
		`User ID=[username];`
		`Password=[password];`

Oracle (Oracle Provider)	Oracle	`Provider=OraOLEDB.Oracle;`
		`User ID=[username];`
		`Password=[password];`
		`Data`
		`Source=[OracleInstanceName];`

Microsoft SQL Server	Microsoft SQL Server	`Provider=SQLOLEDB.1;`
		`Persist Security Info=False;`
		`Data Source=[serverName];`
		`Initial`
		`Catalog=[databaseName];`
		`User ID=[username];`
		`Password=[password];`

Microsoft Access 97 (Microsoft Jet 3.5 Provider)	Microsoft Access	`Provider=Microsoft.Jet.`
		`OLEDB.3.5;`
		`Data Source=[databaseName];`
		`User ID=[username];`
		`Password=[password];`

Template Name	Database Type	Properties
Microsoft Access 2000 (Microsoft Jet 4.0 Provider)	Microsoft Access	`Provider=Microsoft.Jet.` `OLEDB.4.0;` `Data Source=[databaseName];` `User ID=[username];` `Password=[password];`
UDL file		`File Name=[filename]`

9. **Click the Test button to confirm that your connection is properly set up.**

An alert box informs you whether the connection was successful. The two most common causes of an error are incorrect usernames and passwords. Try connecting to the database using the client that's supplied with the database. This verifies that you have the correct user, password, and database names.

10. **Click OK to close the alert box, and then click OK to close the OLE DB Connection dialog box.**

The database connection is created.

Using data link properties

To enter data link properties to create an OLE DB connection in ASP.NET, follow these steps:

1. **In the Databases panel, click the plus (+) button, and select OLE DB Connection from the drop-down list.**

2. **Click the Build button in the OLE DB Connection dialog box that appears.**

The Data Link Properties dialog box appears.

3. **On the Provider tab, select the appropriate Microsoft OLE DB Provider for your database type.**

Most applications use a provider beginning with "Microsoft OLE DB Provider for."

4. **On the Connection tab, enter the connection information for your database.**

The database server administrator provides this information.

5. **Click the Test Connection button to confirm that your connection is properly set up.**

An alert box tells you whether the connection was successful.

6. **Click OK to close the alert box, and then click OK to close the OLE DB Connection dialog box.**

   You are connected to the database.

Building an SQL Server Connection

Many ASP.NET developers use SQL Server as their database backend. As a result, the SQL Server database connection has its own connection type.

To create a .NET SQL Server database connection in ASP.NET, follow these steps:

1. **In the Databases panel, click the plus (+) button and select SQL Server Connection from the drop-down list that appears.**

2. **Enter a name for the database connection in the Connection Name field.**

   Dreamweaver uses this name to reference your database connection. The name can only consist of letters, numbers, or an underscore: No other characters are allowed.

3. **In the Connection String field, build a connection string for your database.**

   For example, to connect to a database named Thor on an SQL server named Poseidon, with the username dbadmin and a password of pass, the connection string would be

   ```
   Persist Security Info=False;Data Source=Poseidon;Initial
         Catalog=Thor;User ID=dbadmin;Password=pass;
   ```

   The Persist Security Info parameter tells the ASP.NET functions to forget the password after using it to log in instead of keeping it in memory.

4. **Click the Test button to confirm that your connection is properly set up.**

   An alert box tells you whether the connection was successful.

5. **Click OK to close the alert box, and then click OK to close the SQL Server Connection dialog box.**

   The database connection is created.

Editing an ASP.NET Database Connection

If you need to edit an ASP.NET database connection, follow these steps:

1. **In the Databases panel, right-click the database connection you want to edit and choose Edit Connection from the drop-down list that appears.**

The OLE DB Connection or SQL Server Connection dialog box appears, depending on which database connection type you're editing.

2. **Edit the connection properties as necessary.**

3. **Click the Test button to confirm that your connection is set up properly.**

4. **Click OK to close the alert box that appears, and then click OK to close the connection dialog box.**

The connection has been edited.

Deleting an ASP.NET Database Connection

To delete an ASP.NET database connection in Dreamweaver, follow these steps:

1. **In the Databases panel, right-click the database connection you want to delete and choose Delete Connection from the drop-down list that appears.**

An alert box appears to confirm that you want to delete the selected connection.

2. **Click Yes to close the alert box.**

The database connection is deleted and removed from the list of connections in the Databases panel.

**Book VII
Chapter 4**

Configuring ASP.
NET Database
Connections

Chapter 5: Configuring JSP Database Connections

In This Chapter

✔ Gathering database connection information

✔ Adding a database connection

✔ Connecting to a remote database

✔ Editing or deleting a database connection

*J*avaServer Pages (JSP) is a popular Java-based application server technology used to create dynamic Web pages. This chapter shows you how to create a database connection for your JSP pages and edit or delete the connection after you create it. You also find out what you need to know about the option settings that you're likely to use for this connection.

Before you begin, be sure that you have a site opened and have the test server configured. (See Book VII, Chapter 1 for instructions.)

Gathering Database Connection Information

Dreamweaver enables you to connect to a variety of databases by modifying the database driver and *connection string* (URL) for each type of database. Before you can set up a connection to your database, make sure that you have the following information on hand:

✦ The location of the database server as a host name or an IP address. If the database resides on the same machine as the application server, this could be `localhost`.

✦ The database username.

✦ The database password.

✦ The name of the database instance. Because a database can host several distinct groups of tables, the instance provides a way to indicate which set of tables to use.

If your database resides on your own server, you must download the Java JDBC driver from the database vendor site (such as Oracle or IBM). If you don't download the driver, when you try to connect to the database, you receive a Java error that the connection method is missing.

Adding a JSP Database Connection

JSP pages use a standard interface for connecting to databases called Java Database Connectivity (JDBC) drivers. The JDBC driver for your database translates the information traveling between your JSP program and your database, enabling the two to communicate with one another.

Dreamweaver offers six different drivers for connecting to a database in JSP through JDBC, as well as an option for creating a custom JDBC connection. Here are Dreamweaver's built-in JSP database connection types:

✦ Custom JDBC Connection

✦ IBM DB2 App Driver (DB2)

✦ IBM DB2 Net Driver (DB2)

✦ MySQL Driver (MySQL)

✦ Oracle Thin Driver (Oracle)

✦ Inet Driver (SQLServer)

✦ Sun JDBC-ODBC Driver (ODBC Database)

For the first option, Custom JDBC Connection, you enter all the necessary information to create the custom database connection. For the rest of the database types, Dreamweaver fills in the appropriate driver name and provides a URL template that you can replace with the information for your database. Table 5-1 shows the driver and URL fields for Dreamweaver's database connection types. Each of these drivers corresponds to a specific database.

Table 5-1	Database Connection Types and Their Respective Drivers and URLs	
Database	*Driver*	*Connection URL*
Custom JDBC Connection	Custom	Custom
IBM DB2 App Driver (DB2)	COM.ibm. db2.jdbc.app. DB2Driver	`jdbc:db2:[database name]`
IBM DB2 Net Driver (DB2)	COM.ibm. db2.jdbc.net. DB2Driver	`jdbc:db2://[host name]: [server port]/[database name]`
MySQL Driver (MySQL)	org.gjt.mm.mysql. Driver	`jdbc:mysql://[host name]/ [database name]`

Database	Driver	Connection URL
Oracle Thin Driver (Oracle)	oracle. jdbc.driver. OracleDriver	`jdbc:oracle:thin: @[host name]:[port]:[sid]`
Inet Driver (SQLServer)	com.inet.tds. TdsDriver	`jdbc:inetdae:[host name]: [port]?database=[database]`
Sun JDBC-ODBC Driver (ODBC Database)	sun.jdbc.odbc. JdbcOdbcDriver	`jdbc:odbc:[odbc dsn`

When you create a JSP connection to your database, replace the `[host name]` and `[database name]` shown in Table 5-1 with your database's values. For example, if you're creating a connection to a local MySQL database named `test`, use the following connection URL:

`jdbc:mysql://127.0.0.1/test`

Java Runtime Environment installation

You must have the Java SE (JRE) installed prior to using a JDBC driver. Visit Sun's site at `http://java.sun.com/javase` if you haven't installed the JRE.

If you're deploying your code to a remote server, be sure that the JDBC driver is installed there too, or your application won't work when you upload it.

Installing the JDBC driver

Although Dreamweaver includes everything you need to use the Java JDBC driver classes for several databases, it doesn't include the code for the JDBC drivers.

To install the appropriate JDBC driver for your database, follow these steps:

1. **Download the Java .jar file for your database.**

Java packages are distributed as .jar files. See Table 5-2 to find out where to download the file you need.

Table 5-2	JDBC Database Driver Download Locations	
Database	*Driver*	*Web Site*
IBM DB2 App/ Net Driver	COM.ibm.db2.jdbc.app. DB2Driver	www-306.ibm.com/ software/data/ db2/express/down load.html
MySQL Driver Connector/J	org.gjt.mm.mysql.Driver	www.mysql.com/ products/ connector/j/
Oracle Thin Driver	oracle.jdbc.driver. OracleDriver	www.oracle.com/ technology/soft ware/tech/java/ sqlj_jdbc/ htdocs/jdbc_10201. html
Inet Driver (i-net Gate)	com.inet.tds.TdsDriver	www.inetsoftware. de/Download.htm

You can also go to Sun's JDBC Data Access API Drivers page at http:// developers.sun.com/product/jdbc/drivers for more.

2. **Copy the Java .jar file to the configuration/JDBCDrivers subdirectory under the Dreamweaver CS4 install directory.**

3. **Restart Dreamweaver.**

After you install the database driver, you can create a dynamic page and the database connection in JSP, as described in the next section.

Creating a New JSP Document

Because pages that work with a database are dynamic, Dreamweaver requires you to create a dynamic page before you can add a database connection.

Follow these steps to create a new dynamic JSP page:

1. **Choose File⇨New.**

   The New Document window appears.

2. **Select JSP from the Page Type list.**

3. **Select a document type definition (DTD) from the DocType drop-down list.**

   Accept the default XHTML 1.0 Transitional setting to create an XHTML-compliant page.

4. Click Create.

Your new JSP page is ready to use.

Dreamweaver allows you to add a database connection now that the dynamic JSP page exists.

Connecting to a Database

After you create a dynamic JSP page (as described in the previous section), follow these steps to create a database connection in JSP:

1. Open the Databases panel by choosing Window⇨Databases.

2. Click the plus (+) button and select a database connection type from the drop-down list.

You can choose from the database types listed in Table 5-1. After you make a selection, a connection dialog box named for the type of connection appears. The Driver and URL fields are prefilled for all the standard database driver types. The fields in the custom connection dialog box are all blank.

3. Enter a database connection name in the Connection Name field.

Dreamweaver CS4 uses this name to reference your database connection. The name can have letters, numbers, or an underscore. No other characters are allowed.

4. Enter the JDBC database driver in the Driver field.

The field is prepopulated for every database type except the Custom JDBC Database. If you're setting up a custom connection, you can usually find the Java class name in the driver's documentation. The class name tells Dreamweaver what Java code to call to access the database. For example, using the MySQL driver, the class name is `org.gjt. mm.mysql.Driver`.

If you're using a JDBC driver, you should have already downloaded it. If you click the Test button and you get a `Class not found` alert, you need to download the class. See Table 5-2 for a list of download locations.

5. In the URL field, replace the bracketed values with the information for your database.

If you're creating a custom connection, refer to the documentation that came with your JDBC driver for the format of this connection string.

The URL field contains all the information required to log in to the database in one long string. For example, for the MySQL driver, it lists the following URL:

```
jdbc:mysql://[hostname]/[database name]
```

In this example, replace the bracketed values [*hostname*] and [*data base name*] with the information for your database.

6. **Enter the database username in the User Name field.**

The server's administrator should provide this information.

7. **Enter the database password in the Password field.**

The password goes with the username from the previous step.

8. **Choose the Using Driver on This Machine radio button.**

This setting determines if the local machine or the remote application server's driver is used to connect to the database. If you're running Mac OS X, you can ignore this setting because Mac OS X computers always use the remote application server to connect.

9. **Click the Test button to confirm that your connection is set up correctly.**

A dialog box confirms a successful connection or displays an error message if it couldn't connect.

If you received a Class was not found error message when you clicked the Test button, you don't have the driver installed for that type of database. Download the Java package that corresponds to the type of database driver. Refer again to Table 5-2, which lists where to find popular drivers on the Internet.

10. **Click OK in the Connection Test dialog box.**

The dialog box closes.

11. **Click OK.**

Dreamweaver creates the database, and the database connection dialog box closes.

JDBC allows you to create an ODBC database connection with the Sun JDBC-ODBC driver using a Data Source Name (DSN). See Book VII, Chapter 3 for more information on using DSNs. You need to make sure that you've set up the DSN before you use it.

Editing a JSP Database Connection

Sometimes you need to go back to your database connection and make a change. Here's how to edit the JSP database connection in Dreamweaver:

1. **Open the Databases panel by choosing Window➪Databases.**

2. **Right-click the database connection you want to edit and select Edit Connection from the list that appears.**

The database connection dialog box opens.

3. **Edit the connection properties as necessary.**

4. **Click the Test button to confirm that your connection is set up correctly.**

5. **Click OK to close the alert box.**

6. **Click OK to close the database connection dialog box.**

   Dreamweaver saves the changes to your database connection.

Deleting a JSP Database Connection

Deleting database connections in Dreamweaver CS4 is similar to editing them. To delete a JSP database connection in Dreamweaver, follow these steps:

1. **Open the Databases panel by choosing Window⇨Databases.**

2. **Right-click the database connection you want to delete and select Delete Connection from the list that appears.**

   An alert box appears to confirm your deletion.

3. **Click Yes to close the alert box and delete the connection.**

   The database connection is deleted and removed from the list of connections on the Databases panel.

Chapter 6: Configuring ColdFusion Database Connections

In This Chapter

✔ **Pulling together database connection information**

✔ **Understanding how ColdFusion connects to databases**

✔ **Adding a database connection**

✔ **Editing or deleting a database connection**

ColdFusion is Adobe's application server technology. What is distinct about ColdFusion compared to other app servers is that it uses a tag-based approach to programming compared to scripts or more traditional programming syntax. As a result, Web designers with no previous programming experience can often pick up ColdFusion more quickly than other languages.

Some examples of ColdFusion applications include event registration, catalog searches, directories, calendars, and even interactive training. ColdFusion applications are moderately complex; they execute on the Web server as CGI scripts. In this chapter, we explain how to set up a database connection in ColdFusion using Dreamweaver. You also find out how to add, edit, and delete a database connection.

Pulling Together Database Connection Information

ColdFusion is highly flexible in its ability to connect to different types of data sources, especially databases. Although ColdFusion supports a wide array of database types, some key pieces of information to create a connection to a database are common among all the database types. To make a connection to a database in ColdFusion, you need to know the following information:

◆ Type of database you are connecting to (for example, SQL Server, Oracle, Access, and so on)

◆ Host name of the database server, or IP address if no host name is available

◆ Username and password to access your database

◆ Name or file location of the database to which you are trying to connect

Understanding How ColdFusion Connects to Databases

ColdFusion is designed to connect to databases at the server level, which means a database connection must be set up on the ColdFusion server itself. This task traditionally requires a ColdFusion administrator's assistance. After the connection is set up, your ColdFusion application can use it. This connection differs from other Web application platforms in that many other Web applications' database connections are created from within your Web application and don't require prior setup on the application server.

ColdFusion uses Java Database Connectivity (JDBC) to connect with databases. If you're unable to find an appropriate database driver included with ColdFusion, you can enter the JDBC driver information directly.

Although the design of how ColdFusion connects to databases has stayed consistent, newer versions of ColdFusion provide greater flexibility in configuring database connections than earlier versions. Specifically, you can create ColdFusion database connections within Dreamweaver directly on the ColdFusion server.

Adding a ColdFusion Database Connection

You can connect ColdFusion to a database a couple different ways, depending on which version of ColdFusion you're running. If you're running ColdFusion 8 or MX 7, you can set up the database connection within Dreamweaver. However, if you're using ColdFusion version 6.0 or earlier, you must use the ColdFusion Administration Web site on the ColdFusion server to configure your database connection.

Before you create a ColdFusion database connection, you must first create a new ColdFusion document and specify an RDS (Remote Development Services) login. (RDS is a security component of ColdFusion used to manage access to files and databases.) Creating the new ColdFusion document tells Dreamweaver the platform of the connection you're trying to set up, and ensures you have the correct document type to use the new database connection. The RDS login tells Dreamweaver how to communicate with the ColdFusion server to publish files.

If you'd like more info on configuring the ColdFusion server, check out www. adobe.com/devnet/coldfusion/configuration.html.

Creating a new ColdFusion document

To create a new ColdFusion document, perform the following steps:

1. **Choose File⇨New.**

The New Document dialog box opens.

2. **Select Blank Page from the Category list.**

3. **Select ColdFusion from the Page Type list.**

4. **Optionally, specify a layout from the Layout list.**

   For this example, we keep the default <none> selected.

5. **Select a document type definition from the DocType drop-down list.**

   This setting makes your page XHTML-compliant. You usually want to stick with the default option, XHTML 1.0 Transitional.

6. **Click Create.**

   A new, blank ColdFusion document is created.

Now that you have created a new ColdFusion document, you can establish a database connection for Dreamweaver to use.

Specifying RDS login information

Prior to setting up the first database connection for a Dreamweaver site, you must specify a Remote Development Services (RDS) password for the ColdFusion server. This password allows Dreamweaver to interact directly with the ColdFusion server to exchange database connection information. If you haven't already entered the RDS password, a checklist appears in the Databases panel, as shown in Figure 6-1. If you installed the ColdFusion server, use the password from the installation; otherwise, contact the administrator of the ColdFusion server.

Book VII Chapter 6

Configuring ColdFusion Database Connections

Figure 6-1: A checklist for using ColdFusion database connections.

To set up the RDS connection, do the following:

1. **Open the Databases panel by choosing Window➪Databases.**

   A checklist appears in the panel.

2. **Click the RDS Login link in the fourth step of the checklist.**

A Login to ColdFusion Remote Development Services (RDS) dialog box appears.

3. **Enter the RDS password for your ColdFusion server.**

The ColdFusion server administrator provides the password.

4. **Click OK to close the dialog box.**

A list of existing database connections appears in the Databases panel.

Configuring a database connection with the ColdFusion Administrator

If you're using a version of ColdFusion prior to version 7, you must use the ColdFusion Administrator to create the database connection. This method works on all versions of ColdFusion, including the current one. The biggest advantage to configuring through Dreamweaver is not having to open up a separate browser window to access the administration pages.

To create a database connection in ColdFusion, follow these steps:

1. **Open the Databases panel by choosing Window⇨Databases.**

2. **Click the Modify Data Sources button (which looks like a yellow cylinder with a pencil; refer to Figure 6-1).**

Dreamweaver opens a new Web browser window with the Administrator Login page of the ColdFusion server, shown in Figure 6-2.

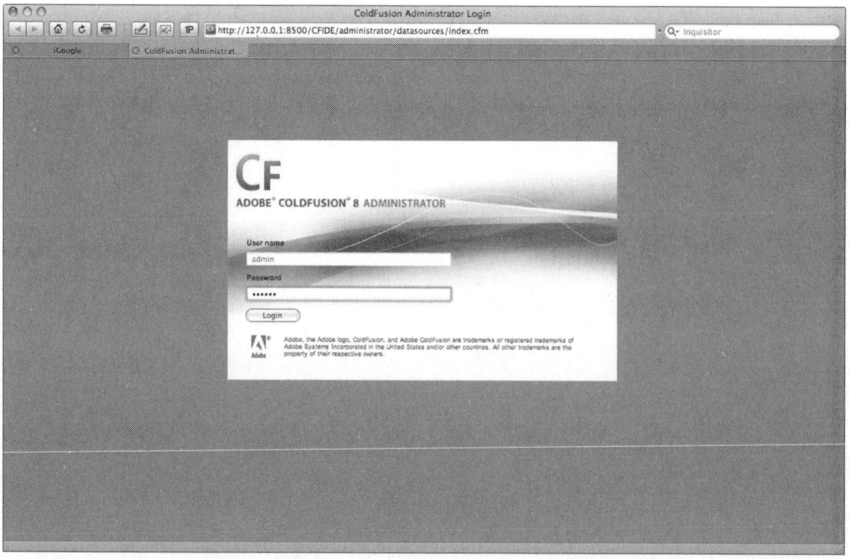

Figure 6-2: The login page for the ColdFusion Administrator console.

3. Enter the ColdFusion Administrator password in the text box next to the Login button.

The ColdFusion server administrator must provide this password.

4. Click the Login button.

After you submit the password, your Web browser is redirected to the Data & Services⇨Data Sources page, as shown in Figure 6-3.

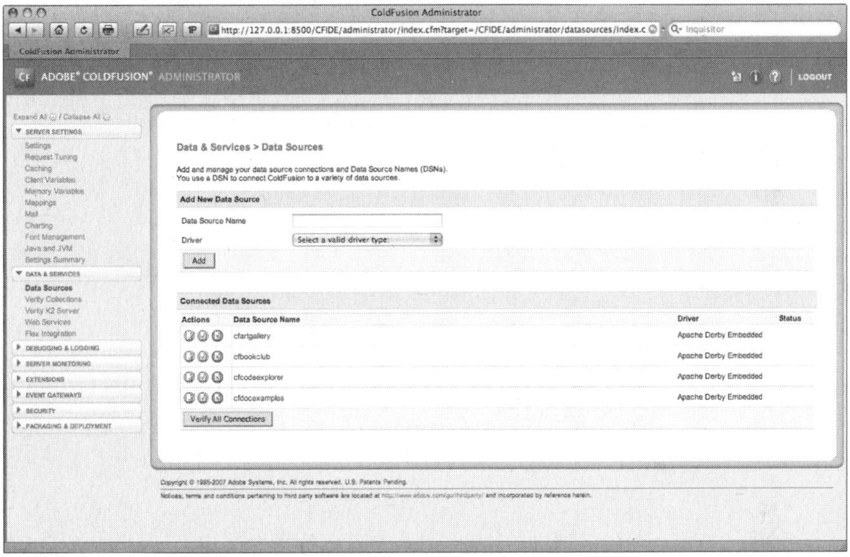

Figure 6-3: Adding a database connection to Cold Fusion.

5. Enter a name for the database connection in the Data Source Name field.

ColdFusion uses this name to reference your database connection. The name can be made up of letters, numbers, or the underscore character only. Additionally, you can't use the names *service*, *jms_provider*, *comp*, or *jms* — these are reserved by ColdFusion.

6. Select the appropriate database driver type from the Driver drop-down list.

7. Click the Add button.

You are directed to the next step of the creation process, as shown in Figure 6-4.

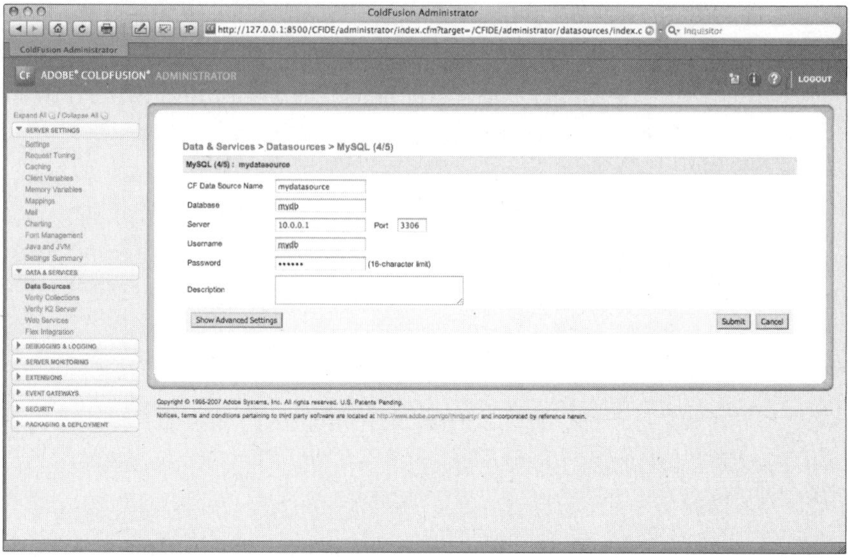

Figure 6-4:
The Add
Data Source
page for
a MySQL
connection.

8. **Enter your database connection information.**

   This information includes the database name, server, username, password, and a description.

9. **Click the Submit button.**

   You are directed back to the Data & Services➪Data Sources page. If your connection settings contain any errors, ColdFusion displays the errors in red text at the top of the page. A green success message at the top of the page indicates a successful configuration.

   In either case, the connection is created. If an error still exists, the connection appears with a yellow background, and the error details show in the Data Source Name column in the Connected Data Sources table. The error details disappear after you fix the error.

Your new database connection appears in the Dreamweaver Databases panel. If the connection doesn't appear immediately, click the Refresh button to update Dreamweaver's list of available connections.

Configuring a database connection in Dreamweaver

If you would prefer to create the ColdFusion database connection (version 8 or MX 7) inside Dreamweaver, do the following:

1. **Open the Databases panel by choosing Window➪Databases.**

2. **Click the plus (+) button and select the appropriate database connection type from the drop-down list.**

   A dialog box appears for the database connection type you selected, similar to Figure 6-5.

3. **Enter the connection information for your database.**

   This information includes username, password, server name, and database name.

4. **Click the Test button to confirm that your connection is set up correctly.**

   A dialog box tells you whether the connection was successful.

5. **Click OK again to close the database server connection dialog box.**

   The database connection is created on the ColdFusion server.

Editing a ColdFusion Database Connection

You can edit a ColdFusion database connection in one of two ways through the ColdFusion Administrator Web console or directly inside Dreamweaver.

Using Dreamweaver

You can edit a ColdFusion Database Connection inside Dreamweaver by following the instructions below:

1. **In the Databases panel, right-click (Windows) or Control+click (Mac) the database connection you want to edit and select Edit Connection from the list that appears, as shown in Figure 6-6.**

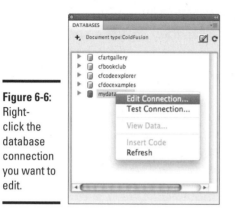

Figure 6-6:
Right-
click the
database
connection
you want to
edit.

The connection dialog box opens.

2. **Edit the connection properties as necessary.**

3. **Click the Test button to confirm that your connection is set up correctly.**

   An alert box tells you the connection was successful.

4. **Click OK to close the alert box.**

   The alert box closes, and you return to the connection dialog box.

5. **Click OK to close the connection dialog box.**

   Dreamweaver saves the changes to your database connection.

Using the ColdFusion Administrator

This method for editing a database connection works for all versions of ColdFusion and Dreamweaver. To edit a ColdFusion database connection in Dreamweaver through the ColdFusion Administrator Web console, do the following:

1. **In the Databases panel, click the Modify Data Sources button.**

   Dreamweaver opens a new Web browser window with the Administrator Login page of the ColdFusion server.

2. **Enter the ColdFusion Administrator password in the text box and click the Login button.**

   After you submit the password, your Web browser redirects to the Data & Services⇨Data Sources page.

3. **Select the database connection you want to edit by clicking its name in the Connected Data Sources table.**

   You're redirected to a page showing the selected database connection's settings.

4. **Edit the connection information for your database.**

   This information includes username, password, server name, and database name.

5. **Click the Submit button.**

   ColdFusion tests your connection. If an error occurs, an error message in red text appears at the top of the page. If the connection is set up properly, a green success message is displayed.

   In either case, the connection is created. If an error still exists, the connection appears with a yellow background, and the error details show in the Data Source Name column in the Connected Data Sources table until the error is fixed.

Deleting a ColdFusion Database Connection

To delete a ColdFusion database connection in Dreamweaver, follow these steps:

1. **In the Databases panel, click the Modify Data Sources button.**

   Dreamweaver opens a new Web browser window with the Administrator Login page of the ColdFusion server (refer to Figure 6-2).

2. **Enter the ColdFusion Administrator password in the text box and click the Login button.**

   The password is submitted, and your Web browser redirects to the Data & Services➪Data Sources page of the ColdFusion Administrator Web console (refer to Figure 6-3).

3. **Select the database connection you want to delete by clicking the red circle icon to the left of the connection's name in the Connected Data Sources table.**

   A dialog box appears, confirming that you want to delete the selected data source.

4. **Click OK.**

   The dialog box closes and the Data & Services➪Data Sources page updates. The deleted connection no longer appears in the Connected Data Sources table.

5. **Click Logout to close your session in the ColdFusion Administrator console.**

   If no Logout button is available, simply close the window.

Chapter 7: Dealing with Database Issues

In This Chapter

✔ **Database connection troubleshooting**

✔ **Resolving permission problems**

✔ **Addressing error messages**

✔ **Avoiding database errors**

*Y*ou've spent a good bit of time working to create your database and configure Dreamweaver for connecting with it. But when you go to try to connect the two in a data-oriented matrimony, all you get are messages like the following:

Error. Cannot connect to database.

Connection error. Unable to locate database. See your system administrator.

Give it up, dude. You can't get there from here.

The majority of error messages that you may encounter when working with databases center around connectivity. These errors principally break down like this:

✦ Invalid host, username, or password

✦ The driver files are missing

✦ A file's permission settings prevent reading a file-based database such as Access

✦ The remote host doesn't support the database driver you're using

Within the database, errors you can encounter include

✦ Attempting to insert a duplicate record into a database with a unique constraint

✦ Creating a table that already exists

✦ Not having proper database access rights within the database, including read, modify, and create permissions

✦ Attempting to insert data that is different from the data type of a column

✦ Misspelling a table or column name

✦ Not including the same number of values as table columns

This chapter shows you how to troubleshoot database problems and resolve permissions issues.

Troubleshooting Basic Database Access

Depending on the type of database you're using, you can troubleshoot a database problem in several ways. First, ping the database to verify connectivity. Then if that's successful, validate your settings for username, password, and host name, making sure they're correct. The following sections give you the details on how to do these troubleshooting tasks.

Verifying contact with the database server

If your database is on a remote server, you should start your troubleshooting by verifying that your computer can reach the database server. The following steps show how to use the ping command to verify connectivity:

1. **Open a command prompt on the Mac or PC.**

To reach the command prompt on a PC, choose Start⇨Run, enter **cmd** in the Run dialog box that appears, and click OK.

To reach the command prompt on a Mac, start the Terminal application by choosing Applications⇨Utilities.

2. **On the command line, enter** ping [*host name*] **where** [*host name*] **is the name of the database server.**

For example, if your database is on a host called `leakypipes.com`, you'd enter the following command:

```
ping leakypipes.com
```

3. **Analyze the output from ping to determine whether it was successful.**

If the ping attempt is successful, you see output like this:

```
Pinging leakypipes.com [24.94.201.11] with 32 bytes of
    data:
Reply from 24.94.201.11: bytes=32 time<10ms TTL=64
Reply from 24.94.201.11: bytes=32 time<10ms TTL=64
```

Unsuccessful output looks something like this:

```
Pinging 12.3.2.4 with 32 bytes of data:
Request timed out.
Request timed out.
```

4. **Press Ctrl+C (Windows) or Ctrl+click (Mac) to stop executing the ping command.**

If your ping was unsuccessful, make sure you have the right information for your host name, are connected to your network correctly, and that the database server isn't down for maintenance.

Validating your database username and password

After verifying contact with the database server (as described in the previous section), the next step is to make sure that your username and password are correct. To eliminate any possible driver issues with Dreamweaver CS4, use your database client to test this information. Each particular database has a different protocol.

MySQL databases

For MySQL running locally on your machine, use the `mysql` command-line client to verify the username and password. Specify your database connection information like this:

```
mysql -u[username] -p[password] -h[host name]
```

For MySQL databases running on a Web host, use the Web control panel provided by your ISP to check on users and passwords. Also, make sure that you have enabled remote connectivity to your MySQL database. Many providers have a MySQL Remote Access utility in which you can grant your IP address permission.

Access and SQL Server

For Access or SQL Server databases, try connecting from Access or SQL Server through ODBC. For both Access and SQL Server, make sure that you have your DSN set up correctly. Also make sure that the remote server has the DSN set up. See the "Problematic Permissions: IIS and File-Based Databases" section for more information on accessing the DSN definition through the Windows Control Panel.

Oracle

For Oracle, use the `sqlplus` command-line tool to verify the username and password. Specify your connection information as follows:

```
sqlplus [username]/[password]@[db_descriptor]
```

The syntax is `sqlplus username@database`. Oracle also provides a utility called `tnsping` that attempts to ping the database server based on its Oracle database descriptor.

IBM Universal Database

Before you test your username and password, make sure you have the DB2 Runtime Client and the ODBC to DB2 driver installed. For the IBM client, verify your login using the Command Center. To test connectivity from the Command Center, follow these steps:

1. **Start the Command Center by choosing Start⇨Programs⇨db2⇨ Command Line Tools⇨Command Center.**

    The Command Center launches. If this folder isn't in your Program Files list, you don't have the client installed.

2. **Click the Scripts tab.**

3. **Enter a simple query, such as the following, into the Query field:**

    ```
    connect to sample;
    ```

4. **Click the Execute icon at the top left.**

If you're able to execute your query without an error, you know that your database details are correct.

Problematic Permissions: IIS and File-Based Databases

Although file permissions are necessary to keep your computer and servers secure, they can thwart your development process when you're working with a local Web server and a database, both of which execute with limited permissions to help keep systems secure. The unfortunate reality is that you very well may run into a permission problem or two when developing and deploying your database-driven Web sites. Permissions apply to both directories and individual files, including database files. When access permission prevents your Web server from reading the database file, you get error messages that don't always clearly point to the problem. Also, verifying that permissions are set correctly on more than one computer can be time-consuming.

IIS permission problems are likely to rear their ugly heads when you publish your site or attempt to use Live Data view on a dynamic page. (See Book IX, Chapter 1 for more on Live Data view.) The same problems can happen whether you're running Windows Vista or XP; however, the Windows administrative tools you can use to fix them vary slightly.

IIS usually runs as the limited access account on Windows called `IUSR_ [computer name]`. For example, if your computer name is `server`, your limited access account name is `IUSR_server`. IIS may take on increased permissions for a Web page if the page allows a user to log in to a specific account. In that case, you still need to be sure that the login account allows access to the database file.

Oracle names

Your Oracle database may require access through an Oracle names file called `tnsnames.ora`. You can use the Oracle Network Configuration tool to set up this file, or the Oracle database administrator may supply it. To verify that your Oracle names configuration is correct, use the Oracle command `tnsping`.

The `tnsping` command takes the name of your database as an argument and pings the database server that the configuration points to. If there's a problem resolving the name or reaching the server through the network, you receive an error message. If not, you know that your naming files are configured correctly and that the database is available over the network.

The default for users who don't log in is `IUSR_[computer name]` unless it's been changed.

You receive an error message if the Web server and database driver can't read the database file as the `IUSR_server` user. Both the database file and the directory containing the database file must have read and write permissions. If the path to the database file uses a share name, regardless of whether the share is on the local computer or a remote computer, make sure that the file share has the proper permission to access the database file as `IUSR_[computer name]`.

To check or change the database file permissions, follow these steps:

1. Log in as a user with Administrator access.

Windows won't allow you to make changes if you don't have the Administrator privilege. If you don't have this, you need to log out and log back in with the Administrator account.

2. Open the folder that contains your database file.

You specified this directory when creating the database.

To find out where the file is located, check the ODBC data sources from the Windows Control Panel's Data Source (ODBC) program. It's located in the Administrative tools folder.

3. Right-click the database file and select Properties.

The filename usually has the .mdb extension.

4. Click the Security tab.

5. Verify that either the `IUSR_[computer name]` or the special user `Everyone` is listed in the Name column. If either account is listed, skip ahead to Step 10. Otherwise, proceed to the next step to add the `IUSR_[computer name]` account.

The user Everyone means that any user, including the IUSR_ [computer name] user, receives the permission granted to it.

6. **Click the Add button to open the Users, Computer, or Groups dialog box.**

7. **Select your computer name from the list.**

   Don't worry if it's grayed out. That just means your computer name is the only choice because you're not part of a Windows domain.

8. **Select IUSR_[computer name] from the list of names.**

   For example, select IUSR_GILLIGAN if your computer name is Gilligan.

9. **Click Add and then click OK.**

   You return to the file's Properties dialog box.

10. **While IUSR_[computer name] is highlighted, click the Allow check box for Full Control in the Permissions section.**

    Clicking Full Control is a shortcut for clicking all the other permission check boxes. This ensures that the file can be used by the Web application.

11. **Click OK.**

    The file's permissions are set to allow access.

Repeat these steps for the directory that contains the database file.

If you want to restrict Web users from browsing the folder that contains your database file, if it's within your Web root folder, you can clear the Read permission for the database folder. This still allows your application to read the file (because it already knows where the file's located), but prevents users from browsing the directory. Of course, placing the database file outside of the Web root folder automatically means the file can't be viewed through the browser.

Troubleshooting Microsoft Error Messages

When working with IIS and a file-driven database such as Access or SQL Server, a common set of errors can sometimes crop up. They involve the interaction between the Web server and the database when requesting dynamic pages. In this section, I look at these common error messages:

✦ 80004005: Data source name not found. (Another variation is 80004005: Microsoft Jet database engine cannot open the file (*unknown*).)

✦ 80040e07: Data type mismatch in criteria expression.

✦ 80040e10: Too few parameters.

✦ 80040e14: Syntax error in INSERT INTO statement.

- ✦ 80040e21: ODBC error on Insert or Update.
- ✦ 800a0bcd: Either BOF or EOF is true.

For each of these errors, the following sections summarize the root cause and the action you need to take to fix it.

80004005: Data source name not found

Another variation is "80004005: Microsoft Jet database engine cannot open the file (*unknown*)". This error generally means that you can't access the database file either because of permissions or because another process is already using the file. Verify that you've set the permissions correctly and that you don't have the database open in another program such as Access. See Microsoft's page for more troubleshooting tips at `http://support.microsoft.com/kb/306345/EN-US/`.

80040e07: Data type mismatch in criteria expression

This error means that you've attempted to enter a value into a database column that isn't the correct type and can't be converted automatically (for example, inserting a string like `midwest` into a number column). The solution is to supply the correct type of data or change the column's data type.

80040e10: Too few parameters

This error indicates that one of the columns you've specified to add data to doesn't exist in the database. To fix this error, check the spelling of your commands and fields. Verify that each column exists. Create a new column in the table to match the data you're trying to insert if it doesn't already exist.

80040e14: Syntax error in INSERT INTO statement

This error may indicate that you've used an invalid character in the name of a table or column. Spaces and special characters such as punctuation symbols aren't permitted. Also, in an Oracle database, you can see this error when using the distinct keyword in a select statement. See `http://support.microsoft.com/default.aspx?scid=kb;EN-US;238164` for patch instructions.

80040e21: ODBC error on Insert or Update

This error indicates that the field you're inserting into isn't large enough to hold the value you're inserting. For example, if you have a string column with a length of five characters and attempt to insert `Tuesday`, you get this error. To correct the error, either increase the size of the column or reduce the size of the string you're inserting.

800a0bcd: Either BOF or EOF is true

You're attempting to display an element from a recordset that doesn't exist in the database table. To resolve this error, verify that each element of your recordset has a corresponding column in the database table using the Server Behaviors tool for the deployments. The Server Behaviors panel allows you to expand your recordset; click the plus button to reveal the fields of the recordset.

Troubleshooting JSP Database Connections

The most common error you are likely to encounter when working with a Java Database Connection (JDBC) database is that the JDBC driver isn't loaded on your machine or your server. If this happens, you receive an error ending in `class not found`. Search the database vendor's Web site for the JDBC driver (see Book VII, Chapter 5 for download URLs for the most popular ones). Dreamweaver is not capable of including them all because literally hundreds of JDBC drivers are available. After installing the driver, restart Dreamweaver so it can detect the presence of the driver. (See Book VII, Chapter 5 for more on setting up JSP database connections.)

Identifying Problems within the Database

When working with database data, sometimes you may accidentally ask the database to do something it can't do, or something that you don't have permission to do. For each of these scenarios, you encounter an error, regardless of which database you're using:

✦ Creating an object that already exists always causes an error unless your database supports a `replace` keyword. It's a good idea to *drop* (delete) objects such as tables before creating them to avoid creation errors.

✦ Inserting a row with a key that's already been used causes an error. To avoid this problem, either create the table without a unique requirement (if that's okay with your data) or check that the value you're trying to insert doesn't already exist in the table. You can use a simple `select` statement to do this.

✦ Misspelled table or column names cause problems. Use the database object browser to check all your column and table names before using them.

✦ Data type and size problems can also creep up in your pages. Always validate the database column type before inserting data into it. Each development model provides functions for checking the length and type of data for a variable. A little checking before your page goes live (and before your users get creative with entering data) can prevent annoying errors.

General Troubleshooting

In general, testing your queries outside of Dreamweaver is a great way to make sure that you can connect to your database and that your SQL queries are correct. If your query works with the database client, you can focus on the code that is creating and executing the query. A *query* tells the database the information you're looking for. We discuss queries in detail in Book IX, Chapter 2.

Verify permission on the database file if you're using a file-based database on both your local computer and the server or with your ISP account. You must also verify that the Web server is set to execute whichever type of code you've chosen as your dynamic site type. In general, make sure that a simple dynamic page is executable before attempting database operations. If the file is executable, you see a blank page or whatever test code you place in the file. If it isn't executable, you likely see the contents of the file with any processing.

Book VIII
Making Pages Dynamic

The 5th Wave   By Rich Tennant

"You know, a lot of symphony orchestras are putting their music online these days as a way to reach new audience members."

Contents at a Glance

Chapter 1: Preparing Dynamic Content Sources

In This Chapter

✔ **Exploring your database in Dreamweaver**

✔ **Creating parameters for your form data**

✔ **Adding URL parameters to Web page requests**

✔ **Keeping track of users with session variables**

✔ **Using a database as your data source**

A dynamic Web site has content that is rendered dynamically when a user visits a site. In the previous book, I discussed how to configure Dreamweaver CS4 to work with application servers and databases. Now, it's time to start working with the data itself.

When you're preparing dynamic content sources, as described in this chapter, you're actually creating code and working with variables and sessions that help you manage your Web site more efficiently. A *data source* is a source of information from which you can extract data to display in your dynamic Web pages. This data can come from several sources in Dreamweaver:

✦ A form submission from another Web page

✦ URL parameters that are part of the Web page request

✦ A session variable that you set on another Web page

✦ A database table column

✦ Other advanced sources, such as JavaBeans properties

Before you can use a data source in your dynamic Web pages, you need to define it by using the Bindings panel. This chapter shows you how to define several data sources — form parameters, URL parameters, session variables, and databases — and make them available for use in your dynamic Web pages.

This chapter also explains how to use the Databases panel to navigate your database and make sure that you're using the right column names.

Exploring Your Database in the Databases Panel

The Databases panel lists the tables and fields for an active database connection. After connecting to your database, you can view its structure and data within the Dreamweaver Databases panel, which displays your database in a tree-like structure. You can view a database table much more easily in Dreamweaver than you can by working directly through a command-line SQL client.

To explore your database visually in the Databases panel, follow these steps:

1. **Open the Databases panel by choosing Window⇨Databases.**

This panel displays all the database connections defined for your site (see Figure 1-1). Any databases with a properly configured connection display with a plus sign before them. You can explore an accessible database only.

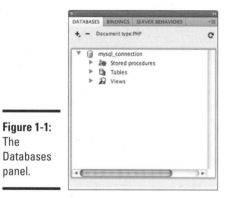

Figure 1-1:
The
Databases
panel.

If no database appears in the panel, you have to create a database connection, which you find out how to do in Book VII.

2. **Click the arrow before the database to view the object types associated with that database.**

The tree view expands to show these database object types:

- **Stored Procedures:** A *stored procedure* is code that is stored within the database itself. Because the stored procedure runs directly on the database server, it can be faster at complex analysis of database data. Stored procedures can also be useful for validating data.

- **Tables:** Database tables are the grid-like structures that contain the actual data. We discuss these more in Book VII, Chapter 1. As you start out with databases, you work probably work primarily with tables.

- **Views:** *Views* are tables that are based on a database query. They are read-only.

3. **Click the arrow before a database category — Stored Procedures, Tables, or Views — to see what your database contains for that category.**

4. **Click the name of the object to expand the details again.**

   You see different information, depending on which database category you select in Step 3:

   - **Stored Procedures:** Listing the stored procedure's parameters and return values.

   - **Tables:** Lists the table's columns and those columns' data types (see Figure 1-2).

   - **Views:** Lists the view's columns and those columns' data types.

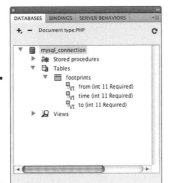

Figure 1-2:
The Data-
bases panel
showing the
columns of
a table.

For database tables, you can view the data in the table by right-clicking the table name in the Databases panel and selecting View Data from the context menu. A window appears that lists the table data.

Defining Form Parameters

The whole point of dynamic Web pages is to not return the same page each time a page is requested. One tool that's used to mix up what's returned is a form parameter. A *form parameter* allows you to pass values between web pages. You can define a form parameter by following these steps:

1. **Open an existing or create a new Web document using the app lan-guage of choice (PHP, ASP, ASP.NET, or JSP).**

2. **Pick a spot for the data-driven form and then choose Insert⇨Form⇨Form.**

See Book II, Chapter 7 for the lowdown on creating forms.

3. **Choose Window⇨Bindings to display the Bindings panel.**

   Before you create any bindings, you see the Dynamic Page setup checklist in the Bindings panel.

4. **Click the plus (+) button, and from the list that appears, select Form Variable or the appropriate form item for your dynamic page type.**

   Options appear on the list based on your dynamic page type. Table 1-1 lists the option names to select for each page type.

Table 1-1   Add a Binding Menu Form Item Name Based on the Dynamic Page Type

Dynamic Page Type	Menu Item Name
ASP	Request Variable > Request.Form
ColdFusion	Form Variable
JSP	Request Variable
PHP	Form Variable

The Form Variable dialog box displays, as shown in Figure 1-3.

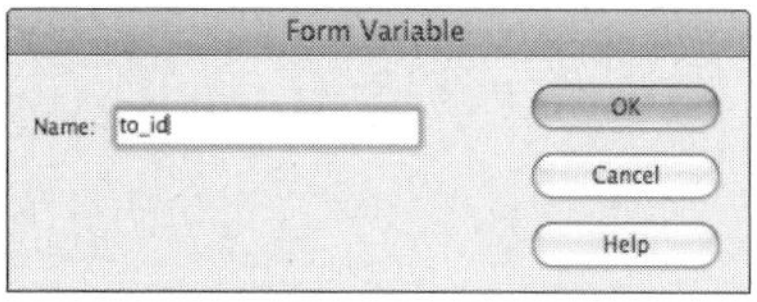

Figure 1-3:
The Form
Variable
dialog box.

Form Variable

Name: to_id

OK
Cancel
Help

Post or get?

When you add a form to your page (as described in Book II, Chapter 7), you need to keep track of how you submit your form data to the server. You have two methods to choose from:

✔ The POST method, which sends parameters in the body of the request

✔ The GET method, which places the data in the URL as parameters

You can use either GET or POST methods, but you need to be consistent about which you use between the page that submits the values and the page that processes them. Also, be sure you know the type of request when you tell Dreamweaver about your form input.

5. **Enter the name of the form variable in the dialog box and click OK.**

The form parameter name is normally the name of the HTML form field or object that the parameter uses to obtain its value. For example, the data field I want to display is the recipient `id` of a message (called `to`). I named the form variable `to_id` in the dialog box.

The form parameter appears in the Bindings panel, as shown in Figure 1-4.

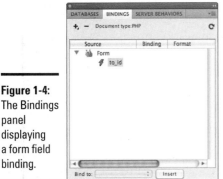

Figure 1-4:
The Bindings panel displaying a form field binding.

After you define the form parameter as a data source, you can insert the parameter in your document by selecting it in the Bindings panel. See Book VIII, Chapter 3 for details.

Defining URL Parameters

URL parameters are a simple way of passing information to the Web server as part of the Web page request. When the Web server receives the request, the URL parameter is included in that request. This allows dynamic pages to be generated based on a specific parameter from a prior page. In the URL, a question mark (?) separates the Web site location from the parameters. Here's an example:

```
http://www.example.com/?username=kramer&password=nextdoor
```

In this example, the Web site is `www.example.com`. The two parameters are `username` (which has a value of `kramer`) and password (which has a value of `nextdoor`). An equal sign (=) separates each parameter from its value. If more than one parameter exists, as in this example, an ampersand (&) separates the parameters. Passing these values to the server is important because it allows the server to determine if the username and password are valid. Depending on how the application is written, username and password validation might determine access to subsequent pages.

When a server processes a Web page request that contains URL parameters, the server makes those parameter values available to the dynamic page before returning the page to the Web browser, where the user sees the updated page displayed.

Dreamweaver uses URL parameters automatically when you submit a form by using the HTTP GET method. The GET method specifies that the parameters are appended to the URL when the page request is sent to the Web server. URL parameters are also frequently used to pass a value to the Web server, such as an action to take, when the user clicks a link. For example, you may have a URL parameter called action that takes the values insert, update, and delete based on the action that the link indicates. Note that you can pass more than one URL parameter at a time to a Web site.

To define a data source binding for a URL parameter, follow these steps:

1. **Create a new PHP, ASP, ASP.NET, or JSP page (or open an existing one).**

2. **If you don't already have the Bindings panel displayed, choose Window⇨Bindings.**

   Before you create any bindings, you see the Dynamic Page setup checklist in the Bindings panel.

3. **Click the plus (+) button and select the URL item for your dynamic page type from the list that appears.**

   Dreamweaver uses different names for this field based on your dynamic page type. Table 1-2 lists the appropriate URL item for your page type.

Table 1-2   Add a Binding Menu for URL Parameters Based Aon the Dynamic Page Type

Dynamic Page Type	URL Item Name
ASP	Request Variable > Request.QueryString
ColdFusion	URL Variable
JSP	Request Variable
PHP	URL Variable

The URL Variable dialog box appears, as shown in Figure 1-5.

4. **Enter the name of the URL variable in the dialog box and click OK.**

   The URL parameter name is normally the name of the HTML form field or the object used to obtain its value.

   Figure 1-5 shows the new binding called search.

   The form parameter appears in the Bindings panel (shown in Figure 1-6).

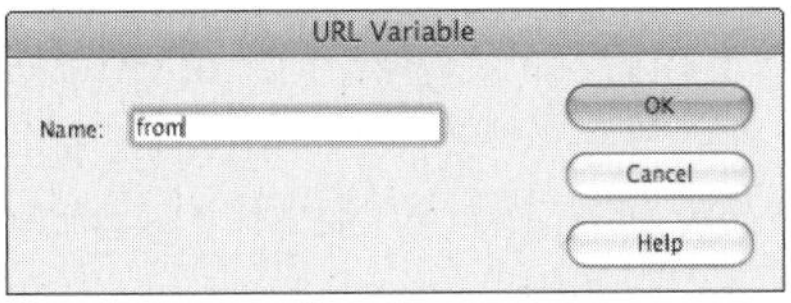

Figure 1-5:
The URL
Variable
dialog box
for a form
field called
`from`.

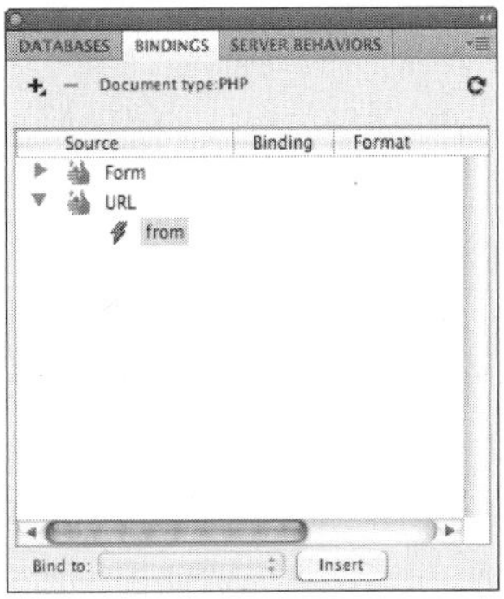

Figure 1-6:
The Bindings
panel after
adding the
URL binding.

After you define the URL as a data source, you can insert the URL in your document from the Bindings panel. See Book VIII, Chapter 3 for details.

Defining Session Variables

Session variables store information that the user enters and makes that information available to any page during the user's visit, or *session.* For example, if a user logs in to the Web site, a session variable saves that authentication information, making it available to every page on the Web site throughout the user's visit. Without a session variable, the user has to reenter the login information every time she visits a new page on the site.

The session variable remains in effect until the user ends the session or a timeout period expires. Because the session is tracked on the server, the information stored in session variables is also stored on the Web server. Only a small unique identifier, called a *cookie,* is stored on the Web browser's computer. (If you'd like more info on cookies, check out `www.cookie central.com/c_concept.htm`.)

You have to use Code view to add a session variable to a page. Follow these steps to define the session variable in the page and add it to the Bindings panel:

1. **Create a new dynamic page or open an existing page that contains a session variable.**

2. **If you don't already have the Bindings panel displayed, choose Window⇨Bindings.**

3. **Click the plus (+) button and select Session Variable from the list that appears.**

Unlike the other binding types, Dreamweaver uses the name *Session Variable* on this list for every dynamic page type.

The Session Variable dialog box displays, as shown in Figure 1-7.

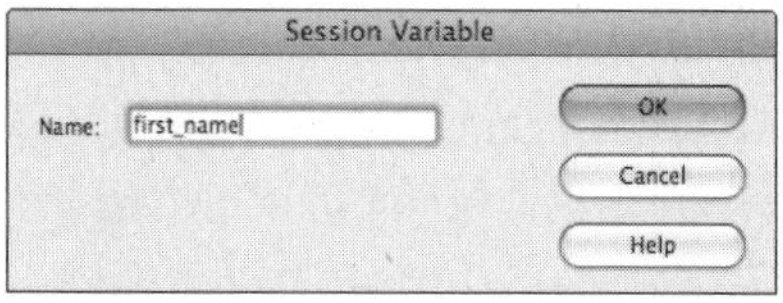

Figure 1-7:
The Session
Variable
dialog box.

4. **Enter the name of the session variable in the dialog box and click OK.**

Figure 1-8 shows the new binding called `first_name`.

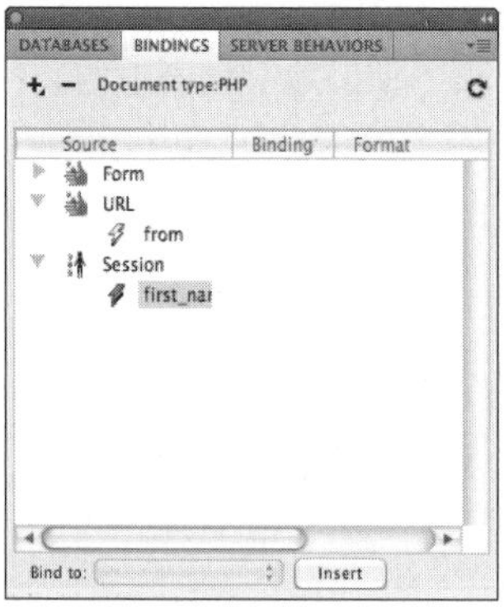

Figure 1-8:
The Bindings
panel
displays
a session
variable
binding.

After you define the session variable as a data source, you can insert your session variable in your document from the Bindings panel. See Book VIII, Chapter 3 for details.

Using a Database as Your Data Source

If you want to use a database as a data source for your dynamic Web site, you build a *query* to gather specific data from the database to use in your page. For example, you might build a query to retrieve all the information about a user before presenting the page so the user can update the data. The data that results from that query is called a *recordset.* After you create a recordset, you can display information from your database in your page.

Understanding recordsets

The recordset lets Dreamweaver process more than one piece of data in a dynamic page. The other data sources that we cover in this chapter (form parameters, URL parameters, and session variables) work with a single piece of data. Because recordsets are the results of database queries, they can contain more than just a single piece of data. This allows displaying an entire list of results on a page.

Recordsets contain one or more results. Each result has one or more columns. Working with recordsets can be complex because of the variable number of results. To make accessing the data for a recordset as fast as possible, the database server stores the results in its memory.

You can create database queries using a graphical table linking tool or by using the standard database language called Structured Query Language (SQL). (Don't confuse the SQL language with Microsoft's database product, called Microsoft SQL Server.) SQL provides a standard format for specifying how information in a database is linked together and then filtered. SQL is specifically designed to describe the relationships between data and how to filter matching rows. Dreamweaver includes a simple-query building tool called SQL Builder to help build simple queries.

Microsoft's ASP.NET coding platform calls a recordset a *dataset.* Despite the different names, they're really the same thing. When working with ASP.NET document types, you can think of the terms *recordset* and *dataset* as interchangeable wherever you run into them.

Defining a recordset

Although you build the queries for a recordset with SQL, Dreamweaver enables you to create a recordset without writing an SQL query. It lets you select fields graphically from a table and column listing.

Before you can define a recordset, you need to establish a database connection in Dreamweaver. See Book VII for details on setting up a database connection.

To define a simple recordset in Dreamweaver, follow these steps:

1. **Create a new dynamic page or open an existing page.**

2. **In the Bindings panel, click the plus (+) button and select Recordset (Query) from the list that appears.**

The Recordset dialog box opens. Depending on your dynamic page type, the dialog box may look slightly different.

If you want to write your own SQL queries for a recordset, use the Advanced Recordset dialog box. You can open this version of the dialog box by clicking the Advanced button in the Recordset dialog box.

3. **In the Name field, enter a name for your recordset.**

Remember to use only letters, numbers, and underscores for names to be sure that the name is compatible with your dynamic page type. In the example in Figure 1-9, we accepted the default name *Recordset1*.

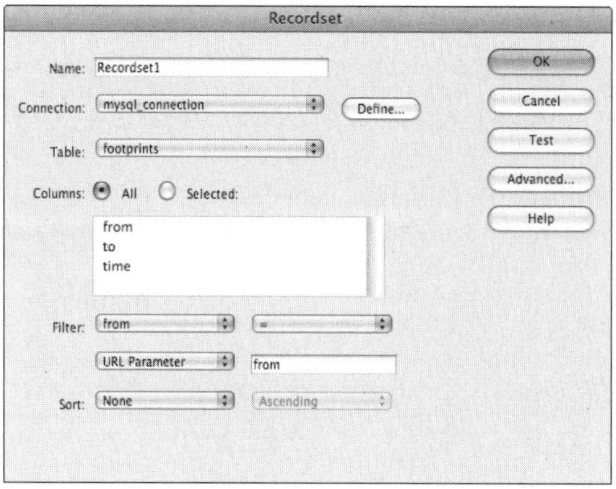

Figure 1-9:
The Record-
set dialog
box is set
to compare
the
database
column
value
against
the URL
parameter.

Recordset	
Name: Recordset1	OK
Connection: mysql_connection ⬍ Define...	Cancel
Table: footprints ⬍	Test
Columns: ● All ○ Selected:	Advanced...
from	Help
to	
time	
Filter: from ⬍ = ⬍	
URL Parameter ⬍ from	
Sort: None ⬍ Ascending ⬍	

4. **Select a database connection from the Connection drop-down list.**

In the example, I selected the `mysql_connection` connection.

5. **Select the database table from the Table drop-down list.**

The database table serves as a foundation for retrieving data for a database query. The Columns field updates to display the columns in your selected table. By default, all the columns are included in the recordset.

In the example shown in Figure 1-9, I choose the `footprints` table.

6. **If you want to specify which columns to include, choose the Selected radio button and select the desired columns.**

If you choose the Selected radio button, you can select multiple columns that you want to include from the Columns listing by Ctrl+clicking (Windows) or ⌘+clicking (Mac OS X) them.

7. **(Optional) If you want to filter the records, do the following:**

   - **In the first Filter drop-down list:** Select a table column to filter. You can compare the database field against one of the previously defined bindings to limit the results of the query.

   - **In the second list:** Select a conditional expression (such as =, <, or >) with which to compare the data from the column that you select in the first drop-down list.

   - **In the third list:** Select the data source for comparison. Your choices include any previously bound values.

   - **In the fourth list:** Enter a value to compare to the database column.

   For example, Figure 1-9 shows the Recordset dialog box comparing a column value (`from`) and a URL parameter.

8. **If you want to sort the records, select the table column that you want to sort by from the first Sort drop-down list. In the second drop-down list, specify whether you want the records sorted in ascending or descending order.**

9. **Click the Test button to verify that the query works correctly.**

   Dreamweaver executes your query and displays the rows in the Test SQL Statement window.

   If your query uses a filter, Dreamweaver displays the Test Value dialog box and prompts you to enter a value to use in the filter before executing the Test query. Enter a filter value typical of what you expect your query to encounter when it's executed as part of the Web page, and then click OK.

10. **If the test returns the records that you expect, click OK.**

    The recordset now appears in the Bindings panel, as Figure 1-10 shows.

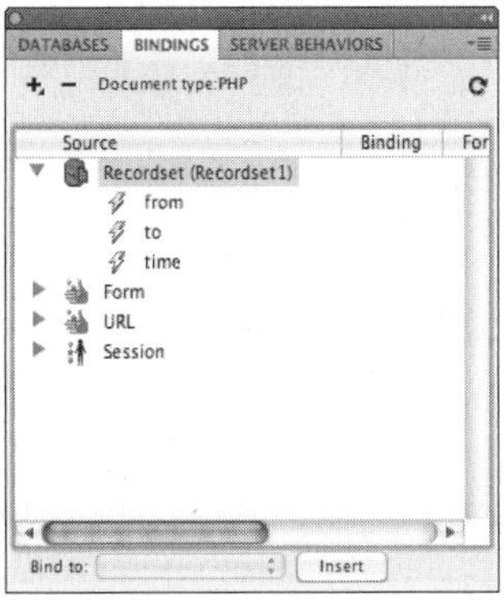

Figure 1-10:
The Bindings panel reflects the new recordset.

Chapter 2: Using Dynamic Content in Your Web Pages

In This Chapter

✔ Adding dynamic content to your page

✔ Formatting dynamic content

✔ Showing multiple records from a recordset

✔ Navigating through your records

✔ Showing and hiding regions of your page

*1*f you are a code monkey, you can use PHP, ASP.NET, or some other backend programming language and hand-code dynamic pages for your Web site. However, writing all of the database integration by hand involves a steep learning curve. Fortunately, Dreamweaver comes to the rescue by allowing you to bind, or connect your Web pages with backend data without becoming a geek in the process.

To make dynamic pages as flexible as possible and yet still organized, Dreamweaver CS4 places all *bindings* (references) to external data before you use it in your dynamic page. After the data is bound, you can select the exact format to display it in. You can even hide portions of pages depending on the values of bindings. After you master these concepts, you're ready to build complex dynamic Web pages.

Displaying and Formatting Dynamic Content

When you want to insert dynamic text on your page, your key tools are the Bindings panel and the Server Behaviors panel.

To insert dynamic text, open the Bindings panel (choose Window➪Bindings), locate the item that you want to use, and drag the item to your page.

Then, if you want to format the new dynamic text, you can use the Server Behaviors panel (choose Window➪Server Behaviors). The following sections describe in more detail how to add, format, and test dynamic content.

Before you can add dynamic text to your pages, you need to establish a database connection (as described in Book VII) and define a data source (as described in Book VIII, Chapter 1).

Adding dynamic text

To insert dynamic text on your page, follow these steps:

1. **In your document, place your cursor where you want to insert the dynamic text.**

2. **In the Bindings panel, locate the data source that you want to use.**

You can choose from any existing data sources, such as recordsets, URL parameters, form parameters, and session variables. (See Book VIII, Chapter 1 for more on these data sources.)

3. **Drag the data source to your document.**

The dynamic text appears on your page, enclosed by curly brackets { }. For example, if you add a URL parameter named username to your page, it looks like this in the Document window:

    {Recordset1.username}

This dynamic text entry is also added to the Server Behaviors panel, as shown in Figure 2-1.

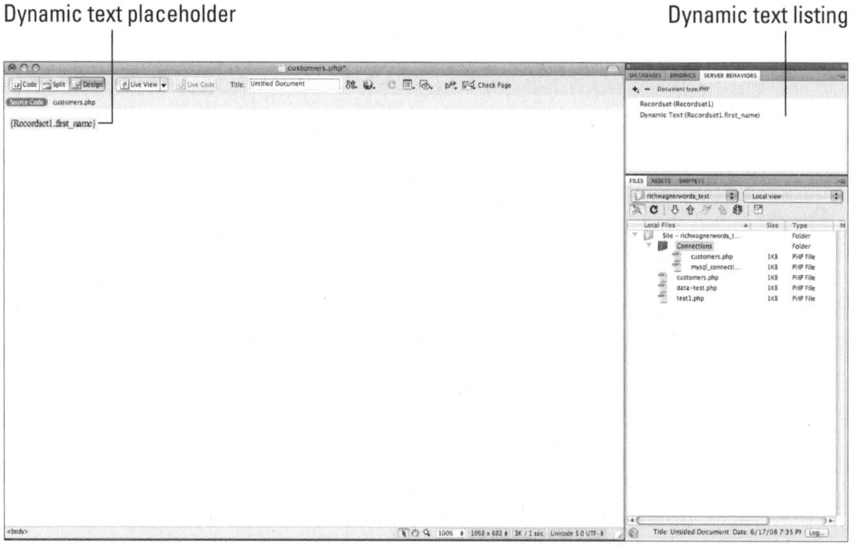

Dynamic text placeholder

Dynamic text listing

Figure 2-1:
The dynamic text placeholder in the Document window and the dynamic text listing in the Server Behaviors panel.

Formatting your dynamic content

After you get dynamic text on your page, you can modify how it appears. For example, if you're displaying a numeric field as money, you generally want it to appear in a format like $2.43. It doesn't look very professional to list a price as $1.1 or $1.154. Fortunately, you can modify the display format of server behavior dynamic text fields.

The formatting options that Dreamweaver provides for dynamic data display depend upon what dynamic page type you're using. In general, you can find functions that change the case (upper or lower) of strings, format numbers, and format dates and times.

To change the formatting of dynamic text, follow these steps:

1. **In the Server Behaviors panel, double-click the dynamic text that you want to format.**

   The Dynamic Text dialog box appears with your dynamic text already selected.

2. **Select the appropriate formatting option from the Format drop-down list.**

   For example, if you want to transform the value to uppercase, select the AlphaCase-Upper option, as Figure 2-2 shows. Or if you want to format a numeric field so that it shows dollars and cents, select Currency – 2 Decimal Places.

Figure 2-2:
The Dynamic Text dialog box.

You can download more formats for dynamic text by selecting Edit Format List at the bottom of the Format drop-down list.

3. **You can safely leave the Code field alone.**

The Code field tells you the actual code that Dreamweaver is using to produce the dynamic text. It's populated automatically when you select a data source.

4. **Click OK to close the Dynamic Text dialog box.**

Dreamweaver applies the formatting that you select in Step 2 to your text.

Testing your dynamic text

If you think that you have your page the way that you want it, the next step is to test it out. You can test the page by using Dreamweaver's Preview in Browser command or Live Data view (both are described in Book VIII, Chapter 3).

Live Data view is a little easier to use because it gives you a dialog box for entering parameter values. For example, you can enter URL parameter values in this dialog box instead of having to manually add them to the URL like this:

```
http://127.0.0.1/url_case.php?username=jack%20bauer
```

Note that %20 is the safe way to provide a blank space in a URL.

To use Live Data view to test your dynamic text, open your document and follow these steps:

1. **Choose View↷Live Data Settings.**

The Live Data Settings window appears.

2. **Click the plus (+) button to add a new entry to the URL Request list.**

3. **Enter the name of the URL parameter in the Name column.**

The name must match the name of the parameter from the URL. For example, we entered first_name to match the name of the URL parameter in Figure 2-3.

4. **Enter a sample value in the Value field and then click OK.**

For our example, we entered Jackson, as shown in Figure 2-3.

This value simulates an actual value sent to your script when it runs. To find out how to format dynamic content, see the earlier section, "Formatting your dynamic content."

5. **Choose View↷Live Data.**

Your Document window updates to show the processing of the page's dynamic content. For example, in Figure 2-4, the URL parameter username is replaced with Jackson.

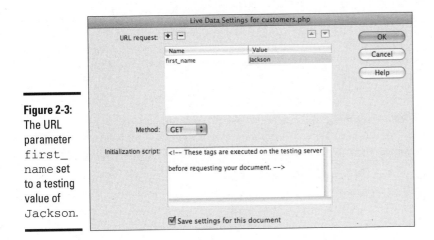

Figure 2-3:
The URL parameter `first_ name` set to a testing value of `Jackson`.

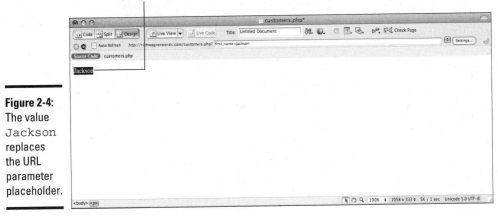

Figure 2-4:
The value `Jackson` replaces the URL parameter placeholder.

You can update the parameter value in the URL box at the top of the Document window. Click the Refresh icon to update the document, or check the Auto Refresh box to update the value live.

Working with Database Recordsets

You can display database recordsets much as you display simple dynamic data (as described in the earlier sections of this chapter) when you're working with a recordset that has one row in its results. You can even use the Dynamic Text server behavior to display a field from a recordset. (If you have more than one row in your recordset, the behavior shows just the first row.)

Things get a bit more complex when your recordset has several rows that you want to include. The dynamic page must be able to apply formatting for each row in a recordset. Dreamweaver lets you specify the format for your results, gives you navigation tools, and uses HTML tables to display the recordsets neatly.

Repeating regions on your page

The Repeat Region server behavior lets you display multiple records from a single recordset on the same page. Select an area, or *region*, of the page that you want to repeat and specify the number of times that you want to repeat it. The Repeat Region server behavior then populates the contents of each repeated region with values from the recordset.

To add a repeat region to your page, follow these steps:

1. **Select the data fields on the page that you want to repeat.**

   For example, we're working with a recordset that's defined to return all the entries from the `customers` table, which has four fields: `first_name`, `last_name`, `city`, and `state`. In Figure 2-5, the four dynamic text fields appear highlighted.

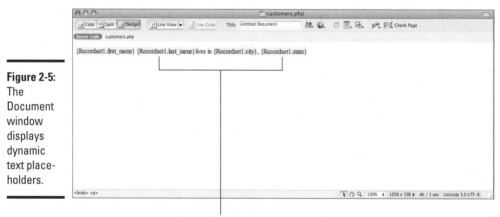

Figure 2-5: The Document window displays dynamic text place-holders.

Repeating regions

2. **In the Server Behaviors panel, click the plus (+) button and select Repeat Region from the drop-down list that appears.**

   The Repeat Region dialog box appears, as shown in Figure 2-6.

3. **From the Recordset drop-down list, select the recordset that you want to use.**

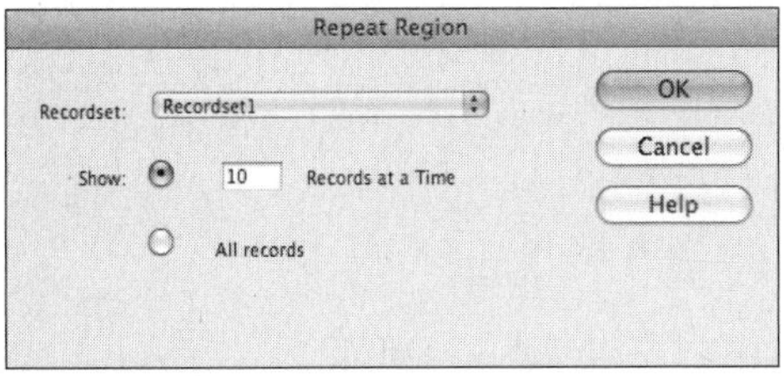

Figure 2-6:
The Repeat
Region
dialog box.

Repeat Region

Recordset: [Recordset1   ‡]   OK

Show: ⦿ [10] Records at a Time   Cancel

       ○ All records   Help

4. **In the Show area, select the number of records that you want to show on the page.**

   The default displays ten records, but you can pick a different number. You can also display all records by clicking the All Records radio button. In our example, we selected two records.

5. **Click OK to close the Repeat Region dialog box.**

   A gray box appears around the repeating fields with the text *Repeat* on a tab (see Figure 2-7). A repeat region (Recordset) also shows up in the Server Behaviors listing.

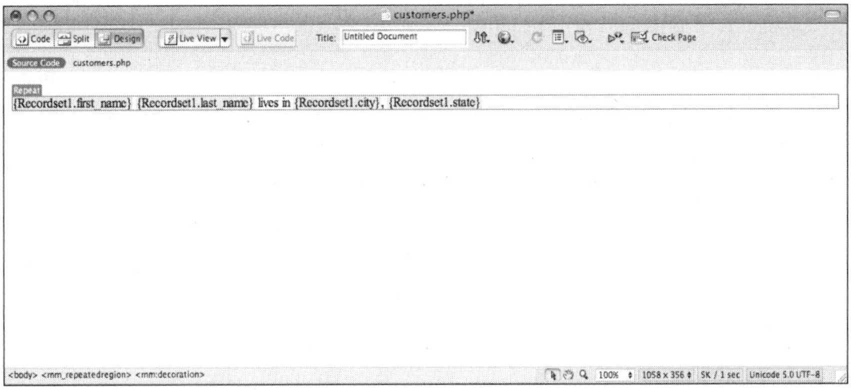

Figure 2-7:
A repeat
region in
Design
view.

customers.php*

Code | Split | Design | Live View ▾ | Live Code | Title: Untitled Document | Check Page

Source Code customers.php

Repeat
{Recordset1.first_name} {Recordset1.last_name} lives in {Recordset1.city}, {Recordset1.state}

\<body> \<mm_repeatregion> \<mm:decoration>   100% ‡ 1058 x 356 ‡ 5K / 1 sec Unicode 5.0 UTF-8

A repeat region is an invisible element in the Dreamweaver designer. To view invisible elements on your page, choose View➪Visual Aides➪Invisible Elements.

6. **Choose View➪Live Data to view the page with actual data from the database.**

   Figure 2-8 shows that the multiple records in this result cause the repeated region to appear five times.

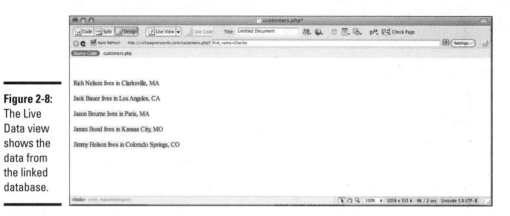

Figure 2-8:
The Live
Data view
shows the
data from
the linked
database.

Fields that appear highlighted in Live Data view are dynamic text. In other words, the text disappears when you turn off Live Data view. (See Book VIII, Chapter 3 for more on Live Data view.)

Repeating regions in HTML tables

To make your data easier to read, you can integrate an HTML table and a repeating region. The bulk of these steps work the same as the last example, but the dynamic text is placed into a table row:

1. **Open a new dynamic page and create a recordset or open an existing page with a defined recordset.**

   You can use the default recordset name of `Recordset1`.

2. **Insert a table by choosing Insert➪Table.**

3. **Enter the number of rows and columns you want in the Rows and Columns fields.**

   You should limit the number of rows to 2.

4. **Click OK.**

   The table appears in the Document window (see Figure 2-9).

5. **Enter the names of the fields in the column headers of the table.**

   I entered `First Name`, `Last Name`, `City`, and `State`.

6. **Select the first column of the table's second row.**

   This is where you'll place the first field of the dynamic text.

7. **Open the Server Behaviors panel by choosing Window➪Server Behaviors.**

8. **Click the plus (+) button and choose Dynamic Text.**

   The Dynamic Text dialog box appears.

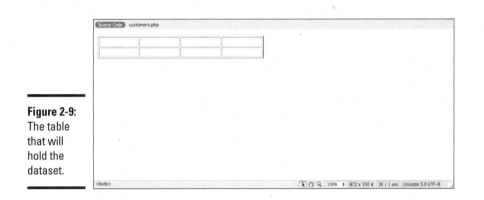

Figure 2-9:
The table
that will
hold the
dataset.

9. **Expand the recordset.**

   All the database table columns display.

10. **Select the column from Step 6.**

    You can leave format and code alone because you just want to display these fields as they are in the database.

11. **Click OK.**

    Your dynamic field appears on your page enclosed by curly brackets {} (in our example, it's `Recordset1.first_name`). The dynamic text entry is added to the Server Behaviors list.

12. **Select the second column of the second table row.**

13. **Repeat Steps 6 through 12 for each of the remaining fields.**

14. **Select the rows in the table with both dynamic text fields.**

15. **Click the plus (+) sign in the Server Behaviors panel and choose Repeat Region.**

    The Repeat Region dialog box appears.

16. **Click OK.**

    The default displays ten records, but you can pick a different number or display all records by selecting the All Records radio button.

    A gray box appears around the repeating fields with the text *Repeat* on a tab. The repeat region (`Recordset1`) also shows up in the Server Behaviors listing.

    Figure 2-10 shows the repeated regions defined on the table row.

17. **Choose View⇨Live Data to view the actual data from the database.**

    Figure 2-11 shows that the two records in this result cause the repeated region to display twice.

**Book VIII
Chapter 2**

**Using Dynamic
Content in Your
Web Pages**

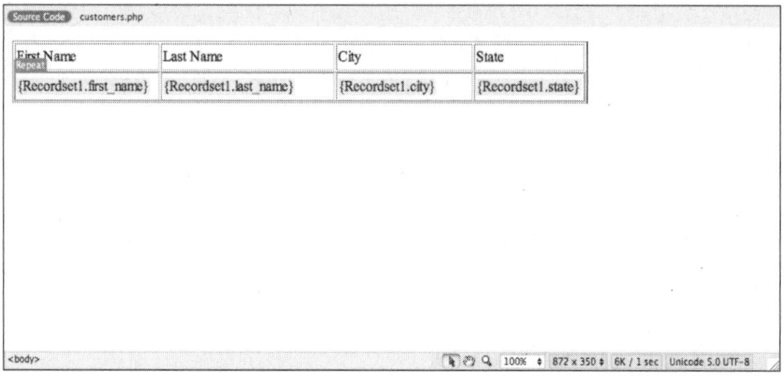

First Name	Last Name	City	State
{Recordset1.first_name}	{Recordset1.last_name}	{Recordset1.city}	{Recordset1.state}

Figure 2-10:
The repeat region for `Recordset1`.

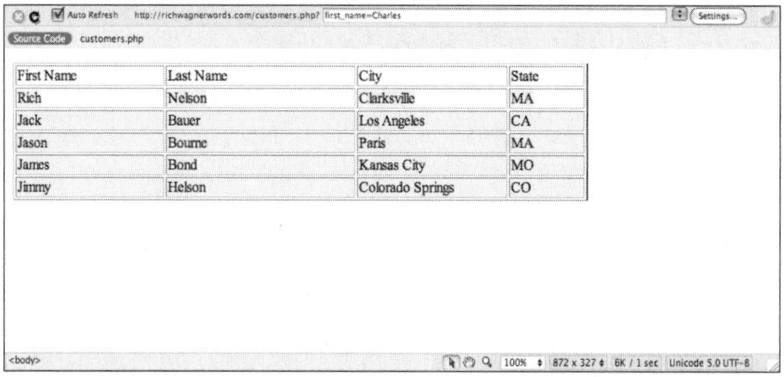

First Name	Last Name	City	State
Rich	Nelson	Clarksville	MA
Jack	Bauer	Los Angeles	CA
Jason	Bourne	Paris	MA
James	Bond	Kansas City	MO
Jimmy	Helson	Colorado Springs	CO

Figure 2-11:
The Live Data mode shows the database data presented in an HTML table.

Adding a recordset navigation bar

Dreamweaver provides paging functions in the Server Behaviors panel for the Web user to go to the first page, last page, next page, and previous page of multi-page repeating regions. You can associate these behaviors with text or with images that you select on the page itself, such as the forward and backward arrows.

When applying a Navigation server behavior to a dynamic Web page, you can display only one recordset on the page because you can't specify to which recordset the navigation applies.

To help users keep track of which record they're viewing in a multi-page record-set, you can add a Record Count server behavior. You can display the total number of records, the first record on a page, and the last record on a page.

Before you can add a Recordset Navigation server behavior, you must have a Repeat Region server behavior on your page (as described in the previous section). Although you can individually add a Navigation server behavior to your page, the easiest way to build navigation for a recordset is to use a navigation bar.

Follow these steps to add the navigation bar to your page:

1. **In the Document window, place the pointer where you want to insert the navigation bar.**

2. **Choose Insert⟹Data Objects⟹Recordset Paging⟹Recordset Navigation Bar.**

The Recordset Navigation Bar dialog box appears (see Figure 2-12).

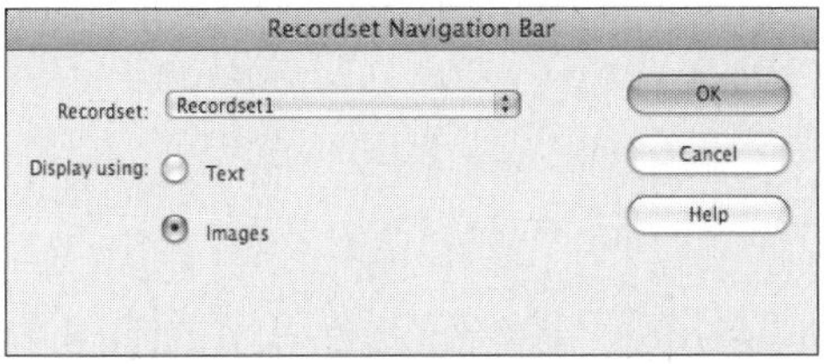

Figure 2-12: The Recordset Navigation Bar dialog box.

3. **Select the recordset that you want to control from the Recordset drop-down list.**

4. **Select Text or Images to indicate the type of navigation bar.**

I'm in a graphical mode, so I'm choosing Images for my example.

5. **Click OK.**

The navigation bar appears on your page, as shown in Figure 2-13.

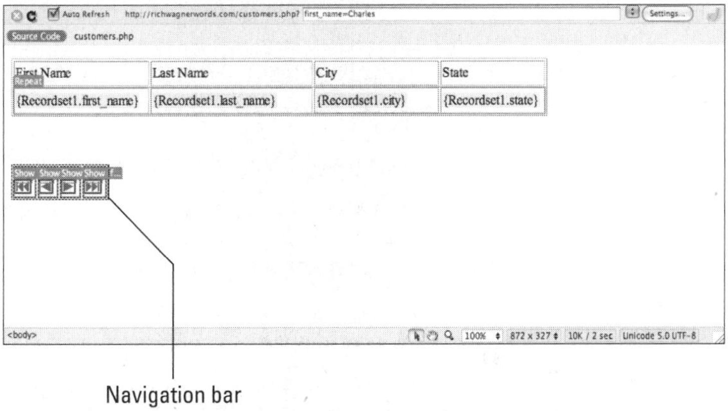

Figure 2-13: The Recordset Navigation bar is displayed.

Navigation bar

Book VIII
Chapter 2

Using Dynamic
Content in Your
Web Pages

Showing and hiding regions on your page

The Show Region server behavior lets you show or hide areas of your document based on certain conditions. For example, a page that displays personal information about users should only be visible by the site administrator. Here's a rundown of the six Show Region server behaviors:

+ Show If Recordset Is Empty

+ Show If Recordset Is Not Empty

+ Show If First Page

+ Show If Not First Page

+ Show If Last Page

+ Show If Not Last Page

For example, the Show If Not First Page and Show If Not Last Page server behaviors let you display previous and next links only when you have a next or previous page that you can jump to.

To apply one of the server behaviors to your page, open your document and follow these steps:

1. **In Design view, select the region that you want to show or hide.**

   To select the region, drag the pointer while clicking the mouse.

2. **In the Server Behaviors panel, click the plus (+) button and then select an option from the Show Region submenu that appears.**

   You can choose from the six Show Region server behaviors.

3. **In the dialog box that corresponds to the type of region you're showing, select the recordset that you want to apply the server behavior to.**

4. **Click OK.**

   The server behavior is applied to the selected region.

Adding Dynamic Form Elements to Your Page

In the same way that you use the Bindings panel to insert dynamic text on your Web page (as described at the beginning of the chapter), you can also integrate dynamic text as default values for form elements. Dreamweaver supports using dynamic data for all the major form elements, including text boxes, check boxes, radio selections, and list/menu boxes.

To insert a dynamic form element on your page, follow these steps:

1. **Choose Insert➪Form➪Form to insert a form on your page.**

See Book II, Chapter 7 for the lowdown on creating forms.

2. **Choose Insert➪Form and then select a form element that would be effective in displaying your data.**

Be sure to give it a distinct ID that you can reference later.

The form element appears on the page.

3. **In the Server Behaviors panel, click the plus (+) button and select a dynamic form type from the Dynamic Form Elements menu.**

Figure 2-14 shows the Dynamic Text Field dialog box.

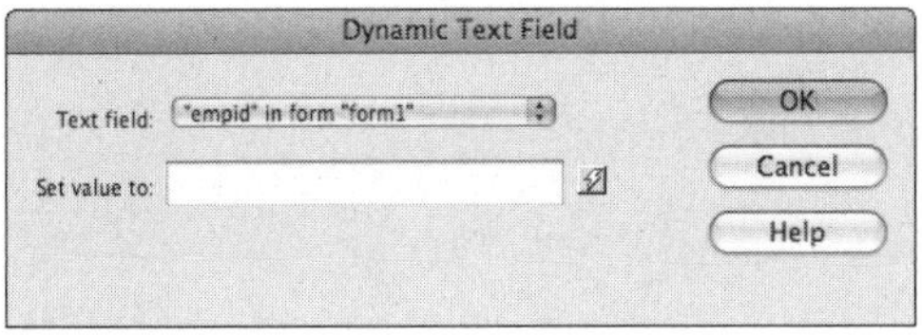

Figure 2-14:
The
Dynamic
Text Field
dialog box.

4. **In the Text field drop-down, select the form element you created back in Step 2.**

5. **Click OK.**

The text field now gets its default value from the data source.

Chapter 3: Previewing and Testing Your Dynamic Pages

In This Chapter

✔ Testing your dynamic pages by using Live Data mode

✔ Previewing your dynamic pages in a Web browser

*W*hen you work with static HTML files inside Dreamweaver CS4, previewing your Web site is easy. Just click the Preview in browser button and have at it. But when you are working with dynamically created pages, previewing your work is much trickier — at least, it seems like it should be. Fortunately, Dreamweaver comes to the rescue by providing built-in support in the form of Live Data previews. In this chapter, you find out how to preview and test your dynamic pages by using Live Data mode or a Web browser.

For your pages to work on a remote server, you must transfer your files to the remote folder. See Book V, Chapter 4 for details on publishing your site.

Viewing Live Data in Your Dynamic Web Pages

A great way to test the functionality of your dynamic Web site is to use Dreamweaver's Live Data mode. When you use the Live Data mode while developing a page in Dreamweaver, Dreamweaver connects to your Web server, pulls the dynamic data for the page from the database, and then uses that data to replace the dynamic data placeholders on your page.

For details on adding dynamic data to your page, see Book VIII, Chapter 2.

In order for the Live Data mode to work correctly, you must simulate any input that usually comes from the user. You also need any supporting files such as server-side includes so that the Web server can execute the dynamic code without errors.

Understanding how Live Data mode works

Here are the specific tasks that Dreamweaver performs when you use Live Data mode:

1. Transfers your dynamic page to the server temporarily.

2. Requests the page from the server.

3. The Web server executes the dynamic page code that may contain calls to database functions.

4. Integrates the page request results into the page and displays them in Design view.

5. Deletes the temporary file from the server.

Figure 3-1 shows how a Web page looks with placeholders. Figure 3-2 shows how the same Web page looks with Live Data mode.

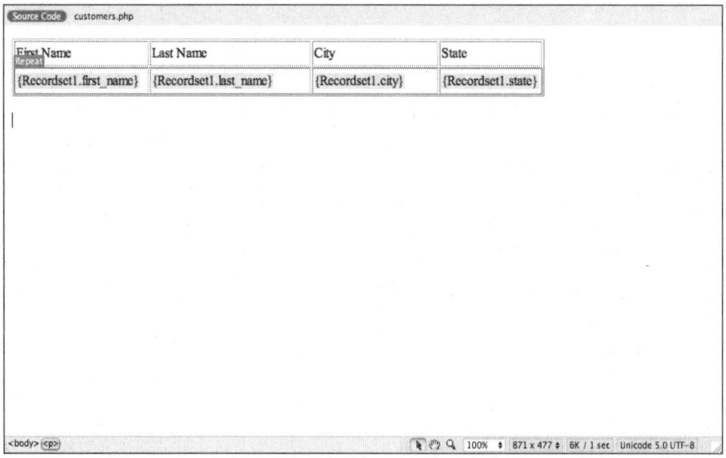

Figure 3-1:
This page, not in Live Data mode, contains placeholders for fields in a customer database.

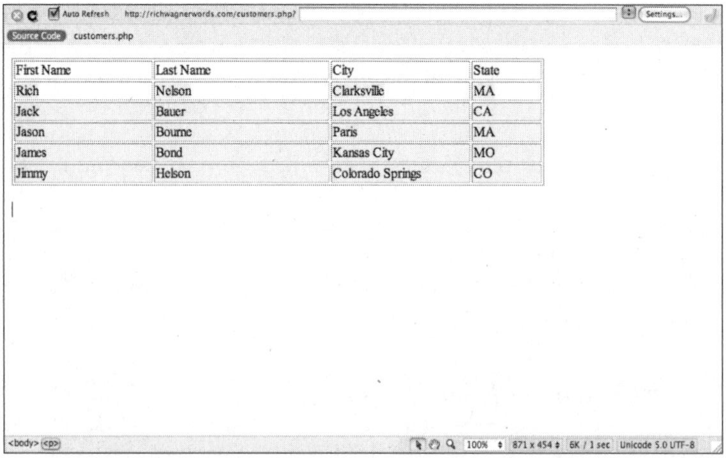

Figure 3-2:
Live Data mode replaces the placeholders with actual data.

In order for Live Data mode to work properly, Dreamweaver has to know how to get the page that you're previewing to the server and how to request that page from the server, specifically the URL path. These paths are set up as part of your testing server (see Book VII, Chapter 1).

You can manually refresh your Live Data page by clicking the Refresh button in the Live Data toolbar. You may find refreshing your Live Data page useful if you've changed any data in the database. You can see how those changes affect your page.

Uploading dependent files to the testing server

Some dynamic Web pages rely on dependent files to work properly. *Dependent files* are files that your Web page references and a browser loads when it displays the page. If a dependent file is missing, your page may generate an error or there may be images missing when the browser displays the page. Dependent files can include

+ **Code files:** These files include JSP .jar classes, ASP .asp files, and ColdFusion .cfm files.

+ **CSS files:** The files include style sheet details such as how different classes of text appear. See Book III, Chapter 1 for more information.

+ **Image files:** Image files include those such as JPG or GIF files. Depending on your image tags, you may not need to have the images on the testing server. In any case, missing images won't cause your page to fail to load.

+ **Server-side includes:** Code that is included from a file as the dynamic Web page code executes. An `include` statement is replaced by the contents of the included file when the page is processed on the Web server.

Dreamweaver doesn't know which dependent files to send to the testing server, so you need to upload the appropriate files manually. Follow these steps to upload your dependent files to the testing server:

1. **Choose Window⇨Files to open the Files panel.**

The Files panel displays files for each portion of your site, including the local, remote, and testing servers.

2. **Click the Expand/Collapse button, as Figure 3-3 shows.**

The expanded view displays two file views at the same time. By default, the local files always appear on the right half of the screen.

3. **Click the Testing Server button (see Figure 3-4).**

The file view on the left displays the Testing Server files, as shown in Figure 3-4.

4. **Select the dependent files from the Local Files list.**

You can select multiple files by holding the Ctrl (Windows) or ⌘ (Mac) key while clicking the files.

5. **To upload the dependent files to the testing server, click the Put Files button (which you can see in Figure 3-4).**

   The files display in the Testing Server file list, and your dynamic page code can now access them during Live Data viewing.

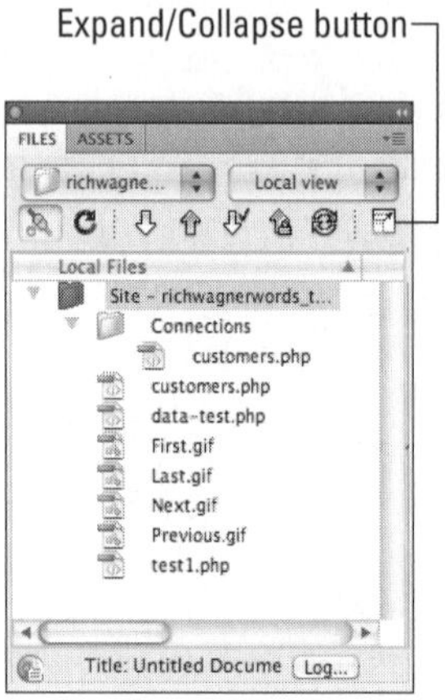

Expand/Collapse button

Figure 3-3:
The Expand/
Collapse
button.

Testing Server button   Put Files button

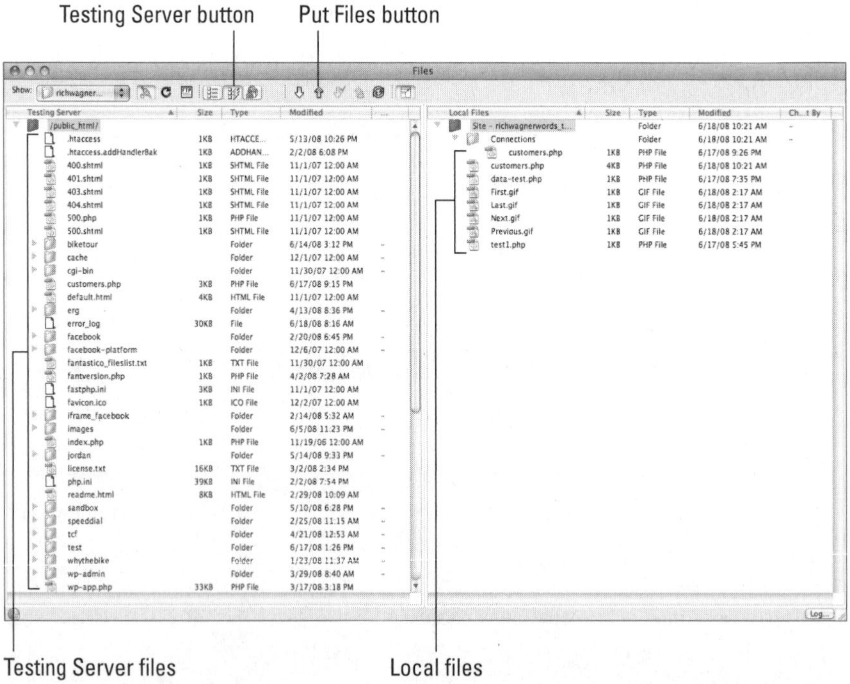

Figure 3-4:
The
expanded
file view.

Testing Server files   Local files

Providing parameters for user input

Sometimes your dynamic page code generates different output based on the user's input, such as a username or a value that indicates a database row (such as a user ID). If your dynamic page code processes user input results, such as a form submission, you may need to update the Live Data settings to supply the value (simulate the user's input). If you don't update the Live Update settings, your page may issue a warning that it can't find any data to display. Follow these steps to add parameters for user input:

1. **Choose View⇨Live Data Settings.**

The Live Data Settings dialog box appears with an empty list of parameters.

2. **To simulate the user input for each parameter, click the plus (+) button.**

An empty row appears in the Name and Value columns.

3. **In the Name column, enter the name of the parameter, and in the Value column, enter the value that you want to send to your dynamic Web page for that parameter.**

For example, if you have a parameter called user_id and want to send the value chucky_chase, you enter fields like the ones in Figure 3-5.

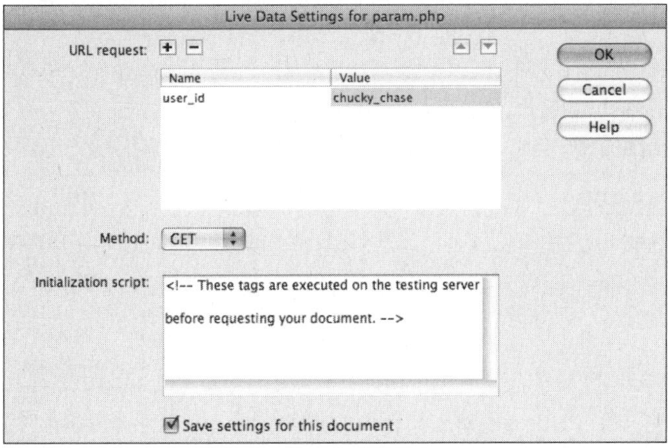

Figure 3-5:
The Live
Data
Settings
dialog box.

4. **From the Method drop-down list, select a form submission method.**

Your form submits its results by using either a GET or a POST method; select that same method from the Method drop-down list. See Book II, Chapter 7 for details on the GET and POST methods.

5. **(Optional) Set session variables in the Initialization Script text area.**

See Book VIII, Chapter 1 for the lowdown on session variables.

6. **Click OK.**

Your page uses the value in the parameter when updating its Live Data mode.

Troubleshooting problems in Live Data mode

Sometimes your Live Data mode may not work right the first time. If your view doesn't work as planned, troubleshooting suggestions can help you figure out the problem.

The most common problem that you may encounter in Live Data mode happens when you have missing dependent files. Here are some troubleshooting tips to try to resolve this problem:

✦ In the Files panel, verify that every file your script needs, including any database-related files, is present in the Testing Server file listing.

✦ In the Testing Server category of the Site Definition dialog box, verify that your testing server folder points to a location on your testing server that can process the dynamic files — in other words, it's within the document root of the Web server).

To do so, open the Site Definition dialog box by choosing Site⇨Manage Sites, choosing your site, and clicking the Edit button.

Verify that the URL prefix maps to the Web address that matches the testing server folder.

Table 3-1 shows some example folders and their corresponding URLs.

Table 3-1	Typical Paths and URLs	
Web Server	**Folder**	**URL**
IIS on Windows	C:\Inetpub\wwwroot\ testapp\	`http://local-host/testapp`
Apache on Windows	C:\Program Files\Apache Group\Apache2\htdocs\ testapp	`http://local-host/testapp`
Apache on Linux	~jon/testapp	`http://example.com/ ~jon/testapp`

If you want to make sure that your testing server folder and URL agree outside of Dreamweaver, place a simple HTML file in your testing server folder. For example, you can use index.htm with these contents:

```
<html>
<body>Smiles everyone, smiles.</body>
</html>
```

You can then verify the URL by pasting the URL prefix plus `index.htm` into your browser's address bar. You should see a page with the content supplied. If you don't, double-check your paths because you have a problem somewhere.

✦ Verify the directory's permissions to be sure that the Web server can read it. If you're using Windows, verify that the folder permissions allow the Web server to execute and read the directory. See Book VII, Chapter 7.

Previewing a Dynamic Web Page in Your Browser

You may find using Live Data mode great for testing your dynamic pages, but Live Data doesn't fully mimic the way that your page looks in a browser. Live Data mode won't go through multiple pages of results from the database. As a result, you should debug and test your application inside of your Web browser.

To preview a Web page in your local Web browser, open the page in Dreamweaver and press F12 (⌘+F12 on a Mac). You don't need to copy any files to a temporary folder on the testing server because Dreamweaver can do the copying for you automatically, or your browser can use the files in the local folder.

Follow these steps to tell Dreamweaver that you want to use a temporary copy of your files when previewing with your browser:

1. **Choose Edit⇨Preferences to open the Dreamweaver Preferences dialog box.**

The Dreamweaver Preferences dialog box appears.

2. **Click the Preview in Browser category.**

The option for previewing appears, as shown in Figure 3-6.

3. **Select the Preview Using Temporary File check box.**

This option tells Dreamweaver to create a temporary copy of the file when previewing the page in a browser.

Of course, you can also use this dialog box if you want to change the default browser that you use for previewing your pages. See Book V, Chapter 1 for details.

4. **Click OK.**

Now the browser uses a temporary file when previewing your page.

The same requirements for dependent files that apply to Live Data also apply to the browser-based preview: Make sure that you specify in the Files panel all the files that you need to display your page. (See the section "Uploading dependent files to the testing server," earlier in this chapter, for details.)

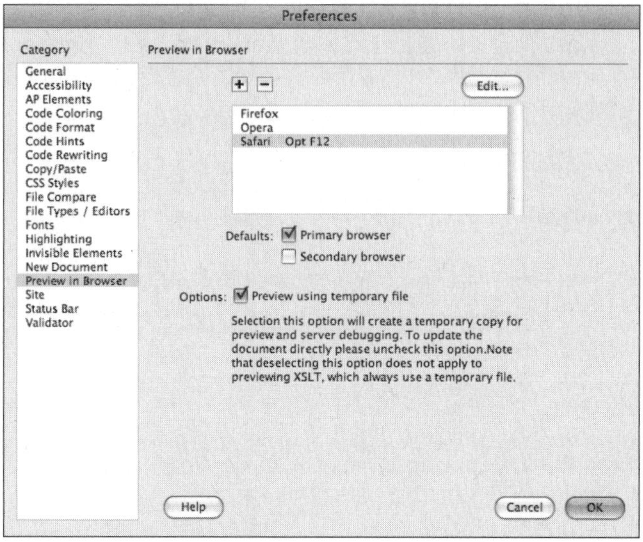

Figure 3-6:
The Preview in Browser category of the Preferences dialog box.

If you get a dialog box asking if you want to update the copy of the file on the testing server, click OK.

Working on dynamic pages without Live Data

I know it's not nearly as fun, but if you can't access your testing server or you simply like to work without Live Data, you can still develop and work with your dynamic page. Dreamweaver uses placeholders to represent where actual data would appear if you were in Live Data mode. These placeholders appear surrounded by curly brackets { } to set them apart from the rest of your page.

Chapter 4: Building Dynamic Forms

In This Chapter

✔ **Understanding dynamic forms**

✔ **Inserting dynamic form elements**

✔ **Making form objects dynamic**

*W*hen you work with application servers like PHP and ASP, you can display dynamic pages based on data from databases. However, you may also want to build dynamic forms as well — providing values for the form fields and capturing the updated data to the backend database when the form is submitted.

Making forms dynamic allows users to update information because the existing values come up as the defaults when the form displays. You must start with a regular form and its elements before making the default values dynamic. We show you how to make text boxes, check boxes, radio buttons, and lists/menus dynamic in this chapter.

The elements that actually make up a form can be supplied with dynamic data. To create a dynamic form, you must define a source for the dynamic data first by creating a binding. The binding tells Dreamweaver what dynamic information your program can reference. These sources can be anything from URL parameters to values for a database recordset. (See Book VIII, Chapters 1 and 2 for more on bindings.)

For more detailed information on the form objects (text fields, check boxes, radio buttons, lists, and menus) described in the following sections, refer to Book II, Chapter 7.

Inserting Text Fields

Text fields allow you to capture basic text information from the user. Dynamic text fields are very useful when users are updating their information because the current values become the defaults for the update screen. To make an existing text field dynamic, follow these steps:

1. **Select a text field in a form on your page.**

See Book II, Chapter 7 for the lowdown on creating forms and text fields.

Figure 4-1 shows an example of an inserted text field.

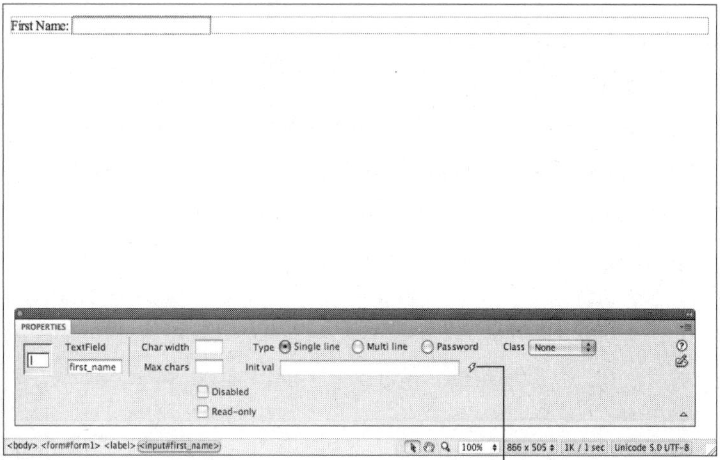

Figure 4-1:
An inserted text field in a form.

The Bind to Dynamic Source button

2. **In the Properties inspector, click the Bind to Dynamic Source button next to the Init Val field.**

The Dynamic Data dialog box appears, as shown in Figure 4-2. It lists the available data sources in the Field area.

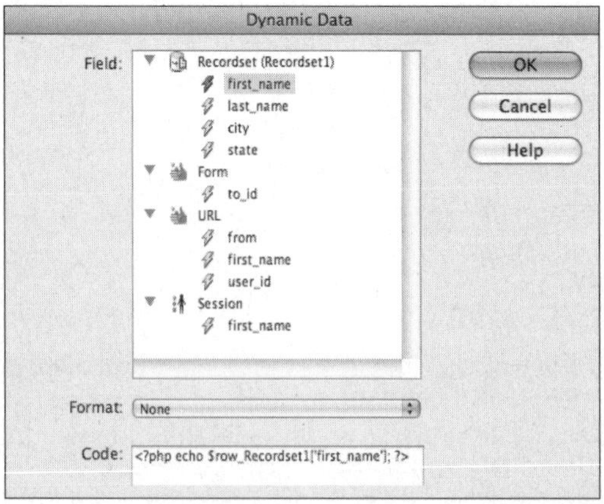

Figure 4-2:
The Dynamic Data dialog box.

3. In the Field area, select the data source that will supply the default value for the text field.

For example, in Figure 4-2, we selected the `first_name` Recordset item. This data source provides the initial value for the text field on the page.

Click the plus sign next to the category of the field (such as Recordset) to expand it before selecting a data source. Leave the Format set to None to display the text exactly as it is in the source.

A recordset can be used as the data source for the dynamic value, but if the recordset returns more than one row, only the first value is used.

4. Click OK.

Figure 4-3 displays the placeholder that's created for the dynamic text on the page: in this case, `Recordset1.first_name`.

Placeholder

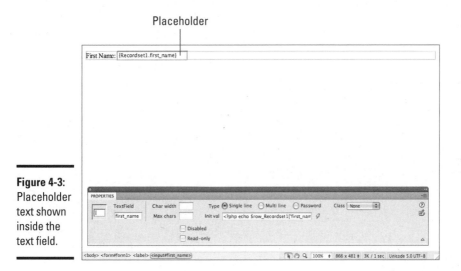

Figure 4-3: Placeholder text shown inside the text field.

Adding Check Boxes

An HTML check box allows a user to select more than one value from a list of check box values. Dynamic check boxes have their default state of checked or not checked set by the value of a binding. Use bindings for tasks such as defaulting the check box values to their current settings for an update screen.

Check boxes are most commonly used when working with Boolean data fields with a true/false value. However, you can also use a check box based on whether a field is equal to the value you specify.

To make a check box dynamic, follow these steps:

1. **Select a check box in a form on your page.**

See Book II, Chapter 7 for the lowdown on creating forms and check boxes.

2. **In the Properties inspector, click the Bind to Dynamic Source button.**

The Dynamic CheckBox dialog box appears (see Figure 4-4). The default value for the CheckBox drop-down list is the current check box.

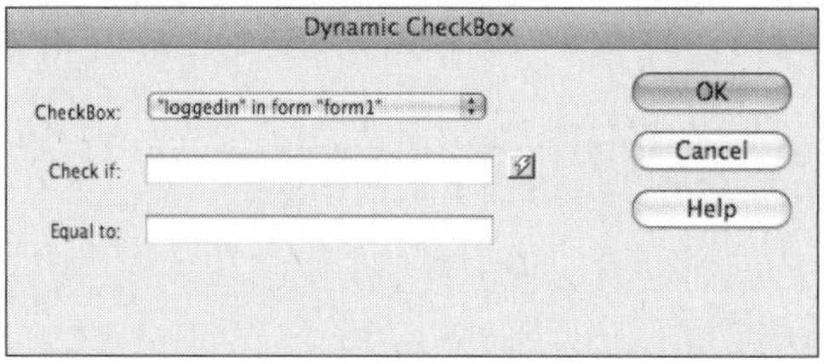

Figure 4-4:
The
Dynamic
CheckBox
dialog box.

3. **Click the Bind to Dynamic Source button next to the Check If field.**

The Dynamic Data dialog box appears, displaying the available data sources (refer to Figure 4-2).

4. **Select the data source field to use for the default value comparison and then click OK.**

After you click OK, you return to the Dynamic CheckBox dialog box and Dreamweaver automatically fills in the Check If field.

5. **In the Equal To field, enter the value the field must have for the check box to be selected.**

If the Check If value is the same as the Equal To value, the check box is selected by default.

6. **Click OK.**

Now when you use Live Data view (see Book VIII, Chapter 3) or preview the page in a browser (press F12 or ⌘+F12 on a Mac), the check box appears selected or deselected, based on the value from the data source you selected in Step 4.

You can repeat the same process for each check box in the same group.

Working with Radio Buttons

Use HTML radio buttons when you want users to select only one choice from a set of options. Radio buttons are typically used in groups (for example, AM or PM when selecting a time). Making a group of radio buttons dynamic means that the default value can come from a binding.

To make the default selection dynamic for a group of radio buttons, follow these steps:

1. **In a form on your page, click any of the radio buttons in a radio button group.**

   This selects all the radio buttons in the group so you can view the group's properties.

   See Book II, Chapter 7 for the lowdown on creating forms and radio buttons.

2. **In the Properties inspector, click the Bind to Dynamic Source button.**

   The Dynamic Radio Group dialog box appears, as shown in Figure 4-5.

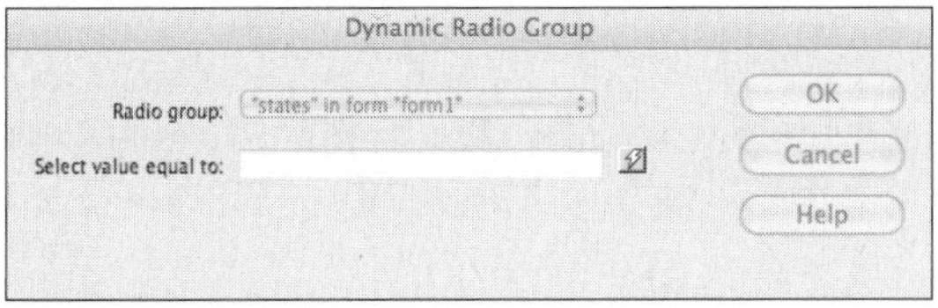

Figure 4-5:
The
Dynamic
Radio Group
dialog box.

3. **Click the Bind to Dynamic Source button next to the Select Value Equal To field.**

   The Dynamic Data dialog box appears, displaying the available data sources (refer to Figure 4-2).

4. **Choose a data source field to use for the default selection value.**

   The Select Value Equal To field is compared to the checked value for each radio group button to determine the default selection.

   You need to expand the category of the field, such as URL, before selecting a data source. In this example, we selected the language URL parameter. The radio group preselects a radio button only if its value matches the value in this field. Dreamweaver automatically fills in the Select Value Equal To field after you select a binding.

5. **Click OK.**

   You return to the Dynamic Radio Group dialog box.

6. **Click OK.**

   Now when you use Live Data view (see Book VIII, Chapter 3) or preview the page in a browser, a radio button is selected based on the value from the data source you selected in Step 4.

You need apply the dynamic formatting only once per radio group because a radio group can have only one value at a time selected.

Book VIII
Chapter 4

Building Dynamic Forms

Inserting Lists and Menus

An HTML form list (or menu) provides a convenient way for a user to select one or more items from the drop-down menu or list. It also dictates that only supplied values can be selected (unlike text fields, where the user can enter anything). You can insert the menu as either a drop-down list or as a scrollable list, which is also called a *list menu*. A list or menu could be used to select which categories you're interested in receiving. Dynamic lists and menus make updating that list simpler by using your current selection values as defaults when updating.

To set the default dynamic values for a menu or list, follow these steps:

1. **Select the menu or list in a form on your page.**

See Book II, Chapter 7 for the lowdown on creating forms, menus, and lists.

2. **In the Properties inspector, click the Bind to Dynamic Source button.**

The Dynamic List/Menu dialog box opens.

3. **Select the desired recordset from the Options from Recordset list.**

4. **In the Values and Labels lists, choose the desired field from the recordset.**

5. **Click the Bind to Dynamic Source button to the right of the Select Value Equal To field.**

The Dynamic Data dialog box appears (refer to Figure 4-2).

6. **You can optionally specify that a particular item is selected by entering a value equal to the menu item's value, in the Select Value Equal To box.**

7. **Click OK.**

When you use Live Data view (see Book VIII, Chapter 3) or preview the page in a browser, the items on the dynamic menu or menus are generated and selected based on the data source value you selected in Step 4.

Figure 4-6 displays a drop-down menu populated with values in Live Data mode.

Figure 4-6:
The menu is populated with values from the recordset.

Chapter 5: Advanced Dynamic Data Presentation

In This Chapter

✓ Working with ColdFusion components

✓ Adding Web services to your site

✓ Putting custom server behaviors to work

ColdFusion allows you to add complex dynamic functionality to your pages without worrying about how the component does its magic. Then, Web services allow you to use a remote server to process portions of your Web page. You can use Web services to do something like returning a temperature based on the input of a zip code. Your site doesn't need to know how to perform the calculation itself, just how to access the server. Additionally, you can customize Dreamweaver's tools for inserting code into your dynamic sites.

Using ColdFusion Components

ColdFusion Components (CFCs) are bits of ColdFusion code that you can use over and over again in your site. Think of CFCs as storage containers that keep your ColdFusion code organized and accessible. CFCs provide access to many more features than you'd have if you simply included ColdFusion code from a file. Here are some of those features and benefits:

✦ **Extendibility:** You can add code to CFCs.

✦ **Security:** You can limit access to portions of the code.

✦ **Speed:** CFCs are faster than other code because they're compiled.

✦ **Documentation:** CFCs automatically generate documentation.

In order to use CFCs, you need to use ColdFusion (version 7 or higher).

By creating a CFC for code that you use throughout your site, you can reduce the amount of work you need to do to maintain the site. Like a Dreamweaver template, if you need to change that code, you only need to make the change in one spot, and the code updates throughout the site.

In order to use ColdFusion components, you either need to install ColdFusion on your local computer or have access to a Remote Development Server (RDS) connection. You have to also specify the testing server URL prefix in the Site Definition dialog box that Dreamweaver uses to display pages after transferring those images to the server. Finally, you should feel comfortable working directly with ColdFusion code.

Building Web pages that use ColdFusion components

Dreamweaver comes with preinstalled ColdFusion components, which you can find in the Components panel (choose Window➪Components). When you select a CFC, Dreamweaver places the code to run the CFC into your page so that you have a solid starting point from which you can modify the code.

To include a ColdFusion component call in your Web page, follow these steps:

1. **Create or open a new ColdFusion page.**

2. **Click the Show Code View button.**

   Unlike server behaviors, ColdFusion Components don't appear in Design view. Work directly with Code view to see the added Component code.

3. **In the Components panel, select CF Components from the drop-down list.**

   Dreamweaver lists the component packages in the Components panel, as shown in Figure 5-1.

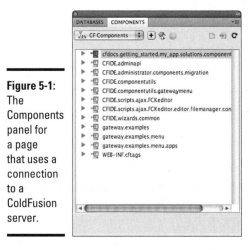

Figure 5-1: The Components panel for a page that uses a connection to a ColdFusion server.

4. Click the arrow beside a component to expand a components package.

The components within that package are listed, along with its functions in a subtree (see Figure 5-2).

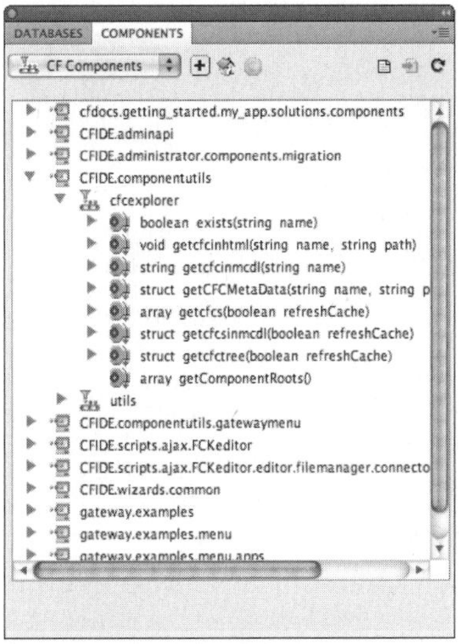

Figure 5-2:
The Components panel listing the component and its functions.

5. Select the function that you want to invoke from your page and then drag that function to the point in the code where you want to place it.

The code from the function is inserted in the Document window. You use the `<cfinvoke>` tag to call ColdFusion Components, as shown in Figure 5-3.

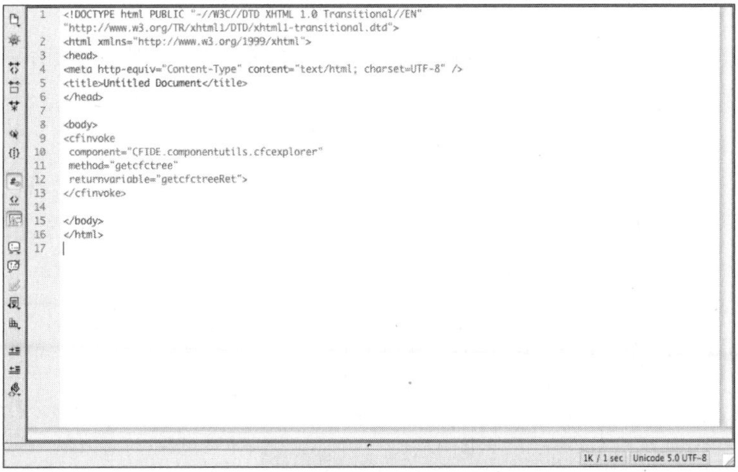

Figure 5-3:
Calling the `getcf ctree` function in the Document window.

You can also insert code by right-clicking (Windows) or Control+clicking (Mac) the function name and selecting Insert Code. Or, you can click the Insert Code button on the Components toolbar.

6. If your function needs parameters, you can add them to the `cfinvoke` tag by adding a parameter value pair.

For example, to add the username parameter with a value of Cosmo Crumer, use this code:

```
username="Cosmo Crumer"
```

7. Choose File⇨Save to save your changes.

You now have your changes saved to the local folder.

8. To see your code in action, choose File⇨Preview in the Browser⇨ *Name of Browser.*

Because the site contains dynamic code, you can't see the output without the ColdFusion server processing it.

Creating ColdFusion components

Although you can certainly create your ColdFusion components the old-fashioned way — by writing them entirely in ColdFusion code — you can make the process much easier by letting Dreamweaver help you out by doing it in a more interactive fashion.

To create a ColdFusion component in Dreamweaver, follow these steps:

1. Create a new ColdFusion page or open an existing one.

2. In the Components panel, select CF Components from the drop-down list.

The available components appear in the main portion of the panel.

3. Click the plus (+) button next to the drop-down list.

The Create Component dialog box appears, as shown in Figure 5-4.

4. Fill in the following fields in the Component section:

- **Display Name:** Enter a descriptive name for your component.

- **Hint:** Enter a brief description of what your component does. This field automatically appears in the documentation for your component.

- **Extends:** You can leave this field blank. Use this field to base your component on an existing component.

- **Component Directory:** Click the Browse button to specify where you want to save the component. Select a directory by using the Web application root folder, usually C:\Inetpub\wwwroot, or a subfolder.

- **Name:** Enter a filename for your component in the Name field. The name follows general naming rules — only letters, numbers, and underscores. Don't add the .cfc file extension to the name.

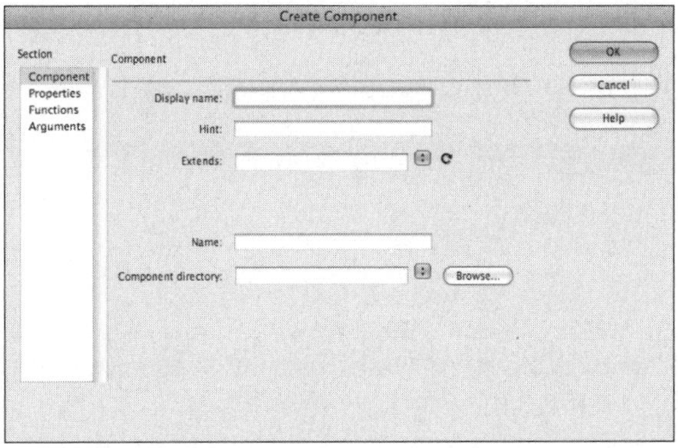

Figure 5-4:
The Create
Component
dialog box.

5. **To define properties (variables for the component), select Properties from the Section list. Click the plus (+) button to add properties:**

   - **Name:** Enter a name for your property in the Name field. The name follows general naming rules — only letters, numbers, and underscores.

   - **Display Name:** Enter a descriptive name for your property.

   - **Hint:** Enter a brief description of what your property stores. This field automatically appears in the documentation for your component.

   - **Type:** Select the type of data your property stores.

6. **To define a function, select Functions from the Section list on the left side of the dialog box.**

7. **Click the plus (+) button and then fill in the following fields, which are shown in Figure 5-5:**

   - **Name:** Enter a descriptive name for your function.

   - **Display Name:** Enter the same name that you enter in the Name field. This display name gives you the option to make a longer, more descriptive version of the name.

   - **Hint:** Enter a summary of what your function does. This summary appears in the automatic documentation for your component.

   - **Access:** Select an access type from the drop-down list. Selecting Remote makes your function available as a Web service.

   - **Return Type:** Select a return type from the drop-down list. All the ColdFusion data types appear in the list.

   You can leave the Roles text box blank and the Output check box deselected.

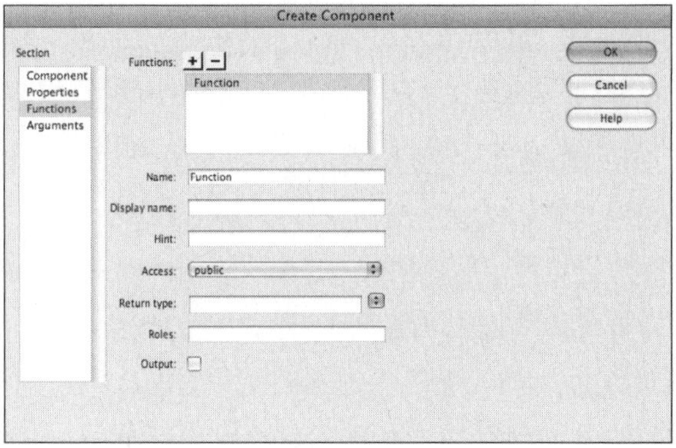

Figure 5-5:
Defining a
function in
the Create
Component
dialog box.

8. **To define an argument for your function, select Arguments from the Section list on the left side of the dialog box.**

9. **Select the function from the Available Functions drop-down list.**

   Each function can have as many arguments as you want.

10. **Click the plus (+) button and then fill in the following fields, which are shown in Figure 5-6:**

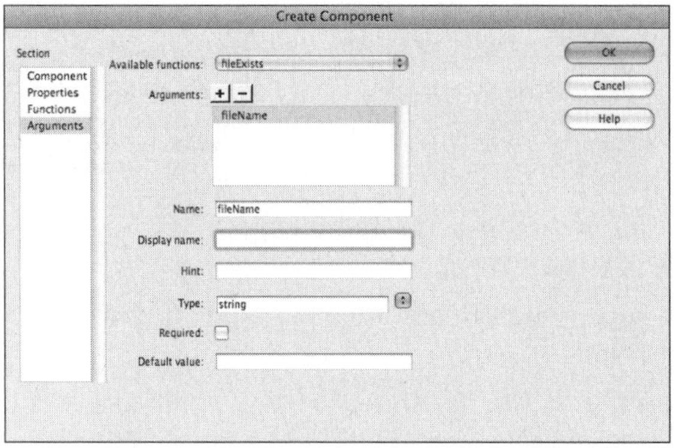

Figure 5-6:
Defining an
argument
for the
`file`
`Exists`
function.

- **Name, Display Name, Hint, and Type:** You can enter these fields as you do in the Functions section (see Step 7).

- **Required:** If you need the argument when calling the function, click the Required check box.

- **Default Value:** To supply a default value, enter it in the Default Value field. The function uses this value if calling code doesn't supply a value when calling the function.

Conditional code block execution

Sometimes, you may have a chunk of code that you don't always want to execute. For example, you want the code to display an error message only after an error.

To specify that you want a code block to execute based on a condition, you can use this syntax:

```
<@ if (condition1) @>
    codeblockif
[<@ elseif (condition2) @>
    codeblockifelse]
[<@ else @>
    codeblockelse]
<@ endif @>
```

Here's a closer look at this syntax:

✔ Replace condition1 and condition2 with any JavaScript expression that evaluates to true or false.

✔ Replace the labels that start with codeblock with the code that you want to run for that condition.

✔ You absolutely need only the `if` portion (the brackets [ ] represent optional parts).

✔ You can have more than one `elseif` portion of a statement.

✔ The else portion executes only if none of the other conditions is true.

---

11. **Click OK to close the dialog box.**

Dreamweaver creates the component as a `.cfc` file and saves it in the directory that you specify in Step 4.

To ensure that Dreamweaver can use your custom component, upload the `.cfc` file to your remote server.

To remove a component, delete the .cfc file from your RDS server. Dreamweaver only lists components it finds on the RDS testing server.

Creating Custom Server Behaviors

Server behaviors are blocks of code that send a request to the server and then receive data in return. Dreamweaver provides many server behaviors in the Server Behaviors panel (choose Windows⇨Server Behaviors), but you can also add more.

You can use Adobe Exchange (www.adobe.com/cfusion/exchange) to add packages of server behaviors. You can also create your own server behaviors by using the Server Behavior Builder. If you're planning to create your own server behavior, first check the Exchange site to see if the server behavior that you want to create already exists.

To create a custom server behavior, you have to

✦ Write the code that performs the action of the server behavior.

✦ Specify where to place the code within the HTML page.

✦ Determine parameters and prompts (prompting the developer for details about how the code works when it's used in your page) for them.

With the Server Behavior Builder, you enter the code block that you want the custom server behavior to insert into a page. You can use any runtime code valid for your server model. For example, if you choose ColdFusion as the document type for your custom server behavior, you have to write ColdFusion code running on a ColdFusion application server. After you build the custom server behavior, you can access it from the Server Behaviors panel.

To create your own custom server behavior with the Server Behavior Builder, follow these steps:

1. **In the Server Behaviors panel, click the plus (+) button and then select New Server Behavior from the list that appears.**

The New Server Behavior dialog box appears, as shown in Figure 5-7.

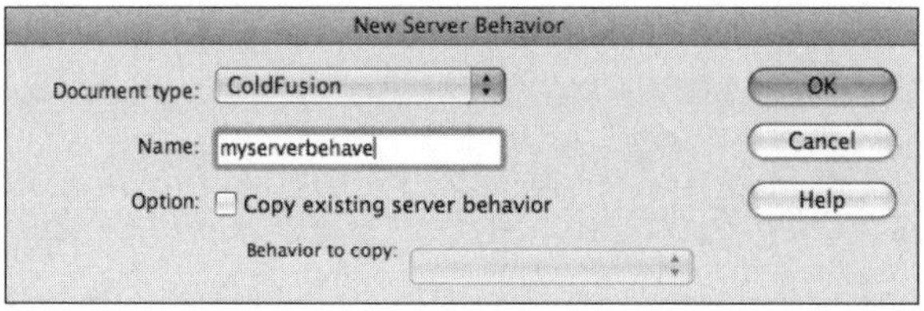

Figure 5-7:
The New
Server
Behavior
dialog box.

2. **Select from the drop-down list the document type to which you want to add this server behavior.**

3. **Enter a name for your server behavior in the Name field.**

The name can use only letters, numbers, and underscores.

4. **Click OK.**

The Server Behavior Builder dialog box appears (see Figure 5-8).

5. **Click the plus (+) button.**

The Create a New Code Block dialog box appears.

6. **Enter the name of your block in the Name field and then click OK.**

The name is added to the code block list.

7. **Enter the code to perform your action in the Code Block text area.**

You can create the code blocks directly within the Server Behavior Builder, or you can copy and paste the code from other sources. Each code block that you create in the Server Behavior Builder must be a single tag or script block. If you need to insert multiple tag blocks, split them into separate code blocks.

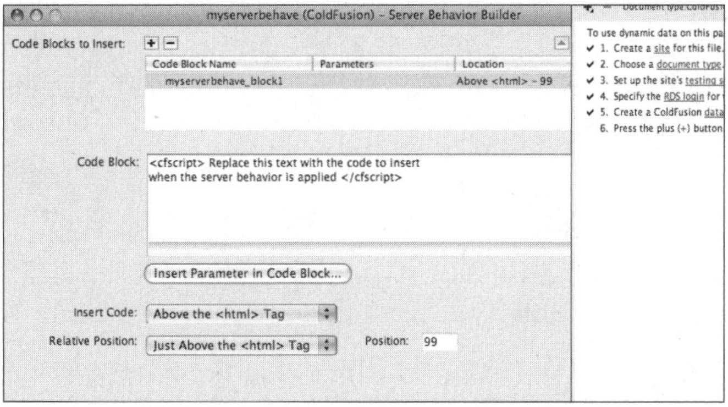

Figure 5-8:
The Server Behavior Builder dialog box.

8. **If you want to include runtime parameters in a code block, select the point in the code block where you want to insert the parameter. Otherwise, skip ahead to Step 13.**

   To include parameters in your code that you supply when you include the stored procedure in a page during the page's design, you first need to mark where the parameters go in your code by using the following format:

   ```
   @@parameter_name@@
   ```

9. **Click the Insert Parameter in Code Block button.**

   The Insert Parameter in Code Block dialog box appears, as shown in Figure 5-9.

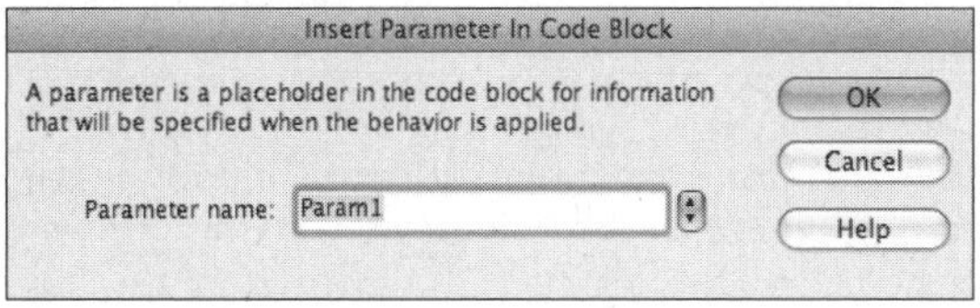

Figure 5-9:
You can define parameter names in this dialog box.

10. **Enter the name in the Parameter Name field and click OK.**

    The usual naming rules apply.

After you click OK, the parameter name placeholder appears in the code at the point that you select in Step 9.

11. (Optional) Repeat Steps 8 through 10 to add more parameters.

12. From the Insert Code drop-down list, select a location where you want to embed the code block.

The Insert Code drop-down list lets you select where to place the code relative to the document, including

- Above the <html> Tag

- Below the <html> Tag

- Relative to a Specific Tag

- Relative to the Selection (the point in the current page that's selected)

The Relative to Selection position applies if you do not wish to define a tag to position the code block against.

13. Select the relative position versus the selection of the code from the Relative Position drop-down list.

Depending on which selection you make for the Insert Code selection in Step 12, you see a different listing of relative locations in the Relative Position drop-down list. For example, if you select Above the <html> Tag, you get the following options:

- The Beginning of the File

- Just Before the Recordsets

- Just After the Recordsets

- Just Above the <html> Tag

- Custom Position

Because selecting the After the <html> Tag for Insert code rules out placing the code at the beginning of the file, you don't have that code placement as an option for that selection.

The Custom Position applies if the designer specifies a tag to position the code block against.

14. To create additional code blocks, repeat Steps 5 through 13.

Remember that you can have only one block of code in the Code Block text area. You can create more code blocks within the server behaviors if you need them.

15. Click Next.

The Generate Behavior dialog box appears.

16. Click OK.

Your server behavior displays in the Server Behaviors panel.

Book IX

Developing Applications Rapidly

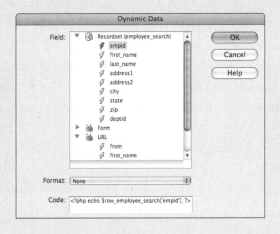

Contents at a Glance

Chapter 1: Building Master and Detail Pages

In This Chapter

- ✔ Developing master and detail pages at the same time
- ✔ Building your master and detail pages separately
- ✔ Putting together master and detail pages for ASP.NET
- ✔ Making sure your master and detail pages work

Simple sets of data can be expressed in a simple table, much like a traditional spreadsheet. But sometimes you don't wish to display complete details on a given table. For example, suppose you wish to display a master list of employees. However, you only wish for the full address and department details to be displayed for an employee when that record is selected. Dreamweaver enables you to do this by setting up what is known as a *master-detail relationship*.

You can use Dreamweaver to build master and detail Web pages, which are a popular way to display information on your Web site. A *master page* displays a list of records and corresponding links for each record. A user can click a link to see further information about a record on its associated *detail page*.

Depending on your programming language, you can either build the set of master and detail pages all in one operation, or you can separately build the master pages and then the detail pages. You can find out more about both methods in this chapter.

The examples in this chapter use a simple Employee table, which you can see in Table 1-1. The first value, the `empid`, is a special field called a *key*. It always has a unique value. Therefore, if you query for a record in a table by using the key, you always get only the row that you're looking for because no two rows have the same key.

Table 1-1	The Employee Table
Column Name	*Type of Data*
empid	Integer
firstname	20 character string
lastname	20 character string
address1	25 character string
address2	25 character string
city	20 character string
state	2 character string
zip	10 character string
deptid	Integer

Building Master and Detail Pages in One Operation (PHP, ASP, JSP, ColdFusion)

For PHP, ASP, JSP, and ColdFusion, you can build sets of master and detail pages all in one operation. You can use the same method for all these languages. Creating both the master and detail pages at the same time is generally easier, but Dreamweaver gives you the flexibility of creating them separately, too.

To create a master and detail page set for PHP, ASP, JSP, or ColdFusion, follow these steps:

1. **Create a new or open an existing dynamic page.**

A blank page opens in Dreamweaver; this page becomes your master page in the language that you selected.

2. **Define a recordset for the page.**

For the lowdown on creating a recordset, check out Book VIII, Chapter 1.

The recordset provides the data that's displayed on both the master and detail pages. Make sure that you include all the table columns that you need to create your master page, including the unique key (the record ID column) for each record and all the table columns that you need to create your detail page. Typically, you show more columns on the detail page than on the master page.

For the example in this chapter, we created an employee_records recordset and included all the columns in the employee table (see Table 1-1).

3. **Save your changes to the master page.**

The new recordset appears in the Bindings panel, and connection code is automatically added to the dynamic page, as shown in Figure 1-1. This page allows a listing of employees to display on the master page.

4. **Choose Insert⇨Data Objects⇨Master Detail Page Set to insert the master and detail pages all in one operation.**

The Insert Master-Detail Page Set dialog box appears (see Figure 1-2). You specify the properties for the master page in the top half of this dialog box and the properties for the detail page in the lower half.

5. **From the Recordset drop-down list, select the recordset that you want to use for the master page.**

For this example, I selected `employee_records`.

After you select a recordset, Dreamweaver fills in the rest of the fields with the columns from the recordset.

6. **In the Master Page Fields area, select which records you want to appear on the master page.**

Click the plus (+) button to add a field and click the minus (–) button to remove a field. In Figure 1-2, we selected the `first_name` and `last_name` fields. These fields appear on the master page in a table format.

Typically, fewer fields appear on the master page than the detail page.

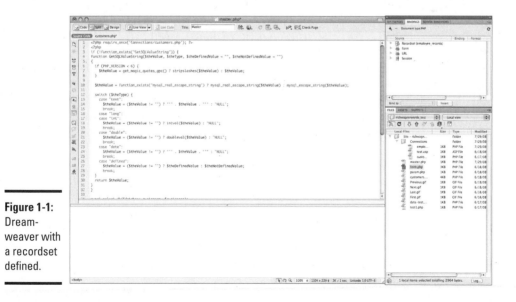

Figure 1-1:
Dream-
weaver with
a recordset
defined.

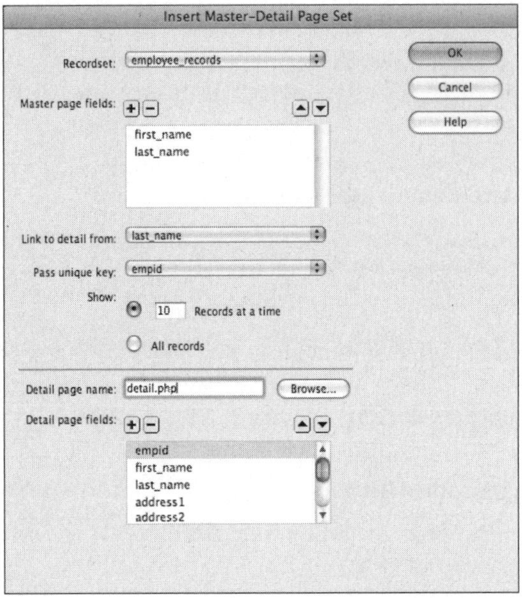

Figure 1-2:
The Insert
Master-
Detail Page
Set dialog
box.

7. **From the Link to Detail From drop-down list, select the field in the recordset that you want to serve as the link to the detail page.**

This field is the one that a user clicks on to display details for a given employee.

For example, I selected the `last_name` field to serve as the link to the detail page for each record.

8. **From the Pass Unique Key drop-down list, select which field contains the values that you want to pass on to the detail page so it can identify the records.**

Typically, you select the key field of the table. This key field tells the detail page which record to display for the user. For our example, we selected the `empid` field.

9. **Specify the number of records that you want to show at one time on the master page.**

In the example, we chose to show 10 records at a time.

10. **In the Detail Page Name text box, enter a name for the detail page or click the Browse button to select an existing file.**

For the example, we specify `detail.php`. Dreamweaver automatically uses this name when it creates the detail page.

11. **In the Detail Page Fields area, select which records you want to appear on the master page.**

Click the plus (+) button and minus (–) button to change the fields that appear on the detail page.

Typically, more fields appear on the detail page than the master page. For the example, we selected all the fields in the table.

As you can see, Figure 1-2 shows the configuration of the Insert Master-Detail Page Set dialog box based on the example values.

12. Click OK.

Dreamweaver creates the master and detail pages and includes dynamic content and server behaviors in both.

The Document window contains the automatically generated objects (a repeated region, navigation objects, record, counter, and link to the detail page), as shown in Figure 1-3.

The detail.php is created automatically for you. You can click the detail.php tab in the Document window to see the layout (see Figure 1-4).

13. Modify the design of the master and detail pages.

You can modify your dynamic fields just as you'd edit any other object.

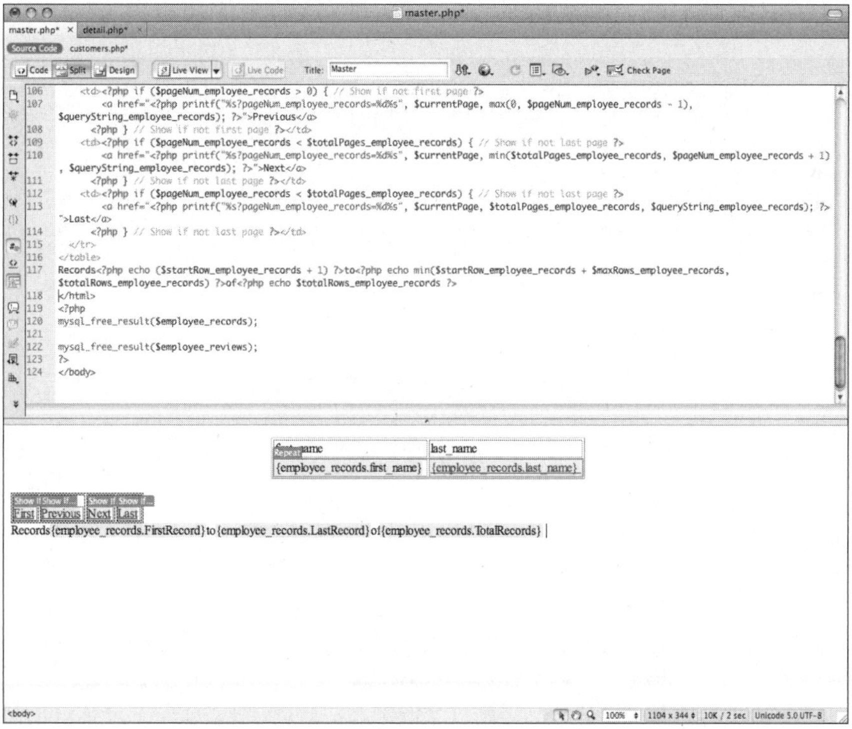

Figure 1-3:
The document shows a repeated region, navigation objects, record counter, and a link to the detail page.

Figure 1-4:
The detail page is created automatically by Dreamweaver.

When you finish designing the pages, you're ready to preview your work in a browser. See the section "Testing Your Master and Detail Pages," later in this chapter for details.

For ASP.NET, you need to build the master and detail pages separately (as described in the section "Developing Master and Detail Pages for ASP.NET," later in this chapter). You can't build these pages at the same time in one operation for ASP.NET.

Developing Master and Detail Pages Block by Block

You can develop a master page block by block for PHP, ASP, JSP, and ColdFusion. Although you usually create the master and detail pages at the same time, you can create them block by block to have complete control over the placement of the blocks.

Creating the master page

To create a dynamic master page, follow these steps:

1. **Create a page and define a recordset.**

Turn to Book VIII, Chapter 1 to find out how to define a recordset.

2. **In the Document window, place the insertion point where you want the records to appear on the page.**

3. **Choose Insert⇨Data Objects⇨Dynamic Data⇨Dynamic Table.**

   The Dynamic Table dialog box opens, as shown in Figure 1-5.

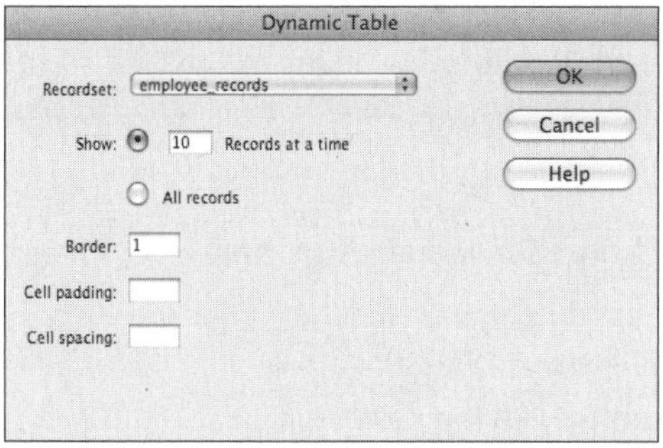

Figure 1-5:
The
Dynamic
Table dialog
box.

4. **From the Recordset drop-down list, select the name of the recordset that you want to appear on the master page.**

5. **Specify the number of records that you want to show at one time on the master page.**

   In the example, we wanted to show 10 records at a time.

6. **Optionally, specify border, cell padding, and cell spacing.**

7. **Click OK to close the dialog box.**

   The master table is created and added to your document.

If you don't want users to see some of the columns on the master page, delete the column from the table by following these steps:

1. **In Design view, click anywhere on the master page.**

2. **Put the pointer near the top of the column so that the column's entries are outlined in red. Then click to select the column.**

3. **Click the Delete button to delete the column from the table.**

Setting up links to open a detail page

After you create the master page (as the preceding section describes), you need to create links that open the detail page and communicate which record the user selected so that only the detail for that record displays.

To set up links to open a detail page, follow these steps:

1. **Open the master page in the Document window.**

2. **In the table, select the placeholder for the dynamic content on which you want to create a link.**

3. **In the Properties inspector, click the folder button next to the Link field.**

   The Select File dialog box appears (see Figure 1-6).

4. **Browse to and select the detail page.**

5. **Click the Parameters button to the right of the URL field.**

   The Parameters dialog box opens.

   Figure 1-7 shows the dialog box.

6. **Click the plus (+) button to add a parameter.**

   This parameter tells the detail page which row to display. Select the key value column as this parameter.

7. **In the Name column, enter the column name.**

   You can also click the Dynamic lightning bolt button and select it from the dialog box.

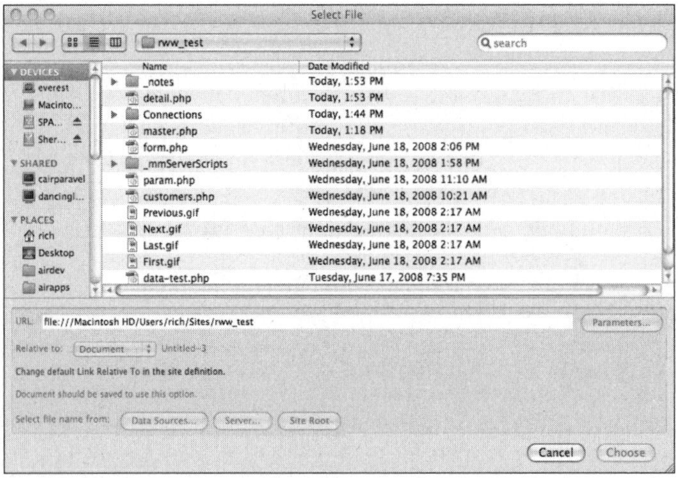

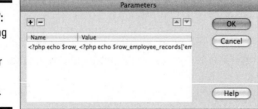

Figure 1-6: Use the Select File dialog box to configure which page to link to and which parameters to send.

Figure 1-7: Configuring the URL parameter and its recordset.

8. **Click in the Value column and then click the Dynamic (lightning bolt) button.**

   The Dynamic Data dialog box displays. This is where you select the column from the recordset.

9. **Expand the recordset, click the key field, and then click OK.**

   In this case, the key field is `empid`.

   After you click OK, the Parameters dialog box displays the new parameter and the code that places it into the page dynamically, as shown in Figure 1-7.

10. **Click OK to close the Parameters dialog box.**

    The URL field in the Select File dialog box is pre-populated with the new parameter.

    Each dynamic page type has different code that appears because each programming language uses a slightly different syntax to display a URL variable dynamically. Fortunately, because Dreamweaver is generating the code for you, you don't need to know the syntax differences.

11. **Click Choose to close the Select File dialog box.**

    You return to the Document window. The name of the detail page appears in the Link field in the Properties inspector. The placeholder for the dynamic content is now a link.

12. **Save your changes to the master page.**

    You now have a complete master page.

Read on to find out how to make the detail page.

Building detail pages

To create a detail page for PHP, ASP, JSP, and ColdFusion page types, follow these steps:

1. **Create a new or open an existing PHP, ASP, JSP, or ColdFusion page.**

2. **In the Bindings panel, click the plus (+) button and select Recordset (Query) from the menu that appears.**

   The simple Recordset dialog box appears.

   If you want to write your own SQL statements, click the Advanced button to display the advanced Recordset dialog box.

3. **In the Name text box, enter a name for your recordset.**

   You can use only letters, numbers, and underscores in the name.

4. **Select a database connection for obtaining the data that you want to display.**

5. **Select a table name for obtaining the data that you want to display.**

   After you select a table name, the database columns appear in the Columns list.

6. **Select which columns should provide the record data to display.**

   Typically, your detail page uses more columns than your master page. You want the recordset for your detail page to contain at least one column (generally the id field) that matches the column that you use for the master page.

7. **Complete the Filter sections as follows:**

   - **The first Filter field:** Select the database column name that contains values to match against the URL parameter (specified in the "Setting up links to open a detail page" section earlier in this chapter). You use the filter to find and display the record specified by the URL parameter passed from the master page.

   - **The second Filter field:** Select the equals (=) symbol, if it's not already selected. This requires the fields to be equal, which they must be to display only the record that is detailed.

   - **The third Filter field:** Select the URL parameter.

   - **The fourth Filter field:** Enter the name of the URL parameter that you want the master page to pass to the detail page.

   The recordset (see Figure 1-8) now returns only the data for the employee who's been selected on the master page.

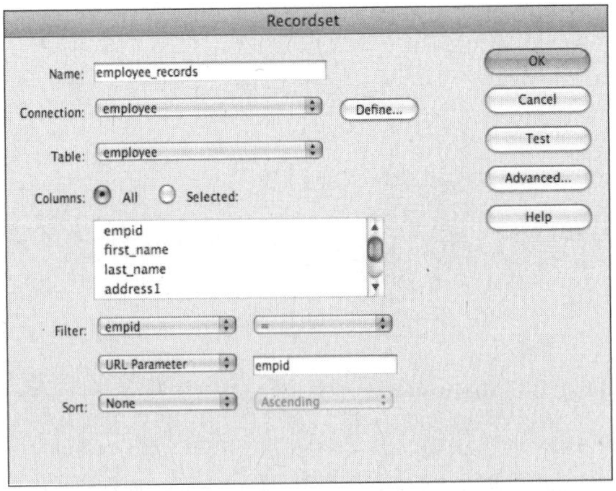

Figure 1-8:
Defining
a detail
recordset.

8. **Click the Test button.**

The Test Value dialog box appears.

9. **Enter a value in the Test Value field and click OK.**

This value represents which detail record displays. This test helps you check that the detail page brings back the data you expect.

A table displaying data from the recordset appears.

10. **Click OK.**

The Test SQL Statement window closes.

11. **In the Recordset dialog box, click OK.**

12. **To bind the columns in the recordset to the detail page, select the columns in the Bindings panel and drag those columns onto the detail page.**

Your detail page can now process requests from the master page. Figure 1-9 shows the Document window after adding fields from the recordset.

See the section "Testing Your Master and Detail Pages," later in this chapter, to find out how to preview your master and detail pages in a browser.

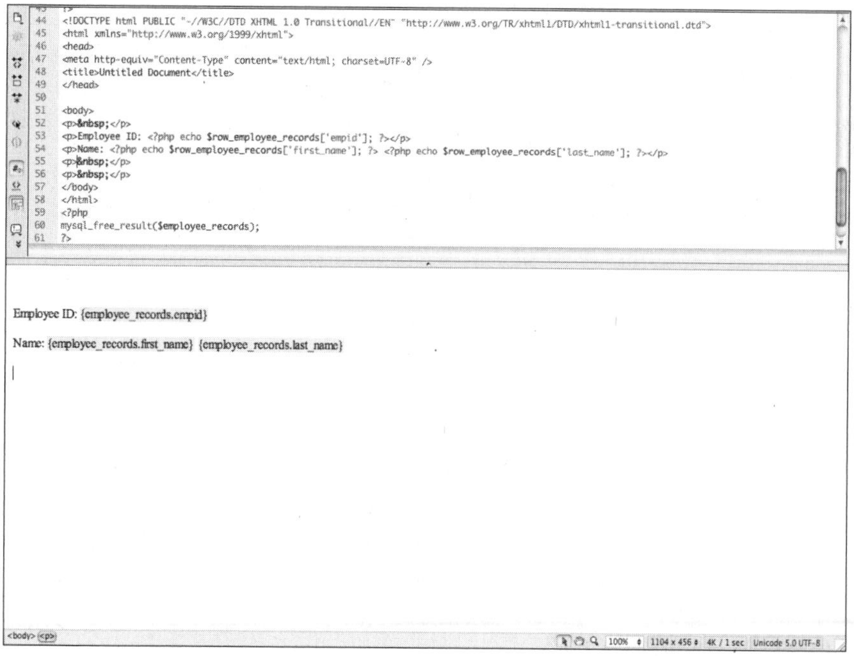

Figure 1-9: The Document window after dragging several fields from the recordset onto it.

Developing Master and Detail Pages for ASP.NET

For ASP.NET, you can use the DataSet Web control to specify table columns and the DataGrid Web control to list the database records to display on the master page. The Web controls provide an easy way to display database data with controls for paging between multiple pages of records.

You need to define a database connection for the site before you create the master page. See Book VII for details.

Creating a master page

To create an ASP.NET master page, follow these steps:

1. **Create a new or open an existing ASP.NET page in Dreamweaver.**

2. **In the Bindings panel, click the plus (+) button and select DataSet (Query) from the menu that appears.**

   The DataSet dialog box appears.

3. **Complete the DataSet dialog box and then click OK.**

   Make sure to include all table columns that you need to create your master page, including the unique key (Record ID column) for each record.

   A dataset is essentially the same thing as a recordset; see Book VIII, Chapter 1 for more information on recordsets.

   The new dataset appears in the Binding panel.

4. **In the Server Behaviors panel, click the plus (+) button and select DataGrid from the menu that appears.**

   The DataGrid dialog box opens.

5. **Select the dataset source from the DataSet drop-down list and click OK.**

   You can leave the default column type as Simple Data Field.

Creating links that open the detail page

After you create the ASP.NET master page (as described in the preceding section), you need to create links that open the detail page and communicate which record the user selected. To open an ASP.NET detail page and display the specified record, follow these steps:

1. **Open the master page in the Document window.**

2. **In the Server Behaviors panel, double-click DataGrid.**

   The DataGrid dialog box appears.

3. **In the Columns list, select the column that you want to serve as the link to the detail page.**

   You can use any field that identifies the record for expanding the detail of the record.

4. **Click the Change Column Type button.**

5. **Select Hyperlink from the pop-up menu.**

   The Hyperlink Column dialog box appears.

6. **In the Hyperlink Text section, specify the text that you want to display in the hyperlink column.**

   Here are your choices:

   - **Static Text:** Select this radio button if you want to use a generic description for this column. Enter text for the link, such as `Details`.

   - **Data Field:** Select this radio button if you want to add text for a link based on a hyperlink column. Then from the drop-down list, select a data field in your dataset. In the example, we selected the `last_name` column.

   - **Format String:** This field is automatically generated and shows the format of the URL text.

7. **In the Linked Page section, specify the URL for the hyperlink column text.**

   Here are your choices:

   - **Static Text:** Select this radio button if you want to use a generic link for this column. Enter the URL for the link, such as `Details.aspx`.

   - **Data Field:** Select this radio button if you want to add a link for data displayed in the hyperlink column. Then from the drop-down list, select a data field in your dataset. In the example, we selected the `first_name` column.

   - **Format String:** This field is automatically generated and shows the format of the URL link.

   The URL opens the detail page and uniquely identifies the record to display on the detail page.

8. **In the Linked Page section, click the Browse button next to the Format String box.**

9. **Locate and select which detail page you want to display.**

Note the following when selecting your link page:

- When you select a detail page, Dreamweaver adds information to the URL that specifies a parameter to use to identify the record.

- Dreamweaver automatically names this parameter based on your database field name, but you can change the name to something else if you want to.

- In any case, be sure to note the name of this URL parameter because you need that name when you create the detail page (which you can read about in the following section, "Creating a detail page").

- Dreamweaver uses a {0} placeholder to indicate where it places the value of the unique identifier when someone accesses the page.

10. **Click OK to close the Hyperlink Column dialog box.**

11. **Click OK.**

The DataGrid dialog box closes. The DataGrid on your page is updated.

Creating a detail page

After you create a master page for ASP.NET (as described in the two previous sections), you need to create a detail page to display the record. To do so, you need to define a dataset for the record and bind its columns to the detail page.

When creating the detail page, you need to know the database column name that you want to reference and the URL parameter that the master page uses to find and display that column's record on the detail page. If you don't remember the URL parameter name, open the master page, go to the Bindings panel, and look under the DataSet listing.

To create an ASP.NET detail page, create a new ASP.NET page in Dreamweaver and follow Steps 2 through 12 in the earlier section, "Building detail pages." Note that although the earlier steps show you how to fill out the Recordset dialog box, the steps are the same for the DataSet dialog box, which you fill out when creating an ASP.NET detail page.

Testing Your Master and Detail Pages

After you create a master and detail page set, you need to test those pages. Follow these steps to preview the pages in a browser:

1. **Open the master page.**

2. **Choose File⇨Preview in Browser⇨***Name of Browser.*

3. **When Dreamweaver asks you if it's okay to copy the file to the testing site, click OK.**

Your browser launches with your master page (see Figure 1-10).

4. **Click a hyperlink to view the associated detail page for that record.**

In the employee example, the linked field is the employee's last name. When you click a link, the browser page changes to expand the record and display the detail page.

WARNING!

Be sure that both your master page and detail page transfer to the testing server. If not, when you click a link in the master page, you get a `Page not found` error message.

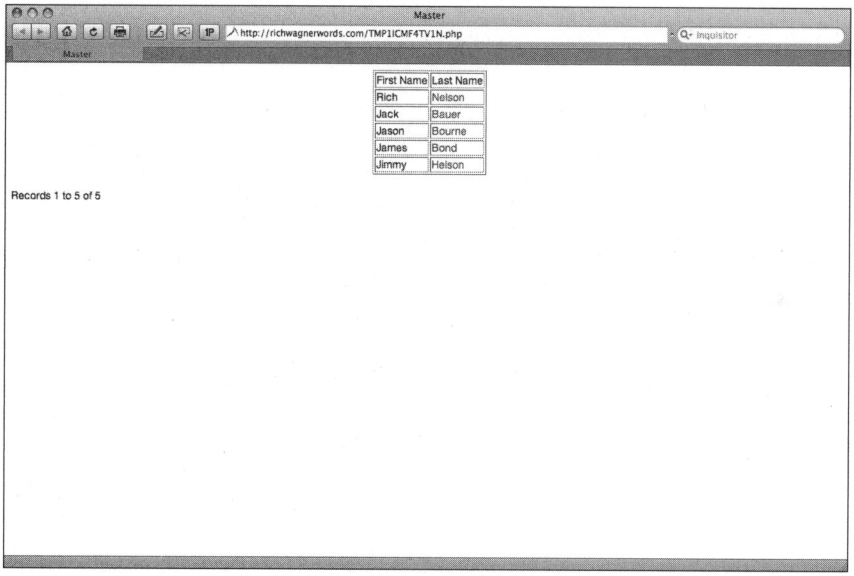

Figure 1-10:
The browser displays the master page that uses the data from the databases.

Chapter 2: Creating Search and Results Pages

In This Chapter

✔ Developing search and results pages for most language types

✔ Developing search and results pages for ASP.NET

Y ou can use Dreamweaver to build *search pages,* which allow users to search your database, and *results pages,* which display the search results. Search pages are frequently used with dynamic database-driven Web pages to provide a shortcut to the information the user is looking for. For example, online stores usually give you the ability to search their products.

A basic search page contains a form with a search field and a submit button. Users enter search parameters in the form and click the submit button. The results page then receives the search parameters, searches the database for records that meet the search criteria, builds a recordset to hold the records it finds, and then displays the contents of the recordset for the users.

If you allow just one search parameter, Dreamweaver can create the recordset for you with a filter. However, if you have more than one search parameter, you need to work directly with an SQL statement and send a parameter to it. This chapter shows you how to build search and results pages for a single search parameter.

Creating the Search Page

At a minimum, search pages consist of a form text field and a Submit button. The following steps show you how to create a basic search page:

1. **Create a new or open an existing PHP, JSP, ASP, or ColdFusion document.**

2. **Insert a form by choosing Insert⇨Form⇨Form.**

    An empty form displays in the Document window. The form's boundaries display as thin red lines.

    If the form isn't visible, enable Invisible Elements by choosing View⇨ Visual Aids⇨Invisible Elements.

3. **Add a text area search field by choosing Insert⇨Form⇨Text Field.**

   The Input Tag Accessibility Attributes dialog box displays (see Figure 2-1).

4. **Enter `search_field` in the ID box.**

   You can ignore the remaining options.

5. **Click OK to close the dialog box.**

   The text field is added to your page.

6. **Position your cursor just after the text field and then choose Insert⇨Form⇨Button to add a Submit button to your form.**

   You can also just click on Button on the insert menu to automatically add the new button right after the text field.

7. **In the Input Tag Accessibility Attributes dialog box, enter** search_btn **as the ID value.**

8. **Click OK to close the Input Tag Accessibility Attributes dialog box.**

9. **Select the Submit button in the document.**

10. **In the Properties inspector, change the Value text to `Search`.**

    The form should now look like Figure 2-2, which has all the basic elements that are required to request a search.

11. **Select the form by clicking the form tag in the Tag selector.**

    This selects the form element so that you can modify its properties.

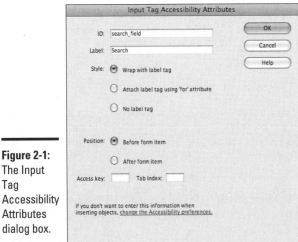

Figure 2-1:
The Input
Tag
Accessibility
Attributes
dialog box.

12. **In the Action field in the Properties inspector, enter a filename for the results page (the page that will process the database search request), or click the Folder button to select a file.**

You create this file when defining the results page, as described in the next section. For example, we entered `results.php`, as shown in Figure 2-3.

13. **Select POST from the Method drop-down list.**

You have now completed the search page. After the user fills out the form and clicks the Submit button, the information is passed on to the results page as a *form parameter.* Read on to find out how to create the results page.

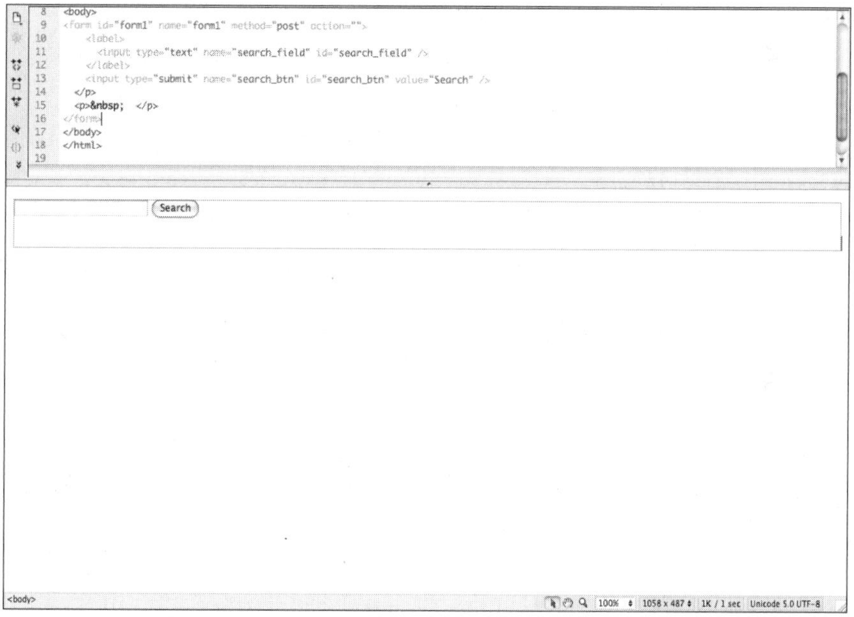

Figure 2-2: The form with a Search text field and a Submit button.

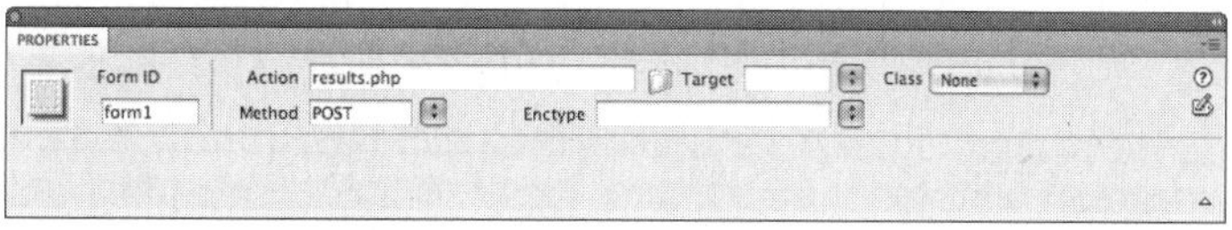

Figure 2-3: The Properties inspector for a form.

Building the Results Page

The complexity of building your results page is directly related to the number of search parameters users can specify. If you allow only one search parameter, you don't have to modify the SQL query when building the results page. This is the type of search that we describe in this chapter.

The results page receives the search parameters from the form, plugs that data into a recordset filter, and then displays the results from the recordset on the page. The search page can optionally link to another page to expand details for a search result. For example, searching a catalog of products produces a list of matching products. If you then click on one of the products, you see the full detail page for just that product.

In the following sections, you find out how to build the recordset that holds the results as well as the page that displays those results.

Building the recordset

To create the recordset that performs the search in the results page, follow these steps:

1. **Create a new or open an existing PHP, JSP, ASP, or ColdFusion document.**

2. **In the Bindings panel, click the plus (+) button and then select Recordset from the drop-down list that appears.**

The Recordset dialog box displays. You need to create a recordset to query the database with the search parameters.

3. **Enter the name of the recordset in the Name field.**

Choose a name that describes the recordset data. For example, we entered `employee_search` (see Figure 2-4), which indicates that the recordset relates to a search.

4. **From the Connection drop-down list, select a connection to the database you want the user to search.**

You must have an active database connection to create the recordset. See Book VII for details on setting up a database connection.

Depending on your dynamic page type, the Recordset dialog box may appear slightly different from Figure 2-4. For example, ColdFusion calls the Connection field a data source and includes optional Username and Password fields for the database. However, these differences don't change the following steps.

5. **In the Table drop-down list, select the database table to be searched.**

For this example, I selected the `employee` table. The Columns list updates after you select a table.

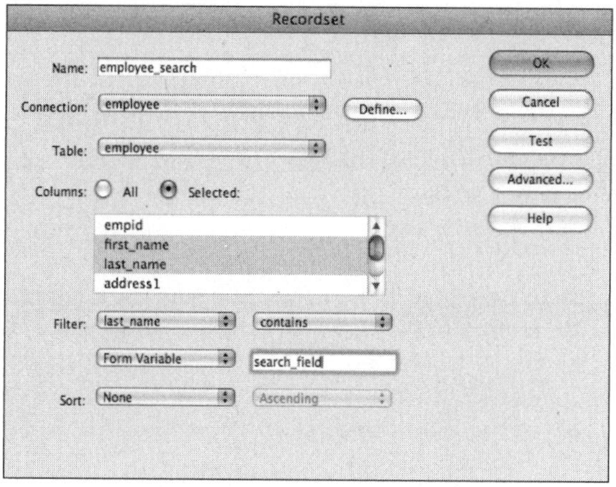

Figure 2-4:
The
Recordset
dialog box
configured
to search
the last
name field
of the
employee
table.

6. **If you want to include only some of the table's columns in the recordset, click the Selected radio button and then select the columns to include.**

   Select the columns to display by Ctrl+clicking (Windows) or ⌘+clicking (Mac) them from the Columns list.

   I selected the `first_name`, `last_name`, and `city`, `state`, and `deptid` columns.

7. **To create the database filter for the search, complete the fields in the Filter area as follows:**

   - For the first Filter field, select the database column you want to search. For example, to search the `last_name` column of the employee table, I selected `last_name`.

   - For the second Filter field, select how to filter your results: Contains, Begins With, Ends With, or Numeric Comparisons. Use the `Contains` item.

   - For the third Filter field, select `Form Variable` if your form uses the `POST` method, or URL Parameter if it uses the `GET` method. For this example, I selected `Form Variable` because the HTML form on the search page uses the `POST` method.

   - For the fourth Filter field, enter the name of the search field from the search page, which in this is `search_field`.

   Dreamweaver uses the conditions you specify to filter the search results. If a record doesn't meet the conditions that you've specified, the record is excluded from the recordset. For example, if there are records for employees with the last names `Phillips` and `Davis` searching on the last name field for names containing the letters *il,* the filter returns only the record for `Phillips`.

Figure 2-4 shows the completed Recordset dialog box for the example. This recordset returns records that contain the search parameter in the last name. For example, if you can only remember that a name contains the letters *il*, you could use this recordset to find the name.

8. **Click the Test button to execute the query and verify that it returns the data you expected.**

   The Test Value dialog box displays.

9. **In the Test Value field, enter a value that represents which record to display and then click OK.**

   In my example, I entered Bo.

   The Test SQL Statement window appears (see Figure 2-5), displaying data from the recordset.

10. **To change the order of the results, select a database column to sort by and choose Ascending or Descending from the Sort drop-down menu in the Recordset dialog box.**

11. **Click OK to close the Test SQL Statement window.**

   You return to the Recordset dialog box.

12. **If the test produced the correct results, click OK to close the Recordset dialog box.**

   If your test didn't produce the results you wanted, check the filtering parameters versus the actual data in the database table.

   The recordset is added to the Bindings panel list.

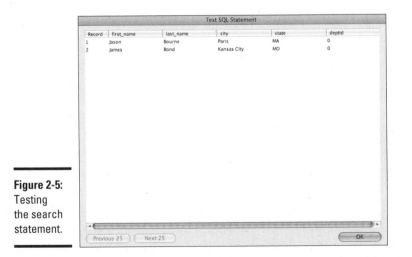

Figure 2-5:
Testing
the search
statement.

After you close the Recordset dialog box, Dreamweaver inserts the code that performs a search based on the search parameter passed from the search page. Only records that match the search criteria become part of the recordset. This code is hidden when you're working on the page in Design view, but you can see it by highlighting the recordset in the Bindings panel.

Displaying the results

After you create a recordset that holds the search results, you need to display the data for the user on the results page. Dreamweaver provides several tools for displaying recordsets, but the easiest is the dynamic table.

To create a dynamic table that displays results, follow these steps:

1. **In your results page, place the insertion point where you want the records displayed on the page. Then choose Insert⇨Data Objects⇨Dynamic Data⇨Dynamic Table.**

   Be sure to insert the table after the yellow code blocks because they must execute first to generate the recordset. The Dynamic Table dialog box opens.

2. **From the Recordset drop-down list, select the recordset you created in the preceding section.**

   For example, we selected the `employee_search`, as shown in Figure 2-6.

3. **Specify how many records to show at one time on the results page.**

   Optionally, specify which border, cell padding, and cell spacing to use.

4. **Click OK to close the dialog box.**

   Dreamweaver inserts a dynamic table that displays the search results. Figure 2-7 shows the dynamic table for the example.

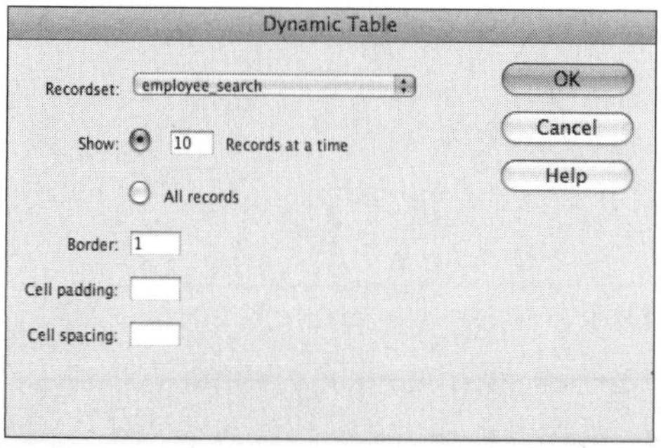

Figure 2-6:
The
Dynamic
Table dialog
box.

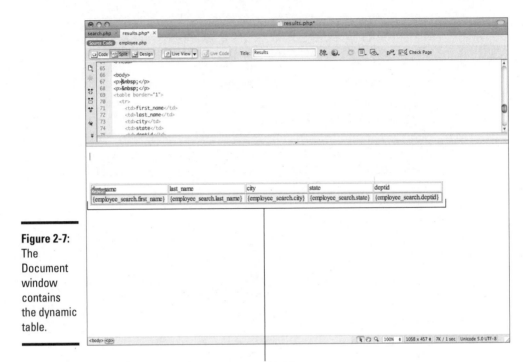

Figure 2-7:
The Document window contains the dynamic table.

Dynamic table

Testing Your Search and Results Pages

After you create your search and results pages, it's a good idea to test them to make sure they work properly as described in the following steps for all dynamic page types:

1. **Open the search page.**

2. **Choose File⇨Preview in Browser⇨*Name of Browser.***

3. **If Dreamweaver asks you if it's okay to copy the file over, click OK to copy files to your testing site.**

Your browser launches with your search page (see Figure 2-8).

4. **Enter a search term in the Search field.**

5. **Click the Submit button.**

The browser page changes to the results page, as shown in Figure 2-9.

ASP.NET system requirements

In order to get output that works with ASP.NET, keep in mind these system requirements:

✓ Make sure you have the latest version of Microsoft's database software component, which is called MDAC. MDAC is available from Microsoft's site at `http://msdn.microsoft.com/data/mdac/downloads/default.aspx`. Download and install the most recent version available.

✓ Install the .NET Framework to allow IIS to process .NET files. Download it from Microsoft at `http://msdn.microsoft.com/netframework/downloads/updates/default.aspx`.

✓ Upload the DreamweaverCtrls.dll Dreamweaver .NET component file. To publish this file on your test or remote server, click the blue up arrow in the Components panel. This places the file in the bin directory of your Web root. Without this file, Dreamweaver-generated code produces errors.

Regardless of which language you choose, if you run into an error, don't panic. Searching for the error with Google or checking the Dreamweaver knowledgebase usually turns up a solution in short order.

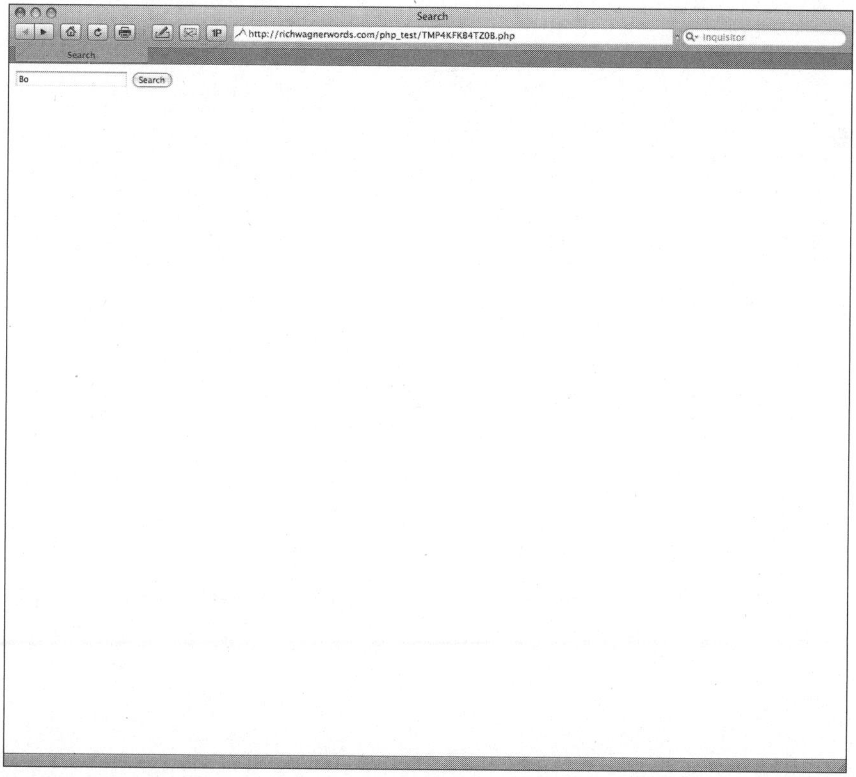

Figure 2-8:
The browser displaying the search page to retrieve all names that contain *Bo*.

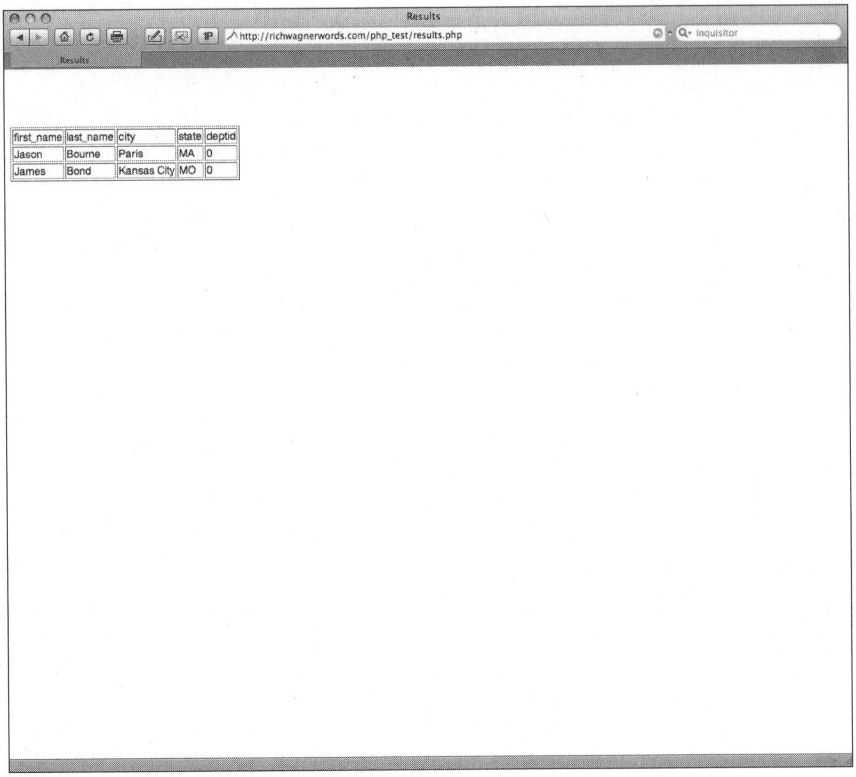
Results
http://richwagnerwords.com/php_test/results.php
Results
first_name last_name city state deptid
Jason Bourne Paris MA 0
James Bond Kansas City MO 0

Figure 2-9: Two records are found containing the search text.

WARNING!

Be sure that both search and details pages transfer to the testing server. If they don't, you get a Page Not Found error when you click a link in the search page.

Chapter 3: Building Record Insert Pages and Restricting Site Access

In This Chapter

✔ Developing a record insert page in one step

✔ Putting together a record insert page a piece at a time

✔ Making sure your record insert page works

✔ Building a login form

✔ Restricting access to pages

So far in this mini-book, we've been focusing on displaying data that is already in a database. However, in many cases, you also want to allow for the ability to add data from a Web page. If so, you'll want to create a *record insert page.*

Every record insert page must have

✦ A database connection

✦ A database table to model the insert fields after

✦ A form that collects data

✦ A submit button

When designing the record insert page, you typically arrange the fields on the form in a table and include labels to identify each field. When users open the record insert page in their Web browsers, they just fill in the form fields. When they finish, they click the submit button, and — presto! — the record is added to the database.

Dreamweaver gives you two methods to add data to a database table from a dynamic Web page. You can do it all in one step by using the Insert Record dialog box. Dreamweaver also supports creating a record insert page by adding the server behaviors a block at a time. We describe both methods in this chapter, as well as show you how to test your completed record insert page.

Creating the Record Insert Page in One Operation

You can add the basic building blocks of a record insert page in a single operation by using the Record Insertion Form application object. The application object adds an HTML form and an Insert Record server behavior to the page.

You must have an active database connection before you can build a record insert page. See Book VII for details on setting up a database connection.

To build the record insert page with the Record Insertion Form application object, follow these steps:

1. **Create a new or open an existing document.**

Add the data entry form here.

2. **Choose Insert⇨Data Objects⇨Insert Record⇨Record Insertion Form Wizard.**

The Record Insertion Form dialog box appears, as shown in Figure 3-1.

3. **Select the database connection from the Connection drop-down list.**

For example, I selected the `employee` connection (see Figure 3-2).

The database connection field varies slightly between the different dynamic document types. For example, ColdFusion includes a Username and Password field.

4. **From the Table drop-down list, select the database table that you want to insert the record into.**

For example, we selected the employee table in Figure 3-2.

After you select a table, Dreamweaver updates the Form Fields section with the columns in the table.

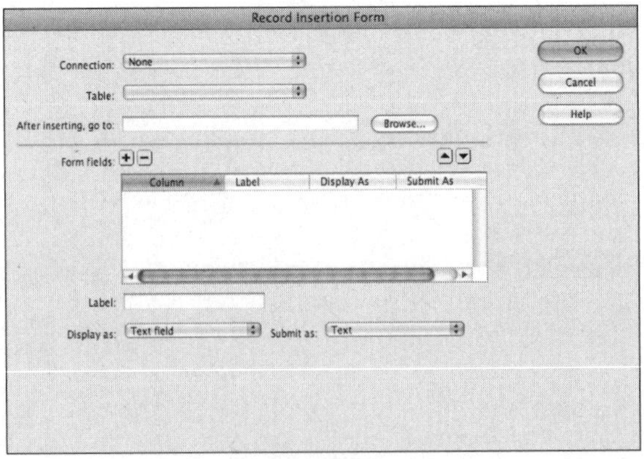

Figure 3-1:
The Record Insertion Form dialog box as it first appears.

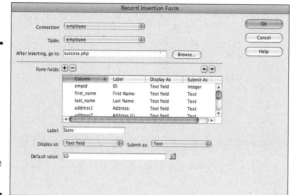

Book IX
Chapter 3

Building Record
Insert Pages and
Restricting Site
Access

Figure 3-2:
The Record
Insertion
Form dialog
box after
configuring
for the
`employee`
data table.

5. **In the After Inserting, Go To text box, enter the page that you want to go to after the record is added. Alternatively, click the Browse button to select a file.**

   For example, we selected a page named success.php. This page simply says that the insert was successful.

   For the ASP.NET dynamic page type, you can also specify a page that you want to go to upon failure or display a debugging page. The rest of the dialog box works the same with ASP.NET as the other page types.

6. **To remove unwanted columns from the record insert page, select the columns that you want to remove in the Form Fields section and click the minus (–) button.**

   The Form Fields section lists the columns that appear on the record insert page. In these fields, the user can enter data before submitting the insert request.

7. **If you're happy with the default settings in the Form Fields section, skip to Step 8. However, if you want to make changes to how a field appears on the record insert page, select the field from the list and fill in the following fields:**

   • **Label:** In this text box, change the Label field to a more descriptive label for the contents of the database field. For example, you can give the `first_name` field a friendlier label, such as `First Name`.

   • **Display As:** Select a form type from the Display As drop-down list. The default setting is Text Field. The Display As list includes all the basic form types, including check boxes, menus, and radio buttons. If you select one of the types that requires additional configuration — such as radio groups — a configuration dialog box appears.

- **Submit As:** From this drop-down list, select the data format that you want to place in the database field. The choices include Text, Numeric, Double, Date, Checkbox Y/N, Checkbox 1/0, and Checkbox -1,0. The data format that you choose here needs to match the database column's type.

- **Default Value:** Specify a default value for any field by entering that value in this field. Because many of the employees are located in South Dakota, I enter SD as a default value.

  To specify a dynamic data source for the default value, click the Bind to Dynamic Source (lightning bolt) button and select a binding. This process works the same as specifying a dynamic source for a regular form object.

  Figure 3-2 shows the Record Insertion Form dialog box for the Employee table example.

8. **If you want to change the order in which the fields display in the form, select a field and click the up or down arrow.**

You need to order table fields together with similar fields (for example, you'll probably want to group all the address fields together).

9. **Click OK to close the dialog box.**

Dreamweaver automatically adds the form and the submit button to your page. Figure 3-3 shows the example form in the Document window along with a submit button labeled Insert Record.

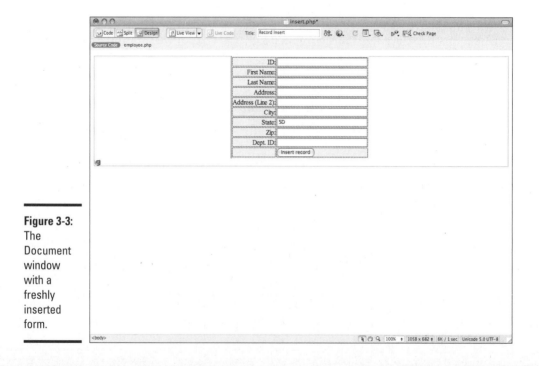

Figure 3-3:
The Document window with a freshly inserted form.

You can modify the appearance of the form by using the usual Dreamweaver functions for changing fonts, colors, and alignment. The form elements must stay within the boundaries of the form. To continue working on your form elements, see Book II, Chapter 7.

Book IX
Chapter 3

Building Record
Insert Pages and
Restricting Site
Access

Click the Insert Record entry in the Server Behaviors panel to edit the server behavior (such as adding additional columns to the insert) in the Record Insertion Form dialog box (refer to Figure 3-1).

Building a Record Insert Page Block by Block

You can add the basic building blocks of an insert page separately by using the form tools and the Server Behaviors panel. Although creating your record insert page using the Record Insertion dialog box is faster, building block by block allows complete control over placement of blocks on your page.

When creating an insert page manually, you create a form for the user to enter the data and then add an Insert Record server behavior to process the form submission, as the following sections describe.

Adding the form

To add the HTML form, follow these steps:

1. **Create a new page or open an existing page.**

2. **Insert a form by choosing Insert⇨Form⇨Form.**

   If you can't see the form, enable invisible elements by choosing View⇨ Visual Aids⇨Invisible Elements.

3. **To select the form, click the form's boundaries or click the `<form>` tag in the bottom-left corner of the Document window.**

   Selecting the form lets you modify that form's properties in the Properties inspector.

4. **In the Properties inspector, enter a name for the form in the Form Name field.**

   You probably want to use something descriptive, such as `insert_form`. Don't set the Action or Method fields because the Insert Record server behavior sets these fields for you.

5. **Add a text field by choosing Insert⇨Form⇨Text Field.**

   You can also add other form objects, depending on the type of data that you want to insert into the database table. See Book II, Chapter 7 for more on the different form objects.

6. **In the Input Tag Accessibility Attributes dialog box, enter a descriptive ID and a text label.**

7. **Optionally, you can tweak the Style and Position settings as desired.**

8. **Click OK.**

9. **Press Enter (Windows) or Return (Mac) to enter a new line to place the element on a separate line.**

   You can also use a table element to align your fields (see Book II, Chapter 7).

10. **For each column that you allow the user to add data to, repeat Steps 5 through 8.**

    For the `employee` table example, we added each of the fields, but arranged them in a slightly different order on the form.

11. **Insert a submit button on the page by choosing Insert⇨Form⇨Button.**

    If the Input Tag Accessibility Attributes dialog box appears, leave the Label field empty and then click Cancel.

12. **With the button selected, change the Value text in the Properties inspector to Insert.**

    The example form looks like Figure 3-4.

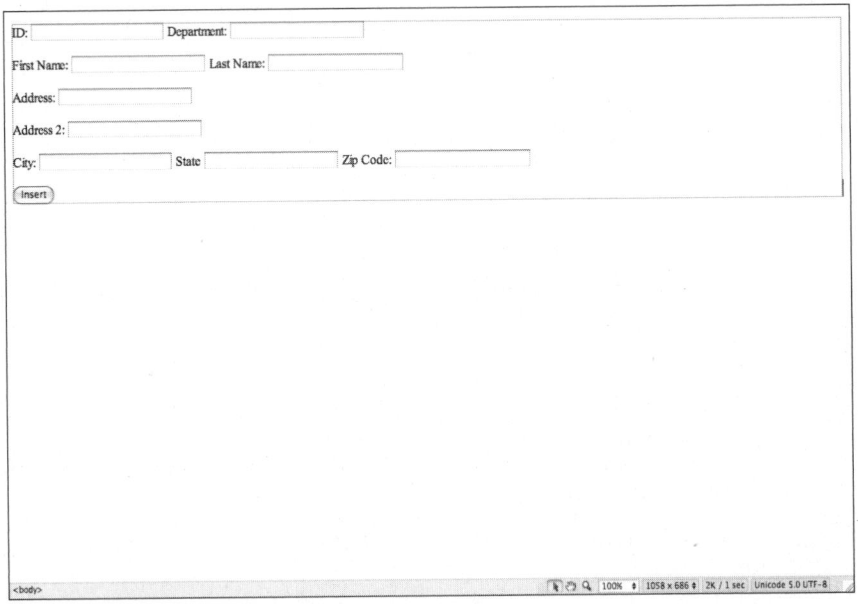

Figure 3-4:
The
completed
form.

Adding the Insert Record server behavior

**Book IX
Chapter 3**

Building Record
Insert Pages and
Restricting Site
Access

You have to add the Insert Record server behavior to your page so that it can process the data in the form submission.

You must have an active database connection before you can add the Insert Record server behavior. See Book VII for details on setting up a database connection.

To add the Insert Record server behavior, follow these steps:

1. **In the Server Behaviors panel, click the plus (+) button and select Insert Record from the drop-down menu that appears.**

   The Insert Record dialog box appears on-screen.

2. **Select your form from the Submit Values From drop-down list.**

3. **From the Connection drop-down list, select a database connection that contains the table that you want to insert data into.**

4. **From the Insert Table drop-down list, select the database table that you want to insert a record into.**

   The database columns appear in the Columns section, as shown in Figure 3-5.

   Depending on your dynamic page type, the Insert Record dialog box may appear slightly different. For example, ColdFusion calls the Connection field a data source and includes options for Username and Password database fields. However, these differences don't change the following steps.

Figure 3-5:
The Insert Record dialog box can pick which fields supply values from the form to the database table.

5. **If you want to modify the associated database column or data type of a field, select the column from the column list and then modify the following fields in the dialog box:**

   - **Value:** Select the form field from the Value drop-down list. Each form field appears in the list.

   - **Submit As:** Select the data type from the Submit As drop-down list. The data type that you select here should mirror the database column data type. The types include text, integer, date, and check box formats.

   Dreamweaver automatically links the form fields that have the same name as the database field.

6. **For each field that you need to change, repeat Step 5.**

7. **In the After Inserting, Go To text field, enter the page that you want to go to after inserting the record. Or click the Browse button and select a file.**

   For the ASP.NET dynamic page type, you have a choice also for the On Failure, Go To text box and a Display Debugging Information check box. You fill in these fields to display debugging information or redirect a user if the record insert fails. The rest of the dialog box works the same as the other document types.

8. **Click OK.**

   Dreamweaver adds the server behavior to the page. You now have a complete page. Users can fill out the fields on the page and then click the submit button.

You can make any visual changes to the form by using Dreamweaver's tools for changing fonts, colors, and placement.

Testing Your Record Insert Page

After you create a record insert page (which you can read about in the "Building a Record Insert Page Block by Block" section, earlier in this chapter), you probably want to test your page. Follow these steps to do so:

1. **Open the Record Insert page.**

2. **Choose File⇨Preview in Browser⇨*Name of Browser*.**

3. **When Dreamweaver asks you if it's okay to copy files to your testing site, click OK.**

   Your browser launches and displays the Record Insert page.

4. **Enter some sample data into the fields.**

Figure 3-6 shows some test data for the Employee table.

5. **Click the Insert Record button.**

When the data is added successfully, the browser opens the success page.

Be sure that both your Record Insert page and success page transfer to the testing server. If not, when you click the button on the insert page, you get a `Page Not Found` error message.

The success page in our example simply contains the text `Inserted Successfully`.

If you want to double-check that the insert really worked, follow these steps:

1. **Open the Databases window.**

2. **Expand the database you are working with by clicking the arrow.**

3. **Expand the Tables item to display the table you are working with.**

4. **Right-click the table on the page.**

5. **Choose View Data from the popup menu.**

The View Data dialog box appears, shown in Figure 3-7.

In the dialog box, you can see that the data was inserted correctly into the table.

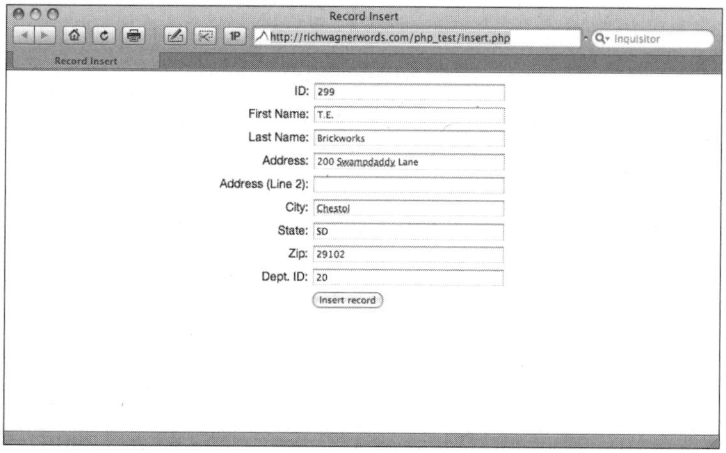

Book IX
Chapter 3

Building Record
Insert Pages and
Restricting Site
Access

Figure 3-6:
Entering
data into
the Record
Insert page.

[Screenshot: Record Insert browser window at http://richwagnerwords.com/php_test/insert.php with fields:]

ID: 299
First Name: T.E.
Last Name: Brickworks
Address: 200 Swampdaddy Lane
Address (Line 2):
City: Chestol
State: SD
Zip: 29102
Dept. ID: 20
(Insert record)

Figure 3-7:
The View Data dialog box shows the newly inserted data.

Building a Login Page

A login page enables registered users to log in to a Web site. Dreamweaver comes with a sample page design of a login page, or you can design your own.

If you want to use Dreamweaver's Login page design, choose File⇨New to open the New Document window. Then select Page Designs from the Category list, select UI: Login from the Page Designs list, and click Create.

The following sections show you how to complete these steps to build your own login page.

Setting up a database table

If you set up a registration page, as described earlier in the chapter, you've already created this table.

Creating the HTML form on the login page

If you want to design your own login page, first you need to create a new page and add an HTML form with a username text box, a password text box, and a submit button. This process is similar to the process of adding a form to a registration page.

Adding a Log In User server behavior to the page

After adding a form to your login page (as described in the preceding section), the final step is to add the Log In User server behavior, which checks to make sure the user entered a valid username and password.

Book IX
Chapter 3

Building Record
Insert Pages and
Restricting Site
Access

To add the Log In User server behavior to your login page, open the page and follow these steps:

1. **In the Server Behaviors panel, click the plus (+) sign and choose User Authentication⇨Log In User.**

   The Log In User dialog box displays.

2. **In the Get Input From Form field, select the form used on the login page.**

3. **In the Username Field and Password Field text boxes, select the appropriate form fields.**

4. **For ColdFusion only, enter your username and password.**

5. **In the Table drop-down list, select the database table that you will check the form fields against.**

6. **From the Username Column and Password Column drop-down lists, specify the table columns for username and password.**

   For example, the users table that we selected in Step 5 contains username and password columns, so we selected those columns.

7. **In the If Login Success, Go To text box, enter the name of the page to open if the user successfully logs in.**

   Or you can click the Browse button and select the page.

8. **In the If Login Fails, Go To text box, enter the name of the page to open if the user is unable to log in.**

   Or you can click the Browse button and select the page.

9. **Indicate whether you want to grant access to this page based just on username and password, or based on authorization level as well.**

   Having multiple authentication levels provides more flexibility for segregated access to information but also comes at the cost of added complexity (and time administering your user's levels and categorizing information). Most people can get by without setting up multiple access levels to their sites.

10. **Click OK.**

Your login page is now complete.

Restricting Access to Your Pages

If you have a Web page that you don't want all users to be able to view, you can restrict access to it. To do this, you add the Restrict Access to Page server behavior to the page so that only authorized users can view the page. If an unauthorized user attempts to open the restricted page, the user is redirected to another page.

Here are a few examples of when restricted access may be useful:

✦ You have a page that you only want users with Administrator privileges to be able to view.

✦ You want to make sure that users log in before they can view a specific page.

✦ You want to review newly registered users before allowing them to access members-only pages.

To restrict access to a page, you need to do the following tasks:

✦ Add Restrict Access to a Page server behavior to that page.

✦ If you want to use authorization levels to further restrict page access, you need to add a column to your user database table to maintain information about which access privileges each user is entitled to.

Follow these steps to restrict access to a page:

1. **Open the page you want to restrict access to.**

2. **In the Server Behaviors panel, click the plus (+) sign and select User Authentication⇨Restrict Access to Page.**

   The Restrict Access to Page dialog box opens.

3. **In the Restrict Based On area, select one of the following options:**

   • **Username and Password:** Select this option if you only want users with a valid username and password to access the restricted page. Use it when you aren't concerned about access levels (or just aren't using them).

   • **Username, Password, and Access Level:** Select this option if you only want users with specific access privileges to be able to view the page. Specify one or more authorization levels for the page — for example, Administrator.

4. **In the If Access Denied, Go To text box, enter the name of the page to open if an unauthorized user attempts to open the restricted page.**

5. **Click OK.**

Dreamweaver adds a server behavior to the page ensuring that only authorized users can access the page.

Chapter 4: Developing Record Update and Delete Pages

In This Chapter

✔ Creating record update pages

✔ Trying out your record update page

✔ Deleting records by using delete pages

✔ Putting your delete page to the test

So far in this mini-book, we've shown you how to browse, search, and insert data. But, before you go away thinking you've discovered everything you need to know, we need to tell you — in the words of a late night television commercial — *But wait, there's more!*

The record update and delete operations are the last two database functions commonly used in dynamic database sites. For example, suppose that employees at your company can view their employee data online. Over time, they may want to change their employment details or have fun changing the data of their office mates. Or perhaps a mean ol' H.R. administrator may need the ability to delete an employee record all together. Boo! In any case, you need to give users the ability to update and delete database records from a Web page, which is what this chapter is all about.

Building an Update Page

Before users can update a record, they need to be able to search for the record that they want to update. Therefore, you need to create a search page and a results page. (We're worn out from talking about how to do that, so see Book IX, Chapter 2 for full details on how to create and work with search and results pages.) Additionally, you need to create an update page that enables users to enter the data for updating the record. Here's a closer look at the three pages that you need to create:

✦ **Search page:** This page allows the user to search for a record that he wants to update. For example, in the case of an employee record, the search page simply searches the employee that's logged in because employees can't modify other employee information.

✦ **Results page:** This page displays the record in a form. The form defaults to the values currently in the database (before the update) and has an update button.

✦ **Update page:** This page performs the update and tells the user when an update is successful.

Here's how the update process works:

1. The user enters search criteria in the form on the search page and then clicks the Submit button.

2. The browser displays the results of the search on the results page.

3. The user selects a record to update on the results page and clicks the Submit button.

4. The browser displays the update page.

The first step in the update process is to create a search and results page set. If you haven't already created these pages, check out Book IX, Chapter 2 for details. Then read the following sections for details on building the update page.

Creating link to the update page

After you create the search and results pages, you need to create a link on the results page to open the update page and display the selected record in an HTML form.

However, before you begin, quickly create a blank dynamic page of the desired type and save it as update.php (the three-letter file extension varies based on the app server you are working with). This is a blank placeholder page for now that will eventually be used to update a record from the results page.

After you have created a blank dynamic page, open the results page that you created based on the instructions back in Book IX, Chapter 2 and follow these steps:

1. **Select the placeholder for the dynamic content on which you want to create a link.**

For example, we selected the `last_name` field to use as the link field, as shown in Figure 4-1. The field placeholder appears as `{employee_search.last_name}`.

2. **In the Properties inspector, click the folder button to the right of the Link field.**

3. **In the Select File dialog box, select the update page that you just created.**

For example, we selected update.php as the update page. For other language types, use the appropriate file extension (such as .asp) rather than .php.

4. **Click the Parameters button.**

The Parameters dialog box appears.

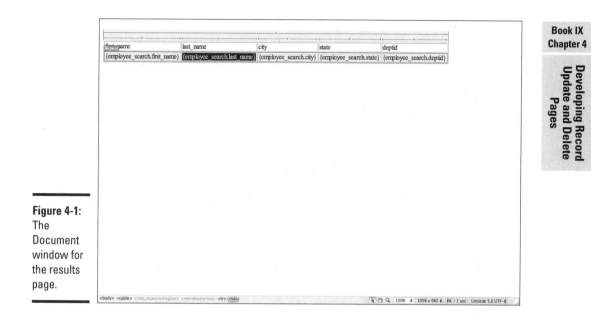

Figure 4-1:
The
Document
window for
the results
page.

5. **Enter the key field from your database record in the Name column.**

The *key field* is a field that always has a unique value. For example, we entered `empid` because this field contains a unique ID for each employee.

6. **Click the Value column to the right of the Name.**

The box is highlighted.

7. **Click the Bind to Dynamic Source (lightning bolt) button to the right of the highlighted box.**

The Dynamic Data dialog box appears, as shown in Figure 4-2.

8. **Select the key field from the recordset and then click OK.**

After you click OK, the Values field in the Parameters dialog box updates to contain the URL parameter.

9. **Click OK to close the Parameters dialog box.**

The Select File dialog box appears with an updated value in the URL field. The value in this field varies depending on your dynamic page type. Figure 4-3 shows the results for a PHP page.

10. **Click Choose to close the Select File dialog box.**

The Document window shows the new link.

11. **Save the results page.**

The results page is now complete.

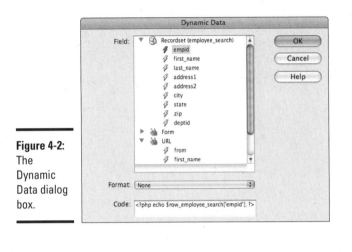

Figure 4-2:
The Dynamic Data dialog box.

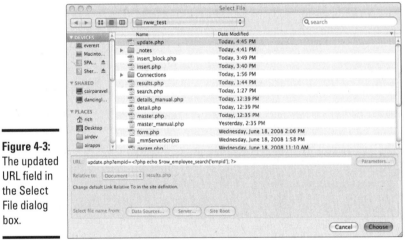

Figure 4-3:
The updated URL field in the Select File dialog box.

Putting the update page together

The update page must read the URL parameter from the results page and store it in a recordset. The recordset provides the default values for the form that enables users to change values. The following sections show how to create the recordset and the form.

Creating the recordset to store the URL parameter

To create the recordset, follow these steps:

1. **Open the results page you created in the previous section.**

You must have an active database connection to create the recordset. See Book VII for details on creating a database connection.

2. **In the Bindings panel, click the plus (+) button and select Recordset (Query) from the menu that appears.**

   The Recordset dialog box appears.

3. **Enter the name of the recordset in the Name field.**

   Use a name that describes the recordset data. For example, we entered `employee_update` to indicate that the recordset relates to an update. (Impressive thinking, eh?)

4. **Select a database connection from the Connection drop-down list.**

   Depending on your dynamic page type, the Recordset dialog box may appear slightly different. ColdFusion, in particular, calls the Connection field a data source and includes optional Username and Password fields for the database. However, these differences don't change the following steps.

5. **In the Table drop-down list, select the database table that you want to update.**

   After you select a table, the Columns list shows the columns in that table.

6. **Click the Selected radio button if you want to include only some of the columns from the table for updating. Or, if you want to include all, leave as is and skip to Step 8.**

7. **In the Columns list, select the columns that you want to update.**

   To select multiple columns, Ctrl+click (Windows) or ⌘+click (Mac).

8. **Configure the Filter area so that the database column is compared against the URL parameter from the results page:**

   • From the first list, select the key column. For example, we selected `empid`, which is the key column for the `employee` table.

   • From the second list, select the equals sign (=). This selection limits the result set to only the record that you want to update. You can update only one record at a time.

   • From the third list, select URL Parameter.

   • From the fourth list, enter the name of the URL parameter defined in the results page. For example, we entered `empid`, the exact same name as the database key column name.

     If your form's field has a different name in the Properties inspector, use that name as the parameter name.

The new recordset retrieves the information needed to update the specific records that the user has selected to update. When the update page is requested, it uses the record ID parameter sent to the page to filter the recordset. The Recordset dialog box for the example looks like Figure 4-4.

9. Click OK.

The recordset is added to the Bindings panel list. Now when the user selects a record on the results page, the update page builds a recordset containing only the selected record.

Adding a form to the update page

After creating the recordset for the update page (which you can read about in the preceding section), you need to create the form that enables the user to modify the record data. Dreamweaver can do the work for you with the Record Update Form Wizard. This wizard automatically creates the form in the Document window and adds the appropriate server behaviors to allow updates.

If you already have used the Insert Record Form Wizard, you'll find this wizard very similar.

Follow these steps to add an HTML form to your update page:

1. Choose Insert➪Data Objects➪Update Record➪Record Update Form Wizard.

The Update Record Form dialog box appears.

Only one application object can exist on the same page. You can't have an update application object and a delete application object on the same page.

2. Select the database connection from the Connection drop-down list.

3. Select the database table that you want to update from the Table to Update drop-down list.

4. From the Select Record From drop-down list, select the recordset that you created, as described in the preceding section.

This list should default to the recordset that you created in the preceding section.

5. From the Unique Key Column drop-down list, select a key column to identify the record in the database table.

For example, we selected `empid`. Leave the Numeric check box selected if the key fields are numeric.

6. In the After Updating, Go To text box, enter the page that you want to open after the record is updated. Alternatively, click the Browse button to select a file.

For example, we selected a page called success.php, which simply displays a success message. If you have not already done so, you can create the page before or after entering the filename for it.

7. To remove unwanted columns from the update page, select the columns in the Form Fields section and click the minus (–) button.

By default, Dreamweaver includes all the columns of the table in the form on the update page.

The Form Fields section lists the columns in which the user can enter data before submitting the update request. For our example, the `empid` field is manually removed because it's an auto-generated key field. Removing this field eliminates the risk of the user changing the key value to a duplicate value.

8. If you're happy with the default settings in the Form Fields section, skip to Step 10. However, if you want to make changes to how a field displays on the update page, select the field from the list and fill in the following fields in the dialog box:

- **Label:** Enter a descriptive label for each database field. This label appears on the form next to the field. By default, Dreamweaver uses the column name as the label. So, for example, rather than use the default label of `first_name`, you could change it to First Name, which is a little friendlier.

- **Display As:** Select a form type for the field. The Display As list includes all the basic form types, including check boxes, radio buttons, and menus. If you select one of the types that needs additional configuration, such as radio groups, a configuration dialog box appears.

- **Submit As:** Select the data format for the database field. The *data format* is the type of data that the database column is expecting. The default matches the current datatype in the database. Your choices include Text, Numeric, Double, Date, Checkbox Y/N, Checkbox 1/0, and Checkbox -1,0.

- **Default Value:** Specify a default value for the field. The value that you enter in the Default Value field is the initial value that appears in the form for the particular field. If you don't enter a value here, Dreamweaver uses the current value from the database for the initial value.

  If you want, you can change the dynamic data source for the default value by clicking the Bind to Dynamic Source (lightning bolt) button and selecting a binding. The value defaults to the value from the recordset. If the data type is a menu, radio group, or check box, another dialog box opens to configure the choices available to the user. For example, a check box has a setting to determine whether it should be automatically checked when the update page opens.

9. **Repeat Step 8 for each field that you want to modify in the Form Field list.**

The dialog box for the example looks like Figure 4-5.

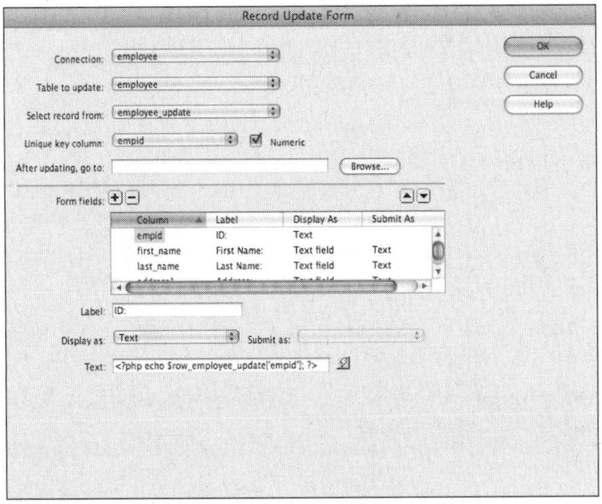

Figure 4-5:
The Record Update Form dialog box after configuring an update.

10. **If you want to change the order in which the fields appear in the form, select a field and click the up or down arrows.**

Table fields should be grouped with similar fields (for example, address fields should all be placed together).

11. **Click OK to close the Record Update Form dialog box.**

The new form appears as a basic table on your update page. Figure 4-6 shows the form created for the example. You can modify the appearance of form objects as you can any other object in Dreamweaver, but remember to not move them outside the form's boundaries. (See Book II, Chapter 7 for more on form objects.)

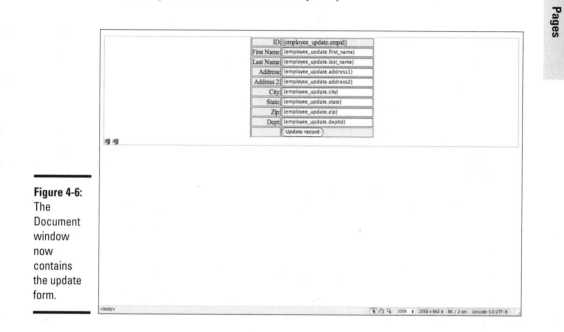

Figure 4-6:
The
Document
window
now
contains
the update
form.

Testing Your Update Page

You can test your results page by previewing it in a browser. Before doing so, make sure the latest versions of your search, results, and update pages are on your server. After you've done that, follow these steps:

1. **Open the search page in Dreamweaver.**

2. **Choose File⇨Preview in Browser⇨*Name of Browser*.**

3. **Enter search criteria in the box and click the Search button.**

The results page is displayed with the matching records (see Figure 4-7).

4. **Select a record to update by clicking the link for that record.**

In our example, the last name for each employee is linked to the update page.

The browser opens the update page for that record. For example, we clicked the Jason Bourne link on the results page, and the browser displayed the update page with the record for Jason, as shown in Figure 4-8.

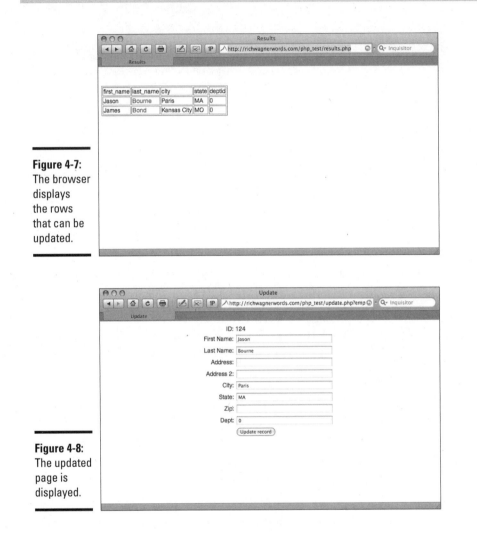

Figure 4-7:
The browser
displays
the rows
that can be
updated.

Figure 4-8:
The updated
page is
displayed.

Be sure that both your search results page and update page transfer to the testing server. If both don't transfer, when you click a link in the update results page, you get a `Page Not Found` error message.

5. **Enter a new value for one or more of the fields on the update page.**

   For example, we added address info, as shown in Figure 4-9.

6. **Click Update Record.**

   Your changes are saved to the database, and the success page appears in the browser (see Figure 4-10).

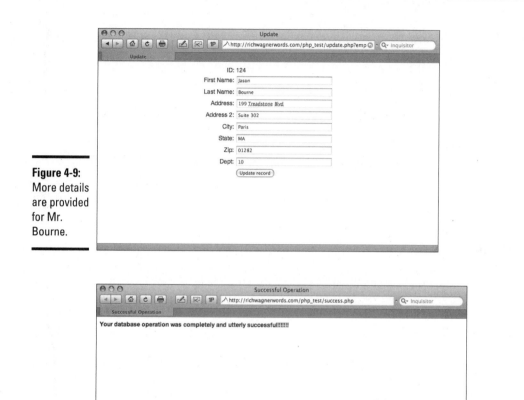

Figure 4-9:
More details
are provided
for Mr.
Bourne.

Figure 4-10:
Success!

What's more, to verify the update was saved, you can navigate back to the update results page to verify the new value.

Building Pages to Delete a Record

The typical process for deleting records from a database consists of a few steps. First, users select which record to delete. After they select a record, a confirmation page opens, asking them to confirm the delete request to prevent deleting a record accidentally. Finally, a page opens that indicates the record was successfully deleted from the database.

In order for users to be able to delete a record, they first need to be able to find that record in the database. Therefore, you need to create a search page and results page that enable users to search for the record. See Book IX, Chapter 2 for details.

The following sections detail how to build the pages that allow a user to delete a record from the database.

Creating delete links to open the confirmation page

After you create a search page and results page, you need to create a Delete link for each record in the results table that users can click to open a *confirmation page,* which is a page that asks them to confirm the deletion.

However, before you begin, quickly create a blank dynamic page of the desired type and save it as `confirm.php` (the extension varies based on the app server you are working with). You'll add content to this file in a moment, but for now, you just need to link to it.

To create the links to the confirmation page, open the results page and follow these steps:

1. **Select the last column in the results repeated region.**

2. **Choose Insert➪Table Objects➪Table➪Insert Columns to the Right.**

    An empty column appears at the end of the table. The empty column is very skinny.

3. **Select the new column's lower cell, which is part of the repeated region.**

4. **Type** Delete.

5. **Select the text you just entered to apply a link to the text.**

6. **In the Properties inspector, enter the name of the confirmation page in the Link field.**

Defining the URL parameter to pass to the confirmation page

After you create a delete link that opens the confirmation page (which you can read about in the preceding section), you want to modify that link so that it passes the identity of the record that the user wants to delete. To define the URL parameter that identifies which record to delete, follow these steps:

1. **Follow Steps 1 through 6 in the "Creating delete links to open the confirmation page" section, earlier in this chapter.**

    The deletion process follows a parallel pattern to the record update.

2. **Click the plus (+) button to add another parameter.**

   An empty row appears in the list.

3. **Enter the name of a column that describes which record is about to be deleted on the confirmation page.**

   For the `employee` table example, we am using the last name field. In a real-world situation, you would probably want to add more fields to confirm the deletion. But for this purpose, the last name field works fine.

   Figure 4-11 shows the two parameters for the `employee` table.

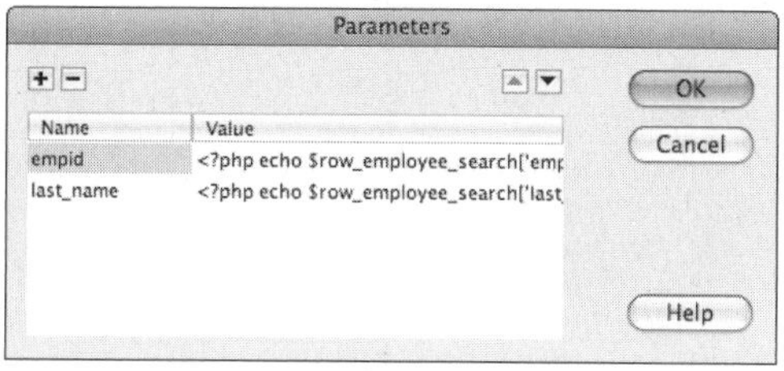

Figure 4-11:
The
Parameters
dialog box
with the key
field and
descriptive
field.

4. **Click OK to close the Parameters dialog box.**

   The Select File dialog box appears with an updated value in the URL field. The value in this field varies depending on your dynamic page type.

5. **Click OK to close the Select File dialog box.**

   The Document window shows the new link.

6. **Save the results page.**

   The results page is complete. The delete link now appears on the page, as shown in Figure 4-12.

Building the confirmation page

The Confirmation page simply displays enough information to identify the record that's about to be deleted. This page consists of a form with a confirmation button.

To create a page that confirms the record deletion, you need to send two parameters to the confirmation page:

✦ The record ID

✦ A field to display the name of that record

This page saves you from having to create another recordset with a filter to look up information that's already been retrieved from the database.

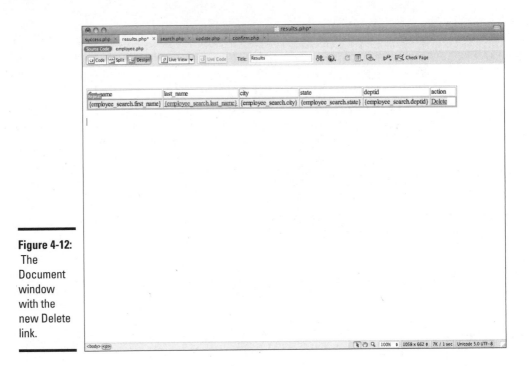

Figure 4-12:
The
Document
window
with the
new Delete
link.

Follow these steps to create the confirmation page:

1. **Open up your confirmation page.**

   We opened up confirm.php.

2. **In the Bindings panel, click the plus (+) button and select URL Parameter from the list that appears.**

   The URL Variables dialog box appears.

3. **In the Name field, enter the name of the database column that is the key.**

   For the example, we entered empid because we need to create a binding for the URL parameter empid.

4. **Click OK.**

   The binding is created.

5. **Repeat Steps 3 and 4 for the last name parameter.**

   For the example, we also created a last_name parameter.

6. **Choose Insert⇨Form to add a form.**

7. **Choose Insert⇨Form⇨Hidden Field to add a hidden field to store the record ID.**

   The user doesn't need to see the empid, but that ID needs to be part of the form submission.

8. **With the hidden field selected, enter the name of the variable in the Hidden Field text box in the Properties inspector.**

For example, we entered `empid_field`.

9. **Click the Bind to Dynamic Source (lightning bolt) button next to the Value field.**

The Dynamic Data dialog box appears.

10. **Select the type of binding (URL Parameter, for example) from the bindings list.**

For the example, we selected the `empid` URL parameter. You can leave the other fields set to their defaults.

11. **Click OK to close the Dynamic Data dialog box.**

In the Properties inspector, Dreamweaver updates the Value field with dynamic code to place the URL parameter into the hidden form field.

12. **Click in the hidden field in the form and type** Do you wish to delete the record for ?

This text tells users they're about to delete a record.

13. **Position your cursor just before the question mark and then select Dynamic Text from the plus (+) menu of the Server Behaviors panel.**

The Dynamic Text dialog box appears, as shown in Figure 4-13.

14. **Select the `empid` URL Parameter from the list and then click OK.**

If you're using a different column as the key, select that parameter instead.

15. **Choose Insert⇨Form⇨Button to add a Submit button to your form.**

The Input Tag Accessibility Attributes dialog box appears.

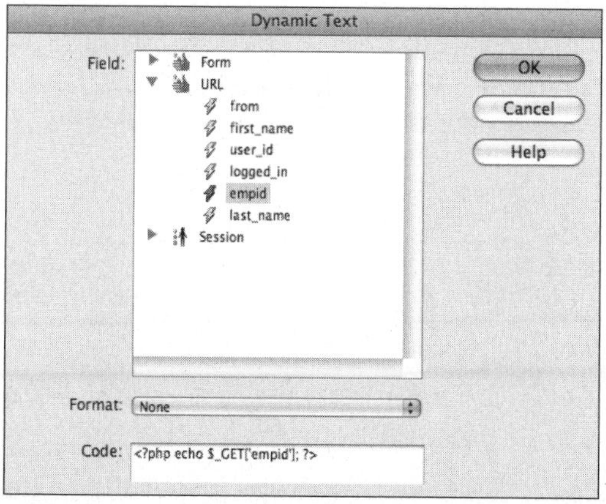

Figure 4-13:
The
Dynamic
Text dialog
box.

16. **Type** delete_btn **in the ID field.**

17. **Click OK to close the dialog box.**

18. **Select the button.**

19. **In the Properties inspector, enter Delete in the Value field.**

The button's text changes to Delete, as shown in Figure 4-14.

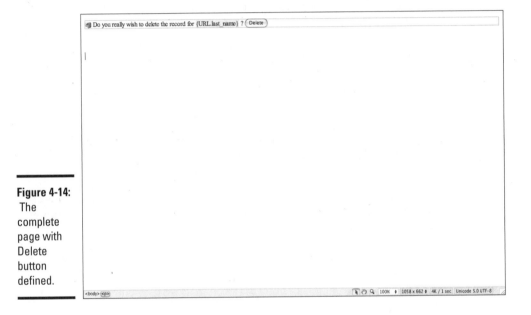

Figure 4-14:
The complete page with Delete button defined.

20. **Save the page.**

Use the name that you selected when creating the Delete link (see "Creating delete links to open the confirmation page," earlier in this chapter).

But wait, there's more! The page isn't complete yet because it can't actually process the deletion. You need to add logic to delete the record, as described in the following section.

Adding logic to delete the record

Dreamweaver adds the logic to perform the database deletion with the Delete Record server behavior. To add this behavior to the HTML form, follow these steps:

1. **In the Server Behaviors panel, click the plus (+) button and select Delete Record from the menu that appears.**

   The Delete Record dialog box appears.

2. **Select Primary Key Value from the First Check If Variable Is Defined drop-down list.**

3. **Select the appropriate database connection from the Connection drop-down list.**

   This field may appear differently depending on your dynamic page code type.

4. **Select the table that you want to delete from the Table drop-down list.**

5. **Select the primary key column from the Primary Key Column drop-down list.**

   We left the Numeric check box checked in our example because the empid record is a numeric field.

6. **Select `Form Variable` from the Primary Key Value drop-down list.**

   Form Variable is the hidden field value from the form submission.

7. **In the text field next to the Primary Key Value drop-down list, enter the name of the field that contains the key value.**

   Again, we entered empid_field for the example.

8. **In the After Deleting, Go To text box, enter the page that you want to open after deleting the record.**

   We entered success.php for the example. You can make this page as simple as the statement Deleted Successfully. The Delete Record dialog box for the example looks like Figure 4-15.

9. **Click OK to close the dialog box.**

   Dreamweaver adds the new server behavior to the page.

The deletion pages are complete.

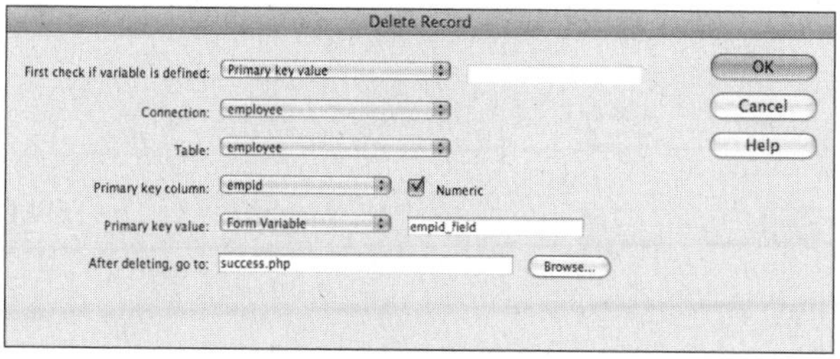

Figure 4-15:
The Delete
Record
dialog box
set to delete
an entry.

Delete Record			
First check if variable is defined:	Primary key value		OK
Connection:	employee		Cancel
Table:	employee		Help
Primary key column:	empid	☑ Numeric	
Primary key value:	Form Variable	empid_field	
After deleting, go to:	success.php	Browse...	

Testing Your Delete Page

To test your delete page, follow these steps:

1. **Open the search page that you already created in Dreamweaver.**
2. **Choose File⇨Preview in Browser⇨*Name of Browser*.**
3. **If Dreamweaver asks you if it's okay to copy files to your testing site, click OK.**

   WARNING!

   Be sure that both your updated results page and the new confirmation page transfer to the testing server. If they don't both transfer, when you click a link in the delete results page, you will get a `Page Not Found` error message. If they don't transfer, copy or upload them to the server before continuing.
4. **Enter search criteria in the text box and click the Search button to display records.**

   The modified results page is displayed, which now allows the user to select a record that she wants to delete.

   Your browser opens and displays a list of records that you can delete. For example, Figure 4-16 lists the employee records that we can delete.

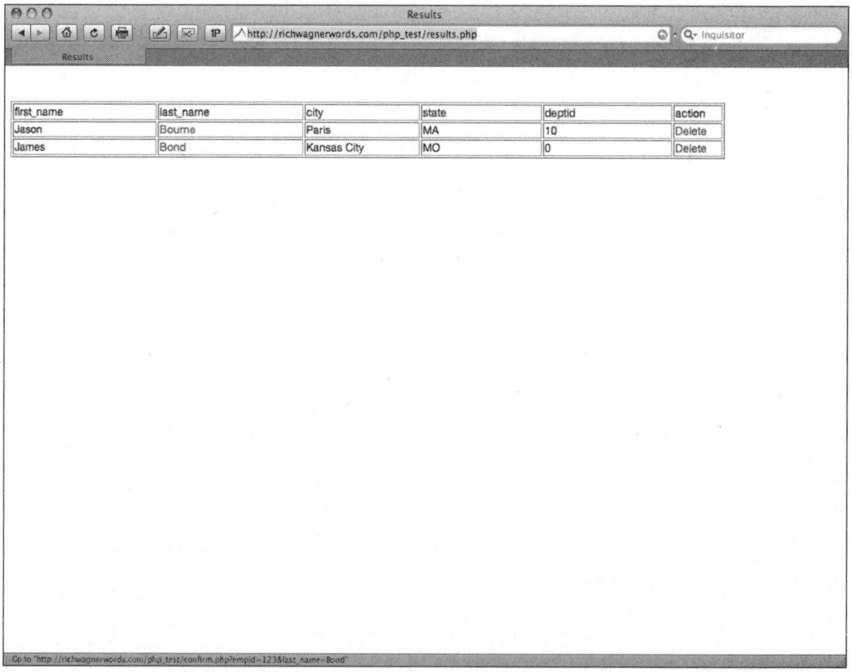
Results
http://richwagnerwords.com/php_test/results.php
Inquisitor
Results
first_name
last_name
city
state
deptid
action
Jason
Bourne
Paris
MA
10
Delete
James
Bond
Kansas City
MO
0
Delete
Go to "http://richwagnerwords.com/php_test/confirm.php?empid=123&last_name=Bond"

Figure 4-16: The browser displays records.

5. **Click the Delete link next to the row that you want to delete.**

   The browser page displays the delete confirmation page. Figure 4-17 shows the delete confirmation page for the example.

6. **Click the Delete button.**

   The browser displays the success page if the operation is successful.

To verify the record deletion, you can navigate back to the delete results page to make sure the record doesn't appear on that page anymore.

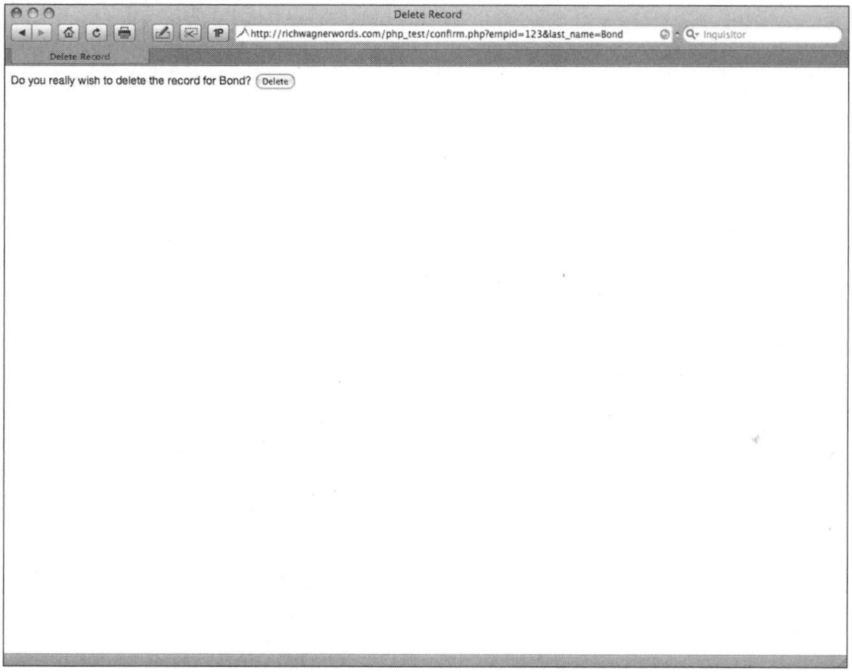

Figure 4-17: The deletion confirmation page shows the employee last name of Bond.

Index

Notes

BUSINESS, CAREERS & PERSONAL FINANCE

Accounting For Dummies, 4th Edition*
978-0-470-24600-9

Bookkeeping Workbook For Dummies†
978-0-470-16983-4

Commodities For Dummies
978-0-470-04928-0

Doing Business in China For Dummies
978-0-470-04929-7

E-Mail Marketing For Dummies
978-0-470-19087-6

Job Interviews For Dummies, 3rd Edition*†
978-0-470-17748-8

Personal Finance Workbook For Dummies*†
978-0-470-09933-9

Real Estate License Exams For Dummies
978-0-7645-7623-2

Six Sigma For Dummies
978-0-7645-6798-8

Small Business Kit For Dummies, 2nd Edition*†
978-0-7645-5984-6

Telephone Sales For Dummies
978-0-470-16836-3

BUSINESS PRODUCTIVITY & MICROSOFT OFFICE

Access 2007 For Dummies
978-0-470-03649-5

Excel 2007 For Dummies
978-0-470-03737-9

Office 2007 For Dummies
978-0-470-00923-9

Outlook 2007 For Dummies
978-0-470-03830-7

PowerPoint 2007 For Dummies
978-0-470-04059-1

Project 2007 For Dummies
978-0-470-03651-8

QuickBooks 2008 For Dummies
978-0-470-18470-7

Quicken 2008 For Dummies
978-0-470-17473-9

Salesforce.com For Dummies, 2nd Edition
978-0-470-04893-1

Word 2007 For Dummies
978-0-470-03658-7

EDUCATION, HISTORY, REFERENCE & TEST PREPARATION

African American History For Dummies
978-0-7645-5469-8

Algebra For Dummies
978-0-7645-5325-7

Algebra Workbook For Dummies
978-0-7645-8467-1

Art History For Dummies
978-0-470-09910-0

ASVAB For Dummies, 2nd Edition
978-0-470-10671-6

British Military History For Dummies
978-0-470-03213-8

Calculus For Dummies
978-0-7645-2498-1

Canadian History For Dummies, 2nd Edition
978-0-470-83656-9

Geometry Workbook For Dummies
978-0-471-79940-5

The SAT I For Dummies, 6th Edition
978-0-7645-7193-0

Series 7 Exam For Dummies
978-0-470-09932-2

World History For Dummies
978-0-7645-5242-7

FOOD, GARDEN, HOBBIES & HOME

Bridge For Dummies, 2nd Edition
978-0-471-92426-5

Coin Collecting For Dummies, 2nd Edition
978-0-470-22275-1

Cooking Basics For Dummies, 3rd Edition
978-0-7645-7206-7

Drawing For Dummies
978-0-7645-5476-6

Etiquette For Dummies, 2nd Edition
978-0-470-10672-3

Gardening Basics For Dummies*†
978-0-470-03749-2

Knitting Patterns For Dummies
978-0-470-04556-5

Living Gluten-Free For Dummies†
978-0-471-77383-2

Painting Do-It-Yourself For Dummies
978-0-470-17533-0

HEALTH, SELF HELP, PARENTING & PETS

Anger Management For Dummies
978-0-470-03715-7

Anxiety & Depression Workbook For Dummies
978-0-7645-9793-0

Dieting For Dummies, 2nd Edition
978-0-7645-4149-0

Dog Training For Dummies, 2nd Edition
978-0-7645-8418-3

Horseback Riding For Dummies
978-0-470-09719-9

Infertility For Dummies†
978-0-470-11518-3

Meditation For Dummies with CD-ROM, 2nd Edition
978-0-471-77774-8

Post-Traumatic Stress Disorder For Dummies
978-0-470-04922-8

Puppies For Dummies, 2nd Edition
978-0-470-03717-1

Thyroid For Dummies, 2nd Edition†
978-0-471-78755-6

Type 1 Diabetes For Dummies*†
978-0-470-17811-9

---

* Separate Canadian edition also available
† Separate U.K. edition also available

Available wherever books are sold. For more information or to order direct: U.S. customers visit www.dummies.com or call 1-877-762-2974.
U.K. customers visit www.wileyeurope.com or call (0)1243 843291. Canadian customers visit www.wiley.ca or call 1-800-567-4797.

 WILEY

INTERNET & DIGITAL MEDIA

AdWords For Dummies
978-0-470-15252-2

Blogging For Dummies, 2nd Edition
978-0-470-23017-6

**Digital Photography All-in-One
Desk Reference For Dummies, 3rd Edition**
978-0-470-03743-0

Digital Photography For Dummies, 5th Edition
978-0-7645-9802-9

**Digital SLR Cameras & Photography
For Dummies, 2nd Edition**
978-0-470-14927-0

**eBay Business All-in-One Desk Reference
For Dummies**
978-0-7645-8438-1

eBay For Dummies, 5th Edition*
978-0-470-04529-9

eBay Listings That Sell For Dummies
978-0-471-78912-3

Facebook For Dummies
978-0-470-26273-3

The Internet For Dummies, 11th Edition
978-0-470-12174-0

Investing Online For Dummies, 5th Edition
978-0-7645-8456-5

iPod & iTunes For Dummies, 5th Edition
978-0-470-17474-6

MySpace For Dummies
978-0-470-09529-4

Podcasting For Dummies
978-0-471-74898-4

**Search Engine Optimization
For Dummies, 2nd Edition**
978-0-471-97998-2

Second Life For Dummies
978-0-470-18025-9

**Starting an eBay Business For Dummies
3rd Edition†**
978-0-470-14924-9

GRAPHICS, DESIGN & WEB DEVELOPMENT

**Adobe Creative Suite 3 Design Premium
All-in-One Desk Reference For Dummies**
978-0-470-11724-8

**Adobe Web Suite CS3 All-in-One Desk
Reference For Dummies**
978-0-470-12099-6

AutoCAD 2008 For Dummies
978-0-470-11650-0

**Building a Web Site For Dummies,
3rd Edition**
978-0-470-14928-7

**Creating Web Pages All-in-One Desk
Reference For Dummies, 3rd Edition**
978-0-470-09629-1

**Creating Web Pages For Dummies,
8th Edition**
978-0-470-08030-6

Dreamweaver CS3 For Dummies
978-0-470-11490-2

Flash CS3 For Dummies
978-0-470-12100-9

Google SketchUp For Dummies
978-0-470-13744-4

InDesign CS3 For Dummies
978-0-470-11865-8

**Photoshop CS3 All-in-One
Desk Reference For Dummies**
978-0-470-11195-6

Photoshop CS3 For Dummies
978-0-470-11193-2

Photoshop Elements 5 For Dummies
978-0-470-09810-3

SolidWorks For Dummies
978-0-7645-9555-4

Visio 2007 For Dummies
978-0-470-08983-5

Web Design For Dummies, 2nd Edition
978-0-471-78117-2

Web Sites Do-It-Yourself For Dummies
978-0-470-16903-2

Web Stores Do-It-Yourself For Dummies
978-0-470-17443-2

LANGUAGES, RELIGION & SPIRITUALITY

Arabic For Dummies
978-0-471-77270-5

Chinese For Dummies, Audio Set
978-0-470-12766-7

French For Dummies
978-0-7645-5193-2

German For Dummies
978-0-7645-5195-6

Hebrew For Dummies
978-0-7645-5489-6

Ingles Para Dummies
978-0-7645-5427-8

Italian For Dummies, Audio Set
978-0-470-09586-7

Italian Verbs For Dummies
978-0-471-77389-4

Japanese For Dummies
978-0-7645-5429-2

Latin For Dummies
978-0-7645-5431-5

Portuguese For Dummies
978-0-471-78738-9

Russian For Dummies
978-0-471-78001-4

Spanish Phrases For Dummies
978-0-7645-7204-3

Spanish For Dummies
978-0-7645-5194-9

Spanish For Dummies, Audio Set
978-0-470-09585-0

The Bible For Dummies
978-0-7645-5296-0

Catholicism For Dummies
978-0-7645-5391-2

The Historical Jesus For Dummies
978-0-470-16785-4

Islam For Dummies
978-0-7645-5503-9

**Spirituality For Dummies,
2nd Edition**
978-0-470-19142-2

NETWORKING AND PROGRAMMING

ASP.NET 3.5 For Dummies
978-0-470-19592-5

C# 2008 For Dummies
978-0-470-19109-5

Hacking For Dummies, 2nd Edition
978-0-470-05235-8

Home Networking For Dummies, 4th Edition
978-0-470-11806-1

Java For Dummies, 4th Edition
978-0-470-08716-9

**Microsoft® SQL Server™ 2008 All-in-One
Desk Reference For Dummies**
978-0-470-17954-3

**Networking All-in-One Desk Reference
For Dummies, 2nd Edition**
978-0-7645-9939-2

**Networking For Dummies,
8th Edition**
978-0-470-05620-2

SharePoint 2007 For Dummies
978-0-470-09941-4

**Wireless Home Networking
For Dummies, 2nd Edition**
978-0-471-74940-0